YO-CZE-925

SERVICE OPERATIONS MANAGEMENT

McGraw-Hill Series in Quantitative Methods for Management

Consulting Editor

Martin K. Starr, Columbia University

Bowen and Starr: *Basic Statistics for Business and Economics*
Byrd and Moore: *Decision Models for Management*
Dannenbring and Starr: *Management Science: An Introduction*
Fitzsimmons and Sullivan: *Service Operations Management*
Gohagan: *Quantitative Analysis for Public Policy*
Heyman and Sobel: *Stochastic Models in Operations Research, Volume I: Stochastic Processes and Operating Characteristics*
McKenna: *Quantitative Methods for Public Decision Making*
Sobol and Starr: *Statistics for Business and Economics: An Action Learning Approach*
Swanson: *Linear Programming: Basic Theory and Applications*
Zeleny: *Multiple Criteria Decision Making*

SERVICE OPERATIONS MANAGEMENT

James A. Fitzsimmons
Robert S. Sullivan

Professors of Management
University of Texas, Austin

McGraw-Hill Book Company

New York St. Louis San Francisco Auckland Bogotá Hamburg
Johannesburg London Madrid Mexico Montreal New Delhi
Panama Paris São Paulo Singapore Sydney Tokyo Toronto

To our parents
to whom we owe everything

This book was set in Times Roman by Progressive Typographers.
The editors were Donald G. Mason and Scott Amerman;
the production supervisor was Phil Galea.
New drawings were done by Danmark & Michaels, Inc.
R. R. Donnelley & Sons Company was printer and binder.

SERVICE OPERATIONS MANAGEMENT

Copyright © 1982 by McGraw-Hill, Inc. All rights reserved.
Printed in the United States of America. Except as permitted under the United States
Copyright Act of 1976, no part of this publication may be reproduced or
distributed in any form or by any means, or stored in a data base or
retrieval system, without the prior written permission of the publisher.

1234567890 DODO 898765432

ISBN 0-07-021215-5

Library of Congress Cataloging in Publication Data

Fitzsimmons, James A.
   Service operations management.

   (McGraw-Hill series in quantitative methods for management)
   Includes bibliographies and index.
   1. Service industries—Management. 2. Operations research. I. Sullivan, Robert S. II. Title.
III. Series
HD9980.5.F55   658.5   81-13680
ISBN 0-07-021215-5   AACR2

CONTENTS

Preface   xiii

Part 1   The Nature of Service Operations

1   The Postindustrial Era   3
Postindustrial Society   4
    Development of a Postindustrial Society · Characteristics of Postindustrial Society
The Challenge for Service Operations Managers   11
Topics for Discussion   14
Selected Bibliography   14

2   The Operations Function in Service Systems   15
Service Classification   16
The Service Package   16
Distinctive Characteristics of Service Operations   20
    Consumer as a Participant in the Service Process · Production and Consumption Occur Simultaneously · Time Perishable Capacity · Site Selection Dictated by Location of Consumers · Labor Intensiveness · Intangibility · Difficulty in Measuring Output
An Open-Systems View of Service Operations   26
Summary   28
Topics for Discussion   28
Selected Bibliography   28

Part 2 Decision Models for Service Operations

3 Evaluation of Service Operations — 33
- The Evaluation Process — 34
  - Objectives of Evaluation · Establishing the Evaluation System
- Cost-Benefit Analysis — 39
  - Cost-Benefit Analysis and Cost Effectiveness Compared · Time Value of Money · Conducting a Cost-Benefit Study · Benefit-Cost Study of Defensive Driving Program · Cost-Effectiveness Study of Kidney Disease Treatment
- Summary — 50
- Topics for Discussion — 51
- Exercises — 51
- Caselettes: River City Planning Commission — 53
  - Miserly County Transportation Authority — 53
- Selected Bibliography — 57

4 Management Systems Simulation — 58
- Basic Concepts — 58
  - Models · Analyzing Mathematical Models · Why Use Systems Simulation?
- The Process of Systems Simulation — 62
  - Simulation Methodology · Monte Carlo Simulation · Generating Random Variables · Discrete-Event Simulation
- Summary — 72
- Topics for Discussion — 73
- Exercises — 73
- Caselettes: Krohler Supermarkets — 76
  - Coquille Refinery Corporation — 78
- Selected Bibliography — 80

5 Linear Programming Models in Services — 81
- Constrained Optimization Models — 82
- Formulating Linear Programming Models — 84
  - Diet Problem · Shift Scheduling Problem · Workforce Planning Problem · Transportation Problem
- Optimal Solutions and Computer Analysis — 92
  - Graphical Solution of LP Models · LP Model in Standard Form · Computer Analysis and Interpretation
- Sensitivity Analysis — 98
  - Objective-Function Coefficient Ranges · Right-Hand-Side Ranging
- Goal Programming — 101
- Summary — 104
- Topics for Discussion — 104
- Exercises — 104

	Caselettes: Munich Delicatessen	110
	Sequoia Airlines	111
	Selected Bibliography	113

6 Forecasting for Service Operations — 115

Importance of Forecasting for Service Operations — 116
   Wide Fluctuations in Demand · Intangibility of
   Services · Simultaneous Production and
   Consumption of Services
Considerations in Choosing a Forecasting Method — 117
   Costs Surrounding a Forecast Model ·
   Required Accuracy · Relevancy of Past Data ·
   Forecasting Horizon · Pattern of Data
Forecasting Methods — 121
   Time Series Models · Causal Models · Subjective Models
Summary — 136
Topics for Discussion — 136
Exercises — 137
Caselettes: Oak Hollow Evaluation Center — 138
   Gnomial Functions, Inc. — 140
Selected Bibliography — 141

Part 3 Designing the Service System

7 Design of Service Delivery Systems — 145

Types of Service Operations — 146
   Project · Batch (Job Shop) · Line (Flow Shop) ·
   Ongoing Process
Approaches to Service System Planning and Design — 148
   Production-Line Approach · Consumer Participation ·
   Isolating the Technical Core
Technological Innovation in Services — 154
Summary — 156
Topics for Discussion — 157
Caselette: ALCOVE Corporation — 157
Selected Bibliography — 159

8 Service Facility Location — 160

Location Considerations — 161
   Geographic Structure · Number of Facilities ·
   Optimization Criteria
Estimation of Spatial Demand — 166
   Define the Target Population · Select an Areal Unit ·
   Estimate Spatial Demand · Map Spatial Demand
Facility Location Techniques — 167
   Single Facility · Locating a Retail Outlet · Multiple Facility

viii CONTENTS

Substitution of Communication for Transportation	175
Marketing Intermediaries	176
Summary	176
Topics for Discussion	177
Exercises	177
Caselettes: Health Maintenance Organization (A)	179
Athol Furniture, Inc.	179
Selected Bibliography	182

9 Design and Layout of Service Facilities — 184

Design — 185
Nature and Objectives of Service Organizations · Land Availability and Space Requirements · Flexibility · Aesthetic Factors · The Community and Environment · Construction and Operating Costs

Facilities Layout — 191
Product Layout · The Line Balancing Problem · Process Layout · The Relative-Location Problem · Computerized Relative Allocation of Facilities Technique (CRAFT)

Summary	203
Topics for Discussion	204
Exercises	204
Caselettes: Health Maintenance Organization (B)	206
Health Maintenance Organization (C)	207
Esquire Department Store	207
Selected Bibliography	209

10 Work Design: The Design of Service Personnel Activity — 211

Environmental Changes — 212
Rising Levels of Education · Service Employee Associations and Unions · Inflation–Minimum-Wage Cycle · Equal Employment Opportunity · Technological Innovation

Job Rationalization — 214
Time Study · Work Sampling · Work Methods Charts · Job Rationalization in Summary

Job Enlargement and Job Enrichment — 222
Hierarchy of Needs · Two-Factor Theory · Individual Differences

Work Design for Service Organizations — 227
Professional Service Organizations · Routine Service Organizations

Summary	230
Topics for Discussion	231
Exercises	231
Caselette: County General Hospital	231
Selected Bibliography	233

11 The Queuing Phenomenon   235

Queuing Systems   235
The Inevitability of Waiting   236
The Psychology of Waiting   237
  Waiting as Psychological Punishment · Waiting as a
  Ritual Insult · Waiting as a Social Interaction
Economics of Waiting   239
Essential Features of Queuing Systems   241
  Calling Population · Arrival Process · Queue
  Configuration · Queue Discipline · Service Process
Summary   253
Topics for Discussion   253
Caselette: Thrifty-Rent-A-Car   254
Selected Bibliography   255

12 Queuing Models and Capacity Planning   257

Analytical Queuing Models   258
  Standard $M/M/1$ Model · Finite-Queue $M/M/1$ Model ·
  $M/G/1$ Model · Standard $M/M/c$ Model · Finite-Queue
  $M/M/c$ Model · General Self-Service $M/G/\infty$ Model
General Relationships between System Characteristics   268
Capacity Planning Criteria   269
  Average Consumer Waiting Time · Probability of Excessive
  Waiting · Minimize the Sum of Consumer Waiting Costs and
  Service Costs · Probability of Sales Lost because of
  Inadequate Waiting Area · Expected Profit on Last Unit of
  Capacity Should Just Exceed Expected Loss
Summary   276
Formulas for Selected Queuing Models   276
  Definition of Symbols · I. Standard $M/M/1$ Model ·
  II. Finite-Queue $M/M/1$ Model · III. Standard $M/G/1$ Model ·
  IV. Standard $M/M/c$ Model · V. Finite-Queue $M/M/c$ Model ·
  VI. Self-Service $M/G/\infty$ Model
Topics for Discussion   280
Exercises   280
Caslettes: Houston Port Authority   282
         Cedar Valley Community College   283
Selected Bibliography   284

Part 4 Managing Service Operations

13 Utilization of Service Capacity   287

Strategies for Altering Demand   287
  Partitioning Demand · Price Incentives · Promoting Off-Peak
  Demand · Developing Complementary Services ·
  Reservation System

	Strategies for Controlling Supply	295
	Daily Workshift Scheduling · Weekly Workshift Scheduling with Days-Off Constraint · Increasing Consumer Participation · Creating Adjustable Capacity · Sharing Capacity · Cross-Training Employees · Using Part-Time Employees · Scheduling Part-Time Tellers at a Drive-In Bank	
	Summary	303
	Topics for Discussion	303
	Exercises	304
	Caselettes: River City National Bank	305
	Gateway International Airport	307
	Selected Bibliography	310

14 Service Vehicle Scheduling and Routing — 312

	Taxonomy of Vehicle Routing	313
	Techniques for Vehicle Routing	315
	Pin and String Method · Savings Concept of the Clarke-Wright Algorithm · The Clarke-Wright (C-W) Algorithm · Using the C-W Algorithm with No System Constraints · Using the C-W Algorithm with One System Constraint	
	Vehicle Scheduling Program: VSP/X	326
	Data Input Requirements for VSP/X · Capabilities of VSP/X	
	Other Issues Involving Vehicle Routing Programs	329
	Summary	330
	Topics for Discussion	330
	Exercises	331
	Caselettes: The Daley Monthly Car Pool	332
	Airport Services, Inc.	333
	Selected Bibliography	335

15 Project Management: Planning, Scheduling, and Controlling Service Activities — 337

	Project Management: A Conceptual Framework	338
	Characteristics of Project System · The Project Management System	
	Traditional Techniques for Project Management	339
	Gantt Project Charts · A Critique of Gantt Charts	
	Network Techniques for Project Management	341
	Network Techniques: A Brief History · Constructing a Project Network · Critical Path Analysis · Estimating Activity Durations · The PERT Assumption: A Critique · Problems with Implementing Critical Path Analysis	
	Summary	354
	Topics for Discussion	355
	Exercises	355
	Caselettes: Whittier County Hospital	358
	Info-Systems, Inc.	360
	Selected Bibliography	361

16 Measuring and Controlling Service Quality — 363
- Service Process Control — 365
  - Designing Quality into the Service · Measuring Service Performance · Quality Control Charts · Characteristic Curves
- Planning for Service Quality — 377
  - Personnel Programs for Quality Assurance · Quality Improvement Program
- Service Liability — 379
- Summary — 380
- Topics for Discussion — 380
- Exercises — 381
- Caselette: Clean Sweep, Inc. — 383
- Selected Bibliography — 386

17 Management Information Systems: The Nervous System of Service Organizations — 387
- Computers: Some Basic Concepts — 388
  - Computer Hardware · Computer Software
- Trends Affecting Management Information Systems — 390
  - Advances in Computer Hardware Technology · Advances in Computer Software · Reduced Costs of Computer Systems · Increased Number of Computer Systems Companies · Computer Orientation of Personnel and Consumers · Increased Number of Computer Installations · The Information Explosion
- Overview of Management Information Systems — 392
  - Nature of Management Information · Value of Management Information · MIS: A General Framework · How Effective Managers Use MIS
- MIS in Service Organizations: Some Brief Examples — 397
  - Hospital Information System · Investment Management Information System · Funeral Home Information System · Professional Rodeo Information System · Real Estate Information System · Airlines Information System
- Summary — 400
- Topics for Discussion — 400
- Caselette: Lemon County Commissioner's Court — 401
- Selected Bibliography — 402

18 Inventory Management — 404
- Inventory Theory — 405
  - Functions of Inventory · Characteristics of Inventory Systems · Relevant Costs of an Inventory System
- Inventory Control Systems — 407
  - Fixed-Order-Quantity System · Fixed-Interval System · (s, S) Inventory Control System · The ABC's of Inventory Control
- Inventory Models — 410

Simple Economic Order Quantity · Inventory Management under Uncertainty
An Example of a Computer-Based Inventory System 416
Summary 417
Topics for Discussion 417
Exercises 418
Caselette: Elysian Cycles 419
Selected Bibliography 421

Part 5 Transition

19 Service, Culture, and Society 425
Information and Communications Technology 425
From Consumer to Prosumer 426
A Service Society 428
Improving Service Sector Productivity 428
Capstone Case: The University Student Union 429

Tables

A	Single-Payment Present Worth Factors	435
B	Uniform-Series Present Worth Factors	436
C	Areas of a Standard Normal Distribution	437
D	Uniformally Distributed Random Numbers	438

Index 439

PREFACE

We are living in the postindustrial era. Consequently, the focus of both production and consumption in our economy has dramatically shifted away from manufacturing and toward services. Consider the following statistics:

1. In 1978, services accounted for 55 percent of the GNP, and that is without considering government services. When these services are included, the figure jumps to 68 percent.
2. In 1978, over 70 percent of the entire workforce was employed in service jobs.
3. Since 1974, two out of every three BBA and MBA graduates accepted jobs in the service sector.
4. Forecasts to 1985 indicate that in the private sector, two out of every three newly created jobs for college graduates will be in service-producing industries.

We contend that service organizations have unique characteristics that warrant separate study. For example, service firms are far more people-oriented than manufacturing firms: customers generally participate in the service process, often with direct and uncensored interactions with employees and facilities. Also, in service organizations, the production function cannot be divorced from the marketing function, since production and consumption occur simultaneously and since services cannot be inventoried. Therefore, variations in demand create challenges in establishing and utilizing capacity that involve facilities design and layout, work design, workshift scheduling, and vehicle routing. Analogies between services and manufacturing (e.g., a hospital is like a job shop) can be superficial and misleading because they tend to ignore the unique people-processing and people-changing nature of services. Within this service context, new and creative approaches to the study of operations management must be found.

This innovative textbook covers conventional operations management topics such as facility layout, job design, and quality control, but from a service operations perspective. These topics are covered in sufficient detail to satisfy AACSB (American Assembly of Collegiate Schools of Business) requirements in production management. Additional topics, such as evaluation, facility location, queuing, vehicle scheduling, and management information systems, are included because of their particular importance to the management of service operations. The material is integrated about the central issue of capacity utilization and consumer participation in the service process. Because of the nature of service operations, each topic is a blend of both the behavioral and quantitative points of view.

The textbook has been written so that instructors familiar with conventional POM texts can easily make the transition to service operations management. This opportunity will enable them to revitalize and enhance the relevance of their courses to the needs of their students.

A very comprehensive Instructor's Manual to accompany this text is available to adopters from the publisher. It contains extensive instructional support materials for each chapter, in addition to the answers to exercises and cases. It also contains sample test questions and transparency masters for instructors who use visual classroom support materials.

We have been influenced by many individuals in writing this textbook: professors who prepared us for a life of teaching and learning; students at the University of Texas who have responded with enthusiasm and willingness to contribute their insights; our families, who have been supportive of early-morning and late-night writing sessions. In particular, we are indebted to Mona Fitzsimmons for her fine editorial assistance, which at times took great patience.

We were very fortunate to have our manuscript reviewed by colleagues who did not hesitate to provide detailed comment and critical analysis. Their insights have been incorporated in the text in many places. Special thanks and acknowledgment go to the following people for their valuable reviews: Harold C. Allen, of the University of South Florida, Richard F. Gonzalez, of Michigan State University; Michael P. Hottenstein, of The Pennsylvania State University; Robert A. Millen, of Northeastern University; Richard A. Reid, of The University of New Mexico; and Brian Talbot, of The University of Michigan. We are particularly pleased that Martin K. Starr, of Columbia University, was so supportive of this project and that he recognized the need for a text dealing exclusively with service operations.

Two students have been particularly helpful in bringing this textbook project to fruition. James H. Vance prepared most of the end-of-chapter caselettes. Michelle D. Smith not only typed the manuscript but also sketched the illustrations.

Finally, we wish to thank George Kozmetsky for encouraging us to address the management issues of the postindustrial society.

James A. Fitzsimmons
Robert S. Sullivan

PART ONE

THE NATURE OF SERVICE OPERATIONS

CHAPTER
ONE

THE POSTINDUSTRIAL ERA

In the early 1900s, only three in every ten workers in the United States were employed in services. The remaining workers were active in agriculture and industry. By 1950, employment in services accounted for 50 percent of the workforce. Services now employ seven out of every ten workers. During the past 80 years we have witnessed a complete reversal in the work activity of the population.

Economists studying economic growth would not be surprised by these events. Colin Clark argues that, as nations become industrialized, there is an inevitable shift of employment from one sector of the economy to another.[1] As productivity increases in one sector, the labor force moves into another sector. This observation, known as the Clark-Fisher hypothesis, leads to a classification of economies by noting the activity of the majority of the workforce.

Table 1.1 describes five stages of economic activity. Many economists, including Clark, limited their analysis to only three stages, of which the tertiary stage was simply services. We have taken the suggestion of Nelson N. Foote and Paul K. Hatt and subdivided the service stage into three categories.[2]

Today the overwhelming number of countries in the world are still in the primary stage of development. These economies are based on extracting natural resources. Their productivity is low and, except for the OPEC countries, their income is subject to fluctuations based on the prices of raw materials. In Africa and Asia more than 70 percent of the labor force is engaged in farming.

---

[1] Colin Clark, *The Conditions of Economic Progress,* 3d ed., The Macmillan Co., London, 1957.

[2] Nelson N. Foote and Paul K. Hatt, "Social Mobility and Economic Advancement," *American Economic Review,* May 1953, pp. 364–378.

Table 1.1 Stages of economic activity

Primary (Extractive):	*Quaternary* (Trade and commerce):*
Agriculture	Transportation
Mining	Retailing
Fishing	Communications
Forestry	Finance and insurance
Secondary (Goods-producing):	Real estate
Manufacturing	Government
Processing	*Quinary* (Refining and extending human capacities):*
Tertiary (Domestic services):*	Health
Restaurants and hotels	Education
Barber and beauty shops	Research
Laundry and dry cleaning	Recreation
Maintenance and repair	Arts

* Services.

In Europe, Japan, and the Soviet Union the major portion of the labor force is employed in goods production.

In the United States the service sector accounts for two-thirds of the total employment and more than one-half the gross national product. The United States can no longer be considered an industrial society but, instead, the first postindustrial or service society.

What are the characteristics of a postindustrial society? What challenges will be faced by the operations manager in a service society? These questions are investigated in this introductory chapter.

POSTINDUSTRIAL SOCIETY

Describing where our society has been, its current condition, and its most likely future is the task of social historians. Daniel Bell, a professor of sociology at Harvard University, has written extensively on this topic. The material that follows is based on his work.[3]

Development of a Postindustrial Society

To place the concept of a postindustrial society in perspective, we need to compare its features with preindustrial and industrial societies.

Preindustrial society The condition of most of the world's population today is one of subsistence. Life is characterized as a game against nature. Working with muscle power and tradition, the labor force is engaged in agriculture, min-

---

[3] Daniel Bell, *The Coming of Post-Industrial Society: A Venture in Social Forecasting,* Basic Books, Inc., New York, 1973.

ing, and fishing. Life is conditioned by the elements, such as the weather, the quality of the soil, and the availability of water. The rhythm of life is shaped by nature, and the work pace varies with the seasons. Productivity is low, with little evidence of technology. Social life revolves around the extended household. The combination of low productivity and large population results in a high percentage of underemployment. Many seek positions in services, but of the personal or household variety. Preindustrial societies are agrarian and structured around tradition, routine, and authority.

Industrial society The predominant activity is one of goods production. The focus of attention is on making more with less. Energy and machines multiply the output per workhour and structure the nature of work. Division of labor is the law creating routine tasks and the notion of the semiskilled worker. Work is accomplished in the artificial environment of the factory with people tending machines. Life becomes a game played against a fabricated nature—a world of cities, factories, and tenements. The rhythm of life is machine-paced and dominated by rigid working hours and time clocks. It is a world of schedules and the acute awareness of the value of time. Efficiency is the watchword. The standard of living becomes measured by the quantity of goods. The complexity of coordinating the production and distribution of goods results in the creation of large bureaucratic and hierarchical organizations. These organizations are designed with certain roles for their members, and the operation tends to be impersonal, with persons treated as things. The individual is the unit of social life in a society that is considered the sum total of all the individual decisions being made in the marketplace. Of course, the unrelenting pressure of industrial life is softened by the countervailing force of labor unions.

Postindustrial society If the standard of living in an industrial society is defined by the quantity of goods, the postindustrial society is concerned with the quality of life, as measured by services such as health, education, and recreation. The central figure is the professional person because information is the key resource, not energy or physical strength. The game now is played among persons. Social life becomes more difficult because political claims and social rights multiply. Society becomes aware that independent actions of individuals can combine to create havoc for everyone, as seen in traffic congestion and environmental pollution. The community rather than the individual becomes the social unit.

The transformation from industrial to postindustrial society occurs in many ways. First, there is a natural development of services, such as transportation and utilities, to support industrial development. As labor-saving devices are introduced into the production process, more workers become engaged in nonmanufacturing activities, such as maintenance and repair. Second, the growth of population and mass consumption of goods increases wholesale and retail trade along with banking, real estate, and insurance. Third, as income increases, the proportion spent on the necessities of food and home decreases

Table 1.2 Comparison of societies

Society	Game	Predominant activity	Use of human labor	Unit of social life	Standard of living measure	Structure
Preindustrial	Against nature	Agriculture Mining	Raw muscle power	Extended household	Subsistence	Routine Traditional Authoritative
Industrial	Against fabricated nature	Goods production	Machine tending	Individual	Quantity of goods	Bureaucratic Hierarchical
Postindustrial	Among persons	Services	Artistic Creative Intellectual	Community	Quality of life in terms of health, education, recreation	Interdependent Global

and the remainder creates a demand for durables and then services. This observation of Christian Engel, a German statistician of the nineteenth century, explains the growth in personal services, such as those offered in restaurants, hotels, travel, and entertainment. However, a necessary condition for the good life is health and education. In our attempts to eliminate disease and increase the span of life, health services become a critical feature of modern society. Higher education becomes the condition for entry into postindustrial society, which requires professional and technical skills of its population. Finally, the claims for more services and social justice lead to a growth in government. Concerns for environmental protection require governmental intervention and illustrate the interdependent and even global character of postindustrial problems. Table 1.2 summarizes the features that characterize these three stages of economic development—preindustrial, industrial, and postindustrial.

Characteristics of Postindustrial Society

What are the important considerations for the management of service operations in the postindustrial society? Service operations management is the process of creating a service from resources composed of labor, material, technology, and information. The person responsible for this conversion process is called an operations manager. Daniel Bell has identified five dimensions of the postindustrial society:[4]

---

[4] Daniel Bell, "Five Dimensions of Post-Industrial Society," *Social Policy*, vol. 4, no. 1, July–August 1973, pp. 103–110.

1. The creation of a service economy
2. The preeminence of the professional and technical class
3. The primacy of theoretical knowledge
4. The planning of technology
5. The rise of a new intellectual technology

We will address each of these dimensions and note their implications for operations managers.

Creation of a service economy Increased productivity in the manufacturing and agriculture sectors has created a higher level of disposable income in the population, which has led to increased purchases of services as shown in Figure 1.1. The result has been an evolution of the United States economy from one geared primarily to manufacture goods to an economy engaged in the creation of services. We can see from Table 1.3 that the growth of services has been significant, rising from 54.7 percent of the economy in 1947 to 65.6 percent in 1975.

Furthermore, if we consider employment, the present economy of the United States is described best as a service economy. As seen in Table 1.4, more than two-thirds of the employed population currently are engaged in ser-

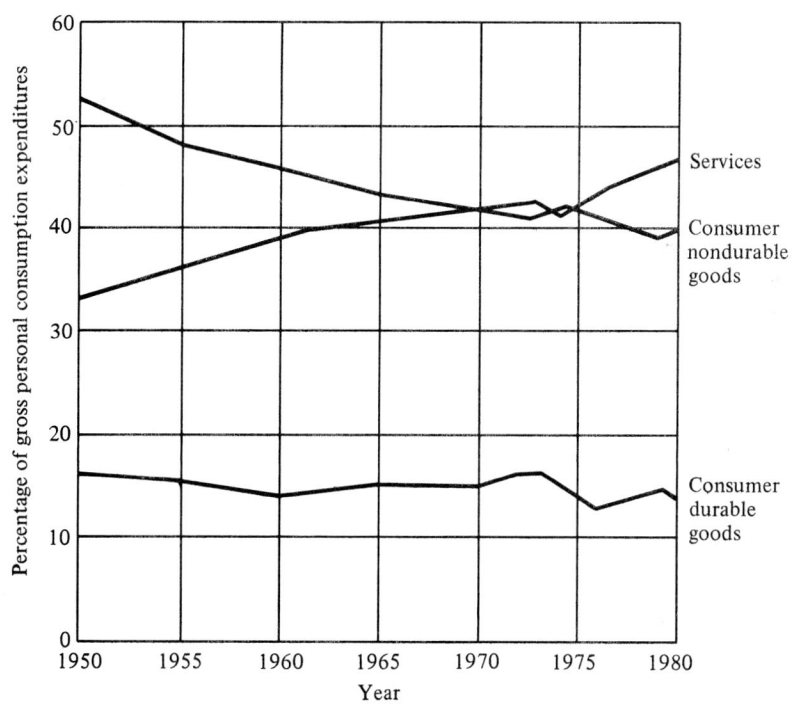

Figure 1.1 Relative importance of services and goods in personal consumption expenditures. [*Economic Report of the President, U.S. Government Printing Office, Washington, January 1981.*]

Table 1.3 Gross national product originating in the services sector, 1947 and 1975
Percentage of current dollar

	Proportion of U.S. GNP	
Sector	1947	1975
Transportation	5.8%	3.7%
Communications	1.3	2.5
Utilities	1.6	2.4
Wholesale trade	6.7	7.9
Retail trade	12.2	10.0
Finance, insurance, real estate	10.0	13.8
Miscellaneous services	8.7	12.0
Government	8.4	13.2
Total	54.7%	65.5%
Total excluding government	46.3%	52.3%

Source: U.S. Service Industries in World Markets, Department of Commerce, December 1976.

Table 1.4 Employment (in thousands) by sector and industry

	1947	1968	1980	Percentage change 1947–1968	Percentage change 1968–1980
Total	51,770	80,780	99,600	56	23
Goods-producing total	26,370	28,975	31,600	9.8	9
Agriculture, forestry, and fisheries	7,890	4,150	3,180	(−48)	(−23)
Mining	955	640	590	(−33)	(−9)
Construction	1,980	4,050	5,480	10	35
Manufacturing:	15,540	20,125	22,358	29	11
Durable	8,385	11,850	13,275	41	12
Nondurable	7,160	8,270	9,100	15.5	10
Service-producing total	25,400	51,800	67,980	104	31
Transportation and utilities	4,160	4,500	5,000	8	10
Trade (wholesale and retail)	8,950	16,600	20,500	85.5	23
Finance, insurance, and real estate	1,750	3,725	4,640	113	24
Services (personal, professional, business)	5,050	15,000	21,000	135	40
Government:	5,470	11,850	16,800	117	42
Federal	1,890	2,735	3,000	45	10
State and local	3,580	9,110	13,800	150	52

Note: Figures are not always exact because of rounding.
Source: The U.S. Economy in 1980, Bureau of Labor Statistics Bulletin 1673 (1970). The data for 1968 and 1980 are from Table A-16, p. 49. The figures for 1947 are adapted from chart data in Bulletin 1673 by Lawrence B. Krause.

vice-producing activity. The trend of increasing employment in services is well established, and the United States leads the other industrial nations of the world in the trend. This change in the structure of the economy is analogous to the earlier shift in employment from agriculture to manufacturing during the industrial revolution. The current change, although not as dramatic, will also have a pronounced effect on society. In particular, future operations managers will most likely be employed in the service industries rather than in manufacturing.

The preeminence of the professional and technical class Changes in the pattern of employment will have implications upon where and how people live, upon educational requirements, and consequently upon the kinds of organizations that will be important to society. Industrialization created the need for the semiskilled worker who could be trained in a few weeks to perform the routine tasks attending machines. The service economy has caused a shift to white-collar occupations in health, education, and government. In the United States, the year 1956 was a watershed. For the first time in the history of industrial society, the number of white-collar workers exceeded the number of blue-collar workers, and the gap is widening. The most interesting growth has been in the managerial and professional-technical fields, jobs that require a college education. Figure 1.2 shows a breakdown of employment by occupational groups. An educated member of the workforce has expectations for a job more challenging than that of the semiskilled worker. Those higher expectations have important implications for the design of service jobs.

The primacy of theoretical knowledge The coordination of machines and people for the production of goods was central to the industrial society. Postindustrial society, however, is structured around knowledge. In fact, the acquisition of knowledge has become a formal process called *research and development* (R&D). The leading manufacturing industries of today (computers, electronics, optics, and pharmaceuticals) are all dependent upon theoretical work prior to production. Of all the manufacturers in the twentieth century, United States Steel Corporation is representative of firms in the early years, General Motors dominated the fifties and sixties, and Internationa Business Machines represents the modern research-based firm. The contrasting attitudes these firms have toward R&D illustrate the emerging emphasis on theoretical knowledge. The interdependent and complex world of today requires the application of theory to all activities, from government planning to product innovation. Operations managers must be able to deal with abstract concepts in the decision-making process and to plan consciously for innovation.

The planning of technology A modern society depends upon technology and innovation to ward off stagnation, to increase productivity, and to create higher living standards. But advances in technology often have deleterious side effects, as evidenced by the once extensive use of DDT, a pesticide that saved

10 THE NATURE OF SERVICE OPERATIONS

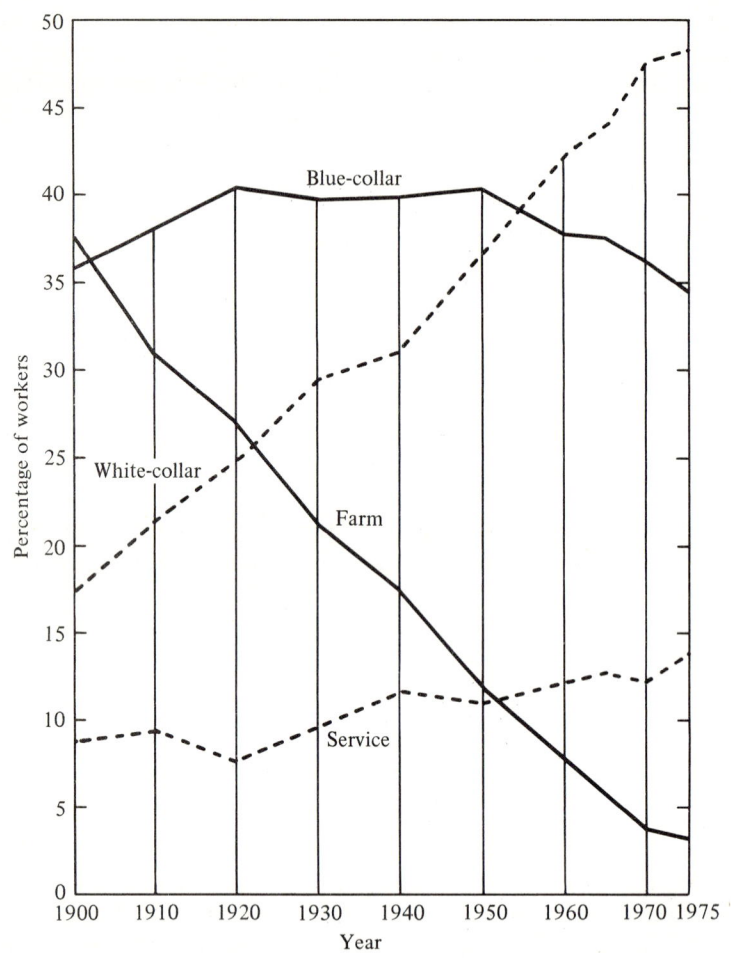

White-collar workers:
  Professional and technical
  Managers, officials, and proprietors
  Clerical and kindred
  Sales workers

Manual workers:
  Craftsmen and foremen
  Operatives
  Laborers, except farm and mine

Service workers:
  Private household workers
  Service, except private household

Farm workers:
  Farmers and farm managers
  Farm laborers and foremen

Figure 1.2 Occupational distribution of the labor force. [*Computed from Historical Statistics of the United States, Colonial Times to 1970, part 1, U.S. Department of Commerce and the Bureau of the Census, September 1975.*]

crops but destroyed wildlife in the process. For this reason, new technology is assessed before its introduction to identify possible second- or third-order consequences that are unintended. For example, before the banking industry introduces the concept of electronic funds transfers to replace checkbooks and credit cards, it must consider the effect it will have on eliminating *float*. Float is the dollar value of checks that have been written but not collected. From the consumer's viewpoint, float is a desirable feature of the present system. It represents an extension of credit because paper checks take days before they clear the banking system.

The rise of a new intellectual technology The management of organized complexity (the complexity of large organizations or social systems) is the challenge of the postindustrial society. The technology for assisting managers of large-scale systems, with many interacting variables, which must be coordinated to achieve specific goals, is available today. This intellectual technology is the marriage of the computer with problem-solving algorithms. These algorithms are logical steps, programmed for the computer to search out the best solutions to a problem. A search that might take days manually is accomplished in microseconds by the computer.

The modern operations manager needs to be comfortable using these new problem-solving tools because the systems of today are too complex to trust to intuition alone.

THE CHALLENGE FOR SERVICE OPERATIONS MANAGERS

The nature of postindustrial society creates many challenges for the service operations manager. Most importantly, the shift to employment in services has been accompanied by a substantial reduction in output per worker as compared with manufacturing or agriculture. Furthermore, much of the growing economic importance of services is attributable to the generally faster rate of price increases that has characterized services as compared with goods. Figure 1.3 illustrates the inflationary pressure of the service sector. An explanation lies in the productivity growth of the two sectors, goods and services; that is, the output per worker in the goods sector has increased more rapidly than the output per worker in the service sector. Productivity, often stated as output per worker, is a measure of economic efficiency. As labor is enhanced by machines (technology), skill (education), or organization (information), productivity increases. Figure 1.4 shows how productivity in the post office increased only marginally during the decade of the sixties because during this period mail was being delivered in much the same way year after year. However, during this period United States industry was introducing labor-saving machines and computer information processing systems. The result was substantial increases in output per industrial worker. Furthermore, postal services became highly inflationary during this per-

12 THE NATURE OF SERVICE OPERATIONS

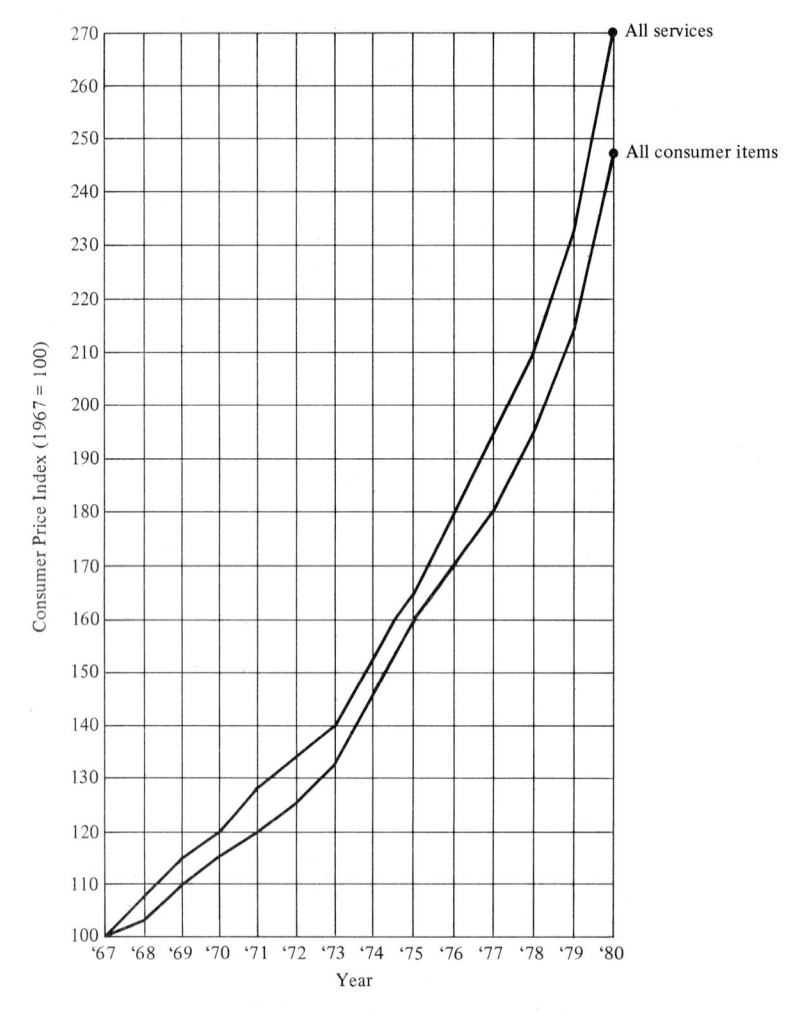

Figure 1.3 Cost of goods and services. [*Economic Report of the President, U.S. Government Printing Office, Washington, January 1981.*]

iod because the salaries of postal workers rose at rates even higher than those of the salaries of industrial workers, but with no corresponding increase in output.

Therein lies the challenge for service operations managers—to develop new management insights that will increase productivity in service organizations. Productivity will be increased in many ways, but the following three hold much promise. First, appropriate technology developed in manufacturing should be transferred to service operations. Examples are inventory control systems and techniques for process analysis. However, caution must be exercised in some areas, such as job design, because of the face-to-face contact with consumers. Second, the innovative use of computer-based information

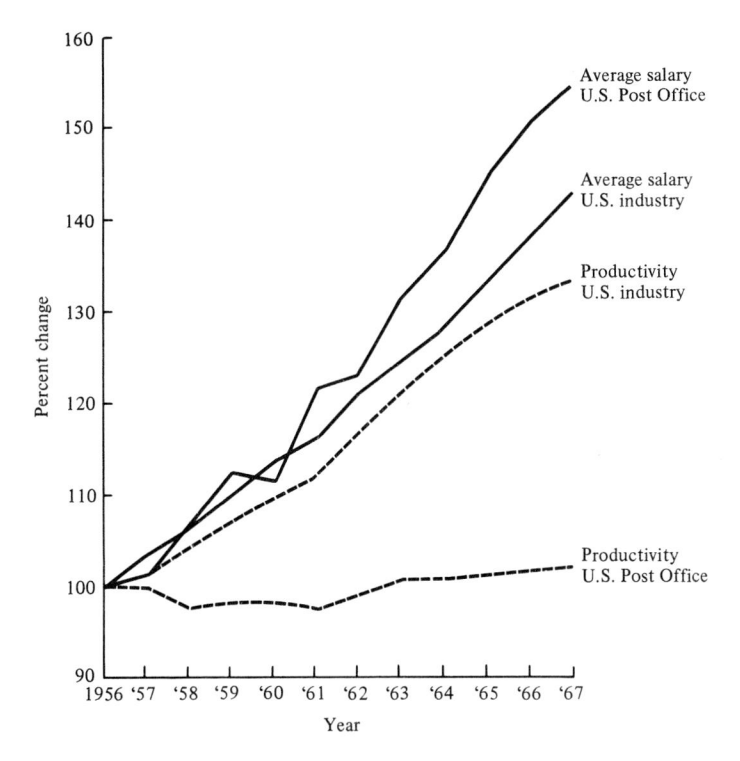

Figure 1.4 Comparison of average salary and productivity for United States industry and U.S. post office. [*Post office salary. Post Office Department Annual Report; Post Office productivity (weighted), Robert R. Nathan Associates; United States industry data, Economic Report of the President, February 1968. Reproduced from C. C. McBride, "Post Office Mail Processing Operations," in Analysis of Public Systems, A. W. Drake, R. L. Keeney, and P. M. Morse (eds.), MIT Press, Cambridge, Mass., 1972.*]

systems will be particularly important in services. These systems will be used both on-line, for example, as reservation systems, or off-line to perform analysis, such as considering sites for facility location. Finally, productivity can be enhanced by recognizing the consumer as a productive resource in the service process.

We believe that this challenge cannot be met by simply adapting the present product-oriented operations management techniques to a people-oriented endeavor. On the other hand, it is equally shortsighted to fall back on the misconception that hospitals (or other service organizations) are so unique as to be immune to the application of knowledge gained in the manufacturing sector. What is needed is a new perspective, in particular an enlarged system view that focuses on the unique characteristics of service organizations but, when appropriate, borrows from the knowledge gained in manufacturing over the past 100 years.

We will begin by considering the operations function in service organizations. The distinctive characteristics of service operations will suggest the critical problem of managing service capacity and the need to integrate the functions of marketing and operations in services. Also, from these distinctive characteristics we shall realize that all decisions are influenced by the role of the consumer as a participant in the service process.

TOPICS FOR DISCUSSION

1. Illustrate how a person's lifestyle is influenced by the type of work the person does. For example, contrast a farmer, factory worker, and social worker.
2. Is it possible for an economy to be based entirely on services?
3. Speculate on the nature of the society that may evolve from the postindustrial society.
4. Explain why a manager of a service operation may face a more complex and difficult task than a manager of a manufacturing operation.
5. Discuss the problems of measuring service productivity.
6. Give an example of how computers have been used effectively in a particular service.
7. Give an example of a service that uses the consumer as a productive resource.

SELECTED BIBLIOGRAPHY

Bell, Daniel: "Five Dimensions of Post-Industrial Society," *Social Policy*, vol. 4, no. 1, July–August 1973, pp. 103–110.
——: *The Coming of Post-Industrial Society: A Venture in Social Forecasting*, Basic Books, Inc., New York, 1973.
Clark, Colin: *The Conditions of Economic Progress*, 3d ed., The Macmillan Co., London, 1957.
Foote, Nelson N., and Paul K. Hatt: "Social Mobility and Economic Advancement," *American Economic Review*, May 1953, pp. 364–378.
Fuchs, Victor R.: *The Service Economy*, National Bureau of Economic Research, New York, 1968.
Gartner, Alan, and Frank Riessman: *The Service Society and the Consumer Vanguard*, Harper and Row Publishers, Inc., New York, 1975.
Gershung, J. I.: *After Industrial Society*, The Macmillan Co., New York, 1978.
Gersuny, C., and W. Rosengren: *The Service Society*, Schenkman Publishing Co., Cambridge, Mass., 1973.
Ginzberg, Eli, and George Vojta: "The Service Sector of the U. S. Economy," *Scientific American*, vol. 244, no. 3, March 1981, pp. 48–55.
Lewis, R.: *The New Service Society*, Longman, New York, 1973.
Ofer, Gus: *The Service Sector in Soviet Economic Growth: A Comparative Study*, Harvard University Press, Cambridge, Mass., 1973.
Service Industries: Trends and Prospects, U.S. Department of Commerce, Domestic and Industrial Business Administration, August, 1975.
Sorrentino, C.: "Comparing Employment Shifts in Ten Industrialized Countries," *Monthly Labor Review*, vol. 94, no. 10, October 1971, pp. 3–11.
Toffler, Alvin: *The Third Wave*, William Morrow and Co., Inc., New York, 1980.

CHAPTER
TWO

THE OPERATIONS FUNCTION IN SERVICE SYSTEMS

From the very beginning with the scientific management movement of Frederick W. Taylor, the roots of operations management were in the factory. The fundamental techniques of operations management, such as inventory control, scheduling, and quality control, result from problems confronted in the factory. How transferable are these techniques to the environment of service systems?

In this chapter we discuss the distinctive features of service operations that set these organizations apart from manufacturing. We feel the service environment is sufficiently different to question the naive application of traditional factory-based techniques to services. Ignoring the differences will result in failure. But more importantly the recognition of these special features will provide insights for enlightened and innovative managment. Advances in service operations management will only result from an appreciation of the service-system environment.

This appreciation begins with a realization that a service is a package of explicit and implicit benefits performed within a supporting facility and using facilitating goods. These multiple facets of a service operation are central to the design and control of a service delivery system. The service-package concept is introduced and example criteria for its evaluation are given. The distinctive characteristics of service operations are discussed in detail and the implications for management noted. On the basis of these characteristics the role of the service operations manager is viewed from an open-system perspective. That is, the service operations manager must deal with the environment because the system is not closed or isolated from the consumer, as in manufacturing. Because services are so heterogeneous, we begin with a scheme to classify services.

SERVICE CLASSIFICATION

Concepts of service operations management should be generally applicable to all service organizations. Unfortunately, service organizations are quite heterogeneous, which makes generalization difficult. A classification scheme can help organize our discussion of service operations.

Yeheskel Hasenfeld and Richard A. English developed a typology of human service organizations by considering their predominant functions and the types of clients served. Human service organizations can be seen either as people changing or as people processing. The authors define these organizational functions as follows:

> People-changing organizations attempt to alter directly the attributes or behavior of their clients through the application of various modification and treatment technologies. People-processing organizations, on the other hand, attempt to change their clients not by altering basic personal attributes, but by conferring upon them a public status and relocating them in a new set of social circumstances. They do so through the use of a classification-disposition system, which may define the clients, for example, as "acceptable for admission," "juvenile delinquent," or "underachiever."[1]

The nature of the clients served is based on their perceived functioning in society. Some organizations are charged with the role of maintaining and enhancing the well-being of people who are already functioning adequately. Other organizations are asked to ameliorate or remedy the ill or deviant state of people who are seen as malfunctioning in society or as requiring involuntary service.

To this typology we have added another dichotomy to include the services found in the marketplace. These services are referred to as facilitating services because typically they are used as a means to some end. For example, insurance is a means of reducing financial risk or perhaps a method of providing a comfortable retirement. From a consumer perspective, the facilitating service may be viewed as doing something for the consumer and human services as attempting to do something to the consumer. Figure 2.1 presents this service classification from a consumer perspective, together with a partial list of examples in each category.

THE SERVICE PACKAGE

Service operations managers have difficulty in identifying their product. This problem is partly due to the intangible nature of services. But it is the presence of the consumer in the process that creates a concern for the total service experience. Consider the following examples. For a restaurant the atmosphere is

---

[1] Yeheskel Hasenfeld and Richard A. English (eds.), *Human Service Organizations*, The University of Michigan Press, Ann Arbor, Mich., 1975, p. 5.

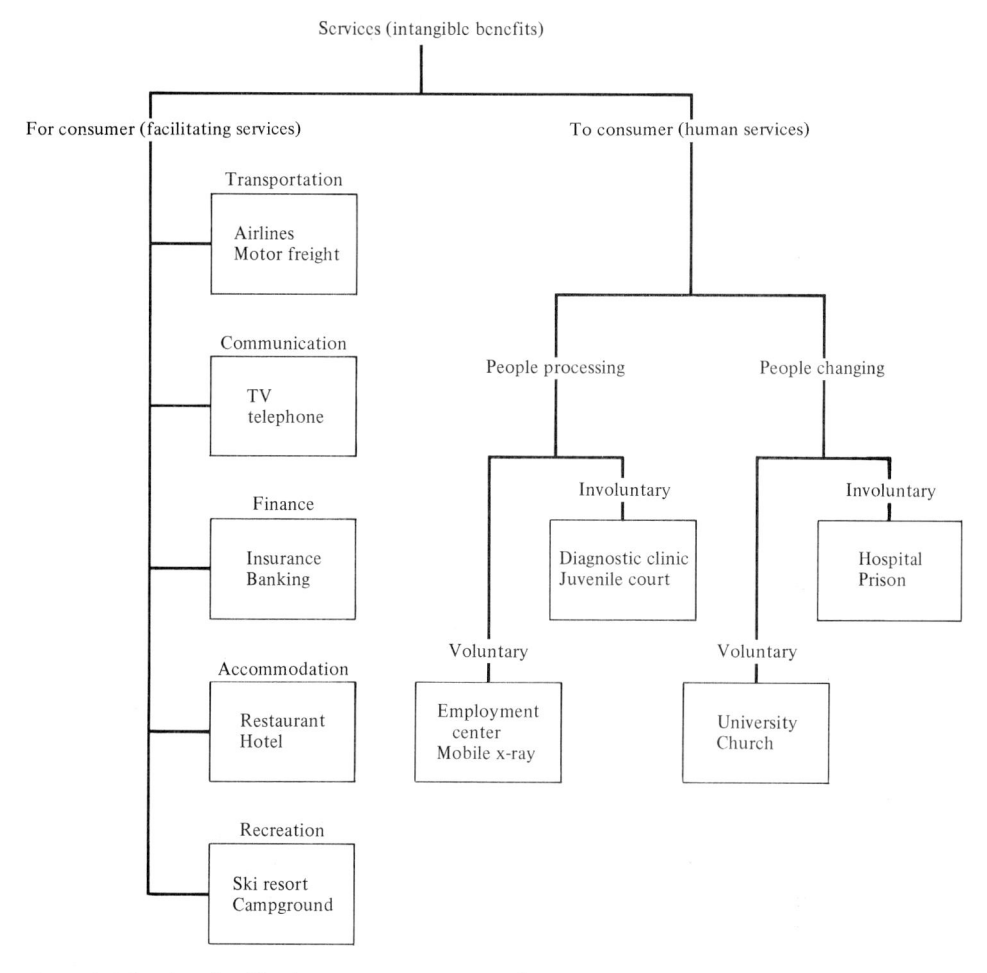

Figure 2.1 Service classification—consumer perspective.

just as important as the meal. For some diners the meal may be only a vehicle for getting together with friends. An opinion of a bank can be quickly formed on the basis of cheerfulness of a teller or on the length of the time waiting in line.

The service package is defined by a bundle of goods and services provided in some environment. This bundle consists of the following four features:

1. *Supporting facility*. The physical resources that must be in place before a service can be offered. Examples are a golf course, ski lift, hospital, or airplane.
2. *Facilitating goods*. The material purchased or consumed by the buyer or items provided by the consumer. Examples are golf clubs, skis, food items, replacement auto parts, legal documents, or medical supplies.
3. *Explicit services*. The benefits that are readily observable by the senses and

Table 2.1 Criteria for evaluating the service package

Supporting facility

1. *Architectural appropriateness:*
   Renaissance architecture for university campus.
   Unique recognizable feature of blue tile roof.
   Massive granite facade of downtown bank.
2. *Interior decorating:*
   Is the proper mood established?
   Quality and coordination of furniture.
3. *Facility layout:*
   Is there a natural flow of traffic?
   Are adequate waiting areas provided?
   Is there unnecessary travel or backtracking?
4. *Supporting equipment:*
   Does the dentist use a mechanical or air drill?
   What type and age aircraft does the charter airline use?

Facilitating goods

1. *Consistency:*
   Crispness of french fries.
   Portion control.
2. *Quantity:*
   Small, medium, or large pizza.
   Free checks.
3. *Selection:*
   Variety of replacement mufflers.
   Menu items available.
   Rental skis.

Explicit services

1. *Training of service personnel:*
   Is the auto mechanic NIASE certified?
      (National Institute for Automotive Service Excellence)
   To what extent are paraprofessionals used?
   Are the physicians trained in American medical schools?
2. *Comprehensiveness:*
   Fast-food restaurant compared with cafeteria.
   General hospital compared with neighborhood clinic.
   College vs. university.
   Motel with meeting rooms, restaurant, and swimming pool.
3. *Consistency:*
   Airline's on-time record.
   Professional Standards Review Organization (PSRO) for doctors.
4. *Availability:*
   Twenty-four-hour banking service.
   Location of fire stations.
   Access to unemployment office by public transportation.

Table 2.1 Criteria for evaluating the service package
(Continued)

Implicit services

1. *Attitude of service personnel:*
   Cheerful flight attendant.
   Police officer issuing traffic citation with tact.
   Surly service person in restaurant.
2. *Privacy and security:*
   Attorney advising client in attorney's office.
   Magnetic key card for motel room.
3. *Convenience:*
   Use of appointments.
   Free parking.
4. *Atmosphere:*
   Restaurant decor.
   Use of standardized forms.
   Sense of confusion rather than order.
5. *Waiting:*
   Joining a drive-in banking queue.
   Telephoning someone and being placed on hold.
   Enjoying a martini in the restaurant bar.
6. *Status:*
   College degree from Ivy League school.
   Box seats at sporting event.
7. *Sense of well-being:*
   Large commercial aircraft.
   Well-lighted parking lot.

that consist of the essential or intrinsic features of the service. Examples are the quality of instruction, smoothness of ride, or response time of the fire department.

4. *Implicit services.* Psychological benefits which the consumer may sense only vaguely or extrinsic features ancillary to the service. Examples are the status of a degree from an Ivy League school, privacy of a loan office, or worry-free auto repair.

The service package consists of the preceding four features, all of which are experienced by the consumer and form the basis of his or her perception of the service. It is important that the service operations manager offer a total experience for the consumer consistent with the desired service package. Take, for example, a budget hotel. The supporting facility is a concrete-block building with austere furnishings. Facilitating goods are reduced to the minimum of soap and paper. The explicit service is a comfortable bed in a clean room. Implicit services might include a swimming pool, black and white television, and a nearby restaurant. Deviations from this service package, such as adding bellhops, would destroy the bargain image. Table 2.1 contains a list of criteria for evaluating the service package.

The importance of the facilitating goods in the service package can be used to classify services across a continuum from pure services to various degrees of mixed services. For example, psychiatric counseling with no facilitating goods would be considered a pure service. Automobile maintenance usually contains more facilitating goods than a haircut. Making general statements about service operations management is difficult with such variations in the nature of services. However, the more important the facilitating good, the more like manufacturing the service operation becomes.

DISTINCTIVE CHARACTERISTICS OF SERVICE OPERATIONS

Many attempts have been made to define services. Consider for example the listing approach:

> Benefits or satisfactions which are offered for sale or are provided in connection with the sale of goods. Examples are amusements, hotel service, electric service, transportation, the services of barber shops and beauty shops, repair, and maintenance.

or a description:

> A service system is an organized system of apparatus, appliances, and/or employees for supplying some accommodation and activities required by the public or the performance of any duties or work for another.

or possibly a definition by exclusion:

> A market transaction by an enterprise or entrepreneur where the object of the market transaction is other than the transfer of ownership of a tangible commodity.

None of these approaches is satisfactory for an operations manager because nothing can be learned from them about the essential characteristics of a service. A study of service operations must begin with an understanding of the environment of service organizations.

In service operations a distinction must be made between inputs and resources. For services inputs are the customers themselves. Customers typically arrive at their own discretion with unique demands on the service system. Resources are the facilitating goods, labor, and capital at the command of the service manager. Thus, to function, the service system must interact with the customer input system. This view of service operations is necessary because of the characteristics of services. A discussion of the characteristics of services and their implications for operations management follows.

Consumer as a Participant in the Service Process

The presence of the consumer as a participant in the service process requires an attention to facility design that is not found in manufacturing. The fact that automobiles are made in a hot, dirty, noisy factory is of no concern to the eventual buyers. Contrast, however, the pleasant surroundings of the dealer's showroom. The presence of the consumer requires attention to the physical surroundings of the service facility. For the consumer, service is an experience conducted in the environment of the service facility. The quality of service is enhanced if the service facility is designed from the consumer's perspective. Attention to interior decorating, furnishings, layout, noise, and even color can influence the consumer's perception of the service. Compare the feelings invoked by picturing yourself in a stereotypical bus station with those picturing yourself in an airline terminal.

An important consideration in providing a service is the realization that the consumer can play an active part in the process. A few examples will illustrate that the knowledge, experience, motivation, and even honesty of the consumer directly affect the performance of the service system:

1. The popularity of supermarkets and discount stores is predicated on the fact that consumers are willing to assume an active role in the retailing process.
2. The accuracy of a patient's medical record can greatly influence the effectiveness of the attending physician.
3. The education of a student is determined largely by the student's own effort and contributions.

This strategy is best illustrated by the fast-food restaurants that have eliminated serving and cleaning-up personnel. The customer not only places the order directly from a limited menu but also is expected to clear the table after the meal. Naturally the customer expects faster service and less expensive meals to compensate for these inputs. However, the service provider benefits in many subtle ways. First of all there are fewer personnel to supervise and to pay fringe benefits to. But more importantly the customer provides the input just at the moment it is required; thus, capacity to serve varies more directly with demand rather than being fixed. Therefore, the service provider can employ customer labor to achieve higher utilization of capacity.

In an educated society, such as in the United States where self-reliance is valued, this strategy has received great acceptance. The consumer, instead of being a passive buyer, becomes a contributor to the gross national product.

Production and Consumption Occur Simultaneously

The fact that services are consumed and created simultaneously and, thus, cannot be stored is a critical feature in the management of service operations. The inability to inventory services precludes using the traditional manufacturing strategy of relying on inventory as a buffer to absorb fluctuations in demand. Inventory for a manufacturer serves as a convenient system boundary, separating internal operations of planning and control from the external environment. Thus, the manufacturing facility can be operated at a constant level of output that is most efficient. The factory is operated as a closed system, with inventory decoupling the productive system and consumer demand. Services operate as open systems, with the full impact of demand variations transmitted to the system.

Inventory can also be used to decouple the stages in a manufacturing process. For services the decoupling is achieved through customer waiting. Inventory control is a major issue in manufacturing operations; in service operations the corresponding problem is customer waiting or queuing. The problems of selecting service capacity, facility utilization, and use of idle time are all balanced against customer waiting time.

The simultaneous production and consumption also eliminate many opportunities for quality control intervention. Unlike manufacturing, where the product is inspected before delivery, services must rely upon other measures to ensure the consistency of output. Limiting the discretion of service employees through the use of standard procedures is one possibility.

Time Perishable Capacity

A service is a perishable commodity. Consider an empty airline seat, a hospital bed not used, or an hour without a patient in the day of a dentist. In each case an opportunity loss has occurred. Because a service cannot be stored, it is lost forever when not used. The utilization of service capacity would not be a problem, if only demand were constant. Alas, this is hardly the case. The demand for services is just as, or more, variable than that for products.

Consumer demand for service typically exhibits cyclic behavior with considerable variation between the peaks and valleys. The custom of eating lunch between noon and 1 p.m. places a real burden on restaurants to accommodate the noon rush. The practice of day-end mailing by business contributes to the fact that 60 percent of all letters are received at the post office between 4 and 8 p.m.[2] The demand for emergency medical service in Los Angeles was found to vary from a low of 0.5 calls per hour at 6 a.m. to a peak of 3.5 calls per hour at 6 p.m.[3] This peak-to-valley ratio of 7 to 1 was also true for fire alarms during an average day in New York City.[4]

For recreational and transportation services, seasonal variation in demand

---

[2] R. C. Cohen, R. McBridge, R. Thornton, and T. White, *Letter Mail System Performance Design: An Analytical Method for Evaluating Candidate Mechanization,* Report R-168, Institute for Defense Analysis, Washington, D. C., 1970.

[3] James A. Fitzsimmons, "The Use of Spectral Analysis to Validate Planning Models," *Socio-Economic Planning Sciences,* vol. 8, no. 3, June 1974, pp. 123–128.

[4] E. H. Blum, *Urban Fire Protection: Studies of the Operations of the New York City Fire Department,* R-681, New York City Rand Institute, New York, January 1971.

creates surges in activity. Flights from New York City to Miami are often booked months in advance for the Christmas holidays.

Faced with variable demand and a perishable capacity to provide the service, the operations manager has three basic options:

1. Smooth demand by:
    a. Using reservations or appointments
    b. Using price incentives (e.g., giving telephone discounts for evening and weekend calls)
    c. Demarketing peak times (e.g., advertising "Shop early and avoid the Christmas rush.")
2. Adjust service capacity by:
    a. Using part-time help during peak hours
    b. Scheduling workshifts to vary workforce needs to demand (e.g., telephone companies staff their operators to match call demand)
    c. Increasing the consumer self-service content of the service
3. Allow customers to wait

This last option can be viewed as a passive consumer contribution to the service process. By waiting, the consumer permits greater utilization of service capacity. The airlines explicitly recognize this by charging standby passengers a reduced price for their tickets.

Site Selection Dictated by Location of Consumers

There are no distribution channels in the traditional sense for services. The consumer and provider are brought together for a service to be performed. Either the consumer comes to the service facility (restaurant) or the service provider goes to the consumer (ambulance service). Of course, there are exceptions; banking by mail and university courses offered via television are examples. In fact, opportunities for innovation in service systems abound in this area.

The time and cost of travel is reflected in the economics of site selection. The result is many small service centers located close to prospective consumers. Of course, the tradeoff is between the fixed cost of the facility and the travel costs of the consumers. The more expensive the facility, the larger or more densely populated must be the market area. For example, many a major-league baseball team has had trouble surviving in a medium-size city.

The resulting small size of operation and the multisite locations of services create several management challenges.

Economies of scale limited Sizing a service operation to its immediate geographical market area removes the opportunity to gain economies of scale found in manufacturing. Manufactured products are distributed to consumers. The distribution of products permits the construction of large facilities with high-volume processes to achieve low unit costs. However, some franchised food services have centralized many of their common functions (e.g., purchasing, advertising, and food preparation) to achieve similar economies of scale.

Control of decentralized operations Unlike manufacturing, services are performed in the field, not in the controlled environment of a factory. For fast-food restaurants control can be achieved by limiting the discretion of employees. Discretion is limited by prepacking the servings, designing special equipment (e.g., a french-fry scoop that measures the portion), and serving only a few items. More sophisticated services, such as health care, must rely on extensive training, licensing, and peer review.

For services that travel out to the customer (e.g., telephone installers, delivery services, maintenance, and repair) the problems of routing, dispatching, and scheduling become important.

Labor Intensiveness

In service organizations, labor is the important resource that determines the effectiveness of the organization. Not unlike manufacturing, services have a problem of technological obsolescence. However, it is the skills of the labor force that age as new knowledge makes current skills obsolete. In an expanding organization, recruitment of new labor provides some of the benefits of the new knowledge. However, in a slow-growth or stable organization in which seniority is important, the only successful strategy may be continuous retraining. The problem of aging labor skills is particularly acute in the professional service organization, where extensive formal education is a prerequisite to employment.

The interaction between consumer and employee in services creates the possibility of a more complete human work experience. The personal nature of services is in stark contrast to the depersonalization of work found in manufacturing. In services work activity is people- rather than thing-oriented. Even the introduction of automation may strengthen personalization by eliminating the relatively routine impersonal tasks and thereby permitting increased personal attention to the remaining work. However, personal attention creates opportunities for variability in the service provided. This is not inherently bad unless consumers perceive significant quality variation. A consumer expects to be treated fairly and given the same service others receive. The development of standards and employee training in proper procedures is the key to ensuring consistency in service provided. It is rather impractical to monitor the output of each employee except via customer complaints.

The direct consumer-employee contact has implications for industrial (service) relations as well. Auto workers with grievances against the firm have been known to sabotage the product on the assembly line. Hopefully, the final inspection will ensure that any such cars are corrected before delivery. However, a disgruntled service employee can do irreparable harm to the organization because the employee is the firm's sole contact with consumers. The service operations manager thus is concerned about the employees' attitudes as well as their performance. J. Willard Marriott, founder of the Marriott Hotel chain, has said, "in the service business you can't make happy guests with unhappy employees."[5] Through training and genuine concern for employee welfare, the organizational goals can be internalized.

Intangibility

Services are ideas and concepts; products are things. It follows that service innovations are not patentable. To secure the benefits of a novel service concept, the firm must expand extremely rapidly and preempt competitors. Franchising has been the vehicle to secure market areas and establish a brand name. Franchising allows the parent firm to sell its idea to a local entrepreneur while retaining some control.

The intangible nature of services also presents a problem for consumers. When buying a product the consumer is able to see, feel, and test its performance before purchase. For a service the consumer must rely upon the reputation of the service firm. In many service areas the government has intervened to guarantee minimal service performances. Through the use of registration, licensing, and regulation, the government can assure consumers that the training and test performance of some service providers meet certain standards. Thus, we find that public construction plans must be approved by a registered professional engineer, a doctor must be licensed to practice medicine, and the telephone company is a regulated utility. However, in its efforts ostensibly to protect the consumer, the government may be stifling innovation, raising barriers to entry, and generally reducing competition.

Difficulty in Measuring Output

Measuring the output of a service organization is a frustrating task for several reasons. For example, counting the number of customers served is seldom useful because it does not account for the quality of service performed. The problem of measurement is further complicated by the fact that many service systems do not have a single important criterion, such as maximizing profit, upon which to base an evaluation of their performance. More importantly, can a system's performance be based on evaluating output alone when this assumes a homogeneous input? A more definitive evaluation of service performance is a measure of the change in each consumer from input to output state, a process known as transactional analysis.

---

[5] G. M. Hostage, "Quality Control in a Service Business," *Harvard Business Review*, vol. 53, no. 4, July–August 1975, pp. 98–106.

AN OPEN-SYSTEMS VIEW OF
SERVICE OPERATIONS

Clearly, service organizations are sufficiently unique in their structure to require more than simple adaptation of production management techniques to achieve effective management results. The distinctive characteristics suggest enlarging the system view to include the input process in the service management system. Generally the input process has been considered outside of the operations management system as part of the uncontrolled environment, even when its influence on the performance of the system is substantial. We begin our discussion of this view of services with some brief system definitions.

Systems A group of interrelated elements forming a collective entity.

The distinction between a closed and open system depends upon how one views the environment.

Closed systems A closed system is a system that has no environment; that is, no outside systems impinge significantly upon it. Nonliving systems, such as electromechanical devices, are closed systems.

Open systems An open system is one that has an environment; that is, it contains other systems with which it relates, exchanges, and communicates. All living systems including organizations are open systems.

From the above discussion a definition of service operations emerges.

Service operations A service operation is an open transformation process of converting inputs (consumers) to desired outputs (satisfied consumers) through the appropriate application of resources (facility, material, labor, information, and the consumer as well).

This open-systems view of service operations is illustrated in Figure 2.2. We see the role of the service operations manager includes the functions of both production and marketing.

When considering service operations, the traditional separation of the production and marketing functions, with inventory as the interface, is neither possible nor appropriate. Marketing will perform two important functions in controlling the input: (1) educating the consumer to play a role as an active participant in the service process and (2) promoting smoothing of demand to match service capacity. Several strategies that might accomplish demand smoothing are: (1) giving economic incentives (e.g., telephone-company rate structure), (2) appealing to convenience (e.g., making appointments for haircuts to avoid customer waiting), and (3) demarketing peak hours (e.g., giving

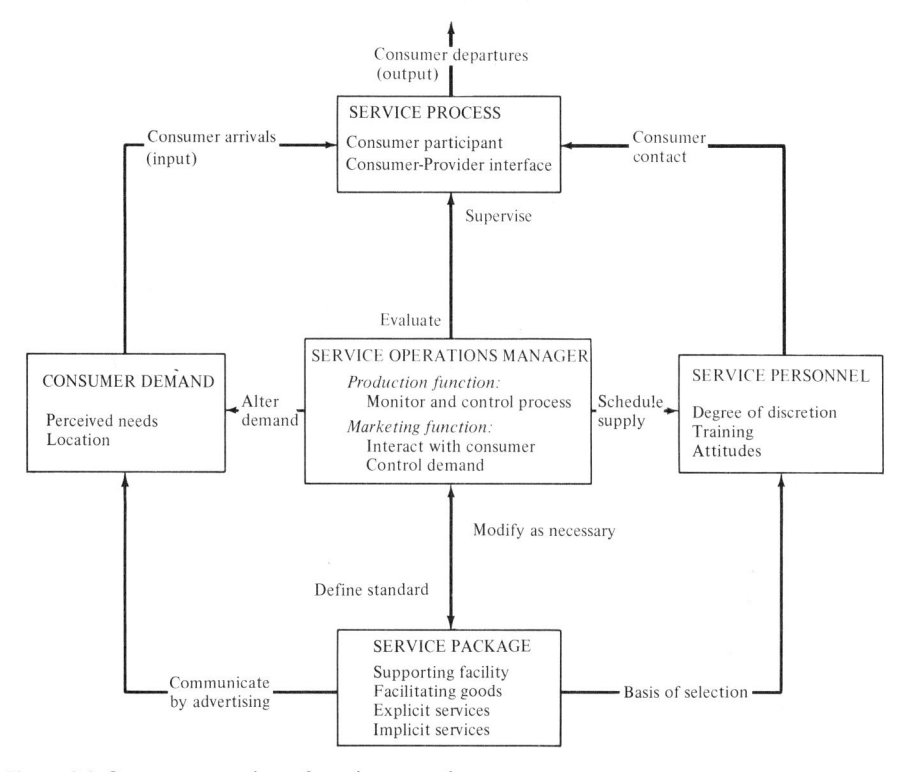

```
                    Consumer departures
                         (output)
                    ┌──────────────────┐
                    │ SERVICE PROCESS  │
    Consumer arrivals│ Consumer participant │ Consumer
        (input)     │ Consumer-Provider interface │ contact
                    └──────────────────┘
                         Supervise

                         Evaluate
                ┌────────────────────────────┐
 CONSUMER DEMAND│ SERVICE OPERATIONS MANAGER │  SERVICE PERSONNEL
                │ Production function:       │
 Perceived needs│  Monitor and control process│ Schedule  Degree of discretion
 Location       │ Marketing function:        │  supply   Training
                │  Interact with consumer    │          Attitudes
                │  Control demand            │
                └────────────────────────────┘

                     Modify as necessary

                     Define standard
                    ┌──────────────────┐
                    │  SERVICE PACKAGE │
     Communicate   │ Supporting facility │
     by advertising│ Facilitating goods  │ Basis of selection
                   │ Explicit services   │
                   │ Implicit services   │
                    └──────────────────┘
```

Figure 2.2 Open-systems view of service operations.

triple stamps on Wednesdays). By necessity the operations and marketing functions are merged into one for service organizations.

For services, the process is the product. The presence of the consumer in the service process negates the closed-system perspective taken in manufacturing. Techniques to control operations in an isolated factory producing a tangible good are inadequate for services. No longer is the process machine-paced and the output easily measured for compliance with specifications. Instead consumers arrive with different demands on the service. Service employees interact directly with the consumer, with little opportunity for management intervention.

Furthermore, consumer impressions of service quality are based on the total service experience, not just on the explicit service performed. A concern for employee attitudes and training becomes a necessity in service systems to ensure service quality. The entire service process, when viewed from the consumer perspective, raises concerns ranging from the aesthetic design of the facility to pleasant diversions in waiting areas.

An open-system concept of services also allows one to view the consumer as a resource. Permitting the consumer to participate actively in the service process can be a method of increasing productivity.

SUMMARY

The management of an open system requires different techniques and sensitivities from those of a closed system. Service managers are faced with nonroutine operations, with only indirect control possible. In services it is the human element which is central to effective operations. For example, the unavoidable interaction between service provider and consumer is a source of great opportunity, as in direct selling. However, this interaction can seldom be fully controlled and, thus, service quality may suffer. For this reason, in service organizations the attitude and appearance of service personnel are important considerations. For services the presence of the consumer in the process materially alters what is viewed as the product. The unique characteristics of intangibility, perishability, and simultaneous provision and consumption introduce special challenges for operations management. In many respects the service operations manager adopts a style of management different from that of his manufacturing counterpart.

TOPICS FOR DISCUSSION

1. Is the United States becoming a self-service, or do-it-yourself, economy? What are the implications for society?
2. Classify service systems by the extent of required customer contact in the performance of the service. What are the operations management implications?
3. In what ways would the management style of a service operations manager differ from that of a manufacturing manager?
4. What are some possible measures of performance for a fire department? For a fast-food restaurant?
5. Are economies of scale possible in services?
6. Take some service you are familiar with and identify the seven "distinctive characteristics of service operations" for this service.
7. What factors are important for a manager to consider when attempting to enhance the service organization's image?
8. Service systems are generally more open than manufacturing systems. What are the underlying causes of this difference?

SELECTED BIBLIOGRAPHY

Blum, E. H.: *Urban Fire Protection: Studies of the Operations of the New York City Fire Department,* R-681, New York City Rand Institute, New York, January 1971.

Cohen, R. C., R. McBridge, R. Thornton, and T. White: *Letter Mail System Performance Design: An Analytical Method for Evaluating Candidate Mechanization,* Report R-168, Institute for Defense Analysis, Washington D. C., 1970.

Fitzsimmons, James A.: "The Use of Spectral Analysis to Validate Planning Models," *Socio-Economic Planning Sciences,* vol. 8, no. 3, June 1974, pp. 123–128.

Fuchs, Victor R.: *The Service Economy,* National Bureau of Economic Research, New York, 1968.

Gartner, Alan, and Frank Riessman: *The Service Society and the Consumer Vanguard,* Harper and Row, Publishers, Inc., New York, 1974.

Hasenfeld, Yeheskel, and Richard A. English (eds.): *Human Service Organizations,* The University of Michigan Press, Ann Arbor, Mich., 1975.

Hostage, G. M.: "Quality Control in a Service Business," *Harvard Business Review,* vol. 53, no. 4, July–August, 1975, pp. 98–106.

Sasser, Earl W., Paul R. Olsen, and Daryl D. Wyckoff: *Management of Service Operations,* Allyn and Bacon, Inc., Boston, 1978.

van Gigch, John P.: *Applied General Systems Theory,* 2d ed., Harper and Row, Publishers, New York, 1978.

PART TWO

DECISION MODELS FOR SERVICE OPERATIONS

CHAPTER
THREE

EVALUATION OF SERVICE OPERATIONS

Evaluation is the process of judging the value or worth of some thing or some activity. In the marketplace the values of goods or services are reflected in their prices. But what is the value of public education, national defense, or vaccination against a communicable disease? These services are not exchanged in the marketplace, and, thus, no price is established for their worth. Only their cost is known. These examples also illustrate a particular feature of public goods: when one person consumes more, others need not consume less because it is a collective good. For example, in the case of vaccination the entire community benefits, not just the person treated. The goal of public policy is to adopt programs and services which generate the greatest surplus of benefits over costs.

Cost-benefit analysis is a formal and systematic approach for the evaluation of public projects. Direct and indirect benefits of a project are translated into dollars. The present value of the stream of benefits is compared with the program costs to measure the economic worth of the project. Programs can then be ranked and funded on the basis of their net present value. Cost-benefit analysis is the evaluation system that is the most widely used in practice and is fully explored later in this chapter.

Evaluation systems are built on the systems concept:

Objectives are defined for the program.
The system's boundary is identified.
The focus is on program outputs or results.
The performance is quantified.
Models are used to relate inputs to outputs.

The systems concept is both an orientation and an ideal that are difficult to achieve in reality. A future projection of system performance is really a probability distribution. Many benefits are difficult to quantify, let alone to be given a dollar value (e.g., the loss of life). An evaluation system such as cost-benefit analysis is not an exact science, but the process does focus the debate on issues of substance.

Cost-benefit analysis need not be limited to the public sector. Many private-sector programs fall outside the marketplace: for example, expenses for the annual picnic, advertising to improve the corporate image, or financial support of the United States Olympic team. Finally, cost-benefit analysis need not be restricted to program investment decisions. Cost-benefit analysis can be used in an operational setting to evaluate program continuation or termination. In fact, a variation of cost-benefit analysis called *zero-based budgeting* requires that every program be rejustified on an annual basis.

The process of evaluation is first discussed in general by considering possible objectives of evaluation. These objectives range from consumer protection to rationalizing a course of action. A program to establish an evaluation system is discussed next, in which cost-benefit analysis may be only one of several techniques that could be selected for the program analysis phase. Cost-benefit analysis is examined and compared with cost effectiveness. The time value of money is discussed and procedures for calculating the present value of future dollars are developed. The procedure for conducting a cost-benefit analysis is developed and illustrated by a cost-benefit study and a cost-effectiveness analysis.

THE EVALUATION PROCESS

The process of evaluation results in choices being made. Assessments of alternative courses of action are made to determine their ability to meet desired goals. Evaluation need not be limited to the study of alternative proposals, but can be focused on an operating service system to determine if it is meeting the planned objectives. Evaluation is different from quality control, which is a process to ensure consistency in output. Evaluation is the cornerstone of planning and of making judgments on how best to achieve goals.

Objectives of Evaluation

Many situations can arise that call for the evaluation of service operations. Evaluations are performed to aid the design phase, to rationalize courses of action, and to provide consumer protection in public services.

Service system design Cost effectiveness, a variation of cost-benefit analysis, has been used in the design of emergency medical systems to determine the number of emergency vehicles needed to serve a community. Essentially vehicles are added to the fleet until the incremental cost does not provide sufficient incremental benefit.[1] Cost-benefit analysis was first conceived a a method to justify capital expenditures for water projects, such as dams and locks. A similar analysis can also be used to justify discontinuing services. In both cases all the benefits created by the project are not obvious and translating the benefits into dollars is a creative process.

Rationalize courses of action Evaluation aids decision making by scoring alternative proposals for comparison and eventual selection. But more importantly, evaluation forces the decision maker to demonstrate how a particular alternative will produce the desired results. The formal evaluation process focuses on explicit details, such as assumptions, projections, and supporting data. A cost-benefit study contains many judgments that should be reviewed by others, perhaps disinterested parties.

Once an alternative is chosen for implementation, the cost-benefit justification can be used to evaluate its progress. If the expected benefits are not forthcoming or if costs become excessive, then termination can be considered before all capital is committed. Dam projects have recently come under close scrutiny, and several partially constructed dams have been abandoned because the anticipated benefits were questionable.

Consumer protection The intangible nature of services makes it difficult for consumers to judge their worth. Unlike products that can be seen and touched to establish quality, many services are purchased on faith. The potential for abuse is great. Thus, either the government or professional groups themselves have established minimum standards of professional conduct, performance, and education required to be considered competent to deliver the service. For example, physicians must be licensed to practice medicine, professional engineers must be registered to approve the plans for public structures, and public accountants must be certified to audit the financial accounts of organizations. This concern for minimal competency extends beyond the traditional professions to include nearly all service purveyors, from lawyers to barbers.

The evaluation process consists of updating and administering examinations and, through peer review, revoking the license to practice of those who fail to maintain professional standards. A hidden cost of this evaluation system is the stifling of innovation and the creation of a barrier to entry. The loss of competition that results does contribute to the high cost of services.

A very different approach to consumer protection is used by many hospitals. A computer processing service collects data from similar hospitals across the nation. Measures of activity, such as the number of caesarean sections performed, are calculated and compared with those from other hospitals to iden-

---

[1] James A. Fitzsimmons and Robert S. Sullivan, "Establishing the Level of Service for Public Emergency Ambulance Systems," *Socio-Economic Planning Sciences,* vol. 13, no. 5, September 1979, pp. 235–239.

tify deviations from the norm. Administrators are thus alerted to the possibility of excessive surgery by the medical staff. Of course, reasonable explanations may exist for these deviations, but the evaluation process raises the questions. This approach is similar to quality control systems discussed in Chapter 16, except, in this case, the service is compared with those of other providers rather than to internal standards.

Establishing the Evaluation System

An evaluation system requires careful design, with the participation of the consumers and producers of the service. In this way agreement can be reached concerning objectives of the service and the criteria for measuring performance. Figure 3.1 contains a flowchart of the steps in developing an evaluation system. Perhaps the most important step is "Evaluation System Review," which reflects the dynamic nature of an open-service delivery system that must adapt to environmental changes to survive. The evaluation system must keep pace with changes in system objectives and performance criteria, for example, the changing concerns for environmental protection and the changing social agenda represented by affirmative action programs. Each step in the evaluation system will be described in turn.

Define the system boundary The environment is comprised of external conditions that are assumed to be given because they are not under the control of the decision maker. The boundary that separates the system from the environment is thus defined in terms of control. Marketing tells us that the success of a firm is determined in part by its ability to influence the environment. Advocates of systems thinking encourage us to push back the boundaries of the system in order to consider the problem at a higher level, or total-systems view. The total-systems view enlarges the scope of study to include more alternatives for consideration. For example, if transportation planners concentrate on highway construction to the exclusion of other modes of travel, they would never consider innovations such as piggyback rail systems (i.e., hauling truck trailers long distances on railcars). Of course, there is a limit to pushing back the boundary because the total system may eventually become too complex for comprehension. But too narrow a system definition handicaps imaginative thinking.

Identify system objectives Setting objectives is inextricably tied to the definition of system boundaries. For example, our transportation planner, who is trying to relieve traffic congestion with a limited view of the world, might feel the objective is finding the best route for a new freeway. An expanded-system view would suggest the objective of providing quick and safe transportation for commuters.

Who is the client? This is an important question when considering the system objectives. In fact, there are usually many clients with different goals. Con-

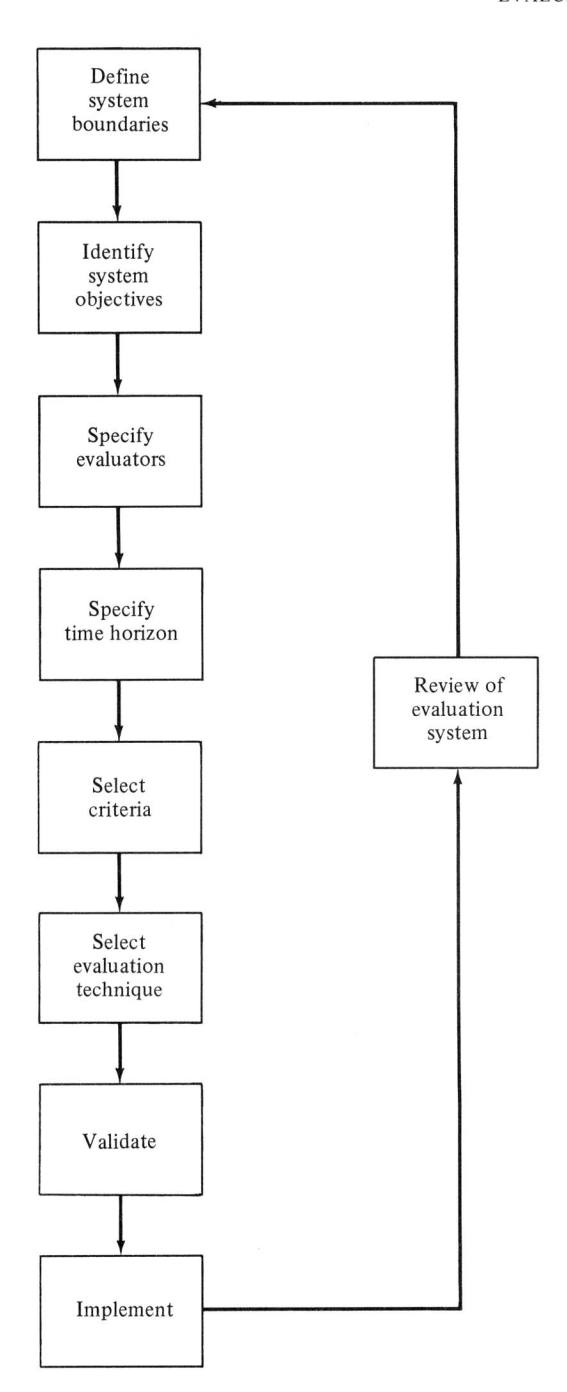

Figure 3.1 Evaluation system paradigm.

sider a prison. Possible clients include the prisoners, guards, criminal justice system, and society at large. These clients have different and conflicting goals. For example, the prisoners may be interested in rehabilitation, the guards in the working conditions, the criminal justice system in recidivism, and society in protection.

Because of these concerns, developing system objectives can be facilitated by consumer involvement. In the public sector this is accomplished by appointing citizen representatives to serve, for example, on urban planning commissions and hospital boards.

Specify the evaluators Selecting the evaluators is dependent upon the purpose of the evaluation system. For system design, the planners themselves and their supervisors will conduct the evaluation. A review of proposed projects is usually conducted by bodies with fiscal responsibility, such as boards of directors or the U.S. Office of Management and Budget. Consumer protection activities must be performed by external evaluation. Consultants are often used in this capacity because they are able to make comparisons with other similar clients and can act as disinterested parties.

Specify the time horizon The period of evaluation can range from an ongoing effort of monitoring performance in the quality control sense to the ad hoc blue-ribbon committee investigating some accident. Periodic evaluations are more common, such as educational accreditation, professional relicensing, and military readiness exercises.

Select criteria Criteria for evaluating system performance must first of all be consistent with the desired objectives. An example from the Soviet Union illustrates the problems that can arise. Five-year production plans for the manufacture of pipe in the U.S.S.R. are stated in tons. Thus, we find no incentive to develop plastic pipe as a substitute for cast iron, although it has superior properties. The criteria selected must also be credible to the organizational members if they are to provide motivation and incentive. Criteria that are measurable are preferred to such judgmental characteristics as clean and pleasant. For services multiple criteria are very appropriate. However, using several measures of performance complicates any attempt to make judgments and comparisons. The problem of aggregating these measures is referred to as multiattribute utility theory.

Select evaluation technique The more sophisticated the evaluation technique is, the greater the need for extensive data. A naive approach may be taken initially and updated later as data become available. Or a simple technique like cost-effectiveness analysis may be chosen because the evaluator is unwilling to place a dollar value on human life. Elaborate techniques also cost more to implement and usually take more time to complete. The major determinants become data availability, budget, and time.

Validation The success of the evaluation system is judged in several ways.

1. *Appropriateness.* Is the system adequate to do the intended job?
2. *Acceptability.* Does the client use the system?
3. *Accuracy.* Does the system measure performance and make predictions within acceptable tolerances?
4. *Timeliness.* Are the results of the evaluation current enough to influence decision making?
5. *Effectiveness.* Does the evaluation help the organization meet its goals?

Implementation Involvement of the client is important for successful implementation. Implementation is a function of the relationship between the two parties involved. The ingredients of this relationship are captured by a concept of "trust" discussed by C. W. Churchman and A. H. Schainblatt.[2] Trust exists when:

1. The two parties have faith in each other's recommendations.
2. Each party is sensitive to the motivation, aspirations, and values of the other party.
3. Each party understands its own decision-making process as well as that of the opposite side.
4. The "implementor" is involved in the formulation of goals in order that the recommendations and programs bear a relationship to the needs of the recipients.
5. The recipients are involved in the preparation of the plans and programs so that they bear a relation to the recipients' perceptions of needs and scales of values.
6. The agent promoting change is capable of placing himself or herself in the position of the recipients and of thinking like them.

This implementation strategy above could be labeled *mutual understanding,* as differentiated from the common strategies of persuasion or communication.

COST-BENEFIT ANALYSIS

Perhaps the most widely used evaluation technique is *cost-benefit analysis.* Initially developed to evaluate water resource projects, the analysis is now used throughout government and in the corporate world. As the name implies, the technique is an economic analysis of a program's projected costs and benefits that allows decision makers to evaluate the worth of capital expenditures.

---

[2] C. W. Churchman and A. H. Schainblatt, "The Researcher and the Manager: A Dialectic of Implementation," *Management Science,* vol. 11, no. 4, December 1965, pp. B69–B87.

A related concept called *cost effectiveness* is very similar to cost-benefit analysis, but some important distinctions exist. Cost effectiveness has its roots in the military, where it was used to evaluate alternative weapon systems. The term "cost effective" has become synonymous with the concept of technological efficiency.

Cost-Benefit Analysis and Cost Effectiveness Compared

Cost-benefit analysis is concerned with measuring the economic efficiency of proposed projects. Expected benefits are converted to dollars and compared with the proposed cost of the project. Dividing the benefit by the cost, the benefit-cost ratio, yields a measure that can be used in making comparisons. Only projects resulting in a benefit-cost ratio greater than 1 are considered economically justified. Thus, at the very least, cost-benefit analysis can eliminate from further consideration projects that cannot pay their own way. More importantly, projects with different objectives can be compared on the relative merit of their economic contribution. Thus, a decision maker with a limited budget can allocate funds across different departments to those projects that generate the greatest amount of benefit per dollar.

Cost effectiveness serves a different purpose because it begins with a given objective and proceeds to calculate the costs of alternative ways of achieving this goal. Thus, cost effectiveness is limited to making comparisons among different ways of reaching some objective. However, the problem of converting benefits to dollars is avoided because effectiveness can be measured in nonmonetary terms, such as lives saved. Cost effectiveness also gives no assurance that a proposal is economically justified, only that the proposal selected is an efficient approach to achieving the objective desired.

These distinctions can be made clear with a simple example. Suppose the drug Dilantin has just become available and will allow an epileptic person to work and earn $50 per day. If a daily dosage costs $10 and the person would be unable to work without it, the benefit-cost ratio is 50 divided by 10 ($=5$). From an economic standpoint, the investment is clearly justified by the benefit. Instead, consider the objective of providing a day of good health for the epileptic person to be used in any manner desired, not just working. A cost-effectiveness ratio for the drug Dilantin would be one day divided by $10 ($=0.1$). The ratio would have the units "days of good health per dollar." Now it is a matter of subjective judgment whether or not the benefit is worth the cost.

For purposes of analysis, cost effectiveness can be considered a version of cost-benefit analysis in which benefits are not converted to dollars. Thus, the following discussion will not distinguish between the two approaches.

Time Value of Money

If invested in a 10 percent simple-interest-bearing account, $1 today is worth $1.10 one year from now. Present dollars are worth more than future dollars because money has a time value. The interest that money earns is payment for postponing the opportunity for current use of the money. Because the benefits $1 can buy must be forgone for one year, $1 promised one year from now is not as valuable as $1 today. However, if 10 percent interest is a good measure of this lost opportunity, then approximately $0.91 now is equivalent to $1 one year hence.

This attitude towards money precludes direct comparison of dollars received or spent at different time periods. To deal with this problem, a process called *present-value analysis* is performed, in which future dollars are brought back to the present time by the use of an agreed upon interest, or discount, rate. Future dollars are thus reduced in value, or discounted.

Single-payment present worth If interest is reinvested, then a principal amount P will yield a future total sum S in n years at i interest rate per year according to the following compound-interest formula.

$$S = P(1 + i)^n \qquad (1)$$

Solving for P, we can determine the present value of a sum S to be paid in n years:

$$P = \frac{S}{(1 + i)^n} \qquad (2)$$

The term $1/(1 + i)^n$ is referred to as the *single-payment present worth factor* SP_{PW} that, multiplied by a future sum S, makes it equivalent to a present sum P. These factors tabulated for a number of possible discount factors and years are found in Table A at the back of the book.

Example 3.1: Single-payment present worth calculations The following diagram shows a number of future payments. Assuming the payments are received at the end of the year as shown, determine the total present value of this stream of benefits using a discount rate of 10 percent.

$$P = 200 \; SP_{PW} \binom{i = 0.10}{n = 1} + 300 \; SP_{PW} \binom{i = 0.10}{n = 5}$$
$$+ 400 \; SP_{PW} \binom{i = 0.10}{n = 8}$$
$$= 200 \, (0.9091) + 300 \, (0.6209) + 400 \, (0.4665)$$
$$= 181.82 + 186.27 + 186.6$$
$$= \$549.69$$

42 DECISION MODELS FOR SERVICE OPERATIONS

Uniform-series present worth Benefits could occur in the form of an annuity, or series of equal payments. For example, consider the present value of three payments of $100 each over the next three years at interest rate i. Using the single-payment approach, the present value would be calculated as

$$P = \frac{\$100}{(1+i)} + \frac{\$100}{(1+i)^2} + \frac{\$100}{(1+i)^3}$$

$$= \$100 \left[\frac{1}{(1+i)} + \frac{1}{(1+i)^2} + \frac{1}{(1+i)^3} \right]$$

$$= \$100 \left(\frac{1}{1+i} \right) \left[1 + \frac{1}{(1+i)} + \frac{1}{(1+i)^2} \right]$$

The bracketed term is the partial sum for the series $1 + X + X^2 + \cdots + X^{n-1}$, where $X = 1/(1+i)$ is less than 1. This series has a sum defined by

$$S_{n-1} = \frac{1 - X^n}{1 - X} = \frac{(1+i)^n - 1}{i(1+i)^{n-1}} \tag{3}$$

Thus in general, the present value of an annuity A of n-years duration with interest rate i is calculated as

$$P = A \left[\frac{(1+i)^n - 1}{i(1+i)^n} \right] \tag{4}$$

The bracketed term in equation (4) above is called the uniform-series present worth factor US_{PW}, and values for this factor are found in Table B at the back of the book.

Example 3.2: Uniform-series present worth calculations The diagram below shows a $100 three-year annuity that will begin in five years. Again, assume payments are made at the end of the year and the discount rate is 10 percent. What is the present value of this uniform series of benefits?

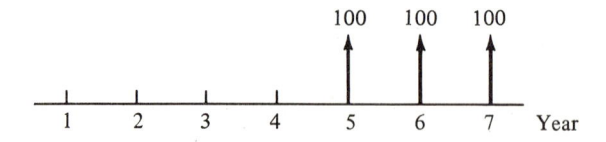

Two equivalent approaches to this calculation are possible. First we find the present value of the annuity for year 4 and then, using a single-payment present worth factor, bring this sum back to the present.

$$P = 100 US_{PW} \binom{i = 0.10}{n = 3} SP_{PW} \binom{i = 0.10}{n = 4}$$

$$= 100(2.487)(0.6830)$$

$$\approx \$169.86$$

Alternatively we can find the present value of a seven-year $100 annuity and subtract out a four-year $100 annuity.

$$P = 100 US_{PW} \begin{pmatrix} i = 0.10 \\ n = 7 \end{pmatrix} - 100 US_{PW} \begin{pmatrix} i = 0.10 \\ n = 4 \end{pmatrix}$$

$$= 100 \left[US_{PW} \begin{pmatrix} i = 0.10 \\ n = 7 \end{pmatrix} - US_{PW} \begin{pmatrix} i = 0.10 \\ n = 4 \end{pmatrix} \right]$$

$$= 100 (4.868 - 3.170)$$

$$\approx \$169.80$$

Selection of discount rate One of the most controversial aspects of cost-benefit analysis is the selection of the discount rate. On the surface it seems straightforward. This discount rate should represent the worth of money if used for other purposes. For a firm the rate of return on equity or the cost of capital could be used. For government two approaches have been suggested. One is the opportunity cost of capital in the private sector, measured by the going market rate of interest. Another is the ill-defined social rate of time preference, which is a measure of the nation's willingness to postpone consumption in favor of future generations. In practice a wide range of discount rates have been used. For example, the Army Corps of Engineers has been criticized for adopting a very low discount rate, but their projects, such as dams, accrue benefits in the distant future. It has been said that high discount rates favor the aged and low rates favor the middle-aged. For a particular project the discount rate selected can easily make the difference between its selection or rejection.

Effects of discount rate on project selection The following example will be used to demonstrate the effect of the discount rate on present value calculations. Two projects A and B are being considered for funding from a $10,000 budget. The diagram of benefits and costs for project A is below:

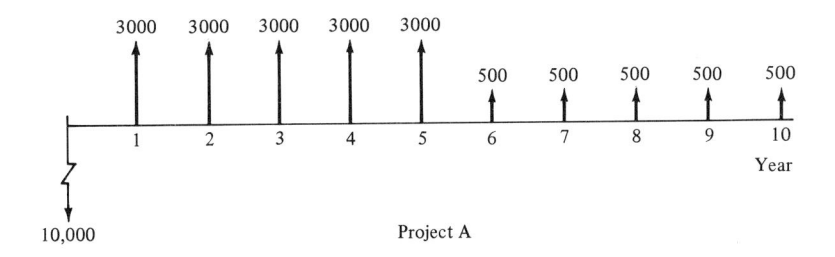

Project A

The net present value of benefits less costs is calculated by means of the function below:

$$NPV = 3000 \; US_{PW}\left(\substack{i \\ n=5}\right)$$
$$+ 500 \left[US_{PW}\left(\substack{i \\ n=10}\right) - US_{PW}\left(\substack{i \\ n=5}\right)\right] - 10{,}000$$

The diagram of benefits and costs for project B is below:

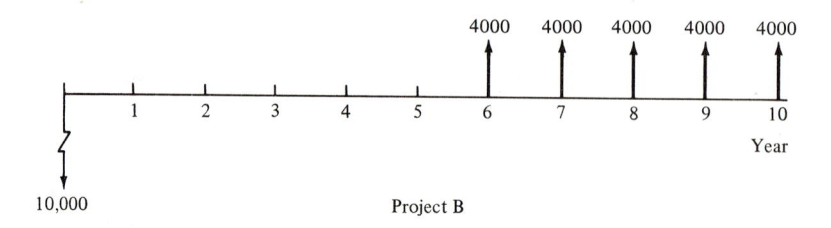

Project B

The net present value of benefits less costs is calculated by means of the function below:

$$NPV = 4000 \left[US_{PW}\left(\substack{i \\ n=10}\right) - US_{PW}\left(\substack{i \\ n=5}\right)\right] - 10{,}000$$

Table 3.1 contains the calculations of net present value for discount rates from 0 to 20 percent. Figure 3.2 illustrates the sensitivity of project selection to discount rate as summarized below:

Discount rate	Project selection decision
$0 \le i < x$	Select B over A
$x \le i < y$	Select A over B
$y \le i < z$	Reject B
$z \le i$	Reject A and B

Table 3.1 Net present value of benefits − costs

Discount rate i	$US_{PW}\left(\substack{i \\ n=10}\right)$	$US_{PW}\left(\substack{i \\ n=5}\right)$	Project A	Project B
0.00	....	....	$7,500	$10,000
0.05	7.722	4.329	4,683	3,572
0.10	6.144	3.791	2,549	−589
0.15	5.019	3.352	889	−3,332
0.20	4.192	2.991	−426	−5,196

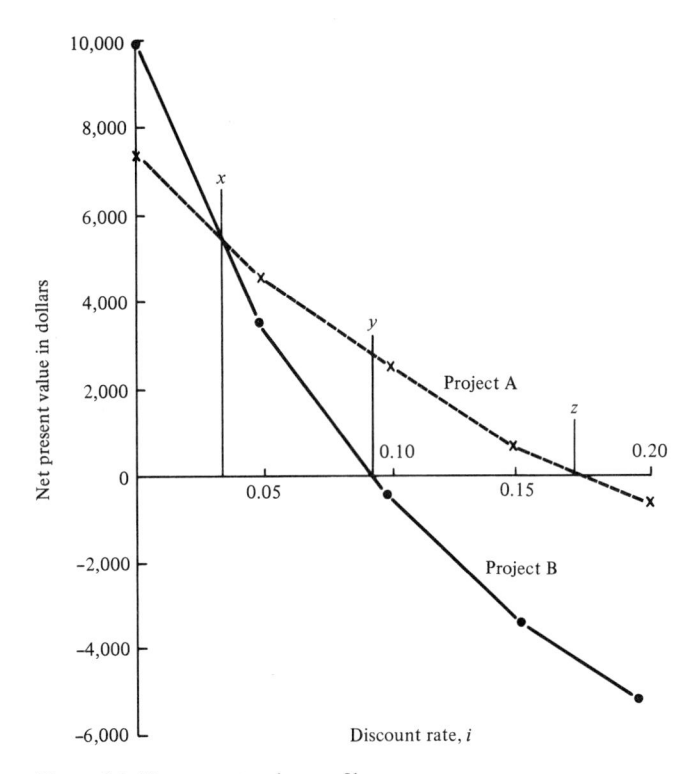

Figure 3.2 Net present value profiles.

Accounting for inflation With inflation, the value of $1 today is worth $0.95 next year at 5 percent inflation. On the other hand, $1 invested at 10 percent interest yields $1.10 in one year. With 5 percent inflation the real value of the dollar in one year is slightly less than $1.05. The effective interest rate i_e is determined as follows, with inflation rate r and interest rate i:

$$1 + i_e = (1 + i)(1 - r)$$
$$i_e = i - r - ir \tag{5}$$

When r is small,

$$i_e \simeq i - r$$

For our example above the effective interest rate is:

$$i_e = 0.10 - 0.05 - 0.005$$
$$= 0.045$$
$$\simeq 0.05$$

Conducting a Cost-Benefit Study

A common error in cost-benefit analysis is comparing total rather than marginal costs and benefits. The analysis should consider the effect of change from the status quo both in new benefits and in new costs. The present situation, if continued into the future unchanged, is called the *baseline,* to which a program is compared to calculate incremental costs and benefits.

The projections of future costs and benefits from a proposed program are based on a causal model. For example, in one cost-benefit study the projected reduction in motorcycle fatalities from wearing helmets was based on the experience in Australia. In the two years following the introduction of a law requiring the wearing of helmets, the state of Victoria, Australia, experienced a 40 percent reduction in fatalities compared with other states without such a law.[3] Unfortunately, data from other sources that did not support an optimistic effect were ignored.

This example illustrates the problem of credibility when the study is so dependent on the judgment of an analyst who usually is interested in showing the program in its best light. Cost-benefit studies need to be reviewed by disinterested parties to question the validity of benefit projections and the omission of possible costs or negative benefits.

Treating benefits Cost-benefit studies are noted for their comprehensiveness. All costs and all benefits are identified and accounted for in the analysis. Evaluating benefits in dollars provides a challenge because many worthwhile benefits have no market value. This problem is illustrated best when a dollar value must be placed on a human life. Benefits are classified as direct, indirect, intangible, and negative.

Direct benefits Averted costs that are currently borne and represent tangible savings are direct benefits. For a dam project the projected value of flood damage avoided would be a direct benefit. The measure of direct benefits is usually taken to be the total resource costs currently incurred that would be saved.

Indirect benefits Avoiding the loss of earnings due to premature death or disability are examples of indirect benefits. In this calculation consumption by survivors is not subtracted from gross earnings to arrive at net earnings. Standard life tables are employed, separately for men and women, to arrive at the expected working life of the population cohorts affected by the program. Estimates of earnings are calculated by applying labor-force participation rates, employment rates, and average earnings to these population cohorts. Current data for this calculation are available from the federal government.[4]

---

[3] *Disease Control Programs* (A), Case Clearing House, no. 9-112-007, Boston.

[4] An example calculation is contained in Dorothy P. Rice and Barbara S. Cooper, "The Economic Value of Human Life," *American Journal of Public Health,* vol. 57, no. 11, November 1967, pp. 1954–1966.

Another example of indirect benefits is the increased commercial activity around a new airport site, which results in attracting industry and creating employment opportunities.

Intangible benefits Avoiding pain, suffering, and grief are examples of intangible benefits that have no market value. Protecting an endangered species, maintaining clean air and water, and avoiding the destruction of natural beauty are other examples. To be explicitly included in the analysis, a dollar value must be placed on these intangibles. The question is what society would be willing to spend to achieve these benefits. Some success has been reported in the health care field, where medical expenses are used to estimate the willingness of people to pay to avoid the manifestations of a disease.

Intangible benefits are by no means unimportant, as seen by the decisions to drop the development of the supersonic transport because of noise pollution and to halt the construction of a dam because of endangering the snail darter.

Human life The most important intangible benefit of all is the value of human life. A frequently used approach to evaluate the economic worth of life is to determine the present value of the average person's expected future earnings. This approach, discussed earlier under indirect benefits, has serious shortcomings because programs benefiting the aged would be discriminated against and the value of women would be considerably underestimated.

An alternative approach is to look at the implied value society places on life by investigating policy decisions involving investments in auto safety, airport landing systems, and factory safeguards. Other possible approaches include determining the insurance premium a person is willing to pay and the probability of being killed while engaged in some dangerous occupation. All of these approaches are inadequate.

Assessing the change in probability of death for all affected members of society is perhaps the best way of evaluating the impact of a program on human life. This concept leads the analysis from cost-benefit to cost effectiveness, where the measure of performance becomes years of life gained.

Negative benefits The consequences of a particular program may have negative economic impacts. For example, constructing a flood control dam on a river could result in creating a reservoir where once farm land was cultivated. Negative benefits should be made explicit and subtracted from positive benefits in determining the program's contribution.

Selection criteria Cost-benefit studies are evaluated on the basis of net welfare improvement, or the total benefit of the gainers minus the combined cost of the losers. In making comparisons among competing programs, this selection criterion is operationalized by calculating the net present value or benefit-cost ratio. The net present value is simply the present value of all benefits less the present

Table 3.2 Cost-benefit comparisons

	Projects			
Criteria	A	B	C	A and C
Present value of benefits	$50,000	$60,000	$12,000	$62,000
Present value of costs	20,000	25,000	5,000	25,000
Net present value	30,000	35,000	7,000	37,000
Benefit-cost ratio	2.5	2.4	2.4	2.48

value of all costs. Net present value measures the size of the program's net contribution.

Dividing the present value of all benefits by the present value of costs yields a benefit-cost ratio. This ratio must exceed 1 for a project to be economically viable. The benefit-cost ratio is particularly useful for comparing projects with different-size investments. The larger the ratio, the more desirable the project.

Table 3.2, summarizes the analysis of three hypothetical projects. Project A is the preferred project on the basis of the benefit-cost ratio criterion. However, if the budget does not permit a $20,000 investment, then project C becomes attractive, but it only generates $7,000 in net welfare improvement. If a budget of $25,000 is available, then funding a combination of projects A and C is preferred to funding project B alone.

Sensitivity analysis Making distinctions in benefit-cost ratios, as illustrated in Table 3.2, is folly. All the assumptions and projections of future benefits would suggest that benefit-cost ratios of 2.4 and 2.5 are not significantly different. Net present value ought to be reported as a probability distribution, and benefit-cost ratios as ranges rather than point estimates. Future benefits are based on probability estimates that could be analyzed using experimental methods to arrive at a distribution of net present value. At least the analysis should report the sensitivity of the benefit-cost ratio to a range of discount rates.

Benefit-Cost Study of Defensive Driving Program

A western community is considering programs to reduce the increasing number of automobile accidents that are resulting in the injury and death of its citizens. A proposal has been made to require drivers to take a 10-hour defensive driving course every third year, when they renew their license. The program consists of five 2-hour video cassettes that can be played at home on the television. Drivers without televisions that will play cassettes will be able to check out a unit from the motor-vehicle office. Upon returning the cassettes and player, the driver will be examined and, if passed, will be issued a renewed license. The program will require an initial investment of approximately $6,500,000 to purchase the cassette players, prepare the instructional programs, and record the video cassettes. The project will be conducted during a six-year period to ensure that everyone has been exposed to the concepts of defensive driving. Annual expenditures of $100,000 are anticipated to cover extra personnel costs to administer the program.

A projection of the current trend in fatalities and injuries will be used as a baseline from which change will be measured. The projections shown in Table 3.3 for the next six years were obtained from the state highway patrol and are based on an anticipated 5 percent annual rate of increase. The estimated reduction in fatalities and injuries resulting from the defensive driving program is based on the experience of a local military installation. When the post commander required all military personnel and their dependents to take a defensive driving course, the annual number of fatalities and injuries fell by 3 percent. Because of the three-year license renewal cycle the projected reduction is only 1 percent for 1980 and increases to 2 percent for 1981 and 3 percent thereafter. These reductions in fatalities and injuries are then converted to dollar amounts. Information from the Department of Transportation indicates that, for the average person, the value of lost earnings due to premature death is $200,000. Every fatality avoided was thus given a value of $200,000. The value for avoiding an injury is estimated to be $67,000. This figure includes the direct cost of medical care and the indirect loss of earnings resulting from the injury. Using a discount rate of 8 percent, the present value of the benefits and program costs are calculated. The assumption is made that benefits occur at the end of the year and costs at the beginning. Adding the present value of the benefits and dividing by the present value of the program costs yields a benefit-cost ratio of 1.4.

A program with such an unimpressive benefit-cost ratio needs to be examined closely before any commitments are made. Of particular concern is the assumption that defensive driving instruction results in a reduced number of accidents. For example, if the rate of reduction never reaches the projected 3

Table 3.3 Benefit-cost calculations for defensive driving program

	Baseline		Estimated program benefits		Value of benefits		
Year	Projected fatalities	Projected injuries	Reduction in fatalities	Reduction in injuries	Lost earnings due to premature fatality	Direct and indirect cost of injuries	Program costs
1980	100	800	1	8	$ 200,000	$ 536,000	$6,500,000
1981	105	840	2	17	400,000	1,139,000	100,000
1982	110	882	3	26	600,000	1,742,000	100,000
1983	116	926	3	28	600,000	1,876,000	100,000
1984	122	972	4	29	800,000	1,943,000	100,000
1985	128	1021	4	31	800,000	2,077,000	100,000
Present value at 8% discount rate					$2,494,020	$6,865,740	$6,899,300

percent level but remains at 2 percent, the benefit-cost ratio becomes less than 1. However, benefits from such a program should last indefinitely and we have only considered the first six years.

Cost-Effectiveness Study of Kidney Disease Treatment[5]

Two possible means for prolonging the life of persons with kidney disease are kidney transplant and the use of dialysis equipment. Because of the difficulty of placing a value on human life, the evaluation of these two treatment approaches will be conducted using cost-effectiveness analysis. Effectiveness will be measured by the expected number of years of life added by either transplantation or dialysis. However, dialysis presents a problem because of the restrictions imposed upon the life of the patient. The life of the dialysis patient is regularly interrupted for hours at a time while the patient is attached to the artificial kidney machine. Dependence on the machine restricts travel and diet. Because of these drawbacks associated with dialysis, one year of life gained from transplantation was given a weight of 1.25 to reflect the improved quality of life. A further complication with dialysis is the large cost differential between treatment at home and treatment in a hospital center.

Table 3.4 shows the cost of providing each treatment and the expected number of years of life gained. These values were obtained from medical experts familiar with each mode of treatment. The figure of 17.2 years for transplant consists of 13.3 added years from a transplanted kidney followed by 3.9 more years on dialysis after eventual failure of the transplant. The adjusted figure of 20.5 years results from weighting the first 13.3 years by the factor 1.25. The cost-effectiveness calculations show the clear superiority of kidney transplants. However, the availability of kidneys for transplant is not addressed.

SUMMARY

Evaluation is a process for making judgments leading to the selection of a course of action. The systems concept which focuses on objectives, outputs, and models relating inputs to outputs is the foundation of the evaluation process. A general model for an evaluation system was developed with a concern for: system boundary, objectives, evaluators, time horizon, selection criteria, validation, and implementation.

Cost-benefit analysis is explored in detail as an evaluation system. Cost effectiveness is shown to be a useful variation of cost-benefit analysis but limited to one accepted goal. The procedures for present value analysis are explored because the value of money is time dependent.

Conducting a cost-benefit study is an art requiring assumptions relating

---

[5] Adapted from Warren F. Smith, "Cost-Effectiveness and Cost-Benefit Analysis for Public Health Programs," *Public Health Reports,* vol. 83, no. 11, November 1968, pp. 904-905.

Table 3.4 Cost-effectiveness calculations for kidney disease treatment

Treatment	Cost	Years of life gained	Cost per year gained	C-E ratio, years gained/$10,000
Dialysis:				
Center	$104,000	9	$11,600	0.9
Home	38,000	9	4,200	2.4
Transplant:				
Unadjusted	44,500	17.2	2,600	3.9
Adjusted	44,500	20.5	2,200	4.6

Source: Adapted from Warren F. Smith, "Cost-Effectiveness and Cost-Benefit Analysis for Public Health Programs," *Public Health Reports*, vol. 83, no. 11, November 1968, p. 905.

inputs to outputs and future projections, often based on little or no data. The monetary value of the most important benefit, human life, is difficult, at best, for people to agree upon. Giving a monetary value to intangible benefits is an impossible task. Thus, we are left with trying to compare costs with benefits converted to dollars and always feeling the benefits are understated. Cost effectiveness avoids the problem of evaluating benefits in monetary terms, but does not escape the need for judgment on the part of the decision maker.

TOPICS FOR DISCUSSION

1. When is cost-effectiveness analysis more appropriate than cost-benefit analysis?
2. Are negative benefits possible in a cost-benefit analysis? Give an example.
3. Suggest a method of determining the value society places on a human life.
4. Describe an example where cost-benefit analysis is appropriate for a private firm.
5. How can cost-benefit ratios be misinterpreted?
6. Public school systems have been criticized for the falling SAT scores of their graduates. Why may this measure be insufficient evidence of poor school performance?
7. Give an example of an evaluation system other than cost-benefit or cost-effectiveness analysis.
8. Give an example where systems thinking has enlarged the system boundary to include innovative alternatives.

EXERCISES

3.1 A firm is considering buying a new computer for $50,000. Presently the firm leases a computer for $8,000 per year which will be renegotiated after five years and will be $6,000 per year thereafter (assume payments at end of year). Assume the new computer will have a 10-year life and the discount rate is 8 percent.
  (a) What is the present value of the lease payments for the next 10 years?
  (b) Should the computer be purchased? Discuss.

3.2 The Big Sky Commuter Airline operates a fleet of airplanes serving communities in the Pacific Northwest. Besides carrying passengers, it delivers lightweight commodities and provides an overnight special-delivery mail service. Because of recent visibility problems, Big Sky is planning to equip its aircraft with new navigation equipment. It is considering the two models below:

	Model Z26	Model X2R1
Expected life	10 years	10 years
Initial cost	$27,000	$21,000
Annual maintenance	$ 1,500	$ 2,000

(a) If a discount rate of 10 percent and present value analysis are used, which model should be selected?

(b) Before the final commitment is made, Big Sky learns of an economy model that sells for $16,000. This model has an expected life of only five years, but the supplier has offered to provide free maintenance. From a present value perspective, is this alternative worth considering?

(c) How would your analysis be changed if inflation were projected to continue at an annual rate of 4 percent?

3.3 The Twin Towers Hotel is considering replacing its central air conditioning system because of the rising cost of electricity (expected to continue into the future at a rate of 10 percent per year). It is considering two replacement possibilities: an energy-efficient electric model and a solar model requiring no significant amount of electricity.

	Electric model	Solar model
Initial cost	$145,000	$200,000
Salvage value	70,000	30,000
Annual electric expense	5,000	0
Annual maintenance expense	1,000	3,000
Expected life	10 years	20 years

(a) State the assumptions of your analysis.

(b) Using a discount rate of 15 percent and present value analysis, which model should be selected?

3.4 The Bayview City Council is considering the following projects for funding next year's capital improvement budget.

Project	Present value of costs	Present value of benefits
1. Enlarge city park.	$2,000,000	$3,200,000
2. Add to city maintenance garage.	1,200,000	1,740,000
3. Modernize city health clinics.	500,000	750,000
4. Expand power-generating capacity.	7,000,000	8,600,000
5. Improve traffic signals.	600,000	800,000
6. Pave streets.	900,000	1,200,000
7. Extend water and sewer lines.	1,400,000	2,000,000

(a) Using cost-benefit analysis, rank order the projects according to their economic contribution.

(b) If the capital improvement budget is limited to $10,000,000, recommend those projects that will maximize total benefits.

3.5 Select some project and classify the benefits as direct, indirect, and intangible. Illustrate how you would measure these benefits in dollar terms.

3.6 Design a system that can be used by the legislature to evaluate the performance of the state university. Address each of the steps shown in the evaluation system paradigm of Figure 3.1.

3.7 Design an evaluation system for the customer service division of the telephone company.

CASELETTE: RIVER CITY PLANNING COMMISSION

As a consultant to the River City Planning Commission you have been asked to suggest the most cost-effective means of reducing railroad-crossing accidents in the community. A survey of railroad grade crossings in the city is shown in Table 3.5. The crossings are grouped into four categories on the basis of the number of tracks, daily automobile traffic, and frequency of trains. Table 3.6 contains information on preventive devices, including an equation which forecasts accidents on the basis of crossings characteristics.

Table 3.5 Railroad crossings

Category	Number of tracks, A	Daily traffic, 1000s, B	Number of trains, C	Number of crossings in city
1	1	10	5	50
2	1	4	5	20
3	2	8	10	40
4	2	2	10	30

Table 3.6 Protective devices

Protective device	Equation forecasting accidents per crossing for next decade	Installation cost, $
Crossbucks	$-6 + 3.0A + 2.5B + 4.0C$	100
Flashing lights	$3 + 2.0A + 0.5B + 1.0C$	2,000
Automatic gates	$-2 + A + 0.1B + 0.2C$	10,000
Grade separation	No accidents	500,000

Questions

1. If the planning commission has a $1,000,000 budget to allocate to crossing devices, what would be your recommendation for the most cost-effective use of these funds? Specify what crossing devices to install for each category of crossing.
2. How many accidents will be prevented in the next decade, if currently all crossings are unprotected and 8000 accidents have occurred in the past decade?
3. If the planning commission insisted on one grade separation, which crossing category would you recommend?

CASELETTE: MISERLY COUNTY TRANSPORTATION AUTHORITY

Helen Weals, financial analyst with the Miserly County Transportation Authority, has been given the task of making preliminary assessments of the feasibility of several possible construction programs that have been proposed by MCTA's engineering staff as alternative solutions to a serious congestion problem in the area.

Within the area under study, the most densely populated part of Miserly County is located along the western bank of the Portage River below the foothills of the Gabriel Mountains. Because there is little development in the hilly terrain, the populated area comprises a linear corridor about 8 miles long, with the central business district, county government offices, and a branch of the state university clustered in the middle of the corridor where Whittier Creek empties into the river. The urbanized area is generally 1 mile wide, slightly more in the downtown area, with higher population densities concentrated parallel to the river between $\frac{1}{4}$ and $\frac{1}{2}$ mile west of the riverbank. The present population in the study area is approximately 360,000.

The main transportation facilities serving this urban corridor are a freeway and a divided thoroughfare. The freeway, which has two main lanes serving each direction of travel, was constructed by the State Highway Department 15 years ago and runs parallel to the riverbank about $\frac{1}{4}$ mile away from the river throughout the study area. There is a connection in the downtown area to the only major bridge crossing within one hour's drive where motorists can enter the adjacent state.

The divided thoroughfare also has two lanes serving each direction and runs parallel to the freeway about $\frac{1}{2}$ mile to the west; other major streets connect this thoroughfare with the freeway at intervals of about $\frac{1}{2}$ mile along the length of the corridor. MCTA runs a small fleet of buses (four at 10-minute intervals and an average operating speed of 12 miles per hour) along the thoroughfare from one end of the study area to the other, and the ridership is close to 25,000 people daily. These riders are mostly people who work, shop, or go to school in the downtown area.

MCTA's problem arises out of the congestion which occurs every morning and afternoon on the freeway and the thoroughfare. Average speeds in the predominant directions of flow (inbound to downtown in the morning and outbound in the afternoon) have dropped to around 15 miles per hour on both facilities; speeds in the opposite directions have only dropped to 30 miles per hour. Although the primary concentration of employment is in the downtown area, there are manufacturing plants located along the riverbank and MCTA's engineers attribute the surprisingly large counterflow to workers at these plants in the outlying areas. An additional problem deals with the lack of adequate parking space downtown. The engineers have estimated that there is an 800-space shortage at the present time; in five years the shortage should be approximately twice that level.

MCTA Engineering has devised three possible programs to deal with the current problems and to provide expanded transportation service in the future, as described below:

1. In conjunction with the State Highway Department, MCTA would expand the freeway to a total of six lanes, expand the thoroughfare by adding one lane in each direction, and construct a cluster of parking garages downtown that would contain 1600 spaces. The parking garages would take two years

to design, finance, and construct. The thoroughfare could be rebuilt in three years. Because of some uncertainty in the state's priorities, MCTA feels there is a 45 percent probability that the freeway could be finished in four years and a 55 percent probability that it would take six years.
2. MCTA would expand the bus fleet to ten vehicles, operating five buses on the thoroughfare and five on the freeway (where the buses would stop at specially constructed shelters at each cross-street interchange). The thoroughfare's median would be rebuilt as a two-lane roadway for buses only, while the state would construct in the freeway median a single-lane roadway for buses traveling in the direction of peak flow. The bus purchases could be made in two years, and MCTA believes that the thoroughfare could be rebuilt by that same time. The state has assured MCTA that the freeway median could be rebuilt within two years at an initial cost of $2,000,000, and it anticipates annual maintenance expenses of $50,000 beginning the following year.
3. MCTA would initiate a car-pool matching program for employees and students who travel to the downtown area and, at the same time, impose a parking surcharge of $1 per car within the area. This surcharge would be levied on any car with fewer than three occupants parking within a commercial or public lot or garage during a $2\frac{1}{2}$-hour period in the morning when the major employee and student influx occurs. The engineering staff feels this program could be implemented within six months.

As shown in Table 3.7 MCTA Engineering has developed a schedule of economic information associated with each alternative program, which Ms. Weals must use in making her assessment. The benefits include all those which the engineers feel are directly attributable to both MCTA's and the state's actions; however, the costs in the table represent MCTA's total costs and only the state's engineering and administrative costs.

Owing to the uncertainty involved in the state's freeway construction timetable in alternative 1, Ms. Weals has asked for and received assurances from the highway engineers that only the construction funds are subject to change. Their concurrence in MCTA's estimates of likely timetables is heartening, and Ms. Weals has been told that, no matter when the completion date actually is, the Highway Department will spend 35 percent of the construction budget of $15,000,000 during the last year of work, 40 percent the year before that, and 25 percent the year before that. They estimate annual maintenance costs of $200,000 beginning in the year after the project's completion; however, they also feel that MCTA underestimated the annual benefits of its role in alternative 1. Upon further questioning, Ms. Weals is told that an additional $4.1 million could be expected on an annual basis beginning in the year after completion, primarily owing to gas and time savings.

Ms. Weals realizes that there are secondary benefits to the local economy from spending construction monies within the study area, because workers will use their paychecks to purchase goods and services from local merchants. She

Table 3.7 Project costs and benefits

Year	Item	Alt 1	Alt 2	Alt 3
	Costs			
1	Engineering, administrative	$ 220,000	$ 160,000	$ 190,000
2	Engineering, administrative	100,000	20,000	110,000
	Construction expenditures	7,000,000	6,500,000	
	Debt service	960,000	900,000	
	Bus purchases	....	600,000	
	Maintenance, operating expenditures	20,000	135,000	
3	Engineering, administrative	60,000	15,000	90,000
	Debt service	1,900,000	900,000	
	Construction expenditures	6,000,000	....	
	Maintenance, operating expenditures	35,000	480,000	
4	Engineering, administrative	10,000	15,000	80,000
	Debt service	1,900,000	900,000	
	Maintenance, operating expenditures	60,000	520,000	
5	Engineering, administrative	10,000	15,000	80,000
	Debt service	1,900,000	900,000	
	Maintenance, operating expenditures	70,000	540,000	
	Benefits			
1	Parking surcharge revenue	....	....	$ 250,000
	Cumulative gas-time savings	....	....	750,000
2	Parking surcharge revenue	....	....	300,000
	Cumulative gas-time savings	$ 15,000	$ 225,000	1,700,000
	Transit-revenue increase	....	90,000	10,000
3	Parking surcharge revenue	....	....	250,000
	Cumulative gas-time savings	135,000	930,000	2,350,000
	Transit-revenue increase	5,000	150,000	12,000
4	Parking surcharge revenue	....	....	175,000
	Cumulative gas-time savings	1,400,000	1,425,000	2,750,000
	Transit-revenue increase	5,000	235,000	14,000
5	Parking surcharge revenue	....	....	105,000
	Cumulative gas-time savings	2,270,000	1,950,000	3,000,000
	Transit-revenue increase	5,000	375,000	14,000

Note: Assume all costs and expenditures occur at the beginning of each year and all benefits are received at the end of each year. Also, assume that the beginning of year 1 is less than one month away and that the intervening period of time may be safely ignored.

feels that it is important to include these in her analysis, but is not sure how to account for them. After some consultation with university economists and chamber of commerce officials, she decides to use a multiplier of 1.75 for all construction expenditures and place these equivalent benefits in the same year that the construction funds are spent by either MCTA or the state.

Ms. Weals decides to estimate the benefit-cost ratios of each alternative by discounting all of the associated costs and benefits to the present. The state uses a discount rate of 7 percent for its studies, but MCTA uses 10 percent. She decides to use one figure consistently for each alternative, but also to figure the ratios under each discount rate for comparison. MCTA finances its projects by means of revenue bonds with a 15-year life; the state pays in lump sums from the highway trust fund when billed by the contractor(s).

Questions

1. Assuming the figures in year 5 remain constant over a lifetime of 15 years for each program, what are the benefit-cost ratios for the three programs under the different discount rates?
2. Can you compare these alternatives on the basis of cost effectiveness? Why?

SELECTED BIBLIOGRAPHY

Blum, Henrik.: "Evaluating Health Care," *Medical Care,* vol. 12, no. 12, December 1974, pp. 999–1011.
Churchman, C. W., and A. H. Schainblatt: "The Researcher and the Manager: A Dialectic of Implementation," *Management Science,* vol. 11, no. 4, December 1965, pp. B69–B87.
Dorfman, Robert (ed.): *Measuring Benefits of Government Investments,* The Brookings Institution, Washington, 1965.
Fitzsimmons, J. A., and R. S. Sullivan: "Establishing the Level of Service for Public Emergency Ambulance Systems," *Socio-Economic Planning Sciences,* vol. 13, no. 5, September 1979, pp. 235–239.
Grant, E. L., and W. G. Ireson: *Principles of Engineering Economy* (5th ed.), The Ronald Press Co., New York, 1970.
Hinrichs, H. H., and G. M. Taylor (eds.): *Program Budgeting and Benefit-Cost Analysis,* Goodyear Publishing Co., Santa Monica, Calif., 1969.
Keeney, R. L., and H. Raiffa: *Decision Analysis with Multiple Objectives,* John Wiley and Sons, Inc., New York, 1976.
Klarman, Herbert E.: "Application of Cost-Benefit Analysis to Health Systems Technology," *Technology and Health Care Systems in the 1980's,* Conference Series, San Francisco, HEW Publication No. HRA-74-3016, January 1972, pp. 225–250.
Lindblom, C. E.: "The Science of Muddling Through," *Public Administration Review,* vol. 19, Spring 1959, pp. 79–88.
Prest, A. R., and R. Turvey: "Cost-Benefit Analysis: A Survey," *Economic Journal,* December 1965, pp. 683–735.
Rice, Dorothy P., and Barbara S. Cooper: "The Economic Value of Human Life," *American Journal of Public Health,* vol. 57, no. 11, November 1967, pp. 1954–1966.
Savas, E. S.: "On Equity in Providing Public Services," *Management Science,* vol. 24, no. 8, April 1978, pp. 800–808.
Smith, Warren F.: "Cost-Effectiveness and Cost-Benefit Analysis for Public Health Programs," *Public Health Reports,* vol. 83, no. 11, November 1968, pp. 899–906.
Wildavsky, Aaron: "The Political Economy of Efficiency: Cost-Benefit Analysis, Systems Analysis, and Program Budgeting," *Public Administration Review,* December 1966, pp. 292–310.

CHAPTER
FOUR

MANAGEMENT SYSTEMS SIMULATION

Service operations often are analyzed by means of mathematical representations of management systems. In subsequent chapters, we shall discuss mathematical relationships associated with linear programming models, forecasting models, location models, waiting-line models, workshift scheduling models, vehicle routing models, and network models. Information may be derived from some mathematical models by the use of analytical tools, such as calculus. But for other models, systems simulation is a more versatile and powerful approach.

In this chapter we present some basic concepts about management systems simulation. We begin with a discussion of several types of models, especially mathematical models. Techniques for analyzing mathematical models are presented, and advantages and disadvantages of systems simulation are highlighted. Steps required for successfully using systems simulation are outlined and illustrated with an example. The purpose of this chapter is to provide an appreciation of the value of simulation for analyzing management systems.

BASIC CONCEPTS

Models

We know that a system is made up of interrelated entities, such as personnel, consumers, and equipment. We also know that managers often have questions about the behavior of existing systems or want to predict the behavior of proposed systems. These managers may use models to help them in their analyses.

A model, of course, is anything that represents a system or displays the characteristics of a system. By analyzing a model, managers are able to discern the behavioral characteristics of the real system.

Figure 4.1 gives a classification of models. Schematic models are used to display interrelationships between elements in a system. Organizational charts and process flow diagrams are examples of schematic models. Scaled-down physical models (also called iconic models) are used to study physical characteristics, such as the layout of a facility. Analog models use some physical entities that behave like other entities. For example, a slide rule is an analog calculator that makes use of the relationship between length and logarithms.

Most management models are mathematical representations of systems. These are called mathematical models because they express relationships in terms of symbols and numbers. For example, consider a model for a simple inventory system. Here, annual inventory cost is related to inventory holding cost and to inventory replenishment cost. An analysis of these cost relationships results in the determination of the best order quantity. This is a mathematical model of the annual inventory cost.

Mathematical models can be classified as being either static or dynamic. In static models, attributes of the system have reached steady-state conditions. This means that the state of the system is not changing in response to time. But in dynamic models, attributes change during a specified time interval. The values of attributes in a dynamic model are time dependent.

Finally, mathematical models can be classified as being either deterministic or stochastic. With deterministic models, relevant values are assumed to be constants and known. For example, we assume a specific value for demand

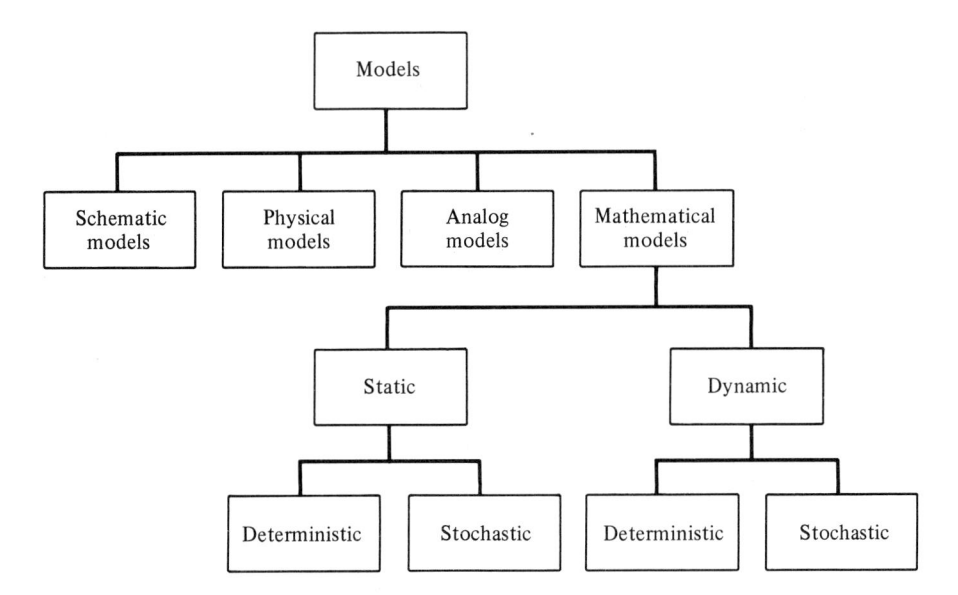

Figure 4.1 Classification of models.

when using a simple inventory model. However, in stochastic models probability distributions are associated with the realization of values. This means that some of the factors in the model are random variables.

Analyzing Mathematical Models

There are two general approaches for analyzing mathematical models: analytical techniques and systems simulation. Analytical techniques such as calculus and linear programming generally are used to solve for values in the model. When these values are "optimal," the analytical solutions are said to be normative. The solutions tell us the best values for decision variables in the model. For example, we can use calculus to derive the best order quantity formula for inventory management. This formula yields an order quantity that gives the minimum annual inventory cost.

There also are formulas that describe the steady-state conditions of a system. For example, we can determine the average queue length and the average waiting time associated with some waiting-line systems. These formulas describe the state toward which the system tends in the long term.

In the models described above, analytical techniques are used to solve for values. But most of these models are relatively simple, and this facilitates the use of analytical methods. For more complex models such methods may be economically impractical and analytical solutions may even be impossible to develop.

Systems simulation is an alternative method for analyzing mathematical models. It refers to experimenting with a model in a manner that allows inferences to be made about the system of interest. The condition of the system is traced from one state to another and values describing the system are recorded. Therefore, systems simulation is a method for observing the system during a compressed time interval. Table 4.1 lists examples of applications of systems simulation within service organizations. These examples show the versatility of simulation for analyzing a broad spectrum of systems.

Systems simulation can be classified as being continuous, discrete-event, or hybrid. In continuous simulation the state of the system evolves in an uninterrupted fashion. For example, the water level in a reservoir changes continuously and is related to the rates at which water enters and leaves. In fact, many continuous systems simulation models focus upon rates of change. And the rates may be modeled by means of sets of differential or difference equations.

J. W. Forrester pioneered in the applications of continuous systems simulation. Using his specially designed computer language called DYNAMO,[1] Forrester first simulated an industrial system. Sets of difference equations were used to represent the various flows through an organization. This first venture by Forrester was called *Industrial Dynamics*.[2] The same approach later was

---

[1] See the bibliography for selected references in computer simulation languages.
[2] J. W. Forrester, *Industrial Dynamics*, M.I.T. Press, Cambridge, Mass., 1961.

Table 4.1 Examples of applications of systems simulation

Application	Purpose
1. Aircraft maintenance	To investigate new operating procedures for scheduled and emergency maintenance
2. Location of ambulance facilities	To investigate the costs and benefits associated with various permanent locations
3. Scheduling of bank tellers	To investigate various heuristic methods for developing teller workshift schedules
4. Design of computer systems	To investigate the effectiveness and costs associated with various computer-system configurations
5. Deployment of fire stations	To investigate various alternative fire department deployment strategies
6. Investment analysis	To investigate the financial implications of various investment alternatives
7. Utilization of hospital facilities	To investigate various heuristic methods for scheduling the use of facilities and personnel
8. Scheduling of police patrols	To investigate the effectiveness of various methods for deploying police patrols
9. Project analysis	To assist in planning, scheduling, and controlling activities required for carrying out a project
10. Routing of school buses	To investigate the effectiveness of various routes and to anticipate equipment needs and operating expenses
11. Utilization of recreation facilities	To investigate policies for using recreation facilities and to anticipate the impact upon the facilities
12. Management of wilderness areas	To investigate the effects of alternative management practices on the quality of recreational experiences

adapted to "view" cities (*Urban Dynamics*)[3] and the entire earth (*World Dynamics*).[4] The results provided by the DYNAMO simulations, of course, are sensitive to the flow rates used and the assumed interdependencies in the system.

While continuous simulation allows for uninterrupted changes in the condition of the system, discrete-event simulation focuses upon events that occur at particular instants in time. These events might be the arrival of a customer or the completion of service. When an event occurs, the state of the system changes. For example, a customer arrival increases the number of customers in the system, while a customer departure (service completion) reduces the number in the system. After each event occurs descriptors of the state of the system are recorded. Many waiting-line systems common to service organizations can be analyzed using discrete-event simulation. GPSS and SIMSCRIPT, two of the most widely used computer simulation languages, focus upon discrete events.

[3] J. W. Forrester, *Urban Dynamics*, M.I.T. Press, Cambridge, Mass., 1969.
[4] J. W. Forrester, *World Dynamics*, M.I.T. Press, Cambridge, Mass., 1971.

62 DECISION MODELS FOR SERVICE OPERATIONS

Hybrid simulation is a combination of continuous simulation and discrete-event simulation. It allows for some continuously evolving conditions in the state of the system, as well as for discrete events that occur at specified points in time. There are not many computer languages that allow for hybrid simulation. One such language, SLAM, is gaining in popularity owing to its flexibility and to the ease with which it can be learned. Hybrid simulation can bring a new dimension of reality to modeling service systems.

Why Use Systems Simulation?

We mentioned before that systems simulation is appropriate where analytical solutions are impractical or impossible. This often is the case with complex models that include large amounts of detail and that are dynamic and stochastic. Simulation is so flexible that any desired level of detail and complexity can be included in the model.

Systems simulation also helps to answer "what-if" questions about existing or proposed systems. For example, what if another teller is added in a bank lobby? What if some tellers handle only depositors? What if an automatic (self-service) teller is placed outside the lobby? The response of the system to these changes can be "observed" over an extended period by means of a simulation. And no changes in the real system are needed to make these observations.

Despite the obvious advantages of systems simulation, the method does have some drawbacks. Unlike some analytical methods, simulation does not provide optimal values for decision variables. And it does not use simple formulas that yield steady-state conditions of a system. In this regard, simulation is at a disadvantage when compared with analytical methods.

Another disadvantage is that the costs associated with systems simulation can be high. These include the costs for model development and for running the simulation on the computer. Development costs can be high owing to the complexity and degree of detail of most simulations. This also accounts for high computer cost. And simulation generally does not have a fixed running period (period of observations) on the computer. A longer running period yields more precise estimates about the behavior of the system, but achieving a desired accuracy can be costly in computation time. These costs must be compared with the potential benefits in a decision of whether or not to use systems simulation for analyzing a service system.

THE PROCESS OF SYSTEMS SIMULATION

Simulation Methodology

Figure 4.2 presents the process of systems simulation. It begins with a description of the problem of interest. For example, the problem might involve customer service in a bank lobby. The description of the problem defines the limits of the system to be included in the simulation.

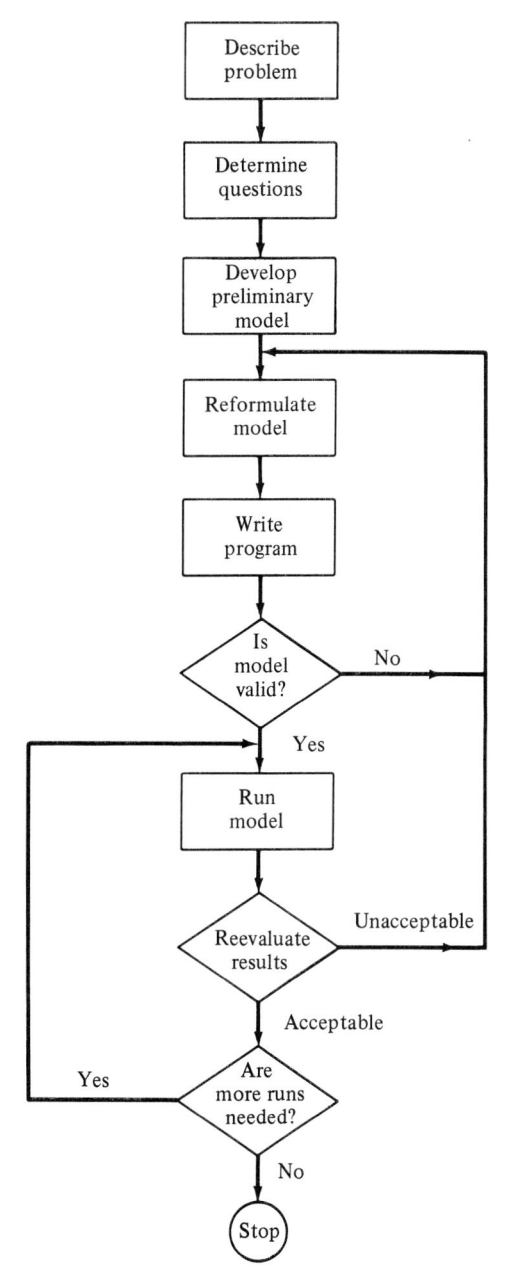

Figure 4.2 The process of systems simulation.

Once the problem has been described and the system boundaries have been delineated, we then specify the questions that we would like to answer. How long do customers have to wait? How many tellers are needed? Should an automatic teller be installed? The questions that we specify are important for determining the structure of the simulation model.

Sample data are used to develop a preliminary model of the system. This is a rough model and may be somewhat simplistic. The purpose of the preliminary model is to stimulate reconsideration of the problem and the questions to be answered. Perhaps the problem had been stated too broadly, or perhaps some interesting questions had been overlooked. The preliminary model also can help in formulating hypotheses about the system. The model should be constructed so that various hypotheses can be tested.

The preliminary model leads to a reformulated and refined model. Simultaneously, more data are collected to be used in the simulation. The reformulated model is sufficiently detailed to address all the questions of interest, and the model is in a format so that it can be programmed for the computer. At this step the type of simulation (continuous, discrete-event, or hybrid) must be decided upon, the variables and parameters of the model must be identified, and the mathematical relationships must be determined.

Writing the computer program can be an arduous task. An appropriate computer language must be selected, and then the mathematical relationships must be translated into proper computer statements. There are many techniques and tricks for programming that can be learned only from practice. A key aspect of good programming is efficiency; this involves making good use of computer memory and time.

Once the model has been programmed, it then must be validated. There are two types of validation, *internal* and *external*. Internal validation refers to whether the calculations are being done the way we intended in the model. This basically is a check on the internal mechanics of the program to make sure they correspond with those of the reformulated model. How can internal validity be checked? An obvious method is to carry out a few hand calculations of the model to see if they agree with the computer output.

External validity refers to the accuracy of the model compared with the real system. Can this model be used to observe the behavior of the real system? Does it accurately predict the behavior of the system? Various measures calculated from the model may be compared with actual observations of the system. If the model does not give acceptable results, then it must be reformulated again.

Once the programmed model has been validated, it then is used to simulate the system. Many simulation runs may be needed to observe the system under different conditions. If at any time the results of the runs are not satisfactory, the model may be further reformulated. Consequently, the process of simulation can be ongoing, with many changes and improvements in the model being made. The simulation process ends when all the runs of the model have been completed.

Monte Carlo Simulation

Typically, systems simulation is used to analyze complex models that cannot be solved practically by means of analytical methods. These models often are stochastic to account for the realities of the system. We know that stochastic

Table 4.2 Pseudo-random numbers*

0.65481	0.32533	0.60527	0.73407
0.90124	0.04805	0.59466	0.41994
0.74350	0.68953	0.45973	0.25298
0.09893	0.02529	0.46670	0.20539
0.61196	0.99970	0.82512	0.61427
0.15474	0.74717	0.12472	0.58021
0.94557	0.10805	0.29529	0.19255
0.42481	0.77602	0.39333	0.33440
0.23523	0.32135	0.20106	0.57546
0.04493	0.45753	0.42941	0.21615

* These pseudo-random numbers were calculated using the congruence method. A description of this method is given by G. Gordon, *Systems Simulations*, 2d ed., Prentice-Hall, Inc., Englewood Cliffs, N.J., 1978.

models include random variables that have associated probability distributions. Monte Carlo simulation is a method that enables us to include random variables in mathematical models.

Monte Carlo simulation relies upon sampling values from the probability distributions associated with the random variables. Values of the random variables are selected at random from the appropriate distributions and then are used in the simulation. These observations of the random variables are made repetitively to imitate the behavior of the variables.

There are several methods that can be used to select observations of random variables from their probability distributions. These methods use *random numbers*. A random number R is a special random variable that is uniformly distributed between 0 and 1. This means that all values in the interval [0, 1] have equal likelihood of being selected for R. Random numbers also are independently distributed. That is, the value that R takes is not affected by past values of R.

Most computer-based simulations use *pseudo-random* numbers. These are values that behave like random numbers, although they actually are calculated by means of numerical methods. While pseudo-random numbers are not truly random, they have the appearance of being random. That is, they pass most of the statistical tests used for identifying random numbers. Pseudo-random numbers have the advantage of not requiring large amounts of storage in the computer. They also facilitate the exact replication of experiments by allowing for the same stream of numbers to be realized. Table 4.2 gives some pseudo-random numbers generated on a computer.

Generating Random Variables

How are random numbers used to obtain observations of random variables? To illustrate this, assume that our model includes the service time given to consumers. Also assume that service time is a discrete random variable. Table 4.3

Table 4.3 Probability distribution of service time and uniform random-number assignment

Service time, min	Probability	Cumulative distribution	Random-number assignment
1	0.02	0.02	$0.00 \leq R < 0.02$
2	0.03	0.05	$0.02 \leq R < 0.05$
3	0.15	0.20	$0.05 \leq R < 0.20$
4	0.30	0.50	$0.20 \leq R < 0.50$
5	0.20	0.70	$0.50 \leq R < 0.70$
6	0.15	0.85	$0.70 \leq R < 0.85$
7	0.08	0.93	$0.85 \leq R < 0.93$
8	0.05	0.98	$0.93 \leq R < 0.98$
9	0.02	1.00	$0.98 \leq R < 1.00$

lists the probability distribution of service time, the cumulative distribution, and the random-number assignment. The cumulative distribution gives the likelihood of service time being less than or equal to specific values. The probabilities must go from 0 to 1. We also know that the random number R is uniformly distributed in the interval [0, 1]. This relationship between the cumulative distribution and R is the basis for generating observations of random variables.

We now can make some observations of service time by using the cumulative distribution and the random numbers. This approach for generating observations of random variables, known as the *inverse transformation method,* is straightforward:

1. Select the first random number R from Table 4.2.
2. Equate the cumulative distribution to the random number. For example, in Table 4.3 find the interval for random-number assignment within which R lies.
3. Find the value of service time that equates the cumulative distribution to the random number. This value is the observation used in the simulation.

The steps described above are illustrated graphically in Figure 4.3. The first random number is $R = 0.65481$. The cumulative probability (y axis) is set equal to R and the associated service time is read on the x axis. For $R = 0.65481$ the service time is five minutes. To make another observation of service time, we move to the next random number $R = 0.90124$. This has an associated service time of seven minutes. If we repeat this process many times, 2 percent of the observations of service time will be one minute, 3 percent will be two minutes, and so forth. Why does this happen?

The previous example assumed that service time was a discrete random variable. The same approach can be used to generate the observations from continuous random variables. The inverse transformation method is widely used with Monte Carlo simulation. But for some random variables there are more efficient approaches. The details of the various methods for generating

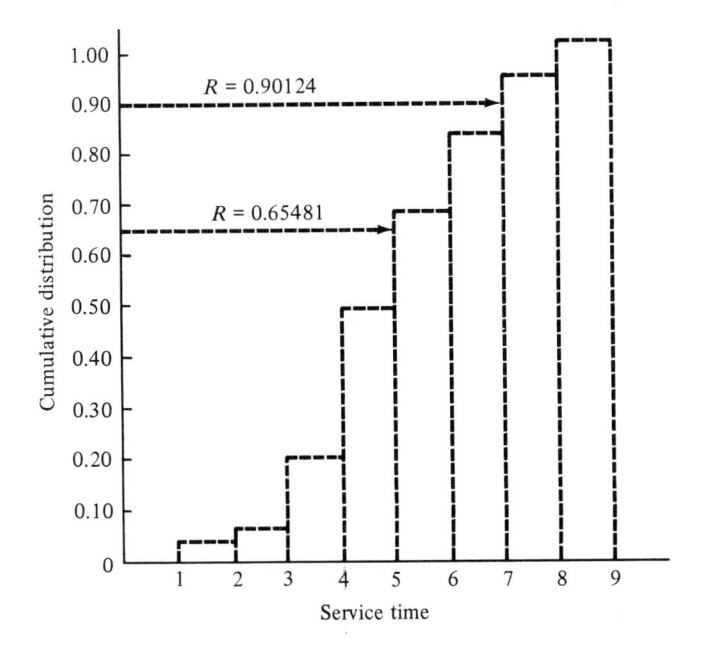

Figure 4.3 Cumulative distribution of service time.

observations of random variables are discussed in most books dealing with simulation.

Discrete-Event Simulation

Discrete-event simulation focuses upon events that change the state of the system. Frequently, these events are the arrivals and departures of consumers, and they occur at instants of time.

Figure 4.4 depicts the general flow of a discrete-event simulation. First, event times are generated, perhaps by means of Monte Carlo techniques. A clock that begins at time 0 is set equal to the next chronological event time. If the next event is an arrival, then the consumer will either enter service or wait in line, depending upon the status of the server. If the next event is a departure (service completion), then either another consumer will enter service or the server will become idle, depending on the status of the waiting line. The state of the system is updated in response to the event, and the clock time is compared with a prespecified maximum time. If the clock time is greater than or equal to the maximum time, then summary statistics describing the system are calculated and printed, and the simulation is stopped. Otherwise, the clock moves to the next event time.

Example 4.1: Airline ticket counter We shall use discrete-event simulation to observe the system state of an airline ticket counter. The system has a

68 DECISION MODELS FOR SERVICE OPERATIONS

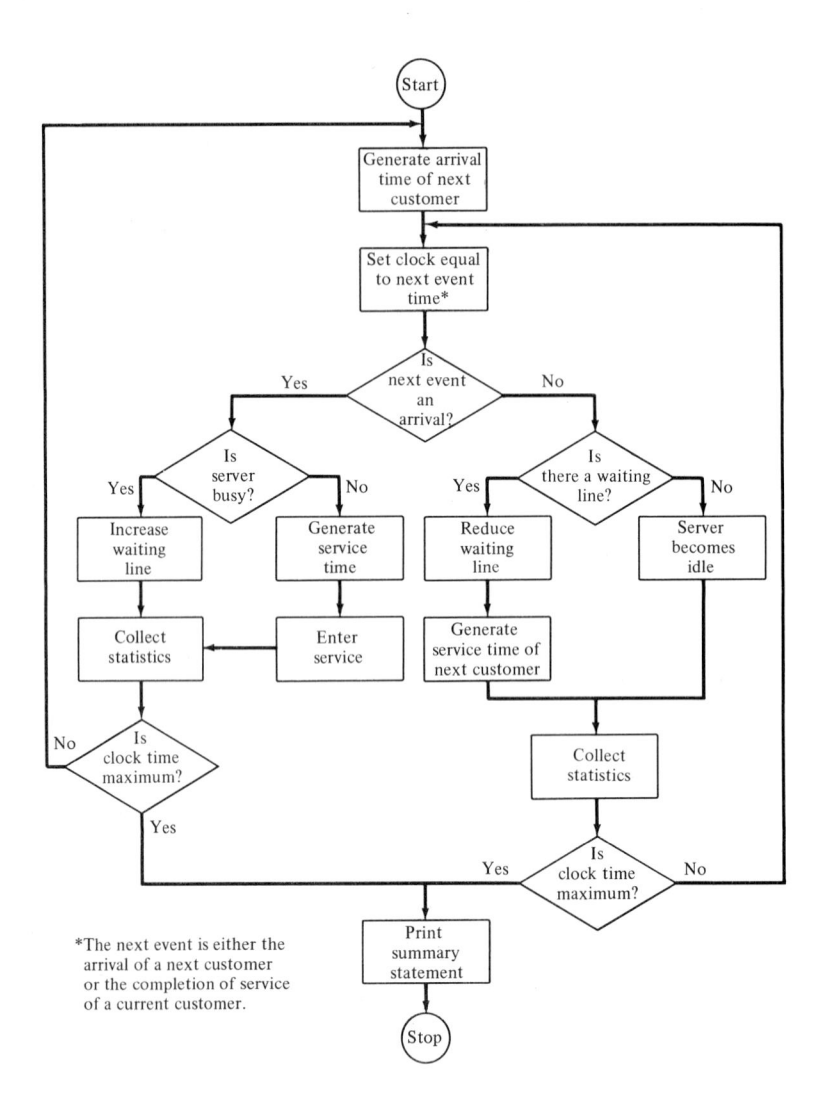

Figure 4.4 An example of a discrete-event simulation flowchart.

single ticket agent and customers are served on a first-come, first-served basis. In this simulation we are concerned with the number of customers waiting, their waiting time, and the status of the ticket agent (busy or idle).

Table 4.4 gives the service times and interarrival times of the first 10 customers. Interarrival time is the time between successive arrivals and is used to determine actual arrival time. The service times and interarrival times may have been generated from appropriate probability distributions by means of Monte Carlo methods.

Table 4.4 Service times and interarrival times for first 10 customers

Customer	Time, min	Interarrival time, min
1	4	5
2	3	4
3	6	4
4	4	5
5	2	3
6	5	4
7	4	5
8	6	5
9	4	4
10	5	3

The simulation begins at time 0. Table 4.5 gives the times that each customer arrives, enters service, and departs service. For example, the first customer arrives at time 5, immediately enters service, and departs at time 9. However, customer 4 arrives at time 18 and finds the server busy. This customer enters service at time 19 and departs at time 23. The total time waiting in line for the 10 customers is 8 minutes. This gives an average waiting time of 0.8 minute per customer.

Table 4.6 lists in chronological order the times of all events in the simulation. We see that the ticket agent was idle for a total of 7 minutes out of the 50-minute simulation. This is a 14 percent idleness. Also, the maximum number of customers waiting in line was 1, and this occurred for 8 minutes out of the 50-minute simulation. This gives an average waiting line of 0.16 customers (0.16 × 1 + 0.84 × 0).

Table 4.5 Simulation of first 10 customers
Time, min

Customer	Arrival time	Time service begins	Time service ends	Time in line	Time in system
1	5	5	9	0	4
2	9	9	12	0	3
3	13	13	19	0	6
4	18	19	23	1	5
5	21	23	25	2	4
6	25	25	30	0	5
7	30	30	34	0	4
8	35	35	41	0	6
9	39	41	45	2	6
10	42	45	50	3	8

Table 4.6 Chronological listing of events

Event time	Event	Number of customers in line	Idle time of ticket agent
0	Start	0	
5	Arrival 1	0	5
9	Departure 1	0	
9	Arrival 2	0	0
12	Departure 2	0	
13	Arrival 3	0	1
18	Arrival 4	1	0
19	Departure 3	0	
21	Arrival 5	1	0
23	Departure 4	0	
25	Departure 5	0	
25	Arrival 6	0	0
30	Departure 6	0	
30	Arrival 7	0	0
34	Departure 7	0	
35	Arrival 8	0	1
39	Arrival 9	1	0
41	Departure 8	0	
42	Arrival 10	1	0
45	Departure 9	0	
50	Departure 10	0	

Example 4.2: A bank check processing operation[5] Commercial banks process huge volumes of checks every day. One important aspect of processing is collecting from the banks on which the checks are drawn. This may take anywhere from a few hours to several days, depending upon the locations of the banks involved. Some checks that are not processed by a specific deadline are held over to the next day for collection.

Bank officials are concerned with the float associated with the check-collecting operations. Float is the dollar value of checks that have been written but not collected. The size of the float is important because there is an opportunity cost for not collecting on the checks. The money could have earned interest. Bank officials would like to institute check processing procedures that reduce the size of the float and consequently the associated opportunity cost.

Monte Carlo simulation was used to study alternative decision rules for processing checks at a major city bank. At this bank an average of one-half million checks arrive daily and these are worth between $1 and $2 billion. For a check to be collected it must be processed and presented before specific deadlines during the day. Checks processed after the deadlines are held over to the next day.

---

[5] Adapted from L. Moore and B. Taylor III, "Experimental Investigation of Priority Scheduling in a Bank Check Processing Operation," *Decision Sciences,* vol. 8, no. 4, October 1977, pp. 692–710.

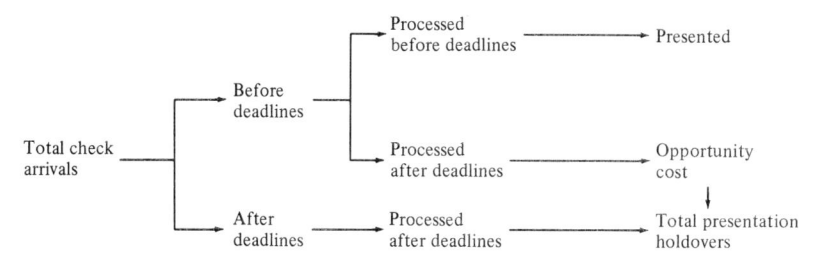

```
                         Processed
                      ┌─ before deadlines ──────── Presented
                      │
             ┌─ Before ─┤
             │ deadlines│
Total check  │          │  Processed                Opportunity
arrivals ────┤          └─ after deadlines ──────── cost
             │                                       │
             │                                       ↓
             │  After       Processed                Total presentation
             └─ deadlines ── after deadlines ─────── holdovers
```

Figure 4.5 Relationship between check arrivals and opportunity cost. [*Reprinted with permission from L. Moore and B. Taylor, III, "Experimental Investigation of Priority Scheduling in a Bank Check Processing Operation," Decision Sciences, vol. 8, no. 4, October 1977, p. 694.*]

Figure 4.5 depicts the relationship between the arrival of checks and the opportunity cost associated with float. The bank was experiencing a $300-million carryover from one day to the next, but it was not known how much of this was due to checks that arrived after the deadline. These checks, of course, could not be processed in time. The primary concern was with checks that arrived before the deadline and were held over.

The simulation study focused on the computer sorter that processed the checks. There are two types of inputs to the computer sorter: (1) checks completely encoded at the time of arrival with the dollar amount entered in magnetic ink and (2) items that were encoded after arrival and sorted according to final sending point. Checks of the first type are called *whole deposits* and checks of the second type are referred to as *1260* (the identification number of the encoder used).

About 142 trays of checks arrive at the computer sorter each day. One tray contains approximately 3500 checks. About twice as many whole-deposit trays arrive as *1260* trays. The computer can process 50,000 checks per hour.

Simulation was used to investigate a modified system for sorting checks on the computer. There were many detailed differences between the modified system and the existing system. However, an important aspect of the modified system was a priority scheme based upon the dollar value of checks. For example, the order in which trays are presented to the computer would be "$1001 and over" checks first, "$501–$1000" checks second, and "$500 and under" checks last. That is, the highest-dollar-value checks would be be given priority for processing.

The computer sorter system was studied by means of discrete-event simulation. Some of the relationships used to describe the systems were:

1. The processing time of a tray on the computer sorter was assumed to be normally distributed with a mean of 4.2 minutes and a standard deviation of 0.2 minutes.
2. The time between tray arrivals was assumed to be exponentially distrib-

uted, with mean time dependent upon the time of day. The mean interarrival times used are as follows:

Time	Mean interarrival time, min
Midnight–6 a.m.	19.4
6–8 a.m.	7.0
8–3 p.m.	5.9
3–5 p.m.	7.0
5 p.m.–midnight	22.6

3. Probabilities associated with tray type were 0.67 for whole-deposit trays and 0.33 for *1260* trays.
4. The number and dollar value of each category of checks in an arriving tray were assumed to be normally distributed. The mean values were estimated for each category of checks.

The check processing system was structured as a discrete-event simulation. A sample size of 40 simulation runs (days) was determined to be appropriate for investigating the modified sorting system. The simulation indicated that the float carried from one day to the next could be reduced by an average of $67 million with the modified system. Because $1 million in float had a $275-per-day opportunity cost, the modified system would reduce the opportunity cost by an average of $18,400 per day. This simulation model provided useful insights about the check processing system. It also enabled management to study the proposed modified system before any changes actually were made.

SUMMARY

Simulation is a versatile and powerful approach for analyzing management systems. It is particularly appropriate for deriving information from mathematical models that cannot be solved by means of analytical methods. Frequently, these models are complex and detailed, and they may include both the dynamic and stochastic features of the system.

Constructing a model to be analyzed by means of systems simulation requires considerable expertise. Not only does it require detailed knowledge about the system, it also requires mathematical model building skills, statistical expertise, and perhaps some computer programming skills. Developing and using a systems simulation model can be very expensive. And the costs of systems simulation must be compared with the potential benefits in a decision of whether or not to use this approach. In many situations, simulation is an excellent approach for analyzing management systems.

TOPICS FOR DISCUSSION

1. Compare and contrast static models with dynamic models for management decision making.
2. What are the advantages and disadvantages of Monte Carlo simulation compared with analytical methods?
3. List and discuss five applications of systems simulations to service organizations. Why was simulation used instead of analytical methods?
4. In your own words describe the simulation methodology.
5. Why are random numbers used to generate random variables? What is a pseudo-random number?
6. Compare and contrast discrete-event simulation with continuous simulation.
7. Give several service-related examples where discrete-event simulation would be a valuable decision-making tool. Discuss how the simulation study might be conducted.
8. Monte Carlo simulation and analytical methods sometimes are used together to approach various managerial problems. Suggest why and how these approaches might be combined.

EXERCISES

4.1 You have been asked by a retail association to develop an inventory control program for use on microcomputers. The program development requires the completion of the following three activities in sequence. You are concerned about the likelihood of finishing the project in the 10 days you promised.

Activity	Description	Expected time, days	Deviation from expected time, days	Probability
A	Write program.	5	+2	0.1
B	Debug program.	2	+1	0.2
C	Write user manual.	3	0	0.3
			−1	0.4

Using the Monte Carlo method, simulate 10 program development experiences. On the basis of your simulation results, what is the probability of finishing the project in 10 days as promised?

4.2 A textbook publishing company is considering the release of the following three books next year. Because of a cash flow problem the company is interested in predicting the expected gross profit from these books.

Book	First-year expected sales	Profit per copy sold	Deviation from expected sales, %	Probability
A	2,000	$5	80	0.1
B	5,000	2	90	0.2
C	10,000	1	100	0.4
			110	0.2
			120	0.1

Using the Monte Carlo method, simulate 10 realizations of the first year's sales experience and calculate the expected profit.

4.3 Constructing a distribution of demand during the reorder lead time is complicated if the lead time itself is variable. Consider the following distributions for a reorder point inventory system.

Daily demand	
Demand	Probability
0	0.1
1	0.2
2	0.3
3	0.3
4	0.1

Lead time	
Days	Probability
1	0.1
2	0.5
3	0.4

(a) What is the range of possible demands during the variable lead time?
(b) Develop a flowchart for a Monte Carlo simulation model that will generate a histogram of demand during lead time.
(c) Using the random numbers in Table D at the back of the book, simulate 10 demands during lead time.

4.4 The coast guard maintains a lighted buoy in the harbor entrance to warn ships of a dangerous reef. The flashing beacon contains two high-intensity quartz halogen bulbs. The supplier has provided the following data on bulb life:

Life, months	Probability
1	0.05
2	0.15
3	0.20
4	0.30
5	0.20
6	0.10

The estimated cost of dispatching a motor launch with a crew to the buoy to remove and replace the weatherproof cover over the bulbs is $50. Bulbs cost $10 each. The time involved in replacing a bulb is negligible. Coast guard regulations require that both bulbs work all the time.

(a) Develop a Monte Carlo simulation model that will help the coast guard decide between the following bulb replacement policies; (1) Replacing only the bulb that burns out or (2) replacing both bulbs when one burns out.
(b) Using the table of random numbers, simulate five years of activity. Discuss some questions of experimental design that this problem raises.
(c) Can you think of other policies to test?

4.5 The project network for installing a new computer is shown in Figure 4.6, with data on activity times and their deviations.

(a) What is the expected project duration time?
(b) Develop a Monte Carlo simulation model that can be used to generate a distribution of project completion times.
(c) Using Table D at the back of the book, simulate 10 project completion experiences. Is your expected project duration the same as calculated in part *a* above?
(d) Explain how you might determine an appropriate number of simulation runs to ensure a good estimation of the project duration distribution.

4.6 Sea Dock, a private firm, operates an unloading facility located in the Gulf of Mexico for supertankers delivering crude oil for refineries in the Port Arthur area of Texas. Sea Dock is interested in using a Monte Carlo simulation model of its operation to test the effect of different queue disciplines on average tanker waiting time. It wishes to institute the queue discipline "select from those

Activity	Expected time, days	Deviation from expected activity time, days	Probability
A	3	+2	0.2
B	5	+1	0.3
C	2	0	0.4
D	4	−1	0.1
E	3		
F	4		
G	2		
H	4		
I	3		
J	2		

Figure 4.6 Project network for new computer installation.

tankers that are waiting the smallest tanker for unloading next" in place of the current first-come, first served (FCFS) rule. This rule results from observing 100 tanker arrivals and realizing that unloading time is a function of the tanker size.

Hours between arrivals	Frequency
11	25
12	50
13	25
	100

Tanker size	Unloading time, hr	Frequency
A	7	40
B	8	30
C	9	20
D	10	10
		100

(a) Develop a flowchart for a Monte Carlo simulation model that could test the effect of different queue disciplines on Sea Dock's operation.

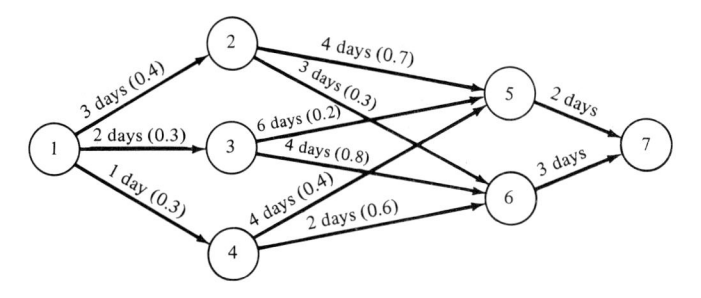

Figure 4.7 Travel network.

(b) Explain why the proposed queue discipline (or any other possible queue discipline) will have no effect on the average waiting time in the system on the basis of the data from the sample of 100 tanker arrivals.

4.7 Consider the travel network shown in Figure 4.7 in which the probabilities of selecting a route from each node are shown in parentheses.

(a) Develop a Monte Carlo simulation model to determine the expected trip time from node 1 to node 7.

(b) Simulate 10 trips and calculate the expected trip time.

4.8 Dr. Swift has the following appointment schedule for Saturday morning:

Appointment time	Expected duration, min
9:00	10
9:15	20
9:30	30
10:00	10
10:15	30
10:45	20
11:00	10
11:15	30

His secretary has researched past records and determined the following distributions:

Arrival time	Frequency	Appointment duration, % of expected time	Frequency
20 min early	10	80	5
10 min early	20	90	25
Just on time	50	100	30
10 min late	10	110	25
Not show up	10	120	15
	100		100

Two days ago Dr. Swift received a telegram from New York advising him that his mother is seriously ill. He has made reservations to fly east on Saturday afternoon at 2 o'clock. In order to get to the airport on time, he knows that he must leave the office by noon.

(a) Develop a Monte Carlo simulation model to assist Dr. Swift in determining the probability of completing his morning appointments in time to make the flight.

(b) Simulate the appointment experiences for 20 mornings and calculate the probability of leaving the office by noon.

(c) How might you check on the appropriateness of the sample size for your simulation?

(d) How might Dr. Swift improve his chances of making the flight?

CASELETTE: KROHLER SUPERMARKETS

The management of Krohler Supermarkets, a national chain, has become aware of decreasing profit margins from its stores during the previous year. Three factors contributed to this earnings decline: (1) rapidly increasing labor costs, (2) increasing costs of wholesale merchandise and inability to increase retail prices because of governmental controls and consumer resistance, and (3) increasing price competition from their major national competitors. Even though earnings have declined significantly, sales volume has been increasing from year to year, but at a lower rate in the immediate past year than in previous years.

Merchandise typically accounted for the largest proportion of a store's operating costs (roughly 80 percent), with the inventory control and stocking functions being critical to this aspect of managing operations. Inventory was ordered each week from a central warehouse by means of a fixed-interval system. Stocking consisted primarily of placing the commodities on display, pricing each item, controlling pilferage, and removing damaged goods.

Labor costs were the second largest factor in supermarket operations (roughly 10 percent). More than 40 percent of the store's wages went to people manning the "front end," which included cashiers and baggers. About 33 percent of the wages went to the stockers, and the balance went to people in the meat, produce, bakery, or deli departments or to the store supervisors. Krohler management personnel felt that a prime area in which to reduce overall operating costs would be the labor requirements, but they were unwilling to reduce their service level to the consumer because of the negative effect it would have on their competitive stance in the supermarket industry.

Krohler's small industrial engineering department had recommended to the management that an investigation be made of the potential savings associated with implementing automatic point-of-sale (APOS) systems at the checkout counters. These APOS systems combined electronic cash registers and optical scanning devices which interacted with an in-store minicomputer that could substantially boost labor productivity, as well as provide greater control over inventory levels and ordering requirements. Since almost every commodity Krohler carried was labeled with a unique manufacturing code (called the Universal Product Code), the system functioned by having a checker pull an item across the optical scanner so the code could be read. The price of the item would be obtained immediately from the minicomputer's memory, displayed on the register, and tallied into the customer's bill. At the same time, the computer would compute any applicable sales tax and note the sale of all items in its inventory control program for later summarization of daily stock levels and order requirements. If a particular item did not have the code attached to it (for example, a bag of apples, deli specialties, or nonuniform packages of meats), the cashier would enter the price and an item code manually into the register. In addition to the time savings anticipated in checking out individual customers, the industrial engineering department pointed out that a significant amount of time would be saved in closing out a register (counting the cash and reconciling opening and closing balances with the intervening sales) and also in not having to price each item on the shelves.

With the existing manual system in place, the basic functions of front-end personnel, including cashiers and baggers, were: (1) enter the merchandise cost into the register, (2) enter applicable sales taxes, (3) total the cost of purchases and taxes, (4) receive payment (cash, check, food stamps, discount coupons, etc.) and make change, (5) bag the items purchased, and (6) assist a customer in removing the bag(s) from the store. Miscellaneous tasks also included check cashing, looking up prices on unmarked items, weighing and pricing produce, and responding to any customer questions.

In a typical Krohler Supermarket, there would be 10 checkout counters placed in a row at the store front, with one designated as an "express" lane to serve customers with 10 items or less. However, because sales fluctuated greatly by day and by hour, management tried very hard to match the number of counters open with expected demand so that both a high level of customer service and a high level of checkout-counter productivity would be maintained. Customer-service level was defined as the percentage of time that more than a certain number of customers were either being served or waiting in line to be checked out. A general rule of thumb used by Krohler management was that the percentage of time that more than three customers waited in line (including the person being served) should be held to 5 percent or less. Checkout-counter productivity was measured on the basis of sales dollars per manned checkout-counter hour.

As one means of examining the possible savings associated with an APOS system versus the existing manual system, Krohler's industrial engineering department was given the task of simulating the store operations with the two systems. Assume you are part of the study team and develop responses to the following questions:

1. What specific questions should a simulation of the two different systems address?
2. What data must be collected before a simulation could be performed?

Given your responses to the above questions, develop a flowchart of a simulation model which could be used to study the operation of an APOS system at a typical Krohler supermarket.

CASELETTE: COQUILLE REFINERY CORPORATION

The Coquille Refinery Corporation is contemplating building a crude-oil storage and docking facility on the southern coast of France. They plan to import crude oil by ship from the Middle East and distribute this crude oil by pipeline to refineries in the area.

The construction of this facility represents a substantial capital investment. Furthermore, the cost of such a facility is principally determined by its crude-oil storage capacity. You have been asked to study the problem and recommend an appropriate storage capacity; bear in mind that too large a capacity represents an unnecessary expense, but too small a capacity will result in costly later additions to the facility.

A long-term contract has been made with the Middle East supplier to furnish an average daily supply of 300,000 barrels of crude oil. Because its fleet of ships consist of 200,000-barrel tankers, the supplier expects that the arrival of its tankers will follow the distribution below:

Tanker arrivals per day	Probability
0	0.1
1	0.5
2	0.2
3	0.2

A review of past production records of refineries in the area suggests the following distribution of crude-oil demand per day:

Barrels per day	Probability
100,000	0.1
200,000	0.2
300,000	0.3
400,000	0.4

Questions

1. Consider the following issues before you simulate:
   (a) What is the expected daily demand for crude oil? Why must this be so?
   (b) What assumptions concerning the timing of crude-oil receipts and deliveries would require the greatest oil storage capacity?
   (c) What assumption concerning receipts and deliveries would require the least oil storage capacity?
   (d) Give a reason based on systems-analysis considerations why backorders should be filled from the next day's receipts rather than considered as lost sales.
2. Develop a Monte Carlo simulation model for Coquille that will generate information useful for resolving the storage capacity problem and simulate 10 days of capacity.
3. Assume a computer program was written to simulate 10,000 days of activity under the assumptions listed in question 1b. From the results of such a simulation the following distribution of oil in storage, after a day's receipts, is determined. (Note: Negative figures represent backorders.)

Oil in storage, in thousands	Probability
−300	0.01
−200	0.04
−100	0.06
0	0.07
⋮	⋮
1000	0.09
1100	0.08
1200	0.07
1300	0.05
1400	0.03
1500	0.02
	1.00

(a) What level of crude-oil safety stock should be carried to ensure 95 percent protection against stockouts (stockouts 1 in 20 days)?
(b) If Coquille decides to use the above safety stock, what should be the oil storage capacity to ensure 90 percent protection against overruns (i.e. sufficient capacity to accommodate completely receipts 9 days out of 10)?
4. Note two ways one might determine if the simulation run length of 10,000 days is adequate.
5. Make a list of cost factors that would influence the final selection of oil storage capacity.

SELECTED BIBLIOGRAPHY

Forrester, J. W.: *Industrial Dynamics,* M.I.T. Press, Cambridge, Mass., 1961.
———: *Urban Dynamics,* M.I.T. Press, Cambridge, Mass., 1969.
———: *World Dynamics,* M.I.T. Press, Cambridge, Mass., 1971.
Gordon, G.: *Systems Simulation,* 2d ed., Prentice-Hall, Inc., Englewood Cliffs, N.J., 1978.
Moore, L. J., and B. W. Taylor: "Experimental Investigation of Priority Scheduling in a Bank Check Processing Operation," *Decision Sciences,* vol. 8, no. 4, October 1977, pp. 692–710.
Naylor, T., and N. Durham: *The Design of Computer Simulation Experiments,* Duke University Press, Durham, N.C., 1969.
Pritsker, A. A. B., and C. D. Pegden: *Introduction to Simulation and SLAM,* Halsted Press, New York, 1979.
Smith, V. K., D. B. Webster, and A. H. Norman: "The Management of Wilderness Areas: A Simulation Model," *Decision Sciences,* vol. 7, no. 3, July 1976, pp. 524–536.

CHAPTER
FIVE

LINEAR PROGRAMMING MODELS IN SERVICES

Linear programming (LP) is a general computer-based modeling tool for making resource allocation decisions that transcend all aspects of service operations management. Linear programming is not computer programming. The programming refers to planning that uses mathematical models consisting of linear expressions.

A model is a selective abstraction of reality. Modeling is an art, because judgements are made in the selection of the important features of reality for the problem at hand. Modeling is also a science because decision variables must be identified and objectives must be clarified.

The use of models, such as linear programming, springs from the belief that the decision-making process can be enhanced by applying the scientific method. Scientists study nature and conduct controlled experiments to understand better the phenomena of interest. Decision models are the laboratory of managers interested in testing the outcomes of decisions before their actual implementation. In this way potential disasters may be avoided and the decision-making process may be improved through a better understanding of the environment.

This chapter emphasizes the art of formulating linear programming models and interpreting computer output. The mathematical details of model manipulation are not discussed. The availability of computer programs to solve LP models is extensive, and users need not be concerned about the mechanics of how optimal solutions are found, anymore than one needs to know the theory of the internal combustion engine to drive an automobile. The chapter concludes with a discussion of an extension of LP called *goal programming*. Goal programming is useful when dealing with the multiple objectives that are unavoidable in public services decision making. In the following section we discuss the concept of an optimum solution to a constrained model.

CONSTRAINED OPTIMIZATION MODELS

In everyday life we are faced with making decisions in which the potential set of alternatives is restricted by money, time, physical limitations, or some other element. For example, suppose we wish to buy a car this week, we can qualify for a $6000 loan, and we want a vehicle with at least a 30-miles-per-gal EPA rating. The set of possible cars is constrained by time, budget, and mileage performance. These constraints are restrictions that reduce the allowable set of solutions to our problem. In this manner constraints actually help us make decisions by limiting our search for a solution to candidate cars that meet the stipulated requirements.

If economy were our goal, then we might measure this by calculating the cost per mile for each car meeting our constraints. The car with the least cost-per-mile value would be considered the optimum solution to our constrained decision problem.

Constrained optimization problems are common to service operations. For example, a potential location for a service facility is constrained by available sites. Scheduling telephone operators is constrained by the variations in demand for service and personnel policies regarding split shifts.

Linear programming models are a special class of constrained optimization models. In linear programming all relationships are expressed as linear functions. All linear programming models are of the following algebraic form:

Maximize (or minimize) $c_1 x_1 + c_2 x_2 + \cdots + c_n x_n$

subject to the system constraints

$$a_{11} x_1 + a_{12} x_2 + \cdots + a_{1n} x_n \begin{Bmatrix} \leq \\ = \\ \geq \end{Bmatrix} b_1$$

$$a_{21} x_1 + a_{22} x_2 + \cdots + a_{2n} x_n \begin{Bmatrix} \leq \\ = \\ \geq \end{Bmatrix} b_2$$

$$\vdots$$

$$a_{m1} x_1 + a_{m2} x_2 + \cdots + a_{mn} x_n \begin{Bmatrix} \leq \\ = \\ \geq \end{Bmatrix} b_m$$

and nonnegativity constraints

$$x_1, x_2, \ldots, x_n \geq 0$$

Note that each system constraint is limited to only one of the conditions ≤ or = or ≥ (strictly > or < are not permitted). This problem structure contains the following characteristics:

1. *Decision variables.* The variables $x_1, x_2, \ldots, x_n$ are called decision variables that take on real values greater than or equal to zero. These variables represent actions the decision maker can take, such as assign 10 telephone operators to the Tuesday afternoon shift. Notice the decision to do nothing is represented by all zero-valued decision variables.
2. *Objective function.* The function $c_1 x_1 + c_2 x_2 + \cdots + c_n x_n$ is called the objective function, which is either maximized (e.g., profits) or minimized (e.g., costs) depending upon the nature of the coefficients $c_1, c_2, \ldots, c_n$. The problem states that this function is made as large or small as possible provided a system of constraints are met.
3. *Constraint functions.* As numerical values are assigned to the decision variables $x_1, x_2, \ldots, x_n$ to influence the objective function, these values are also assigned to each constraint function. The model requires that numerical values be assigned such that no constraint is violated. The numbers $b_1, b_2, \ldots, b_n$ taken together are called the *right-hand sides* (RHS). These numbers indirectly limit the possible values of the decision variables. These RHS are typically resource constraints, such as total worker hours available.
4. *Parameters.* Coefficients in the objective function and RHS values are parameters. Parameters are entities whose values remain fixed during the problem solution, but could be changed later. Examples are unit profit contributions for the objective-function coefficients or availability of resources for RHS values.
5. *Constants.* The coefficients $a_{11}, a_{12}, \ldots, a_{1n}$ represent the consumption of the first RHS resource per unit of each decision variable. These coefficients reflect a constant rate of resource use, for example, the amount of protein per pound in different foods.

Example 5.1: Stereo Warehouse The retail outlet of Stereo Warehouse, a discount hi-fi store, is planning a special clearance sale. The showroom has 400 square feet of floor space available for displaying this week's specials, a model X receiver and series Y speakers. Each receiver has a wholesale cost of $100, requires 2 square feet of display space, and will sell for $150. The wholesale cost for a pair of speakers is $50; they require 4 square feet of display space and will sell for $70. The budget for securing the stereo items is limited to $8000. The sales potential for the receiver is considered to be no more than 60 units. However, the budget-priced speakers appear to have an unlimited appeal. The store manager desiring to maximize gross profit must decide how many receivers and speakers to stock.

This problem can be formulated as an LP problem in the following manner:

Let x = number of receivers to stock

y = number of speakers to stock

Maximize $50x + 20y$ gross profit

subject to
$$2x + 4y \leq 400 \quad \text{floor space}$$
$$100x + 50y \leq 8000 \quad \text{budget}$$
$$x \leq 60 \quad \text{sales limit}$$
$$x, y \geq 0$$

The decision variables x and y appear in both the objective function and the constraint functions to ensure that the optimum solution does not violate the resource limits. For example, if one receiver is stocked, the gross profit contribution is $50; however, the available floor space is reduced by 2 square feet, the budget is reduced by $100, and potential x sales are now limited to 59. The solution to this problem will increase the values of x and y until some, but not necessarily all, the resources are depleted. The solution of Stereo Warehouse is deferred until a later section.

Before leaving the topic of constrained optimization models, a few caveats are in order. When a constrained optimization model is solved, the solution is called *optimal,* meaning the best values for the decision variables have been found. However, this so-called optimal solution is with respect to the model and may not be optimal with regard to *reality.* Recall that the model is only an abstraction of reality and cannot include all the elements of reality. There can be a vast difference between the optimal solution of the model and what is finally implemented by the decision maker for reasons ranging from political considerations to personal preference. An optimal site selection for company headquarters could be vetoed by the corporate president, who refuses to live in the selected city. However, when used with care, linear programming models provide an excellent vehicle to lay out the problem in explicit detail for all to see and to question. Constraints can be modified, added, or eliminated and objective functions can be changed. Furthermore, the cost of pursuing a nonoptimal solution can be determined.

Next, we discuss the art of formulating LP models and consider examples of classic LP model structures.

FORMULATING LINEAR PROGRAMMING MODELS

The ability to recognize a potential linear programming problem and to structure it for computer solution is an art acquired from experience. However, some exposure to examples of classical forms of LP models can help. For example, recognizing that a problem is like the classical "diet problem" suggests the likely mathematical structure that will evolve. Experience with formulating LP problems suggests that the following strategy can be helpful.

1. Draw a diagram or construct a table showing the relationships in the problem, including the parameters and constraints.
2. Identify and invent symbolic notation for the decision variables.
3. State the objective in words.
4. Express each constraint in words, identify the right-hand-side values, and note the direction of the inequality.
5. Write out the complete model in algebraic form. Begin with the objective function, then list the right-hand sides, followed by the inequality signs, and finish by filling in the left-hand algebraic expressions for each constraint.
6. Note the nonnegativity conditions for the decision variables.
7. Using possible solutions, test the problem for internal consistency and completeness.

These guidelines are followed in formulating the example problems.

Diet Problem

This class of problems is illustrated by a selection of various food items for a meal that meets certain nutritional requirements. Given that each food item selected contributes to the nutritional requirements at different rates, the objective is to find a mixture that minimizes costs.

Example 5.2: Lakeview Hospital The dietitian at Lakeview is preparing a special milk shake as a treat for cardiac care patients recovering from surgery. The dietitian is concerned that the level of cholesterol will not exceed 175 units and the level of fat will not exceed 150 units. Protein content should be at least 200 units and the calorie content should exceed 100 units. The dietitian has selected three possible ingredients: skim milk, ice cream, and sugar. One unit of skim milk costs 15 cents and contributes 50 units of cholesterol, no fat, 70 units of protein, and 30 calories. One unit of ice cream costs 25 cents and contributes 150 units of cholesterol, 100 units of fat, 10 units of protein, and 80 calories. One unit of sugar costs 10 cents and contributes 90 units of cholesterol, 50 units of fat, no protein, and 200 calories. How many units of each ingredient should be included in the milk shake if costs are to be minimized?

The information from the problem statement is organized and displayed in Table 5.1. The problem suggests the following decision variables:

Let
M = units of skim milk in the shake
C = units of ice cream in the shake
S = units of sugar in the shake

The object is to minimize the total cost of the milk shake. Table 5.1 identifies the constraints as being cholesterol content less than or equal to

Table 5.1 Lakeview Hospital diet problem
Units of nutritional element per unit of ingredient

Nutritional element	Skim milk	Ice cream	Sugar	Nutritional requirement
Cholesterol	50	150	90	≤ 175
Fat	0	100	50	≤ 150
Protein	70	10	0	≥ 200
Calories	30	80	200	≥ 100
Cost per unit, cents	15	25	10	

175 units, fat content less than or equal to 150 units, protein content equal to or more than 200 units, and calorie content equal to or more than 100 units. The algebraic expression of the model becomes:

Minimize $\quad 0.15M + 0.25C + 0.10S$

subject to
$$50M + 150C + 90S \leq 175 \quad \text{cholesterol}$$
$$100C + 50S \leq 150 \quad \text{fat}$$
$$70M + 10C \geq 200 \quad \text{protein}$$
$$30M + 80C + 200S \geq 100 \quad \text{calories}$$
$$M, C, S, \geq 0$$

Notice that the problem as formulated could yield a solution using skim milk alone (i.e., $M = 3.5$, $C = 0$, and $S = 0$). Because such a solution would hardly be considered a milk shake, additional constraints should be added to the problem to preclude this from occurring.

Shift Scheduling Problem

This problem arises when an operation must be staffed over a period of time during which the requirements for service vary. The objective is to schedule staff assignments to meet the requirements during the period using the minimum number of people.

Example 5.3: Gotham City Police Patrol Unable to hire new police officers because of budget limitations, the Gotham City Police Commissioner is trying to utilize the force better. The minimum requirement for police patrols for weekdays is noted below:

Time period	Patrol officers, minimum
Midnight–4 a.m.	6
4–8 a.m.	4
8–noon	14
12–4 p.m.	8
4–8 p.m.	12
8–midnight	16

LINEAR PROGRAMMING MODELS IN SERVICES

Patrol officers are assigned in pairs to a patrol car and they work an eight-hour shift. Currently patrol officers report for duty at midnight, 8 a.m., and 4 p.m. The commissioner believes a better use of officers could be achieved if they were also permitted to report for duty at 4 a.m., noon, and 8 p.m. Of course, this might require some patrol officers to switch partners after four hours of duty. How many patrol officers should report for their eight-hour shift at each of the six reporting times? The assignments must minimize the total number of officers and still meet the minimum staffing requirements.

Figure 5.1 shows with shading the periods of overstaffing that result from the current practice of patrol officers reporting for eight-hour shifts at three reporting times (i.e., $x_1 = 6$, $x_3 = 14$, and $x_5 = 16$). The decision variables for the staffing problem are defined as:

Let x_i = number of officers scheduled to report at reporting time i for $i = 1, 2, 3, 4, 5, 6$

The problem is directed at minimizing the total number of patrol officers with constraints on the minimum number required for each four-hour time interval during the day. The algebraic expression of the model also accounts for the implied constraint that once a patrol officer reports for duty, that officer remains on duty for a complete eight-hour shift.

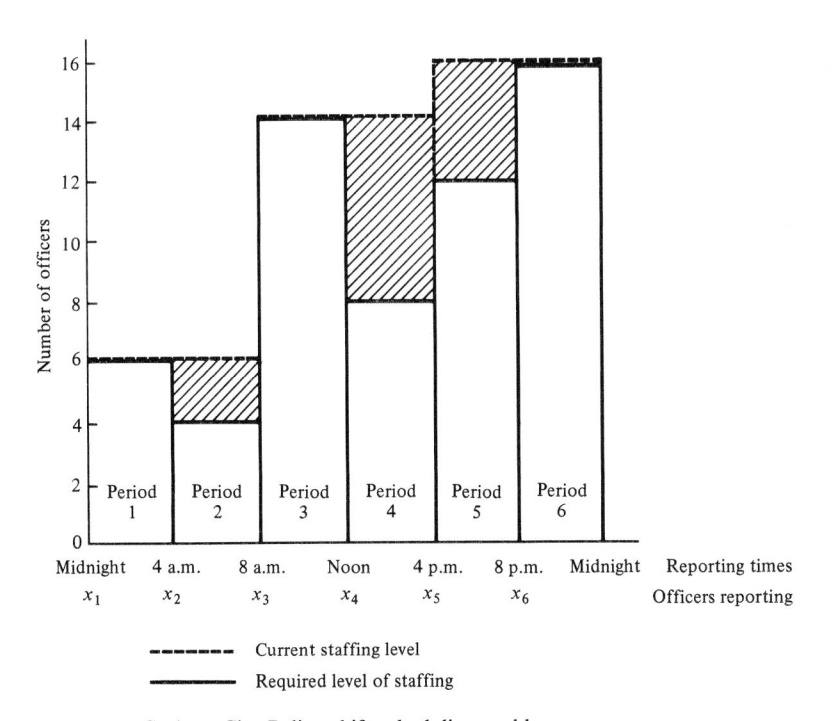

Figure 5.1 Gotham City Police shift scheduling problem.

88 DECISION MODELS FOR SERVICE OPERATIONS

$$\text{Minimize} \quad x_1 + x_2 + x_3 + x_4 + x_5 + x_6$$

$$\begin{aligned}
\text{subject to} \quad x_1 + x_6 &\geq 6 && \text{period 1} \\
x_1 + x_2 &\geq 4 && \text{period 2} \\
x_2 + x_3 &\geq 14 && \text{period 3} \\
x_3 + x_4 &\geq 8 && \text{period 4} \\
x_4 + x_5 &\geq 12 && \text{period 5} \\
x_5 + x_6 &\geq 16 && \text{period 6}
\end{aligned}$$

Notice that each decision variable appears in exactly two constraints to account for the eight-hour shift. For example, patrol officers reporting at 4 a.m. contribute to the staffing requirements for both the second and third time interval because each time interval is four hours in duration. Because we are dealing with numbers of patrol officers, the decision variables must be restricted to integer values. Fortunately, because of the problem structure, the linear programming solution will be integer. A linear programming model that has all constraints with coefficients of 1 will yield an integer solution. In general, however, a linear programming solution yields nonnegative real (integer or fractional) numbers.

Workforce Planning Problem

Employee turnover is common among service occupations, such as bank tellers and airline attendants. Furthermore, new employees require some training period before they are ready to meet the public. The level of staff required also varies in response to changes in consumer demand, such as summer or holiday vacation periods for airlines. Workforce planning involves the identification of when and how many people to recruit to meet future staffing requirements and to replace employees who leave. The objective is to meet staff requirements in a dynamic setting at minimum personnel cost.

Example 5.4: Last National Drive-In Bank Last National must decide how many new bank tellers to hire and train over the next six months. The teller requirements expressed as number of teller hours needed are 1500 in January, 1800 in February, 1600 in March, 2000 in April, 1800 in May, and 2200 in June. One month of training is necessary before a teller can be assigned duty; thus, tellers must be hired one month before they are actually needed. Also, each trainee requires 80 hours of simulated job experience supervised by a regular teller during the month of training. Hence, for each trainee, 80 fewer hours are available from regular tellers. Each experienced teller works 160 hours per month whether needed or not. Last National has 12 experienced tellers available at the beginning of January. Past experi-

LINEAR PROGRAMMING MODELS IN SERVICES

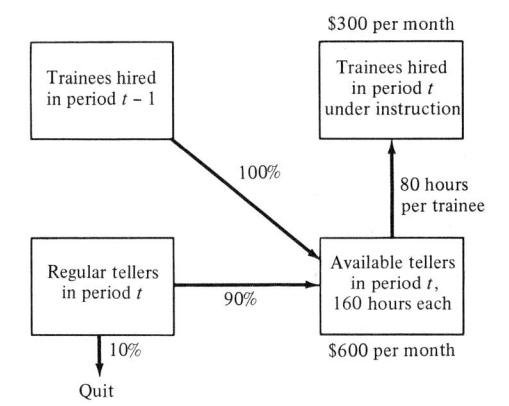

Figure 5.2 Monthly teller transition diagram.

ence has shown that by the end of each month, approximately 10 percent of the experienced tellers have quit their jobs. Regular tellers receive a salary of $600 per month and trainees are paid $300 during their month of training. How many tellers should be hired for each of the next six months?

Figure 5.2 captures the essential relationships for this time-phased planning model. The decision variables are the number of trainees to hire for each period and, in addition, the number of tellers available at the beginning of each period.

Let T_t = number of trainees hired at the beginning of period t
for $t = 1, 2, 3, 4, 5, 6$

A_t = number of available tellers at the beginning of period t for $t = 1, 2, 3, 4, 5, 6$

The objective is to minimize the total personnel costs over the six-month planning horizon. Two sets of constraints are required. One set represents the required teller hours for each month. Another set of constraints expresses the number of available tellers from one period to the next, with new hires and employee turnover accounted for. The following model will make use of some shorthand algebraic notation:

Minimize $\sum_{t=1}^{6} (600A_t + 300T_t)$

subject to
$160A_1 - 80T_1 \geq 1500$ January
$160A_2 - 80T_2 \geq 1800$ February
$160A_3 - 80T_3 \geq 1600$ March
$160A_4 - 80T_4 \geq 2000$ April

$$160A_5 - 80T_5 \geq 1800 \qquad \text{May}$$

$$160A_6 - 80T_6 \geq 2200 \qquad \text{June}$$

$$A_1 = 12$$

$$0.9A_{t-1} + T_{t-1} - A_t = 0 \qquad \text{for } t = 2, 3, 4, 5, 6$$

$$A_t, T_t \geq 0 \text{ and integer} \qquad \text{for } t = 1, 2, 3, 4, 5, 6$$

Note that, in using this model, only the value for January hiring is of immediate interest. The trainee hires for the other months can be treated as estimates for now. Prior to the start of February the model is run again with the requirements for January dropped and the July requirements added. In this manner each hiring decision is based on a six-month projected requirement plan, which permits a gradual adjustment in the size of the workforce. Also, as in the police patrol example, the decision variables must be restricted to integers. Unfortunately, this problem structure does not necessarily yield integer results. This problem illustrates a special class of linear programming models, called *integer programming*, which requires a special computer code that guarantees integer results.

Transportation Problem

Transportation problems are a special class of LP models called *networks*. The problem structure also ensures integer solution. The problem is essentially one of shipping goods from origins or supply points to destinations or demand points. Each destination has a particular demand, and each origin a particular supply. The number of origins need not equal the number of destinations. To facilitate solution, a dummy origin or destination is added to balance the total demand and supply. Given a unit shipping cost between every pair of origin and destination, the objective becomes one of minimizing total shipping cost. This problem structure also arises in nontransportation situations, such as assigning personnel to jobs.

Example 5.5: Lease-A-Lemon Car Rental Lease-A-Lemon has discovered an imbalance in the distribution of rental cars in its northeast territory. A surplus of cars exists in the following cities: 26 in New York, 43 in Washington, and 31 in Cleveland. Shortages exist in the following cities: 32 in Pittsburgh, 28 in Buffalo, and 26 in Philadelphia. The table below shows the distances in miles to transfer a car between the cities:

	Pittsburgh	Buffalo	Philadelphia
New York	439	396	91
Washington	296	434	133
Cleveland	131	184	479

LINEAR PROGRAMMING MODELS IN SERVICES

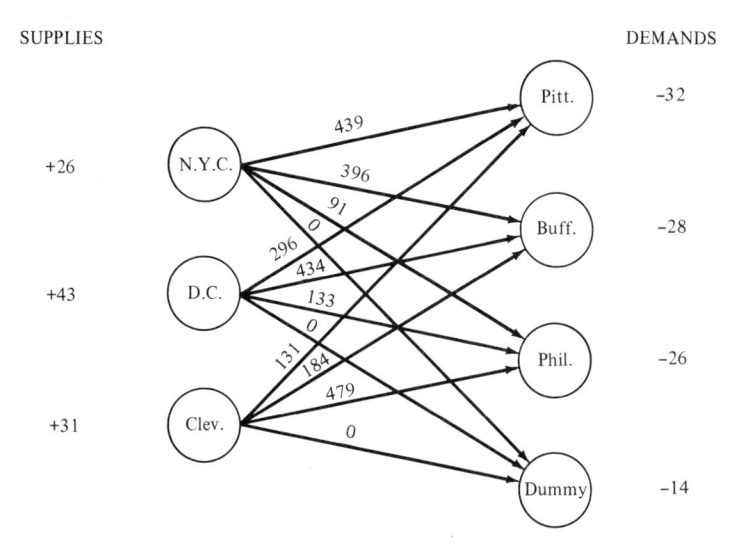

SUPPLIES

DEMANDS

+26 N.Y.C. 439, 396, 91, 0

+43 D.C. 296, 434, 133, 0

+31 Clev. 131, 184, 479, 0

Pitt. −32

Buff. −28

Phil. −26

Dummy −14

Figure 5.3 Lease-A-Lemon car redistribution network.

Develop a plan to redistribute the cars at minimum cost on the basis of a transportation charge of $1 per mile.

Figure 5.3 is a network representation of the problem with origin nodes showing positive supply and destination nodes showing negative demand. The supply and demand are balanced with the addition of a dummy destination node showing a −14 (i.e. 86 − 100) demand. The dummy represents cars not redistributed and, thus, has unit transportation costs of zero. The decision variables are the number of cars sent from each supply city to each demand city. To facilitate the model formulation, a unit transportation cost parameter is also defined below:

Let x_{ij} = number of cars sent from city i to city j for
$i = 1, 2, 3$ and $j = 1, 2, 3, 4$

c_{ij} = unit cost in dollars to transport a car from city i to city j for $i = 1, 2, 3$ and $j = 1, 2, 3, 4$

The objective is to minimize total redistribution cost. Two sets of constraints are required: one set limits the supply from each origin and the other set limits the demand at each destination. The constraints will all be equalities because supply and demand are balanced.

Minimize $\sum_{i=1}^{3} \sum_{j=1}^{4} c_{ij} x_{ij}$

subject to

$$x_{11} + x_{12} + x_{13} + x_{14} = 26$$
$$x_{21} + x_{22} + x_{23} + x_{24} = 43$$
$$x_{31} + x_{32} + x_{33} + x_{34} = 31$$
$$x_{11} + x_{21} + x_{31} = 32$$
$$x_{12} + x_{22} + x_{32} = 28$$
$$x_{13} + x_{23} + x_{33} = 26$$
$$x_{14} + x_{24} + x_{34} = 14$$

$$x_{ij} \geq 0 \quad \text{for all } i, j$$

Notice the characteristic structure of the constraints that is common to all transportation problems. The appearance of only coefficients of 1 in the constraints assures an integer solution.

OPTIMAL SOLUTIONS AND COMPUTER ANALYSIS

The Stereo Warehouse problem is used to illustrate graphically the nature of LP models and their solutions. Because the problem has only the two decision variables x and y, we can draw a picture of the model and see how an optimal solution is achieved. This geometric representation of the model is also used to explain the computer-generated solution.

Graphical Solution of LP Models

Recall the formulation of the Stereo Warehouse model, where x and y represent the number of receivers and speakers to be stocked. In this formulation, Z represents the value of the objective function.

Maximize	$Z = 50x + 20y$	gross profit
subject to	$2x + 4y \leq 400$	floor space
	$100x + 50y \leq 8000$	budget
	$x \leq 60$	sales limit
	$x, y \geq 0$	nonnegativity

The set of inequalities or constraints defines a region of permissible values of x and y. Notice that letting $x = 0$ and $y = 0$ satisfies all the inequalities, as it should, because that is the "do-nothing" alternative. However, our interest is finding the best, or optimal, values of x and y that maximize the objective function. For a two-variable problem, the permissible or *feasible* region can be identified if we plot each constraint inequality. The procedure for drawing the feasible region follows:

1. Assign one variable to the x axis and the other variable to the y axis.
2. Notice that the nonnegativity constraints on the variables limit the feasible region to the first quadrant (upper right-hand corner).
3. Temporarily change each inequality constraint to an equality.
4. Plot each constraint as an equation using the x and y intercepts (i.e., assume $x = 0$ and solve for the y intercept, then repeat for $y = 0$ to find the x intercept, and draw a straight line joining these two axis intercepts).
5. Identify the feasible side of the inequality. This can be accomplished by substituting $x = 0$ and $y = 0$ into the inequality constraint, unless (0, 0) happens to be on the line; then some other arbitrary point must be selected. If the inequality is satisfied, then the side containing $x = 0$ and $y = 0$ should be shaded; otherwise the opposite side of the line is shaded (i.e., represents a feasible region).
6. Notice that each constraint further reduces the feasible region into a geometric figure called a *convex polygon*.

The above procedure is followed for Stereo Warehouse to create the feasible region shown in Figure 5.4. Notice for the first constraint that the x intercept ($y = 0$) is $\frac{400}{2} = 200$ and the y intercept ($x = 0$) is $\frac{400}{4} = 100$. Also notice that the test point $x = 0$, $y = 0$ satisfies all three constraints, and, thus, the shaded area is either below or to the left of each constraint. Furthermore, notice that any point (combination of x and y values) within the feasible region simultaneously satisfies all three constraints and the nonnegativity condition.

The optimal solution to the problem can now be found graphically. Recall that the objective is to make Z as large as possible provided the values of x and y are in the feasible region. If we let Z take on a trial value, say 2000, then we can plot Z as a straight line, using the intercept approach. For $Z = 2000$, the x intercept ($y = 0$) is $\frac{2000}{50} = 40$ and the y intercept ($x = 0$) is $\frac{2000}{20} = 100$. In Figure 5.5 we see the objective function $Z = 2000$ plotted on the graph of the feasible region. As the value of Z is increased to 3000, 3600, and finally 3800, we find the objective function moves out from the origin in parallel lines, or contours. The maximum value of $Z = 3800$ occurs at point C (i.e., $x = 60$, $y = 40$), a corner of the polygon. If Z moves out any further, no point on the contour line will be common to the feasible region. We have just demonstrated an axiom of linear programming. An optimal solution to a LP model will always occur at a corner or *extreme point*, of the feasible region. In the special case in which the slope of the objective function is identical to a constraint, the optimal solution will also include any point between the extreme points along the constraint line.

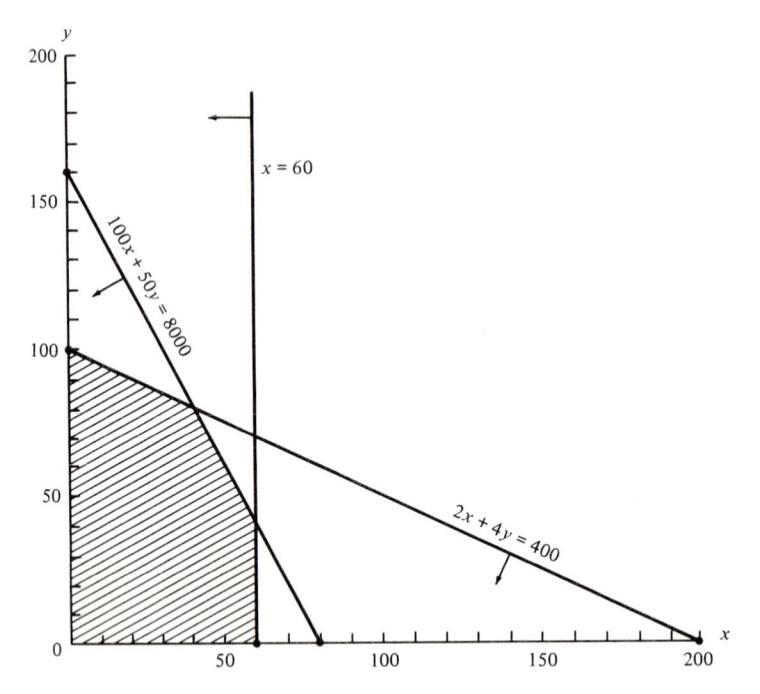

Figure 5.4 Stereo Warehouse feasible region.

LP Model in Standard Form

Realizing that an optimal solution will be found at an extreme point reduces our search for a feasible region to a finite set of points. Furthermore, each extreme point is defined as the simultaneous solution of a pair of constraints stated as equations.

A formal way of restating an inequality constraint as an equation in linear programming models is accomplished with the use of a *slack* or *surplus* variable. For constraints of the ≤ variety a nonnegative slack (i.e., resources not used) variable is added to the left-hand side. For example, the Stereo Warehouse floor-space constraint would be restated as:

$$2x + 4y + s_1 = 400$$

The slack variable s_1 would represent available floor space not used by the receivers and speakers stocked. For constraints of the ≥ variety, a nonnegative surplus (i.e., results produced in excess of requirements) variable is subtracted from the left-hand side. For example, in the Gotham City Police Patrol problem the first-period patrol-officer requirement constraint would be restated as:

$$x_1 + x_6 - \bar{s}_1 = 6$$

The surplus variable $\bar{s}_1$ would represent the number of patrol officers assigned to the first period in excess of the requirement of six patrol officers.

LINEAR PROGRAMMING MODELS IN SERVICES **95**

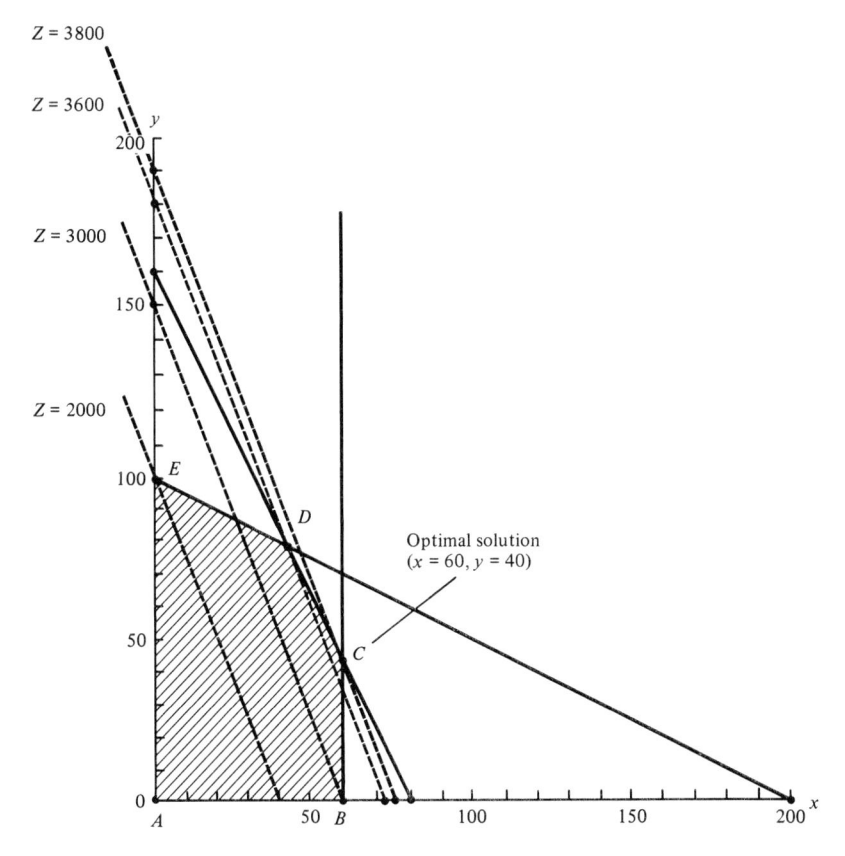

Figure 5.5 Stereo Warehouse optimal solution.

The Stereo Warehouse model is reformulated below using the following slack variables:

s_1 = square feet of floor space not used

s_2 = dollars of budget not allocated

s_3 = number of receivers that could have been sold

Maximize $\quad Z = 50x + 20y$

subject to
$$2x + 4y + s_1 = 400$$
$$100x + 50y + s_2 = 8000$$
$$x + s_3 = 60$$
$$x, y, s_1, s_2, s_3 \geq 0$$

The Stereo Warehouse problem is solved by examining each extreme point identified by the letters A, B, C, D, and E in Figure 5.5. Table 5.2 contains the

96 DECISION MODELS FOR SERVICE OPERATIONS

Table 5.2 Stereo Warehouse extreme-point solutions

Extreme point	Nonbasic variables	Basic variables	Variable value	Objective-function value Z
A	x, y	s_1	400	0
		s_2	8000	
		s_3	60	
B	s_3, y	s_1	280	3000
		s_2	2000	
		x	60	
C	s_3, s_2	s_1	120	3800
		y	80	
		x	60	
D	s_1, s_2	s_3	10	3600
		y	80	
		x	40	
E	s_1, x	s_3	60	2000
		y	100	
		s_2	3000	

analysis of these extreme points. At each extreme point, variables with positive values are labeled *basic* and variables with zero values are labeled *nonbasic*. Notice that the number of basic variables equals the number of constraints in the problem. This result is always true for LP problems except in the special case in which a basic variable is also zero-valued (a situation referred to as a *degenerate* solution). Also, notice that when a slack variable is nonbasic, its corresponding constraint is binding (i.e., all the resource is used).

The computer solution of LP problems evaluates the extreme points in a systematic way. This computer procedure is called the *simplex algorithm*. In our Stereo Warehouse example, the simplex algorithm starts at point A, proceeds to extreme point B (because variable x contributes more to the objective function than y), and stops at extreme point C, the optimum. The algorithm is able to identify optimality, and, thus, all extreme points need not be examined. The details of the simplex algorithm are not discussed here but can be found in any of the operations research texts listed in the Selected Bibliography at the end of this chapter.

Computer Analysis and Interpretation

The computer input for the Stereo Warehouse example is shown in Figure 5.6. Notice the use of .LE. instead of the ≤ symbol. The word RNGOBJ stands for "range objective-function coefficients" and RNGRHS stands for "range the right-hand side" of the constraints. All LP computer programs have the ability to perform a sensitivity analysis on the problem parameters.

The computer solution to the Stereo Warehouse problem is shown in Figure 5.7. Each variable, including the slacks for constraints 1, 2, and 3, is given a

LINEAR PROGRAMMING MODELS IN SERVICES

```
        VARIABLES
         X Y
        MAXIMIZE
         50 X + 20 Y
        CONSTRAINTS
1.       2X + 4Y .LE. 400
2.       100X + 50Y .LE. 8000
3.       X .LE. 60
        RNGOBJ
        RNGRHS
        OPTIMIZE
```

Figure 5.6 Computer input for Stereo Warehouse.

number for future reference. The status of each variable at optimality is either B (basic) or NB (nonbasic). The activity level or value of each variable is given. The nonbasic variables have, of course, zero value.

The opportunity cost of the nonbasic slack variables has an important managerial interpretation. Recall that a nonbasic slack variable means that the corresponding constraint is binding at optimality. For the Stereo Warehouse problem, the budget constraint of $8000 and the limit of 60 units for receiver sales are restricting the profit to a maximum of $3800. The floor-space constraint is no problem because at optimality 120 square feet (value of s_1) of the available 400 square feet are not being used. If profits are to be increased, more of these limiting resources must be obtained. The opportunity cost of $10 for constraint 3 represents the increase in the objective function value if one more unit of x could be sold. Notice that, if the RHS of constraint 3 is increased by 1, the following constraint equations are binding (s_2 and s_3 are omitted because they are nonbasic):

$$100x + 50y = 8000$$

$$x = 61$$

The solution of the above simultaneous equations yields $x = 61$ and $y = 38$. Substituting these values into the objective function provides a revised profit of $3810, an increase of $10. A similar analysis explains the $0.40 increase in the objective-function value if the RHS of the budget constraint is increased by $1 to $8001.

These opportunity costs are often referred to as *shadow prices* because they represent the imputed price of the limited resource. These shadow prices

```
                    SUMMARY OF RESULTS

VAR   VAR      ROW  STATUS    ACTIVITY      OPPORTUNITY
NO    NAME     NO                LEVEL         COST
 1    X                B      60.0000000        --
 2    Y                B      40.0000000        --
 3    --SLACK   1      B     120.0000000        --
 4    --SLACK   2     NB          --          .4000000
 5    --SLACK   3     NB          --         10.0000000

        MAXIMUM VALUE OF THE OBJECTIVE FUNCTION =     3800.000000
```

Figure 5.7 Computer results for Stereo Warehouse.

98 DECISION MODELS FOR SERVICE OPERATIONS

can be used by the manager to decide on the value of securing more resources. For example, if money could be borrowed for less than 40 cents on the dollar during the period of the sale, the difference would become additional profit.

Most computer programs use the convention that if a unit increase in the RHS value improves the objective function (increases it for maximization or decreases it for minimization), then the shadow price is positive and represents the amount of objective-function change. However, in some problems increasing an RHS could result in impairing the objective function. For example, if the protein constraint in the Lakeview Hospital diet problem is increased, the objective function could increase, contrary to the minimization desired. The shadow price would be negative for this constraint if it is binding at optimality.

Finally, notice that the shadow price of a resource in excess (corresponding slack variable is basic) is considered zero. In the Stereo Warehouse problem the value to the manager of securing additional floor space is zero because all the available floor space is not used.

SENSITIVITY ANALYSIS

What happens to the optimal solution of an LP problem if the values of the model parameters change? This question is of great interest to a decision maker in an uncertain environment. Sensitivity of the solution with respect to the objective-function coefficients is discussed first, and then constraint RHS ranging is analyzed.

Objective-Function Coefficient Ranges

The permissible range of each objective-function coefficient is shown in Figure 5.8. The coefficient for the y variable (CJ = 2) may range from a low of 0 to a high of 25. The x-variable coefficient (CJ = 1) has a range of 40 to infinity. Within these ranges the optimal solution remains at extreme point C, shown in Figure 5.9. As shown, the objective-function slope changes with different coefficient values and essentially pivots about extreme point C.

```
                        RNGOBJ
                        ******
            (OPTIMALITY RANGE FOR COST COEFFICIENTS)
                      BASIC VARIABLES ONLY

  CJ    XIN      MIN CJ        ORIGINAL CJ      MAX CJ        XIN
                 --------      ------------     -------
                 Z-LOWER             Z          Z-UPPER

  2      4       0.0000         20.000          25.000          5
                 3000.0         3800.0          4000.0

  1      5       40.000         50.000          *INF*
                 3200.0         3800.0
```

Figure 5.8 Objective-function coefficient sensitivity results.

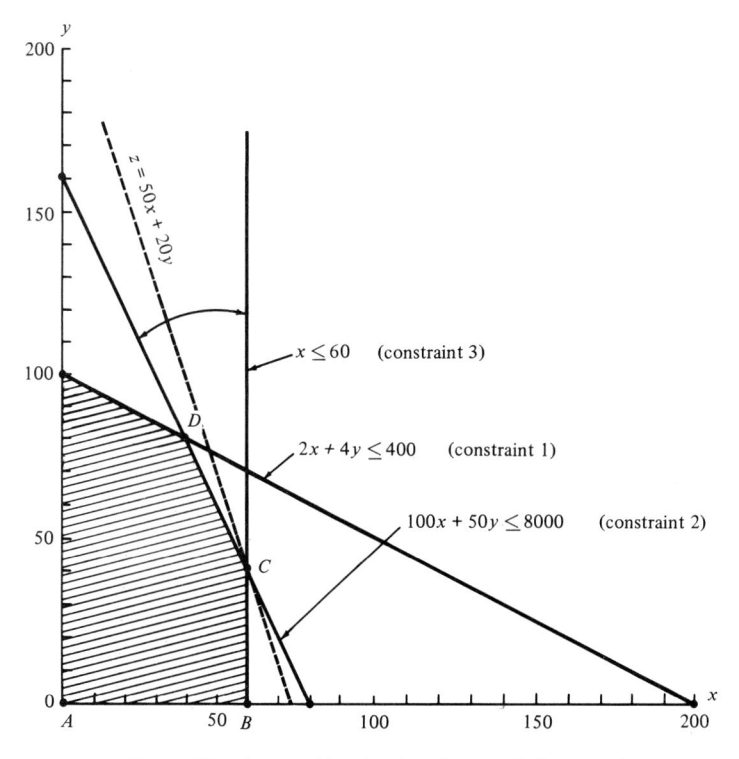

Figure 5.9 Stereo Warehouse objective-function coefficient ranging.

Notice that, with a y coefficient of 0, the objective function lies along the line segment BC of constraint 3. When the y coefficient is 25, the objective function lies along the line segment DC, parallel to constraint 2. The column labeled "XIN" in Figure 5.8 gives the variable number that would enter the solution if the coefficient exceeds the range. For example, if the y coefficient exceeds 25, variable number 5 (s_3) enters the solution. This means the optimal solution will move from extreme point C to D in Figure 5.9. If the y coefficient falls below 0 (i.e., goes negative), variable number 4 (s_2) enters the solution. This means the optimal solution will move from extreme point C to B. A similar analysis can be made for the x objective-function coefficient.

Figure 5.8 also gives the value of the objective function at the extremes of each coefficient range. The decision maker must be cautioned that the range for each coefficient is limited to changing one parameter at a time holding all others fixed.

Right-Hand-Side Ranging

The allowable RHS ranges for each of the two binding constraints is shown in Figure 5.10. The RHS for the second constraint (BI = 2) ranges from 6000 to 9500. The third constraint right-hand side (BI = 3) ranges from 40 to 80. Within these ranges the optimal solution contains the basic variables s_1, x, and y. The

100 DECISION MODELS FOR SERVICE OPERATIONS

```
                         RNGRHS
                         ******
           (OPTIMALITY RANGE FOR RIGHT-HAND-SIDE CONSTANTS)
                      NON-SLACK RESOURCES ONLY

 BI    XOUT      MIN  BI       ORIGINAL BI       MAX  BI      XOUT
                 -------       -----------       -------
                 Z-LOWER            Z            Z-UPPER


  2     2        6000.0          8000.0          9500.0         3
                 3000.0          3800.0          4400.0

  3     3        40.000          60.000          80.000         2
                 3600.0          3800.0          4000.0
```

Figure 5.10 Right-hand-side-ranging results.

value of these variables will change as reflected in the changes in the objective-function value. It should be noted that the shadow price for each resource applies *only* in the appropriate range. For example, recall that the shadow price for constraint 3 is a $10-per-unit increase in the RHS. Notice that the objective-function value increases from $3800 to $4000 when the RHS increases from 60 to 80 [i.e., $(80 - 60) \cdot (10) = 200$]. Likewise the objective-function value is reduced by $200 when the RHS of constraint 3 is decreased from 60 to 40.

Notice in Figure 5.11 what happens graphically when the RHS of con-

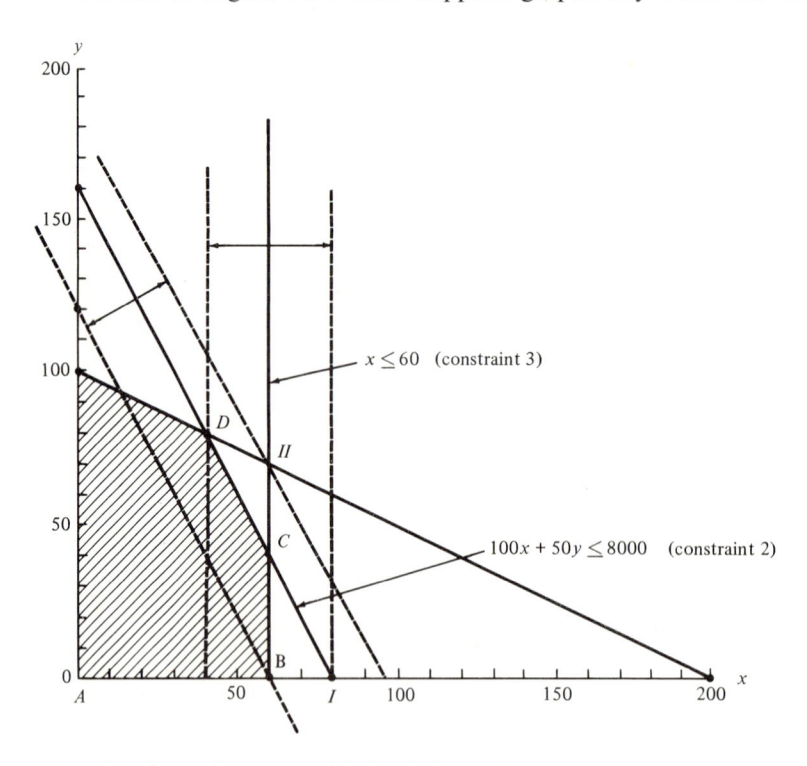

Figure 5.11 Stereo Warehouse right-hand-side ranging.

straint 3 is changed. As the RHS is increased, the extreme point C moves along the line segment CI until C becomes coincident with I at a RHS = 80. The values of the basic variables at extreme point I are $s_1 = 240, x = 80$, and $y = 0$. This is a degenerate solution because variable $y = 0$ but still remains in the basis. Note under the "XOUT" column of Figure 5.10 that variable 2, or y, leaves the basis if the RHS of constraint 3 exceeds 80.

If the RHS of constraint 3 is reduced, the extreme point C moves along the line segment CD until C becomes coincident with D at RHS = 40. The values of the basic variables at extreme point D are $s_1 = 0, x = 40$, and $y = 80$. This is a degenerate solution because variable s_1 is leaving the basis. Again from Figure 5.10 note under the "XOUT" column that variable 3, or s_1, leaves the basis if the RHS of constraint 3 falls below 40. A similar analysis for binding constraint 2 can be made to show graphically the movement of extreme point C along the line segment BII as the RHS is changed from 6000 to 9500.

The concept that the resource shadow price is limited to the RHS range is important in postoptimality analysis. For example, in the Stereo Warehouse problem suppose additional money can be obtained at a cost less than the shadow price of 40 cents per dollar. The question of how much to obtain at this price is answered by the RHS range on the budget constraint. Secure $9500 − $8000, or $1500, additional financing to maximize profits. The same caution raised earlier about treating the sensitivity analysis as being limited to changing one parameter at a time, holding all others fixed, is true for RHS ranging.

GOAL PROGRAMMING

Linear programming models allow for only one objective, and all constraints must be met absolutely. Many problems, particularly in the public sector, have multiple objectives in different units of measure. This makes the construction of a consolidated single objective difficult, if not impossible. For example, an emergency ambulance system could have the following objectives:

1. Maintain an average response time of approximately four minutes.
2. Ensure that 90 percent of all calls receive aid in less than 10 minutes.
3. Try not to exceed a budget of $100,000 per year.
4. Allocate calls to ambulance crews in an equitable manner.

Goal programming is a variation of linear programming which permits multiple and conflicting goals with different dimensions. Multiple goals are rank-ordered and treated as *preemptive priorities*. In the solution procedure, higher-ranked goals are not sacrificed to achieve lower-ranked goals. The solution approach is equivalent to solving a series of nested LP problems in which higher-ranked goals become constraints on lower-ranked goals. Where linear programming optimizes a single objective, goal programming minimizes the deviations from goals. This solution approach is known as "satisficing" because not all goals will necessarily be met but instead the goals will be achieved as closely as possible.

The objective function will contain only deviational variables (i.e., plus or minus deviations from goals), which can also be given *deviational weights* to distinguish relative importance within a priority level. The objective is always to minimize the sum of the deviations at each priority level, with consideration given to the hierarchy of preemptive priorities. All constraints are stated as equalities and contain both plus and minus deviational variables in addition to decision variables. To illustrate a goal programming model, the Stereo Warehouse example is reformulated as a goal program.

Example 5.6: Stereo Warehouse as a goal program

Let x = number of receivers to stock
y = number of speakers to stock
d_1^- = amount by which profit falls short of \$999,999
d_1^+ = amount by which profit exceeds \$999,999
d_2^- = amount by which floor space used falls short of 400 square feet
d_2^+ = amount by which floor space used exceeds 400 square feet
d_3^- = amount by which budget falls short of \$8,000
d_3^+ = amount by which budget exceeds \$8,000
d_4^- = amount by which sales of receivers falls short of 60
d_4^+ = amount by which sales of receivers exceeds 60
P_k = priority level with rank k

Minimize $Z = P_1 d_4^+ + P_2(d_1^- + 2d_3^+) + P_3(d_2^- + d_2^+)$

subject to
$$50x + 20y + d_1^- - d_1^+ = 999{,}999 \quad \text{profit goal}$$
$$2x + 4y + d_2^- - d_2^+ = 400 \quad \text{floor space goal}$$
$$100x + 50y + d_3^- - d_3^+ = 8{,}000 \quad \text{budget goal}$$
$$x + d_4^- - d_4^+ = 60 \quad \text{sales-limit goal}$$

$x, y, d_1^-, d_1^+, d_2^-, d_2^+, d_3^-, d_3^+, d_4^-, d_4^+ \geq 0$

This formulation has translated the profit objective into a goal at the second priority level. Notice that only d_1^- is included in the objective function to be minimized. Minimizing d_1^-, the underachievement of the goal, forces the profit to approach 999,999, a very large number. The floor space used for display now becomes a third priority in which both deviational variables are minimized. In other words, we want to use approximtely 400 square feet. The goal programming model permits a previous absolute constraint on available space to be treated as a more realistic approximate requirement. Exceeding the budget is to be avoided because only d_3^+ is found in the objective function. The deviational weight of 2 indicates that meeting the budget is twice as important as maximizing profit. Finally, exceeding the sales limit of 60 receivers is found at the first priority. This illustrates how system or physical constraints are treated in goal

```
VARIABLES
X Y DM1 DP1 DM2 DP2 DM3 DP3 DM4 DP4
MINIMIZE
1000DP4 + 100DM1 + 200DP3 + DM2 + DP2
CONSTRAINTS
1.  50X + 20Y + DM1 - DP1 ,EQ, 999999
2.  2X + 4Y + DM2 - DP2 ,EQ, 400
3.  100X + 50Y + DM3 - DP3 ,EQ, 8000
4.  X + DM4 - DP4 ,EQ, 60
OPTIMIZE
```

Figure 5.12 Goal programming model of Stereo Warehouse for solution using LP program.

programming. Thus, the typical LP absolute constraints, such as ≤ or ≥, have their appropriate deviational variable at the first priority level. The goal hierarchy ensures that no solution will violate these system constraints.

Figure 5.12 illustrates the computer input for the Stereo Warehouse goal programming model for solution using a regular LP program. To ensure that the goal hierarchy is not violated, the priority ranks have been given increasingly large weights (i.e., $P_1 = 1000$, $P_2 = 100$, and $P_3 = 1$). The variables labeled "DM" represent underachievement deviations (d^-) and the variables labeled "DP" represent overachievement deviations (d^+).

The goal programming solution to Stereo Warehouse is found in Figure 5.13. Notice that the values for the decision variables x and y are identical to the previous LP solution. When the value for DM1 is subtracted from its RHS of 999,999, the profit is found to be $3800, as before. The deviational variable DM2 takes on a value of 120, indicating the underachievement of our goal to use approximately 400 square feet of floor space. Our budget of $8000 is completely exhausted because DP3 = 0. The deviational variable DM4 is nonbasic or zero, as required to achieve the constraint on receiver sales. In summary, all goals are met except the desire to utilize 400 square feet of floor space. The objective-function value is of little consequence because it is simply the sum of all weighted deviations. Unfortunately the opportunity costs, or shadow prices, are of no interest because the objective function has no economic meaning.

```
                    SUMMARY OF RESULTS

VAR     VAR         ROW STATUS          ACTIVITY
NO      NAME        NO                  LEVEL
1       X           --      B           60,0000000
2       Y           --      B           40,0000000
3       DM1         --      B           996199,0000000
4       DP1         --      NB          --
5       DM2         --      B           120,0000000
6       DP2         --      NB          --
7       DM3         --      NB          --
8       DP3         --      NB          --
9       DM4         --      NB          --
10      DP4         --      NB          --

MINIMUM VALUE OF THE OBJECTIVE FUNCTION  =  99620020,000000
```

Figure 5.13 Computer results of the goal programming model of Stereo Warehouse.

SUMMARY

Linear programming is one of the most popular computer-based modeling techniques available to the modern service operations manager. Computer programs are widely available in both batch and interactive modes. The power of LP to find optimal solutions and to conduct sensitivity analysis is invaluable to the decision maker. Furthermore, the structure of the constrained optimization model fits well the real world of the service operations manager.

The art of formulating LP models is developed through examples and practice using a systematic approach. Many example LP models illustrate the general problem-solving nature of linear programming. We find that the discipline of formulating LP models helps decision makers clarify objectives and identify resource constraints.

The procedure for solving LP models is demonstrated by the use of graphics. Because no one solves real LP models by hand, the interpretation of computer solutions is stressed. Again, using graphics, the concepts of shadow prices and sensitivity analysis are demonstrated. Because many service operations managers are faced with multiple objectives, the concept of goal programming is introduced. With goal programming, the manager attempts to satisfy goals rather than optimize a single objective.

TOPICS FOR DISCUSSION

1. Give some everyday examples of constrained optimization problems.
2. How can the validity of linear programming models be evaluated?
3. The simplex algorithm is basically a systematic procedure for solving a series of simultaneous equations. Comment.
4. Why can the number of nonnegative variables in a LP solution never exceed the number of constraints?
5. Interpret the meaning of the opportunity cost for a nonbasic decision variable that did not appear in the LP solution.
6. Explain graphically what has happened when a degenerate solution occurs in a LP problem.
7. Using Figure 5.9, analyze the x objective-function coefficient that ranges from a value of 40 to infinity.
8. Using Figure 5.11, explain what happens to the LP solution as the RHS of binding constraint 2 ranges from $6000 to $9500.
9. Linear programming is a special case of goal programming. Explain.
10. What are some limitations in the use of linear programming?

EXERCISES

5.1 The Economy Cab Company wants to mix two fuels (A and B) for its taxi cabs in order to minimize operating costs. The company needs at least 3000 gallons in order to operate its cabs next month. There are only 2000 gallons of fuel A available, and fuel B is unlimited in supply. The mixed fuel must have an octane rating of at least 80.

When fuels are mixed, the amount of fuel obtained is just equal to the sum of the amounts put in, if no spillage or evaporation is assumed. The resulting octane rating is just the average of the individual octanes, weighted in proportion to the respective volumes. Fuel A costs 20 cents per gallon and has an octane rating of 90; fuel B costs 10 cents per gallon and has an octane rating of 75.

(*a*) Formulate this blending problem (a variation on the diet problem) as a linear programming model to minimize the cost of the blended fuel.

(*b*) Using the graphical method, determine the amount of each fuel required for an optimum blend.

5.2 Springdale has been ordered by a federal district court to desegregate its school system. The city is divided into seven school districts and is served by three elementary schools, one junior high, and one high school. The table below gives the distance from each district to each elementary school and the number of minority and white children in each district. Ideally minorities should represent 40 percent of the enrollment in each elementary school. However, to achieve perfect desegregation is not practical, and, thus, the school board is willing to settle for a percentage of minorities in each school that is no less than 30 percent or more than 50 percent. Each school has a capacity of 400 students. Formulate a linear programming model to minimize the total number of student miles traveled by bus. Do not solve.

District	Distance to school, mi A	B	C	Minorities in district	Whites in district
1	10	18	32	90	40
2	0	25	38	110	20
3	20	13	24	50	60
4	8	22	33	70	70
5	35	0	16	40	130
6	26	14	24	30	120
7	38	7	0	10	160
Total				400	600

5.3 The computer input for the Lakeview Hospital example is shown in Figure 5.14, with M, C, and S defined as units of skim milk, ice cream, and sugar. The results of the computer solution are given in Figure 5.15.

(*a*) What is the cost of the milk shake?

(*b*) How many units of each ingredient are required for this minimum-cost milk shake? If you feel this mixture is unacceptable as a milk shake, suggest a constraint that would guarantee an acceptable milk shake.

(*c*) What would be the cost of including 1 unit of ice cream in the mixture? Explain why this cost is less than 25 cents.

(*d*) What is the cholesterol, fat, protein, and calorie content of this milk shake?

```
      TITLE
      LAKEVIEW HOSPITAL
      REGULAR
      VARIABLES
      M C S
      MINIMIZE
      .15M + .25C + .10S
      CONSTRAINTS
   1. 50M + 150C + 90S ,LE, 175
   2. 100C + 50S ,LE, 150
   3. 70M + 10C ,GE, 200
   4. 30M + 80C + 200S ,GE, 100
      RNGOBJ
      RNGRHS
      OPTIMIZE
```

Figure 5.14 Computer input for Lakeview Hospital.

106 DECISION MODELS FOR SERVICE OPERATIONS

```
                    SUMMARY OF RESULTS

VAR   VAR      ROW STATUS      ACTIVITY          OPPORTUNITY
NO   NAME       NO              LEVEL              COST
 1    M         --   B        2.8571429              --
 2    C         --   NB           --               .1907143
 3    S         --   B         .0714286              --
 4  --SLACK      3   NB           --               .0019286
 5  --SLACK      4   NB           --               .0005000
 6  --SLACK      1   B        25.7142857             --
 7  --SLACK      2   B       146.4285714             --

  MINIMUM VALUE OF THE OBJECTIVE FUNCTION =        .435714
```

Figure 5.15 Lakeview Hospital computer solution.

The sensitivity analysis of objective-function coefficients and right-hand-side parameters are shown in Figures 5.16 and 5.17.

(*e*) What are the ranges of acceptable unit costs for skim milk and sugar for their optimal solution?

(*f*) What ingredient enters the solution if either cost exceeds its upper limit?

(*g*) What are the acceptable ranges for the minimum limits on the levels of protein and calories in the milk shake?

(*h*) What ingredient leaves the solution if the protein requirement falls to zero?

5.4 The computer input for Gotham City Police Patrol is shown in Figure 5.18, with x_j defined as the number of patrol officers reporting for duty at the beginning of period j. The results of the computer solution are given in Figure 5.19.

(*a*) How many patrol officers are required to meet the staffing requirements? Is this solution an improvement over the current practice of patrol officers reporting at only three times during the day?

(*b*) In what period is there an excess of patrol officers? As police chief how could you make full use of their time?

(*c*) Using Figure 5.1 in the text, sketch in the results of this optimum staffing schedule.

(*d*) What does an opportunity cost of zero for variable x_4 suggest to you?

(*e*) A police officer, unhappy about reporting for duty at midnight, suggested the following schedule: $x_1 = 0$, $x_2 = 8$, $x_3 = 6$, $x_4 = 2$, $x_5 = 10$, $x_6 = 6$. Show that this schedule is both feasible and optimal.

5.5 The computer input for Last National Drive-In Bank is shown in Figure 5.20, with A_j and T_j representing the number of tellers available and trainees hired at the beginning of period j. The results of the computer solution are given in Figure 5.21.

```
                           RNGOBJ
                           ******
               (OPTIMALITY RANGE FOR COST COEFFICIENTS)
                         BASIC VARIABLES ONLY

 CJ    XIN       MIN CJ        ORIGINAL CJ       MAX CJ        XIN
                 ------                           ------
                 Z-LOWER           Z            Z-UPPER

  1     4      1.50000E-02        .15000        1.4850           2
               5.00000E-02        .43571        4.2500

  3     5      4.44089E-16        .10000         .60377          2
                 .42857            .43571         .47170
```

Figure 5.16 Lakeview Hospital objective-function coefficient sensitivity analysis.

LINEAR PROGRAMMING MODELS IN SERVICES 107

```
                              RNGRHS
                              ******
             (OPTIMALITY RANGE FOR RIGHT-HAND-SIDE CONSTANTS)
                        NON-SLACK RESOURCES ONLY

  BI    XOUT       MIN  BI        ORIGINAL BI       MAX  BI      XOUT
                   -------        -----------       -------
                   Z-LOWER             Z            Z-UPPER


   3      1        0.0000           200.00          233.33          3
                   5.00000E-02       .43571          .50000

   4      3        85.714           100.00          157.14          6
                    .42857            .43571         .46429
```

Figure 5.17 Lakeview Hospital right-hand-side sensitivity analysis.

```
     TITLE
     GOTHAM CITY POLICE PATROL
     REGULAR
     VARIABLES
     X1 X2 X3 X4 X5 X6
     MINIMIZE
     X1+X2+X3+X4+X5+X6
     CONSTRAINTS
  1. X1+X6.GE.6
  2. X1+X2.GE.4
  3. X2+X3.GE.14
  4. X3+X4.GE.8
  5. X4+X5.GE.12
  6. X5+X6.GE.16
     RNGOBJ
     RNGRHS
     OPTIMIZE
```

Figure 5.18 Computer input for Gotham City.

```
                         SUMMARY OF RESULTS

   VAR   VAR      ROW STATUS     ACTIVITY        OPPORTUNITY
   NO    NAME     NO               LEVEL            COST
    1    X1        --      B      2.0000000          --
    2    X2        --      B      6.0000000          --
    3    X3        --      B      8.0000000          --
    4    X4        --      NB        --            0.0000000
    5    X5        --      B     12.0000000          --
    6    X6        --      B      4.0000000          --
    7    --SLACK    1      NB        --            1.0000000
    8    --SLACK    2      B      4.0000000          --
    9    --SLACK    3      NB        --            1.0000000
   10    --SLACK    4      NB        --            0.0000000
   11    --SLACK    5      NB        --            1.0000000
   12    --SLACK    6      NB        --            0.0000000


       MINIMUM VALUE OF THE OBJECTIVE FUNCTION =         32.000000
```

Figure 5.19 Gotham City computer solution.

108 DECISION MODELS FOR SERVICE OPERATIONS

```
TITLE
LAST NATIONAL DRIVE IN BANK
REGULAR
VARIABLES
A1 A2 A3 A4 A5 A6 T1 T2 T3 T4 T5 T6
MINIMIZE
600A1+600A2+600A3+600A4+600A5+600A6+
300T1+300T2+300T3+300T4+300T5+300T6
CONSTRAINTS
 1,  160A1-80T1,GE,1500
 2,  160A2-80T2,GE,1800
 3,  160A3-80T3,GE,1600
 4,  160A4-80T4,GE,2000
 5,  160A5-80T5,GE,1800
 6,  160A6-80T6,GE,2200
 7,  A1=12
 8,  .9A1+T1-A2=0
 9,  .9A2+T2-A3=0
10,  .9A3+T3-A4=0
11,  .9A4+T4-A5=0
12,  .9A5+T5-A6=0
RNGOBJ
RNGRHS
OPTIMIZE
```

Figure 5.20 Computer input for Last National Bank.

(a) The activity levels did not turn out to be integer-valued, as would be required. How many trainees would you recommend be hired in each of the coming six periods?

(b) Is your recommendation in part a feasible? By how much has the objective-function value increased?

(c) Give a reason why you are not surprised to find T_6 is nonbasic.

(d) How much overstaffing results from this solution?

5.6 The computer input for Lease-A-Lemon Car Rental is shown in Figure 5.22, with x_{ij} representing the number of cars to send from city i to city j. The results of the computer solution are given in Figure 5.23.

(a) What is the recommended schedule of car movements?

SUMMARY OF RESULTS

VAR NO	VAR NAME	ROW NO	STATUS	ACTIVITY LEVEL	OPPORTUNITY COST
1	A1	--	B	12.0000000	--
2	A2	--	B	11.6743204	--
3	A3	--	B	11.3555291	--
4	A4	--	B	12.9310345	--
5	A5	--	B	12.5000000	--
6	A6	--	B	13.7500000	--
7	T1	--	B	.8743204	--
8	T2	--	B	.8486408	--
9	T3	--	B	2.7110583	--
10	T4	--	B	.8620690	--
11	T5	--	B	2.5000000	--
12	T6	--	NB	--	913.4454340
13	--SLACK	1	B	350.0543688	--
14	--SLACK	2	NB	--	2.7155172
15	--SLACK	3	NB	--	3.6519025
16	--SLACK	4	NB	--	3.9747940
17	--SLACK	5	NB	--	4.0861358
18	--SLACK	6	NB	--	7.6680679

MINIMUM VALUE OF THE OBJECTIVE FUNCTION = 46865.356923

Figure 5.21 Last National Bank computer solution.

LINEAR PROGRAMMING MODELS IN SERVICES **109**

```
    TITLE
    LEASE-A-LEMON CAR RENTAL
    REGULAR
    VARIABLES
    X11 X12 X13 X14 X21 X22 X23 X24 X31 X32 X33 X34
    MINIMIZE
    439X11+396X12+91X13+0X14+296X21+434X22+133X23+0X24
    +131X31+184X32+479X33+0X34
    CONSTRAINTS
1.  X11+X12+X13+X14=26
2.  X21+X22+X23+X24=43
3.  X31+X32+X33+X34=31
4.  X11+X21+X31=32
5.  X12+X22+X32=28
6.  X13+X23+X33=26
7.  X14+X24+X34=14
    RNGOBJ
    RNGRHS
    OPTIMIZE
```

Figure 5.22 Computer input for Lease-A-Lemon.

(*b*) Is this solution degenerate?

(*c*) This model consisted of seven equality constraints. In the simplex solution procedure an artificial variable is added to each of these equality constraints. The opportunity cost associated with each constraint (artificial variable) gives the unit change in the objective function if the RHS is increased by 1. Explain why constraint 2 has a zero opportunity cost. Why are the opportunity costs for constraints 1, 2, and 3 negative or zero and the opportunity costs for constraints 4, 5, and 6 positive? What is special about constraint 7?

5.7 A certain company is planning the introduction of a new product that will be promoted by specially trained agents. The new product campaign is to be guided by the following considerations: (1) the training session for special agents should be as close to 20 working days as possible; (2) sales

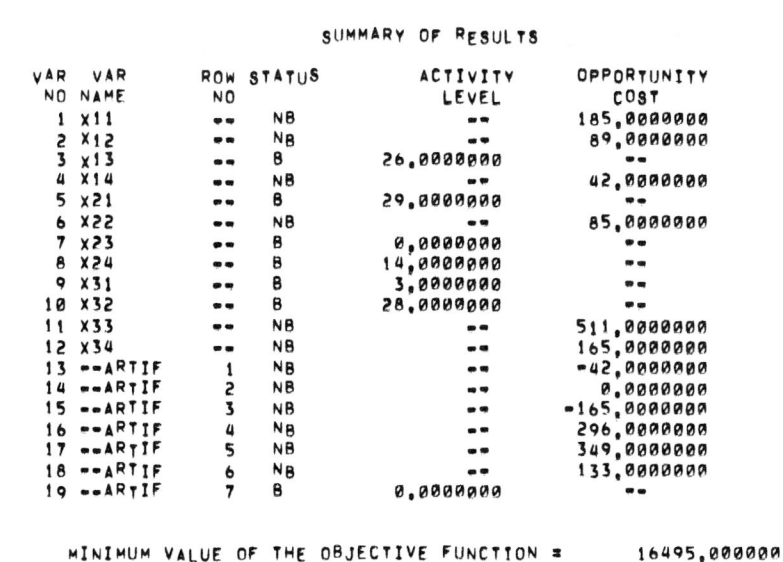

```
                    SUMMARY OF RESULTS

VAR   VAR       ROW STATUS      ACTIVITY      OPPORTUNITY
 NO   NAME       NO              LEVEL           COST
  1   X11        --     NB         --          185.0000000
  2   X12        --     NB         --           89.0000000
  3   X13        --     B        26.0000000        --
  4   X14        --     NB         --           42.0000000
  5   X21        --     B        29.0000000        --
  6   X22        --     NB         --           85.0000000
  7   X23        --     B         0.0000000        --
  8   X24        --     B        14.0000000        --
  9   X31        --     B         3.0000000        --
 10   X32        --     B        28.0000000        --
 11   X33        --     NB         --          511.0000000
 12   X34        --     NB         --          165.0000000
 13   --ARTIF    1      NB         --          -42.0000000
 14   --ARTIF    2      NB         --            0.0000000
 15   --ARTIF    3      NB         --         -165.0000000
 16   --ARTIF    4      NB         --          296.0000000
 17   --ARTIF    5      NB         --          349.0000000
 18   --ARTIF    6      NB         --          133.0000000
 19   --ARTIF    7      B         0.0000000        --

    MINIMUM VALUE OF THE OBJECTIVE FUNCTION =      16495.000000
```

Figure 5.23 Lease-A-Lemon computer solution.

during the first quarter, hopefully, will be near 5 million units; and (3) under no circumstances can training costs exceed $600,000. Write the objective function and constraints if the sales target is considered twice as important as the training-time target. Training cost is $20,000 per day and each day of training will produce 150,000 units of sales during the first quarter. The decision to be made concerns the number of days that should be spent on training sales agents.

Let x = the days devoted to training. Define other variables as necessary and formulate a goal programming model.

5.8 Tennis World carries three lines of its Toe-brand tennis racket: the Student, the Weekender, and the Professional. The more expensive the line, the greater the markup, but the more expensive lines also require more floor space for increasingly elaborate displays. Pertinent data are summarized in the table below:

Tennis racket	Cost per racket to Tennis World	Tennis World markup, %	Display space per racket, sq ft
Student	$10	10	1
Weekender	15	20	2
Professional	30	50	5

In deciding the optimal merchandizing plan, the following goals are stated in their order of preference: (1) avoid overrunning the purchasing budget of $2000; (2) achieve a gross margin (sum of markups for each racket) of at least $500; (3) avoid using more than 300 square feet of floor space for displays; and (4) ensure that all the purchasing budget is spent. Formulate a goal programming model to determine the number of each type of tennis racket to stock. Recall the following retailing relationship: selling price = cost + (markup)(cost).

CASELETTE: MUNICH DELICATESSEN

Among the most popular items served by the Munich Deli is its bratwurst. This sausage is based on an original old-world recipe that combines beef, chicken, lamb, and assorted spices in a pure-animal casing. By Department of Agriculture regulations, the Munich Deli must display on its label certain content information and adhere to those content specifications in the processing and packaging of this sausage. Because of its popularity Munich Deli can sell all the bratwurst it can make. Potential variability of the costs of the major ingredients, however, causes a continuing problem for the processing manager, who must determine the amounts of each ingredient to mix into the sausage.

Bratwurst is prepared in 100-pound batches. According to the label (which cannot be altered except through a lengthy and costly procedure), each batch consists of at least 30 percent lamb by weight, with no specific requirement on beef or chicken. Moreover, the label indicates that each batch, by weight, is at most 24 percent fat, at least 12 percent protein, and at most 64 percent water and other elements.

A recent Department of Agriculture study has shown that the major ingredients in bratwurst contain the label-controlled elements in the following proportions:

	Percentage of weight		
Element	Beef	Chicken	Lamb
Fat	20	15	25
Protein	20	15	15
Water and others	60	70	60

It can be reasonably assumed that the spices and casing add an insignificant amount to the total sausage weight and almost nothing in terms of the elements being controlled.

The principal ingredients are available currently at costs of $1, $0.50, and $0.70 per pound of beef, chicken, and lamb, respectively. At these costs there seem to be unlimited supplies. Thus, the processing manager at Munich Deli must decide how much of each principal ingredient to mix into each batch of bratwurst to meet labeling requirements at the lowest cost.

A preliminary analysis suggests that this decision problem can be formulated as a linear programming model, with

x_1 = number of pounds of beef per batch

x_2 = number of pounds of chicken per batch

x_3 = number of pounds of lamb per batch

Formulate this problem as a linear programming problem.

Questions

1. Suppose that the early, unseasonably cold weather reduces the production of lamb and the price for new supplies of lamb rises to 85 cents per pound. What effect will this situation have on the optimum contents of the sausage found originally? What effect will this situation have on Munich Deli's production costs for each batch of bratwurst?
2. The Agriculture Department is considering adopting new regulations, restricting the water content in all sausage. For what range of values of water content would Munich Deli continue to use the same ingredients in their sausage as in the original optimum (i.e., the same basic variables)?
3. Suppose that a meat supplier advises Munich Deli of the availability of veal tongues. Reference to the original recipe for bratwurst reveals that veal tongues could be used, and technically this ingredient is already covered on the sausage label under the generic category "beef and beef by-products." Unlike the regular beef originally considered, these tongues are 30 percent fat, 15 percent protein, and 55 percent water, all by weight. The meat supplier is willing to sell Munich Deli these tongues for 40 cents per pound. Should this new ingredient be included in the optimal sausage composition? Why?

CASELETTE: SEQUOIA AIRLINES

Sequoia Airlines is a well-established regional airline, serving California, Nevada, Arizona, and Utah. Sequoia competes against much larger carriers in this regional market, and its management feels that the price, frequency of flight service, capability to meet schedules, baggage handling, and image projected by the flight attendants are the most important marketing factors airline passengers consider in deciding to use any particular carrier.

In every one of these areas, Sequoia is attaining its desired objectives. However, maintaining its flight attendant staff at desired levels has been difficult in the past, and many times it has had to ask flight attendants to work hours in excess of normal owing to worker shortages. This has resulted in excessive personnel costs because of overtime premiums and some morale problems among the flight attendants. One reason for the worker shortage is a higher-than-industry average turnover rate, due to experienced attendants being hired away by other airlines. This is not totally due to morale problems, as that cause seems to become important only during seasonal peak demand periods, when shortages are particularly bad. By interviewing the existing personnel, Sequoia has discovered that other, competing regional carriers (whose training programs are not as highly developed) have been hiring a significant proportion of the staff away from Sequoia by offering slightly higher direct salaries, attractive indirect-benefit packages, and a guarantee of minimum flying hours in off peak demand periods.

As a beginning, Sequoia's management has asked for a six-month hiring and training analysis of the flight attendant staff requirements, beginning next month (July). Investigation of the operations schedule indicates that 14,000 attendant hours are needed in July; 16,000 in August; 13,000 in September; 12,000 in October; 18,000 in November; and 20,000 in December. Sequoia's training program for new personnel requires an entire month of in-class preparation before they are assigned to regular flight service. As junior flight attendants, they remain on probationary status for one additional month. Periodically, there is some personnel movement from the working flight attendant staff to the staff that supervises the training of new employees. Figure 5.24 indicates the relationships and the percentages of interstaff movements which research has shown to be historically true.

Normally, when no personnel shortages occur, each junior flight attendant works an average of 140 hours per month and is paid a salary of $1050 during the probationary period. During the training period, each new employee is paid $750. The experienced flight attendants receive an average salary of $1400 per month, and they work an average of 125 hours per month. Each instructor receives a salary of $1500 per month.

The poorly kept secret of Sequoia's personalized training program is limiting the number of trainees to no more than five per instructor. Instructors not needed in a particular month (surplus) may be used as flight attendants. To ensure a high level of quality in flight service, Sequoia requires that the proportion of junior-flight-attendant hours not exceed 25 percent of any month's total (junior plus experienced) attendant hours.

In May, Sequoia hired 10 new employees to enter the training program, and this month they hired 10 more. At the beginning of June there were 120 experienced flight attendants and 6 instructors on Sequoia's staff.

LINEAR PROGRAMMING MODELS IN SERVICES **113**

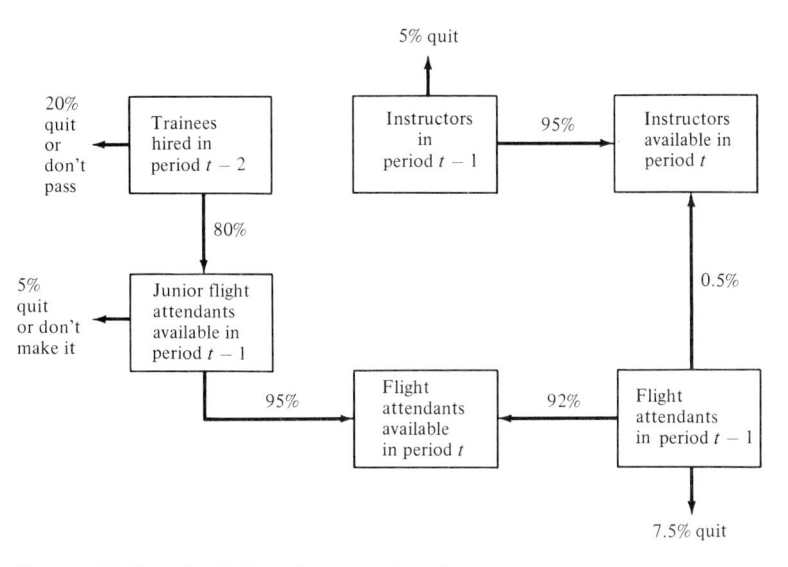

Figure 5.24 Sequoia Airlines flight-attendant flows.

Let T_t = number of trainees hired at the beginning of period t, $t = 1, 2, 3, 4, 5, 6$

J_t = number of junior flight attendants available at the beginning of period t, $t = 1, 2, 3, 4, 5, 6$

F_t = number of experienced flight attendants available at the beginning of period t, $t = 1, 2, 3, 4, 5, 6$

I_t = number of instructors available at the beginning of period t, $t = 1, 2, 3, 4, 5, 6$

S_t = number of surplus instructors available as flight attendants at the beginning of period t, $t = 1, 2, 3, 4, 5, 6$

Questions

1. For the forecast period (July–December) determine the number of new trainees that must be hired at the beginning of each month so that total personnel costs in the flight attendant staff and training program are minimized.
2. How would you deal with the noninteger results?
3. Discuss how you would use the LP model to make your hiring decision for the next six months.

SELECTED BIBLIOGRAPHY

Budnick, Frank S., Richard Mojena, and T. E. Vollmann: *Principles of Operations Research for Management,* Richard D. Irwin, Inc., Homewood, Ill., 1977.

Eppen, Gary D., and F. S. Gould: *Quantitative Concepts for Management,* Prentice-Hall, Inc., Englewood Cliffs, N.J., 1979.

Hillier, Frederick S., and Gerald J. Lieberman: *Introduction to Operations Research,* 3d ed., Holden-Day, Inc., San Francisco, 1980.

Lee, Sang M.: *Goal Programming for Decision Analysis,* Auerbach Publishers, Inc., Philadelphia, 1972.

Taha, Hamdy A.: *Operations Research: An Introduction,* The Macmillan Co., New York, 1971.

Wagner, Harvey M.: *Principles of Operations Research,* 2d ed., Prentice-Hall, Inc., Englewood Cliffs, N.J., 1975.

CHAPTER
SIX

FORECASTING FOR SERVICE OPERATIONS

Forecasting is the cornerstone of management decision making; every aspect somehow relies upon forecasts. These forecasts are the predictions or projections of possible occurrences often associated with various alternative courses of action. Consequently, forecasting links the current activities of managers with the potential realities of the future.

Why are forecasts necessary? Of course, they reduce the uncertainties associated with decision making by enabling managers to anticipate the future. But they also enable managers to recognize explicitly the risks inherent in decision making. Such risks might be measured in part by the magnitude of the dispersion of possible outcomes. The ability of managers to arrive at reasonably accurate forecasts determines the amount of risk associated with alternative actions. It thereby influences the decision process.

Managers require forecasts for every aspect of the operations function. They are used in the short term for controlling inventories and for developing workshift schedules and vehicle routes. With medium-term decisions, forecasts are used for capacity planning. This may involve identifying facilities, equipment, and personnel requirements. In the long term, forecasts may be used to investigate new services, changes in the mix of services, and changes in technology that may affect the service delivery system.

This chapter provides an overview of forecasting for service operations management. Time series forecasting models are given the most emphasis because of their widespread use. However, causal models and subjective models also are discussed. Students should develop an appreciation of the role of forecasting in management decision making. Additionally, they should understand the mechanics of several popular forecasting models.

IMPORTANCE OF FORECASTING FOR SERVICE OPERATIONS

Forecasting is important for all management decision making. But it has special significance for service operations. Consider some of the unique characteristics of service organizations and their implications for forecasting.

Wide Fluctuations in Demand

Demand for many services is highly seasonal. This is particularly evident for holiday-related services, such as airline transportation and hotel accommodations. However, demand for services varies not only with the month of the year, but also with the day of the week and the hour of the day. Consequently, a forecasting model may have to focus on small time intervals. Forecasts of demand by hour of the day may be needed for workshift scheduling, for vehicle routing, for capacity planning, and for other fundamental operating decisions.

Intangibility of Services

Forecasting demand for services requires a quantifiable measure of demand volume. But demand often is not restricted to a single service. Demand may be for a service in conjunction with convenience, with a pleasing atmosphere, and with other intangibles that affect consumers' perceptions. Demand is for a service package that has many components. This makes measuring demand for services very difficult. Consider, for example, a fast-food restaurant. Can demand be measured by the amount of food sold? Should we consider lost customers who depart owing to long waiting lines? Should we consider the different attitudes of customers toward the service package? A forecasting model requires data that accurately measure the volume of demand for the service package.

Simultaneous Production and Consumption of Services

Services are produced and consumed simultaneously. Consequently, the capacity to provide the service must be available when demand occurs. If capacity is not available, then some consumers will have to wait, perhaps in line. Others may not be willing to wait and will depart the system without receiving the service. Both situations result in consumer ill will, which often has a high penalty cost. Similarly, there is a penalty associated with having capacity available when anticipated demand is not realized. In this case, employees on the payroll may be idle while waiting for consumers. These situations point out the urgency of accurate demand forecasting for service organizations. Forecasting is needed so that capacity can be appropriately adjusted to demand levels.

Demand forecasting is important for decision making at all levels within service organizations. But most forecasting models require a history of relevant data, perhaps collected on an hourly basis. This presumes an ability to recognize relevant data, to collect the data, and to transform the data into a form that can be used for forecasting. The ability to collect relevant data is one of several important considerations in choosing a forecasting method.

CONSIDERATIONS IN CHOOSING A FORECASTING METHOD

Many forecasting models have been developed during the past three decades. As we might expect, the trend has been toward more sophisticated models that make use of computer-based information systems. With so many forecasting models available, it can be difficult for managers to select an appropriate technique.

Several factors deserve consideration when selecting a forecasting model. These include (1) the cost surrounding the forecasting model, (2) the required accuracy, (3) the relevancy of past data, (4) the forecasting lead time, and (5) the underlying pattern of behavior. We shall look at each of these factors in more detail.

Costs Surrounding a Forecasting Model

A forecasting model involves both developmental costs and operating costs. The developmental costs are associated with constructing the model, validating its ability to forecast, writing and debugging the required computer programs, and educating analysts and managers in using the model. For some well-established models, developmental costs may be low. But, for models tailored to the specific needs of managers, these costs can be very high, running into tens of thousands of dollars.

The operating costs of a forecasting model are the costs of making a forecast once the model is developed. These costs are affected by the amount of data needed and the computation time. With some models new forecasts can be made for only a few cents. But other models can require huge amounts of data and be very expensive. As we would expect, the accuracy of forecasts is related to the cost of the model.

Required Accuracy

The quality of a forecasting model ultimately is judged by its ability to predict future occurrences. Therefore, accuracy is a primary concern in selecting a

118 DECISION MODELS FOR SERVICE OPERATIONS

model. But what is an acceptable level of accuracy? We might spend large amounts of money on a model that yields very accurate forecasts. Or we might choose a less-sophisticated and cheaper model that is not extremely accurate.

As you may surmise, there is a tradeoff in costs of choosing a forecasting model. There are real, out-of-pocket expenses associated with developing and using a forecasting model. Generally the less-expensive models yield less-accurate forecasts, and there are costs associated with inaccuracies in the forecast. These costs might involve excessive inventories, lost customers, excessive capacity, or lost opportunities. Is it worthwhile to spend more on an accurate forecasting model than incur the potential costs of a less-expensive but poor forecast? Figure 6.1 depicts the relevant costs and their relation to forecasting accuracy. Although selecting the model is a matter of managerial judgment, primary consideration is given to the cost tradeoffs.

We mentioned that forecasting accuracy refers to how well the forecast predicts future occurrences. There are several conventional measures of accuracy, and these focus on forecast error. This is the deviation of the forecast from the actual occurrence. The most common measures of accuracy are the mean absolute deviation (MAD) and the mean square deviation (MSD). MAD is calculated by taking the *absolute value* of the deviation associated with each forecast, summing these absolute values, and then dividing the sum by the number of forecasts. MSD is calculated by squaring the deviation associated with each forecast, summing these squared values, and then dividing the sum by the number of forecasts.

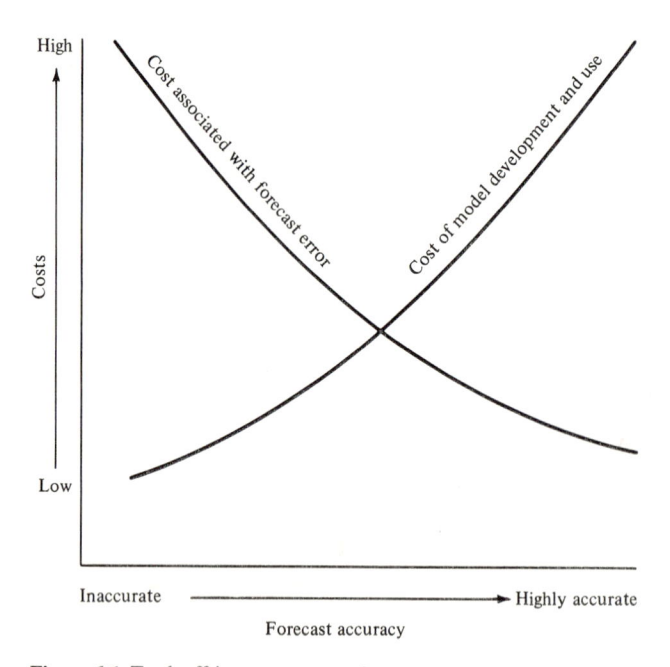

Figure 6.1 Tradeoff in costs versus forecast accuracy.

While MAD and MSD both measure accuracy, they respond differently to the individual forecasting errors. MAD gives equal weight to all forecasting errors. However, MSD is affected much more by extremely large errors. This, of course, results from squaring the deviations.

Relevancy of Past Data

Many forecasting models require the assumption that past behavioral patterns and past relationships will continue in the future. These models use those patterns and relationships in projecting future occurrences. This presumes a level of stability between the past and the future.

But what happens if this stability is not present? It means that past data will not be relevant in developing forecasts. In this case, subjective approaches may be more appropriate. Such approaches may also rely heavily upon the opinions of knowledgeable persons. When past data are not relevant, forecasts are likely to be developed by means of subjective methods that do not project past behavioral patterns into the future.

Forecasting Horizon

The forecasting horizon refers to the length of time into the future that the forecasts are made. By convention, this horizon is categorized as short term (less than three months), medium term (between three months and two years), and long term (greater than two years). Most forecasting models have been developed for short- or medium-term horizons and may provide satisfactory forecasts for one or two periods in the future. But the forecasts deteriorate in accuracy when used for longer horizons. An obvious reason for this is that many models use past data that may be relevant for the near future, but that have less relevance for the longer term.

Pattern of Data

We mentioned that many forecasting models rely upon the assumption that past behavioral patterns and past relationships will continue in the future. These models assume that actual occurrences are determined by some underlying, known pattern plus some random influences. Therefore,

$$\text{Actual value} = \text{pattern} + \text{randomness}$$

The random influences are unpredictable and account for forecast errors.

All forecasting models do not work equally well for all patterns of data. Therefore, it is important to select a model that is appropriate for the particular situation. The four most common patterns of data are constant, trend, seasonal, and cyclic. Figure 6.2 depicts data that are relatively constant over time, but that have some randomness. Figure 6.3 shows data that increase at a constant rate over time. These data have an increasing trend. Figure 6.4 depicts

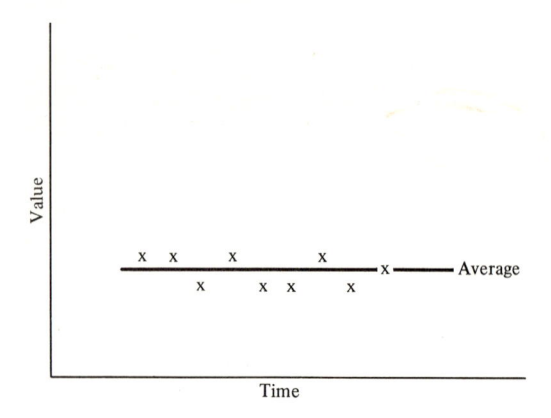

Figure 6.2 Constant pattern of data.

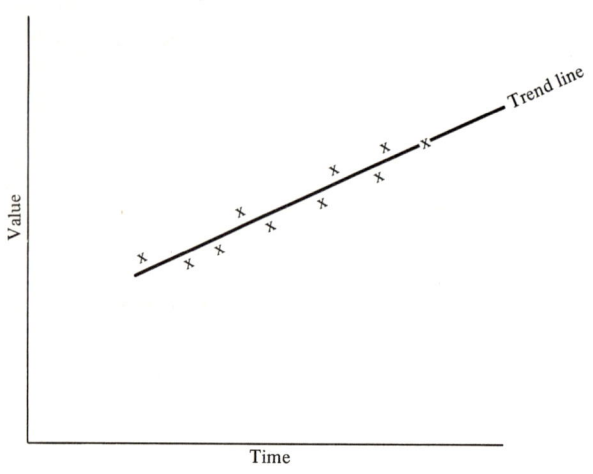

Figure 6.3 Trend pattern of data.

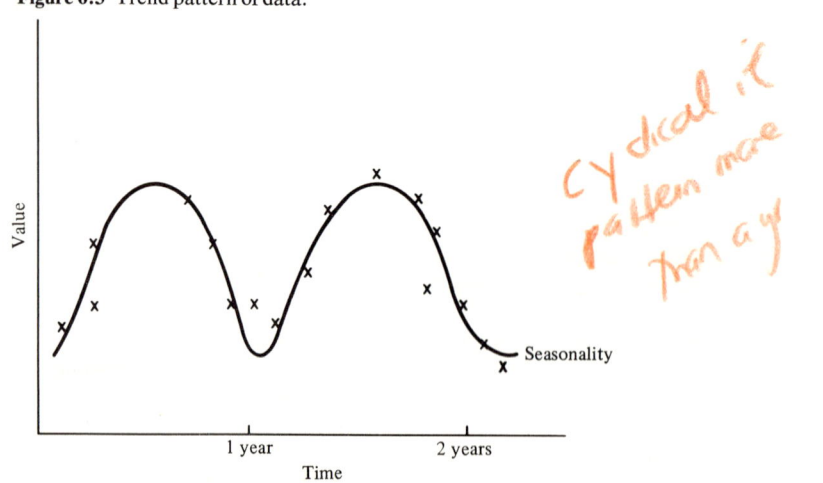

Figure 6.4 Seasonal pattern of data.

data that repeat in short cycles. For example, airline travel peaks during each holiday season. This seasonality can be anticipated every year. When data repeat in cycles that are longer than a year, the pattern is called cyclic. Some economists have identified long cycles in the United States economy and in the economies of the world. These have been used to forecast repetitive recessionary periods.

FORECASTING METHODS

While it is possible to categorize forecasting techniques in many different ways, we shall focus on three classifications: time series models, causal models, and subjective models. These classifications are not necessarily mutually exclusive. For example, causal models can include time as a variable and subjective models can use the results of causal models and time series models. Nevertheless, we shall discuss each classification separately. Table 6.1 summarizes the characteristics of several popular methods in each classification.

Time Series Models

Time series models presume that the value of actual occurrences follows an identifiable pattern over time. This means that the value is functionally related

Table 6.1 Characteristics of forecasting methods

Method	Data required	Relative cost	Forecast horizon	Application
Time series models:				
Moving average	N most recent observations	Very low	Short term (1 period)	Inventory control
Exponential smoothing	Smoothing constant, previous smoothed value, and most recent observation	Very low	Short term (1 to 3 periods)	Inventory control and demand forecasting
Causal models:				
Regression	All past data for all variables	Moderate	Medium term	Demand forecasting
Econometrics	All past data for all variables	Moderate to high	Medium to long term	Economic conditions
Subjective models:				
Delphi	Survey results	High	Long term	Technological forecasting
Cross-impact analysis	Correlations between events	High	Long term	Technological forecasting
Historical analogies	Several years data for a similar situation	High	Medium to long term	General economic conditions

122 DECISION MODELS FOR SERVICE OPERATIONS

to the time period. The N-period moving average is an elementary time series model. However, exponential smoothing models generally are considered to be better.

N-period moving average This method uses the average of the N most recently observed data as a forecast. For example, a five-period moving average uses the five most recent observations. N (the number of periods) must be large enough to encompass a full cycle of data, if such cycles exist.

Consider the data in Table 6.2. We can begin with January 1977 to construct a five-period moving average. The first average uses the data from January through May. This yields an average of 1516.60. The average, 1516.60, is associated with the midpoint of the N periods used. In this case it is associated with March. To update the average, we remove the January observation and add the June observation. This yields an average of 1597.00 that is associated with April.

The N-period moving-average method presumes stability between the past and the future. The averaging process smooths out randomness in the data and leaves a relatively constant pattern. Consequently, the average itself is used as the forecast.

The N-period moving average once was very popular for short-term forecasting, especially for inventory control. It requires N pieces of data, and each is given a weight of $1/N$ in the averaging process. Yet, this may be contrary to our intuition. We might expect more recent data to be better indicators of the future. The N-period moving average requires adjustment to handle data that exhibit trends and seasonality.

Table 6.2 Revenue passenger miles for Pan American Airways, 1977

Period	t	Actual revenue passenger miles, in millions	Five-period moving average, in millions
January	1	1588.00	
February	2	1228.00	
March	3	1462.00	1516.60
April	4	1585.00	1597.00
May	5	1720.00	1792.80
June	6	1990.00	1950.80
July	7	2207.00	2030.40
August	8	2252.00	2064.20
September	9	1983.00	1971.00
October	10	1889.00	1848.00
November	11	1524.00	
December	12	1592.00	

Source: Civil Aeronautics Board, *Air Carrier Traffic Statistics,* January–December 1977.

Exponential smoothing Exponential smoothing is the most popular time series forecasting method. In its simplest form, it handles data that exhibit a relatively constant pattern. But extensions of exponential smoothing can be used for trend and seasonal data.

Exponential smoothing is similar to the N-period moving average in that it "smooths out" randomness in the data. The method requires a smoothing constant, α (alpha), which is the weight given the most recent observation. Generally, α is given a value between 0.1 and 0.3.

The smoothed value calculated at time t is derived from the observed value at time t and the previous smoothed value:

$$S_t = S_{t-1} + \alpha(A_t - S_{t-1}) \tag{1}$$

where S_t is the smoothed value calculated at period t and A_t is the actual observed value at period t. The term $(A_t - S_{t-1})$ is the forecast error that is used to adjust the previous smoothed value. Equation (1) also can be written as

$$S_t = \alpha(A_t) + (1 - \alpha)S_{t-1} \tag{2}$$

We see that A_t is given a weight α in determining S_t, and we can easily show that A_{t-1} is given a weight $\alpha(1 - \alpha)$. More generally, observation A_{t-n} is given a weight $\alpha(1 - \alpha)^n$. This is the basis for the name *exponential* smoothing. All past observations are considered in calculating S_t, but older data are given less weight. This is an important positive feature of the exponential smoothing method.

Table 6.3 illustrates the calculation of smoothed values using $\alpha = 0.1$. Note that we have assumed that S_1 equals A_1 to begin the process. With $\alpha = 0.1$, $S_2 = 0.1(1305.00) + 0.9(1651.00)$, which yields $S_2 = 1616.40$.

Table 6.3 Exponentially smoothed values and forecasts
Pan American Airways revenue passenger miles, 1978
($\alpha = 0.1$)

Period	t	Actual revenue* passenger miles A_t, in millions	Smoothed value S_t, in millions	Forecast F_t, in millions	$\|A_t - F_t\|$, in millions
January	1	1651.00	1651.00	. . . .	
February	2	1305.00	1616.40	1651.00	346.00
March	3	1617.00	1616.46	1616.40	0.60
April	4	1721.00	1626.91	1616.46	104.54
May	5	2015.00	1665.72	1626.91	388.09
June	6	2297.00	1728.85	1665.72	631.28
July	7	2606.00	1816.57	1728.85	877.15
August	8	2687.00	1903.61	1816.57	870.44
September	9	2292.00	1942.45	1903.61	388.39
October	10	1981.00	1946.30	1942.45	38.55
November	11	1696.00	1921.27	1946.30	250.30
December	12	1794.00	1908.55	1921.27	127.27

* Data from Civil Aeronautics Board, *Air Carrier Traffic Statistics*, January–December 1978.

124 DECISION MODELS FOR SERVICE OPERATIONS

This simple smoothing process assumes that the underlying pattern of data is relatively constant. Therefore, the smoothed value calculated at period t is used as the forecast for period $t + 1$:

$$F_{t+1} = S_t$$

where F_{t+1} is the forecast for period $t + 1$. The mean absolute deviation (MAD) for February through December is 365.47.

Figure 6.5 depicts actual values and the forecasts calculated with $\alpha = 0.1$ and $\alpha = 0.2$. We should expect a higher value of α to result in forecasts that respond more rapidly to recent data. Consequently, the forecasts would be less smooth.

Exponential smoothing with trend adjustment The simple exponential smoothing model just described can be extended to handle trends in the data. The trend is the average rate at which the data change from one period to the next.

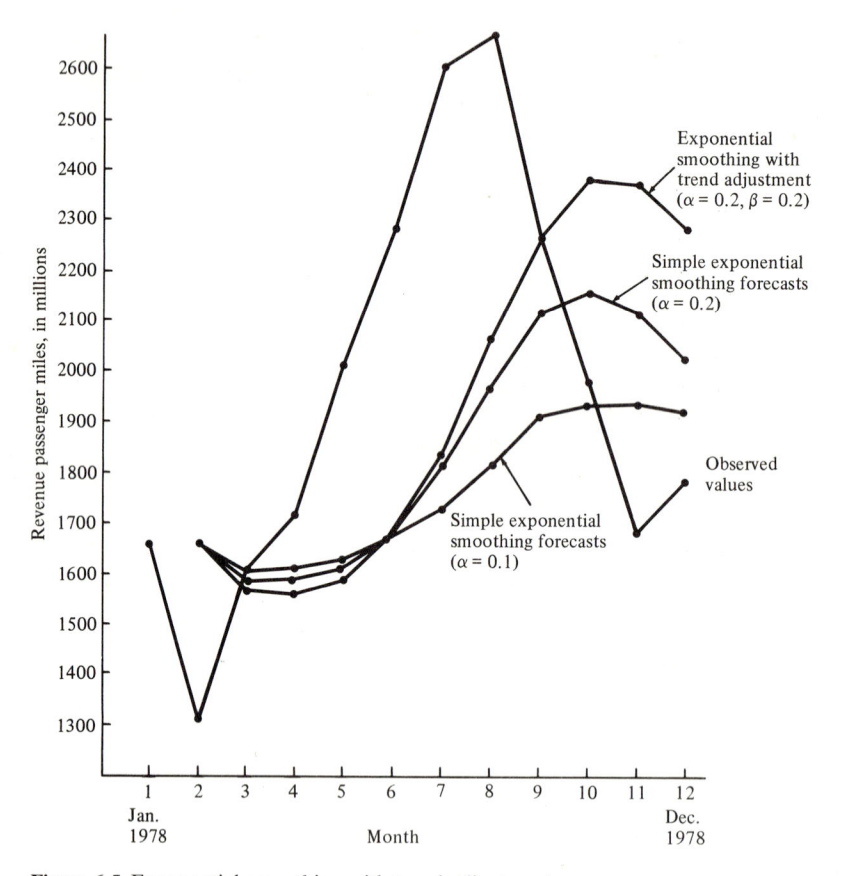

Figure 6.5 Exponential smoothing with trend adjustment.

For a particular period t, this trend is estimated by $(S_t - S_{t-1})$. The changes in the trend from period to period can be smoothed in a manner similar to smoothing actual observations.

Let β (beta) be the smoothing constant for the trend. β need not be the same as α, but it generally is set between 0.1 and 0.3. The smoothed trend calculated at period t is given by

$$T_t = \beta(S_t - S_{t-1}) + (1 - \beta)T_{t-1} \tag{3}$$

The smoothed data calculated at period t now must include the trend factor.

$$S_t = \alpha A_t + (1 - \alpha)(S_{t-1} + T_{t-1}) \tag{4}$$

And our forecast for period $t + 1$ is the smoothed value plus the trend.

$$F_{t+1} = S_t + T_t \tag{5}$$

How can we develop forecasts for n periods into the future? Simply multiply the trend by the appropriate number of periods.

$$F_{t+n} = S_t + nT_t \tag{6}$$

Table 6.4 illustrates the calculations for exponential smoothing with trend adjustment. T_1 is assumed to be zero to begin the calculations. We set $\alpha = 0.2$ and $\beta = 0.2$. T_2 is calculated as follows:

$$T_2 = 0.2(1581.80 - 1651.00) + 0.8(0)$$

$$= -13.84$$

The forecast for March (period 3) is given by

Table 6.4 Exponential smoothing with trend adjustment
Pan American Airways revenue passenger miles, 1978
($\alpha = 0.2$, $\beta = 0.2$)

Period	t	Actual revenue* passenger miles A_t, in millions	Smoothed value S_t, in millions	Trend T_t	Forecast F_t, in millions	$\|A_t - F_t\|$, in millions
January	1	1651.00	1651.00	0.00	....	
February	2	1305.00	1581.80	−13.84	1651.00	346.00
March	3	1617.00	1577.77	−11.88	1567.96	49.04
April	4	1721.00	1596.91	−5.67	1565.89	155.11
May	5	2015.00	1675.99	11.28	1591.24	423.76
June	6	2297.00	1809.21	35.67	1687.27	609.73
July	7	2606.00	1997.10	66.11	1884.88	721.12
August	8	2687.00	2187.97	91.06	2063.21	623.79
September	9	2292.00	2281.63	91.58	2279.03	12.97
October	10	1981.00	2294.77	75.89	2373.21	392.21
November	11	1696.00	2235.73	48.91	2370.66	674.66
December	12	1794.00	2186.51	29.28	2284.63	490.63

* Data from Civil Aeronautics Board, *Air Carrier Traffic Statistics*, January–December 1978.

126 DECISION MODELS FOR SERVICE OPERATIONS

$$F_3 = S_2 + T_2$$
$$= 1581.80 - 13.84$$
$$= 1567.96$$

Figure 6.5 contains a plot of forecasts developed using exponential smoothing with trend adjustment. MAD calculated for February through December is 412.63. This is slightly poorer than the forecasts developed without the trend adjustment. The trend appears not to be an important element of the pattern of data.

Exponential smoothing with seasonal adjustment The simple exponential smoothing model can be extended to handle seasonal patterns in the data. The process involves "deseasonalizing" the data. The deseasonalized data then is smoothed in the conventional way and finally "reseasonalized" to arrive at a forecast.

Assume that the data repeats itself every L periods. That is, L is the length of a season. Frequently, L will be 12 months. Data are deseasonalized by using a *seasonality index* associated with each period. The index I_t is initially estimated by normalizing the first L periods of data. This is achieved by determining the mean for periods 1 through L and then dividing each of the first L values by the mean. Algebraically, the initial value of the index for period t is given by

$$I_t = \frac{A_t}{\bar{A}} \tag{7}$$

where $\bar{A} = (A_1 + A_2 + \cdots + A_L)/L$.

The above process yields initial indices for each of the L periods. These indices are used to deseasonalize data. This is achieved by dividing the actual value by the appropriate index calculated one full season before. The deseasonalized data are then smoothed in the conventional way:

$$S_t = \alpha \frac{A_t}{I_{t-L}} + (1 - \alpha)S_{t-1} \tag{8}$$

The forecast for period $t + 1$ is the smoothed value S_t reseasonalized by the appropriate index. In this case, it would be with the index I_{t-L+1}, because we are forecasting one period ahead.

$$F_{t+1} = (S_t)(I_{t-L+1}) \tag{9}$$

The process described above would be fine if the seasonality indices were stable. But these were estimated on the basis of only the first L periods. As new data become available, the indices can be adjusted by means of the smoothing process.

At period t, we calculate S_t and observe A_t. Therefore, a new observation of the seasonality index for period t is (A_t/S_t). We let γ (gamma) be the weight given this most recent observation of the index. Generally this weight is set equal to a value between 0.2 and 0.5. The smoothed estimate of the seasonality index is given by

$$I_t = \gamma \frac{A_t}{S_t} + (1 - \gamma)I_{t-L} \tag{10}$$

Table 6.5 illustrates the calculations for exponential smoothing with seasonal adjustment. The value of γ is 0.3 and the value of α is 0.2. The length L was set equal to 12, because this seemed likely to be a full season. $\bar{A}$ was calculated to be 1971.87. Therefore, I_1 equals $(1651)/(1971.83)$, which is 0.837. Other indices for periods 2 through 12 are similarly calculated.

For this example, the first 12 observations are used to give initial estimates of the seasonality indices. Therefore, we cannot begin to calculate new

Table 6.5 Exponential smoothing with seasonal adjustment
Pan American Airway revenue passenger miles, 1978–1979
($\alpha = 0.2$, $\gamma = 0.3$)

Period	t	Actual revenue* passenger miles A_t, in millions	Smoothed value S_t, in millions	Index I_t	Forecast F_t, in millions	$\|A_t - F_t\|$, in millions
			1978			
January	1	1651.00	....	0.837	....	
February	2	1305.00	....	0.662	....	
March	3	1617.00	....	0.820	....	
April	4	1721.00	....	0.873	....	
May	5	2015.00	....	1.022	....	
June	6	2297.00	....	1.165	....	
July	7	2606.00	....	1.322	....	
August	8	2687.00	....	1.363	....	
September	9	2292.00	....	1.162	....	
October	10	1981.00	....	1.005	....	
November	11	1696.00	....	0.860	....	
December	12	1794.00	1794.00	0.910	....	
			1979			
January	13	1806.00	1866.59	0.876	....	
February	14	1731.00	2016.38	0.721	1235.35	495.65
March	15	1733.00	2035.76	0.829	1653.53	79.47
April	16	1904.00	2064.91	0.888	1776.79	127.21
May	17	2036.00	2050.40	1.013	2110.11	74.11
June	18	2560.00	2079.84	1.185	2388.53	171.47
July	19	2679.00	2069.29	1.314	2748.75	69.75
August	20	2821.00	2069.46	1.363	2819.80	1.20
September	21	2359.00	2061.47	1.157	2405.48	46.48
October	22	2160.00	2079.17	1.015	2071.05	88.95
November	23	1802.00	2082.35	0.862	1788.33	13.68
December	24	1853.00	2073.22	0.905	1894.55	41.55

* Data from Civil Aeronautics Board, *Air Carrier Traffic Statistics*, January–December 1979. Values may differ slightly owing to rounding off of the index.

128 DECISION MODELS FOR SERVICE OPERATIONS

smoothed data until period 13, and these are used to develop forecasts for period 14. To begin the process, we assume that S_{12} equals A_{12}. Therefore,

$$S_{13} = 0.2 \frac{A_{13}}{I_1} + 0.8 S_{12}$$

$$= 0.2 \frac{1806.00}{0.837} + 0.8 (1794)$$

$$= 1866.59$$

The forecast for period 14 (February 1979), is

$$F_{14} = (S_{13})(I_2)$$

$$= (1866.59)(0.662)$$

$$= 1235.35$$

At this point the seasonality index associated with January can be revised.

$$I_{13} = 0.3 \frac{A_{13}}{S_{13}} + 0.7 (I_1)$$

$$= 0.3 \frac{1806}{1866.59} + 0.7 (0.837)$$

$$= 0.876$$

The mean absolute deviation (MAD) for February through December 1979 is 101.87. This is a considerable improvement over the simple and trend models. An obvious reason for this is that the airlines business does exhibit definite seasonal patterns.

Exponential smoothing can be extended to include both trend and seasonality adjustments. The procedure is similar to that described above, except that the trend is included. The values are calculated using the following formulas:

$$S_t = \alpha \frac{A_t}{I_{t-L}} + (1 - \alpha)(S_{t-1} + T_{t-1}) \qquad (11)$$

$$T_t = \beta (S_t - S_{t-1}) + (1 - \beta) T_{t-1} \qquad (12)$$

$$I_t = \gamma \frac{A_t}{S_t} + (1 - \gamma) I_{t-L} \qquad (13)$$

The forecast for period $t + 1$ is given by

$$F_{t+1} = (S_t + T_t) I_{t-L+1} \qquad (14)$$

Table 6.6 illustrates the calculation of forecasts using $L = 12$, $\alpha = 0.2$, $\beta = 0.2$, and $\gamma = 0.3$. The resulting mean absolute deviation (MAD) for February through December 1979 is 159.89. Figure 6.6 shows the forecasts with only the seasonal adjustment and the forecasts with both seasonal and trend adjustments. Including the trend does not improve the forecasts for this example.

Table 6.6 Exponential smoothing with seasonal adjustment and trend
Pan American Airway revenue passenger miles, 1978–1979
($\alpha = 0.2$, $\beta = 0.2$, $\gamma = 0.3$)

Period	t	Actual revenue* passenger miles A_t, in millions	Smoothed value S_t, in millions	Trend T_t	Index I_t	Forecast F_t, in millions	$\|A_t - F_t\|$, in millions
\multicolumn{8}{c}{1978}
January	1	1651.00	....	....	0.837	....	
February	2	1305.00	....	....	0.662	....	
March	3	1617.00	....	....	0.820	....	
April	4	1721.00	....	....	0.873	....	
May	5	2015.00	....	....	1.022	....	
June	6	2297.00	....	....	1.165	....	
July	7	2606.00	....	....	1.322	....	
August	8	2687.00	....	....	1.363	....	
September	9	2292.00	....	....	1.162	....	
October	10	1981.00	....	....	1.005	....	
November	11	1696.00	....	....	0.860	....	
December	12	1794.00	1794.00	0.00	0.910	....	
\multicolumn{8}{c}{1979}
January	13	1806.00	1866.59	14.52	0.876	....	
February	14	1731.00	2027.99	43.89	0.719	1244.96	486.04
March	15	1733.00	2080.17	45.55	0.824	1699.05	33.95
April	16	1904.00	2136.87	47.78	0.878	1855.31	48.69
May	17	2036.00	2146.20	40.09	1.000	2232.48	196.48
June	18	2560.00	2188.55	40.54	1.166	2546.82	13.18
July	19	2679.00	2188.69	32.46	1.292	2946.00	267.00
August	20	2821.00	2190.96	26.42	1.340	3026.75	205.75
September	21	2359.00	2179.80	18.91	1.138	2577.42	218.42
October	22	2160.00	2188.97	16.96	0.999	2208.93	48.93
November	23	1802.00	2183.75	12.53	0.850	1897.35	95.35
December	24	1853.00	2164.36	6.14	0.894	1998.20	145.20

* Data from Civil Aeronautics Board, *Air Carrier Traffic Statistics,* January–December 1979. Values may differ slightly owing to rounding off of the index.

Exponential smoothing in summary Exponential smoothing is a popular technique for short-term forecasting, especially demand forecasting. Reasons for this popularity include the following:

1. All past data are considered in the smoothing process.
2. More recent data are given more weight than older data.
3. The technique requires only a few pieces of data to update a forecast.
4. The model can be easily programmed and is inexpensive to use.
5. The rate at which the model responds to changes in the underlying pattern of data can be altered by adjusting the smoothing constants.

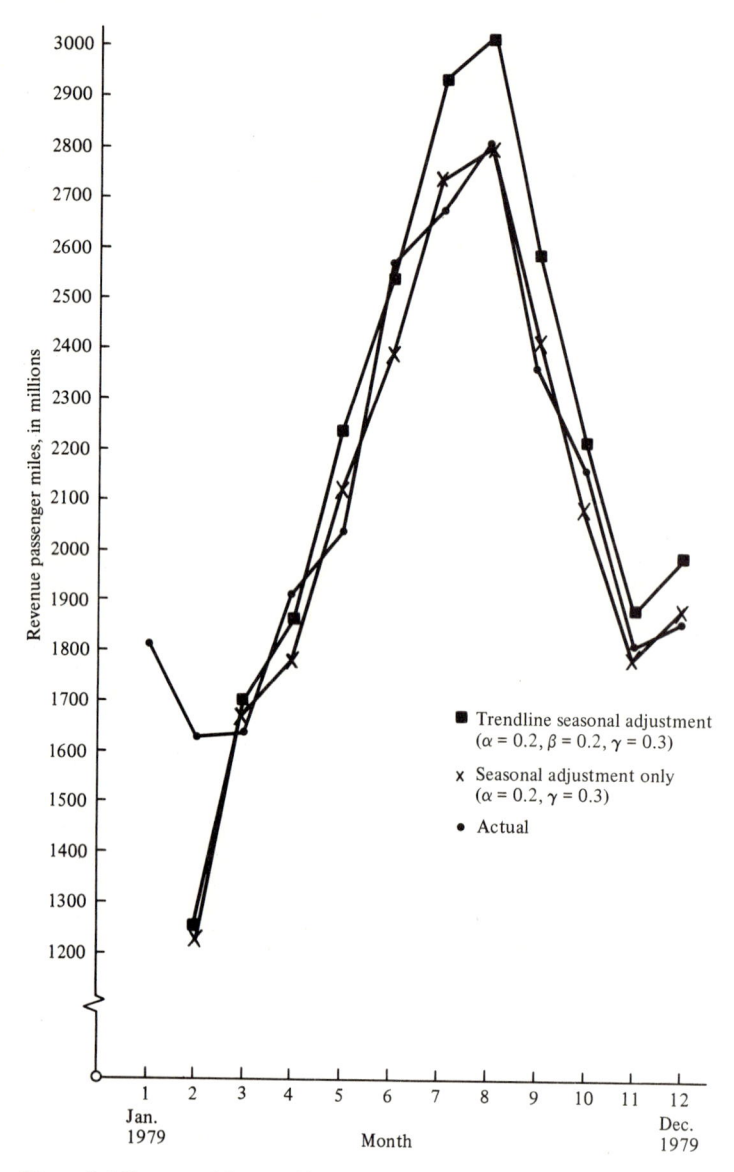

Figure 6.6 Exponential smoothing with seasonal adjustment.

Causal Models

Recall that time series models use the assumption that data follow an identifiable pattern over time. Similarly, causal models presume that an identifiable relationship exists between the item being forecast and other factors. These other factors might include selling price, number of employees, advertising expenditure, and virtually anything else that might influence the item being forecast. As with time series models, it is assumed that the relationships identified from past data will continue in the future.

Causal models can vary greatly in complexity. The simplest models relate the item being forecast to a single factor. However, more complex causal models can use a system of mathematical equations that include dozens of factors.

The cost of developing and using causal models generally is high. Consequently, such models are not frequently used for short-term forecasting. However, they are popular for medium- and long-term horizons.

The most widely adopted causal models use regression analysis. More complicated regression models that include systems of equations are called *econometric models*. We shall briefly discuss each of these forecasting techniques.

Regression models Most students are introduced to regression models in elementary statistics courses. Using conventional statistical terminology, we shall call the item being forecast the *dependent variable Y*. The factors that determine the value of the dependent variable are called *independent variables X_i*. If there are n such factors, then the dependent variable might have the following relationship:

$$Y = a_0 + a_1 X_1 + a_2 X_2 + \cdots + a_n X_n \tag{15}$$

where $a_0, a_1, a_2, \ldots, a_n$ are constant coefficients. If we know the values of the independent variables for some time in the future and the coefficients, then we can use equation (15) to forecast the value of the dependent variable.

Regression techniques enable us to estimate the values of the coefficients in equation (15) from past data. Consider the data given in Table 6.7. We can reasonably assume that the number of new mortgage loans is determined by the prevailing interest rate. That is,

$$Y = a_0 + a_1 X_1 \tag{16}$$

where Y is the number of new loans and X_1 is the interest rate.

Regression enables us to estimate a_0 and a_1 such that equation (16) "fits" the past data. For this case, the regression equation is

$$Y = 83.500 - 3.857 X_1 \tag{17}$$

The coefficient values are calculated using regression equations that can be found in most elementary statistics books. Also, computer programs for regression analysis are readily available.

Figure 6.7 depicts the actual observations and the plot of the regression equation. Notice that the vertical distances of the line from the data points represent "errors," or deviations. The regression line is the only one that minimizes the sum of the square of the deviations. For this reason the regression line also is called the *least squares line*.

In order to use regression models for forecasting, we must be able to deter-

Table 6.7 Number of new home mortgage loans and prevailing interest rates for an urban bank

Quarter	Number of new home mortgage loans	Prevailing mortgage interest rate, %
	1979	
I	43	10.50
II	45	10.75
III	40	10.75
IV	40	11.00
	1980	
I	38	12.00
II	34	12.25
III	34	12.75
IV	31	13.25
	1981	
I	27	14.00
II	33	13.50
III	35	13.25
IV	34	13.25

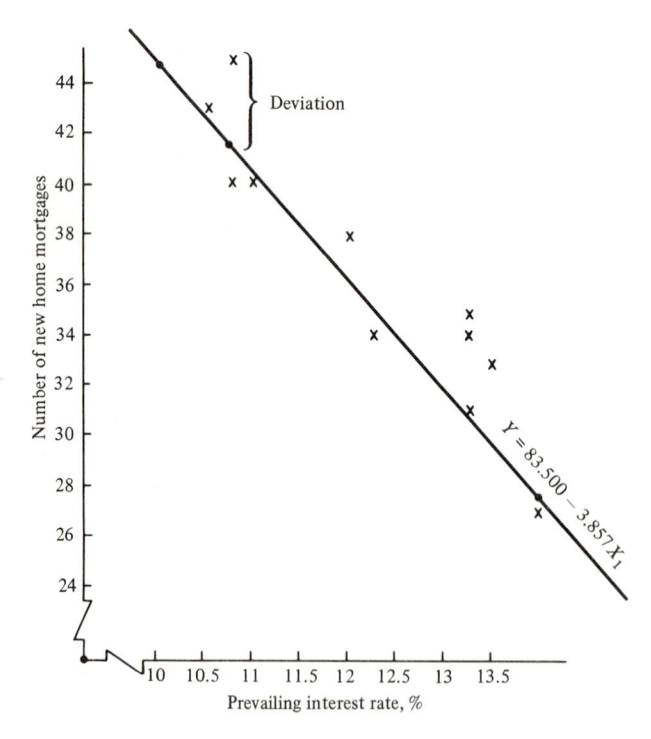

Figure 6.7 Number of new home mortgages versus prevailing interest rate.

mine the future values of the independent variables. For example, assume that the interest rate for the fourth quarter of 1981 is expected to be 13.25 percent. The forecast for the number of new mortgage loans is:

$$Y = 83.500 - 3.857(13.25)$$
$$= 32.156$$

Regression models require a history of data for the dependent variable and for the independent variables. Most regression models give equal weight to all past data in determining the coefficients of the forecasting equation. However, regression techniques have been developed that discount data according to their age. That is, discounted regression models give more weight to recent data in determining the coefficients.

Our example uses a single independent variable. But regression models can include many independent variables that determine the value of the dependent variable. These are called multiple regression models. Also, regression models can include sine and cosine functions of time to express seasonality and cycles. Such cyclical regression models are referred to as Fourier models.

Regression models must be tailored to the specific needs of each organization. Their development can be time-consuming and expensive. Also, interpretation of the statistical results of regression analysis requires some expertise. Consequently, regression models are appropriate for medium- and long-term forecasting horizons.

Econometric models Econometric models are regression models that include a system of equations. These equations relate to one another, and the coefficients of the equations are determined by means of regression techniques.

The Federal Aviation Administration (FAA) uses an econometric model to forecast future growth in air travel. This model consists of a set of simultaneous equations that forecast passenger miles, number of passengers, and fares for scheduled domestic service. The key equation forecasts revenue passenger miles as a function of average fare per revenue passenger mile, income per capita, and several other variables that measure the state of the economy and the prices of alternative modes of transportation.

Econometric models, like the one developed by the FAA, tend to be sophisticated and expensive. Their development and use require considerable expertise in statistics and related economic matters. Consequently, econometric models are used primarily with long-range forecasting horizons.

Subjective Models

Subjective forecasting models generally are used when there is a scarcity of relevant data. This is common with long-term forecasting horizons. Available data may indicate patterns and relationships that will continue in the short term or even in the medium term. But these patterns and relationships are unlikely to persist in the long term. Therefore, there is little relationship between the past and the long-term future.

Subjective forecasting models attempt to bring together opinions and any other information that relate to the item being forecast. Frequently, the information is qualitative in nature. Consequently, these models systematically and logically draw together qualitative expressions in arriving at a forecast.

Many subjective forecasting models have been suggested. The Delphi method is one of the most controversial. Closely related to Delphi is cross-impact analysis. Both of these methods rely upon eliciting the opinions of experts. In contrast, the method of historical analogy focuses upon similar past occurrences. We shall briefly describe each of these subjective forecasting models.

Delphi method The Delphi method was developed at the Rand Corporation by Olaf Helmer. It involves the systematic solicitation and collation of informed judgment. Procedurally, Delphi uses a carefully designed set of questionnaires that are administered sequentially. The method is carried out as follows:

1. An initial questionnaire is administered to experts who are not allowed to interact among themselves. The questionnaire requests estimates of a set of numerical quantities. For example, estimated dates at which technological breakthroughs will be realized are requested.
2. The results of the first questionaire are summarized and fed back to the respondents. The summary might include median values and interquartile ranges.
3. The respondents are asked to revise the previous estimates on the basis of the summary results.
4. On succeeding rounds of the questionnaire, respondents whose estimates deviated markedly from the median are asked to justify their estimates.
5. The justifications also are summarized and fed back to the respondents in another iteration.
6. The process continues until some degree of agreement is achieved among the respondents or until no further revisions occur.

Table 6.8 shows summarized results from two Delphi forecasts. The median and the interquartile range were fed back to respondents to be used for revising their estimates.

The Delphi method can be very time-consuming and expensive. It generally has been associated with technological forecasting, which involves predicting the dimensions of technological change in the distant future. Consequently, Delphi is appropriate for long-term forecasting horizons.

The Delphi method requires a knowledgeable administrator to oversee questionnaire development, to summarize results, and to revise the questionnaires. The qualities of the administrator are important for successfully applying Delphi.

Table 6.8 Summarized responses from Delphi forecasts

	Year selected by respondents as date of probable occurrences		
Event	25%	50%	75%
1. There will be a single National Building Code.	1975	1977	1980
2. Polymers will be created by molecular tailoring, with service ranges in excess of 1000°F.	1971	1976	2000

Source: McGraw-Hill Survey of Technological Breakthroughs and Applications of Significant Technological Developments, McGraw-Hill Book Company, Inc., New York, 1968.

Cross-impact analysis Cross-impact analysis relies upon the premise that future events are directly related to the occurrence of earlier events. A panel of experts studies a set of correlations between events that are presented in matrix form. The correlation between an earlier event and a future event is analyzed to estimate the likelihood of the future event occurring.

As an example, consider a 1982 forecast that examines (1) $3-per-gallon gasoline prices by 1983 and (2) the commercial development of electric cars by 1987. By consensus, it might be determined that, given (1), the probability of (2) is 0.7, and, given (2), the probability of (1) is 0.6. In matrix form, this is

	Probability of event	
Given event	(1)	(2)
(1)	....	0.7
(2)	0.6	....

Assume now that the forecasted probability for commercial development of electric cars by 1987 is 1.0, and the forecasted probability of $3-per-gallon gasoline by 1983 is 0.8. These values are statistically inconsistent with the values in the matrix. The inconsistencies would be pointed out to the experts on the panel, who then would revise their estimates in a series of iterations.

Cross-impact analysis, like Delphi, is generally used for long-term forecasting horizons. It also requires an administrator, whose qualities can affect the forecast.

Historical analogy Historical analogy involves comparative analysis of the introduction and growth patterns of new items with similar, previously introduced items. Forecasts are based upon similarity in developmental patterns over the life of the item.

Historical analogy frequently is used to forecast market penetration for new products and services. It is related to identifying the life cycle of the new item. This, of course, involves the birth, starting up, steady-state operation, rejuvenation, and finally termination of the productive system. But, the specific form of the life cycle is estimated by analogy with that of a similar item.

Historical analogy requires detailed information about the proposed new item and about analogous, previously introduced items. Identifying the appropriate analogous items can require a considerable amount of time, effort, and expense. Also, the data used can often be interpreted in a variety of ways. This can raise concern about the credibility of the forecasts derived. As with other subjective forecasting models, historical analogy is based upon judgments and qualitative factors that may be relevant to the future.

SUMMARY

Forecasting underlies nearly every aspect of management decision making. Short-term forecasting is needed for inventory control, vehicle routing, and workshift scheduling. Medium-term forecasting is needed for capacity utilization decisions. And long-term forecasting is used for planning new services. Virtually every function of management presumes a forecast of future outcomes.

Forecasts are intimately connected with the decision process. Yet, we have a tendency to stress other aspects of the process and assume that viable forecasts will be available. But the quality of the forecasts is determined by the forecasting model selected. Managers should pay attention to the characteristics of any forecasting model that they adopt. An appropriate forecasting model can significantly enhance management decision making.

TOPICS FOR DISCUSSION

1. What characteristics of service organizations make forecast accuracy very important?
2. Forecasting is important for decision making at all levels within organizations. Explain.
3. What costs are associated with forecast model development and use, and what costs are associated with forecast error? How do these costs typically change with more accurate forecasting models?
4. The number of customers at a bank is likely to vary by the hour of the day and by the day of the month. What are the implications of this for choosing a forecasting model?
5. Compare and contrast mean absolute deviation with mean square deviation.
6. Discuss several important factors that influence the choice of a forecasting model.
7. Compare N-period moving-average models with exponential smoothing models.
8. Time series models are the most commonly used forecasting methods. Explain why this is true. Give some service organization examples where time series models would be appropriate.
9. Causal models are often used for medium-term forecasting. Give some service examples of causal relationships that might be incorporated into a forecasting model.
10. Outline the Delphi approach.
11. Cross-impact analysis can be used with the Delphi method. Suggest how this might be accomplished.

FORECASTING FOR SERVICE OPERATIONS **137**

12. In January 1980, Pan American Airways merged with National Airlines. How will this merger affect the results of the exponential smoothing forecasts given in Table 6.6?

EXERCISES

6.1 In September 1981, there were 1035 depositing customers at a bank. The forecast for September (made in August) was for 1065 customers. Use $\alpha = 0.1$ to update the forecast for October.

6.2 You are given the following information:

$$A_5 = 72$$
$$S_4 = 67$$
$$\alpha = 0.1$$

Update the forecast for period 6 using simple exponential smoothing.

6.3 You are given the following information:

$$A_5 = 72$$
$$S_4 = 67$$
$$t_4 = 1.4$$
$$\alpha = 0.1$$
$$\beta = 0.3$$

Update the forecast for period 6 using exponential smoothing with trend adjustment.

6.4 Demand for a certain drug in a hospital has been increasing. For the past six months we observed the following demand:

Month	Demand, units
January	15
February	18
March	22
April	23
May	27
June	26

Use a three-month moving average to make a forecast for July.

6.5 For the data in exercise 6.4, use $\alpha = 0.1$ to make a forecast for July.

6.6 For the data in exercise 6.4, use $\alpha = 0.1$ and $\beta = 0.2$ to make a forecast for July and August. Calculate MAD and MSD for your January through June forecasts.

6.7 In January 1979, revenue passenger miles for Pan American Airways were 1,806,000,000. Update the forecasts in Table 6.3 using $\alpha = 0.1$.

6.8 Refer to exercise 6.7. Update the forecasts in Table 6.4 using $\alpha = 0.2$ and $\beta = 0.2$.

6.9 In January 1980, revenue passenger miles for Pan American Airways were 2,564,000,000. Update the forecasts in Table 6.5 using $\alpha = 0.2$ and $\gamma = 0.3$.

6.10 Refer to exercise 6.9. Update the forecasts in Table 6.6 using $\alpha = 0.2$, $\beta = 0.2$, $\gamma = 0.3$.

6.11 Calculate MAD for exercises 6.7, 6.8, 6.9, and 6.10.

6.12 Refer to exercise 6.11. Why do you believe the forecasts in exercises 6.9 and 6.10 are so poor?

CASELETTE: OAK HOLLOW EVALUATION CENTER

Oak Hollow Medical Evaluation Center is a nonprofit agency offering multidisciplinary diagnostic services to study children in the community who have disabilities or delays in development. The Center can test the patient for physical, psychological, or social problems. Fees for services are based on an ability-to-pay schedule.

The Evaluation Center exists in a highly competitive environment. Many public-spirited organizations are competing for shrinking funds (Proposition 13 syndrome), and many groups, such as private physicians, private and school psychologists, and social service organizations, are also "competing" for the same patients.

As a result of the competitive situation that exists, the Center finds itself in an increasingly vulnerable financial position.

Mr. Abel, director of the Center, is becoming increasingly concerned with the Center's ability to attract adequate funding and to serve community needs. Mr. Abel must now develop an accurate estimate of the future patient load level, staffing requirements, and operating expenses as part of his effort to attract funding for the Center. To this end, the director has approached an operations management professor at the local university for assistance in preparing a patient, staffing, and budget forecast for the coming year. The professor has chosen you to aid her in this project. Tables 6.9 through 6.12 give you some pertinent information.

Assignments

1. Given the information available and your knowledge of different forecasting techniques, you are to recommend a specific forecasting technique(s) for the study. Consider the advantages and

Table 6.9 Annual number of patient tests performed[*]

Test	1975	1976	1977	1978	1979
Physical exam	390	468	509	490	582
Speech and hearing screening	102	124	180	148	204
Psychological testing	168	312	376	386	437
Social-worker interview	106	188	184	222	244

[*] All entering patients are given a physical examination. Patients are then scheduled for additional testing deemed appropriate.

Table 6.10 Annual expenses

Area	1975	1976	1977	1978	1979
Physical and neurological exams	$18,200	$24,960	$ 32,760	$ 31,500	$ 41,600
Speech and hearing	2,040	2,074	3,960	3,950	4,850
Psychological test	6,720	12,480	16,450	16,870	20,202
Social work	3,320	3,948	4,416	5,550	7,592
Subtotal	$30,280	$43,462	$ 57,586	$ 57,870	$ 74,244
Other expenses	46,559	48,887	51,820	55,447	59,883
Total	$76,839	$92,349	109,406	$113,317	$134,127

Table 6.11 Monthly patient demand, September 1978–December 1979

	Physical exams	Speech and hearing test	Psychological testing	Social-worker interview
1978				
September	54	16	42	24
October	67	21	54	31
November	74	22	48	33
December	29	9	23	13
1979				
January	58	20	44	24
February	52	18	39	22
March	47	16	35	20
April	41	14	31	17
May	35	12	26	15
June	29	10	22	12
July	23	8	17	10
August	29	10	22	12
September	65	24	48	27
October	81	29	61	34
November	87	31	66	37
December	35	12	26	14

Table 6.12 Current staffing levels*

Physicians	2 part time, 18 hours per week
Speech and hearing clinician	1 part time, 20 hours per week
Psychologist	1 full time, 38 hours per week
	1 part time, 16 hours per week
Social worker	1 full time, 40 hours per week

* The Oak Hollow Evaluation Center operates on a 50-week year.

disadvantages of your preferred technique and identify additional information, if any, that Mr. Abel would need.
2. Develop forecasts for patient, staffing, and budget levels for next year.

CASELETTE: GNOMIAL FUNCTIONS, INC.

Gnomial Functions, Inc. (GFI) is a medium-sized consulting firm in San Francisco which specializes in developing various forecasts of product demand, sales, consumption, or other information for its clients. To a lesser degree, it has also developed ongoing models for internal use by client companies. When contacted by a potential client, GFI usually establishes a basic work agreement with the firm's top management that sets out the general goals of the end product, primary contact personnel in both firms, and an outline of the project's overall scope (including any necessary time contraints for intermediate and final completion and a rough price estimate for the contract). Following this step, a team of GFI personnel is assembled to determine the most appropriate forecasting technique and to develop a more-detailed work program to be used as the basis for final contract negotiations. This team, which may vary in size according to the scope of the project and the client's needs, will perform the

Table 6.13

Month	DynaSol Industries sales, units	Sales, in thousands	Regional market sales, units	Sales, in thousands
		1978		
September	24	$ 44.736	223	$ 396.048
October	28	52.192	228	404.928
November	31	59.517	230	408.480
December	32	61.437	231	422.564
		1979		
January	30	57.998	229	418.905
February	35	67.197	235	429.881
March	39	78.621	240	439.027
April	40	80.637	265	484.759
May	43	86.684	281	529.449
June	47	94.748	298	561.479
July	51	110.009	314	680.332
August	54	116.480	354	747.596
September	59	127.265	389	809.095
October	62	137.748	421	931.401
November	67	148.857	466	1,001.356
December	69	153.300	501	1,057.320
		1980		
January	74	161.121	529	1,057.320
February	79	172.007	573	1,145.264

tasks established in the work program in conjunction with any personnel from the client firm who would be included in the team.

Recently, GFI has been contacted by a rapidly growing regional firm that manufactures, sells, and installs active solar water-heating equipment for commercial and residential applications. DynaSol Industries has seen its sales increase by more than 200 percent during the last 18 months and wishes to obtain a reliable estimate of its sales during the next 18 months. The company management expected that sales should increase substantially because of competing energy costs, tax-credit availability, and fundamental shifts in the attitudes of the regional population towards so-called exotic solar systems. They also faced increasing competition within the burgeoning market. This situation requires major strategic decisions concerning the company's future. At the time when GFI was contacted, DynaSol had almost reached the manufacturing capacity of its present facility and, if it were to continue growing with the market, would have to expand either by relocating to a new facility entirely or by developing a second manufacturing location. Each involved certain known costs and each had its own advantages and disadvantages. The major unknown, as far as management was concerned, was the growth of the overall market for this type of product and how large a share the company would be able to capture.

Table 6.13 contains the preliminary information available to GFI on DynaSol's past sales.

Assignments

1. Given the information available and your knowledge of different forecasting techniques, your role as a team member is to develop a recommendation for utilizing a specific forecasting technique in the subsequent study. The final contract negotiations are pending, so it is essential that you take into account the advantages and disadvantages of your preferred technique as they would apply to the problem at hand and point out any additional information you would like to have.
2. Assume that you are a member of DynaSol's small marketing department and the contract negotiations with GFI have fallen through irrevocably. The company's top management has decided to use your expertise to develop a forecast for the next six months (and perhaps for the six-month period following that one as well) because it must have some information on which to base a decision to expand its operations. Develop such a forecast and note, for the benefit of top management, any reservations or qualifications you feel are vital to its understanding and use of the information.

SELECTED BIBLIOGRAPHY

Berry, W. L., V. A. Mabert, and M. Marcus: "Forecasting Teller Window Demand With Exponential Smoothing," *Institute for Research in the Behavioral, Economic, and Management Sciences,* Purdue University Paper No. 536, November 1975.

Box, George E. P., and G. M. Jenkins: *Time Series Analysis: Forecasting and Control,* Holden-Day, Inc., San Francisco, 1970.

Bright, James: "Can We Forecast Technology?" *Industrial Research,* March 1968, pp. 55–63.

—— and E. F. Milton (eds.): *A Guide to Practical Technology Forecasting,* Prentice-Hall, Inc., Englewood Cliffs, N.J., 1973.
Brown, R. G.: *Smoothing, Forecasting and Prediction,* Prentice-Hall, Inc., Englewood Cliffs, N.J., 1963.
——: *Statistical Forecasting for Inventory Control.* McGraw-Hill Book Company, New York, 1959.
Buffa, E. S., and J. G. Miller: *Production-Inventory Systems: Planning and Control,* 3d ed., Richard D. Irwin, Inc., Homewood, Ill., 1979.
——: *Modern Production/Operations Management,* 6th ed., John Wiley and Sons, Inc., New York, 1980.
Buffa, F. P.: "The Application of a Dynamic Forecasting Model with Inventory Control Properties," *Decision Sciences,* vol. 6, no. 2, April 1975, pp. 298–306.
Butler, William F., Robert A. Kavesh, and Robert B. Platt: *Methods and Techniques of Business Forecasting,* Prentice-Hall, Inc., Englewood Cliffs, N.J., 1974.
Chambers, J. C., S. K. Mullick, and D. D. Smith: *An Executive's Guide to Forecasting,* John Wiley and Sons, Inc., New York, 1974.
——: "How to Choose the Right Forecasting Technique," *Harvard Business Review,* July–August 1971, pp. 45–74.
Chase, R. B., and N. J. Aquilano: *Production and Operations Management,* rev. ed., Richard D. Irwin, Inc., Homewood, Ill., 1977.
Fusfeld, A. R., and R. N. Foster: "Delphi Technique: Survey and Comment," *Business Horizons,* vol. 14, June 1971, pp. 29–34.
Guerts, Michael D., and I. B. Ibrahim: "Comparing the Box-Jenkins Approach With the Exponentially Smoothed Forecasting Model: Application to Hawaii Tourists," *Journal of Marketing Research,* March 1975, pp. 182–188.
Jenkins, G. M., and D. G. Watts: *Spectral Analysis and Its Applications,* Holden-Day, Inc., San Francisco 1969.
Lanford, H. W.: *Technological Forecasting Methodologies,* American Management Association, New York, 1972.
Mabert, V. A.: "Forecast Modification Based Upon Residual Analysis: A Case Study of Check Volume Estimation," *Decision Sciences,* vol. 9, no. 2, April 1978, pp. 285–296.
——: "Statistical Versus Sales Force–Executive Opinion Short Range Forecasts: A Time Series Analysis Case Study," *Decision Sciences,* vol. 7, no. 2, April 1976, pp. 310–318.
Makridakis, Spyros, Anne Hodgswon, and Steven C. Wheelwright: "An Interactive Forecasting System," *The American Statistician,* vol. 28, no. 4, November 1974, pp. 153–158.
Martino, Joseph P.: *Technological Forecasting for Decision Making,* Elsevier Publishing Co., Inc., New York, 1972.
Mincer, Jacob (ed.): *Economic Forecasts and Expectations,* Columbia University Press, New York, 1969.
Nelson, Charles R.: *Applied Time Series Analysis for Managerial Forecasting,* Holden-Day, Inc., San Francisco, 1973.
O'Neal, C. R.: "New Approach to Technological Forecasting Morphological Analysis," *Business Horizons,* vol. 13, December 1970, pp. 47–58.
Reisman, A., D. Gudapati, R. Chandrasekaran, P. Darukhanavala, and D. Morrison: "Forecasting Short-Term Demand," *Industrial Engineering,* vol. 8, no. 5, May 1976, pp. 38–45.
Rochberg, R.: "Information Theory, Cross-Impact Matrices, and Pivotal Events," *Technological Forecasting and Social Change,* Elsevier Publishing Co., Inc., New York, 1970, pp. 53–60.
Sackman, H.: *Delphi Assessment: Expert Opinion, Forecasting, and Group Process,* R-1283-PR, The Rand Corp., New York, April 1974.
Wheelwright, Steven C., and Spyros Makridakis: *Forecasting Methods for Management,* Wiley-Interscience, New York, 1973.
Whybark, D. C.: "A Comparison of Adaptive Forecasting Techniques," *The Logistics and Transportation Review,* vol. 8, no. 3, 1972, pp. 13–26.

PART THREE

DESIGNING THE SERVICE SYSTEM

CHAPTER
SEVEN

DESIGN OF SERVICE DELIVERY SYSTEMS

Designing a service delivery system is a creative process. It begins with a statement of service objectives. The various alternatives for achieving these objectives then must be identified and analyzed, and finally decisions must be made. Designing a service system involves issues such as facility location, facility layout, job design, consumer involvement, equipment selection, and service capacity. The design process is never finished. Once the system becomes operational, modifications in the service design are introduced as conditions change.

As an example of service system design, consider a copying service. The objectives include pickup and delivery service for commercial customers, self-service for walk-in consumers, photo reduction, offset printing, collating, and binding. Table 7.1 identifies a number of design decisions for this copying service and possible resolutions. As can be seen, the design decisions are interrelated. The selection of the university area site ensures demand for self-service facilities and a pool of part-time help. As the decisions are made, the service takes on a unique character. This copying service will have a youthful, energetic atmosphere, perhaps with stereo music and travel posters on the walls.

The creative design process can be facilitated by an understanding of the various classifications of productive systems. For manufacturing systems four types of operations have been identified: flow shop (production line), job shop (batch process), projects, and process industries. In this chapter the analogous types of service processes will be examined and their particular characteristics identified.

Three major approaches for viewing service system design are suggested. Each approach—the production-line approach, consumer involvement, and isolating the technical core—advocates a particular philosophy. The features

145

Table 7.1 Copying service design considerations

Design decision	Possible resolution
Facility location	Locate near the university.
Layout	Use storefront area for self-service and partition off rear production area.
Job design	Staff reception area with part-time university students, hire experienced offset printer-binder, hire housewife to train as store supervisor.
Consumer involvement	Encourage self-service with price incentives and easy to follow instructions.
Equipment selection	Identify mix of copying machines for flexibility of use and number to avoid excessive consumer waiting.
Facility appearance	Use bright colors and carpeted floor in self-service area.
Facilitating goods	Stock various sizes and weights of paper and a variety of covers and binders.

of these approaches will be examined. The use of technology in services raises a particular design issue because of the consumer participation in the process. The difficulty of introducing technology in service operations is also a service design issue. Our discussion of the overall system design strategy begins with a classification of service by type of operation.

TYPES OF SERVICE OPERATIONS

When considering the design of a service system, it is helpful to keep in mind the four types of operations classifications: project, batch (job shop), line (flow shop), and ongoing process. Table 7.2 briefly describes these four classifications and gives examples from manufacturing and services. Seldom does a service system fall into only one classification. In fact, one approach to service process design combines both the job-shop and flow-shop concepts. During the life of any organization, many opportunities to manage projects occur. The process service operation is unique because it serves by just being available. The characteristics of each of these operation classifications follow.

Project

Most professional services, such as architects, consultants, lawyers, and doctors, manage a number of projects. A project is characterized by a number of interrelated, well-defined activities, each being accomplished according to a required sequence. For example, the design of a building would begin with a study of the site. Consultation with the consumer to arrive at general specifications would follow. Preliminary sketches are then prepared and revised, and a three-dimensional model made from the sketches. After approval, simulta-

DESIGN OF SERVICE DELIVERY SYSTEMS

Table 7.2 Classification of manufacturing and services by type of operation

Type of operation	Operation description	Manufacturing	Service
Project	Long-duration activities, low volume, usually one of a kind	Construction of airport, oil-refinery overhaul	Legal defense, management, consulting
Batch (job shop)	Short-duration activities, low volume, custom product	Tool and die making, cabinet making, printing	Catering, automotive repair, health care
Line (flow shop)	Short-duration activities, high volume, standard product	Light bulbs, appliances, automobiles	Cafeteria, car wash, muffler repair
Ongoing process	Continuous processing of a homogeneous material	Oil refinery, chemical plant, flour mill, paper mill	Police and fire protection (24-hr availability)

neous work can begin on drawings of the structural, electrical, and mechanical components.

The project is completed when all the activities are finished. This important consideration of project completion time is directly affected by a sequence of critical activities.

Batch (Job Shop)

In a job shop operation, services are tailored to the consumer's specifications. As an example, consider the service department for a large automobile dealership. This facility has the equipment and personnel needed to perform a variety of automotive services. Upon arrival consumers confer with a troubleshooter, who prepares a detailed schedule of work for the vehicle.

The ability to perform different combinations and sequences of activities for each consumer is an important feature of a job shop. Such flexibility is gained at the expense of a regular flow of consumers through the service system. For this reason, scheduling work in a job shop is a problem. The topic of job-shop scheduling addresses the problem of sequencing jobs at various operations in the system.

Line (Flow Shop)

A flow shop is appropriate for delivering standardized services. Here the sequence of operations is always the same, like an assembly line. Consider, for example, a cafeteria. Instead of partially assembled cars moving along a conveyor, diners form a line, push their trays ahead of them, and select items for their meal. Services that can be standardized and divided into routine tasks are candidates for line operations. We have all experienced a service line operation, such as a medical examination, university registration, or automobile-license renewal.

Service standardization allows for division of labor and the use of specialized equipment. Labor turnover may be high, but the necessary skills are easily acquired. The line process is also inflexible with regard to output and to changes in services performed. Because of the sequential nature of the activities, the service output is limited to the slowest activity, or bottleneck. An ideal or balanced service line would have tasks assigned so that each activity would take an equal amount of time.

Ongoing Process

Services such as police and fire protection are examples of ongoing processes; they operate on a continuous 24-hour basis. In addition to providing their customary services of extinguishing fires, apprehending criminals, etc., they also provide a service by just being available. Most people feel more secure knowing firemen and policemen are on call. A critical design issue is the deployment of these service resources. One measure of performance is the time required to travel from the service facility to the location of the caller.

APPROACHES TO SERVICE SYSTEM PLANNING AND DESIGN

In Chapter 2, we defined the service package as a bundle of attributes that a consumer experiences. This bundle consists of four features: supporting facility, facilitating goods, explicit service, and implicit service. With a well-designed service system, all of these features are harmoniously coordinated in light of the desired service package. Consequently, the definition of the service package is the key to designing the service system. This design can be approached in one of several ways.

At one extreme, we can deliver services by way of a production-line approach. With this approach, routine services are provided in a controlled environment to ensure consistent quality and efficiency of operation. Another approach for service system design is to encourage active consumer participation in the process. Allowing the consumer to take an active role in the service process can result in many benefits to both consumer and provider. An intermediate approach divides the service into high- and low-consumer-contact operations. This allows the low-contact operations to be designed as a technical core, isolated from the consumer. Figure 7.1 presents a spectrum of approaches as an aid to creative service system design. It should be noted that combinations of these approaches can be used. For example, banks isolate their check processing operations, use self-serve automatic tellers, and provide personalized loan service.

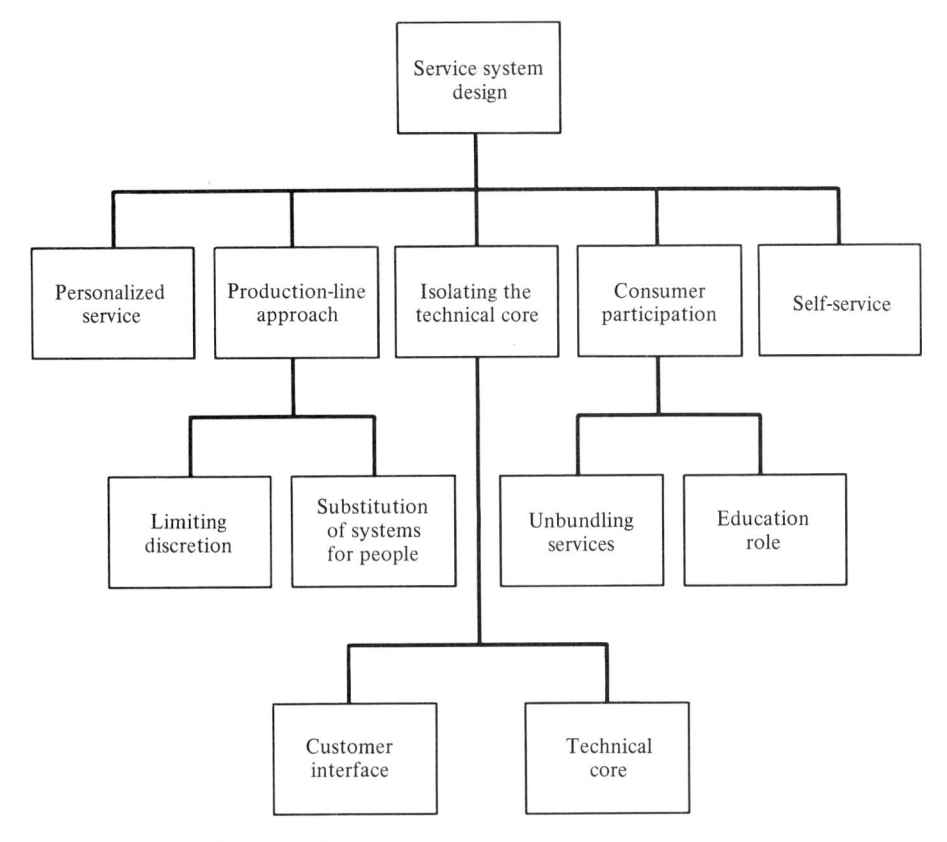

Figure 7.1 Approaches to service system design.

Production-Line Approach

We tend to see service as something personal: it is performed by individuals directly for other individuals. This humanistic perception can be overly constraining and impede innovative service system design. For example, we might benefit from a more technocratic service delivery system. Manufacturing systems are designed with control of the process in mind. The output is often machine-paced. Jobs are designed with explicit tasks to perform. Special tools and machines are supplied to increase worker productivity.

McDonald's provides an example of the technocratic production-line approach to service.[1] Raw materials, such as the hamburger patties, are prepackaged and measured at a central plant; the employees are left with no discretion as to size, quality, or consistency. Furthermore, the storage facilities are de-

---

[1] Theodore Levitt, "Production Line Approach to Service," *Harvard Business Review*, September–October 1972, pp. 41–52.

signed expressly for the predetermined mix of products. No extra space is available for foods and beverages not called for in the service.

The production of french fries illustrates the attention to design detail. The fries come precut, partially cooked, and frozen. The fryer is sized to cook a correct quantity of fries. This is an amount that will be not so large as to create an inventory of soggy fries or so small as to require frequent attention. The fryer is emptied onto a wide, flat tray near the service counter. This location prevents fries from an overfilled bag from dropping to the floor and creating an unclean environment. A special wide-mouthed scoop with a funnel in the handle is used to ensure a consistent measure of french fries. The thoughtful design ensures that employees never soil their hands or the fries, the floor remains clean, and the quantity is controlled. Furthermore, the customer is delivered a generous-looking portion of fries by a speedy, efficient, and cheerful employee.

The entire system is engineered from beginning to end, from prepackaged hamburgers to highly visible trash cans that encourage customers to clear their tables. Every detail is accounted for through careful planning and design of the entire system. The production-line approach to service system design attempts to translate a successful manufacturing concept into the service sector. There are several features of this approach that contribute to its success.

Limited discretionary action of personnel A worker on an automobile assembly line is given well-defined tasks to perform, along with the tools to accomplish them. Employees with discretion and latitude might produce a more personalized car, but with loss of uniformity from one car to the next. Standardization and quality (consistency in output) are the hallmarks of a production line. With some services, we might desire this consistency in service performance for all consumers. For example, specialized services like muffler replacement and pest control are advertised as having the same high-quality service at any of their franchised outlets. Thus, the consumer can expect identical service at any location, just as one product from a manufacturer is indistinguishable from another.

Division of labor The production-line approach suggests that the total job be broken down into groups of tasks. Task grouping permits specialization of labor skills. Not everyone at McDonald's need be a cook. Furthermore, the division of labor allows one to pay only for the skill required to perform the task. Consider, for example, a new concept in health care called the *automated multiphasic testing laboratory*. Patients are processed through a fixed sequence of medical tests as part of the diagnostic workup. Tests are performed by medical technicians using sophisticated equipment. Because the entire process is divided into routine tasks, the examination can be accomplished without the need for an expensive physician.

Substitution of technology for people The systematic substitution of equipment for people has been the source of progress in manufacturing. This approach also can be used in services, as seen by the acceptance of automatic teller machines in lieu of bank tellers. But a great deal can be accomplished by means of the soft technology of systems. Consider, for example, the use of mirrors placed in an airplane galley. This benign device automatically ensures that the flight attendant will be self-motivated to maintain a pleasant appearance. Another example is the greeting-card display that has a built-in inventory replenishment and reordering feature. When the stock gets low, a colored card appears to signal a reorder. Using a portable printer, insurance agents can personalize their recommendations and illustrate the accumulation of cash values. Data about the client are inputted to a distant computer by telephone to calculate the projections.

Service standardization The limited menu at McDonald's guarantees a fast hamburger. Limiting the service options creates opportunities for preplanning and predictability. The service becomes a routine process, with well-defined tasks and orderly flow of customers. Standardization also helps provide uniformity in service quality because the process is easier to control. Franchise services take advantage of standardization to build national organizations and, thus, overcome the problem of demand being limited to only the immediate region around a service location.

Consumer Participation

For most service systems, the consumer is present when the service is being performed. Instead of being a passive bystander, the consumer represents productive labor just at the moment it is needed. Opportunities exist for increasing productivity by shifting some of the service activities onto the consumer.

Depending upon the degree of consumer involvement, a spectrum of service delivery systems is possible from self-service to complete dependence on a service provider. For example, consider the services of a real estate agent. A homeowner has the options of selling the home personally or staying away from any involvement by engaging a real estate agent for a 6 percent commission. An intermediate alternative is the "Gallery of Homes" approach. For a flat fee, say $500, the homeowner lists the home with the Gallery. Home buyers visiting the Gallery are interviewed concerning their needs and are shown pictures and descriptions of homes that might be of interest. Appointments for visits with homeowners are made and an itinerary is developed. The buyers provide their own transportation and the homeowners show their own homes. The Gallery agent conducts the final closing and arranges financing as usual. Productivity gains are achieved by a division of labor. The real estate agent concentrates on duties requiring special training and expertise, while the homeowner and buyer share the remaining activities. The following features illustrate some of the contributions consumers can make in the delivery of services.

Substitution of consumer labor for provider labor The increasing minimum wage has hastened this substitution of consumer labor for personalized services. Hotel bellhops are seen less often and more buffets are being served. Airlines are encouraging passengers to use carry-on luggage. Technology has also helped to facilitate consumer participation. Consider, for example, the use of automatic tellers at banks and the use of long-distance direct dialing. The modern consumer has become a producer, receiving benefits for his or her labor in lower-cost services.

Smoothing service demand Service capacity is a time perishable commodity. For example, in a medical setting it is more appropriate to measure capacity in terms of physician hours available rather than just number of doctors on the staff. This approach emphasizes the permanent loss to the service provider of capacity whenever the server is idle owing to a lack of consumer demand. However, the nature of demand for service is one of pronounced variation by the hour of the day (restaurants), day of the week (theaters), or season (ski resorts). If variations in demand can be smoothed, the required service capacity will be reduced and fuller, more-uniform utilization of capacity can be realized. The result is improved service productivity.

To implement a demand smoothing strategy, participation of consumers is required. They must adjust the timing of their demand to match service availability. Typical methods of accomplishing this are appointments and reservations. In compensation, consumers expect to avoid waiting for the services. Consumers may also be induced to acquire the service in offpeak hours by price incentives (e.g., reduced telephone rates after 5 p.m.).

If attempts to smooth demand fail, high utilization of capacity may still be accomplished by requiring consumers to wait for service. Thus, consumer waiting contributes to productivity by permitting greater utilization of capacity. Perhaps signs such as the following should be posted in waiting areas: "Thank you for waiting. You are helping us to achieve better utilization of our service capacity."

We would expect consumers to be compensated for this input to the service process through lower prices. But what about "free" or prepaid government service? In this situation, waiting is a surrogate for the price that might otherwise be charged the user. The results are a rationing of the limited public service among users and high utilization of capacity. However, using consumers' waiting time as an input to the service process may be criticized on the grounds that individual consumers value their time differently.

The consumer may require training to assume a new and, perhaps, more-independent role as an active participant in the service process. This education role of the provider is a new concept in services. Traditionally the service provider has kept the consumer ignorant and thus dependent on the server.

As services become more specialized, the consumer must also assume a diagnostic role, (e.g., Does the loud noise under my car need the attention of AAMCO or Midas?). Furthermore, an informed consumer may also provide a quality control check, which has been particularly lacking in the professional services. The key to increased service productivity may thus be dependent upon an informed and self-reliant consumer.

Isolating the Technical Core

The manufacture of products is conducted in a controlled environment. The process design is totally focused on creating a continuous and efficient conversion of inputs into products without consumer involvement. Using inventory, the production process is decoupled from the variations in consumer demand.

How can service managers design their operations to achieve the economics of production, when consumers are participating in the process? One suggestion is to separate the service delivery system into high- and no-contact consumer operations.[2] The no-contact, or back-office, operation is then run as a plant: all the production management concepts and automation technology are brought to bear. This separation of activities can result in a consumer perception of personalized service, while in fact achieving economies of scale through volume processing.

The success of this approach depends upon the required amount of consumer contact in the creation of the service and the ability to isolate a technical core of no-contact operations.

Degree of consumer contact Consumer contact refers to the physical presence of the consumer in the system. The degree of customer contact can be measured by the percentage of time the consumer is in the system relative to the total service time. In the high-contact services, shown in Table 7.3, the consumer determines the timing of demand and the nature of the service by direct participation in the process. The perceived quality of service is determined to a large extent by the consumer's experience. The consumer has no direct influence on the production process of low-contact systems because they are not present. Even if a service falls into the high-contact category, it may still be possible to seal off some operations to be run as a factory. For example, the maintenance operations of a public transportation system or the laundry of a hospital are plants within the service system.

Separation of high- and low-contact operations When service systems are decoupled into high- and low-contact operations, each area can be designed separately to achieve improved performance. The different considerations in the design of the low- and high-contact operations are listed in Table 7.4. Notice that high-contact operations require personnel with excellent public relations skills. The daily operations are uncertain because consumers dictate the timing of demand and, to some extent, the service itself. Also observe that low-contact op-

---

[2] Richard B. Chase, "Where Does the Customer Fit in a Service Operation," *Harvard Business Review*, November–December 1978, pp. 137–142.

Table 7.3 Service system classification by customer contact*

High contact	*Pure service:*
	    Health centers
	    Hotels
	    Public transportation
	    Restaurants
	    Schools
	    Personal services

	Mixed service:
	    Branch offices of:
	        Banks
	        Computer companies
	        Real estate
	        Post offices
	        Funeral homes

	Quasimanufacturing:
	    Home offices of:
	        Banks
	        Computer companies
	        Government administration
	        Wholesale houses
	        Post offices

Low contact	*Manufacturing:*
	    Factories producing durable goods
	    Food processors
	    Mining companies
	    Chemical plants

* Used by permission of the *Harvard Business Review.* Exhibits from "Where Does the Customer Fit in a Service Operation" by Richard B. Chase (November–December 1978). Copyright © 1978 by the president and fellows of Harvard College; all rights reserved.

erations need not physically be near the consumer operations. The operations can be scheduled to obtain high utilization of capacity.

Airlines have effectively used this approach in their operations. The reservation clerks and attendants wear uniforms designed in Paris and smiles to match. Baggage handlers are seldom seen and aircraft maintenance is performed at a distant depot and run like a factory.

TECHNOLOGICAL INNOVATION IN SERVICES[3]

The great gains in productivity for agriculture and manufacturing have come from the substitution of technology for human effort. Technology need not be

[3] From Stanford V. Berg, "Determinants of Technological Change in the Service Industries," *Technological Forecasting and Social Change,* vol. 5, 1973, pp. 407–421.

Table 7.4 Major design considerations for high- and low-contact operations*

Design consideration	High-contact operation	Low-contact operation
Facility location	Operations must be near the customer.	Operations may be placed near supply, transportation, or labor.
Facility layout	Facility should accommodate the customer's physical and psychological needs and expectations.	Facility should enhance production.
Product design	Environment as well as the physical product define the nature of the service.	Customer is not in the service environment, so the product can be defined by fewer attributes.
Process design	Stages of production process have a direct, immediate effect on the customer.	Customer is not involved in the majority of processing steps.
Scheduling	Customer is in the production schedule and must be accommodated.	Customer is concerned mainly with completion dates.
Production planning	Orders cannot be stored, so smoothing production flow will result in loss of business.	Both backlogging and production smoothing are possible.
Worker skills	Direct workforce makes up a major part of the service product and so must be able to interact well with the public.	Direct workforce need only have technical skills.
Quality control	Quality standards are often in the eye of the beholder and hence variable.	Quality standards are generally measurable and hence fixed.
Time standards	Service time depends on customer needs, and therefore time standards are inherently loose.	Work is performed on customer surrogates (e.g., forms), and time standards can be tight.
Wage payment	Variable output requires time-based wage systems.	Fixable output permits output-based wage systems.
Capacity planning	To avoid lost sales, capacity must be set to match peak demand.	Storable output permits setting capacity at some average demand level.
Forecasting	Forecasts are short-term, time-oriented.	Forecasts are long-term, output-oriented.

* Used by permission of the *Harvard Business Review*. Exhibits from "Where Does the Customer Fit in a Service Operation" by Richard B. Chase (November–December 1978). Copyright © 1978 by the president and fellows of Harvard College; all rights reserved.

confined to hardware and machines. It also includes innovative systems, such as electronic funds transfer or automated multiphasic health testing. However, unlike manufacturing, where technological innovations are introduced unnoticed by the consumer, technological innovations become an integral part of the service provided the consumer. For example, many airlines have introduced automatic ticketing machines that accept credit cards and issue tickets according to a request entered by the passenger by pushing appropriate buttons.

Because consumers participate directly in the service process, the success of technological innovations is dependent upon consumer acceptance. The impact on consumers is not always limited to a loss of personal attention; consumers may also need to learn new skills (e.g., operate an automatic teller machine) or assume some liability (e.g., loss of float through the use of electronic funds transfer). The contribution of consumers as active participants in the service process must be considered when making changes in the service delivery system.[4]

Service process innovations may be spurred by technological changes in the environment. The laundry and dry-cleaning service has changed in response to synthetic fabrics and "no-iron" sheets. Cleaning synthetic fabrics required new detergents and dry-cleaning solvents. These in turn required the development of a process of injection and metering. The no-iron sheets led to the first sheet folding machine.

The introduction of technology in services is complicated by the need for standardization. For example, all banks in the United States had to agree on the use of the same magnetic ink character imprints on checks to make the check clearing process more efficient. Otherwise, checks of uncooperative banks would need to be hand-sorted. Hand sorting of some checks would severely limit the effectiveness of the technology. The Bank of America took a leadership role in gaining acceptance of the concept. However, the self-interest of banks was a principle motivation for acceptance. The volume of check processing had exceeded manual sorting capacity. Other examples of this needed cooperation occurred in retailing with the acceptance of universal product coding by manufacturers. Retailers could then use sensor equipment to read the code (a series of vertical stripes of different widths). Consequently, they could use a computer to register the sale and update inventory levels simultaneously.

The incentive to innovate in services is hampered because many ideas cannot be patented. An example is the idea of self-serve retailing. Much of the potential for technological and organizational progress is in such areas, so the prospective rewards for innovations are decreased because the innovations may be imitated freely.

SUMMARY

We have found that services can be classified as flow shops, job shops, projects, or ongoing processes. General approaches to the design of service delivery systems have been investigated. These approaches and their combinations provide many opportunities for innovative designs. Finally the difficulty of introducing technology in services was addressed. Specific design decisions,

---

[4] An important exception to the above observation is the use of magnetic-ink-character recognition equipment in banking. This technological innovation did not affect the consumer at all but instead made the "hidden" check clearing process more productive.

such as facility location, facility layout, etc., will now be addressed in the chapters that follow. Approaches to these problems developed for manufacturing operations will be adapted for the design of service systems.

TOPICS FOR DISCUSSION

1. Why is the banking industry having trouble getting consumer acceptance of electronic funds transfer?
2. Give an example where a product innovation by an input supplier has created a change in the method of providing a service.
3. Select a service and identify the high- and low-consumer-contact functions.
4. Isolating the service technical core permits the application of manufacturing technology. Explain.
5. Give an example of a service where isolation of the technical core would be inappropriate.
6. What are some drawbacks of increased consumer involvement in the service process?
7. Franchise services embody the concept of "manufacturing in the field." Comment.
8. What are some other examples of the "production-line approach to services?"

CASELETTE: ALCOVE CORPORATION[5]

ALCOVE Corporation was founded in 1978 by a small group of computer design and systems management personnel to develop hardware and software applications in the burgeoning small (or mini-) computer industry. Located in a major city in the southwestern United States, ALCOVE's formation was the direct result of a part-time research program initiated by the city's leading newspaper to assess the potential of a more-centralized residential distribution system. In particular, the newspaper wanted to investigate the feasibility of developing a vehicular control system that would locate itself accurately enough to deliver papers to residential subscribers. Thus, the corporation's name grew out of the project as an acronym for *A*utomatic *L*ocation *CO*ntrolled *VE*hicles.

By 1980, the principal organizers of ALCOVE Corporation thought the system would be applicable to a number of different delivery operations besides that of newspapers, including other consumer products delivered to retail outlets, laundry and dry-cleaning pickup and delivery, armored-car service, parcel delivery service, industrial or municipal refuse collection, security patrols, postal service, and other home delivery services (pharmacies, appliance repair, etc.). ALCOVE had developed a simple method which would maintain an accurate measure of position along a prescribed route and provide a means of automatically correcting any position errors and also a means of detecting any deviations from the specified route. Owing to the advanced research involved in developing this method, ALCOVE filed a patent application covering its work as a means of protecting the investment (which was roughly $150,000). The prototype system developed for the newspaper consisted of a slightly

---

[5] Adapted from a Harvard Business School case AVCON, Inc., ICCH no. 9-673-109, 1973.

modified version of a standard panel truck, the position sensing device, an on-board minicomputer with input and CRT display terminal, and various pieces of control equipment. The modifications to the panel truck consisted primarily of adding a large window on each side, so the papers could be thrown from the cargo bay to either side, and mounting racks and shelves for the equipment. The prototype was developed for $30,000, composed of the following cost categories:

Stock panel truck	$10,000
Truck modifications (contracted)	12,000
On-board electronics	8,000
Total prototype cost	$30,000

The primary value of having on-board electronics, which (when coupled with the position sensing device and preprogrammed with a specific route or routes) could indicate within 20 feet an appropriate location to throw a paper and, if necessary, guide a driver back to the correct route, is enabling a driver to operate efficiently over a complicated delivery route without reference to maps or to lists and without prior knowledge of the route. ALCOVE believed automated delivery would be more economical than fleet delivery for several reasons—the number of vehicles and drivers required to cover a given amount of territory could be reduced, inexperienced drivers could perform almost as well or as well as experienced drivers, and substantial benefits in the quality of customer service would result. In addition to these advantages, ALCOVE's design team felt that a major benefit of implementing this system for the newspaper would be the availability of computer-ready data for accurate route accounting throughout the distribution system. This latter point was very important to the newspaper because only about 20 percent of the total sales occurred at newsstands. The remaining 80 percent were distributed through individual carriers, who were, in fact, independent retailers. The carriers purchased the papers below cost from a branch distributor and then delivered them. Although many subscription additions and changes were handled centrally and passed on to the branch distributors, carriers quite often solicited new subscriptions which were never known either to the central or to the branch office. Income from the subscriptions handled through the central and branch offices was passed down to the carrier, but the carriers made a higher profit from the subscriptions they handled directly.

Owing to changing economic and social conditions, the news carrier force had evolved from being composed primarily of young people to being composed substantially of adults. Consequently, the newspaper experienced a significant increase in pressure for higher wages and for expanded unionization within the distribution and delivery labor pool. In fact, these labor pressures built to the point where a distribution system strike for higher wages was considered likely if negotiations were not successfully concluded by the end of the year. The newspaper's management was hopeful that ALCOVE's project would provide the solution to a number of these problems.

In tests of the prototype vehicle, ALCOVE demonstrated that the system could deliver an average of 10 papers per minute at an average speed of 12 miles per hour with two throwers in the cargo bay and one driver. They also felt that this system could reduce the newspaper's circulation cost per thousand from around $70 to $55 in the first year of operation and to $50 in the second year.

Questions

1. Compare and contrast the automated delivery system with the manual delivery system presently used by the newspaper.
2. Assess the potential value such a system might have if placed into service; also address the potential difficulties in implementing it.
3. Develop a recommendation to the newspaper management outlining why you would or would not choose to proceed with further development and implementation of the system ALCOVE has developed.

SELECTED BIBLIOGRAPHY

Berg, Stanford V.: "Determinants of Technological Change in the Service Industries," *Technological Forecasting and Social Change,* vol. 5, 1973, pp. 407–421.

Brewer, Garry D.: "On Innovation, Social Change and Reality," *Technological Forecasting and Social Change,* vol. 5, 1973, pp. 19–25.

Chase, Richard B.: "Where Does the Customer Fit in a Service Operation," *Harvard Business Review,* November–December 1978, pp. 137–142.

Kaufmann, Felix: "Hard and Soft Health Technology of the Future," *Technological Forecasting and Social Change,* vol. 5, 1973, pp. 67–74.

Levitt, Theodore: "Production-Line Approach to Service", *Harvard Business Review,* September–October 1972, pp. 41–52.

———: "The Industrialization of Service," *Harvard Business Review,* September–October 1976, pp. 63–74.

Thomas, Dan R. E.: "Strategy is Different in Service Business," *Harvard Business Review,* July–August 1978, pp. 158–165.

CHAPTER
EIGHT

SERVICE FACILITY LOCATION

Services do not move through the traditional product distribution channel (i.e., factory–warehouse–retailer). Instead, either the consumer travels to the service facility or the server moves to the consumer. Examples exist in both the public and private sectors. Students are bused to school and parents travel to shopping centers. Fire trucks are dispatched to a burning building and insurance agents visit your home.

The necessity of bringing the consumer and provider together results in a facility serving a relatively small geographic area. A natural tradeoff exists between the number and cost of facilities and the transportation cost of bringing consumers and providers together. Expensive facilities, such as hospitals, are found in areas that serve a large or populous region. Fast-food restaurants, on the other hand, are found on every street corner and even in less-populated rural areas. However, in all cases the location of the facility with respect to its market is critical for success. Facility location defines the potential market. Service market expansion is accomplished by adding new facilities at geographically dispersed locations, creating a multisite location problem. The essential questions to be answered are:

1. How many facilities should there be?
2. Where should the facilities be located?
3. What should be the capacity of each facility?
4. Which facility should service which consumer?
5. What services should each facility provide?

The multisite location problem is complex. The above questions must be answered simultaneously, because each impacts upon the other. This chapter investigates issues concerning service facility location. It begins with an overview of the problem structure, including travel time models, site selection, decision-making criteria, and the estimation of spatial demand. Facility location models for both single- and multiple-facility systems are also explored. These models are illustrated with both public and private sector examples.

We have assumed that the consumer and provider must be together physically for a service to be performed. However, alternatives do exist if one is willing to substitute communication for transportation or use marketing intermediaries. For example, the bearer of a VISA or MASTERCARD is extended bank credit every time the card is presented to a retailer. Such alternatives will be explored as possible methods of extending services beyond their immediate geographic area.

LOCATION CONSIDERATIONS

Many factors enter into the service facility location decision. Figure 8.1 presents a classification of location problems. The broad categories are geographic structure, number of facilities, and optimization criteria. Let's take a look at each one of these categories in more detail.

Geographic Structure

A traditional classification of location problems is based on the geographic structure. The location can be represented either on a plane or on a network. Location on a plane, or flat surface, is characterized by a solution space that is infinite. Facilities may be located anywhere on the plane and may be identified by an xy cartesian coordinate, as shown in Figure 8.2. Distance between locations is measured in one of two ways. One method is the euclidian metric, or vector, travel distance, defined as:

$$d_{ij} = [(x_i - x_j)^2 + (y_i - y_j)^2]^{1/2} \qquad (1)$$

where d_{ij} = distance between points i and j
x_i, y_i = coordinates of the ith point
x_j, y_j = coordinates of the jth point

The other method is the metropolitan metric, or rectangular displacement, travel distance, defined as:

$$d_{ij} = |x_i - x_j| + |y_i - y_j| \qquad (2)$$

Location on a network is characterized by a solution space that is restricted to the nodes of a network. The arcs of the network represent travel links between these nodes, or centers of activity. Also, distance (time) between pairs of nodes is calculated along the shortest route.

162 DESIGNING THE SERVICE SYSTEM

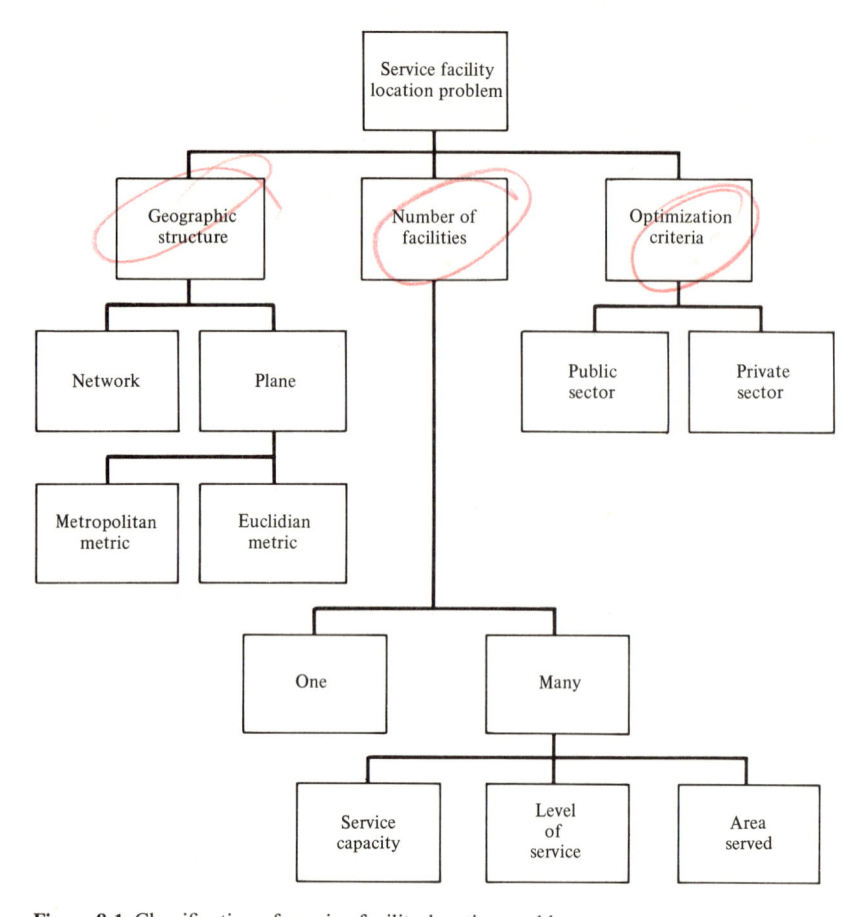

Figure 8.1 Classification of service facility location problems.

The selection of structure and distance metric is often dictated by the problem setting and available data. Networks can more accurately represent the geographic uniqueness of an area (e.g., the travel restrictions caused by a river with few bridges or by mountainous terrain). Unfortunately, the cost of gathering the travel times between nodes on a network can be prohibitive. When locating on a plane that represents an urban area, the metropolitan metric often is used because streets for some cities are arranged in an east-west and north-south pattern. Both the metropolitan and euclidian metrics require an estimate of speed to convert distance traveled to time.

Number of Facilities

The location of a single facility can generally be treated mathematically with little difficulty. Unfortunately, the methods used to site a single facility are not useful for multisite location problems. Finding a unique set of sites is complicated by the problem of assigning demand nodes to sites (i.e., defining service

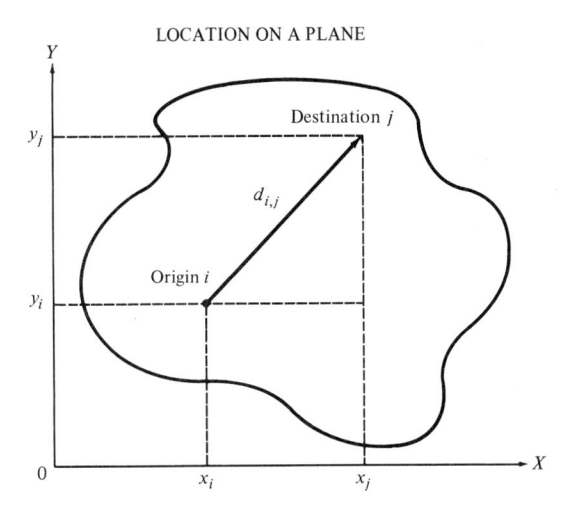

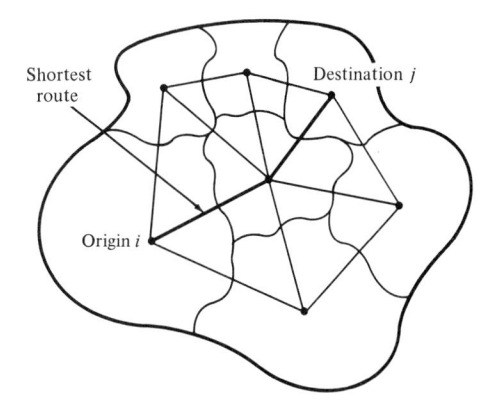

Figure 8.2 Geographic structure.

areas for each site). The problem is further complicated if the capacity at each site varies. For services such as health care, a hierarchy of service exists. Private physicians and clinics offer primary care, general hospitals provide primary care plus hospitalization, and health centers add special treatment capabilities. Thus, the level of service to provide may also be a variable in multisite location studies.

Optimization Criteria

Private and public sector location problems are similar in that they share the objective of maximizing some measure of benefit. However, the location criteria chosen differ because the "ownership" is different. With the private sector, the location decision is governed by the minimization of cost or maximization of profit to the private owners. In contrast, we like to think that public facility decisions are made in response to the needs of society as a whole. The objective is to maximize a societal benefit that may be difficult to quantify.

Private sector criteria Traditional private-sector location analysis focuses on a tradeoff between the cost of building and operating facilities and the cost of transportation. Much of the literature has addressed this problem, which is appropriate for the distribution of products (i.e., the warehouse location problem). However, these models may find some applications in services when the service is delivered to the customer (e.g., consulting, insurance, janitorial service).

For the case when the consumer travels to the facility, no direct cost is incurred. Instead, distance becomes a barrier restricting potential consumer demand for the service. Facilities, such as retail shopping centers, are thus located to attract the maximum number of consumers.

Public sector criteria Location decisions in the public sector are complicated by the lack of agreement on goals and the difficulty of measuring benefits in dollars in order to make tradeoffs with facility investment. Because the benefits of a public service are difficult to define or to quantify directly, surrogate or substitute measures of utility are used.

Average distance traveled by users to reach the facility is a popular surrogate. The smaller this quantity, the more accessible the system is to its users. The problem becomes one of minimizing total average distance traveled, with a constraint on the number of facilities. The problem is additionally constrained by some maximum travel distance for the user. Another possibility is the creation of demand. Here the user population is not considered fixed but is determined by location, size, and number of facilities. The greater the demand created or drawn, the more efficient the system is in filling the needs of the region.

These utility surrogates are optimized with constraints on investment. Cost-effectiveness analysis is usually performed to examine the tradeoffs between investment and utility. The tradeoffs for the surrogates are (1) the decrease in average distance traveled per additional thousand-dollar investment and (2) the increase in demand per additional thousand-dollar investment.

Effect of criteria on location The selection of optimization criteria influences service facility location. For example, William J. Abernathy and John C. Hershey studied the location of health centers for a three-city region.[1] As part of the study they noted the effect of health-center locations with respect to the following criteria:

1. *Maximize utilization.* Maximize the total number of visits to the centers.

---

[1] William J. Abernathy and John C. Hershey, "A Spatial-Allocation Model for Regional Health-Services Planning," *Operations Research,* vol. 20, no. 3, May–June 1972, pp. 629–642.

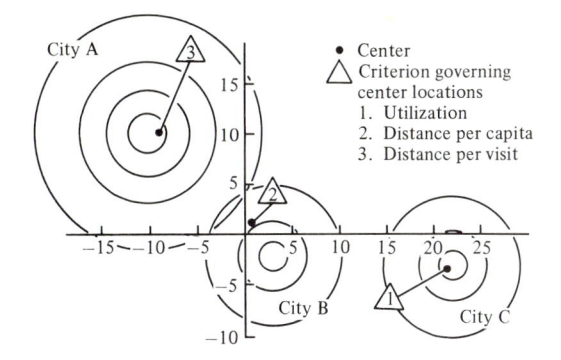

Figure 8.3 Location of one health center for three different criteria. [From W. J. Abernathy and J. C. Hershey, "A Spatial-Allocation Model for Regional Health-Services Planning," *Operations Research*, vol. 20, no. 3, May–June 1972, p. 637.]

2. *Minimize distance per capita.* Minimize the average distance per capita to the closest center.
3. *Minimize distance per visit.* Minimize the average per-visit travel distance to the nearest center.

The problem was structured so that each city had a population with a different mix of health care consumption characteristics. These characteristics were measured along two dimensions: (1) the effect of distance as a barrier to health care use and (2) the utilization rate at immediate proximity to a health care center. Figure 8.3 shows a map of the three cities and the location of a single health care center under each of the three criteria. The three criteria yield entirely different locations because of the different behavioral patterns of each city. For criterion 1 (maximize utilization) the center is located at city C because this city contains a large number of individuals for whom distance is a strong barrier. City B is selected for criterion 2 (minimize distance per capita) because it is centrally located between the two larger cities. City A is the largest population center with the most mobile and frequent users of health care. Criterion 3 (minimize distance per visit) logically selects this city.

Selection of the actual site requires other considerations beyond minimization of travel distance. Available real estate represents a major constraint on the final selection of the site. However, as indicated by Table 8.1, many considerations enter into the final site selection decision.

Table 8.1 Site selection considerations

1. *Access:* Convenient to freeway exit and entrance ramp; Served by public transportation	4. *Parking:* Adequate off-street parking
2. *Visibility:* Set back from street; Sign placement	5. *Expansion:* Room for expansion
3. *Traffic:* Traffic volume on street that may indicate potential impulse buying; Traffic congestion that could be a hindrance (e.g., fire stations)	6. *Environment:* Immediate surroundings should complement the service
	7. *Competition:* Location of competitors
	8. *Government:* Zoning restrictions; Taxes

ESTIMATION OF SPATIAL DEMAND

The quality of service facility location analysis rests upon an accurate assessment of spatial demand for the service (i.e., demand by geographical area). This requires the selection of some geographical unit that partitions the area to be served and of some method of predicting demand from each of these partitions. Census tracts or their smaller divisions, the block or block groups, are popular, but other districts such as ZIP codes or even traffic zones often are used. In many cases the demand for service is collected empirically by searching past records for addresses of users and tallying these by district. The steps followed to define spatial demand will be illustrated by an example of a day care center.[2]

Define the target population The characteristics which define the target population must be established. For example, if a system of day care centers for all families were being established, the target population might consist of families with children under 5 and an employable adult. A private system might also include the ability to pay. In this example the target population is defined as families that receive ADC (Aid to Dependent Children) support with children under 5 and an employable or trainable parent.

Select an areal unit For purposes of accuracy geographical units should be as small as practicable. There are two limits: (1) the areal unit must be large enough to contain a sufficient sample size for estimating demand and (2) the number of areal units must not exceed the computational capacity of computers and facility location techniques. Census tracts are often selected as the areal unit because demographic data on the residents are readily available on computer tapes from the U.S. Census Bureau. In this study, block groups were selected as geographical units because census tracts were too large and single blocks too small.

Estimate spatial demand Demographic data on block-group residents are analyzed statistically to develop equation (3) that predicts the percentage of ADC families in each block group.

$$Y_i = 0.0043X_{1i} + 0.0248X_{2i} + 0.0092X_{3i} \qquad (3)$$

where Y_i = percentage of ADC families in block group i
X_{1i} = percentage of persons in block group i that are less than 18 years old living in a housing unit with more than 1.5 persons per room
X_{2i} = percentage of families in block group i with a single male head and children less than 18 years old

[2] From Lawrence A. Brown, F. B. Williams, C. Youngmann, J. Holmes, and K. Walby, "The Location of Urban Population Service Facilities: A Strategy and Its Application," *Social Science Quarterly*, vol. 54, no. 4, pp. 784–799.

X_{3i} = percentage of families in block group i with a single female head and children less than 18 years old

Once Y_i, a percentage, is estimated for each block group, it is multiplied by both the number of families in the block group and the average number of children per family younger than five years of age. This figure becomes the estimate of the number of children requiring day care service from each block group.

Map spatial demand The block-group demand can be mapped to provide a visual representation of the spatial distribution of day care needs. The spatial demand map is useful in indicating neighborhoods of concentrated demand that are possible candidates for locating day care centers. Furthermore, many facility location techniques require an initial set of locations that are successively improved upon.

FACILITY LOCATION TECHNIQUES

An understanding of the facility location problem can be gained from the results of locating a single facility. For example, consider the problem of locating a beach-mat concession along the beach front at Waikiki. Suppose you wish to find a location that would minimize the average walk to your concession from anywhere on the beach. Furthermore, you have data showing the density of bathers along the beach front, which is related to the size and location of hotels. This problem is shown schematically in Figure 8.4. The objective is:

Minimize $$Z = \sum_{i=0}^{s} w_i(s - x_i) + \sum_{i=s}^{n} w_i(x_i - s) \quad (4)$$

where w_i = relative weight of demand attached to the ith location on the beach
 x_i = location of the ith demand point on the beach in feet from the origin, taken, in this case, to be the west end of the beach
 s = site of the beach-mat concession

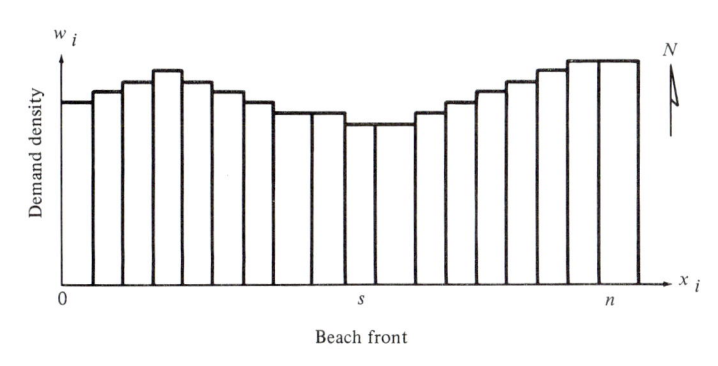

Figure 8.4 Locating a single facility along a line.

The total-distance function Z is differentiated with respect to s and set equal to zero. This yields

$$\frac{dZ}{ds} = \sum_{i=0}^{s} w_i - \sum_{i=s}^{n} w_i = 0$$

or

$$\sum_{i=0}^{s} w_i = \sum_{i=s}^{n} w_i \qquad (5)$$

The above result suggests that the site should be located at the median with respect to the density distribution of bathers. That is, the site is located such that 50 percent of the potential demand is to each side. We probably should have expected this because the median has the property of minimizing the sum of the absolute deviations from it.

The result for locating a site along a line can be generalized for locating a site on a plane if we use the metropolitan travel metric. Total travel distance will be minimized if the coordinates of the site correspond to the intersection of the x median and y median for their respective density distributions.

The selection of a solution technique is determined by the characteristics of the problem, as outlined in Figure 8.1. Our discussion of location techniques is not exhaustive, but a few techniques are discussed to illustrate approaches to the problem. The selected techniques are also representative of approaches that deal with the various problem characteristics: single- vs. multiple-facility location, location on a plane or network, and public vs. private optimization criteria.

Single Facility

Metropolitan metric The location of a single facility on a plane to minimize the weighted travel distances by means of metropolitan travel metric is straightforward. The objective is:

Minimize $\qquad Z = \sum_{i=1}^{n} w_i \{|x_i - x_s| + |y_i - y_s|\} \qquad (6)$

where w_i = weight attached to the ith point (e.g., population)
$\quad x_i, y_i$ = coordinates of the ith demand point
$\quad x_s, y_s$ = coordinates of the service facility
$\quad n$ = number of demand points served

Notice that the objective function may be restated as two independent terms.

Minimize $\qquad Z = \sum_{i=1}^{n} w_i |x_i - x_s| + \sum_{i=1}^{n} w_i |y_i - y_s| \qquad (7)$

Recall from our beach-mat example that the median of a discrete set of values is such that the sum of absolute deviations from it is a minimum. Thus, our optimum site will have coordinates such that x_s is at the median value for w_i ordered

SERVICE FACILITY LOCATION **169**

in the x direction and y_s is at the median value for w_i ordered in the y direction. Because x_s or y_s or both may be unique or lie within a range, the optimal location may be at a point, on a line, or within an area.

Example 8.1: Copying service A copying service has decided to open an office in the central business district of a city. The manager has identified four office buildings that will generate a major portion of its business. Figure 8.5 shows the location of these demand points on an xy coordinate system. Weights are attached to each point and represent potential demand per month in hundreds of orders. Because of the urban location, a metropolitan travel metric is appropriate. The manager would like to determine a location that will minimize the total weighted travel distance of customers.

A site located at the intersection of the x and y medians will solve this location problem. The median is calculated as follows:

$$\text{Median} = \sum_{i=1}^{n} \frac{w_i}{2} \qquad (8)$$

From Figure 8.5 we find that the median has a value of $\frac{16}{2} = 8$. To identify the x-coordinate median for x_s, we sum the values of w_i in the x direction both left to right and right to left. In the top half of Table 8.2 we have ordered the demand points from left to right, as they appear in Figure 8.5 (i.e., 1, 2, 3, 4). The weights attached to each demand point are summed in order until the median value of 8 is reached or exceeded. The x_i value of 2 is circled to indicate the median location. This procedure is repeated with demand points ordered from right to left, as shown in the bottom half of Table 8.2 (i.e., 4, 3, 2, 1). The x_i value of 3 is circled as the median location from

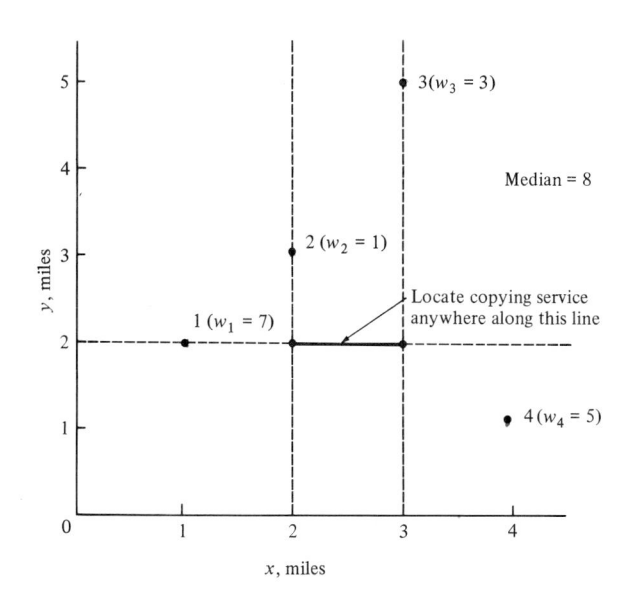

Figure 8.5 Locating a copying service.

this direction. Table 8.3 illustrates the same procedure for identifying the y-coordinate median for y_s. In this case the y_i value of 2 is circled when approached from either direction. This procedure ensures that, if a range of locations is appropriate, it will be readily identified. In this case the location that minimizes total travel distance is a line defined as:

$$2 \leq x_s \leq 3$$

$$y_s = 2$$

Euclidian metric Changing the geographic structure to the straight-line distance between points complicates the location problem. The objective now becomes:

Minimize $$Z = \sum_{i=1}^{n} w_i[(x_i - x_s)^2 + (y_i - y_s)^2]^{1/2} \qquad (9)$$

Taking the partial derivative with respect to x_s and y_s and setting them equal to zero results in two equations. Solving these equations for x_s and y_s yields the following pair of equations that identify the optimal location.

$$x_s = \frac{\sum_{i=1}^{n} \frac{w_i x_i}{d_{is}}}{\sum_{i=1}^{n} \frac{w_i}{d_{is}}} \qquad (10)$$

$$y_s = \frac{\sum_{i=1}^{n} \frac{w_i y_i}{d_{is}}}{\sum_{i=1}^{n} \frac{w_i}{d_{is}}} \qquad (11)$$

where $d_{is} = [(x_i - x_s)^2 + (y_i - y_s)^2]^{1/2}$.

Table 8.2 Median value for x_s

Point i	Location x_i	Σw_i	
Ordering left to right			
1	1	7	= 7
2	②	7 + 1 = 8	
3	3		
4	4		
Ordering right to left			
4	4	5	= 5
3	③	5 + 3 = 8	
2	2		
1	1		

Table 8.3 Median value for y_s

Point i	Location y_i	Σw_i	
Ordering bottom to top			
4	1	5	= 5
1	②	5 + 7 = 12	
2	3		
3	5		
Ordering top to bottom			
3	5	3	= 3
2	3	3 + 1 = 4	
1	②	3 + 1 + 7 = 11	
4	1		

Unfortunately, these equations have no direct solution because x_s and y_s appear on both sides of the equality (i.e., they are contained in the d_{is} term). The solution procedure begins with trial values of x_s and y_s. The formulas are used to calculate revised values of x_s and y_s. The process is continued until the difference between successive values of x_s and y_s is negligible.[3]

Locating a Retail Outlet

When locating a retail outlet, such as a supermarket, the objective is to maximize profit. The decision variables are the location and size of store to build.

A so-called gravity model is used to estimate consumer demand. This model is based on the physical analog that the gravitational attraction of two bodies is directly proportional to the product of their masses and inversely proportional to the square of the distance that separates them. For a service the attractiveness of a facility may be expressed by equation (12).

$$A_{ij} = \frac{S_j}{T_{ij}^\lambda} \qquad (12)$$

where A_{ij} = attraction to facility j for consumer i
S_j = size of the facility j
T_{ij} = travel time from consumer i's location to facility j
λ = parameter estimated empirically to reflect the effect of travel time on various kinds of shopping trips (e.g., convenience shopping would have a relatively large value for λ)

David L. Huff developed a retail location model, using this gravity model to predict the benefit a customer would have for a particular store size and location.[4] Knowing that customers would also be attracted to other competing stores, he proposed the ratio P_{ij}. For n stores, this ratio measures the probability of a customer from a given statistical area i traveling to a particular shopping facility j.

$$P_{ij} = \frac{\dfrac{S_j}{T_{ij}^\lambda}}{\sum_{j=1}^{n} \left(\dfrac{S_j}{T_{ij}^\lambda}\right)} \qquad (13)$$

An estimate of the total annual consumer expenditures at a prospective shopping facility j can then be calculated as below:

$$T_j = \sum_{i=1}^{m} (P_{ij} C_i B_{ik}) \qquad (14)$$

---

[3] This form of the problem is referred to as the *generalized Weber problem* after Alfred Weber who first formulated the problem in 1909.

[4] David L. Huff, "A Programmed Solution for Approximating an Optimum Retail Location," *Land Economics,* August 1966, pp. 293–303.

172 DESIGNING THE SERVICE SYSTEM

where P_{ij} = probability of a consumer from a given statistical area i traveling to a shopping facility j, calculated by means of equation (13)
C_i = number of consumers at area i
B_{ik} = average annual amount budgeted by consumer at area i for product class k
m = number of statistical areas

An iterative procedure, described in Figure 8.6, is used to calculate the expected annual profit for each potential site and possible size of facility. Net operating profit before taxes is calculated as a percentage of sales adjusted for the size of the store. The result is a list of potential sites, with the store size at each that maximizes profit. All that remains is negotiating a real estate deal for the site that comes closest to maximizing annual profit.

Multiple Facility

Location set covering problem The difficulty of evaluating public facility location decisions has resulted in a search for surrogate, or substitute, measures of the benefit of the facility location. One such measure is the distance that the most distant consumer would have to travel to reach the facility. This is known as the maximal service distance. We want to find the minimum number and location of facilities that will serve all demand points within some specified maximal service distance. This is known as the location set covering problem.

Example 8.2: Rural medical clinic location A state department of health is concerned about the lack of medical care in rural areas. A group of nine communities have been selected for a pilot program in which medical clinics will be opened to serve primary health needs. It is hoped that every community will be within 30 miles of at least one clinic. The planners would like to determine the number of clinics required and their locations. Any community can serve as a potential clinic site except community 6 because facilities are unavailable. Figure 8.7 shows a network identifying the cities as numbered circles. Lines drawn between the sites show the travel distances in miles.

The problem is approached by first identifying for each community the other communities that can be reached from it within the 30-mile travel limit. Beginning with community 1, we see from Figure 8.7 that communities 2, 3, and 4 can be reached within the 30-mile travel distance limit. The results of similar inspections for each community are reported in the second column of Table 8.4 as the set of communities served from each site. An equivalent statement could be made that this set, less any communities that could not serve as a site, represents the set of sites that could cover the community in question with service within 30 miles. Thus for community 5, a clinic located at sites 3, 4, or 5 meets the maximal travel limit.

The third column of Table 8.4 represents the set of potential sites that

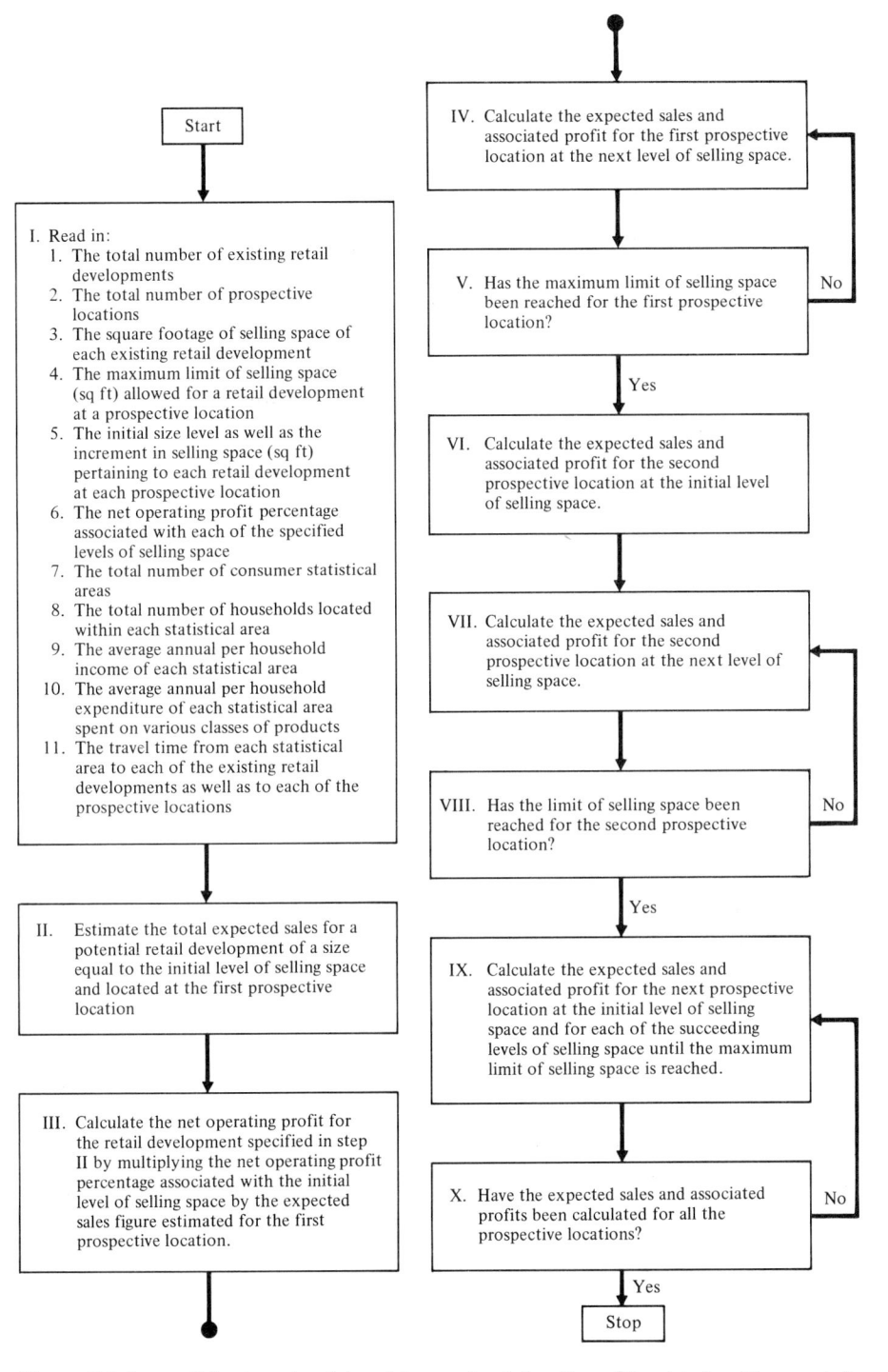

```
                                    ┌─────────────────────────────────────────┐
                                    │ IV. Calculate the expected sales and    │
          ┌─────────┐                │     associated profit for the first     │◄──┐
          │  Start  │                │     prospective location at the next    │   │
          └────┬────┘                │     level of selling space.             │   │
               │                     └──────────────────┬──────────────────────┘   │
               ▼                                        ▼                          │
┌──────────────────────────────────┐  ┌─────────────────────────────────────────┐  │
│ I. Read in:                      │  │ V. Has the maximum limit of selling     │No│
│   1. The total number of existing│  │    space been reached for the first     │──┘
│      retail developments         │  │    prospective location?                │
│   2. The total number of         │  └──────────────────┬──────────────────────┘
│      prospective locations       │                     │ Yes
│   3. The square footage of       │                     ▼
│      selling space of each       │  ┌─────────────────────────────────────────┐
│      existing retail development │  │ VI. Calculate the expected sales and    │
│   4. The maximum limit of selling│  │     associated profit for the second    │
│      space (sq ft) allowed for a │  │     prospective location at the initial │
│      retail development at a     │  │     level of selling space.             │
│      prospective location        │  └──────────────────┬──────────────────────┘
│   5. The initial size level as   │                     ▼
│      well as the increment in    │  ┌─────────────────────────────────────────┐
│      selling space (sq ft)       │  │ VII. Calculate the expected sales and   │
│      pertaining to each retail   │  │      associated profit for the second   │◄──┐
│      development at each         │  │      prospective location at the next   │   │
│      prospective location        │  │      level of selling space.            │   │
│   6. The net operating profit    │  └──────────────────┬──────────────────────┘   │
│      percentage associated with  │                     ▼                          │
│      each of the specified       │  ┌─────────────────────────────────────────┐   │
│      levels of selling space     │  │ VIII. Has the limit of selling space    │No │
│   7. The total number of consumer│  │       been reached for the second       │───┘
│      statistical areas           │  │       prospective location?             │
│   8. The total number of         │  └──────────────────┬──────────────────────┘
│      households located within   │                     │ Yes
│      each statistical area       │                     ▼
│   9. The average annual per      │  ┌─────────────────────────────────────────┐
│      household income of each    │  │ IX. Calculate the expected sales and    │
│      statistical area            │  │     associated profit for the next      │
│  10. The average annual per      │  │     prospective location at the initial │◄──┐
│      household expenditure of    │  │     level of selling space and for each │   │
│      each statistical area spent │  │     of the succeeding levels of selling │   │
│      on various classes of       │  │     space until the maximum limit of    │   │
│      products                    │  │     selling space is reached.           │   │
│  11. The travel time from each   │  └──────────────────┬──────────────────────┘   │
│      statistical area to each of │                     ▼                          │
│      the existing retail         │  ┌─────────────────────────────────────────┐   │
│      developments as well as to  │  │ X. Have the expected sales and          │No │
│      each of the prospective     │  │    associated profits been calculated   │───┘
│      locations                   │  │    for all the prospective locations?   │
└──────────────┬───────────────────┘  └──────────────────┬──────────────────────┘
               ▼                                         │ Yes
┌──────────────────────────────────┐                     ▼
│ II. Estimate the total expected  │                 ┌────────┐
│     sales for a potential retail │                 │  Stop  │
│     development of a size equal  │                 └────────┘
│     to the initial level of      │
│     selling space and located at │
│     the first prospective        │
│     location                     │
└──────────────┬───────────────────┘
               ▼
┌──────────────────────────────────┐
│ III. Calculate the net operating │
│      profit for the retail       │
│      development specified in    │
│      step II by multiplying the  │
│      net operating profit        │
│      percentage associated with  │
│      the initial level of        │
│      selling space by the        │
│      expected sales figure       │
│      estimated for the first     │
│      prospective location.       │
└──────────────────────────────────┘
```

Figure 8.6 Sequential steps in determining optimal location. [*Reprinted with permission from David L. Huff, "A Programmed Solution for Approximating an Optimum Retail Location," Land Economics, August 1966, pp. 293–303.*]

174 DESIGNING THE SERVICE SYSTEM

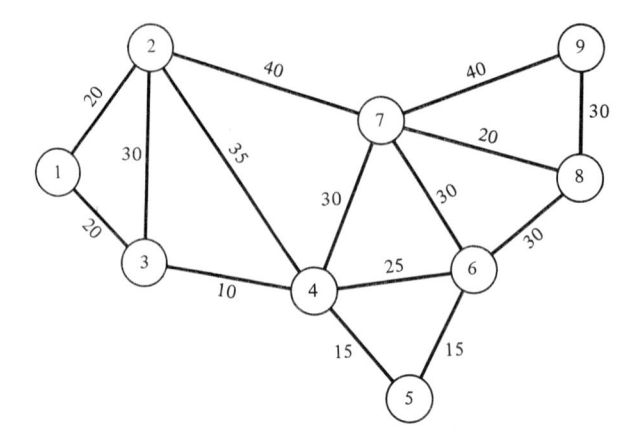

Figure 8.7 Travel network for rural area.

could cover a given community. Several of these sets have been placed in brackets because they represent subsets of other potential locations. For example, because community 2 can only be served by sites 1, 2, or 3, one of these sites must then be selected for a clinic location. Identifying these subsets reduces the problem size while ensuring the restrictions are satisfied. Notice that any site common to two or more of these subsets is an excellent candidate for selection because of our desire to minimize the number of clinics to cover all the communities. In this case, sites 3, 4, and 8 are candidates. From inspection we see that, if sites 3 and 8 are selected, all subsets are accounted for and, thus, all communities can be covered with just these two clinics. We also have identified the service region for each clinic. The clinic located at community 3 will serve communities 1, 2, 3, 4, and 5, and the clinic located at community 8 will serve communities 6, 7, 8, and 9.

The location set covering problem often can yield more than one solution. For example, if the maximal travel distance were set at 40 miles, the following five pairs of clinic site locations would provide coverage: (3, 8), (3, 9), (4, 7), (4, 8), and (4, 9).

Table 8.4 Range of service for potential sites

Community	Set of communities served from site	Potential sites that could serve the community*
1	1, 2, 3, 4	1, 2, 3, 4
2	1, 2, 3	(1, 2, 3)†
3	1, 2, 3, 4, 5	1, 2, 3, 4, 5
4	1, 3, 4, 5, 6, 7	1, 3, 4, 5, 7
5	3, 4, 5, 6	(3, 4, 5)†
6	4, 5, 6, 7, 8	4, 5, 7, 8
7	4, 6, 7, 8	(4, 7, 8)†
8	6, 7, 8, 9	7, 8, 9
9	8, 9	(8, 9)†

* Community 6 cannot serve as a clinic site.
† Subsets of potential sites.

Maximal covering location problem A variation of the location set covering problem is maximal covering. This problem is based on a very appealing objective: maximize the population covered within a desired service distance.

A travel network, such as shown in Figure 8.7, would now be augmented with information on the user population of each community. Richard Church and Charles ReVelle developed a greedy adding (GA) algorithm for solving this problem that builds upon the location set covering analysis.[5] The algorithm starts with an empty solution set and then adds to this set the best facility sites one at a time. The first facility selected covers the largest population. Additional sites are selected that cover the greatest amount of the remaining uncovered population until all the population is covered or the limit on the number of sites is reached.

For example, recall from Example 8.2 that sites 3, 4, and 8 were identified as candidates for the set covering problem. If we assume that each community has an equal population, then the GA algorithm would select site 4 as the first site to maximize population coverage. From Table 8.4 we see that site 4 covers communities 1, 3, 4, 5, 6, and 7. This exceeds the number of communities covered by either site 3 or 8. Site 8 would be selected next because it covers the uncovered communities 8 and 9, while site 3 would only cover the uncovered community 2.

SUBSTITUTION OF COMMUNICATION FOR TRANSPORTATION

An appealing alternative to moving people from one place to another is the use of telecommunications. One proposal that has met with some success is the use of telemetry to extend health care into remote regions. Paramedics or nurse practitioners with communication to a distant hospital are able to provide health care without the need to transport the patient. The banking industry has been promoting direct payroll deposit, which permits employees to have their pay deposited directly into their checking accounts. By authorizing employers to deposit salaries, the employees save trips to the bank. Bankers also benefit by reduced check processing paperwork and congestion at their motor banks.

A study by David A. Lopez and Paul Gray illustrates how an insurance company in Los Angeles decentralized its operations by using telecommunications and strategically locating satellite offices.[6] An examination was made of the benefits and costs to the insurance firm when work was moved to the workers rather than when workers moved to their work. Insurance companies and other information-based industries are good candidates for employer decentralization because their office staff performs routine clerical tasks using the firm's

---

[5] Richard Church and Charles ReVelle, "The Maximal Covering Location Problem," *Papers of the Regional Science Association,* vol. 32, Fall 1974, pp. 101–118.

[6] David A. Lopez and Paul Gray, "The Substitution of Communication for Transportation—A Case Study," *Management Science,* vol. 23, no. 11, July 1977, pp. 1149–1160.

computer data bases. The proposed plan would replace the centralized operation in downtown Los Angeles with a network of regional satellites located in the suburbs where the workers live. The analysis included a location study to determine the size, location, and number of satellites that would minimize the variable costs associated with employee travel and the fixed costs of establishing the satellites. The decentralization plan yielded several benefits to the company: (1) reduced staff requirements, (2) reduced employee turnover and training, (3) reduced salaries for clerical employees, (4) elimination of a lunch program, and (5) increased income from the lease of the headquarters site. Employees whose travel to work was reduced by $5\frac{1}{2}$ miles yielded a net benefit over costs of reduced salary and loss of subsidized lunch. This employee benefit is important in the light of increasing energy expenses for transportation.

It was found that the work of life underwriting and servicing insurance policies could be performed by means of a computer terminal. Phone communications only were required for personal contacts, and few face-to-face meetings were needed. These findings substantiate other studies in Britain and Sweden which indicate that individuals require face-to-face contacts for initial meetings and periodic refreshing. They do not require continual face-to-face contact to reach decisions and to conduct routine business.

MARKETING INTERMEDIARIES

The idea that services are created and consumed simultaneously does not allow for the "channel-of-distribution" concept developed for goods. Because services are intangible and thus cannot be stored, transported, or inventoried, the geographic area for service is restricted. However, service channels of distribution have evolved which use separate organizational entities as intermediaries between the producer and consumer.

James H. Donnelly provides a number of examples that illustrate how some services have created unlimited geographic service areas.[7] The retailer who extends a bank's credit to its customers is an intermediary in the distribution of credit. The fact that Bank of America is a California bank does not limit the use of the VISA card, which is honored worldwide. The health maintenance organization (HMO) performs an intermediary role between the practitioner and patient by increasing the availability and convenience of "one-stop" shopping. Group insurance written through employers and labor unions is an example of the insurance industry using intermediaries to distribute its service.

SUMMARY

The problem of locating service facilities was considered across several dimensions. The analytical difficulty was illustrated by the attempt to locate a single

---

[7] James H. Donnelly, "Marketing Intermediaries in Channels of Distribution for Services," *Journal of Marketing*, vol. 40, January 1976, pp. 55–70.

facility. Changing from a metropolitan travel metric to a euclidean travel metric created a problem for which no direct solution exists. We found that the solution technique for any location problem is dependent upon the criterion chosen.

Estimating spatial demand requires a definition of the target population, selection of the areal unit, and the use of regression analysis. Mapping spatial demand is often the first step in the facility location analysis.

The concept of location set covering is central to understanding the many approaches to the multiple-facility location. Finally, if the requirement for face-to-face interaction between server and consumer is relaxed, then the advantages of substituting communication for transportation becomes possible. In the private sector the use of marketing intermediaries can decouple the provider from the consumer.

TOPICS FOR DISCUSSION

1. Pick a particular service and identify shortcomings in its site selection.
2. How would you proceed to estimate empirically the parameter λ in the Huff retail location model for a branch bank?
3. Why do you think set covering is an attractive approach to public sector facility location?
4. What are the characteristics of a service that would make communication a good substitute for transportation?
5. What are the benefits of using intermediaries in the service distribution channel?

EXERCISES

8.1 A temporary-help agency wants to open an office in a suburban section of a large city. It has identified five large corporate offices as potential customers. The locations of these offices on an XY coordinate grid in miles for the area are: $c_1 = (4, 4)$, $c_2 = (4, 11)$, $c_3 = (7, 2)$, $c_4 = (11, 11)$, and $c_5 = (14, 7)$. The expected demand for temporary help from these customers is weighted as follows: $w_1 = 3$, $w_2 = 2$, $w_3 = 2$, $w_4 = 4$, and $w_5 = 1$. The agency reimburses employees for travel expenses to their assignments. Recommend a location (xy coordinates) for the agency that will minimize the total weighted metropolitan distance for job-related travel.

8.2 Four hospitals located in a county are cooperating to establish a centralized blood-bank facility to serve them all. On an XY coordinate grid of the county the hospitals are found at the following locations: $H_1 = (5, 10)$, $H_2 = (7, 6)$, $H_3 = (4, 2)$, and $H_4 = (16, 3)$. The expected number of deliveries per month from the blood bank to each respective hospital is estimated at 450, 1200, 300, and 1500. Recommend a location for the blood bank that would minimize total distance traveled using the metropolitan metric.

8.3 A small city airport is served by four airlines. The terminal is rather spread out, with boarding areas located on an XY coordinate grid at: $A = (1, 4)$, $B = (5, 5)$, $C = (8, 3)$, and $D = (8, 1)$. The number of flights per day of approximately equal capacity is: $A = 28$, $B = 22$, $C = 36$, and $D = 18$. A new central baggage claim area is under consideration.

(*a*) Recommend a location for the new baggage claim area that will minimize the total weighted distance from boarding areas using the metropolitan metric.

(*b*) Using the result found in part *a* as an initial solution and the euclidean metric find the optimum location.

8.4 A store samples two customers in each of five areas to draw an estimate of consumer spending in its home-appliances department. It is estimated that these customers represent a good sample of the 10,000 customers whom the store thinks it serves. The number of customers in each area is:

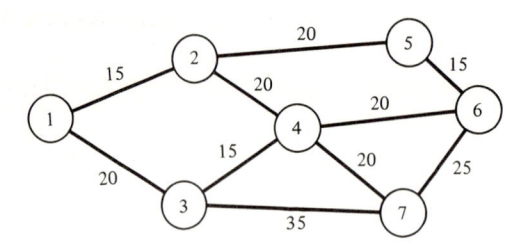

Figure 8.8 Service area network.

$N_1 = 1500$, $N_2 = 2500$, $N_3 = 1000$, $N_4 = 3000$, and $N_5 = 2000$. It is found that the consumers have the following budgets in dollars for home appliances per year: $C_{11} = 100$, $C_{12} = 150$; $C_{21} = 75$, $C_{22} = 100$; $C_{31} = 125$, $C_{32} = 125$; $C_{41} = 100$, $C_{42} = 120$; and $C_{51} = 120$, $C_{52} = 125$. Using the Huff model, estimate annual home-appliance sales for the store.

8.5 Another chain department store opens a branch in a nearby shopping complex. (See Exercise 8.4.) The new store is 3 times larger than the original one. The travel times in minutes from the five areas to the two stores are as follows: $T_{11} = 20$, $T_{12} = 15$; $T_{21} = 35$, $T_{22} = 20$; $T_{31} = 30$, $T_{32} = 25$; $T_{41} = 20$, $T_{42} = 25$; and $T_{51} = T_{52} = 25$. Use the Huff model to estimate the annual consumer expenditures in the home-appliance section of each store, assuming $\lambda = 1$.

8.6 Recall the rural medical clinic (Example 8.2) in the text. Suppose it were required that each community be 25 miles at most from the nearest clinic. How many clinics would now be required and what would be their locations? Give all possible location solutions.

8.7 A rural volunteer fire department has just purchased two used fire engines that a nearby city auctioned off. The time in minutes to travel between communities in the service area is shown on the network in Figure 8.8.

(a) Select all possible pairs of communities in which the fire engines should be located to ensure that all communities can be reached in 30 minutes or less.

(b) What additional consideration could be used to make the final site selection from the community pairs found in part a above?

8.8 You have been asked to help locate a catering service in the central business district of a city. The locations of potential customers on an XY coordinate grid are: $P_1 = (4, 4)$, $P_2 = (12, 4)$, $P_3 = (2, 7)$, $P_4 = (11, 11)$, and $P_5 = (7, 14)$. The expected demand is weighted as follows: $W_1 = 4$, $W_2 = 3$, $W_3 = 2$, $W_4 = 4$, and $W_5 = 1$. Recommend a location that will minimize the total weighted metropolitan distance traveled.

8.9 A community is presently being served by a single self-serve gas station with 6 pumps. A competitor is opening a new facility with 12 pumps across town. Table 8.5 contains the travel times in minutes from the four different areas in the community to the sites and the number of customers in each area.

(a) Using the Huff model and assuming $\lambda = 2$, calculate the probability of a customer traveling from each area to each site.

(b) What proportion of the existing market do you estimate will be lost to the new competitor?

Table 8.5 Travel times to gas stations

Area	1	2	3	4
Old station	5	10	9	15
New competitor	20	8	12	6
No. of customers	100	150	80	50

CASELETTE: HEALTH MAINTENANCE ORGANIZATION (A)

In January 1979, Ms. Joan Taylor, a representative of Life-Time Insurance Company, arrived in Austin, Texas, to establish a health maintenance organization (HMO). The HMO concept would offer Austinites an alternative to the traditional fee-for-service medical care. Individuals could voluntarily join or enroll in the HMO and, for a fixed fee, be eligible for health services. The fee would be paid in advance.

Ms. Taylor had been the administrator of Life-Time's very successful HMO in Buffalo, New York. She had carefully planned the preliminary work required to establish the HMO in Austin. When she arrived, most of the arrangements had been completed. However, the location of the ambulatory health center (clinic) had not been selected.

Preliminary data estimating the number of potential enrollees in the HMO had been determined by census tract. These data are presented below.

Estimated number of enrollees per census tract

Census tract	Enrollees, in thousands	Census tract	Enrollees, in thousands
1	5	13.02	4
2	4	14	5
3	3	15.01	6
4	1	15.02	4
5	2	15.03	5
6	1	16.01	3
7	4	16.02	2
8	1	18.03	5
9	2	20	2
10	4	21.01	4
11	2	21.02	3
12	2	23.01	4
13.01	3	....	

Determine the location of the clinic using the census tract map in Figure 8.9.

CASELETTE: ATHOL FURNITURE, INC.

Athol Furniture, Inc. (AFI) is a growing regional chain of discount furniture and large-appliance stores. Management has targeted the small city of Bluff Lake as the next location for a new retail outlet. Although the total population is currently 21,000, Bluff Lake is expected to grow during the next decade because of increased mining in the surrounding hills.

AFI's marketing department did a general analysis of the market potential of expansion into Bluff Lake, but the task of locating the best site for a store has been given to Mr. Charles Aquirre. After obtaining the market data on Bluff Lake, Mr. Aquirre decides that it would be very appropriate to utilize the Huff

180 DESIGNING THE SERVICE SYSTEM

Figure 8.9 Census-tract map of Austin, Texas.

location model in developing a recommendation for the company's management because there are existing competitors and several potential sites under consideration.

Figure 8.10 is a map of Bluff Lake showing major streets and highways, railroad (AFI will ship its merchandise into the city by rail from a regional warehouse 800 miles away), Crystal River, Bluff Lake, and the census block groups, which are numbered 1 through 12. Table 8.6 gives the number of households, average annual income per household, and average annual furniture/large-appliance expenditure per household for each census block group.

In Figure 8.10, the letters *A* and *B* show the locations of AFI's existing competitors, and Table 8.7 indicates the sizes of these existing stores to the

SERVICE FACILITY LOCATION 181

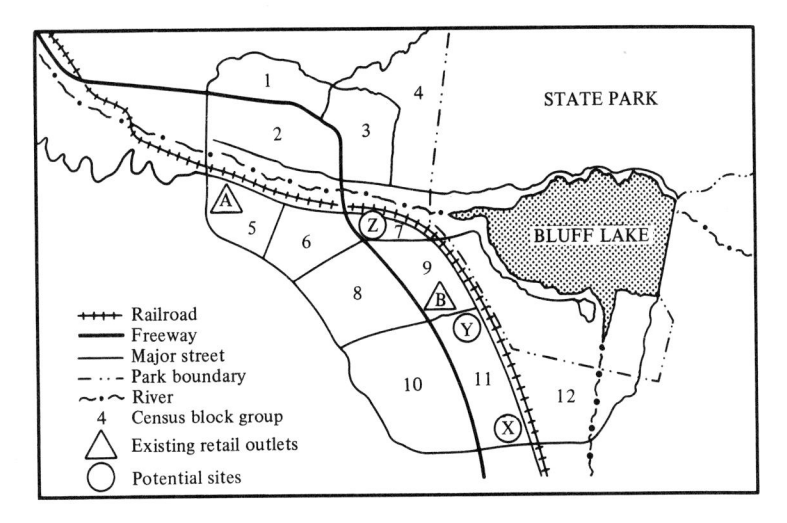

Figure 8.10 Bluff Lake.

nearest 5000 square feet of sales area. The letters X, Y, and Z in Figure 8.10 show the possible sites which Mr. Aquirre feels AFI could use for a retail store. The maximum size limit (sales area) of each potential location is given in Table 8.8.

On the basis of average speeds for the main streets and the highways obtained from the city's planning department, Mr. Aquirre has developed a matrix of travel times between the existing and potential retail sites and the center of each census block group. These travel times in minutes can be found in Table 8.9.

From experience with other AFI locations, Mr. Aquirre has developed a fairly accurate portrayal of the relationship of the store size (sales area) to mar-

Table 8.6 Market data

Census block group	Number of households	Avg annual income	Avg annual furniture/large-appliance expenditures per household
1	730	$12,000–$12,500	$180
2	1130	8,500–9,000	125
3	1035	19,500–20,000	280
4	635	25,000–over	350
5	160	4,500–5,000	75
6	105	4,000–4,500	50
7	125	4,000–4,500	60
8	470	8,000–8,500	115
9	305	6,000–6,500	90
10	1755	18,500–19,000	265
11	900	15,000–15,500	215
12	290	25,000–over	370
	7640		

Table 8.7 Competitors' store sizes

Store	Sales area, sq ft
A	10,000
B	15,000

Table 8.8 Maximum size limit of AFI's potential sites

Site	Maximum sales area, sq ft
X	15,000
Y	20,000
Z	10,000

Table 8.9 Minimum travel time between potential and existing sites and block groups, min

Site	1	2	3	4	5	6	7	8	9	10	11	12
A	7	5	5	9	1	3	4	5	7	10	14	17
B	10	8	8	10	7	3	3	2	1	2	2	5
X	16	14	14	16	13	8	7	6	4	4	2	2
Y	12	10	10	12	9	5	4	3	2	4	2	5
Z	7	5	5	7	4	2	1	4	3	10	10	13

Table 8.10 Relationship of size of store to margin on sales, expenses, and net operating profit, % of sales

Sales area, sq ft	Margin on sales	Expenses	Net operating profit before taxes
10,000	16.2	12.3	3.9
15,000	15.6	12.0	3.6
20,000	14.7	11.8	2.9

gin on sales, expenses, and net operating profit before taxes. This information is shown in Table 8.10.

Questions

1. Utilizing the Huff location model (with $\lambda = 1.00$), recommend a store size and location for AFI that will maximize expected net operating profit before taxes. Assuming that AFI does not wish to consider a store smaller than 10,000 square feet, assess the store sizes, based on increments of 5,000 square feet up to the maximum allowable sales area for each potential site.
2. What is the expected annual net operating profit before taxes for the outlet you have recommended?
3. Briefly state any shortcomings you may perceive in this model.

SELECTED BIBLIOGRAPHY

Abernathy, William J., and John C. Hershey: "A Spatial-Allocation Model for Regional Health-Services Planning," *Operations Research,* vol. 20, no. 3, May–June 1972, pp. 629–642.

Brown, Lawrence A., F. B. Williams, C. Youngmann, J. Holmes, and K. Walby: "The Location of Urban Population Service Facilities: A Strategy and Its Application," *Social Science Quarterly,* vol. 54, no. 4, March 1974, pp. 784–799.

Church, Richard, and Charles ReVelle: "The Maximal Covering Location Problem," *Papers of the Regional Science Association,* vol. 32, Fall 1974, pp. 101–118.

Computer Programs for Location-Allocation Problems, Department of Geography, The University of Iowa, Iowa City, July 1973.

Donnelly, James H.: "Marketing Intermediaries in Channels of Distribution for Services," *Journal of Marketing,* vol. 40, January 1976, pp. 55–70.

Fitzsimmons, James A.: "A Methodology for Emergency Ambulance Deployment," *Management Science,* vol. 19, no. 6, February 1973, pp. 627–636.

Hakimi, S.: "Optimal Locations of Switching Centers and the Absolute Centers and Medians of a Graph," *Operations Research,* vol. 12, no. 3, May–June 1964, p. 450.

Huff, David L.: "A Programmed Solution for Approximating an Optimum Retail Location," *Land Economics,* August 1966, pp. 293–303.

Lopez, David A., and Paul Gray: "The Substitution of Communication for Transportation—A Case Study," *Management Science,* vol. 23, no. 11, July 1977, pp. 1149–1160.

Khumawala, B. M.: "An Efficient Algorithm for the p-Median Problem With Maximum Distance Constraint," *Geographical Analysis,* vol. 5, no. 4, October 1973, pp. 309–321.

ReVelle, C., D. Marks, and J. Leibman: "An Analysis of Private and Public Sector Location Models," *Management Science,* vol. 16, no. 11, July 1970, pp. 692–707.

Savas, E. S.: "On Equity in Providing Public Sources," *Management Science,* vol. 24, no. 8, April 1978, pp. 800–808.

Toregas, C., R. Swain, C. ReVelle, and L. Bergman: "The Location of Emergency Service Facilities," *Operations Research,* vol. 19, no. 6, November–December, 1971, pp. 1363–1971.

CHAPTER
NINE

DESIGN AND LAYOUT OF SERVICE FACILITIES

The importance of facilities design and layout to service organizations stems from the concept of the *service package*, that is, the combination of elements that determine consumers' perceptions of services. For many organizations, consumer perceptions are determined by their interactions with the service facilities. Understandably, the contribution of good design and layout to the service package is often explicitly recognized in the service operations. Consider, for example, any restaurant renowned for its atmosphere. Consider, also, the factors that contribute toward creating that atmosphere. Do they include the heights of ceilings, the use of pillars and partitions, the amount of privacy, the lighting, the view, or the style and quality of furnishings? Clearly, an atmosphere that complements the food also enhances the value of the total service package.

Just as good design and layout can enhance the value of a service package, bad design and layout can impede service operations and hamper the achievement of organizational objectives. An example of the impact of bad design upon senior-citizen housing occurred in San Francisco. Here, a particular apartment complex for the elderly was designed with a single elevator directly accessible from an open side alley. Continuous sabotage of the elevator by neighborhood vandals resulted in monthly repair costs of approximately $9000. Furthermore, because the elevator was frequently inoperable, residents were forced to use a completely enclosed, poorly lit staircase. This made them easy targets for muggers. Life in the apartment complex became a nightmare for the senior citizens, who were in constant fear for their safety. The social objectives underlying the

Figure 9.1 Tack design used by many hotels.

construction of the apartments could not be realized owing to poor facilities design, and residents often seized the first opportunity to move elsewhere.[1]

Service facilities design and layout decisions are interdependent, each influencing the other. Design involves such factors as the shape of a building, the number of stories, the location and number of windows and doors, the types of building materials, and the interior decorating. Layout, on the other hand, involves the relative location of service operations, consumer waiting areas, rest rooms, and other areas within the service facility. The important facets of both design and layout problems shall now be discussed.

DESIGN

Facilities design can have an important effect upon service operations. For example, Figure 9.1 illustrates a "tack" design used by many Holiday Inns. This design requires a small amount of land, is spotted and recognized easily, has a standard layout, and has a capacity that is determined only by the number of floors. Factors that influence design are (1) the nature and objectives of the service organization, (2) land availability and space requirements, (3) flexibility, (4) aesthetic factors, (5) the community and environment, and (6) construction and operating costs.

---

[1] This case was reported on national television. Shortly after the report appeared, remedial steps were taken to improve the living conditions of the residents. Guards were employed and the alley was fenced off to outsiders.

Nature and Objectives of Service Organizations

The operations of many service organizations directly benefit from a particular design. A few examples should serve to illustrate this:

Churches. Churches in some communities are still expected to have a traditional design. For example, a community might want its church to have a bell tower and a choir loft. Any deviations from the traditional design could result in negative repercussions from the community.

Ski lodges. An Alpine aura is created around ski lodges that have peaked snow roofs and large fireplaces.

Funeral homes. Funeral homes are often expected to be dignified and quiet. Traditionally, funeral homes occupy single-story brick structures. Rooms are generally sound-proofed with the floors being richly carpeted.

Theme restaurants. Theme restaurants attempt to provide a particular atmosphere for customers. For example, a Chinese restaurant would benefit from facilities having a traditional Chinese decor. Analogous examples can be found with retailers specializing in various items such as cars, sporting goods, and wedding dresses.

Land Availability and Space Requirements

The amount of suitable land that can be acquired for facilities construction may be limited by finances, zoning laws, geographical terrain, and the like. In some cases, particularly in urban areas, the space requirements for service facilities may exceed the land area that can be acquired. This will influence facilities design. A fundamental principle governing design is that limited construction areas must be utilized efficiently and often intensively. The vertical expansion of cities by way of skyscrapers is a result of the scarcity and high cost of building sites. In contrast to urban facilities design, rural and suburban facilities tend to be single story and spread out (horizontal expansion) owing to an abundance of affordable land. The implications of land availability and space requirements for small service organizations are clear. A McDonald's hamburger restaurant, for example, occupies a single-story, standard-design building in surburban areas. In cities, however, it rents space in multistory buildings that also house offices, retail stores, and other service organizations. The desirability of constructing individual facilities, as compared with renting space in multistory buildings, is directly related to the availability and cost of building sites.

Flexibility

Design flexibility is particularly important when demand volume is subject to change and when service specifications are subject to obsolescence. Changing of demand and of specifications requires facilities that can be appropriately adjusted. For example, a hospital building might be designed with more stories than needed to satisfy current patient needs. Part of the building could remain unfinished until higher patient demand is realized. At that time, the additional floors of the building could be completed and occupied. This same strategy of constructing excess capacity is frequently used by hotels that expect occupancy rates to increase in the future.

The ability to adjust facilities appropriately is important for the economic viability and effectiveness of an organization. And the practicality of such adjustments often is determined by the initial design. Incorporating flexibility into a design may increase the initial cost and the operating cost of a facility. However, attempting to adjust an inherently inflexible design at a later time can be very expensive. It may even be impossible! Decisions with regard to design flexibility center around the costs of flexibility, the likelihood of changes in demand level and service specifications, and the costs involved in making adjustments.

Aesthetic Factors

Facilities that are aesthetically appealing can enhance consumers' attitudes toward a service. They also can improve the attitudes of employees toward their work. The heights of ceilings, the locations of windows and doors, the various shapes of rooms, and the interior decor create an atmosphere that is part and parcel of the service package. For example, consider a customer requesting a personal loan from a bank. Unlike many, this bank has individual loan offices with carpeted floors and upholstered furniture. The customer's perception of the loan service is influenced by the privacy and comfort of the office. Indeed, the office design personalizes the loan service; it contributes an aura of importance to the transactions between the customer and the loan officer.

The Community and Environment

The community and environment within which facilities are to be constructed are becoming increasingly important considerations. Zoning regulations and community action groups are often effective in environmental protection. They seek to control many aspects of facilities design, as well as the types of services being rendered. Computer systems specifically developed to evaluate the impact of proposed large-scale facilities upon the environment also are becoming available. For example, a prototype system has been developed by the Southwest Center for Urban Research to protect the Gulf Coast environment of Chambers County, Texas.[2] This computer-based system can address many criti-

---

[2] See R. Payne, (ed.), *EXXON USA*, vol. 16, no. 3, Public Affairs Department of Exxon Company, Third Quarter, 1977.

cal issues. For example, what will be the impact of new facilities upon the marshlands? How much and what types of solid waste will be created? How much will consumer and employee traffic and its associated pollution increase? Alternative designs for service facilities can readily be evaluated through the use of such computer systems.

Construction and Operating Costs

Construction costs and operating costs are influenced by facilities design. Construction costs are affected by the amount and type of building materials needed to envelop a specified volume. A shape that minimizes surface areas, such as walls and ceilings, also tends to minimize material requirements. In addition, the number of windows and exterior doors needed is reduced.

An increasingly important way that facilities design influences operating costs is by way of energy requirements. The shape and height of a building can affect thermal conductivity (heat exchanges). This, in turn, affects the cost of maintaining the internal environment of the facility. Long before the energy crisis, studies were being conducted to determine the relationship between facilities design and heat losses for schools and hospitals. As an example, Figure 9.2 depicts the heat-loss curves for a 200,000-square-foot building. This is about the

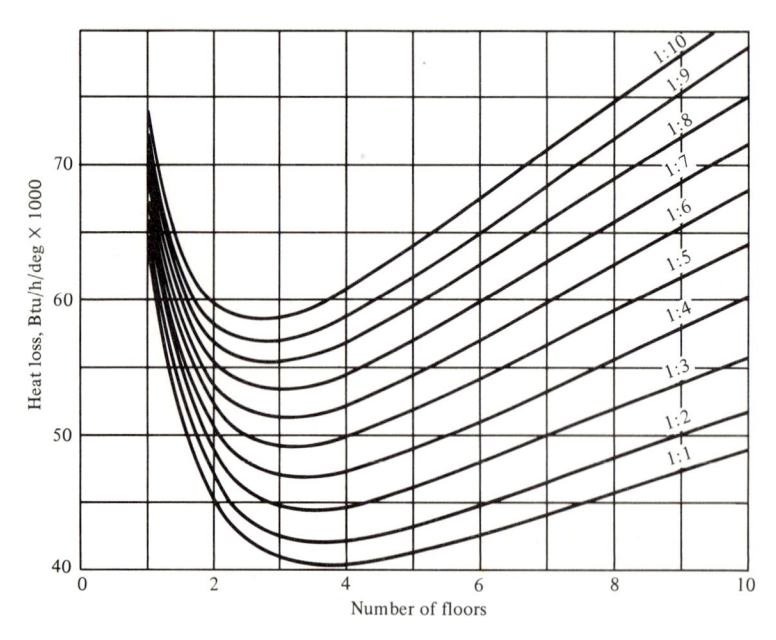

Figure 9.2 Heat-loss curves for a 200,000-sq-ft building as a function of floors and plan ratio (width:length). [*Reprinted with permission from G. A. Atkinson and R. J. Phillips, "Hospital Design: Factors Influencing the Choice of Shape," The Architects Journal Information Library, vol. 139, no. 16, Apr. 15, 1964, pp. 851–855.*]

size of a typical high school or department store. By varying the number of stories and shape (plan ratio), it can be shown that a single-story, narrow building experiences up to 85 percent more heat loss than a four-story, square building. While there are many assumptions that underlie these heat-loss functions, they still serve to illustrate the impact that facilities design can have upon energy consumption.

A comprehensive survey of the effects of building design on energy consumption was conducted by the American Institute of Architects.[3] Figure 9.3 shows the relationships among 13 design subsystems and elements that necessitate energy consumption. These subsystems are:

1. *Site analysis.* The ways in which the natural environment can further the cause of energy conservation and be incorporated in the building design process.
2. *Building orientation.* Locating a structure on site in such a manner as to minimize the effect on the surrounding environment and to conserve energy within the building.
3. *Configuration.* The effect the overall shape of a building has upon energy consumption.
4. *Envelope.* The foundation, walls, and roof as they define a building shape. The building envelope provides the visual image of man's constructed environment.
5. *Space planning.* The inside of a building and the effect the interior and internal structures have on energy conservation.
6. *Transportation.* The effect of stationary pedestrian circulation routes and of mechanical systems, such as elevators and escalators, on energy consumption. Wherever mechanical systems are used, energy consumption increases.
7. *Ventilation.* The controlled intake, circulation, and exhaust of air.
8. *Heating.* The control of internal temperatures during cold seasons. Human comfort must be balanced against practices that conserve energy.
9. *Cooling.* The control of internal temperatures during warm seasons.
10. *Electric power.* Designing the building to be more efficient for electric energy consumption.
11. *Lighting.* The effect design has on the requirements for artificial lighting.
12. *Domestic hot water.* The controlled use of hot water. Hot water is used relatively little by offices; however for domestic structures, lower temperatures and less pumping of water can save energy.
13. *Waste management.* Designing a system to use waste to advantage. This can lead to energy and dollar savings.

---

[3] *Energy Conservation Guideline for Office Buildings,* American Institute of Architects Research Corporation, Washington, 1974.

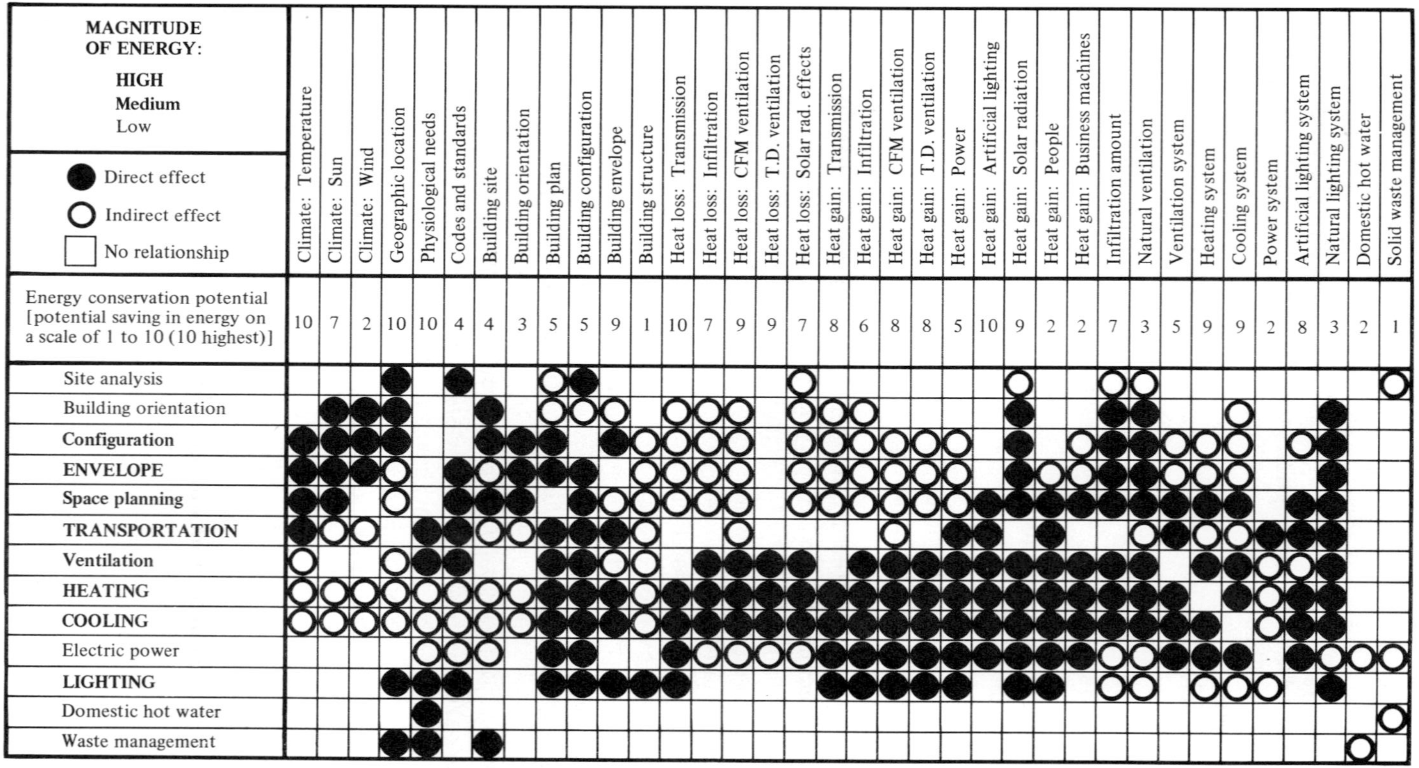

Figure 9.3 Interrelationship matrix: energy savings potential. [Reprinted with permission from American Institute of Architects Research Corporation. *Energy Conservation Guideline for Office Buildings*, Washington, 1974.]

FACILITIES LAYOUT

Layout analysis can be approached from two perspectives. The first assumes that the facilities' shapes and sizes are completely flexible. That is, the design places no constraint upon the relative locations of operations. This may occur, for example, when the layout is to be determined in conjunction with the initial facilities design. This would enable the design to be altered to accommodate a particular layout.

A second perspective is to assume that the facilities already exist. The service operations, then, are to be located within the facilities, the design of which is to some extent unalterable. Such circumstances may restrict the location of certain operations owing to specific requirements for space, ventilation, rest rooms, and the like.

For purposes of discussion, we shall differentiate between two "pure" forms of layout. They are product layout and process layout. It should be borne in mind, however, that most layouts exhibit characteristics of both forms to varying degrees.

Several factors influence the form of layout adopted by service organizations. These include:

1. Volume of demand for services
2. Variability in the types of services provided
3. Degree of personalization of the services
4. Skill and other special attribute requirements of employees
5. Nature of consumer interaction with the service operations, such as self-service
6. Costs of providing the services
7. Implicit and explicit costs to customers
8. Flexibility in adapting to service specification and demand volume changes
9. Consistency (reproducibility) of services provided

The relevance of these factors shall become evident as we discuss the characteristics of each type of layout.

Product Layout

The relative location of operations in a product layout should facilitate the efficient delivery of a limited variety of services to a large number of consumers. If there are several services provided in tandem (one after the other) for consumers, then the operations are arranged in the sequence of their performance. Consider, for example, an auto diagnostic center, where various parts of a vehicle are examined in a specified sequence. The equipment used to perform the examinations are arranged in the sequence in which the operations are to be performed. If some operations are self-service, then they must be located along the normal flow of consumers and at the appropriate points in the sequence.

192 DESIGNING THE SERVICE SYSTEM

The flow diagrams in Figure 9.4 show both series and parallel arrangements of operations that are typical of product layouts. A cafeteria serving line is an example of a series configuration, while provision of several tellers in a bank is an example of a parallel configuration.

The capacity of service operations in a product layout is important because changes are often difficult and costly to make. In some cases, capacity is geared toward peak demand, and workshifts are adjusted appropriately. The number of toll booths open on a highway, the number of cashiers at a fast-food restaurant, and the number of information operators at a telephone company are examples in which workshifts are adjusted to meet demand. Capacity utilization is affected by demand levels and workshifts. This topic is discussed in more detail in Chapter 13.

A product layout is generally associated with a continuous-flow system. That is, consumers proceed without interruption through the service system. There is little variety in the services offered, and the volume of demand often is high. The focal point of control is the rate at which consumers proceed through the system. Efficiency in providing a limited number of services is stressed, sometimes at the expense of depersonalizing the services.

SINGLE SERVER
•••• ◯   (Example: Copying machine)

PARALLEL
••••   (Example: Multiple bank tellers)

SERIES
•••• ◯ •• ◯ •• ◯   (Example: Cafeteria serving line)

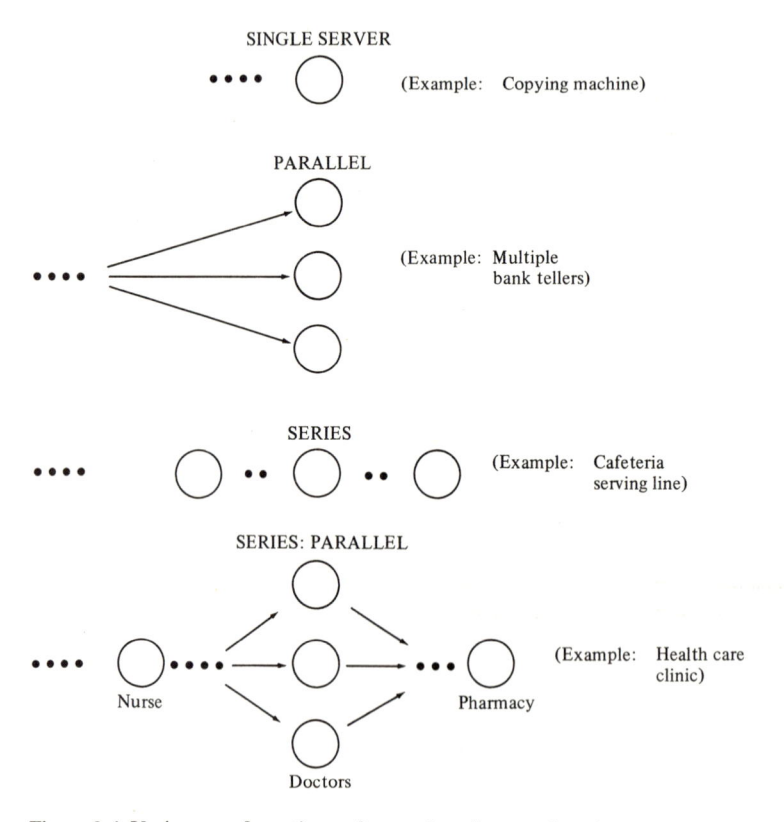

SERIES: PARALLEL
•••• ◯ •••• ◯ ••• ◯   (Example: Health care clinic)
Nurse   Pharmacy
        Doctors

Figure 9.4 Various configurations of operations in a product layout.

Employees associated with continuous-flow systems often possess special skills or attributes, or are trained to operate specialized equipment. They may be technicians. This can be seen, for example, in automotive repair shops specializing in transmissions. Here, mechanics use equipment specifically designed to facilitate transmission replacement. As a result, cars can be repaired much faster and with greater quality assurance.

Self-service operations are becoming increasingly important in product layouts as a means of containing costs. Supermarkets have used self-service for years. More recently, many banks have installed automatic tellers that enable customers to deposit or withdraw funds from their accounts by way of a computer terminal, using a password and magnetically coded plastic card. As labor costs continue to soar and as technology continues its advance, we expect many more service organizations to innovate with self-service operations.

Specialization in a product layout enhances the efficiency of operations and results in relatively low variable costs. However, if skilled labor or specialized equipment is used, then the fixed costs may be high. Consequently, demand level for the services must be high in order to cover the fixed expenses.

Useful visual aids for grasping an overall picture of continous-flow service systems are *process charts* and *operations-flow diagrams*. Both of these tools have their roots in industrial engineering and have been used extensively by manufacturing organizations. While manufacturing focuses on the flow of materials through the production process, service organizations are concerned with the flow of consumers, employees, or information through the various operations. Process charts and operations-flow diagrams are helpful in identifying consumer and employee transit routes, distances traveled by consumers and employees, service times at operations, and locations where consumer attitudes towards the services are likely to be formed.

The following symbols conventionally are used with process charts and operations-flow diagrams.

○ Operation — An operation required in providing a service. The operation may be carried out by employees or equipment for the customer, or it may be a self-service operation.

⇨ Transportation — The movement of customers, employees, or information between operations.

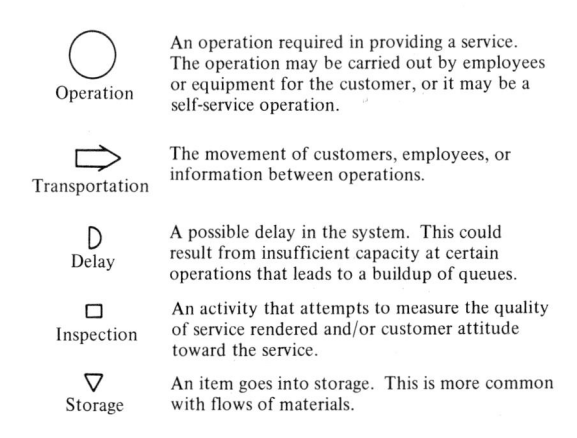

D Delay — A possible delay in the system. This could result from insufficient capacity at certain operations that leads to a buildup of queues.

□ Inspection — An activity that attempts to measure the quality of service rendered and/or customer attitude toward the service.

▽ Storage — An item goes into storage. This is more common with flows of materials.

Figure 9.5 is an example of a process chart for immigrants arriving into the United States at an international airport. We see that the immigrants must

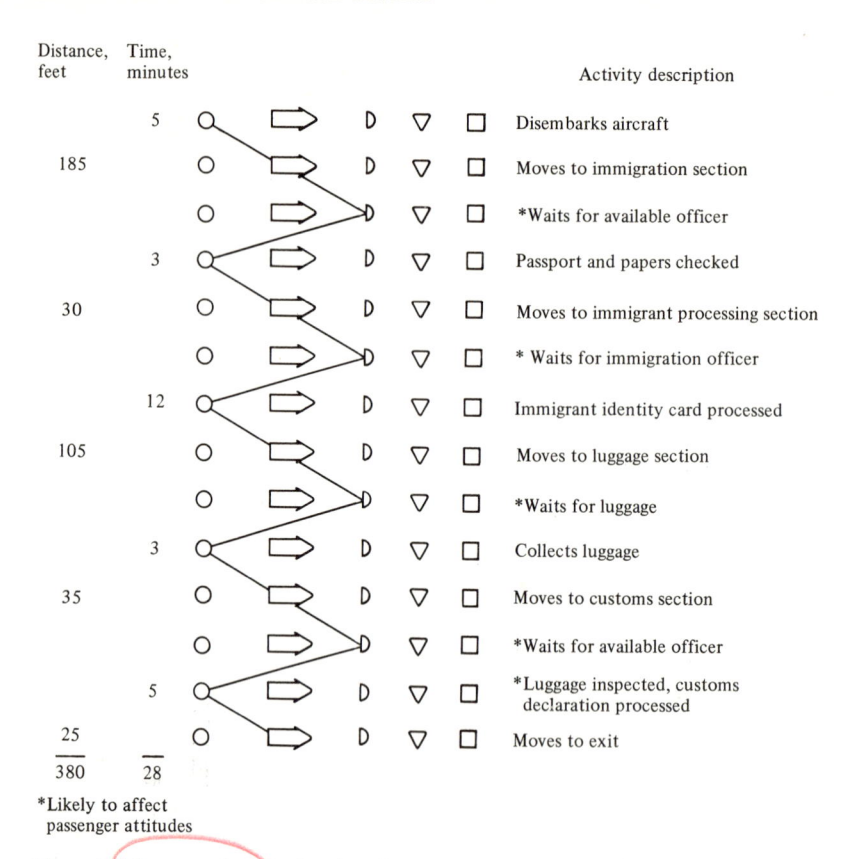

Distance, feet	Time, minutes						Activity description
	5	○	⇨	D	▽	□	Disembarks aircraft
185		○	⇨	D	▽	□	Moves to immigration section
		○	⇨	D	▽	□	*Waits for available officer
	3	○	⇨	D	▽	□	Passport and papers checked
30		○	⇨	D	▽	□	Moves to immigrant processing section
		○	⇨	D	▽	□	* Waits for immigration officer
	12	○	⇨	D	▽	□	Immigrant identity card processed
105		○	⇨	D	▽	□	Moves to luggage section
		○	⇨	D	▽	□	*Waits for luggage
	3	○	⇨	D	▽	□	Collects luggage
35		○	⇨	D	▽	□	Moves to customs section
		○	⇨	D	▽	□	*Waits for available officer
	5	○	⇨	D	▽	□	*Luggage inspected, customs declaration processed
25		○	⇨	D	▽	□	Moves to exit
380	28						

*Likely to affect passenger attitudes

Figure 9.5 Process chart for immigration operations at an airport.

travel 380 feet from the point of disembarking until they exit from customs clearance. However, for 60 feet they are burdened with luggage. We also see that operations require an average of 28 minutes, but there is still the possibility of delays at four locations. Such delays often breed impatience and anxiety on the part of the immigrants. These feelings can become exaggerated for immigrants who fear missing connecting flights. The asterisks on the process chart indicate points where attitudes are likely to be formed. The distances walked and the delays in queues represent the greatest potential for causing dissatisfaction.

Figure 9.6 is an operations-flow diagram for *all* airline passengers arriving from abroad. This has the advantage of giving a visual perspective of the sequence of operations performed for all arriving passengers. In this case, immigrants are processed through a different series of operations than are United States citizens and foreigners holding other types of entrance visas. As with a process chart, the flow diagram can indicate an appropriate sequence of operations, locations where queues are likely to form, and locations where consumer attitudes are likely to be determined. The operations-flow diagram is a valuable

DESIGN AND LAYOUT OF SERVICE FACILITIES

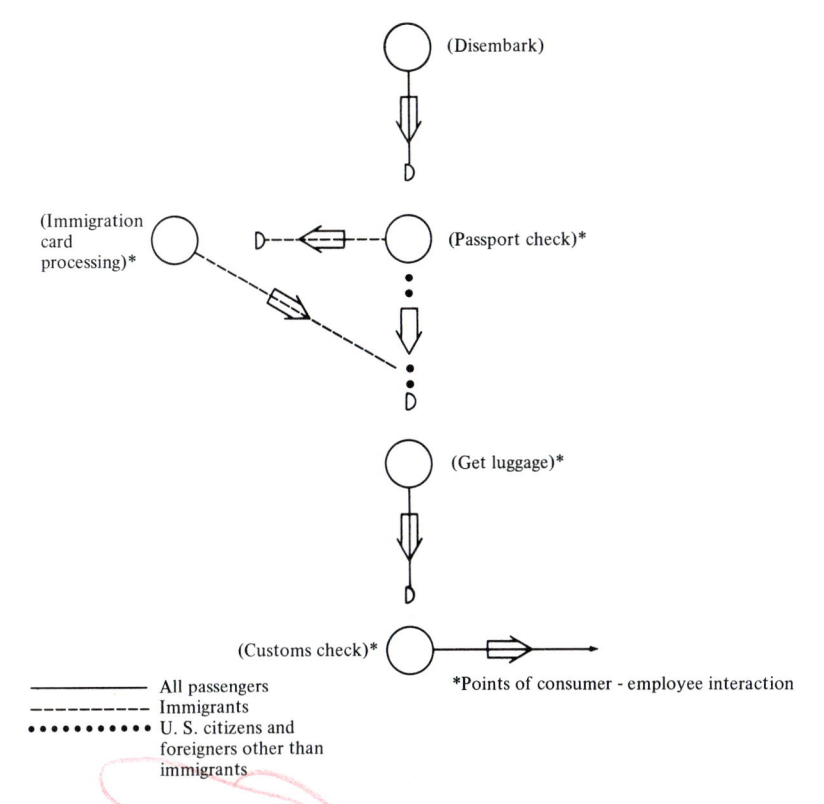

Figure 9.6 Operations-flow diagram—processing of passengers arriving from abroad.

supplement to the process chart for viewing the interaction of elements in a continuous-flow service system.

The Line Balancing Problem

For standardized services in which an inflexible sequence of activities is performed, a line process is appropriate. A cafeteria is an example of the assembly-line concept applied to a service. Instead of partially assembled cars moving along a conveyor, diners form a line, push their trays ahead of them, and select items for their meal. Many routine services, such as muffler and brake repair shops, are not assembly line in nature, but all consumers receive the same well-defined service. Service standardization allows for the division of labor and the use of specialized equipment. Labor turnover may be high, but the skills required are easily acquired. The line process is also inflexible with regard to output and to changes in services performed. Because of the sequential nature of the activities, the service output is limited to the slowest activity, or bottleneck. An ideal or balanced service line would have tasks assigned so that each activity would take an equal amount of time.

Table 9.1 Cafeteria process times

Step	Activity	Average time, sec
1	Select dessert (self-serve).	15
2	Select salad (self-serve).	20
3	Serve vegetables.	30
4	Serve entree.	60
5	Pour drinks.	20
6	Tally and collect payment.	90

Example 9.1: Student union cafeteria The student union cafeteria has been receiving complaints from students about the long lines during the noon hour. Checking with the service personnel, the manager finds the work is unevenly divided among the four workers, as shown in Table 9.1. With this data a flow diagram of the existing system is developed, as shown in Figure 9.7a. As suspected, activity 6 is the bottleneck limiting the cafeteria output to 40 diners per hour.

Output can be increased only if activity 6 can be accomplished in less time. A proposal to add another cashier has been suggested. However, ad-

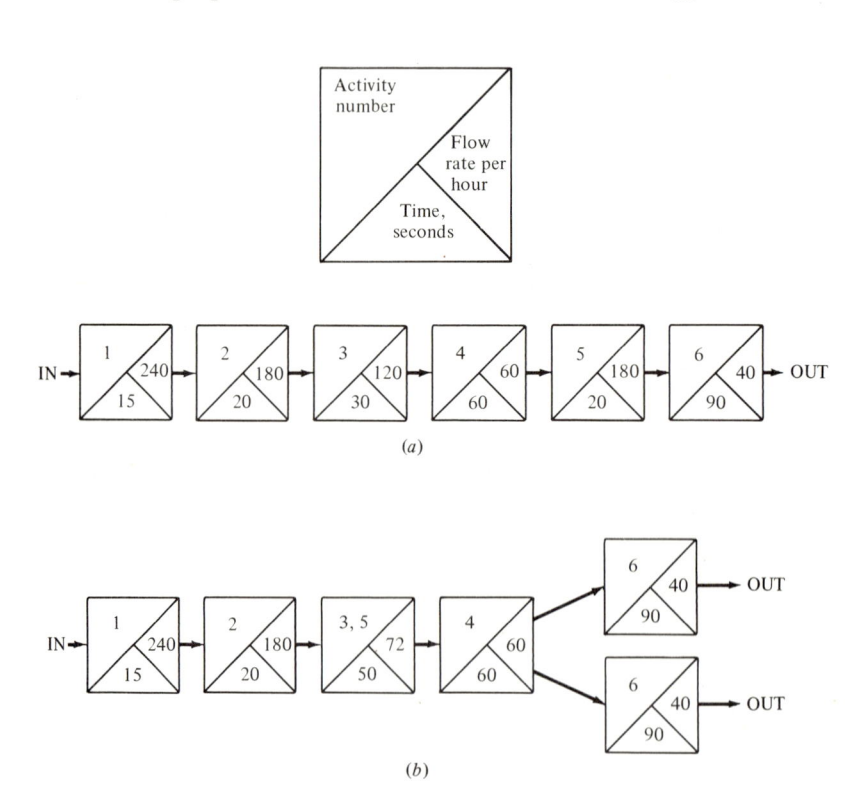

Figure 9.7 (a) Present and (b) proposed cafeteria flow diagrams.

ditional personnel cannot be hired because of budget limitations. Thus, it is suggested that activities 3 and 5 be combined into one job and the freed person be used as the second cashier. The flow diagram of this proposal is shown in Figure 9.7b. With two cashiers in parallel, activity 4, serving the entree, becomes the bottleneck. The cafeteria capacity is increased to 60 diners per hour simply by balancing the line.

Process Layout

A process layout has similar operations grouped together in the same department. The basis for judging similarity can vary depending upon the characteristics of employees and equipment, the types of services being rendered, and the attitudes and expectations of consumers. Consider a hospital setting as an example. Blood, urine, and stool analyses are carried out in the same laboratory because they can be performed by the same technicians using the same or similar equipment. Other departments in the hospital are delineated according to the special characteristics of their patients. Maternity, cancer, and children's wards offer a variety of services, which are directed at the needs of specific groups of patients. Even within individual wards, it may be valuable to group patients according to their particular ailments. Consider the following statement issued by a group of doctors who evaluated a new emergency room: "We would like to see clustered seating in the emergency room waiting area so a three-year-old with a sore throat won't be sitting beside a paranoid schizophrenic acting out his fantasies who is sitting beside someone who's vomiting."

A process layout is generally associated with an intermittent-flow system. This refers to interruption in the flow of consumers through the system. These interruptions result from variability in services demanded and from variability in the sequence in which the services are to be delivered. Consumers arriving at a particular operation likely will find it busy and will have to wait. Control in an intermittent-flow system is directed at scheduling consumers at each operation. Common scheduling rules are first come, first served; emergency; reservation; and shortest processing time.

Process layouts facilitate delivering customized and personalized services. Service specifications can vary in accordance with the requirements of individual consumers. The importance of personalization, of course, stems from the concept of the service package. This includes the degree to which the services conform to each consumer's individual needs.

Flexibility in service delivery is provided by using general purpose equipment and employees who possess broad skills. For a medical example, a general practitioner may attempt to diagnose and treat a wide variety of ailments. However, we would expect the doctor's skill and effectiveness in dealing with a particular ailment to be less than that of a specialist. Analogous examples can be found in the legal, insurance, banking, and investment professions. In all cases, personalization is stressed as a factor that enhances the total value of the service package.

198 DESIGNING THE SERVICE SYSTEM

Most service organizations use a process layout. They need the capacity to provide a wide variety of services, they cater to individual consumer needs, and they are labor intensive with employees possessing broad skills. These characteristics are exhibited by most law offices, outpatient clinics, travel agencies, and insurance companies. Process layouts are appropriate for these types of organizations.

The Relative-Location Problem

Let's assume that a decision has been made to use a process layout and operations have been grouped into departments. We next want to locate departments relative to each other within a building. Some departments may be restricted to specific locations owing to their requirements for windows, ventilation, and rest rooms. But for other departments, there is a choice which centers around the impact that a layout has upon the service package. Questions that need addressing are:

1. How will a particular layout affect the attitudes of consumers? The distances walked, the proximity to rest rooms, and the view from windows are among many factors that may determine these attitudes.
2. How will a particular layout affect the quality of services? For example, the attitudes of employees (especially those that come in direct contact with consumers), the need for communication and other departmental interactions, and the compatibility with the organizational hierarchy may need consideration.
3. What are the costs associated with a particular layout? These include the fixed costs associated with establishing the layout, relevant variable costs associated with providing the services, and the costs to consumers.

The layout problem can be structured in terms of the costs of consumer and employee travel between departments. In this case, an appropriate objective is to determine a layout that minimizes the total cost of travel. Consider a facility that has been divided into n locations. Also, n departments will be assigned to these locations. We would like to determine the assignment that minimizes total travel cost. It can be shown that the number of possible layouts is n factorial. For example, there are 10!, or 3,628,800, possible layouts for a facility with 10 locations and 10 departments. Determining the best layout from so many possibilities is difficult. Clearly, complete enumeration is computationally impractical, even using the most efficient computers. As an alternative, we shall now discuss more popular rule-of-thumb (heuristic) techniques that frequently determine a satisfactory layout.

Example 9.2: Insurance office The home office of an insurance company is concerned only with the distances walked by employees between departments. The objective is to determine the relative location of departments

Table 9.2 Flow of employees between departments for a typical week

Flow matrix:

From\To	A	B	C	D	E	F
A	✕	7	20	0	5	6
B	8	✕	6	10	0	2
C	10	6	✕	15	7	8
D	0	30	5	✕	10	3
E	10	10	1	20	✕	6
F	0	6	0	3	4	✕

Net flow → Triangularized matrix:

From\To	A	B	C	D	E	F
A	✕	15	30	0	15	6
B	✕	✕	12	40	10	8
C	✕	✕	✕	20	8	8
D	✕	✕	✕	✕	30	6
E	✕	✕	✕	✕	✕	10
F	✕	✕	✕	✕	✕	✕

Department area requirements

Dept	Sq ft
A	1000
B	400
C	1750
D	2550
E	3400
F	3000

that minimizes the employee travel between nonadjacent departments. Nonadjacent departments are departments that are not located next to each other.

Operations sequence analysis is a simple heuristic method designed to address the relative-location problem.[4] This method requires a matrix of estimated consumer or employee flow between departments per unit time and a grid whose intersections (vertices) represent locations. Consider the flow matrix for the six-department insurance office given in Table 9.2. Initially, we shall assume that all departments are the same size, even though this is not realistic. The matrix is triangularized since our concern is the number of people traveling between departments and not the direction of travel.

An initial relative location of departments on the grid is given in Figure 9.8a. The initial solution can be arbitrary, or it can be based upon good judgment. For nonadjacent departments, the interdepartmental flows are multiplied by the number of grids separating the departments. These products are then summed to arrive at a flow distance figure that provides a

---

[4] E. S. Buffa, "Sequence Analysis for Functional Layouts," *Journal of Industrial Engineering,* vol. 6, no. 2, March–April, 1955, pp. 12–13.

200 DESIGNING THE SERVICE SYSTEM

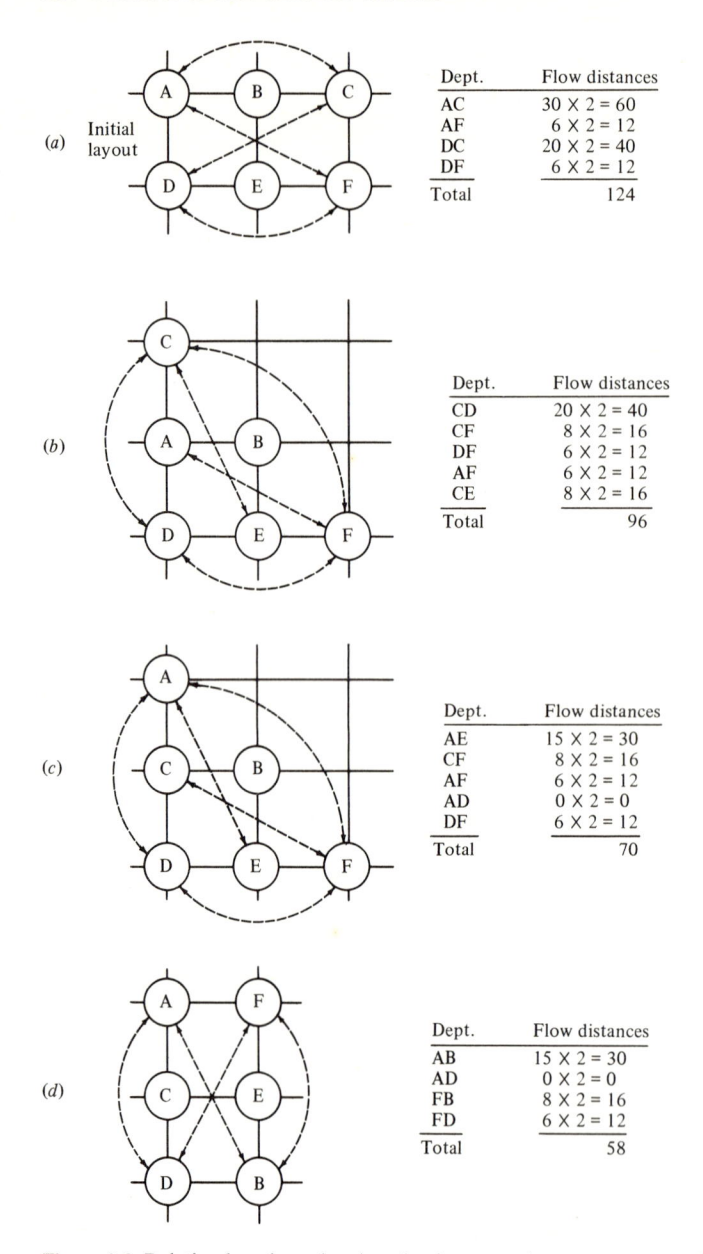

(a) Initial layout

Dept.	Flow distances
AC	30 × 2 = 60
AF	6 × 2 = 12
DC	20 × 2 = 40
DF	6 × 2 = 12
Total	124

(b)

Dept.	Flow distances
CD	20 × 2 = 40
CF	8 × 2 = 16
DF	6 × 2 = 12
AF	6 × 2 = 12
CE	8 × 2 = 16
Total	96

(c)

Dept.	Flow distances
AE	15 × 2 = 30
CF	8 × 2 = 16
AF	6 × 2 = 12
AD	0 × 2 = 0
DF	6 × 2 = 12
Total	70

(d)

Dept.	Flow distances
AB	15 × 2 = 30
AD	0 × 2 = 0
FB	8 × 2 = 16
FD	6 × 2 = 12
Total	58

Figure 9.8 Relative locations developed using operations sequence analysis.

rough measure of the cost associated with employees traveling between departments.

The initial relative location is revised by systematically exchanging the location of certain pairs of departments. As a guideline, we want high-flow departments to be adjacent and low-flow departments to be nonadjacent. Figures 9.8*b* through 9.8*d* give several revised relative locations. Revisions

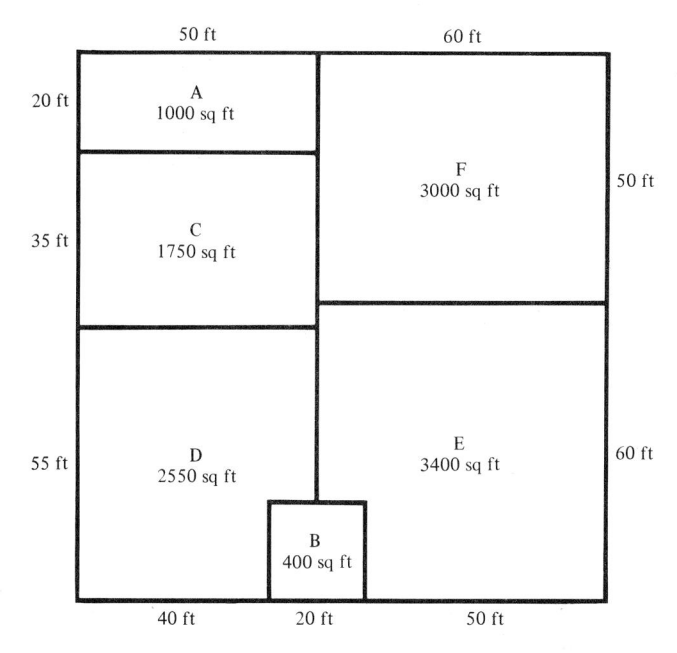

```
                50 ft              60 ft
        ┌─────────────────┬──────────────────┐
  20 ft │        A        │                  │
        │    1000 sq ft   │                  │
        ├─────────────────┤        F         │
        │                 │    3000 sq ft    │ 50 ft
  35 ft │        C        │                  │
        │    1750 sq ft   │                  │
        ├─────────────────┼──────────────────┤
        │                 │                  │
        │                 │                  │
        │        D        │        E         │ 60 ft
  55 ft │    2550 sq ft   │    3400 sq ft    │
        │                 │                  │
        │           ┌─────┤                  │
        │           │  B  │                  │
        │           │400sq│                  │
        └───────────┴─────┴──────────────────┘
              40 ft   20 ft       50 ft
```

Figure 9.9 Final layout within a square building.

can be made until no reduction in flow distance can be found or until a satisfactory flow distance is achieved.

Once a satisfactory relative location is developed, the areas within the facility are allocated to departments. One approach is initially to configure each department as a square and then to modify the configuration appropriately to fit into regularly shaped facilities, such as a rectangular building. Architects, of course, generally would be called upon to develop a final layout. Figure 9.9 is a feasible layout for a square building developed from the results of our operations sequence analysis. Notice that differences in area requirements have changed the adjacency of several departments.

A deficiency of operations sequence analysis is that it only considers the volume of interdepartmental flow and grid distance. Clearly, there are other factors that are important for determining a layout. These might include consumer expectations, the mobility of consumers and employees between locations, and employee preferences.

Computerized Relative Allocation of Facilities Technique (CRAFT)[5]

The logic underlying operations sequence analysis was improved and incorporated into a computer program known as CRAFT. CRAFT uses as inputs an interdepartmental flow (volume) matrix, a cost (cost/unit/unit-distance-

[5] E. S. Buffa, G. C. Armour, and T. E. Vollmann, "Allocating Facilities with CRAFT," *Harvard Business Review*, vol. 42, no. 2, March–April 1964, pp. 136–159.

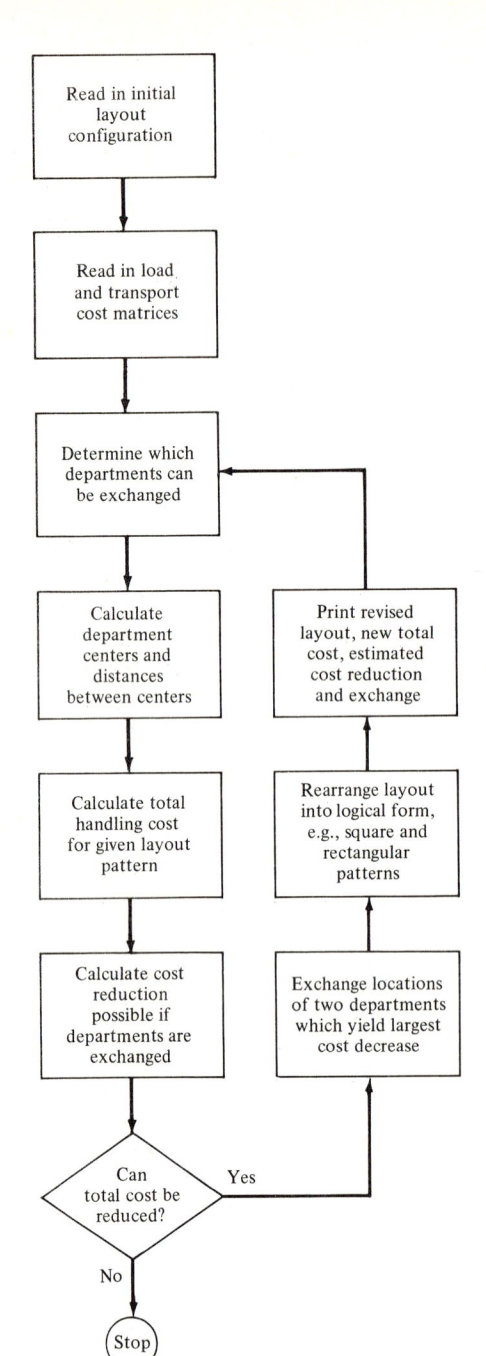

Figure 9.10 Flow diagram for CRAFT logic. [*Reprinted by permission of the Harvard Business Review. Exhibit from "Allocating Facilities with Craft," Elwood S. Buffa, Gordon C. Armour and Thomas E. Vollmann, March–April 1964. Copyright © 1964 by the President and Fellows of Harvard College; all rights reserved.*]

moved) matrix, and an initial layout with exact departmental dimensions. The output of the program is a series of layouts, each having lower total interdepartmental flow costs. There is no guarantee that the final layout provides the minimum total cost. However, comparisons of CRAFT with other available computerized layout methods indicate that it generally provides very good solutions. Also, CRAFT is very efficient in terms of computation time. Figure 9.10 is a condensed flow diagram for the CRAFT logic.

Applications of CRAFT have been reported for determining office, hospital, and public school layouts. In these cases, the objective was to minimize the costs associated with having people travel between departments. Various constraints on departmental locations and subjective preferences also have been included into some CRAFT analyses.

There are several characteristics of CRAFT as it applies to service organizations that should be noted. These include the following:

1. Distances are calculated between the centers of departments. This may be unrealistic, in particular when departments are rectangularly shaped.
2. The resulting departmental shapes may be undesirable for operations that are to be performed. Efficiency of operations and aesthetic factors are affected by the shapes.
3. CRAFT requires the specification of exact departmental dimensions, where in fact a range of dimensions may be acceptable. Modifications of CRAFT to allow for a range of departmental dimensions have been proposed.[6]
4. The interdepartmental flows are assumed to be deterministic and known. If the flows are changing rapidly, then CRAFT may yield unsatisfactory results.
5. The interdepartmental flows are assumed to be independent of the layout. But, situations can be envisioned where the volume of flow between departments is related to the proximity of the departments. In some cases, it may be desirable to encourage some flows (departmental interactions), while discouraging others.
6. Quantifying the costs associated with distances traveled can be difficult. When employees are traveling, the costs can be related to their wages. Subjective weights or penalties can be associated with having consumers traveling between departments.
7. Travel cost is assumed to be linearly related to distance traveled. But there are situations where both distance and consumer and employee characteristics determine the methods of travel and consequently travel costs. Common modes are by foot, elevator, motorized cart, and moving walkways.

SUMMARY

We have observed that most organizations adopt layouts that have characteristics of both the product and process layouts. When there is a distinct sequence of operations that dominates all others in terms of consumer or employee flow, an organization will lean towards adopting a product layout. However, when

---

[6] See P. Lew and P. M. Brown, "Evaluation and Modification of CRAFT for an Architectural Methodology," *Emerging Methods in Environmental Design and Planning*, MIT Press, Cambridge, Mass., 1970, pp. 151–161.

Table 9.3 Characteristics of a product layout and of a process layout

	Product layout	Process layout
Arrangement of operations	Arranged in the sequence in which they are delivered	Grouped according to common characteristics
Variety of services	Little variety	Great variety
Degree of personalization	Impersonal	Highly personalized
Specialization of employees and equipment	Highly specialized	General purpose
Volume of demand	High	Low
Flow through the system	Continuous	Intermittent
Point of control	Flow regulation	Consumer scheduling at operations
Fixed costs (e.g., for equipment)	High	Low
Variable costs	Low	High

there is no discernible dominant sequence, a process layout will be more appropriate. That is, operations will generally be grouped into departments according to some criteria. The relative locations of the departments within the facilities will be determined intuitively or by using available heuristic methods. The important characteristics of the product layout and process layout are summarized in Table 9.3.

TOPICS FOR DISCUSSION

1. Contrast the attention to aesthetics in waiting rooms that you have visited. Did it make a difference in your mood?
2. Give examples of service systems with product and process layouts. Why is one style layout chosen over the other?
3. For a retail store, one might want to maximize interdepartmental flows. Why?
4. Select some service and discuss how the design and layout of the facility met the six factors: objective of organization, land availability, flexibility, aesthetics, environment, and costs.
5. Give examples of service designs and layouts that accentuate the service concept and examples that detract from the service concept. Explain the successes and failures.
6. The CRAFT program is an example of a heuristic programming approach to problem solving. Why may CRAFT not find the optimal solution to a layout problem?

EXERCISES

9.1 The registration procedure for students at most American universities follows a similar pattern. It generally involves obtaining name cards, health clearances, class cards, ID photos, etc. On the basis of your own experience of the procedure and times involved, draw a process chart and flow diagram for registration procedures.

9.2 Getting a physical examination at a doctor's office involves a series of steps. The table below lists the activities and their average times. The activities can occur in any order but the MD consultation must be the last activity. Three nurses are assigned to perform activities 1, 2, and 4.

DESIGN AND LAYOUT OF SERVICE FACILITIES **205**

Activity	Average time, min
1. Medical history	6
2. Blood pressure, wt., temp.	20
3. MD checkup	18
4. Lab work	10
5. MD consultation	12

(a) What is the bottleneck activity and the maximum number of patients that can be seen per hour?

(b) Suggest a reallocation of nursing and/or MD activities that would result in increased service capacity. Draw a process flow diagram. What is the capacity of your improved system?

9.3 A school cafeteria is operated by five persons performing the activities below with average times shown.

Activity	Average time, sec
1. Serve salad and dessert.	10
2. Pour drinks.	30
3. Serve entree.	60
4. Serve vegetables.	20
5. Tally and collect payment.	40

(a) What is the bottleneck activity and maximum service capacity per hour?

(b) Suggest a reallocation of activities that would increase capacity and use only four employees. Draw a process flow diagram. What is the capacity of the improved system?

(c) Recommend a way to maintain the serving capacity found in part b using only three employees.

9.4 The Second Best Discount Store is considering rearranging its stock room to improve customer service. Stock pickers are given customer orders to fill from six warehouse areas. The movement between these areas is noted in the flow matrix below.

	A	B	C	D	E	F
A	....	1	4	2	0	3
B	0	....	2	0	2	1
C	2	2	....	4	5	2
D	3	4	2	....	0	2
E	1	0	3	1	....	4
F	4	3	1	2	0	....

Using the initial layout below, perform an operations sequence analysis to determine a layout that minimizes total flow between nonadjacent departments. Calculate your flow improvement.

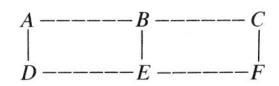

```
A ------- B ------- C
|         |         |
D ------- E ------- F
```

9.5 A convenience store is considering making a change in its layout to encourage impulse buying. The triangular flow matrix below gives the measure of association between different product groups (e.g., beer, milk, and magazines). A plus (+) indicates a high association such as between beer and cigarettes, a minus (−) indicates a repulsion such as between beer and milk, and a zero (0) indicates no association.

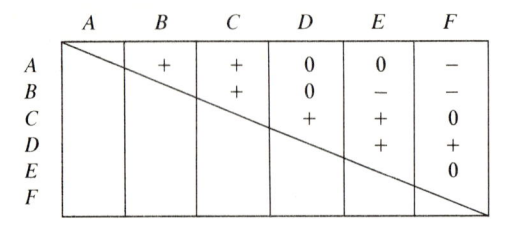

	A	B	C	D	E	F
A		+	+	0	0	−
B			+	0	−	−
C				+	+	0
D					+	+
E						0
F						

Using operations sequence analysis, determine a layout which will encourage impulse buying by placing high-association product groups close to one another.

CASELETTE: HEALTH MAINTENANCE ORGANIZATION (B)

Ms. Taylor, the administrator of the Life-Time Insurance Company HMO, was pleased with the location selected for the ambulatory health center. The center would not only serve as the clinic for the acutely ill, but would also serve as the center for the preventive health services.

An important goal of the HMO was to offer programs which would encourage members to enhance their ability to stay healthy. Various programs had already been planned. These included programs on smoking, proper nutrition, and diet, as well as exercise.

The clinic portion of the health center would be quite large. However, certain constraints in the layout would be necessary. The acutely ill patients would need to be separated from the well members. In addition, local safety regulations prohibited the x-ray department from being adjacent to the main waiting room.

It was very important to Ms. Taylor to minimize the walking distance of both the patients and the HMO personnel. The matrix below provides the expected flow between the departments, based on 40 patients per day.

		A	B	C	D	E	F
Reception	A	....	30	0	5	0	0
Waiting room*	B	10	....	40	10	0	0
Examination	C	15	20	....	15	5	5
Laboratory	D	5	18	8	....	6	3
X-ray*	E	0	4	1	2	....	4
Minor surgery	F	2	0	0	0	1	....

* These areas cannot be adjacent owing to safety regulations regarding possible radiation leakage.

Suggest various layouts and determine which layout would minimize the walking distance between the different areas in the clinic.

CASELETTE: HEALTH MAINTENANCE ORGANIZATION (C)

The administrator of the Life-Time Insurance Company HMO, Ms. Taylor, was anxious to solve potential problems before the clinic opened in Austin. In Buffalo, the pharmacy had been very busy from the beginning. Long waiting times for prescriptions presented a very real problem.

The Buffalo HMO pharmacy was modern, spacious, and well designed. The peak time for prescriptions was between 10 a.m. and 3 p.m. During this period, prescriptions would back up, and the waiting time would increase. After 5 p.m. the staff would be reduced to one pharmacist and one technician. The two had no trouble providing very timely service throughout the evening.

Ms. Taylor became acutely aware of the long waiting time. Several complaints had been lodged. Each person stated that the waiting time had exceeded one hour. However, the pharmacy always maintained a minimum of five persons on duty until 5 p.m.

Ms. Taylor personally studied the tasks of all the pharmacy personnel. She noted the time required to accomplish each task, as shown in the study results below. Because the prescriptions were filled in an assembly line fashion, each person performed only one task.

Activity	Rate per hour
Receive prescriptions.	150
Type labels.	30
Fill prescriptions.*	60
Check prescriptions.*	90
Dispense prescriptions.*	120

* Must be performed by a pharmacist.

Identify the bottleneck activity and suggest how the capacity can be increased.

CASELETTE: ESQUIRE DEPARTMENT STORE

The Esquire Department Store (EDS) established by Mr. Arthur Babbitt, Sr., in 1951 has shown a recent decline in sales. The store manager, young Arthur Babbitt, Jr., has noticed a decrease in the movements of customers between departments. He believes customers are not spending enough time in the department store. This may be due to the present layout which is based on the concept of locating related departments close to each other. Babbitt, Sr., is not convinced. He argues that he has been in business for about 30 years and the loyal customers are not likely to quit shopping here simply because of the layout. He believes they are losing customers because the new store across town seems to attract them away with discount prices.

Babbitt, Jr., explains that the more distance the customer travels between departments, the more products the customer will see. Customers usually have

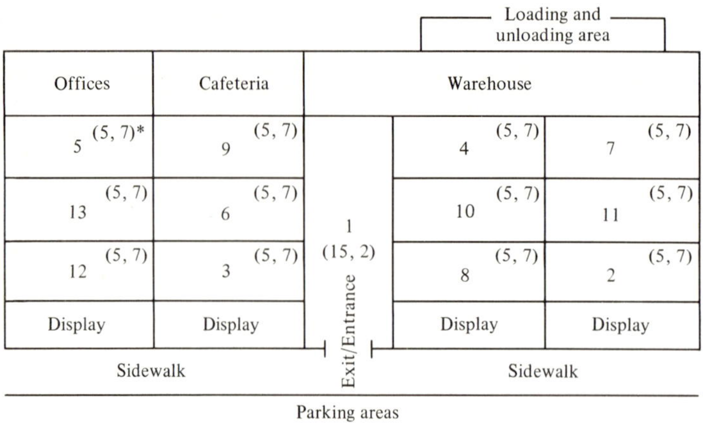

208 DESIGNING THE SERVICE SYSTEM

			Loading and unloading area	
Offices	Cafeteria		Warehouse	
(5, 7)* 5	(5, 7) 9		(5, 7) 4	(5, 7) 7
(5, 7) 13	(5, 7) 6	1	(5, 7) 10	(5, 7) 11
(5, 7) 12	(5, 7) 3	(15, 2) Exit/Entrance	(5, 7) 8	(5, 7) 2
Display	Display		Display	Display
Sidewalk			Sidewalk	

Parking areas

*Figures in parentheses refer to (rows, columns).

Figure 9.11 Current layout of Esquire. See Table 9.4 for department code.

something specific in mind when they go shopping, but exposure to more products may stimulate additional purchases. Thus, it seems to Babbitt, Jr., that the best answer to this problem is to change the present layout to expose the customer to more products. He feels the environment now is different from that of 1951 and the company must display products better and encourage impulse buying.[7]

At this point Babbitt, Sr., interrupts to say, "Son you may have a point here about the store layout. But before I spend money on tearing this place up, I need to see some figures. Develop a new layout and show me how much you can increase the time customers spend in the store."

Babbitt, Jr., returns to his office and pulls out some information that he has gathered about revising the store layout. He has estimated that there are 57 customers entering the store per hour on the average. The store operates 10 hours a day for 200 days a year. He has a drawing of the present layout, which is shown in Figure 9.11, and a chart depicting the flow of customers between departments, which is shown in Table 9.4.

Questions

1. Use the CRAFT computer program to develop a layout that will maximize customer time in the store. Recall that CRAFT is designed to minimize flow, thus Table 9.4 must be converted by first finding the largest flow.
2. What percentage increase in customer store time is achieved by the proposed layout?
3. What other consumer behavior concepts should be considered in the relative location of departments?

[7] Montrose S. Sommers and Jerome B. Kernan, "A Behavioral Approach to Planning, Layout and Display," *Journal of Retailing,* Winter 1965–1966, pp. 21–26, 62.

Table 9.4 Flow of customers between departments, in thousands

	1	2	3	4	5	6	7	8	9	10	11	12	13
1	0	32	41	19	21	7	13	22	10	11	8	6	10
2	17	0	24	31	16	3	13	17	25	8	7	9	12
3	8	14	0	25	9	28	17	16	14	7	9	24	18
4	25	12	16	0	18	26	22	9	6	28	20	16	14
5	10	12	15	20	0	18	17	24	28	30	25	9	19
6	8	14	12	17	20	0	19	23	30	32	37	15	21
7	13	19	23	25	3	45	0	29	27	31	41	24	16
8	28	9	17	19	21	5	7	0	21	19	25	10	9
9	14	8	13	15	22	18	13	25	0	33	27	14	19
10	18	25	17	19	23	15	25	27	31	0	21	17	10
11	29	28	31	16	29	19	18	33	26	31	0	16	16
12	17	31	25	21	19	17	19	21	31	29	25	0	19
13	12	25	16	33	14	19	31	17	22	15	24	18	0

1. Exit-entrance
2. Appliances
3. Audio-stereo-TV
4. Jewelry
5. Housewares
6. Cosmetics
7. Ladies' ready to wear
8. Men's ready to wear
9. Boys' clothing
10. Sporting goods
11. Ladies' lingerie
12. Shoes
13. Furniture

SELECTED BIBLIOGRAPHY

Armour, G. C.: "A Heuristic Algorithm and Simulation Approach to Relative Location of Facilities," *Management Science,* vol. 9, no. 1, September 1963, pp. 294–309.

Atkinson, G. A., and R. J. Phillips: "Hospital Design: Factors Influencing the Choice of Shape," *The Architects' Journal Information Library,* April 1964, pp. 851–855.

Buffa, Elwood S., Gordon C. Armour, and Thomas E. Vollmann: "Allocating Facilities with CRAFT," *Harvard Business Review,* vol. 42, no. 2, March–April 1964, pp. 136–159.

———: "Sequence Analysis for Functional Layouts," *Journal of Industrial Engineering,* vol. 6, no. 2, March–April 1955, pp. 12–13.

Elshafei, Alwalid N.: "Hospital Layout as a Quadratic Assignment Problem," *Operational Research Quarterly,* vol. 28, no. 1, 1977, pp. 167–179.

Energy Conservation Guideline for Office Buildings, American Institute for Architects Research Corporation. Washington, 1974.

Francis, R. L., and J. A. White: *Facility Layout and Location: An Analytical Approach,* Prentice-Hall, Inc., Englewood Cliffs, N.J., 1974.

Hillier, F. S., and M. M. Connors: "Quadratic Assignment Problem Algorithms and the Location of Indivisible Facilities," *Management Science,* vol. 13, no. 1, September 1966, pp. 42–57.

Kaiman, L.: "Computer Programs for Architects and Layout Planners," *Proceedings, American Institute of Industrial Engineers,* 22nd Annual Conference and Convention, Boston, 1971.

Lee, R. C., and J. M. Moore: "CORELAR–Computerized Relationship Layout Planning" *Journal of Industrial Engineering,* vol. 18, no. 3, March 1967, pp. 195–200.

Lew, P., and P. M. Brown: "Evaluation and Modification of CRAFT for an Architectural Methodology," *Emerging Methods in Environmental Design and Planning,* G. T. Moore, (ed.), MIT Press, Cambridge, Mass., 1970, pp. 151–161.

Muther, R., and K. McPherson: "Four Approaches to Computerized Layout Planning," *Industrial Engineering,* vol. 2, 1970, pp. 39–42.

Nugent, C. E., T. E. Vollmann, and J. Ruml: "An Experimental Comparison of Techniques for the Assignment of Facilities to Locations," *Operations Research,* vol. 16, no. 1, January–February 1968, pp. 150–173.

Payne, Richard, (ed.): *EXXON USA,* vol. 16, no. 3, Public Affairs Department of Exxon Company, Third Quarter, 1977.

Sommers, Montrose S., and Jerome B. Kernan: "A Behavioral Approach to Planning, Layout and Display," *Journal of Retailing,* Winter 1965–1966, pp. 21–26, 62.

Volgyesi, A. S.: "Toronto General: The Hospital That Computer Built," *Computer Decisions,* September 1969.

———: "Space-Age Approach to Space Allocation," *Computer Decisions,* May 1970, pp. 32–35.

Vollmann, Thomas E., Christopher E. Nugent, and Robert L. Zartler: "A Computerized Model for Office Layout," *The Journal of Industrial Engineering,* vol. 19, no. 7, July 1968, pp. 321–327.

———, and E. S. Buffa: "The Facilities Layout Problem in Perspective," *Management Science,* vol. 12, no. 10, June 1966, pp. 450–468.

CHAPTER
TEN

WORK DESIGN: THE DESIGN OF SERVICE PERSONNEL ACTIVITY

In previous chapters, we described how the various elements of the service delivery system (SDS) interact to determine the value of a service package and the capacity of a system. We also noted that because service organizations tend to be labor-intensive, employees often are the backbone of the SDS. Employees who interact directly with consumers are in the front lines, so to speak, and consequently have an immediate and uncensored impact upon the service package. This means that the value of employees in a service organization is determined by many factors in addition to skill, such as morale, motivation, personality, and physical appearance. All these factors must be considered in the design of service personnel activity.

Work design for employees can also have a complementary impact upon the tasks that consumers may be required to carry out. Self-busing of trays in fast-food restaurants, presorting of volume mail according to zip code, and self-service in gas stations are examples where tasks previously performed by employees have been passed on to the consumer. This added dimension of work design directly influences the efficiency of the SDS and, consequently, consumer attitudes toward the service package.

For our purpose, work design means the specification of the contents, methods, and relationship of jobs in order to satisfy service requirements and organizational objectives. Closely related to work design is organizational structure; that is, the hierarchy of superior-subordinate relationships and the amount of discretionary power given employees in performing their jobs. Work design has been the focal point of numerous studies, whose research findings fill many volumes. It is an extremely complex subject, involving many variables, and there is no one best approach for all situations. In this chapter, we limit ourselves to an overview of contemporary and topical approaches to work design as they relate to service organizations. To provide a framework for our discussion, we begin with a look at changes in the social environment that influence employee attitudes toward their work.

ENVIRONMENTAL CHANGES

Changes in work environment, indeed changes in basic social conditions, have important implications for work design. A detailed discussion of the causes of such changes is beyond the scope of this book, but we shall describe briefly some important trends that are expected to continue.

Rising Levels of Education

In the early 1960s, about two-thirds of American young people graduated from high school. By 1975, this figure for high school graduates rose to three-fourths. Also, in 1975 more than one-half of all high school graduates entered a degree program at a college or university. What are the implications of these higher levels of education for work design?

Employees' aspirations for pay, job title, and achievement are directly and positively correlated with education. They want to perform tasks commensurate with their level of education; at the same time they are reluctant to do jobs they consider menial or below their capabilities. Some individuals may even prefer unemployment to employment in an undesirable job.

Service Employee Associations and Unions

For many decades, large private and public service organizations have been unionized or have formed local associations. For example, the Teamsters Union has been active in organizing workers in transportation, in warehousing, and in public street and sanitation departments, as well as in many other service organizations. Also, the Service Employees International Union (SEIU) has been successful in organizing employees in hospitals, schools, and social service agencies.

The impact of unions and associations in the public sector has been felt primarily at the state and local levels. During the mid-1960s, unions and associations representing public employees took a dramatic shift toward militancy in their collective bargaining tactics. In 1960, there were only 57,200 worker days lost to strikes by local workers. By 1973, this figure soared to 2,166,300 worker days. Public employees, even those in essential occupations, have been willing to defy public opinion and in many cases the law, in order to strengthen their bargaining positions. An example is the 1978 police strike in Cleveland, Ohio. The point of contention was the dismissal of 13 police officers for refusing to go on single-person daytime patrols in a high-crime area of the city.

The principal bargaining points of unions and associations still focus upon wages and benefits. However, they also include work rules, overtime compensation, training programs, adoption of labor-saving technologies, and the hiring, firing, transfer, and promotion of personnel.

Inflation–Minimum-Wage Cycle

The cycle of inflation and its upward push on the minimum wage has been the nemesis of the United States economy since the early 1970s. Service organizations are particularly hard hit because they tend to be labor intensive, and many rely heavily upon low-wage, low-skill employees. The Federal Minimum Wage Law dates back to 1938, but it was not until the 1961 Fair Labor Standards Act (FLSA) that service organizations began to feel the pinch of higher labor costs. The FLSA extended minimum-wage coverage to employees of laundries, hospitals, dry-cleaning establishments, nursing homes, and schools. In 1968, federal minimum-wage coverage was further extended to include employees in hotels and restaurants. Employees not covered by the federal law often are covered by individual state minimum-wage laws.

Service organizations adjust to increased labor costs in a variety of ways that affect work design. A common remedy is to reduce the workforce and to increase the workloads of remaining employees. A 1977 study of the impact of increased state minimum wage upon the California hotel and restaurant industry indicated the following cuts in staff: cleanup staff 81 percent, kitchen help 63 percent, servers 57 percent, management personnel 10 percent. Other common responses to increased minimum wages are raising prices, reducing hours of operation, using part-time employees to replace full-time workers, introducing labor-saving technologies, encouraging self-service operations, and charging for what were previously free services.

Equal Employment Opportunity

Title VII of the 1964 Civil Rights Act prohibits employers and unions from discriminating on the basis of race, color, religion, sex, or national origin. In particular, it prohibits discrimination with regard to working conditions, compensation, admission to training programs, and the hiring, firing, transfer, and promotion of personnel. Title VII was strengthened by the 1972 Equal Employment Opportunity Act (EEO), which extended coverage to private organizations employing more than 15 people and to state and local governments. In 1973, EEO was amended to protect the handicapped from job discrimination.

EEO has resulted in many minorities and women seeking jobs that were traditionally considered the sole domain of white males. Examples are the jobs of police officers, fire fighters, commercial pilots, and most professional occupations. Noncompliance with EEO has resulted in court action against several service organizations, such as AT&T (1973), United Airlines (1971 and 1973), and the National Broadcasting Company (1971).

Affirmative action programs that attempt to comply with EEO can influence both work design and attitudes of employees. Under such programs, artificial barriers against the employment of minorities and women are removed from employment criteria and from job specifications. For example, tests of strength, endurance, or intelligence may be challenged in the courts unless it can be proven that such standards are necessary to perform tasks relevant to meeting organizational objectives. Using personal appearance, marital status, and age as criteria for job selection or assignment may also be open to challenge.

Some affirmative action programs have been accused of encouraging the employment and advancement of minorities at the expense of white males. Declining morale and resentment on the part of individuals who were passed over have been attributed to such circumstances. A basic unresolved problem for employers is to comply with EEO without alienating those individuals who view themselves as victims of reverse discrimination.

Technological Innovation

Service organizations often are considered unlikely to adopt new technologies because of their labor intensiveness and the variability of service requirements. Manufacturing organizations are known to introduce labor-saving machines to produce higher volumes of standardized products. In contrast, service organizations meet increased demand primarily by augmenting the size of their workforces. Resistance to new technologies in part revolves around preserving the personalized provider-consumer interactions expected of most services. But as the costs of services continue to soar, this resistance likely will weaken. Out of necessity, both consumers and providers will become amenable to a less personalized yet more efficient SDS. Automated health clinics and physical examination centers operated by technicians instead of doctors are examples of areas where efficient technologies are gaining acceptance.

Competitive pressures can also spur the adoption of new technologies. Automatic tellers at banks and computerized reservation services offered by hotels and airlines not only increase operational efficiency, they also enhance consumers' perceptions about the value of the service package. When new technologies are adopted, they affect what tasks must be performed and the manner in which they are to be carried out. That is, technological innovation is an intrinsic element of work design. Its role in service industries is a concern of this chapter.

JOB RATIONALIZATION

Contemporary work design has its roots in the industrial revolution with the pioneering ideas of Charles Babbage (1835), Frederick Taylor (1911), and Frank Gilbreth (1911). Their views moved away from traditional craft-oriented work design and organizational structure toward division of labor, scientific management, and motion study. The approach, often referred to as job rationalization, emphasizes division of labor to permit repetitive-task performance with limited labor skills. The intended result is high productivity with efficient use of resources. Job rationalization also stresses the separation of the functions of management and labor, where management defines jobs by dividing work into small, easily learned tasks that can be performed repetitively. Labor, on the other hand, exercises little or no discretion, performing the tasks according to specifications and in what is viewed as a mechanistic mode.

By the 1940s, human engineering and work simplification became the bywords of industrial engineers. Their efforts focused on worker-machine interfaces and combined motion study, experimental psychology, and work physiology in studying complex and/or strenuous tasks. Job rationalization frequently attempts to motivate employees by means of wage incentives. Wage rates might be based upon skill requirements, performance evaluations, and/or productivity. Various forms of piece-rate compensation schemes have been devised where employee salaries are directly related to output. The compensation plans for hair stylists, insurance agents, auto mechanics, and hotel cleanup help are examples in the service sector, where wages often are linked to productivity.

High volume and efficient production are primary objectives of job rationalization. However, they are sometimes achieved at the expense of employee frustration and dissatisfaction. The real costs that might result from excessive job rationalization relate to high turnover and absenteeism, poor quality work, high training costs, and high costs of supervision. Work design seeks a balance between productivity or efficiency and employee frustration or dissatisfaction.

Following are some specific techniques for work measurement and methods analysis often associated with job rationalization.

Time Study

This is a technique for work measurement that is used to develop standards of performance. It relies upon decomposing repetitive jobs (work cycles) into individual work elements that are small identifiable units of work (e.g., serve a cup of coffee, take an order, etc.). When an employee performs an element, the completion time is determined by means of a stopwatch and is recorded on an observation sheet. The appropriate number of cycles to observe is determined statistically and is based upon the variability of the element times and level of confidence (accuracy) desired.

After all of the element completion times are recorded, the elapsed times are then determined by subtracting the element completion time from the completion time of the predecessor element. The mean of the elapsed time for each element is calculated and then adjusted according to the relative proficiency of the employee involved in the study. That is, a *performance rating* is used to adjust the mean times to make them appropriate for an "average" worker. For example, a poor worker, at 90 percent of normal, would have a time adjusted by 0.90. For an extra-fast worker, at 110 percent of normal, the time would be adjusted by a factor of 1.10. The resulting adjusted times are referred to as *normal element times:*

$$NT_i = R_i(OT_i) \tag{1}$$

where NT_i = normal time of the *i*th work element
OT_i = average observed time of the *i*th work element
R_i = proficiency rating of the employee in performing the *i*th work element expressed as a decimal percentage (e.g., 0.90 for 90 percent of normal)

A final adjustment of the normal element times is generally needed to allow for fatigue, breaks, and other personal needs of the worker. This allowance is expressed as a percentage and often is the same for each work element. The resulting adjusted times are known as *standard element times,* and their sum is the *standard cycle time.* This latter value is used to determine productive capacity, required number of employees, tasks to assign employees, standard costs, employee performance, and compensation plans.

$$ST_i = NT_i(1 + A) \tag{2}$$

$$CT = \sum_{i=1}^{n} ST_i \tag{3}$$

where ST_i = standard time for the *i*th work element
A = allowance expressed as a decimal percentage (e.g., 0.10 for 10 percent)
CT = standard cycle time
n = number of work elements in the work cycle

Table 10.1 is a time-study observation sheet for wrapping silverware in napkins. The work cycle was decomposed into four elements, and then 10 cycles were observed. There are two rows of times associated with each work element. The lower row gives the continuous stopwatch time at which the element was completed. The upper row gives the interval time for the element. The last column gives the normal time calculated for each element.

The standard cycle time is 0.32 minutes per item. Note that the observation sheet has a space to record the times for foreign work elements. These are elements that generally are not considered to be part of the work cycle and consequently are not relevant for setting standard times.

Work Sampling

This is a technique for analyzing repetitive work activities when the work cycles are too long to be analyzed economically by time studies. Observations of an employee are made at randomly selected points in time. The activity that the employee is engaged in is recorded and classified into one of several prede-

Activity: *Folding silverware into napkins* Study no. *13* Observer *C.C.* Date: *1/10/81*

Began timing: *2:32*
Ended timing: *2:35*

Std time *0.32 min/item*

Element description		1	2	3	4	5	6	7	8	9	10	Sum	Avg time	Rating	Norm time
1 Position napkin	T	0.03	0.05	0.05	0.06	0.06	0.06	0.05	0.05	0.05	0.04	0.50	0.050	1.10	0.055
	R	3	28	65	95	25	57	85	13	42	67				
2 Group knife, fork, and spoon	T	0.05	0.08	0.09	0.08	0.08	0.07	0.08	0.09	0.06	0.08	0.76	0.076	1.00	0.076
	R	8	30	74	103	33	64	93	22	48	75				
3 Roll silverware	T	0.07	0.15	0.06	0.06	0.07	0.06	0.06	0.06	0.07	0.07	0.73	0.073	0.90	0.065
	R	15	51	80	9	40	70	99	28	55	82				
4 Place in box	T	0.08	0.09	0.09	0.10	0.11	0.10	0.09	0.09	0.08	0.09	0.92	0.092	1.05	0.097
	R	23	60	89	19	51	80	208	37	63	91				
5	T														
	R														
6	T														
	R														
7	T														
	R														
8	T														
	R														

Cycles

Foreign elements: _____

_____

Normal cycle time *0.293*
+ Allowance (10%) *0.029*
= Std time *0.322*

Note: T = time
R = reading

termined categories that include the possibility of idleness or nonproductive work. Work sampling is based upon the premise that a random sample of an employee's activities is representative of the person's total activities. Therefore, a frequency distribution constructed from the randomly selected observations will be a good approximation to the actual distribution of activities. This frequency distribution can be used to draw inferences about the distribution of an employee's work activities. This, in turn, can assist in determining appropriate workforce levels, allowances for personal needs, and work assignments. It can also be used to set standards of productivity that might underlie a compensation plan.

The appropriate number of observations to record is dependent upon the proportion of time engaged in the activity and the level of confidence desired in estimating a proportion. Standard statistical techniques are used to determine the appropriate sample size. Assume that we want to estimate the proportion of time an employee is involved in nonproductive work. Let P represent the true proportion. We want our estimate to come within a plus or minus K percent of P, and we want to achieve this with a $1 - \alpha$ level of confidence. That is, we want a $1 - \alpha$ probability (usually 0.95 or $\alpha = 0.05$) such that our estimate will fall within the interval $P - K$, $P + K$. The appropriate sample size N is

$$N = \frac{Z^2 \hat{P}(1 - \hat{P})}{K^2} \tag{4}$$

where Z = standard normal deviate associated with a $1 - \alpha$ confidence level
$\hat{P}$ = approximate value of P

$\hat{P}$ can be based upon a small initial sample, or it can be a reasonable guess. When there is no prior information upon which to arrive at $\hat{P}$, then a conservative approach is to set $\hat{P}$ equal to 0.5. This will yield a sample size larger than is necessary to achieve the desired level of confidence.

Work sampling is used extensively to analyze the activities of hospital personnel. The information provided by work sampling can be used for assigning employees to workshifts to meet the changing demand for services.

Consider the following typical categories of nursing activities: (1) direct patient care, (2) indirect patient care, (3) paperwork, (4) communication, (5) escorting and errands, (6) clean up, (7) travel, and (8) nonproductive activities. Assume that we want to estimate the proportion of time nurses are involved in nonproductive activities during the midnight to 8 a.m. shift. We are sure that the true proportion of nonproductive activities is less than 15 percent. Data for analysis will be collected during a 30-day period of observation. Also, our estimate should come within a plus or minus 2 percent of the true proportion with a 95 percent confidence level.

1. How many observations are required?
2. How should the observations be taken?

We can substitute into equation (4) with $K = 0.02$, $\hat{P} = 0.15$, and $Z_{0.05} = 1.96$ (Table C at the back of the book: Areas of a Standard Normal Distribution). This yields a sample size

$$N = \frac{(1.96)^2(0.15)(1 - 0.15)}{(0.02)^2}$$

$$= 1225 \text{ observations}$$

Because these observations are to be collected during 30 days, the number of observations per day is

$$\frac{1225 \text{ observations}}{30 \text{ days}} = 40.83$$

$$\simeq 41 \text{ observations per day}$$

The 41 observations per day are to be taken randomly during the eight-hour (480-minute) workshift. Random-number tables or some other random selection procedure can be used to choose 41 points of observation from the 480 minutes of work. The observation times chosen for a particular day should be independent of those chosen for any other day.

Work Methods Charts

A variety of charts have been devised to provide a graphic portrayal of the flow of work activities and the interactions between workers, consumers, and/or equipment. Worker-machine charts (formerly called man-machine charts) and activity charts are among the most widely used of these graphic techniques.

Worker-machine charts These charts are used to analyze on a time scale the interaction of an employee with equipment when the employee's work-cycle time is less than that of the equipment. The objective is to investigate the possibility of having an employee operate several pieces of equipment by properly scheduling work activities.

Figure 10.1 is a worker-machine chart for a single bank teller serving a two-lane drive-in bank. For simplicity, all randomness in the process is ignored and average times are used. On the average, a customer uses 15 seconds to enter the service area, 48 seconds to be served, and 9 seconds to exit the area. Notice that while the cycle time for a customer averages 72 seconds, the time for the teller is only 48 seconds per customer. Also, observe that while the teller is occupied with a customer in one lane, another customer will be arriving, departing, or waiting in the other lane.

Figure 10.2 is an alternative form of the worker-machine chart. It is appropriate when the number of activities to be portrayed is small enough to be represented by differently shaded bars.

220 DESIGNING THE SERVICE SYSTEM

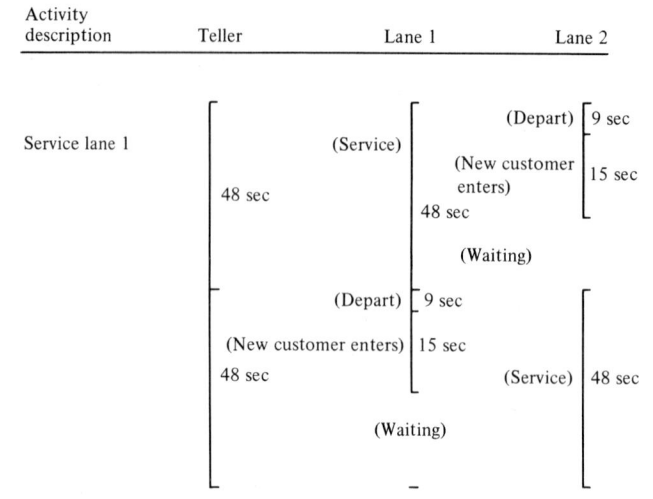

Activity description	Teller	Lane 1	Lane 2
Service lane 1	48 sec (Service)	(Depart) 9 sec (New customer enters) 48 sec (Waiting)	(Depart) 9 sec 15 sec (Waiting)
	(New customer enters) 48 sec	(Depart) 9 sec 15 sec (Waiting)	(Service) 48 sec

Total cycle time: 96 seconds
Idle-teller time per cycle: 0
Working-teller time per cycle: 96 seconds
Idle-lane time per cycle: 48 seconds
Working-lane time per cycle: 144 seconds

Figure 10.1 Worker-machine chart—teller serving two lanes of a drive-in bank.

Activity charts These charts are more general than worker-machine charts in that they show the interactions of a group of workers with equipment and/or customers. The activity chart uses a time scale to show when each worker performs a specific task. The reason for using activity charts is a conjecture that, by properly scheduling the activities, the process can be performed with fewer workers.

Figure 10.3 is an activity chart that depicts two tellers serving three lanes in

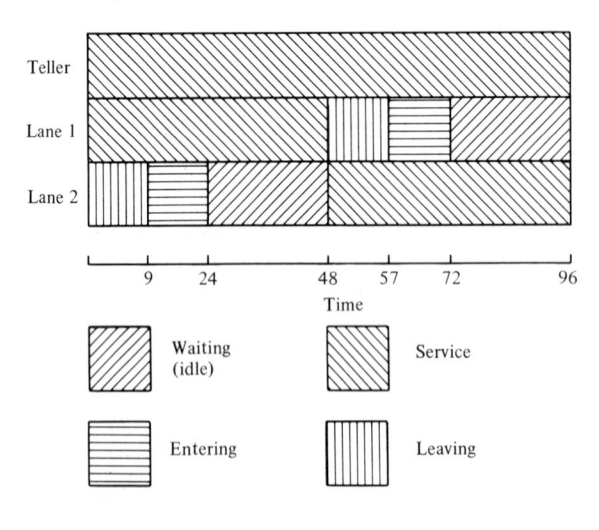

Figure 10.2 Worker-machine chart—alternative form, teller serving two lanes of a drive-in bank. [*Reprinted by permission from B. L. Foote, "A Queuing Case Study of Drive-in Banking," Interfaces, vol. 6, no. 4, August 1976, p. 33. Copyright 1976 The Institute of Management Sciences.*]

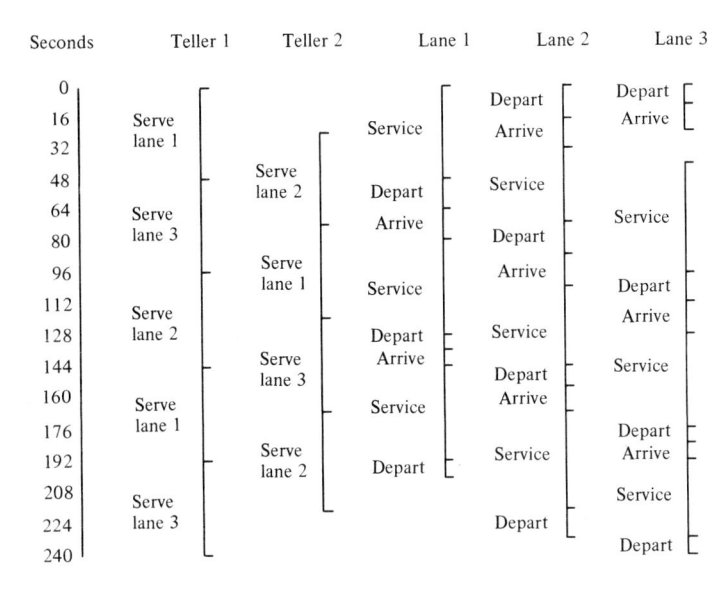

WORK DESIGN: THE DESIGN OF SERVICE PERSONNEL ACTIVITY 221

Seconds	Teller 1	Teller 2	Lane 1	Lane 2	Lane 3
0				Depart	Depart
16	Serve lane 1		Service	Arrive	Arrive
32					
48		Serve lane 2	Depart	Service	
64	Serve lane 3		Arrive		Service
80				Depart	
96		Serve lane 1	Service	Arrive	Depart
112	Serve lane 2				Arrive
128			Depart	Service	
144		Serve lane 3	Arrive		Service
160	Serve lane 1		Service	Depart Arrive	
176					Depart
192		Serve lane 2	Depart	Service	Arrive
208	Serve lane 3				Service
224				Depart	
240					Depart

Figure 10.3 Activities chart—two tellers serving three lanes in a drive-in bank.

a drive-in bank. The tellers are located together in a single station. One lane is serviced directly from the teller station. The other two lanes are served by pneumatic tubes that transmit the banking transactions to and from the teller station. The average service time at each station is 48 seconds per customer. In addition, it takes an average of 15 seconds for a vehicle to enter the service area and 9 seconds to depart. The activity chart shows that this service system rapidly stabilizes with no waiting on the part of the customers and no idleness on the part of the tellers. Teller 1 services lanes in the sequence 1, 3, and 2, and teller 2 services lanes in the sequence 2, 1, and 3. What would happen if the service time were greater or less than 48 seconds?

Job Rationalization in Summary

Job rationalization has its roots in the industrial revolution when efficiency at high levels of production was the primary concern. Table 10.2 contains a synopsis of some common techniques often associated with the job rationalization mode. Frederick Taylor (1911) summarizes the advantages of this scientific approach to work design:

> Science, not rule of thumb.
> Harmony, not discord.
> Cooperation, not individualism.
> Maximum output, in place of restricted output.
> The development of each man to his greatest efficiency and prosperity.

Table 10.2 Summary of techniques for work measurement and methods analysis

Purpose of application	Examples
Time study	
To develop standards of work performance for use in determining productive capacity, in assigning tasks to employees, and in developing compensation plans.	Examining a car's transmission (routine) Setting a table Cleaning a hotel room
Work sampling	
To analyze repetitive work that has long cycles. The distribution of work activities is estimated and used for determining workforce levels, allowances for personal needs, and work assignments.	Secretaries, teachers, etc.
Worker-machine chart	
To analyze on a time scale the interaction of an employee with equipment (or consumers). The objective is to determine the appropriate number of pieces of equipment to assign an employee.	Bank teller operations Telephone answering service operation Chef operations (with ovens) Waiter operations (with customers)
Activities chart	
To analyze the interactions of a worker or group of workers with other workers. The objective is to determine the most efficient scheduling of activities.	Bank teller operations Aircraft overhauling operations Aircraft in-transit operations

Is job rationalization a panacea for work design? How appropriate is it now that we are living in the postindustrial era? In particular, how appropriate is it for designing service jobs where the value of the service package is often determined by the attributes of employees? Figure 10.4 shows how industrial psychologists traditionally view the effects of excessively rationalized jobs. In the following sections, we shall address some of the questions posed above and discuss alternatives to the job rationalization mode.

JOB ENLARGEMENT AND JOB ENRICHMENT

Hierarchy of Needs

The work of E. Mayo (1933) on human relations stimulated interest in workers' relationships with formal organizations. Subsequent research by R. Hoppock (1935), R. L. Kahn (1951), and C. R. Walker (1952) focused on worker satisfaction and morale and their relationships with productivity. These studies had a direct impact upon Abraham Maslow's (1954) theories on worker motivation.

Maslow postulated his famous theory on the hierarchy of worker needs. Within this framework, there are levels of needs of workers, as shown in Figure

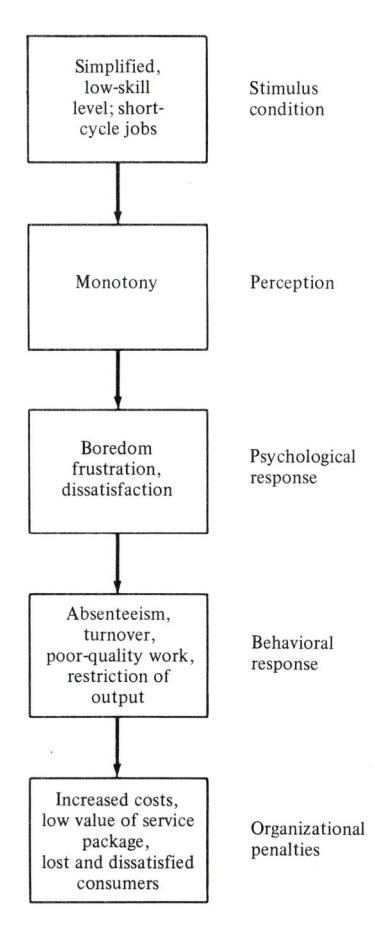

```
┌─────────────┐
│ Simplified, │
│  low-skill  │    Stimulus
│ level; short-│   condition
│  cycle jobs │
└──────┬──────┘
       │
       ▼
┌─────────────┐
│             │
│  Monotony   │    Perception
│             │
└──────┬──────┘
       │
       ▼
┌─────────────┐
│   Boredom   │
│ frustration,│    Psychological
│dissatisfaction│  response
└──────┬──────┘
       │
       ▼
┌─────────────┐
│ Absenteeism,│
│  turnover,  │    Behavioral
│poor-quality work,│ response
│restriction of │
│   output    │
└──────┬──────┘
       │
       ▼
┌─────────────┐
│Increased costs,│
│low value of service│ Organizational
│   package,  │    penalties
│lost and dissatisfied│
│  consumers  │
└─────────────┘
```

Figure 10.4 Effects of excessive job rationalization.

10.5. According to Maslow, only unsatisfied needs can motivate a worker to higher productivity. Also, the lowest level of unsatisfied needs tends to be the dominant motivator. For example, if the physiological, safety and security, and belongingness needs of a worker are satisfied, but self-esteem is not satisfied, then this latter need becomes the worker's central concern. In this case, a worker can be motivated most effectively by enhancing the worker's perception of self-esteem.

Maslow's theory is intuitively appealing. It provides a simple, easy-to-understand structure for explaining worker motivations. But, is it too simple? Subsequent studies on worker motivation indicate that employee attitudes are much more complex. The latter studies led to the development of *job enlargement*.

Job enlargement is a topical approach to work design that centers around expanding the content of jobs to counter employee frustration and dissatisfaction inherent in job rationalization. Jobs can be enlarged in both a horizontal and vertical dimension. The horizontal dimension (also known as horizontal

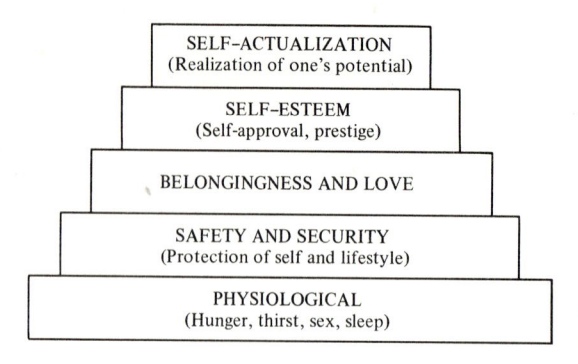

Figure 10.5 Maslow's hierarchy of needs.

loading) refers to the number and variety of tasks assigned to an employee. The vertical dimension refers to the amount of control and discretion a worker has in planning and performing tasks.

Edward E. Lawler (1969) reviewed the results of 10 studies on the use of job enlargement. For each of these studies, job enlargement resulted in higher-quality output. However, in only 4 of the 10 studies did it result in higher productivity. These findings suggest that higher motivation produced by job enlargement is more likely to improve quality than it is to increase productivity.

Lawler also indicates that the vertical dimension of job enlargement is more important for employee motivation than the horizontal dimension. This may result from employees feeling that their abilities are being tested, and then they can exercise self-control. However, both dimensions of job enlargement, jointly instituted, show more consistent improvements in employee motivation than either one instituted alone.

The term "job enrichment" is frequently used synonymously with "job enlargement." However, some industrial psychologists prefer the term "enrichment" because it connotes the psychological aspects of job value as perceived by employees. This value involves the expectation that good performance will result in satisfying higher-order needs, such as self-esteem and self-actualization. Enriched jobs are characterized by:

1. Variety in assigned tasks
2. Employee autonomy and discretion in performing tasks
3. Feedback for employees with regard to performance
4. Completion of a whole and identifiable piece of work that can be associated with the service rendered (end product)

Two-Factor Theory[1]

Frederick Herzberg (1959), a leading advocate of job enrichment, instituted a *two-factor theory* for motivating employees, and this theory has created con-

[1] Adapted from Frederick Herzberg, "One More Time: How Do You Motivate Employees?" *Harvard Business Review*, vol. 46, no. 1, January–February 1968, pp. 53–62.

troversy. Briefly, Herzberg's theory is that the factors involved in producing job satisfaction are separate and distinct from those that lead to dissatisfaction. Factors that lead to satisfaction are known as motivators, and they include achievement, recognition, nature of the work, responsibility, and growth or advancement. Factors that lead to dissatisfaction-avoidance are referred to as "hygiene" factors because they purportedly are necessary for a healthy work environment. The hygiene factors include company policy and administration, supervision, interpersonal relationships, working conditions, salary, status, and security. The two-factor theory asserts that the absence of motivators leads to *nonsatisfaction,* which is distinct from dissatisfaction, and also that the presence of hygiene factors leads to *dissatisfaction-avoidance,* which is distinct from satisfaction.

Figure 10.6 shows the results of studies of factors affecting worker attitudes as reported by Herzberg. The sample was selected from employees in a wide variety of occupations that included hospital maintenance workers, nurses, housekeepers, teachers, accountants, and engineers.

Herzberg suggests the following 10 steps for instituting a job enrichment program that leads to increased employee motivation:

1. Select those jobs in which (*a*) the investment in industrial engineering does not make changes too costly, (*b*) attitudes are poor, (*c*) hygiene is becoming very costly, and (*d*) a difference can be made in performance.

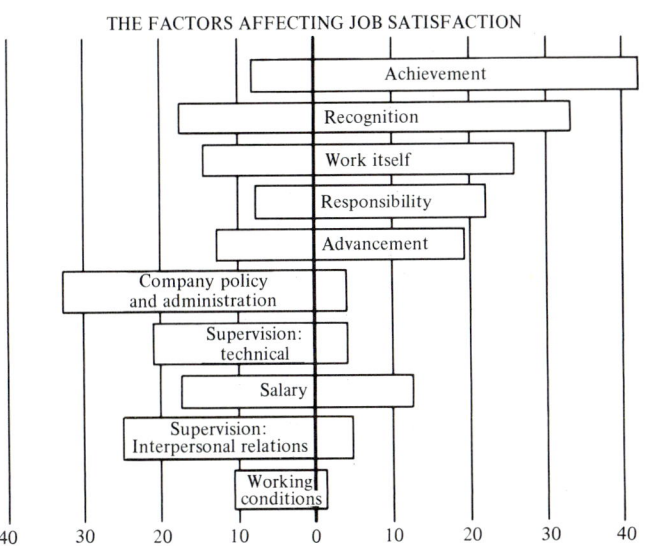

THE FACTORS AFFECTING JOB SATISFACTION

[Chart showing factors: Achievement, Recognition, Work itself, Responsibility, Advancement, Company policy and administration, Supervision: technical, Salary, Supervision: Interpersonal relations, Working conditions, plotted on scale from 40 30 20 10 0 10 20 30 40]

DISSATISFIERS: Percentage of times mentioned in descriptions of events reducing satisfaction

SATISFIERS: Percentage of times mentioned in descriptions of events improving satisfaction

Figure 10.6 The factors affecting job satisfaction. [*Reprinted with permission from Frederick Herzberg, "New Approaches in Management Organization and Job Design," Industrial Medicine and Surgery, vol. 31, no. 11, November 1962, p. 480.*]

2. Approach those jobs with the conviction that they can be changed. Years of tradition have led managers to believe that the content of jobs is sacrosanct and the only direction of action that they can take is to stimulate people.
3. Brainstorm a list of changes that may enrich the jobs, without concern for their practicality.
4. Screen the list to eliminate suggestions that involve hygiene, rather than actual motivation.
5. Screen the list for generalities, such as "give them more responsibility," that are rarely followed in practice. This seems obvious, but the motivator words have never left industry; the substance has just been rationalized and organized out. Words like "responsibility," "growth," "achievement," and "challenge," for example, have been elevated to the lyrics of a patriotic anthem for all organizations. It is the old problem typified by the Pledge of Allegiance to the flag being more important than contributions to the country—of form rather than substance.
6. Screen the list to eliminate any horizontal-loading suggestions.
7. Avoid direct participation by the employees whose jobs are to be enriched. Ideas they have expressed previously certainly constitute a valuable source for recommended changes, but their direct involvement contaminates the process with human relations hygiene and, more specifically, gives them only a sense of making a contribution. The job is to be changed, and it is the content that will produce the motivation, not attitudes about being involved or the challenge inherent in setting up a job. That process will be over shortly, and it is what the employees will be doing from then on that will determine their motivation. A sense of participation will result only in short-term movement.
8. In the initial attempts at job enrichment, set up a controlled experiment. At least two equivalent groups should be chosen, one an experimental unit in which the motivators are systematically introduced over a period of time, and the other one a control group in which no changes are made. Hygiene should be allowed to follow its natural course in each group for the duration of the experiment. Pre- and postinstallation tests of performance and job attitudes are necessary to evaluate the effectiveness of the job enrichment program. The attitude test must be limited to motivator items in order to divorce the employee's view of the job from all the surrounding hygiene feelings.
9. Be prepared for a drop in performance in the experimental group the first few weeks. The changeover to a new job may lead to a temporary reduction in efficiency.
10. Expect your first-line supervisors to experience some anxiety and hostility over the changes you are making. The anxiety comes from their fear that the changes will result in poorer performance for their units. Hostility will arise when the employees start assuming responsibilities for their own performance that the supervisors previously held. The supervisor may then be left with little to do. After a successful experiment, however, the supervi-

sor usually discovers the supervisory and managerial functions that have been neglected or never held because all the supervisor's time was given over to checking the work of subordinates.

Despite Herzberg's empirical findings that tend to support the two-factor theory, controversy persists. In particular, subsequent research relevant to the two-factor theory has produced conflicting results. With some studies that used Herzberg's research methodology, supportive results were achieved. However, for many other studies that used different research methodologies, the two-factor theory was not substantiated. These latter studies support a traditional theory of motivation which asserts that a presence of *both* motivators and hygiene factors contributes to employee satisfaction; and conversely, an absence of motivators and hygiene factors leads to employee dissatisfaction. That is, the impact of motivators and hygiene factors on employee motivation and productivity are not separate and distinct. Consequently, detractors of Herzberg's theory believe that the hygiene factors, as well as the motivators, should be considered in work design to achieve employee satisfaction, increased motivation, and higher productivity.

Individual Differences

The two-factor theory is not the only point of controversy surrounding job enrichment. Some enrichment programs have been very successful, while others have been mediocre at best. This has led many industrial psychologists to postulate that community (environmental) characteristics, individual job differences, and individual employee differences play an important role in determining the success of job enrichment programs. Employee characteristics such as "need for achievement" and "need for social affiliation" have been empirically tested to determine whether they affect employee responses to changes in job design. A study by John E. Stinson and Thomas W. Johnson (1977) indicates that high-need achievers and high-need affiliators are more dissatisfied with highly structured, nonautonomous tasks (i.e., rationalized jobs) than are low-need achievers and low-need affiliators. Such high-need employees tend to respond favorably to job enrichment programs.

Some low-need employees may not be dissatisfied with rationalized jobs. Their outside interests and their needs for security might make them prefer the highly predictable nature of structured work. Consequently, when job enrichment is not feasible or economically practicable, management might attempt to identify low-need employees and assign them highly rationalized jobs.

WORK DESIGN FOR SERVICE ORGANIZATIONS

We have approached work design from two perspectives: from that of an industrial engineer who sees job rationalization leading to greater efficiency at high levels of productivity and from that of an industrial psychologist who sees job rationalization leading to employee boredom and dissatisfaction and consequently to high absenteeism and turnover. Job enrichment programs attempt to counter the ill effects of rationalization by designing factors into work that appeal to the higher-order needs of employees.

Have the engineers or psychologists developed the panacea for work design that we've been seeking? Phrased another way, is there one approach that is universally best, especially as it relates to service jobs? The answer is emphatically no! The unique characteristics of the organization, the employees, the jobs, the services rendered, and the consumers all are important in determining the appropriate rationalization-enrichment mix for a particular situation. To identify the best mix of work design methods, we will look at two different types of service organizations: the professional service organization (PSO) and the routine service organization (RSO).

Professional Service Organizations

PSOs conjure up images of doctors, lawyers, and educators, interacting with their respective patients, clients, and students. But PSOs also rely heavily upon other front-line employees, such as receptionists, assistants, and secretaries. Traditionally, work structure in PSOs is highly enriched. Why is this the case and is it still appropriate?

PSOs are characterized by having a cadre of highly educated employees who are motivated by prestige, self-direction, accomplishment, and the potential for high earnings. These organizations are also unique in that individuals play an important role in image setting and in decision making. That is, the value of the individual to a PSO is often substantial.

Another characteristic of PSOs is the emphasis placed upon personalized service, often with very low volume. The individual qualities of employees, over and above their technical skills, significantly influence the value of the service package. This is seen in the close provider-consumer relationships common to PSOs. Consumers often desire the humanistic touch, and they are willing to pay a premium to get it. The costs of professional services are high, owing in part to the consumers' willingness to pay, but also owing to the very personalized way in which the services are delivered.

The high costs of many professional services leads us to question the appropriateness of their work design. Can PSOs gain anything by rationalizing at least some of their processes? That is, is it preferable to substitute a more routine and perhaps a more technocratic service delivery system for one that may be excessively humanistic? This is a very sensitive question with no clear-cut answer. Consider, for example, health care. Many doctors might argue the need for maintaining the traditional approach for delivering health services that emphasizes the close doctor-patient relationship. Such an approach provides reassurance and psychological comfort to many patients. But there are segments of society, especially those representing the poor, that note the inefficiencies of the traditional health care delivery system. Such inefficiencies, they argue, have resulted in skyrocketing costs that put these services beyond the financial reach of many.

How might some of the advantages of job rationalization be incorporated into PSOs without losing the humanistic element? There is no one best answer, but the following are some avenues that warrant consideration:

1. Conduct a work and organizational audit to:
    a. Identify routine, high-volume operations.
    b. Identify exceptional and disruptive operations.
    c. Identify dominant work flows.
    d. Determine the proportion of time spent in various operations by professionals and by supporting staff.
2. Investigate the implications of eliminating low-volume services, or services that tend to disrupt dominant processes.
3. Identify potential areas for automation. Routine functions generally offer the greatest opportunity.
4. Use paraprofessionals wherever possible to perform tasks presently carried out by the professionals.
5. Stimulate demand for services that have the potential for high volume and that can be routinized.
6. Schedule the contact between consumers and professionals at the end of the service delivery and, when possible, at the beginning. This reassures the consumers that they are receiving personalized treatment.

Routine Service Organizations

RSOs are at the opposite end of the spectrum from PSOs. Typical RSOs are fast-food restaurants, budget hotels, and other service organizations that focus upon providing a standardized, low-cost service to a large number of consumers. In most cases, the personal touch has been eliminated.

Work design in RSOs is appropriate for meeting high volumes of demand very efficiently. Consequently, work is highly rationalized and relies heavily upon having low-skilled, low-paid employees perform a limited variety of repetitive tasks. Jobs are designed so that employees have little or no discretion in determining how they are to be performed. Patrons of RSOs don't expect royal treatment; in fact, they are willing to accept a standardized impersonal service in return for convenient location, speed of delivery, and low cost.

RSOs are often associated with a franchise organization or a chain-store operation. In both cases, a rigid hierarchical organizational structure is common. Local operating managers are monitored by, and have reporting responsibilities to, a central administrative unit. The managers recruit and train low-skilled workers to carry out tasks in accordance with a standard operating manual.

Operating managers who are not franchise holders are generally salaried, but receive bonuses and other rewards based upon productivity as measured by dollar sales. In some exceptional cases, the local operating managers are absorbed into the central administration and thereby afforded the opportunity for advancement up the organizational hierarchy.

Can RSOs gain anything by adopting a program of job enrichment? Experience with enrichment programs certainly indicates that many employees do respond favorably. This is especially true for high-need individuals. And in a highly competitive environment, having motivated and satisfied employees in the front lines can make a difference to consumers.

Previously, we presented Herzberg's suggestions for implementing a job enrichment program. In a more modest vein, it may be desirable for the sake of efficiency and productivity to retain the rationalization mode for many of the processes. But it also may be desirable to temper other processes with elements of job enrichment. Jobs that impact directly upon consumers' perceptions about the value of the service package are prime candidates for enrichment. A consumer survey along with work methods analyses can assist in identifying these jobs. Jobs might also be enriched, providing their redesign does not disrupt the dominant flow of work. But the emphasis for motivating and satisfying employees should first be directed at front-line jobs, which have the greatest potential for influencing the value of the service package.

SUMMARY

We know that service organizations tend to be labor-intensive and that workers play an important role in determining the value of the service package. Consequently, managers should be aware of how work design influences worker performance and attitudes.

We have discussed two basic philosophies of work design: job rationalization and job enrichment. Job rationalization, which has its roots in the industrial revolution, emphasizes routine and repetitive work to increase efficiency. But the job rationalization mode may not consider the social and psychological needs of workers. Consequently, it is attributed with causing worker discontent, high absenteeism, and high turnover.

Job enrichment is a method of work design intended to improve worker attitudes and motivation. The value of jobs to workers is enhanced by satisfying some of the higher-order needs. These might include self-esteem and self-actualization.

We have not suggested that any particular mode of work design is "the best" for service organizations. On the contrary, in designing work, the manager must consider the qualities of workers, the expectations of consumers, and the nature of the service package that is to be conveyed. Some professional service organizations might benefit from job rationalization to improve efficiency, while some routine service organizations might benefit from job enrichment to improve worker attitudes. It is the job of the manager to select the appropriate mix of work-design methods.

TOPICS FOR DISCUSSION

1. How might a manager promote internalization of organizational goals among his personnel?
2. What is the current work ethic?
3. Why does the term "quality of working life" take on new meaning for services?
4. Contrast the management styles for a professional service organization and routine service organization.
5. What is the role of a "checker" in a routine service organization?
6. How does one build in service quality control by organizational design? By job design?
7. Is job rationalization necessarily dehumanizing?
8. Give some examples of methods used to motivate service personnel.
9. Why is it important to design service jobs from a marketing perspective?
10. Contrast the PSO and RSO according to the dimensions of type of product, worker discretion, and role of manager.

EXERCISES

10.1 It is required to estimate the proportion of time when a car wash facility is unused. It is known that the facility is busy for at least 80 percent of the day. A study is conducted for a whole week. If we need an estimate within ±5 percent at a 90 percent confidence level, how many observations are required each day?

10.2 One station attendant serves a full-serve gas station that has a total of three pumps. On the average, a car takes 10 seconds to pull up to a pump; the attendant takes 15 seconds to find out customer needs and begin pumping gas. It takes 40 seconds for the gas to be pumped (attendant is free during this time), and cleaning the windshield takes 15 seconds. Finally, it takes 30 seconds to replace the nozzle back on the pump and for payment to be made. Customers enter the station every 60 seconds (deterministic). Draw a worker-machine chart for a 5-minute observation of this scenario. (A customer goes to an empty pump if available or to any pump otherwise.)

10.3 One of the cleaning staff at the Last Resort Motel was observed making beds at an average rate of eight minutes per bed. The proficiency rating of the staff person is estimated to be 90 percent.

 (*a*) What is the normal time for this task?

 (*b*) If allowance for fatigue and personal needs is 10 percent, what is the standard time for this task?

10.4 The cleaning staff at Last Resort Motel has complained about overwork. Management has decided to conduct a work sampling study to verify their contention that the staff is only busy about 60 percent of the time. The study should yield an estimate of idle time with a ±5 percent degree of accuracy at a 95 percent confidence level.

 (*a*) How many random observations should be taken?

 (*b*) Explain how you would select each observation time during a typical eight-hour day (the study will be conducted for 10 days).

CASELETTE: COUNTY GENERAL HOSPITAL

County General is a large, public hospital serving a major metropolitan area in the growing sunbelt region of the United States. A significant portion of the hospital's budget is consumed by labor costs, and the total number of employees is broken down as follows:

232 DESIGNING THE SERVICE SYSTEM

Administrative and management	18
Professional:	
MDs	67
RNs	145
LVNs	196
Support	368
Total	794

The hospital's top management has been concerned for some time that the labor costs for professional staff, particularly the registered nurses, have not been kept under control as closely as the annual operating plan had envisioned at its inception. In attempting to see how the nursing staff can be better utilized, management has decided to undertake a work sampling study of the registered nurses to see what proportions of their time are actually spent on various tasks.

In designing the study, management established eight general categories of activities for defining the registered nurse's typical workday:

1. Direct patient care
2. Indirect patient care (preparation of medicine, equipment, etc.)
3. Paperwork
4. Communication and teaching
5. Escorting and errands
6. Housekeeping
7. Travel
8. Nonproductive (idle time, meal time, etc.)

Observers who perform the actual sampling will be given lists of specific duties that would define each category and ensure that the study has a high degree of consistency in the allocation of a nurse's daily duties to the correct categories. On the basis of a pilot study, County General's management estimates that the proportions of time spent in each of the above categories are 15, 12, 10, 40, 5, 3, 5, and 10 percent respectively. The study will be conducted over a 14-day period from each of three workshifts, and management wants to ensure that their estimates come within ±2 percent of the true proportions with a 98 percent confidence level.

Questions

1. How many observations will be required to make sure that all the categories have enough data collected to meet the established parameters for accuracy? Assume a normal distribution.
2. The study was accomplished as designed, and the hospital management team was given the summary data shown below:

Category	% of time	Category	% of time
1	13.8	5	3.1
2	12.3	6	4.5
3	11.9	7	3.1
4	39.7	8	11.6

On the basis of your knowledge of hospital functions and the general goal of providing a high level of service to their customers, suggest at least one or two strategies that management might apply to better utilize the time of the registered nursing staff. Describe what effects your strategies might have on time requirements from other staff groups and on the general level of health care in County General.

SELECTED BIBLIOGRAPHY

Bennet, Keith W.: "Lordstown: Putting Some Myths to Rest," *Iron Age*, vol. 211, no. 22, May 1973, p. 33.
Blood, Milton R., and Charles L. Hulin: "Job Enlargement, Individual Differences, and Worker Responses," *Psychological Bulletin*, vol. 69, no. 1, 1968, pp. 41–55.
Chartrand, Phillip J.: "Job Redesign—Progress or Pipedream?" *The Business Quarterly*, vol. 41, no. 4, Winter 1976, pp. 65–77.
Davis, Louis E.: "The Coming Crisis for Production Management: Technology and Organization," *Design of Jobs—Selected Readings*, L. E. Davis and J. C. Taylor (eds.), Penguin Books, Inc., London, 1972, pp. 417–430.
———: "The Design of Jobs," *Industrial Relations*, vol. 6, no. 1, October 1966, pp. 21–45.
———: The Effects of Automation on Job Design," *Industrial Relations*, vol. 2, no. 1, October 1962, pp. 53–71.
———: "Job Design and Productivity: A New Approach," *Personnel*, vol. 33, no. 5, March 1957, pp. 418–430.
———: "Readying the Unready: Post-Industrial Jobs," *Design of Jobs-Selected Readings*, L. E. Davis and J. C. Taylor (eds.), Penguin Books, Inc., London, 1972, pp. 431–447.
———, and Ernst S. Valfer: "Studies in Supervisory Job Design," *Human Relations*, vol. 19, no. 4, November 1966, pp. 339–352.
Emery, F. E., and E. L. Trist: "Socio-Technical Systems," In F. E. Emery (ed.), *Systems Thinking*, Penguin Books, Inc., London, 1969, pp. 281–296.
Ewen, Robert B., Charles L. Hulin, Patricia Cain Smith, and Edwin A. Locke: "An Empirical Test of the Herzberg Two-Factor Theory," *Journal of Applied Psychology*, vol. 50, no. 6, 1966, pp. 544–555.
Farr, James L.: "Incentive Schedules, Productivity, and Satisfaction in Work Groups: A Laboratory Study," *Organizational Behavior and Human Performance*, vol. 17, 1976, pp. 159–170.
———: "Task Characteristics, Reward Contingency, and Intrinsic Motivation," *Organizational Behavior and Human Performance*, vol. 16, no. 2, August 1976, pp. 294–307.
Gibson, Charles H.: "Volvo Increases Productivity Through Job Enrichment," *California Management Review*, vol. 40, no. 4, Summer 1973, pp. 64–66.
Giles, William F.: "Volunteering for Job Enrichment: A Test of Expectancy Theory Predictions," *Personnel Psychology*, vol. 30, 1977, pp. 427–435.
Graen, George B., and Charles L. Hulin: Addendum to "An Empirical Investigation of Two Implications of the Two-Factor Theory of Job Satisfaction," *Journal of Applied Psychology*, vol. 52, no. 4, 1968, pp. 341–342.
Hackman, Richard J., and Greg R. Oldham: "Motivation Through the Design of Work: Test of a Theory," *Organizational Behavior and Human Performance*, vol. 16, 1976, pp. 250–279.
Herzberg, Frederick: "One More Time: How Do You Motivate Employees?" *Harvard Business Review*, vol. 46, no. 1, January–February 1968, pp. 53–62.
Howell, Margaret A.: "Time Off as a Reward for Productivity," *Personnel Administration*, vol. 34, no. 6, November–December 1971, pp. 48–51.
Hulin, Charles L., and Patricia A. Smith: "An Empirical Investigation of Two Implications of the Two-Factor Theory of Job Satisfaction," *Journal of Applied Psychology*, vol. 53, no. 4, 1969, pp. 279–291.
Kilbridge, M. D.: "Do Workers Prefer Larger Jobs?" *Personnel*, vol. 37, no. 5, September–October 1960, pp. 45–48.

Kopelman, Richard E., and Paul H. Thompson: "Boundary Conditions for Expectancy Theory Predictions of Work Motivation and Job Performance," *Academy of Management Journal,* vol. 19, no. 2, June 1976, pp. 237–258.

Lawler, Edward E., III: "Job Design and Employee Motivation," *Personnel Psychology,* vol. 22, no. 4, Winter 1969, pp. 426–435.

Leavitt, Theodore: "Production-Line Approach to Service," *Harvard Business Review,* September–October 1972, pp. 41–52.

Paul, William J., Keith B. Robertson, and Frederick Herzberg: "Job Enrichment Pays Off," *Harvard Business Review,* vol. 47, no. 2, March–April 1969, pp. 61–78.

Prasow, Paul: "Manpower Developments and Requirements in Our New Service Economy," *California Management Review,* Fall 1968, pp. 91–93.

"The Spreading Lordstown Syndrome," *Business Week,* March 4, 1972, pp. 69–70.

Stinson, John E., and Thomas W. Johnson: "Tasks, Individual Differences and Job Satisfaction," *Industrial Relations,* vol. 16, no. 3, October 1977, pp. 315–322.

"Training in Service Occupations," *Monthly Labor Review,* U.S. Bureau of Labor Statistics, May 1966, pp. 523–527.

CHAPTER
ELEVEN

THE QUEUING PHENOMENON

The role of the consumer as a participant in the service process is central to the problem of determining appropriate service capacity. Fluctuations in demand for service are difficult to cope with because the consumption and production of service occur simultaneously. Consumers typically arrive at random and place immediate demands on the available service. If service capacity is fully utilized at the time of arrival, the consumer may be expected to wait patiently in line. Varying arrival rates and service time requirements result in queues (i.e., lines of consumers waiting their turn for service) forming. This queuing phenomenon is a central feature of service operations.

Our investigation of this phenomenon begins with a definition of queuing systems and the inevitability of waiting. The implications of asking people to wait are further studied from a psychological perspective. We shall discover that the perception of waiting is often more important to the consumer than the actual time spent waiting. This suggests that innovative ways should be found to reduce the negative aspects of waiting. The economic value of waiting as a cost for the provider and currency for the consumer is also considered. The features of a service system are discussed in terms of a schematic queuing model and queuing terminology is defined.

QUEUING SYSTEMS

A queue is a waiting line of consumers who require service from one or more servers. The queue need not be a physical line of individuals in front of a server. Instead, it might be students sitting at computer terminals scattered over a college campus or a person being placed on "hold" by a telephone operator. Servers are typically considered individual stations where consumers receive service. The stereotype queue of people waiting in a formal line for service is illustrated by the checkout counters at a supermarket and teller windows at a bank. Yet, queuing systems occur in a variety of forms. Consider the following variations:

1. Servers need not be limited to serving one consumer at a time. Transportation systems, such as buses, airplanes, and elevators, are bulk services.
2. The consumer need not always travel to the service facility; in some systems the server actually comes to the consumer. This approach is illustrated by urban services such as fire, police, and ambulance.

In any service system, a queue forms whenever current demand exceeds the existing capacity to serve. This occurs when the servers are busy so that arriving consumers cannot receive immediate service. Such a situation is bound to occur in any system in which arrivals occur at varying times and service times also vary.

THE INEVITABILITY OF WAITING

Waiting is a part of everyone's life; it can involve an incredible amount of time! For example, a typical day might include waiting at several stop lights, waiting for someone to answer the telephone, waiting for your meal to be served, waiting for the elevator, waiting to be checked out at the supermarket, and the list goes on and on.

In Russia, we find a dramatic example of the role that queuing can play in a person's daily life. As Hedrick Smith observes, the queue is a national pastime.

> Personally, I have known of people who stood in line 90 minutes to buy four pineapples, three hours for a two-minute roller coaster ride, three and half hours to buy three large heads of cabbage only to find the cabbages were gone as they approached the front of the line, 18 hours to sign up to purchase a rug at some later date, all through a freezing December night to register on a list for buying a car, and then waiting 18 more months for actual delivery, and terribly lucky at that. Lines can run from a few yards long to half a block to nearly a mile, and usually they move at an excruciating creep.[1]

There is also a matter of line etiquette as well. Line jumping by serious shoppers is accepted only for ordinary items, but not for scarce ones. Smith continues:

> "People know from experience that things actually run out while they are standing in line," advised one young blonde. "So if the line is for something really good and you leave it for very long, people get very upset. They fly off the handle and curse you and try to keep you from

[1] Hedrick Smith, *The Russians,* Quadrangle Press, New York, 1975, pp. 64–65.

getting back in when you return. It's up to the person behind you to defend your place in line. So it's serious business asking someone to hold your place. They take on a moral obligation not only to let you in front of them later on but to defend you. You have to be stubborn yourself and stand your ground in spite of the insults and the stares. And when you get to the front of the line, if the sales clerks are not limiting the amount, you can hear people, maybe six or eight places back, shouting at you not to take so much, that you are a person with no scruples or that you have no consideration for other people. It can be rather unpleasant."[2]

The Russian queuing experience is far more severe than that found in the United States. However, in any service system waiting is bound to occur. A complete absence of waiting would only be possible in a situation in which consumers are asked to arrive at predetermined intervals and service times are deterministic. Later we will demonstrate that waiting is caused by both the fluctuations in arrival rates and the variability in service times. Thus, delays can be encountered even when arrivals are by appointment, as long as service times vary. This is a common experience for patients waiting in a doctor's office. Waiting also occurs at fast-food restaurants where the variability of service times has been reduced by offering a limited menu, but consumers arrive at random. Therefore, waiting is inevitable and service operations managers must consider how customers in queue are to be treated.

THE PSYCHOLOGY OF WAITING[3]

Waiting is disagreeable because one is forced to be idle and to forego more productive or rewarding pastimes. Indeed, the very act of waiting requires an effort to be patient. Thus, even when consumers have nothing else to do, they detest delays. We shall investigate waiting from the perspective of psychological punishment, ritual insult, and social interaction when waiting with others.

Waiting as Psychological Punishment

Waiting draws attention to time itself because it is an anticipatory state. Waiting is an activity without inherent content; time appears to pass more slowly precisely because it is tentative. The waiting period is often judged to be longer than it actually is, because more attention is paid to time than is ordinarily done during periods of activity. In the absence of anything constructive to do, fantasizing can provide some relief from boredom. However, there are dangers inherent to this. Social customs do not condone gazing aimlessly into space or, worse, appearing to stare at another person. One must remain alert. How often have you honked at the car before you when it failed to move after the traffic signal changed to green?

---

[2] Ibid., p. 67.

[3] Adapted from Barry Schwartz, *Queuing and Waiting*, University of Chicago Press, Chicago, 1975, pp. 167–183.

An alternative to boredom is to engage the consumer in the external world. Background music and magazines found in waiting areas are common diversions. Unfortunately, when the magazines are dated, bland, and tattered from past use, as they frequently are, consumers become only superficially engaged. Consequently, consumers occasionally prepare themselves by bringing a paperback novel or needlepoint to occupy their waiting time more constructively.

A challenging problem is to use waiting time in a constructive manner. When this is not possible, then opportunities for diversion should be provided that minimize the perception of waiting on the part of consumers. Consider the following uses of waiting time:

1. An insightful solution to the problem of waiting for elevators is accomplished by placing mirrors in the hallway. The mirrors give people the opportunity to check their own grooming and also permit the observation of others without looking directly at them.
2. Services that consist of several stages, such as one might find at a diagnostic clinic, can conceal waiting by asking people to walk between successive stages.
3. A constructive use of waiting time is common in dental services when patients are instructed in proper dental hygiene while waiting for the dentist.
4. Restaurants have discovered how profitable waiting for a table can be when they divert customers into the bar.
5. Furnishings in a waiting area can indirectly affect the perception of waiting. The fixed benchlike seating in bus and rail terminals discourages conversation. The light, movable table and chair arrangement found in a European sidewalk cafe brings people together and provides opportunities for socializing.

Waiting as a Ritual Insult

Waiting is an anticipatory condition where the consumer's desires can be consummated only upon the initiative of the server. The server, therefore, has power over the consumer, and waiting acts to reinforce the consumer's subordinate status. To be kept waiting is to acknowledge that one's own time and social worth are less valuable than those of the person who imposes the wait.

Among equals, the ritual apology "Sorry to keep you waiting" follows a greeting to the person having waited. This, of course, is in recognition of the implied insult. However, the powerful are exempt from this ritual observance by which equals protect their dignity. Thus, an apology is seldom provided by the doctor who keeps his patient waiting, and least of all to a clinic patient. The sensitive patient will promptly interpret this as an insult, which will not endear the doctor to him.

The opportunity for service personnel to enlarge their egos at the expense of clients needs to be avoided. Management can approach this problem in a variety of ways:

1. Train employees to be courteous and attentive, perhaps through role playing or sensitivity training.
2. Create an organizational atmosphere that reinforces proper employee attitudes. Management can set the example by showing respect for employees and acknowledging the dignity of the individual.
3. To avoid the appearance of ignoring waiting consumers, train employees to make some initial contact. Airline passengers are greeted at the cabin door and again shortly after takeoff; the flight attendants move through the plane passing out complimentary peanuts.
4. Use the tradition of tipping, the age old incentive to ensure cordial client-employee relations.

Waiting as a Social Interaction

Waiting in line with others adds a new dimension because now an unexpected opportunity for social interaction exists. Appreciating this fact, many airlines provide key club lounges for first-class passengers. For a monthly fee, passengers may obtain the privilege of access to these lounges where one can wait in pleasant surroundings. Relaxing in an atmosphere of dim lights, soft music, and plush leather chairs, conversing with friends, and sipping on a drink, one waits to be informed when the flight is about to be boarded. The popularity of these lounges results from the fact that they make waiting less painful. The attractive features are (1) the opportunity to converse with others, (2) pleasant surroundings, (3) waiting with peers, and (4) removing the anxiety of anticipating the flight boarding call.

One's place in line signifies priority for service. Thus, to wait in a file requires physical protection of one's priority for service. Furthermore, one is constantly reminded of the waiting activity as the line creeps toward the server.

We have found that waiting is more than just a waste of time on the part of the consumer. It consumes psychic energy that results in boredom. Unappreciated waiting may be considered insulting to the consumer. Finally, consumers are sensitive to the environment where they must wait. Service providers should be aware of the psychological aspects of waiting and take appropriate action to alleviate this suffering on the part of their clients as much as possible.

ECONOMICS OF WAITING

The economic cost of waiting can be viewed from two perspectives. For a firm, the cost of keeping an employee waiting may be measured by unproductive wages. For consumers, the cost of waiting is the foregone alternative use of time. To this is added the costs of boredom, anxiety, and other psychic distress.

In a competitive market, excessive waiting or the expectation of long waits can lead to potential lost sales. How often have you driven by a filling station, observed many cars lined up at the pumps, and then decided not to stop? One strategy to avoid lost sales is to conceal the queue from arriving consumers. In the case of restaurants, this is often achieved by diverting people into the bar, a tactic that results in increased sales. Amusement parks, such as Disneyland, require people to pay for their tickets prior to entry into the park when they are unable to observe the waiting lines inside.

The consumer can be considered a resource with the potential to participate in the service process. For example, a patient waiting for a doctor can be asked to complete a medical history record and thereby save valuable physician time (service capacity). The waiting period also could be used to educate the person in good health habits. This can be achieved by making available health publications or film strips. Restaurants are quite innovative in their approach to this problem and actively engage the customer directly in providing the service. For example, after giving your order to a waiter, you are asked to go to the salad bar and prepare your own salad, which you eat while the cook prepares your meal.

Consumer waiting may be viewed as a contribution to productivity by permitting greater utilization of limited capacity. In service systems, higher utilization of facilities is purchased at the price of consumer waiting. Prominent examples can be found in public services such as post offices, medical clinics, and welfare services where high utilization is achieved with long queues.

Yoram Barzel reports the following event to illustrate the economic value of waiting:

> On June 14, 1972, the United States of America Bank (of Chicago) launched an anniversary sale. The commodity on sale was money, and each of the first 35 persons could "buy" a $100 bill for $80 in cash. Those farther down the queue could each obtain similar but declining bonuses: the next 50 could gain $10 each; 75, $4 each; 100, $2 each, and the following 100, $1 each. Each of the next 100 persons could get a $2 bill for $1.60 and, finally, 800 (subsequently, it seems, expanded to 1800) persons could gain $.50 each. The expected waiting time in such an unusual event was unpredictable; on the other hand, it was easy to assess the money value of the commodity being distributed.
>
> First in line were four brothers aged 16, 17, 19, and 24. Since the smallest was 6'2", their priority was assured. "I figured," said Carl, the youngest brother, "that we spent 17 hours to make a $20 profit. That's about $1.29 an hour."
>
> "You can make better than that washing dishes," added another of the brothers. Had they been better informed they could have waited less time. The 35th person to join the line arrived around midnight, had to wait just 9 hours, and was the last to earn $20—$2.22 per hour. To confirm her right, she made a list of all those ahead of her in the line.
>
> "Why am I here?" she asked. "Well, that $20 is the same as a day's pay to me. And I don't even have to declare it on my income tax. It's a gift, isn't it?"[4]

This experience demonstrates that those in line considered their waiting time as the cost of securing a "free" good.

[4] Yoram Barzel, "A Theory of Rationing by Waiting," *The Journal of Law and Economics*, vol. 17, no. 1, April 1974, pp. 73–94.

ESSENTIAL FEATURES OF QUEUING SYSTEMS

Figure 11.1 depicts the essential features of queuing systems. These are (1) calling population, (2) arrival process, (3) queue configuration, (4) queue discipline, and (5) service process.

Services obtain consumers from a calling population. The rate at which they arrive is determined by the arrival process. If servers are idle, then the consumer is immediately attended. Otherwise, the consumer is diverted to a queue, which can have various configurations. At this point, some consumers may *balk* when confronted with a long or slow-moving waiting line and seek service elsewhere. Other consumers, after joining the queue, may consider the delay intolerable, so they *renege*, which means leaving the line before service is rendered. When a server does become available, a consumer is then selected from the queue and service begins. The policy governing the selection is known as the queue discipline. The service facility may consist of no servers (self-service), one or more servers, or complex arrangements of servers in series or parallel. After the service is rendered, consumers depart the facility. At that time, they may either rejoin the calling population for future return or exit with no intentions of returning.

We shall now discuss in more detail each of these five essential features of queuing systems.

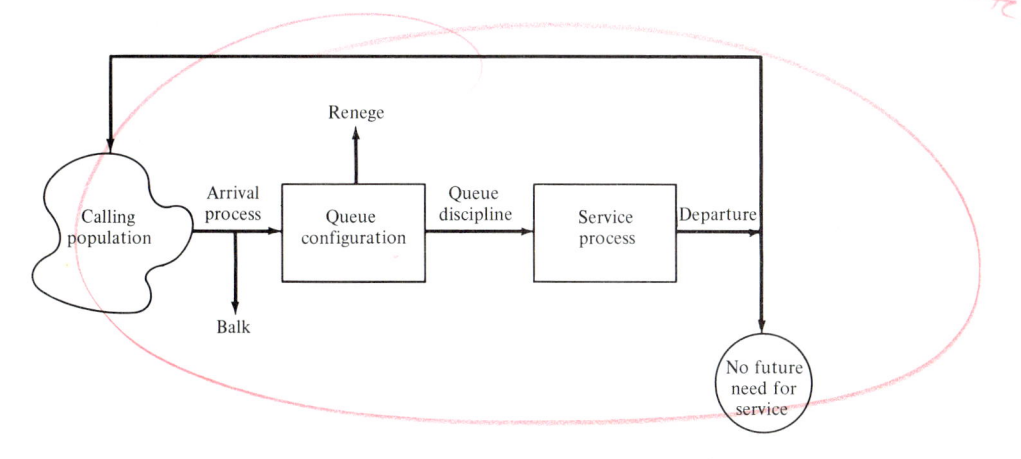

Figure 11.1 Queuing system schematic.

242 DESIGNING THE SERVICE SYSTEM

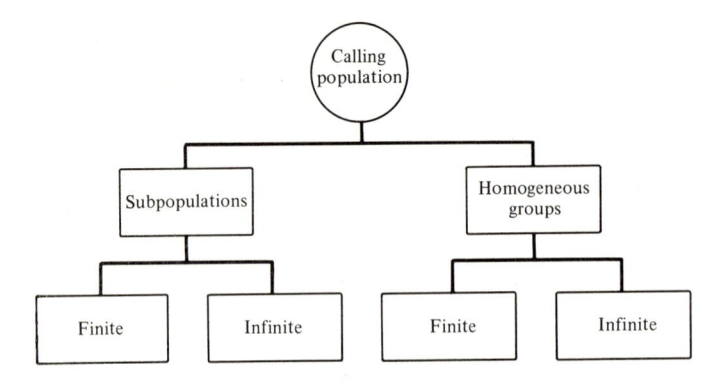

Figure 11.2 Classification of calling population.

Calling Population

The calling population need not be homogeneous but may consist of several subpopulations. For example, the arrivals at an outpatient clinic can be divided into walk-in patients, patients with appointments, and emergency patients. Each patient class will place different demands on services; but more importantly, the waiting expectations of each will differ significantly.

It is possible in some queuing systems for the source of calls to be limited to a finite number of people. Take for example, the demands made upon an office copier by a staff of three secretaries. In this case the probability of future arrivals is dependent upon the number of persons currently in the system seeking service. For instance, the probability of a future arrival becomes 0 once the third secretary joins the copier queue. Clearly, all calling populations are finite. But unless the population is quite small, an assumption of independent arrivals or infinite population usually suffices. In Figure 11.2 a classification of calling population is shown.

Arrival Process

Any analysis of service systems must begin with a complete understanding of the temporal and spatial demand for the service. Typically, data are collected by recording the actual time of arrivals. These data are then used to calculate interarrival times. Many empirical studies indicate that the frequency distribution of interarrival times will have an exponential distribution. The shape of the curve in Figure 11.3 is typical of the exponential distribution. Note the high frequency at the origin and the long tail that tapers off to the right. The exponential distribution can also be recognized by noting that the mean and standard deviation are theoretically equal ($\mu = 2.4$ and $\sigma = 2.6$ for Figure 11.3).

The exponential distribution has a continuous probability density function of the form

$$f(t) = \lambda e^{-\lambda t} \qquad t \geq 0 \qquad (1)$$

where λ = average arrival rate within a given interval of time (e.g., minute, hour, day)
 t = time between arrivals
 e = base of natural logarithms 2.718...

mean = $1/\lambda$
variance = $1/\lambda^2$

The cumulative distribution function is

$$F(t) = 1 - e^{-\lambda t} \qquad t \geq 0 \qquad (2)$$

Equation (2) gives the probability that the time between arrivals will be *t* or less. Note that λ is the inverse of the mean time between arrivals. Thus, for Figure 11.3, the mean time between arrivals is 2.4 minutes, which implies that λ is 0.4167 arrivals per minute (an average rate of 25 patients per hour). The exponential distribution for the data displayed in Figure 11.3 is

$$f(t) = 0.4167 e^{-0.4167 t} \qquad t \geq 0 \qquad (3)$$

and

$$F(t) = 1 - e^{-0.4167 t} \qquad t \geq 0 \qquad (4)$$

Equation (4) can now be used to find the probability that, if a patient has already arrived, another will arrive in the next 5 minutes. We simply substitute $t = 5$, and $F(5) = 1 - e^{-0.4167(5)} = 1 - 0.124 = 0.876$, or an 87.6 percent chance.

Another distribution known as the Poisson has a unique relationship to the exponential distribution. The Poisson distribution is a discrete probability func-

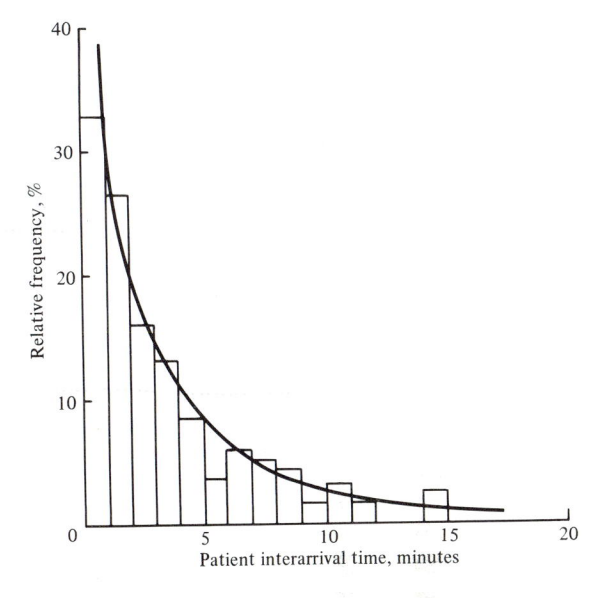

Figure 11.3 Distribution of patient interarrival times for a university health clinic. [*Adapted with permission from E. J. Rising, R. Baron, and B. Averill, "A Systems Analysis of a University Health-Service Outpatient Clinic, Operations Research, September 1972, p. 1038.*]

244 DESIGNING THE SERVICE SYSTEM

Poisson distribution of number of arrivals per hour (top view)

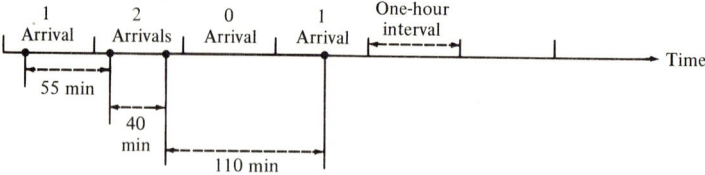

```
  1          2         0         1      One-hour
Arrival   Arrivals  Arrival  Arrival   interval
```

Exponential distribution of time between arrivals in minutes (bottom view)

Figure 11.4 Poisson and exponential equivalence.

tion of the form

$$f(n) = \frac{(\lambda t)^n e^{-\lambda t}}{n!} \qquad n = 0, 1, 2, 3, \ldots \qquad (5)$$

where λ = average arrival rate within a given interval of time (e.g., minutes, hours, days)
t = number of time periods of interest (usually $t = 1$)
n = number of arrivals, $n = 0, 1, 2, \ldots$
e = base of natural logarithms 2.718....

mean = λt
variance = λt

The Poisson distribution gives the probability of n arrivals during the time interval t. For the data of Figure 11.3, an equivalent description of the arrival process is

$$f(n) = \frac{25^n e^{-25}}{n!} \qquad n = 0, 1, 2, \ldots \qquad (6)$$

This gives the probability of 0, 1, 2, ... number of patients arriving during any hour interval. Note that we have taken the option of converting $\lambda = 0.4167$ arrivals per minute to $\lambda = 25$ arrivals per hour.

Figure 11.4 shows the relationship between the Poisson distribution (arrivals per hour) and the exponential distribution (minutes between arrivals). As can be seen, they represent alternative views of the same process.[5] Thus, an exponential distribution of interarrival times with a mean of 2.4 minutes is equivalent to a Poisson distribution of number of arrivals per hour with mean of 25 (i.e., 60/2.4).

Although service demand data are often collected by calculating the interarrival times, they are usually reported as rates per unit time. The demand rate during the unit of time should be stationary with respect to time. Otherwise, the underlying fluctuations in demand rate as a function of time will not be accounted for. This dynamic feature of demand is illustrated in Figure 11.5

---

[5] See Joseph A. Panico, *Queuing Theory*, Prentice-Hall, Inc., Englewood Cliffs, N.J., 1969, for the mathematical equivalence.

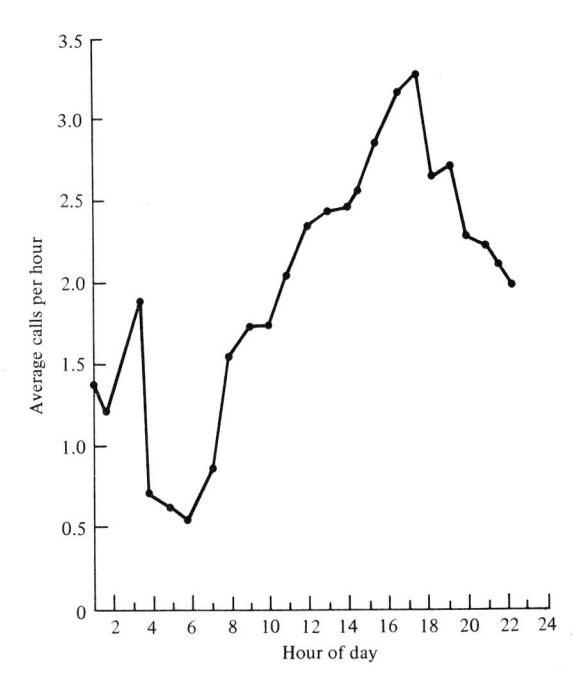

Figure 11.5 Ambulance calls by hour of day. [*Reprinted with permission from James A. Fitzsimmons, "The Use of Spectral Analysis to Validate Planning Models," Socio-Economic Planning, vol. 8, no. 3, June 1974, p. 127. Copyright © 1974, Pergamon Press, Ltd.*]

for hours in a day, in Figure 11.6 for days of the week, and in Figure 11.7 for months of the year.

Variation in demand intensity directly affects the requirements for service capacity. When possible, service capacity is adjusted to match changes in demand, perhaps by varying the staffing levels. Another strategy is to smooth demand by asking customers to make appointments or reservations. Differential pricing is used by the telephone company to encourage callers to use off-peak hours. Movie theaters provide ticket discounts for patrons arriving before 6 p.m. Smoothing demand and adjusting supply are important topics which are covered in depth in Chapter 13. Figure 11.8 presents a classification of arrival processes.

Although our discussion has focused on the frequency of demand as a function of time, the spatial distribution of demand may also vary. This is particularly true of emergency ambulance demand in an urban area which has a spatial shift in demand owing to the temporary population movements from residential areas to commercial and industrial areas during working hours.

Queue Configuration

The queue configuration refers to the number of queues, their locations, their spatial requirements, and their effect on customer behavior. Figure 11.9 illustrates three alternative waiting configurations for a service, such as a bank, post office, or airline counter, where multiple servers are available.

246 DESIGNING THE SERVICE SYSTEM

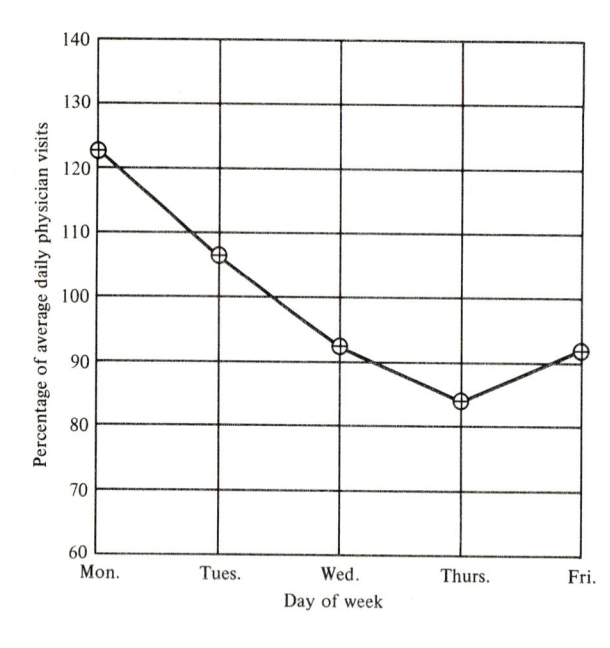

Figure 11.6 Patient arrivals at health clinic by day of week. [*Reprinted with permission from E. J. Rising, R. Baron, and B. Averill, "A Systems Analysis of a University Health-Service Outpatient Clinic," Operations Research, September 1972, p. 1038.*]

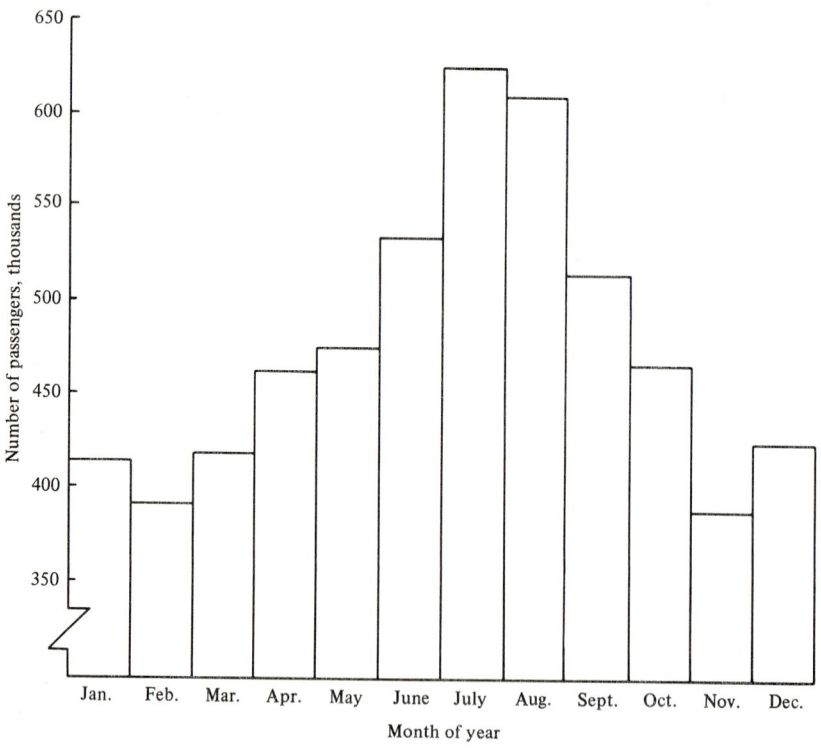

Figure 11.7 International airline passengers by month of year. [*FAA Statistical Handbook of Civil Aviation, 1960.*]

THE QUEUING PHENOMENON **247**

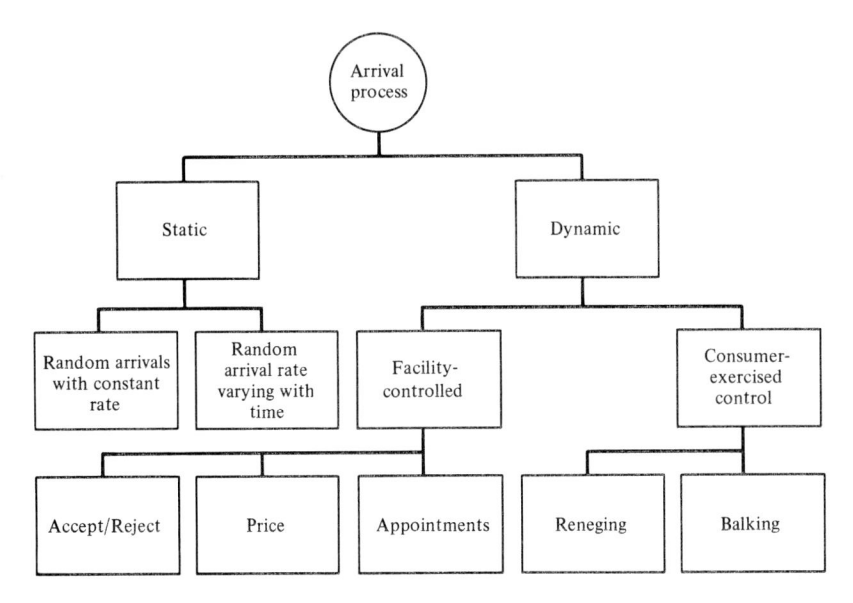

Figure 11.8 Classification of arrival processes.

For the multiple-queue alternative shown in Figure 11.9a, the arriving consumer must decide which queue to join. The decision need not be irrevocable, because one may switch to the end of another line. This line switching activity is called *jockeying*. In any event, watching the line next to you move faster is a source of aggravation. However, the multiple-queue configuration has advantages:

1. The service provided can be differentiated. The use of express lanes in supermarkets is an example. Shoppers with small demands on service can be isolated and processed quickly, and long waits for little service avoided.
2. Division of labor is possible. For example, drive-in banks assign the more experienced teller to the commercial lane.
3. The consumer has the option of selecting the particular server of preference.
4. Balking behavior may be deterred. When arriving consumers experience a long single queue snaked in front of a service, they often interpret this as evidence of a long wait and decide not to join the line.

Figure 11.9b depicts the common arrangement of brass posts with red velvet rope strung between them, forcing arrivals to join one sinuous queue. Whenever a server becomes available, the first person in line moves over to the service counter. This is a popular device found in bank lobbies, post offices, and amusement parks. Its advantages are:

1. The arrangement guarantees fairness by ensuring that a first-come, first-served rule applies to all arrivals.

248 DESIGNING THE SERVICE SYSTEM

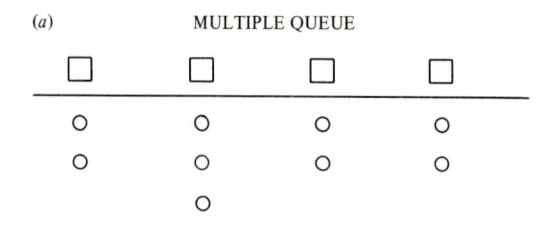

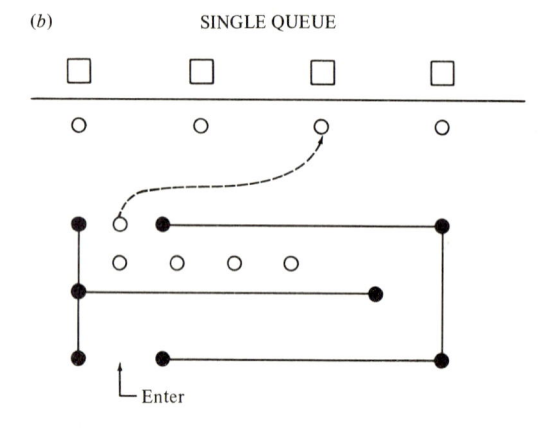

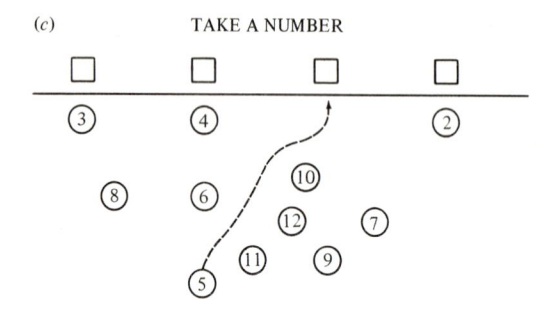

(a) MULTIPLE QUEUE

(b) SINGLE QUEUE

(c) TAKE A NUMBER

Figure 11.9 Alternative waiting-area configurations.

2. There is a single queue, and thus no anxiety is associated with waiting to see if one selected the fastest line.
3. With only one entrance at the rear of the queue, the problem of line cutting is resolved and reneging is made difficult.
4. Privacy is enhanced because the transaction is conducted with no one standing immediately behind the person being served.
5. This arrangement is more efficient in terms of reducing the average time consumers spend waiting in line.

Figure 11.9c illustrates a variation on the single queue in which the arriving consumer takes a number to indicate place in line. With the use of such num-

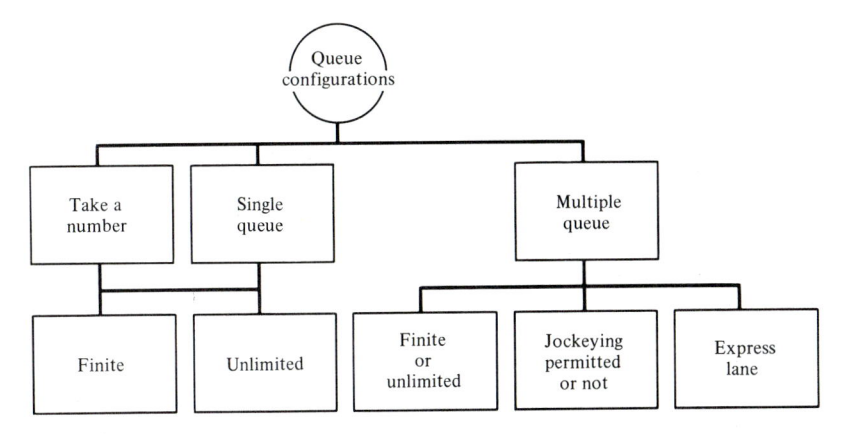

Figure 11.10 Classification of queue configurations.

bers to indicate position in queue, there is no need for a formal line. Consumers are free to wander about, strike up a conversation, relax in a chair, or pursue some other diversion. Unfortunately, they must remain alert to hear their numbers being called or risk missing their turns for service. Bakeries make subtle use of the "take-a-number" system in order to increase impulse sales. Consumers given the chance to browse among the tantalizing pasteries often find they purchase more than the fresh loaf of bread they came for.

If the waiting area is inadequate to accommodate all the consumers desiring service, then they are turned away. This condition is referred to as a finite queue. Restaurants with limited parking may experience this problem to a certain extent. However, a public parking garage is a classic example. Once the last stall is taken, future arrivals are rejected with the word "FULL" until a car is retrieved. Figure 11.10 contains a classification of queue configurations.

Finally, concealment of the waiting line itself may deter customers from balking. Amusement parks often process waiting customers by stages. The first stage is a line outside the concession entrance, the second is an inside vestibule area, and the final stage is the wait for an empty vehicle to convey a party through the amusement.

Queue Discipline

The queue discipline is a policy established by management to select the next consumer from the queue for service. The most popular service discipline is the first-come, first-served (FCFS) rule. This represents an egalitarian approach to serving waiting consumers because all consumers are treated alike. Because no information other than position in line is used to identify the next consumer for service, the rule is considered static.

Dynamic queue disciplines are based on some attribute of the consumer or status of the waiting line. For example, computer installations typically give first priority to waiting jobs with very short processing times. This shortest-processing-time (SPT) rule has the important feature of minimizing the average time a consumer spends in the system.[6] This rule is seldom used in its pure form, because jobs with long operation times would be continually set aside for more recent arrivals with shorter times. By selecting next the job with shortest service time, excessive delays result for jobs with long service times. Typically, arrivals are placed in priority classes on the basis of some attribute, and the FCFS rule is used within each class. An example is the express checkout stand at supermarkets, where orders of less than 10 items are processed. This allows large stores to segment their consumers and thereby compete with the neighborhood convenience stores, which provide prompt service. In a medical setting, the concept known as *triage* is used as a way of giving priority to those who would benefit most from immediate treatment.

The most responsive queue discipline is the preemptive priority rule. Under this rule, the service of a person presently in process is interrupted to serve a newly arrived consumer with higher priority. This is usually reserved for emergency services, such as fire or ambulance services. An ambulance on the way to a hospital to pick up a patient for routine transfer will interrupt this mission to respond to a suspected cardiac-arrest call.

The queue discipline can have an important effect on the likelihood of a waiting consumer reneging. For this reason, information on the expected waiting time might be made available to the arriving consumer and updated periodically for each waiting consumer. This information is usually available to computer center users interested in the status of their jobs waiting in queue to be processed.

Some fast-food chains, like McDonald's, take a more direct approach to avoid consumer reneging. When long lines begin to form, a service person begins to take orders while consumers are still waiting in line. Taking this idea further is the concept of round-robin service used by time-shared computer systems. In this system, a consumer is given partial service and then the server moves on to the next waiting consumer. Thus, consumers alternate between waiting and being served. Figure 11.11 shows a classification of queue disciplines.

Service Process

The distribution of service times, the arrangement of servers, management policies, and server behavior all contribute to service performance. Figure 11.12 contains histograms of several service time distributions in an outpatient clinic. As can be seen, the distribution of service times may be of any form. Conceivably, the service time could be a constant, such as the time to process a car through an automated car wash. However, when the service is brief and simple to perform (e.g., service at a fast-food restaurant, collecting tolls at a bridge, checking out at a supermarket), the distribution of service times frequently is

---

[6] Richard W. Conway, William L. Maxwell, and Louis W. Miller, *Theory of Scheduling*, Addison-Wesley Pub. Co., Reading, Mass., 1967, p. 27.

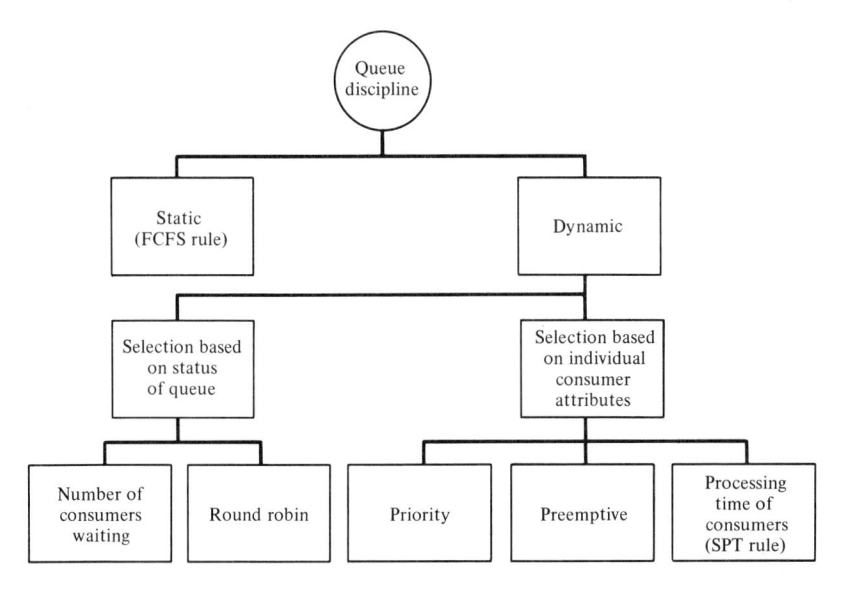

Figure 11.11 Classification of queue disciplines.

exponential (see Figure 11.3). The histogram for second service times, Figure 11.12c, most closely approximates an exponential distribution. The second service times represent those brief encounters in which, for example, the physician prescribes a medication or goes over your test results with you. The distribution of service times is a reflection of the variations in customer needs and server performances.

Table 11.1 illustrates the variety of service facility arrangements that are possible. With servers in parallel, management gains flexibility in meeting the variations in demand for service. Management can effectively vary the service capacity by opening and closing service lines to meet changes in demand. At a bank, additional teller windows are opened when the length of queues becomes excessive. Cross-training employees adds to this flexibility. For example, at supermarkets stockers are often used as cashiers when lines become long at the checkout stands. A final advantage of parallel servers is that they provide redundancy in case of equipment failures.

The behavior of service personnel toward consumers is critical to the success of the organization. Under pressure of long waiting lines, the server may speed up and spend less time with each customer. Unfortunately, a gracious and leisurely manner then becomes curt and impersonal. Sustained pressure to hurry may increase the rate of consumer processing, but it also sacrifices quality. This behavior on the part of a pressured server can have a detrimental effect on other servers in the system. For example, a busy emergency telephone operator may dispatch yet another patrol car before properly screening the call for its critical nature. In this situation, the operator should have spent more time than usual to ensure that the limited resources of patrol cars were being

252 DESIGNING THE SERVICE SYSTEM

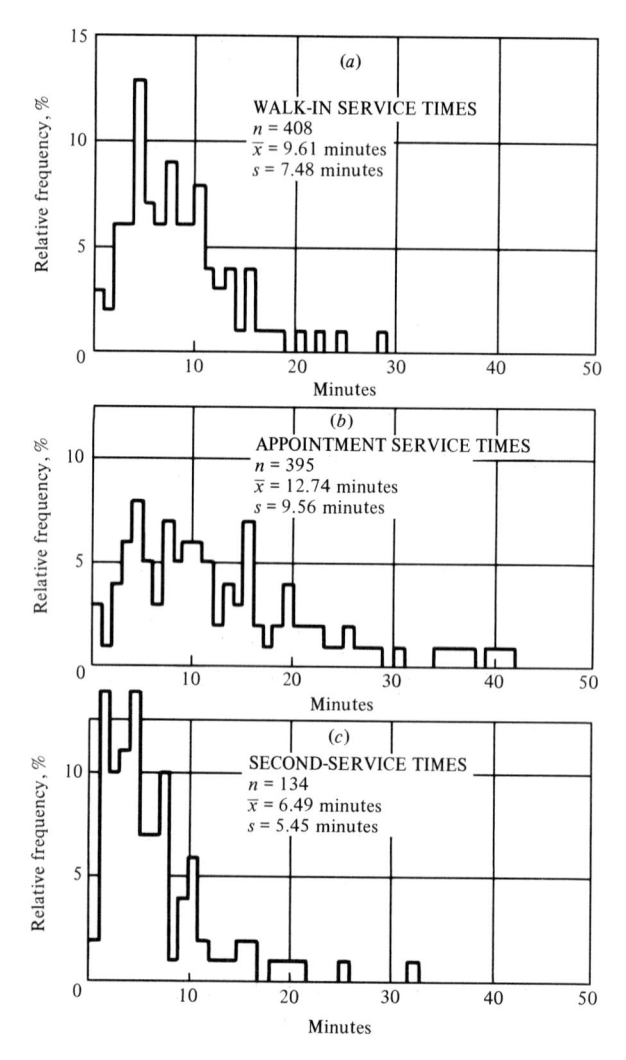

Figure 11.12 Histograms of outpatient-clinic service times. [*Reprinted with permission from E. J. Rising, R. Baron, and B. Averill, "A Systems Analysis of a University Health-Service Outpatient Clinic, Operations Research, September 1972, p. 1038.*]

(a) WALK-IN SERVICE TIMES
$n = 408$
$\bar{x} = 9.61$ minutes
$s = 7.48$ minutes

(b) APPOINTMENT SERVICE TIMES
$n = 395$
$\bar{x} = 12.74$ minutes
$s = 9.56$ minutes

(c) SECOND-SERVICE TIMES
$n = 134$
$\bar{x} = 6.49$ minutes
$s = 5.45$ minutes

Table 11.1 Service facility arrangements

Service facility	Server arrangement
Parking lot	Self-serve
Cafeteria	Servers in series
Toll booths	Servers in parallel
Supermarket	Self-serve first stage, parallel servers second stage
Hospital	Many service centers in parallel and series, not all used by each patient

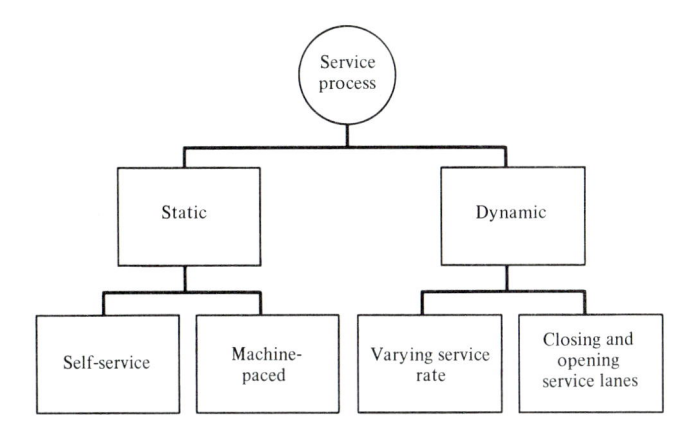

Figure 11.13 Classification of service processes.

dispatched to the most critical cases. Figure 11.13 suggests a classification of service processes.

SUMMARY

An understanding of the queuing phenomenon is necessary before creative approaches to the management of service systems can be considered. An appreciation of the behavioral implications of keeping consumers waiting reveals that the perception of waiting is often more important than the actual delay.

A schematic queuing model identified the essential features of queuing systems as calling population, arrival process, queue configuration, queue discipline, and service process. We have discovered that an understanding of each feature provides insights and identifies management options for improving consumer service.

In the next chapter we will study several analytical queuing models that are useful for predicting consumer waiting times. These models will suggest further insights that will be helpful in capacity planning and scheduling decisions.

TOPICS FOR DISCUSSION

1. Suggest some strategies for controlling the variability in service times.
2. Suggest diversions that could make waiting less painful.
3. Select a bad and good waiting experience and contrast the situations with respect to the aesthetics of the surroundings, diversions, people waiting, and attitude of servers.
4. Suggest ways that service management can influence the arrival times of consumers.
5. At some fast-food restaurants, when the lines become long, an order taker will walk up the line taking orders. What are the benefits of this policy?

CASELETTE: THRIFTY-RENT-A-CAR

Thrifty-Rent-A-Car has become one of the southwest's major rental agencies even though it competes with several national agencies. It is definitely the largest regional company, with offices and outlets in 19 cities and 5 states, located primarily in the airport terminals of those major cities. Thrifty's rental fleet consists almost entirely of fuel-efficient compact and subcompact automobiles. Its clientele utilizes the vehicles for tourism and business purposes, obtaining service at any location with or without prior arrangements. Although Thrifty does lose customers on occasion when the desired vehicles are unavailable at a given location, this "stockout" situation occurs less than 10 percent of the time.

The service counter where customers are processed by Thrifty's personnel is a simple design, which varies only in the number of cubbyholes used to keep various forms within easy reach of the servers. In the smaller markets, Thrifty uses a maximum of three people at one time behind the counter, but in the largest markets, this number could be as many as eight when demand is heaviest. Usually these peak demand times are reflective of the airport's inbound-outbound flight schedule, and, as they occur, one or more attendants may deal exclusively with clients who have made prior arrangements to pick up a vehicle or with those who are returning vehicles. When this situation exists, these attendants hang appropriate messages above their chosen stations to indicate their special service functions to clientele. Because the speed of customer service is an important factor in maintaining its competitive edge, Thrifty's management and service personnel have worked very hard to ensure that each client is processed without unnecessary delay.

Another important factor in Thrifty's competitive stance is its ability to turn incoming vehicles around and have them quickly prepared for new clients. The following is a list of the steps necessary to process a vehicle for turnaround from incoming delivery to outgoing delivery: (1) confirmation of odometer reading, (2) refueling and confirming fuel charge, (3) visual damage inspection, (4) priority assessment, (5) interior cleaning, (6) maintenance assessment, (7) maintenance and checkout, (8) exterior cleaning and polishing, (9) lot storage and refueling, and (10) delivery to customer.

When a client returns a vehicle to any location, one of Thrifty's crew will confirm the odometer reading, drive about 200 meters to the service lot and confirm any fuel charge necessary to refill the car's tank. The crew member will immediately relay the information to all attendants so that the client may complete payment and be released as soon as possible. (If the crew member notices any interior or exterior damage to the vehicle, the attendant will notify the manager on duty; the client must clarify his or her responsibility in the circumstances and may be delayed while this is going on.) After this step, the fleet supervisor assigns a priority status to incoming cars, based upon the company's known (certain) demand and reserve policy (for walk-up clients): high priority treatment for those cars needed within the next six-hour period and normal treatment for everything else. Vehicles assigned a high priority get preferential treatment in servicing.

After the vehicle's interior is thoroughly cleaned and sprayed with a mild air freshener, a mechanic examines the vehicle's maintenance record, gives it a test drive, and notes on a form any maintenance actions deemed necessary. Thrifty has certain policies covering periodic normal maintenance, like oil and filter changes, tire rotation and balancing, lubrication, coolant replacement, engine tune-ups, etc. Major special maintenance actions, such as brake repair, transmission repair or adjustment, or air-conditioning–heating repair, are performed as needed.

Every garage in Thrifty's system is a standard side-by-side three-bay design; two of the bays are always used for normal maintenance and the third is used for either normal or special maintenance. About 20 percent of the time is spent on special maintenance in this third bay. In general, Thrifty uses a team of five mechanics for its garages: one master mechanic (who is the garage manager), two journeyman mechanics, and two apprentices. The apprentices are responsible for all normal maintenance items except the engine tune-up; they are stationed to service every vehicle in each outside bay, and they alternate on vehicles placed in the middle bay. The journeyman mechanics are responsible for all other maintenance and also alternate servicing vehicles in the middle bay.

After servicing, the vehicles are moved outside, where the car wash is located, and a team of two people washes, rinses, and buffs the exterior to ensure that it has a good appearance. Because part of the rinse cycle contains a wax-type liquid compound, the vehicles do not usually require time-consuming wax jobs. From this point, each vehicle's fuel tank is again topped off and the vehicle is placed in the lot for storage. When called for by an attendant, a driver will take the vehicle to the rental area of the airport terminal for the client to pick it up.

Assignment

On the basis of your experience and the description of Thrifty's operations, describe the five essential features of the queuing systems at the customer counter, the garage, and the car wash.

SELECTED BIBLIOGRAPHY

Barzel, Yoran: "A Theory of Rationing by Waiting," *The Journal of Law and Economics,* vol. 17, no. 1, April 1974, pp. 73–94.

Budnick, Frank S., Richard Mojena, and Thomas E. Vollmann: *Principles of Operations Research for Management,* Richard D. Irwin, Inc., Homewood, Ill., 1977.

Conway, Richard W., William L. Maxwell, and Louis W. Miller: *Theory of Scheduling,* Addison-Wesley Pub. Co., Reading, Mass., 1967.

Fitzsimmons, James A.: "The Use of Spectral Analysis to Validate Planning Models," *Socio-Economic Planning,* vol. 8, no. 3, June 1974, pp. 123–128.

Hall, Edward T.: *The Hidden Dimension,* Doubleday and Co., Inc., Garden City, N.Y., 1969.

Panico, Joseph A.: *Queuing Theory,* Prentice-Hall, Inc., Englewood Cliffs, N.J., 1969.

Rising, E. J., R. Baron, and B. Averill: "A Systems Analysis of a University Health-Service Outpatient Clinic," *Operations Research,* September 1972, pp. 1030–1047.

Schwartz, Barry: *Queuing and Waiting,* University of Chicago Press, Chicago, 1975.

Smith, Hedrick: *The Russians,* Quadrangle Press, New York, 1975.

CHAPTER
TWELVE

QUEUING MODELS AND CAPACITY PLANNING

The capacity planning decision involves a tradeoff between the cost of providing service and the cost or inconvenience of consumer waiting. The cost of service capacity is determined by the number of servers available, while consumer inconvenience is measured by waiting time. Figure 12.1 illustrates this tradeoff, under the assumption that a monetary cost can be attributed to waiting. Increasing service capacity typically results in lower waiting costs and higher service costs. If the combined costs constitute our planning criterion, then an optimal service capacity minimizes these combined costs.

Unfortunately, the monetary cost of waiting is often difficult and sometimes impossible to determine. In a hospital the cost of keeping a surgical team waiting for a pathologist's report could be the combined salaries of the team members plus the operating-room cost. But the cost of keeping a patient waiting in a reception room for the doctor is not easily calculated. Furthermore, as noted in Chapter 11, the circumstances affect the perception of waiting.

The tradeoff between consumer waiting and service capacity can be seen in many everyday occurrences. For example, an emergency ambulance seldom is busy more than 30 percent of the time. Such low utilization is required to provide assistance on a moment's notice. Excess ambulance capacity is necessary because the implicit cost of waiting for service may be exorbitant in terms of human lives. However, the usual scene at a post office is lines of impatient people waiting for service. Here a judgment has been made that the implicit cost of waiting is not critical, certainly not life-threatening. The result is harried servers and waiting customers.

258 DESIGNING THE SERVICE SYSTEM

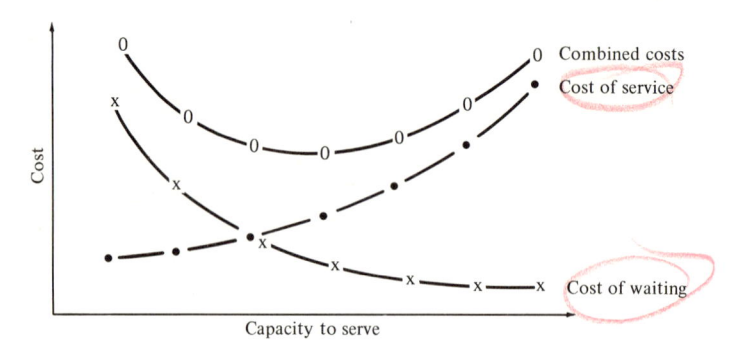

Figure 12.1 Economic tradeoff in capacity planning.

In order to plan for service capacity, it is necessary to predict the degree of consumer waiting associated with different levels of capacity. A number of analytical queuing models have been developed that can be used to make these waiting time predictions. The models are analytical in that for each case a number of formulas have been derived. Given a minimal amount of data, in particular the mean arrival rate and mean service rate, the formulas can generate characteristics of the system, such as the average time a customer should expect to wait. From these calculations, capacity decisions, such as determining the size of a parking lot, can be made. In addition, the queuing models help explain the queuing phenomenon. For example, the models can predict the results of adding servers to a multiple server system or show the effect on waiting time of reducing service time variation. Formulas for selected queuing models are listed at the end of this chapter.

ANALYTICAL QUEUING MODELS

On the basis of our discussion of the queuing phenomenon, it is evident that a large number of different queuing models exist. A popular system proposed by D. G. Kendall classifies parallel-server queuing models and uses the following notation in which three features are identified:

$$A/B/C$$

A represents the distribution of time between arrivals, B describes the distribution of service times, and C is the number of parallel servers. The descriptive symbols used for the arrival and service distributions include the following:

M = exponential interarrival or service time distribution (or the equivalent Poisson distribution of arrival or service rate)
D = deterministic interarrival or service time
E_k = Erlang distribution with shape parameter k (If $k = 1$, then Erlang is

equivalent to exponential and if $k = \infty$ then the Erlang is equivalent to deterministic)

G = general distribution (e.g., normal, uniform, or any empirical distribution)

Thus, $M/M/1$ designates a single-server queuing model with Poisson arrival rate and exponential service times. The Kendall notation will be used to define the class to which a queuing model belongs. Further considerations will be noted that are particular to the model in question. For each queuing model, the assumptions underlying its derivation will be noted. The usefulness of an analytical model for a particular situation is limited by its assumptions. If the assumptions are invalid for a particular application, then one typically resorts to a computer simulation approach.

A final consideration involves the concepts of *transient state* and *steady state*. A system is in a transient state when the values of the operating characteristics depend upon time. In steady state the system characteristics are independent of time and the system is considered in statistical equilibrium. System characteristics are usually transient during the early stages of operation because of their dependence on initial conditions. For example, compare the initial conditions for a department store at opening time on a normal business day and on an end-of-year sale day, when crowds overwhelm clerks. The number in queue will initially be quite large, but given a long enough period of time the system will eventually settle down. Once normal conditions have been reached a statistical equilibrium is achieved in which the number in queue assumes a distribution independent of the starting condition. All the queuing model formulas given at the end of the chapter assume a steady state has been reached. Several popular queuing models and their applications in decison-making settings follow.

Standard *M/M/1* Model

Every queuing model requires specific assumptions with respect to the queuing system features previously discussed in Chapter 11 (i.e., calling population, arrival process, queue configuration, queue discipline, service process). The application of any queuing model, therefore, should include validation with respect to these assumptions. The derivation of the standard $M/M/1$ model requires the following set of assumptions about the queuing system:

1. *Calling population.* An infinite or very large population of callers arriving independently of each other and not influenced by the queuing system (e.g., appointment is not required)
2. *Arrival process.* Negative exponential distribution of interarrival times or Poisson distribution of arrival rate
3. *Queue configuration.* Single waiting line with no restrictions on length and no balking or reneging

4. *Queue discipline.* First-come, first-served
5. *Service process.* One server with negative exponential distribution of service times

Using the selected formulas given at the end of the chapter, performance characteristics can be calculated on the basis of only the mean arrival rate λ and the mean service rate per server μ. These formulas clearly indicate why the traffic intensity $\rho = (\lambda/\mu)$ must always be less than 1 for a single-server model. If this condition were not true and $\lambda = \mu$, the mean values for the operating characteristics would be undefined because all the formulas have denominators of $(\mu - \lambda)$. The system would theoretically never reach steady state. In general, the capacity to serve, represented by μ times the number of servers, must always exceed the demand rate λ.

Example 12.1: Boat ramp A recreational site has one launching ramp for people who trailer their small boats to fish. A study of people arriving to fish indicates a Poisson distribution with mean rate of $\lambda = 6$ boats per hour during the morning launch. A test of the data collected on launch times suggests that an exponential distribution with mean of six minutes per boat (equivalent service rate $\mu = 10$ boats launched per hour) is a good fit. If the other assumptions for a $M/M/1$ model apply (infinite calling population, no queue length restrictions, no balking or reneging, and a FCFS queue discipline), then the formulas may be used to calculate the system characteristics. Traffic intensity at the site is $\rho = 0.6$, which means the ramp is busy 60 percent of the time. Thus, arrivals can expect immediate service without delay 40 percent of the time, or when the ramp is idle. Formula (I.8) at the end of the chapter indicates that expected waiting time in queue is $W_q = 0.15$ hours, or 9 minutes. Expected time in the system on the basis of formula (I.7) is $W_s = 0.25$ hours, or 15 minutes, which is equivalent to adding the expected waiting time of 9 minutes to the mean service time of 6 minutes. Arrivals would expect to find the number in the system, calculated from formula (I.4), to be $L_s = 1.5$ boats; and the expected number in queue, from formula (I.5), to be $L_q = 0.9$ boats. The expected number of boats in queue plus the expected number being launched should add up to the expected number of boats in the system. However, the expected number of boats being launched is not 1, the number of servers, but instead is calculated as follows:

$$\begin{aligned}\text{Expected number} \atop \text{being served} &= {\text{expected number} \atop \text{when idle}} + {\text{expected number} \atop \text{when busy}} \\ &= P_0(0) + P(n > 0)(1) \\ &= (1 - \rho)(0) + \rho(1) \\ &= \rho\end{aligned}$$

Adding $\rho = 0.6$ consumers on the average being served and 0.9 on the average in queue, we get the expected 1.5 consumers in the system.

Note that the number n of consumers in the system is a random variable with a geometric probability distribution given by formula (I.3) at the end of the chapter and repeated below.

$$P_n = (1 - \rho)\rho^n \qquad (I.3)$$

The number of consumers in the system can also be used to identify states of the system. For example, when $n = 0$, the system is idle; for $n = 1$ the server is busy but no queue exists; and for $n = 2$ the server is busy and a queue of 1 has formed. This probability distribution can be very useful for determining the size of a waiting room (number of chairs) required to accommodate arriving consumers with a certain probability of assurance that they will find a vacant chair. For the boat-ramp example let us determine the number of parking spaces needed to assure us that 90 percent of the time a person arriving to fish will find a parking space while waiting to launch. Using the probability distribution for system states repeatedly for increasing values of n, the system state probabilities are accumulated until 90 percent assurance is exceeded. Table 12.1 contains these calculations and indicates that a system state of $n = 4$ or less will occur 92 percent of the time. This suggests that room for four boat trailers should be provided because 92 percent of the time arrivals will find three (four less one being served) or fewer people waiting in queue to launch.

Finite-Queue $M/M/1$ Model

A modification of the standard $M/M/1$ model may be made by introducing a restriction on the allowable number of consumers in the system. Suppose N represents the maximum number of consumers allowed in the system or, in a single-server model, $N - 1$ indicates the maximum number of consumers in the queue. Thus, if the consumer arrives at a point in time when N consumers are in the system, then the arrival departs without seeking service. An example of this type of finite queue is a telephone exchange in which callers are put on hold until such time as all the trunk lines are in use and any further callers receive a

Table 12.1 Calculating required waiting area

n	P_n	P (number of consumers $\leq n$)
0	0.4	0.4
1	0.24	0.64
2	0.144	0.784
3	0.0864	0.8704
4	0.05184	0.92224

busy signal. Except for this one characteristic of finite capacity, all the assumptions of the standard $M/M/1$ model still hold. Note that the traffic intensity ρ can now exceed unity. Furthermore, P_N represents the probability of not joining the system and λP_N is the expected number of customers lost. This particular model is very useful in estimating expected lost sales because of inadequate waiting area or excessive queue length. In the boat-ramp example assume that the waiting area can only accommodate two boat trailers and thus $N = 3$ for the system. Using formulas (II.1) and (II.3) at the end of the chapter, the probabilities of 0, 1, 2, and 3 consumers in the system are calculated below when $N = 3$ and $\rho = 0.6$.

n	Calculation	P_n
0	$\left(\dfrac{1-0.6}{1-0.6^4}\right)(0.6)^0$	0.46
1	$(0.46)(0.6)^1$	0.27
2	$(0.46)(0.6)^2$	0.17
3	$(0.46)(0.6)^3$	0.10
		1.00

Notice that the above distribution totals 1.00 and thus indicates that all possible system states have been accounted for. System state $n = 3$ occurs 10 percent of the time. With an arrival rate of 6 people per hour, 0.6 people per hour (6 × 0.10) will find inadequate waiting space and look elsewhere for a launching site. Using formula (II.4) at the end of the chapter, the expected number in the system is $L_s = 0.9$. This figure is much smaller than the unlimited-queue case because on the average only 90 percent of the arrivals are processed.

M/G/1 Model

For this model any general service time distribution with mean $E(t)$ and variance $V(t)$ may be used. The condition that ρ be less than 1 still applies for the steady state, where ρ now equals $\lambda E(t)$. All the assumptions for the standard $M/M/1$ model except for the generality of the service time distribution apply. Unfortunately, a formula does not exist for determining the system state probabilities. However, the list at the end of the chapter does contain formulas for L_s, L_q, W_s, and W_q. Formula (III.2) is repeated below because the appearance of the service time variance term $V(t)$ provides some interesting insights.

$$L_q = \frac{\rho^2 + \lambda^2 V(t)}{2(1-\rho)} \qquad \text{(III.2)}$$

Clearly the expected number of consumers waiting for service is directly related to the variability of service times. This suggests that consumer waiting can be reduced by controlling the variability in service times. For example, the limited menu of fast-food restaurants contributes to their success because the small variety of foods they offer allows for standardization of service.

Recall that the variance of the exponential distribution is $1/\mu^2$ and notice that substituting this value for $V(t)$ in formula (III.2) yields $L_q = \rho^2/(1 - \rho)$, which is equivalent to formula (I.5) for the standard $M/M/1$ model. Now consider the $M/D/1$ model with a deterministic service time and zero variance. Again, according to formula (III.2), when $V(t) = 0$, then $L_q = \rho^2/[2(1 - \rho)]$. Thus, one-half of the congestion measured by L_q is explained by the variation in service times. This implies that the variability in time between arrivals accounts for the other half of the congestion. Thus, considerable potential exists for reducing congestion simply by using appointments or reservations to control the variability in arrivals. Congestion in a queuing system is caused equally by variability in service times and in interarrival times, so strategies for controlling congestion should address both sources.

Standard $M/M/c$ Model

The assumptions for this model are the same as those for the standard $M/M/1$ model with the stipulation that service rates across channels are independent and equal; that is, all servers are considered identical. As before $\rho = \lambda/\mu$; however, now ρ must be less than c, the number of servers, in order for steady-state results to occur. If we define the system utilization factor as $\lambda/c\mu$, then for any system in steady state the utilization factor must range between 0 and 1. Figure 12.2 illustrates the characteristic curves for L_s as a function of the utilization factor and c, the number of parallel servers. These curves graphically demonstrate the excessive congestion that occurs as one attempts to gain full utilization of service capacity.

The curves can also be used to demonstrate the disproportional gain that occurs when congestion is reduced by adding parallel servers. For example, consider a single-server system ($c = 1$), with 0.8 utilization factor. From Fig-

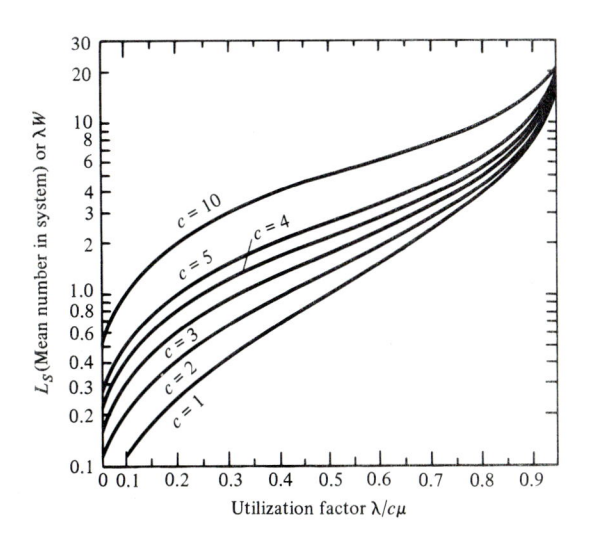

Figure 12.2 $M/M/c$ model curves for L_s.

ure 12.2 the value of $L_s = 4$. By adding another identical server, a two-channel system is created and the utilization factor is reduced by one-half to 0.4. Figure 12.2 gives $L_s \simeq 1$ [actually $L_s = 0.95$, from formula (IV.4)]. A 400 percent reduction in congestion is achieved by only doubling the number of servers. Figure 12.2 suggests that this disproportionate reduction in congestion is most pronounced at high utilization levels. Congestion increases rapidly for utilization factors above 0.8.

Now, instead of creating a two-channel system, just double the service rate of the single-server system and thus reduce the utilization factor to 0.4. Figure 12.2 gives $L_s \simeq 0.67$ for this superserver system. However, this additional gain in reducing L_s is obtained at the cost of increasing the expected number in queue (from $L_q = 0.15$ to 0.27), as seen in Table 12.2. This is not surprising because a single-server system would require more people to wait in line. In a multiple-server system of equal capacity, more people are able to be in service, and thus, fewer wait in line. Therefore, the decision to use one superserver or the equivalent capacity with several servers in parallel depends upon the concern for expected waiting time in queue (L_q/λ) or expected time in system (L_s/λ). As indicated in the earlier discussion of the psychology of waiting, a concern for reducing the waiting time in queue is usually advisable, particularly if people must physically wait in line. Furthermore, once service begins, the consumer's attitude toward time changes because now the consumer is the center of attention. However, the concept of using one large computer system to serve an entire university community is often justified because short turnaround time (time in system) and large memory are of primary importance.

Consolidating the entire service capacity into one superserver is one approach to achieving economies of scale in services. Another approach is the concept of pooling services. Pooling is accomplished by gathering together independent servers at one central location to form a single service facility with multiple servers.

Example 12.2: The secretarial pool A small business school has assigned a secretary to each of its four departments: accounting, finance, marketing, and management. The secretaries type class materials and correspondence

Table 12.2 Effects of doubling service capacity

System characteristic	Single-server baseline system	Two-server system	Single-superserver system
ρ	0.8	0.8	0.4
$(\lambda/c\mu)$*	0.8	0.4	0.4
L_s	4.0	0.95	0.67
L_q	3.2	0.15	0.27

* Utilization factor.

only for their own departmental faculty. The dean has received complaints from the faculty about delays in getting work accomplished, particularly from the accounting faculty. The dean assigns an assistant to collect data on arrival rates and service times. Upon analyzing the data, the assistant reports that secretarial work arrives with a Poisson distribution at an average rate of $\lambda = 2$ requests per hour for all departments except accounting, which has an average rate of $\lambda = 3$ requests per hour. The average time to complete a piece of work is 15 minutes, regardless of its source, and these times are exponentially distributed.

Because of budgeting limitations no additional secretaries can be hired. However, the dean believes the service could be improved if all the secretaries were pooled and instructed to receive work from the entire business school faculty. All work requests would be received at one central location and processed on a first-come, first-served basis by the first secretary that becomes available regardless of departmental affiliation. Before proposing the plan to the faculty, the dean asks the assistant who collected the data to analyze and compare the performance of the existing system with the pooling alternative.

The present system is essentially four $M/M/1$ independent single-channel queuing systems, each with a service rate of $\mu = 4$ requests per hour. The appropriate measure of system performance would be the expected time in the system, or turnaround time from the faculty viewpoint. The difference in arrival rates should explain why the accounting faculty is particularly concerned about delays. Using formula (I.7), we find for the present system of independent departmental secretaries that accounting faculty members experience a $W_s = 1.0$-hour, or 60-minute, average turnaround time and the other departments experience a $W_s = 0.5$-hour, or 30-minute, average turnaround time.

The proposal to pool the secretarial staff creates a multiple-channel single-queue system, or $M/M/4$ in this case. The arrival rate is the combined arrivals (2 + 2 + 2 + 3) from all departments, or $\lambda = 9$ requests per hour. Using formula (IV.1) with $c = 4$ and $\rho = \frac{9}{4}$, the value of P_0 is calculated:

$$P_0 = \frac{1}{\left[\frac{(9/4)^0}{0!} + \frac{(9/4)^1}{1!} + \frac{(9/4)^2}{2!} + \frac{(9/4)^3}{3!}\right] + \frac{(9/4)^4}{4!(1 - 9/16)}}$$

$$= \frac{1}{\left(1 + 9/4 + \frac{81/16}{2} + \frac{729/64}{6}\right) + \frac{6561/256}{24(7/16)}}$$

$$= \frac{1}{7.68 + 2.44}$$

$$= 0.10$$

Using formula (IV.4), the value of L_s is calculated:

$$L_s = \frac{(9/4)^5}{(4-1)!\,(4-9/4)^2}(P_0) + \frac{9}{4}$$

$$= \frac{59{,}049/1024}{6(1.75)^2}(0.10) + 2.25$$

$$= 0.314 + 2.25$$

$$= 2.564$$

$$W_s = \frac{L_s}{\lambda} = \frac{2.564}{9} = 0.28 \text{ hours, or 17 minutes}$$

The substantial reduction in expected turnaround time from 30 minutes (60 minutes for accounting faculty) to 17 minutes should easily win faculty approval.

The benefits from pooling are achieved by better utilization of idle secretaries. Under the departmental system four independent queues existed, which allowed situations to develop where a secretary in one department could be idle, while a secretary in another department could be burdened with a long waiting line of work. If a waiting request could be transferred to the idle secretary, then it would be immediately processed. Switching to a single queue avoids this problem by not allowing a secretary to become idle until the waiting line of requests is empty.

The success of pooling service resources comes from realizing that congestion results from the variation in the rate of arrivals and variation in service times. By taking a total systems perspective of the process, temporary idleness at one location can be used to reduce congestion at another location, caused by a temporary surge in demand or time-consuming requests. Furthermore, server idleness that can be but is not put to use represents lost service capacity and results in a deterioration of service quality, as measured by customer waiting. The concept of pooling need not apply only to servers who are at different locations. The common practice in banks and post offices of having customers form a single queue rather than line up in front of the individual windows represents an application of the pooling concept. Theoretically the average waiting time is reduced from that of permitting multiple queues; however, the single long line may give arriving customers the impression of long waits. This is the reason McDonald's gave for abandoning the idea: it was feared customers would balk upon seeing the long line.

Pooling service facilities at one location should be undertaken with some caution if consumers must physically travel to the facility. In this case the expected travel time to the facility should be included with the expected waiting time in queue when evaluating the proposal. For emergency services, dispersing the servers throughout the service area is generally preferred to locating all services at one central location. An emergency ambulance system is a particularly good example of this need for physically dispersed servers in order to minimize response time.

Finite-Queue $M/M/c$ Model

This model is similar to the finite-queue $M/M/1$ model with the exception that N, the maximum number in the system, must be equal to or greater than c, the number of servers. An arriving consumer is rejected if the number in the system is equal to N or the length of the queue is $N - c$. All the other assumptions for the standard $M/M/c$ model hold except ρ can now exceed c. Because excess consumers are rejected, the system can reach steady state, even when the capacity to serve is inadequate to meet total demand (i.e., $\lambda > c\mu$).

An interesting variation on this model is the no-queue situation, which occurs when no possibility exists for a consumer to wait because a waiting area is not provided. This situation can be modeled as a finite-queue system with $N = c$. A parking lot is an illustration of this no-queue situation. If we consider each parking space as a server, then, at the point when the parking lot is completely full, there no longer exists an opportunity for further service and future arrivals must be rejected. If c equals the number of parking spaces, then the parking lot system can be modeled as a no-queue variation of the finite-queue $M/M/c$ model.

General Self-Service $M/G/\infty$ Model

If there is an infinite number of servers in a multiple-server system or if arrivals serve themselves, a situation is created where no arriving consumer must wait for service. This of course describes exactly the concept that has made the modern supermarket so popular. At least during the shopping portion (excluding checkout), consumers do not experience waiting. The number of consumers in the process of shopping does vary because of random arrivals and differing service times. The probability distribution of the number of consumers in the system can be calculated by means of formula (VI.1). Note that this distribution for P_n is in fact Poisson, with mean or L_s equal to ρ. It is interesting to note that this model is not restricted to an exponential distribution of service times.

The model is also useful as an approximation to describe circumstances where waiting may occur, but only rarely, as in emergency ambulance services. Using the Poisson distribution of number of consumers in the system, the number of servers required to ensure that the probability of someone waiting is quite small can be determined.

> **Example 12.3: Supermarket** The typical supermarket can be viewed as two queuing systems in tandem. The arriving consumer secures a shopping cart and proceeds to serve himself or herself by picking items from the shelves. Upon completing this task, the shopper joins a single queue (a new idea to reduce waiting caused by multiple queues) behind the checkout registers.

The checker tallies the bill, makes change, and sacks the groceries. The shopper then exits the system, perhaps with the assistance of a carryout person. T. L. Saaty's observation that departures from the standard $M/M/c$ queuing system are also Poisson-distributed suggests that the supermarket system can be analyzed as two independent systems.[1] The first subsystem consists of a self-service system $M/M/\infty$, and the second system at the checkout registers is an $M/M/c$ system. Observation of consumer behavior indicates that arrivals are Poisson with a rate of 30 per hour and shopping is completed in 20 minutes on the average with exponential distribution. The shoppers then join the single queue behind the three checkout registers and wait until a register becomes available. The checkout process requires five minutes on the average, with exponential distribution.

For the $M/M/\infty$ model with $\rho = \frac{30}{3}$, formula (VI.2) indicates $L_s = 10$ consumers engaged in the shopping activity on the average.

Using formula (IV.1) with a $p = \frac{30}{12}$, or 2.5, $P_0 = 0.045$. Formula (IV.4) yields $L_s = 6$ customers on the average in the $M/M/3$ checkout subsystem. Thus, on the average there are 16 shoppers in the store.

GENERAL RELATIONSHIPS BETWEEN SYSTEM CHARACTERISTICS

In concluding the discussion of queuing models, it is necessary to point out that there are some general relationships between the average system characteristics that exist across all models. The first two relationships are definitional in nature.

First, the expected number in the system should equal the expected number in queue plus the expected number in service, or

$$L_s = L_q + E(\text{number in service}) \qquad (1)$$

Note that E(number in service) is not the number of servers but equals ρ for all models except the finite queue case.

Second, the expected time in the system should equal the expected time in queue plus the expected time in service, or

$$W_s = W_q + \frac{1}{\mu} \qquad (2)$$

where $1/\mu$ is the reciprocal of the service rate.

The characteristics for a busy system are conditional values based on the probability that the system is busy, or $P(n \geq c)$. Thus the expected number in queue for a busy system is simply the expected number under all system states

---

[1] T. L. Saaty, *Elements of Queuing Theory with Applications*, McGraw-Hill Book Co., New York, 1961.

divided by the probability of the system being busy, or

$$L_b = \frac{L_q}{P(n \geq c)} \quad (3)$$

Similarly the expected waiting time in queue for a busy system is

$$W_b = \frac{W_q}{P(n \geq c)} \quad (4)$$

Furthermore, it has been shown that the following relationship exists between the expected number in the system and the expected time in the system:[2]

$$W_s = \frac{1}{\lambda} L_s \quad (5)$$

and also between the expected number in queue and expected waiting time:

$$W_q = \frac{1}{\lambda} L_q \quad (6)$$

When applying equations (5) and (6) for systems with a finite queue, an effective arrival rate must be used for λ. For a system with a finite queue the effective arrival rate is $\lambda(1 - P_N)$.

These relationships are quite important because they permit derivation of all the system average characteristics from the knowledge of one characteristic obtained by analysis or by collecting data on actual system performance.

CAPACITY PLANNING CRITERIA

Queuing theory indicates that, in the long run, the capacity to serve must exceed the demand for service. If not, at least one of the following adjustments must occur:

1. Excessive waiting by consumers will result in some reneging (i.e., the consumer leaves the queue before being served) and, thus, in some reducing of demand.
2. Excessive waiting, if known or observed by potential consumers, will cause them to reconsider their need for service and will reduce demand.
3. Under pressure of long waiting lines, the servers may speed up, spend less time with each consumer, and, thus, increase service capacity. However, a gracious and leisurely manner now becomes curt and impersonal.
4. Sustained pressure to hurry may result in eliminating time-consuming fea-

---

[2] J. D. C. Little, "A Proof of the Queuing Formula: $L = \lambda W$," *Operations Research*, 1961, vol. 9, pp. 383–387. Also W. S. Jewell, "A Simple Proof of $L = \lambda W$," *Operations Research*, 1967, vol. 15, pp. 1109–1116 and S. Stidham, Jr., "A Last Word on $L = \lambda W$," *Operations Research*, 1974, vol. 22, pp. 417–421.

tures and performing the bare minimum and, thus, increase service capacity.

These uncontrolled situations result from inadequate service capacity, which can be avoided by rational capacity planning.

Several approaches to capacity planning are explored using different criteria for evaluating service system performance. Determining the desired level of service capacity implies a tradeoff between cost of service and cost of customer waiting, as suggested by Figure 12.1. Thus, capacity analysis will utilize the queuing models to predict customer waiting for various levels of service.

Average Consumer Waiting Time

This criterion for capacity planning can be appropriate in several circumstances. For example, a restaurant owner may wish to promote liquor sales in the bar and, therefore, stipulates that consumers must be kept waiting for a table five minutes on the average. It has been suggested that, because a watch face is typically divided into five-minute increments, people waiting in line may not realize how long they have been waiting until at least five minutes have passed. Therefore in designing a drive-in bank facility, it may be advisable to have consumers wait no more than five minutes on the average for service. In a study of a health clinic the appointment system was changed to meet increasing demand, while maintaining the same average waiting time for patients.[3] In these cases the use of the $M/M/c$ model or computer simulation would be appropriate to identify the service level in terms of number of servers that would guarantee the desired expected consumer waiting time.

Example 12.4: Drive-in bank Excessive congestion is a problem during the weekday noon hour at a downtown bank drive-in facility. Bank officials fear consumers may take their accounts elsewhere unless service is improved. A study of consumer arrivals during the noon hour indicates an average arrival rate of 30 per hour with Poisson distribution. Banking transactions take three minutes on the average with exponential distribution. Because of the drive-in facility layout, arriving consumers must select one of the existing three lanes for service. Once in a lane it is impossible to renege or jockey between lanes because of medians separating the lanes. Assuming arriving consumers select lanes at random, the system can be treated as parallel, independent, single-channel queuing systems with the arrival rate divided evenly among the tellers. If the bank officers agree to a criterion that consumers should wait on the average no more than five minutes, how many drive-in tellers are required? Because we are concerned

---

[3] E. J. Rising, R. Baron, and B. Averill, "A Systems Analysis of a University Health-Service Outpatient Clinic," *Operations Research,* September 1972, pp. 1030–1047.

QUEUING MODELS AND CAPACITY PLANNING

Table 12.3 Expected time in queue for bank teller alternatives

No. tellers	λ per teller	μ	W_b, min
3	10	20	6
4	7.5	20	4.8

only with consumers who actually wait, formula (I.9) is appropriate. Table 12.3 indicates that one additional teller is required to meet the service criterion.

Probability of Excessive Waiting

For public services that have difficulty identifying the economic cost of waiting, a service level is often specified. The service level is stated in a manner such that at least P or more percent of all consumers should experience a delay less than T time units. For example, a federal guideline states that the response time for 95 percent of all ambulance calls should be less than 10 minutes for urban systems and less than 30 minutes for rural systems. The Public Utilities Commission gives a similar performance criterion for telephone service. The commission directs that telephone service must be provided at a resource level such that an incoming call can be answered within 10 seconds 89 percent of the time. A probability distribution of delays is required to identify service levels that will meet these probabilities of not exceeding a certain excessive delay. Formulas for these delay probabilities are available for the standard $M/M/c$ model.[4] However, for the case when no delay is desired ($T = 0$), then formula (IV.3) for $P(n \geq c)$ can be used to find a value for c such that the probability of immediate service is at least P percent.

Example 12.5: Self-serve gas station A retail gasoline distributor plans to construct a self-service filling station on vacant property leading into a new housing development. On the basis of the traffic in the area, the distributor forecasts a demand of 48 cars per hour for a typical hour. The distributor believes this demand is equally divided between those seeking regular and unleaded fuels. Time studies conducted at other sites reveal an average self-service time of five minutes for a driver to fill the tank, pay the cashier, and drive away. The service times are exponentially distributed, and past experience justifies assuming an arrival rate with a Poisson distribution. Because of the two types of fuels, the queuing system can be modeled as two independent $M/M/c$ systems in parallel, each with a mean arrival rate of $\lambda = 24$ customers per hour. The distributor believes the success of self-service stations is due to competitive gasoline prices and to the consumers'

---

[4] T. L. Saaty, *Elements of Queuing Theory with Applications,* McGraw-Hill Book Co., New York, 1961.

Table 12.4 Probability of finding all gas pumps in use

c	P_0	$P(n \geq c)$
3	0.11	0.44
4	0.13	0.26
5	0.134	0.11
6	0.135	0.04

desire for fast service. Therefore, the distributor would like to install enough regular and unleaded pumps to guarantee that arriving consumers will find a free pump at least 95 percent of the time. Formula (IV.3) with $\rho = \frac{24}{12} = 2$ is used to calculate the probability of consumer delay for various values of c which indicate the number of pumps that will yield a probability of delay less than 5 percent. These calculations are summarized in Table 12.4. Note that the calculations are begun with a value of $c = 3$ to ensure a feasible system. The results suggest six pumps be installed for regular gas and six for unleaded.

Minimize the Sum of Consumer Waiting Costs and Service Costs

If both consumers and servers are members of the same organization, then the costs of providing service and employee waiting are of equal importance to the organization's effectiveness. This situation arises, for example, when organizations rely on a captive service, such as a secretarial pool or computer service facility. In these cases the cost of employees' waiting time is at least equal to their average salary. In fact, the cost could be considerably more if all the implications of waiting were assessed, such as the frustration of not completing a task or the effect of delays on others in the organization.

The economic tradeoff depicted in Figure 12.1 best describes this situation where the capacity to serve may be increased by adding servers. As servers are added, the cost of service increases but is offset by a corresponding decrease in the cost of waiting. Adding both costs results in a convex total-cost curve that identifies a service capacity with minimum combined costs. The queuing models are used to predict the expected waiting time of employees for different levels of capacity with these values substituted in the total-cost function below.

Assuming linear cost functions for service and waiting and comparing alternatives based on steady-state performance, the total cost per unit of time (hour) is given by

Total cost per hour = hourly cost of service + hourly waiting cost

$$TC = C_s C + C_w \lambda W_s$$
$$= C_s C + C_w L_s \qquad (7)$$

where
C = number of servers
C_s = hourly cost per server
C_w = hourly cost of waiting per customer

Recall that equation (5) converts λW_s, the number of arriving customers per hour times the average waiting time per customer, to its equivalent L_s. For equation (7), waiting is defined as time in system; however, if waiting in queue is more appropriate, then L_q is substituted for L_s. In situations where service is self-serve, such as using a copying machine or computer terminal, waiting in queue might be justified.

Example 12.6: Computer-terminal selection The director of a large engineering staff is considering the rental of several computer terminals that will permit the staff to interact directly with the computer. On the basis of a survey of the staff, the director finds that the department will generate, on the average, 8 requests per hour for service, and the engineers estimate the average computer analysis will require 15 minutes. A computer terminal adequate for these needs rents for $10 per hour. Considering the average salary of the engineering staff, the cost of keeping an engineer idle is $30 per hour. For the basis of a "quick-and-dirty" analysis, the director assumes the requests for service are Poisson distributed and user times are exponentially distributed. Furthermore, the engineering staff is large enough to assume an infinite calling population. Using the $M/M/c$ model, the calculations in Table 12.5 are performed.

Table 12.5 Total cost of computer-terminal alternatives

C	P_0	L_q	$C_s C$	$C_w L_q$	TC
3	0.11	0.88	$30	$26.4	$56.4
4	0.13	0.17	40	5.1	45.1
5	0.134	0.04	50	1.2	51.2
6	0.135	0.01	60	0.3	60.3

Notice that L_q is used instead of L_s in the calculations because the computer terminals are self-serve. The results indicate that four terminals will minimize the combined costs of rent for the terminals and salary for the waiting engineers.

Probability of Sales Lost because of Inadequate Waiting Area

This planning decision deals with the capacity of the waiting area rather than the capacity to serve. An inadequate waiting area may cause potential consumers to balk and to seek service elsewhere. This problem is of particular concern where the waiting area can be seen by arriving consumers, such as the parking lot at a restaurant or the drive at a drive-in bank. Analysis of these systems uses the finite-queue models to estimate the number of balking consumers.

If N represents the maximum number of consumers allowed in the system, then P_N is the probability of a consumer arriving to find the system full. Thus, P_N represents the probability of sales lost because of an inadequate waiting area and λP_N represents the expected number of sales lost per unit of time. The cost of sales lost owing to inadequate waiting area can now be compared with the possible investment in additional space.

Example 12.7: Downtown parking lot A parking lot is a multiple-server queuing system without a queue; that is, the lot can be considered a service system in which each parking space is a server. After the lot is full, subsequent arrivals are rejected because the system has no provision for a queue. Thus, a parking lot is a finite-queuing system with a queue capacity of zero because N equals c. With this model in mind, an enterprising student notices the availability of a vacant lot in the central business district. The student learns from a real estate agent that the owner is willing to rent the property for $50 a day as a parking lot until a buyer is found. After making some observations of traffic in the area, the student finds that approximately 10 cars per hour have difficulty finding space in the parking garage of the department store across the street from this lot. The garage attendant reports that customers spend approximately one hour shopping in the store. For purposes of calculating the feasibility of this venture, the student assumes the arrivals are Poisson-distributed and shopping times are exponentially distributed. The student is interested in what potential business is being lost because the lot has room for only six cars.

This parking lot case can be considered an *M/M/c* queuing system with no provision for a queue. Therefore, the formulas for the finite-queue *M/M/c* model are calculated with $c = N$. Substituting for $c = N$ in formulas (V.1), (V.2), (V.4), and (V.7) yields the following results for the no-queue case. No other formulas are applicable.

$$P_0 = \frac{1}{\sum_{i=0}^{c} \frac{\rho^i}{i!}} \qquad (8)$$

$$P_n = \frac{\rho^n}{n!} P_0 \qquad (9)$$

$$L_s = \rho(1 - P_N) \qquad (10)$$

$$W_s = 1/\mu \quad \text{(Note: } L_q = 0\text{)} \qquad (11)$$

With $\rho = 10$, $P_0 = 0.00035$ and $P_6 = 0.485$, so on the average $\lambda P_6 = 4.85$ potential consumers per hour find the lot full. Therefore, this lot with a capacity of six cars serves approximately one-half the demand.

Expected Profit on Last Unit of Capacity Should Just Exceed Expected Loss

This capacity planning criterion does not rely upon the use of queuing models but, rather, upon an economic principle called *marginal analysis*. This approach is useful when a capacity decision must be made in which there are losses associated both with inadequate capacity and excess capacity. This capacity problem typically arises during the facility design phase, such as when decisions are made concerning the seating capacity of a restaurant or movie theater. In addition to an estimate of the unit profit per consumer and possible loss, the analysis requires a probability distribution for the service demand.

The marginal analysis criterion, as shown below, requires the expected profit on the last sale to exceed the expected loss on the last sale.

$$E(\text{profit on last sale}) \geq E(\text{loss on last sale})$$

$$(\text{unit profit}) \cdot P(\text{profit}) \geq (\text{unit loss}) \cdot P(\text{loss})$$

$$\pi \cdot P(d \geq x) \geq L \cdot P(d < x)$$

$$\geq L \cdot [1 - P(d > x)]$$

$$P(d \geq x) \geq \frac{L}{\pi + L} \tag{12}$$

where π = unit profit from sale
L = unit loss from not making sale
d = demand
x = capacity to serve

Given a probability distribution of demand, equation (12) suggests that capacity should be set such that the probability of demand exceeding capacity is the ratio of unit loss to the sum of unit profit and unit loss.

Example 12.8: Paradise Tours Paradise Tours has been offering a Hawaiian adventure package each summer for the past several years that has attracted a good, though variable-sized group of vacationers from the local university. A review of past records suggests that the demand for this tour is normally distributed with mean of 50, standard deviation of 10, and no trend indicated. Paradise Tours reserves seats with a regularly scheduled airline at a special reduced affinity-group rate. This policy enables the airline to attract small groups not large enough to charter an entire plane. The airline also allows the travel agent to charge a $50 service fee in addition to the ticket price. However, a major concern of Paradise is the $10 charge by the airline for each unsold reserved seat. The airline is concerned about tying up seats during the peak season and also wants to prevent oversubscription by travel agents. Paradise has been reserving 50 seats and finds it has no record of ever paying the $10 overbooking charge. Should it continue this reservation policy?

Using equation (12), the following probability is calculated:

$$P(d \geq x) \geq 10/(50 + 10) = 0.167$$

From Table C at the back of the book, Areas of a Standard Normal Distribution, the z value for 0.167 in one tail is 0.97. Thus the number of seats to reserve is:

$$\text{Reserve seats} = \mu + z\sigma$$
$$= 50 + (0.97)(10)$$
$$\approx 60$$

SUMMARY

When the assumptions are met, analytical queuing models can help service system managers evaluate possible alternative courses of action by predicting waiting time statistics. The models also provide insights that help explain such queuing phenomena as pooling, the effect of finite queues on realized demand, the nonproportional effects on waiting time of adding servers, and the importance of controlling demand as seen by reducing service time variance. The approach to capacity planning is found to be dependent upon the criterion of system performance used. Further, queuing models are useful in the analysis because of their ability to predict system performance. However, if the queuing model assumptions are not met or the system is too complex, then computer simulation modeling is required.

FORMULAS FOR SELECTED QUEUING MODELS

Definition of Symbols

n = number of units in system

λ = mean arrival rate (units per time period)

μ = mean service rate (units per time period)

ρ = traffic intensity (λ/μ)

N = maximum number allowed in system

c = number of servers

P_n = probability of n units in system

L_s = steady-state mean number of units in system

L_q = steady-state mean number of units in queue

L_b = steady-state mean number of units in queue for busy system
W_s = steady-state mean time in system
W_q = steady-state mean time in queue
W_b = steady-state mean time in queue for busy system

I. Standard $M/M/1$ Model[5]

$$P_o = 1 - \rho \tag{I.1}$$

$$P(n > 0) = \rho \tag{I.2}$$

$$P_n = P_o \rho^n \tag{I.3}$$

$$L_s = \frac{\lambda}{\mu - \lambda} \tag{I.4}$$

$$L_q = \frac{\rho \lambda}{\mu - \lambda} \tag{I.5}$$

$$L_b = \frac{\lambda}{\mu - \lambda} \tag{I.6}$$

$$W_s = \frac{1}{\mu - \lambda} \tag{I.7}$$

$$W_q = \frac{\rho}{\mu - \lambda} \tag{I.8}$$

$$W_b = \frac{1}{\mu - \lambda} \tag{I.9}$$

II. Finite-Queue $M/M/1$ Model

$$P_o = \begin{cases} \dfrac{1 - \rho}{1 - \rho^{N+1}} & \text{for } \lambda \neq \mu \\ \dfrac{1}{N + 1} & \text{for } \lambda = \mu \end{cases} \tag{II.1}$$

$$P(n > 0) = 1 - P_o \tag{II.2}$$

$$P_n = P_o \rho^n \quad \text{for } n \leq N \tag{II.3}$$

$$L_s = \begin{cases} \dfrac{\rho}{1 - \rho} - \dfrac{(N + 1)\rho^{N+1}}{1 - \rho^{N+1}} & \text{for } \lambda \neq \mu \\ \dfrac{N}{2} & \text{for } \lambda = \mu \end{cases} \tag{II.4}$$

[5] Note: $0 < \rho < 1.0$.

$$L_q = L_s - (1 - P_o) \tag{II.5}$$

$$L_b = \frac{L_q}{1 - P_o} \tag{II.6}$$

$$W_s = \frac{L_q}{\lambda(1 - P_N)} + \frac{1}{\mu} \tag{II.7}$$

$$W_q = W_s - \frac{1}{\mu} \tag{II.8}$$

$$W_b = \frac{W_q}{1 - P_o} \tag{II.9}$$

III. Standard M/G/1 Model[6]

$$L_s = L_q + \rho \tag{III.1}$$

$$L_q = \frac{\rho^2 + \lambda^2 V(t)}{2(1 - \rho)} \tag{III.2}$$

$$W_s = \frac{L_s}{\lambda} \tag{III.3}$$

$$W_q = \frac{L_q}{\lambda} \tag{III.4}$$

IV. Standard M/M/c Model[7]

$$P_o = \frac{1}{\left(\sum_{i=0}^{c-1} \frac{\rho^i}{i!}\right) + \frac{\rho^c}{c!\left(1 - \frac{\rho}{c}\right)}} \tag{IV.1}$$

$$P_n = \begin{cases} \frac{\rho^n}{n!} P_o & \text{for } 0 \leq n \leq c \\ \left(\frac{\rho^n}{c!c^{n-c}}\right) P_o & \text{for } n \geq c \end{cases} \tag{IV.2}$$

$$P(n \geq c) = \frac{\rho^c \mu c}{c!(\mu c - \lambda)} P_o \tag{IV.3}$$

$$L_s = \frac{\rho^{c+1}}{(c-1)!(c-\rho)^2} P_o + \rho \tag{IV.4}$$

$$L_q = L_s - \rho \tag{IV.5}$$

[6] Note: $V(t)$ = service time variance.
[7] Note: $0 < \rho < c$.

$$L_b = \frac{L_q}{P(n \geq c)} \qquad \text{(IV.6)}$$

$$W_s = \frac{L_q}{\lambda} + \frac{1}{\mu} \qquad \text{(IV.7)}$$

$$W_q = \frac{L_q}{\lambda} \qquad \text{(IV.8)}$$

$$W_b = \frac{W_q}{P(n \geq c)} \qquad \text{(IV.9)}$$

V. Finite-Queue $M/M/c$ Model

$$P_o = \frac{1}{\left(\sum_{i=0}^{c} \frac{\rho^i}{i!}\right) + \left(\frac{1}{c!}\right)\left(\sum_{i=c+1}^{N} \frac{\rho^i}{c^{i-c}}\right)} \qquad \text{(V.1)}$$

$$P_n = \begin{cases} \dfrac{\rho^n}{n!} P_o & \text{for } 0 \leq n \leq c \\[2mm] \dfrac{\rho^n}{c!\,c^{n-c}} P_o & \text{for } c \leq n \leq N \end{cases} \qquad \text{(V.2)}$$

$$P(n \geq c) = 1 - P_o \sum_{i=0}^{c-1} \frac{\rho^i}{i!} \qquad \text{(V.3)}$$

$$L_s = \frac{P_o \rho^{c+1}}{(c-1)!(c-\rho)^2}\left[1 - \left(\frac{\rho}{c}\right)^{N-c} - (N-c)\left(\frac{\rho}{c}\right)^{N-c}\left(1 - \frac{\rho}{c}\right)\right]$$
$$+ \rho(1 - P_N) \qquad \text{(V.4)}$$

$$L_q = L_s - \rho(1 - P_N) \qquad \text{(V.5)}$$

$$L_b = \frac{L_q}{P(n \geq c)} \qquad \text{(V.6)}$$

$$W_s = \frac{L_q}{\lambda(1 - P_N)} + \frac{1}{\mu} \qquad \text{(V.7)}$$

$$W_q = W_s - \frac{1}{\mu} \qquad \text{(V.8)}$$

$$W_b = \frac{W_q}{P(n \geq c)} \qquad \text{(V.9)}$$

VI. Self-Service $M/G/\infty$ Model

$$P_n = \frac{e^{-\rho}}{n!} \rho^n \qquad \text{for } n \geq 0 \qquad \text{(VI.1)}$$

$$L_s = \rho \qquad \text{(VI.2)}$$

$$W_s = \frac{1}{\mu} \qquad \text{(VI.3)}$$

TOPICS FOR DISCUSSION

1. For a queuing system with a finite queue the arrival rate can exceed the capacity to serve. Explain and illustrate with an example how this is feasible.
2. What are some disadvantages associated with the concept of pooling service resources?
3. Capacity planning using queuing models is usually applied to strategic decisions, not day-to-day operations. Explain.
4. Discuss how the $M/G/\infty$ model could be used to determine the number of emergency medical vehicles required to serve a community.
5. Discuss how one could determine the economic cost of keeping customers waiting.

EXERCISES

12.1 A general-purpose auto repair garage has one mechanic who specializes in muffler installations. Customers seeking service arrive at an average rate of two per hour, with Poisson distribution. The average time to install a muffler is 20 minutes, with negative exponential distribution.

(a) Upon arrival at the garage, how many customers should one expect to find in the system?

(b) The management is interested in adding another mechanic when the customer average time in system exceeds 90 minutes. If business continues to increase, at what arrival rate per hour will an additional mechanic be called for?

12.2 The business school is considering replacing the old CDC 3100 with a faster computer. Based on past records, the average student arrival rate is 24 per hour, Poisson-distributed, and the service times are exponentially distributed. The computer selection committee has been instructed to consider only machines that will yield an average turnaround time (expected time in system) of five minutes or less. What is the smallest computer processing rate per hour that can be considered?

12.3 The Lower Colorado River Authority (LCRA) has been studying the congestion at the boat launching ramp near Mansfield Dam. On weekends the arrival rate averages five boaters per hour, Poisson-distributed. The average time to launch or retrieve a boat is 10 minutes, with negative exponential distribution. Assume only one boat can be launched or retrieved at a time.

(a) LCRA plans to add another ramp when the average turnaround time (time in system) exceeds 90 minutes. At what average arrival rate per hour should LCRA begin to consider another ramp?

(b) If there is room to park only two boats at the top of the ramp in preparation for launching, how often will an arrival find insufficient parking space?

12.4 On the average four customers per hour use the public telephone in the sheriff's detention area, and the use has a Poisson distribution. The length of a phone call varies according to a negative exponential distribution with a mean of five minutes. The sheriff will install a second telephone booth when an arrival would expect to wait three minutes or longer for the phone.

(a) By how much must the arrival rate per hour increase to justify a second telephone booth?

(b) Suppose the criterion for justifying a second booth is changed to: install a second booth when the probability of having to wait at all exceeds 0.6. By how much must the arrival rate per hour increase to justify a second booth?

12.5 A company has a central document copying service. Arrivals are assumed to follow the Poisson probability distribution with a mean rate of 15 per hour. Service times are assumed to follow the exponential distribution. With the present copying equipment the average service time is three minutes. A new machine is available which will have a mean service time of two minutes. The average wage of the people who bring the documents to be copied is $3 an hour.

(*a*) If the new machine can be rented for $4 per hour *more* than the old machine, should they rent the new machine? Consider lost productive time of employees as waiting in queue *only* because the copying machine is self-serve.

(*b*) For the *old* copying machine, when a person arrives, what is the probability that person will encounter people already *waiting in line* for service? (Be careful to identify properly the number of customers that might be present for this situation to arise.)

(*c*) Suppose the *new* copying machine is rented. How many chairs should be provided for those waiting in line if we are satisfied when at least 90 percent of the time there will be enough chairs?

12.6 Sea Dock, a private firm, operates an unloading facility located in the Gulf of Mexico for supertankers delivering crude oil for refineries in the Port Arthur area of Texas. Records show that, on the average, two tankers arrive per day with Poisson distribution. Supertankers are unloaded one at a time on a FCFS basis. Unloading requires approximately 8 hours of a 24-hour working day, and unloading times have a negative exponential distribution.

(*a*) Sea Dock has provided mooring space for three tankers. Is this sufficient to meet U.S. Coast Guard regulations requiring that at least 19 out of 20 arrivals should find mooring available?

(*b*) Sea Dock can increase its unloading capacity to a rate of four ships per day by adding additional labor at a cost of $480 per day. Considering the $1000 per day demurrage fee charged to Sea Dock for keeping a supertanker idle (this includes unloading time as well as waiting in queue), should they consider this expansion opportunity?

12.7 Last National Bank is concerned about the level of service at its single drive-in window. A study of customer arrivals during its busy period revealed the following: on the average 20 customers arrive per hour with Poisson distribution and they are given FCFS service, requiring an average of two minutes, with service times having a negative exponential distribution.

(*a*) What is the expected number of customers waiting in queue?

(*b*) If Last National were using an ATM (automatic teller machine) with constant service time of two minutes, what would be the expected number of customers in the system?

(*c*) There is space in the drive for three cars (including the one being served). What is the probability of traffic on the street being blocked by cars waiting to turn into the bank driveway?

(*d*) Last National is considering adding teller stations at the current drive-in facility. It has decided upon $5 per hour as the imputed cost of customer waiting time in the system. The hourly cost of a teller is $10. Average arrival rate of customers has reached 30 per hour. On the basis of the total hourly cost of tellers and customer waiting, how many tellers do you recommend? Assume demand is equally divided among the tellers, with separate waiting lines, and no customer jockeying is permitted.

12.8 Green Valley Airport has been in operation for several years and is beginning to experience flight congestion. A study of airport operations reveals that planes arrive at an average of 12 per hour with Poisson distribution. The single runway can land and clear a plane every four minutes on the average, and service times have negative exponential distribution. Planes are processed on a FCFS basis with takeoffs occurring between landing planes. Planes waiting to land are asked to circle the airport.

(*a*) What is the expected number of airplanes circling the airport waiting in queue for clearance to land?

(*b*) A new ground approach radar system approved by the FAA is being considered as a means to reduce congestion. Under this system, planes can be processed at a *constant* rate of 15 per hour (i.e., the variance is zero). What would be the expected number of airplanes circling the airport waiting in queue for clearance to land if the system were to be used?

(*c*) Assume the cost of keeping an airplane in the air is approximately $70 per hour. If the hourly cost of the proposed radar system were $100 per hour, would you recommend its adoption?

12.9 Lakeside Community College has been using a medium-size computer, donated by a local firm, to support its computer science program. The computer center director notes that students submit batch jobs at an average rate of 20 per hour with Poisson distribution. Jobs are processed on a FCFS basis and take on the average two minutes of CPU time with negative exponential distribution. Students are requested to remain in the ready room as their jobs are processed.

  (a) What is the expected number of students waiting in queue to process their jobs?

  (b) If only three chairs are provided in the ready room for students, what is the probability that a student upon arrival will find no chair available (assume all students will sit given the opportunity)?

  (c) The college plans to consider replacing the computer when increases in demand result in an average waiting time in queue exceeding six minutes. If the computer center keeps track of student average arrival rate per hour, at what point should a new computer be considered?

  (d) Lakeside has an opportunity to get another identical computer for its computation center. Assume the arrival rate is still 20 per hour with Poisson distribution. What is the average number of jobs in the system if the computers operate in parallel to select jobs from a single queue?

  (e) As an alternative, the college decides to dedicate one computer to research computation and the other to teaching. If the demand of 20 jobs per hour is equally divided between research and teaching, on the average, how many jobs are there in the total system?

  (f) What savings in student waiting time could be achieved by pooling the computers?

12.10 Community Bank is planning the expansion of its drive-in facility. Observations of the existing single teller window reveal the following: customers arrive at an average rate of 10 per hour with Poisson distribution and they are given FCFS service with an average transaction time of 5 minutes with transaction times having negative exponential distribution. Community Bank has decided to add another teller and install four remote stations with pneumatic tubes running from the stations to the tellers, located in a glassed-in building. The cost of keeping a customer waiting in the system is represented as a $5 per hour loss of goodwill. The hourly cost of a teller is $10.

  (a) If each teller is assigned two stations exclusively, the demand is assumed equally divided among the stations, and no customer jockeying is permitted, what is the average number of customers waiting in the entire system?

  (b) If instead, both tellers work all the stations and the customer waiting the longest is served by the next available teller, what is the average number of customers in the system?

  (c) What are the hourly savings achieved by pooling the tellers?

CASELETTE: HOUSTON PORT AUTHORITY

The Houston Port Authority has engaged you as a consultant to advise it on possible changes in the handling of wheat exports. Presently a crew of dock workers, using conventional belt conveyors, is assigned to the task of unloading hopper cars containing wheat onto cargo ships bound for overseas. The crew is known to take an average of one-half hour to unload a car. The crew when working an 8 hour shift is paid $80. Hopper car arrivals have averaged 12 per shift. The railroad assesses a demurrage charge from time of arrival to release at a rate of $4 per hour on rolling stock not in service. Partially unloaded cars from one shift are first in line for the following shift.

A chi-square "goodness-of-fit" analysis of the arrival rates for the past months indicates that the assumption of a Poisson distribution is warranted. Data on unloading times for this period may also be assumed to follow a negative exponential distribution.

Because of excessive demurrage charges, a proposal has been made to add another crew. A visit to the work area indicates that both crews will be unable to work together on the same car because of congestion; however, two cars may be unloaded simultaneously with one crew per car.

During your deliberations the industrial engineering staff reports that a pneumatic handling system has become available. This system can transfer wheat from cars to cargo ships at a constant rate of 3 cars per hour, 24 hours per day, with the assistance of a skilled operator earning $8 per hour. Such a system would cost $400,000 installed. The Port Authority uses a 10 percent discount rate for capital improvement projects. The port is in operation 24 hours a day, 365 days a year. For purposes of analysis consider a 10-year planning horizon and prepare a recommendation for the Port Authority.

CASELETTE: CEDAR VALLEY COMMUNITY COLLEGE

Cedar Valley Community College, founded only two years ago, has experienced enrollment beyond expectations. The large number of students in the computer science program has placed such demands on the college's small computer that complaints of excessive turnaround time have reached the president's office.[8]

As computer center director you have been asked to identify what new computer models are available and to recommend a replacement for the existing batch processor. After talking to several computer hardware vendors, you have settled upon a compatible system which has available six models differing only in processing speed and, of course, price.

On the basis of historical records, you estimate that an average program can be processed in one, two, three, four, five, or six minutes, depending on whether model A, B, C, D, E, or F, respectively, is chosen. The rental cost of the particular model depends on its speed; the rental rate per minute is 90 cents/S, where S is the service time for the average program (e.g., model A which completes a program in one minute rents for 90 cents per minute and model B for 45 cents per minute, etc.).

A statistical analysis of the distribution of these historical processing times reveals that they follow a negative exponential distribution. During the past month you installed a time clock to gather information on the time of arrival of computer center users to plan the staffing of the ready desk. A study of these clock times indicates that, on the average, 12 users arrive per hour with Poisson distribution.

The president has suggested that a criterion of minimizing average total cost per hour (rental plus waiting) be used in the analysis. For this analysis the cost of keeping a user waiting for output is estimated to be 50 cents per minute.

---

[8] Turnaround time for batch processing is the elapsed time from submitting a computer job to the time the output is available for pickup.

At your suggestion the president also agrees to an acceptable service level of not exceeding an average five-minute turnaround time.

Which computer model(s) and configuration would you recommend?

SELECTED BIBLIOGRAPHY

Bleuel, W. H.: "Management Science's Impact on Service Strategy," *Interfaces,* vol. 6, no. 1, pt. 2, November 1975, pp. 4–12.

Budnick, Frank S., Richard Mojena, and Thomas E. Vollmann: *Principles of Operations Research for Management,* Richard D. Irwin, Inc., Homewood, Ill., 1977.

Crabill, T. B., D. Gross, and M. J. Magazine: "A Classified Bibliography of Research on Optimal Design and Control of Queues," *Operations Research,* vol. 25, no. 2, March–April 1977, pp. 219–232.

Drake, Alvin W., Ralph L. Keeney, and Phillip N. Morse (eds.): *Analysis of Public Systems,* MIT Press, Cambridge, Mass., 1972.

Foote, B. L.: "A Queuing Case Study of Drive-In Banking," *Interfaces,* vol. 6, no. 4, August 1976, pp. 31–37.

Hillier, F. S., and G. J. Lieberman: *Introduction to Operations Research,* Holden-Day, Inc., San Francisco, 1974.

Parikh, S. C.: "On a Fleet Sizing and Allocation Problem," *Management Science,* vol. 23, no. 9, May 1977, pp. 972–977.

Rising, E. J., R. Baron, and B. Averill: "A Systems Analysis of a University Health-Service Outpatient Clinic," *Operations Research,* September 1972, pp. 1030–1047.

Saaty, T. L.: *Elements of Queuing Theory with Applications,* McGraw-Hill Book Co., New York, 1961.

PART FOUR

MANAGING SERVICE OPERATIONS

CHAPTER
THIRTEEN

UTILIZATION OF SERVICE CAPACITY

Service capacity is a perishable commodity. For example, an empty seat on an airplane represents a potential service that is lost once the aircraft takes off. Unlike products that are stored in warehouses for future consumption, a service is an intangible personal experience that cannot be transferred from one person to another. Instead, a service is produced and consumed simultaneously. And whenever the demand for a service falls short of the capacity to serve, the result is idle servers and facilities. Variability in service demand is quite pronounced. In fact, our culture and habits contribute to these fluctuations. For example, we eat our meals at the same hours and take our vacations in July and August. Studies of hospitals indicate low utilization in the summer and fall months. These natural variations in service demand create periods of idle service but at other times periods of consumer waiting. In this chapter, we shall explore operating strategies that can increase capacity utilization by better matching the supply and demand for services. Figure 13.1 summarizes the strategies commonly used to manage the utilization of service capacity by altering demand and/or controlling supply.

STRATEGIES FOR ALTERING DEMAND

Fluctuations in demand for service need not be accepted as inevitable. Service systems can smooth their demand by using both active and passive measures. Smoothed demand is one in which the cyclical variation has been reduced. While the arrival of consumers will still occur at random intervals, the rate of

288 MANAGING SERVICE OPERATIONS

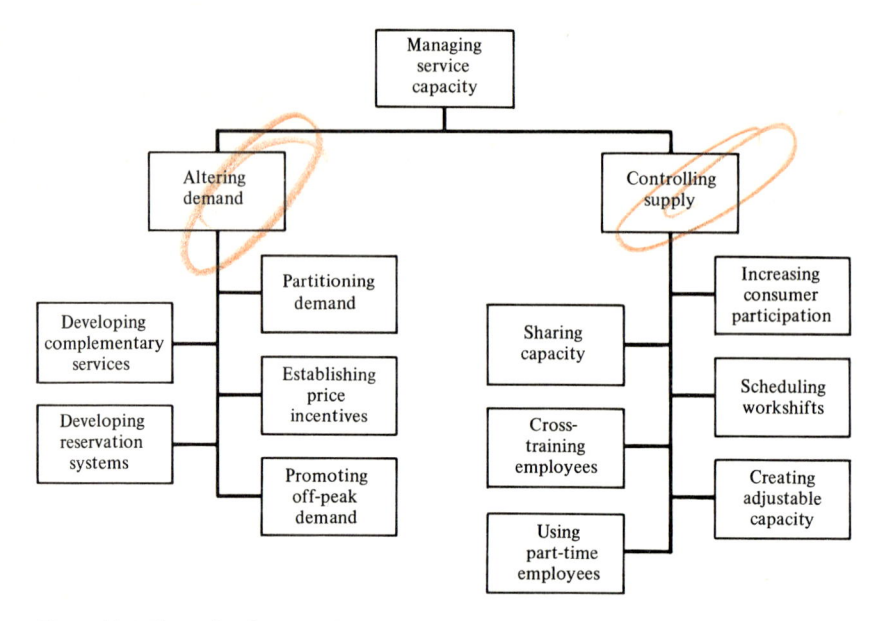

Figure 13.1 Strategies for matching supply and demand for services.

arrivals will be more constant over time. We shall discuss several strategies that might be used for demand smoothing.

Partitioning Demand

Demand for a service is seldom derived from a homogeneous source. Demand for a service is often grouped into random arrivals and planned arrivals. For example, a drive-in bank can expect visits from its commercial accounts on a regular daily basis and random arrivals from its personal account holders.

An analysis by E. J. Rising, R. Baron, and B. Averill[1] of health-clinic demand showed that the greatest number of walk-in patients arrived on Monday and lesser numbers arrived during the remaining week days. While walk-in demand is uncontrollable, appointments are controllable. Therefore, why not make appointments in the latter part of the week to level demand? Using data for the same week in the previous year, the number of walk-in patients for each weekday was subtracted from the daily total. This gave the number of appointment patients needed each day to smooth demand. For the sample week shown in Figure 13.2, this procedure yielded the following number of appointment periods:

---

[1] E. J. Rising, R. Baron, and B. Averill, "A System Analysis of a University Health-Service Outpatient Clinic," *Operations Research,* September 1972, pp. 1030–1047.

Monday	84
Tuesday	89
Wednesday	124
Thursday	129
Friday	114

The daily smoothing of demand was further refined by scheduling appointments at appropriate times during the day. After a two-month shakedown period, smoothing demand yielded the following benefits:

1. The number of patients seen by physicians increased by 13.4 percent.
2. The increased patient demand was met even though there were 5.1 percent fewer physician hours scheduled.
3. The overall time physicians spent with patients increased 5.0 percent because of an increase in the number of appointments.
4. The average waiting time for patients remained the same.
5. A team of sociologists concluded that physician morale increased.

Price Incentives

There are many examples of differential pricing. Consider the following:

1. Weekend and night rates for long-distance telephone calls

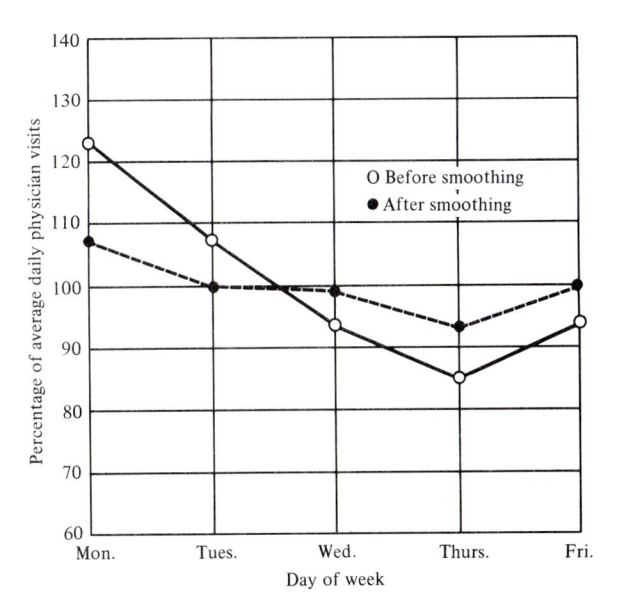

Figure 13.2 Effect of smoothing physician visits. [*Reprinted with permission from E. J. Rising, R. Baron, and B. Averill, "A Systems Analysis of a University Health-Service Outpatient Clinic," Operations Research, September 1972, p. 1035.*]

Table 13.1 Suggested discriminatory fee schedule

Experience type	Days and weeks of camping season	No. of days	Daily fee
1	Saturdays and Sundays of weeks 10 to 15, plus Dominion Day and civic holidays	14	$6.00
2	Saturdays and Sundays of weeks 3 to 9 and 15 to 19 plus Victoria Day	23	2.50
3	Fridays of weeks 3 to 15 plus all other days of weeks 9 to 15 that are not in experience type 1 or 2	43	0.50
4	Rest of camping season	78	Free

2. Matinee or reduced prices before 6 p.m. at movie theaters
3. Off-season hotel rates at resort locations
4. Peak-load pricing by utility companies

Differential pricing has been suggested for federal campsites to encourage better use of this scarce resource. For example, J. C. Nautiyal and R. L. Chowdhary developed a discriminatory pricing system that ensures camping fees will accurately reflect the marginal benefit of the last campsite on any given day.[2]

They identified four different camping experiences on the basis of days and weeks of the camping season. Table 13.1 contains a schedule of daily fees by experience type.

The experience groupings were made on the basis of total daily occupancy in the park, under the assumption that occupancy is directly affected by available leisure time and climate. Campers in each experience group were interviewed to determine their travel costs. It was assumed that the marginal visitor was the camper who had incurred the highest cost in coming to the recreation site. This information was used to develop a demand curve for each experience type. Given the available number of campsites, the campsite fee was determined by means of these demand curves. Table 13.2 shows a comparison of the revenues generated under the existing system with those estimated using discriminatory fees.

Additional benefits of discriminatory pricing can also be realized. For experience type 4, which is free, no regular staff need be maintained at the campsites. However, for the arrangement to work effectively in altering demand, it must be well advertised and include an advance booking system for campsites.

Note the projected increase in demand for experience type 3 because of the substantially reduced fee. The result of off-peak pricing is to tap a latent de-

[2] J. C. Nautiyal and R. L. Chowdhary, "A Suggested Basis for Pricing Campsites: Demand Estimation in an Ontario Park," *Journal of Leisure Research*, vol. 7, no. 2, 1975, pp. 95–107.

Table 13.2 Comparison of existing revenue and projected revenue from discriminatory pricing

Experience type	Existing fee of $2.50		Discriminatory fee	
	Campsites occupied	Revenue	Campsites occupied (est.)	Revenue
1	5,891	$14,727	5,000	$30,000
2	8,978	22,445	8,500	21,250
3	6,129	15,322	15,500	7,750
4	4,979	12,447	....	....
Total	25,977	$64,941	29,000	$59,000

mand for campsites instead of redistributing peak demand to off-peak. Thus, discriminatory pricing fills in the valleys (periods of low demand) instead of leveling off the peaks. The result is overall better utilization of a scarce resource and, for a private sector firm, increased profit provided fees cover variable costs. This experience has been observed by other service organizations also, particularly airlines.

Promoting Off-Peak Demand

Creative use of off-peak capacity results from seeking out different sources of demand. An example is the use of a resort hotel during off-season as a retreat location for business or professional groups. A ski resort during the winter becomes a staging area for backpacking during the summer. Telephone companies promote long-distance dialing, again preferably at night or on weekends when switching equipment is underutilized.

Promoting off-peak demand can be used to discourage overtaxing the facility. The appeal to "shop early and avoid the Christmas rush" is one example.

Developing Complementary Services

Restaurants have discovered the benefits of complementary services by adding a bar. Diverting waiting customers into the lounge during busy periods can be profitable to the restaurant, while also sedating anxious consumers. Movie theaters have traditionally sold popcorn and soft drinks. But recently, they also have added video games to their lobbies. These examples illustrate complementary services offered to occupy waiting consumers.

Convenience stores have expanded their services to include self-service gas pumps and fast-food meals. The concept of holistic medicine, which combines traditional medical attention with nutritional and psychiatric care, is a further example. Developing complementary services is a natural way of expanding one's market. It is particularly attractive if the new demands for service are contracyclical and result in a more uniform aggregate demand (i.e., when the new service demand is high, the original service demand is low.)

Reservation Systems

Taking reservations presells the potential service. As reservations are made, additional demand is deflected to other time slots at the same facility or to other facilities of the same organization. National reservation systems used by motel chains regularly book customers in nearby motels when their first choice is unavailable.

Reservations benefit consumers by reducing waiting and guaranteeing service availability. However, problems do arise when consumers fail to honor their reservations, the all too common no-show. Usually, consumers are not held financially liable for their unkept reservations. We see this with airlines when passengers make several flight reservations to cover contingencies. Of course, only one reservation will be used and the others become no-shows at no explicit cost to the passenger.

Airlines faced with flying empty seats have adopted a strategy of overbooking. By accepting reservations for more than the available seats, airlines hedge against no-shows. However, the airline risks turning away passengers with reservations if it overbooks too many seats. Because of overbooking abuses, the Federal Aviation Agency now requires airlines to reimburse overbooked passengers and to find space on the next available flight. Similarly, many hotels place their overbooked guests at no expense in a nearby hotel of equal quality. A good overbooking strategy should minimize the expected opportunity cost of idle service capacity and the expected cost of turning away reservations.

Example 13.1: Surf Side Hotel During the past tourist season, Surf Side Hotel did not achieve very high occupancy in spite of a reservation system designed to keep the hotel fully booked. Prospective guests apparently were making reservations which, for one reason or another, they failed to honor. A review of front desk records during the current peak period when the hotel was fully booked revealed the record of no-shows given in Table 13.3.

A room that remains vacant owing to a no-show, results in an opportunity loss of the $40 room contribution. From Table 13.3, the expected number of no-shows is calculated to be 3.04. This yields an expected opportunity loss of 3.04 × $40, or $121.60, per night. In order to avoid some of this loss, management is considering an overbooking policy. However, if a guest holding a reservation is turned away owing to overbooking, other costs are incurred. Surf Side has made arrangements with a nearby hotel to pay for the rooms of guests it cannot accommodate. Furthermore, there is a penalty associated with the loss of customer goodwill and the impact this has on future business. Management estimates this total loss to be approximately $100 per guest overbooked. A good overbooking strategy must strike a balance between all these costs. The best overbooking strategy should minimize the expected loss in the long run. Table 13.4 displays the

Table 13.3 Surf Side Hotel no-show experience

No-shows	Frequency	Cumulative frequency
0	7	100
1	19	93
2	22	74
3	16	52
4	12	36
5	10	24
6	7	14
7	4	7
8	2	3
9	1	1

loss associated with each possible overbooking alternative. For each overbooking strategy, the expected loss is calculated by multiplying the loss for each possible no-show possibility by its probability of occurrence and adding the products. For example, for a policy of overbooking by two rooms, the following calculations are made:

0.07(200) + 0.19(100) + 0.22(0) + 0.16(40) + 0.12(80) + 0.10(120) + 0.07(160) + 0.04(200) + 0.02(240) + 0.01(280) = $87.80

From Table 13.4 it appears that a policy of overbooking by two rooms will minimize the expected loss in the long run. If this policy is adopted, front-desk personnel need to be trained to handle overbooked guests in a gracious manner.

Recall from Chapter 12 the relationship shown below:

$$P(d \geq x) \geq \frac{L}{\pi + L} \qquad (1)$$

This ratio also can be used to identify the best overbooking strategy. Let L, the loss, be the $100 opportunity loss associated with an overbooking and π, the profit, be the $40 room contribution. Also let d be the no-show demand based on past experience and x be the number of rooms overbooked. Then the probability that no-shows exceed the number of rooms overbooked should be:

$$P(d \geq x) \geq \frac{100}{40 + 100} \geq 0.71$$

From Table 13.3 an overbooking strategy of two rooms guarantees that 74 percent of the no-shows will be covered. This confirms our earlier decision.

Table 13.4 Overbooking loss table

| | | Reservations overbooked ||||||||||
No-shows	Probability	0	1	2	3	4	5	6	7	8	9
0	0.07	0	100	200	300	400	500	600	700	800	900
1	0.19	40	0	100	200	300	400	500	600	700	800
2	0.22	80	40	0	100	200	300	400	500	600	700
3	0.16	120	80	40	0	100	200	300	400	500	600
4	0.12	160	120	80	40	0	100	200	300	400	500
5	0.10	200	160	120	80	40	0	100	200	300	400
6	0.07	240	200	160	120	80	40	0	100	200	300
7	0.04	280	240	200	160	120	80	40	0	100	200
8	0.02	320	280	240	200	160	120	80	40	0	100
9	0.01	360	320	280	240	200	160	120	80	40	0
Expected loss, $	.....	121.60	91.40	87.80	115.00	164.60	231.00	311.40	401.60	497.40	560.00

STRATEGIES FOR CONTROLLING SUPPLY

For many services demand cannot be smoothed very effectively. Consider, for example, the demand for telephone operators shown in Figure 13.3. These data are the half-hourly call rates during a typical 24-hour day for a metropolitan telephone company. We see that peak volume (2500 calls) occurs at 10:30 a.m., while the minimum volume (20 calls) occurs at 5:30 a.m. The peak-to-valley variation is 125 to 1. No inducements are likely to change this demand pattern substantially. Therefore, control must come from adjusting service supply to match demand. We shall discuss several strategies that can be used to control service supply.

Daily Workshift Scheduling

By carefully scheduling workshifts during the day, the profile of service supply can be made to approximate demand. Workshift scheduling is an important staffing problem for many service organizations faced with cyclical demand, such as telephone companies, hospitals, banks, police departments, and others.

The general approach begins with a forecast of demand by hour that is converted to hourly service staffing requirements. Next, a schedule of tours or shifts is developed to match the staffing requirement profile as closely as possible. Finally, specific service personnel are assigned to tours or shifts. The telephone-operator staffing problem will be used to demonstrate the analysis required for each step. However, the approach can be generalized to any service organization.

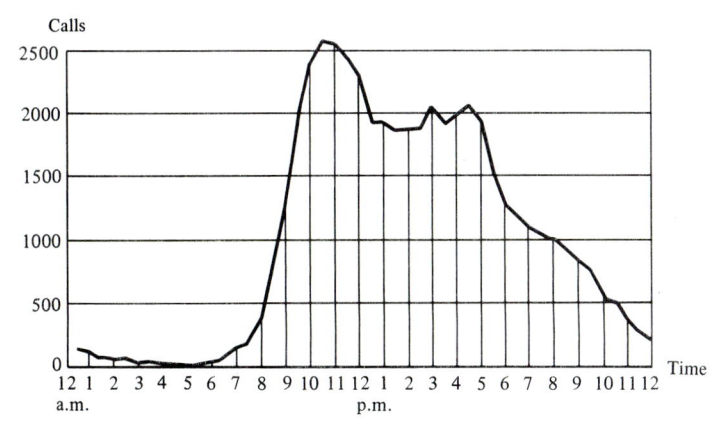

Figure 13.3 Daily demand for telephone operators. [*Reprinted with permission from E. S. Buffa, M. J. Cosgrove, and B. J. Luce, "An Integrated Work Shift Scheduling System," Decision Science, vol. 7, no. 4, October 1976, p. 622.*]

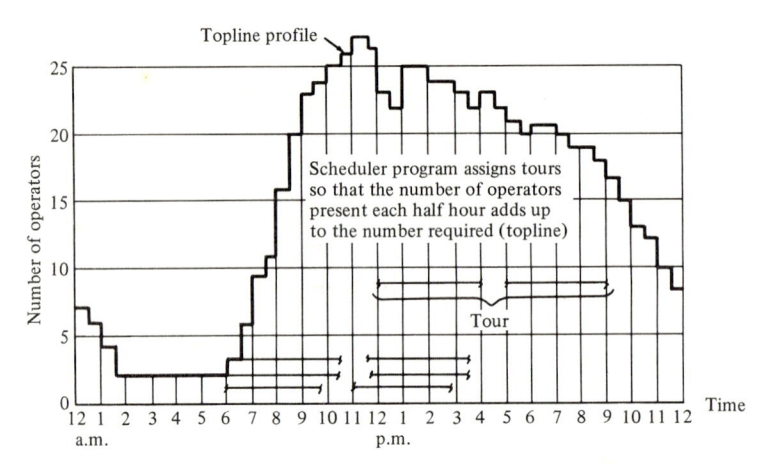

Figure 13.4 Profile of operator requirements and tour assignments. [*Reprinted with permission from E. S. Buffa, M. J. Cosgrove, and B. J. Luce, "An Integrated Work Shift Scheduling System," Decision Science, vol. 7, no. 4, October 1976, p. 626.*]

Forecast demand Daily demand is forecast to account for weekday/weekend variations and seasonal adjustments. Saturday and Sunday call load was found to be approximately 55 percent of the typical weekday load. Summer months were found to be generally lower in demand. Special high-demand days, such as Mother's Day and Christmas, were accounted for.

Convert to operator requirements A profile of half-hour operator requirements is developed on the basis of the forecasted daily demand and call distribution, shown in Figure 13.3. A standard service level, defined by the Public Utilities Commission, requires that an incoming call must be answered within 10 seconds, 89 percent of the time. The half-hour operator requirements are thus determined by means of a conventional queuing model to ensure that the service level is achieved for each half-hour.[3] The result is a profile of operators required by half-hour, as shown in Figure 13.4.

Schedule shifts Tours need to be assigned so that they aggregate to the top-line profile, shown in Figure 13.4. Each tour consists of two working sessions separated by a rest pause or meal period. The set of possible tours is defined by state and federal laws, union agreements, and company policy. A heuristic computer program chooses tours from the permissible set such that the absolute difference between operator requirements and operators assigned is minimized when summed over all half-hour periods. Defining R_i as the number of operators required in period i and W_i as the operators assigned in period i, then the objective can be stated as:

[3] The $M/M/c$ queuing model as described in Chapter 12 is used. This model permits the calculation of probabilities for having a telephone caller wait for different numbers of operators.

Minimize $$\sum_{i=1}^{n} |R_i - W_i| \qquad (2)$$

The schedule-building process is shown schematically in Figure 13.5. At each iteration, one tour at a time is selected from all possible tours. The tour selected at each step is the one that best meets the criterion stated in expression (2) above. Because this procedure favors shorter-length tours, the different shift lengths are weighted in the calculation. The result is a list of tours required to meet forecasted demand, as well as positioning of lunch and rest periods during the tours.

Assign operators to shifts Given the set of tours required, the assignment of operators to these tours is complicated because of the 24-hour, 7-day-week operation. Questions of equity arise regarding the timing of days off and assignment of overtime work, which involves extra pay. Another computer program makes operator assignments according to policies, such as "give at least one day off per week and maximize consecutive days off." The actual assignment of operators to shifts also takes into account employee shift preferences. The result of this final step is a feasible schedule of employees assigned to tours.

Weekly Workshift Scheduling with Days-Off Constraint

Developing workshifts to match the profile of daily demand is only part of the problem. Services such as police and fire protection operate on a seven-day-a-week basis. Employees working five days a week need to be scheduled for time off, usually for two consecutive days each week. Management is interested in

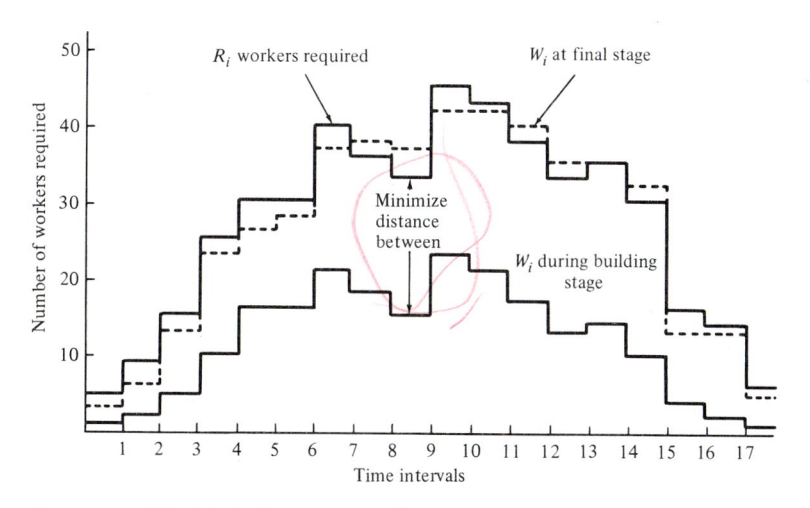

Figure 13.5 Schedule building process. [*Reprinted with permission from E. S. Buffa, M. J. Cosgrove, and B. J. Luce, "An Integrated Work Shift Scheduling System, Decision Science, vol. 7, no. 4, October 1976 p. 622.*]

developing these work schedules and meeting the varying employee requirements for weekdays and weekends with the smallest possible staff.

The problem is to develop work tours to meet a typical week's requirements if a repetitive weekly cycle of activities is assumed. The workforce requirements will vary during the week, with at least N employees required for each weekday and at least n employees required for each weekend day. Clearly, the workforce size W must be sufficient to meet the demand on any given day, so that $W \geq \max(n, N)$. But the capability of a workforce, with employees working five days, must also be sufficient to meet the total number of person days required in a week, or $5W \geq 5N + 2n$. These two relationships define the smallest possible $W \geq \max\{n, N + [2n/5]\}$, where $[x]$ is the smallest integer greater than or equal to x.

Finding enough potential days off becomes a problem if we require days off to be either both weekdays or both weekend days. Because of the odd number of weekdays only $4(W - N)$ weekdays can be paired and used for days off. The number of available weekend days is of course $2(W - n)$. Together we have a pool of $6W - 4N - 2n$ available days to accommodate $2W$ days off for assignment. If the number of available days off is insufficient [i.e., $2W - (6W - 4N - 2n) = 4N + 2n - 4W > 0$], then the workforce W will have to be increased.

This problem can be alleviated by scheduling k employees for either (F, Sa) or (Su, M) days-off assignments. Thus, we reduce the number of (Sa, Su) assignments by k and simultaneously increase the number of (F, Sa) and (Su, M) assignments each by $k/2$. This exchange will add $2k$ days off towards the deficit $4N + 2n - 4W$. The only limit on this procedure is the number of weekend pairs $(W - n)$ initially available. Thus, the value of k will equal $\min\{(4N + 2n - 4W)/2, W - n\}$. Only when $W - n < 2N + n - 2W$, will some deficit remain and a larger workforce W be required. Thus, a further necessary condition on the size of a feasible workforce is $W \geq (2N + 2n)/3$. The smallest possible workforce size is determined by

$$W = \max\{n, N + [2n/5], [(2N + 2n)/3]\} \qquad (3)$$

And the value of k is

$$k = \max\{0, 2(2N + n - 2W)\} \qquad (4)$$

A schedule of tours is developed by forming a matrix of seven columns, one for each day of the week, and W rows, one for each employee tour. The schedule is developed by means of the following three-step algorithm:

1. Assign $k/2$ employees (F, Sa) days off and $k/2$ employees (Su, M) days off.
2. Assign $W - n - k/2$ employees to weekends off.
3. Any remaining employees assign days-off pairs (M, Tu), (Tu, W), (W, Th), and (Th, F) in order, as needed.

This algorithm and other variations to treat the workshift scheduling problem with cyclic demands and day-off constraints are described in an article by K. R. Baker and M. J. Magazine.[4]

Example 13.2: Computer center operations The university computer center is operated on a 24-hour, 7-day-a-week schedule. The day is divided into three 8-hour shifts. The total number of operators required per day is shown below:

Day	Su	M	Tu	W	Th	F	Sa
Operators	3	6	5	6	5	5	5

The computer center director is interested in developing a workforce schedule that will minimize the number of operators required to staff the facility. Employees work five days a week and are entitled to two consecutive days off each week.

For weekdays at least six employees are required ($N = 6$). For weekends the requirement is at least five employees ($n = 5$). Using equation (3), the lower bound on the workforce size W is found:

$$W = \max \{n, N + [2n/5], [(2N + 2n)/3]\}$$
$$= \max \{5, 6 + 10/5, (12 + 10)/3\}$$
$$= \max \{5, 8, 8\}$$
$$= 8$$

The number of employees k to schedule for either a (F, Sa) or (Su, M) day-off assignment is determined by equation (4):

$$k = \max \{0, 4N + 2n - 4W\}$$
$$= \max \{0, 24 + 10 - 32\}$$
$$= 2$$

The shift schedule below is developed using the three-step algorithm.

1. Assign $k/2$ employees (F, Sa) days off and $k/2$ employees (Su, M) days off, where $k/2 = 1$. Thus employee 1 is assigned (F, Sa) and employee 2 (Su, M).
2. Assign $W - n - k/2$ employees to weekends off. Thus $8 - 5 - 1 = 2$ employees are assigned (Sa, Su) days off. These employees are numbers 3 and 4.
3. Any remaining employees assign off-day pairs (M, Tu), (Tu, W), (W, Th), and (Th, F) as needed. Thus employee 5 is assigned (M, Tu), employee 6 is assigned (Tu, W), employee 7 is assigned (W, Th), and employee 8 is assigned (Th, F).

---

[4] K. R. Baker and M. J. Magazine, "Workforce Scheduling With Cyclic Demands and Day-Off Constraints," *Management Science*, vol. 24, no. 2, October 1977, p. 161–167.

300 MANAGING SERVICE OPERATIONS

	Schedule matrix, x = day off						
Operator	Su	M	Tu	W	Th	F	Sa
1	....	....	....	....	....	x	x
2	x	x	....	....	....	....	....
3	x	....	....	....	....	....	x
4	x	....	....	....	....	....	x
5	....	x	x	....	....	....	....
6	....	....	x	x	....	....	....
7	....	....	....	x	x	....	....
8	....	....	....	....	x	x	....
Total	5	6	6	6	6	6	5
Required	3	6	5	6	5	5	5
Excess	2	0	1	0	1	1	0

Increasing Consumer Participation

This strategy is best illustrated by the fast-food restaurants that have eliminated food-serving and table-clearing personnel. The customer not only places the order directly from a limited menu but also is expected to clear the table after the meal. Naturally the customer expects faster service and less expensive meals to compensate for the help. However, the service provider benefits in many subtle ways. Of course, there are fewer personnel to supervise and to pay. But more importantly the customer provides the input just at the moment it is required; thus, capacity to serve varies more directly with demand rather than being fixed.

Some drawbacks to self-service do exist because the quality of labor is not completely under the service manager's control. A self-service gas customer may pump leaded gas into an unleaded tank. The same customer may also fail to check tire pressure and oil levels regularly, which can lead to eventual problems.

Creating Adjustable Capacity

Through design, a portion of capacity can be made variable. Airlines routinely move the partition between first class and coach to meet the changing mix of passengers. At one time Pan American Airlines adjusted the configuration on each flight. However, this idea was eventually abandoned as being too costly and time-consuming for ground crews.

An innovative restaurant, Benihana of Tokyo, arranged its floor plan to accommodate eating areas serving two tables of eight diners each. Chefs are assigned to each area and prepare the meal at the table in a theatrical manner with flashing knives and animated movements. The restaurant can thus effectively adjust its capacity by having only the number of chefs on duty that are needed.

Capacity at peak periods can be expanded by the effective use of slack times. Performing supportive tasks during lulls allows employees to concentrate on essential tasks during rush periods. For example, employees at a restaurant can refill sugar dispensers or clean and tidy the premises when demand is low. This frees them of these tasks during the rush period.

Sharing Capacity

A service delivery system often requires a large investment in equipment and facilities. During periods of underutilization, it may be possible to find other uses of the capacity. Airlines have cooperated in this manner for years. At small airports, airlines share the same gates, ramps, baggage handling equipment, and ground personnel. It is also common for some airlines to lease their aircraft to other airlines during slack periods. The lease agreement includes painting on appropriate insignia and refurbishing the interior.

Cross-Training Employees

Some service systems are made up of several operations. Sometimes when one operation is busy, another operation may be idle. Cross-training employees to perform tasks in several operations creates flexible capacity to meet localized peaks in demand.

The gains from cross-training employees can be seen at supermarkets. When queues develop at the cash registers, the manager calls on stockers to operate registers until the surge is over. Likewise, during slow periods the cashiers are busy stocking shelves. This approach can also help build esprit de corps and give employees relief from monotony.

Using Part-Time Employees

When peaks of activity are persistent and predictable, such as mealtimes for restaurants or paydays for banks, part-time help can supplement regular employees. If the skills and training required are minimal, a ready part-time labor pool is available from high school and college students and others interested in supplementing their primary source of income.

Another source of part-time help is off-duty personnel placed on standby. Airlines and hospitals often pay their personnel to be on standby. Standbys are paid some nominal fee to restrict their activities and to be ready for work when needed.

Scheduling Part-Time Tellers at a Drive-In Bank[5]

Drive-in banks experience predictable variations in activity for different days in the week. Figure 13.6 shows the teller requirements for a typical week based on

[5] From Vincent A. Mabert and Alan R. Raedels, "The Detail Scheduling of a Part-Time Work Force: A Case Study of Teller Staffing," *Decision Science,* vol. 8, no. 1, January 1977, pp. 109–120.

302 MANAGING SERVICE OPERATIONS

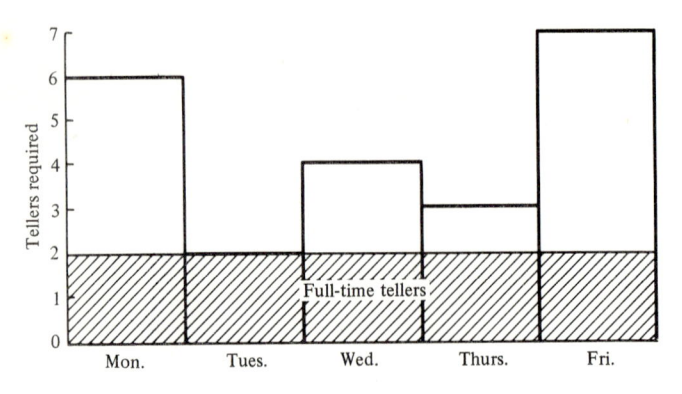

Figure 13.6 Teller requirements.

customer demand variations. The bank usually employed enough tellers to meet peak demands on Friday. However, this policy created considerable idle teller time on the low demand days, particularly Tuesday and Thursday. In order to reduce teller costs, management decided to employ part-time tellers and reduce the full-time staff to a level that just meets the demand for Tuesday and Thursday. Furthermore, to provide equity in hours worked, it was decided that a part-time teller should work at least two but no more than three days in a week.

A primary objective of scheduling part-time workers is to meet requirements with the minimum number of teller days. A secondary objective is to have a minimum number of part-time tellers. The approach is illustrated using bank tellers, but the same procedure can be used for scheduling part-time employees for many other services.

Determine the minimum number of part-time tellers needed Figure 13.6 shows that with two full-time tellers, 12 teller days remain to be covered during the week. Using three-day schedules, we see that five tellers on Friday determines the feasible minimum in this case.

Develop a decreasing-demand histogram From Figure 13.6, note the daily part-time teller requirements. Resequence the days in order of decreasing demand, as shown in Figure 13.7.

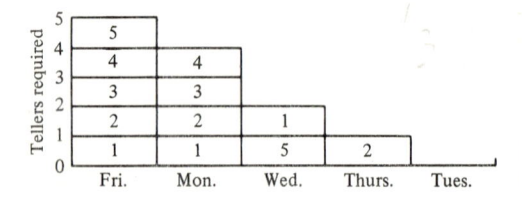

Figure 13.7 Decreasing part-time teller demand histogram.

Table 13.5 Part-time daily work schedule

Teller	Mon	Tue	Wed	Thur	Fri
1	X	....	X	....	X
2	X	....	....	X	X
3, 4	X	....	....	....	X
5	....	....	X	....	X

Assign tellers to the histogram Starting with the first part-time teller, assign that individual to the first block on Friday, the second teller to block two, and so forth, as shown in Figure 13.7. Repeat the sequence with Monday and carry over the remaining tellers into Wednesday. Table 13.5 summarizes the resulting daily part-time work schedule, which consists of two 3-day schedules and two 2-day schedules.

SUMMARY

The inherent variability of demand creates a challenge for managers trying to make the best use of service capacity. The problem can be approached from two perspectives. One strategy focuses on smoothing consumer demand, which permits fuller utilization of a fixed service capacity. Various alternatives for altering demand are available, such as pricing incentives, promoting off-peak use, and developing complementary services and reservation systems.

Another strategy considers the problem from the supply side. Many alternatives have been proposed to adjust service capacity to match demand. Elaborate procedures for workshift scheduling have been developed to adjust capacity to demand. When possible, the part-time employees are used to create variable capacity. Increasing consumer participation in the service process shifts some of the service tasks to the consumer and reduces part of the burden during peak demand periods. Other possibilities include sharing capacity with others, as airlines do by leasing their aircraft during off-season periods. Occasionally capacity can be adjusted, for example by closing and opening dining areas in a restaurant. Cross-training employees can also provide flexible capacity by enabling employees to assist one another during busy periods.

The strategies are presented as two separate views of the problem, one from the demand side and the other from the supply side. Of course, this should not preclude the use of mixed strategies that attempt to mediate the problem from both perspectives.

TOPICS FOR DISCUSSION

1. Explain, from a consumer participation point of view, why airlines find it profitable to offer reduced fares for standby passengers.

2. What are some noneconomic incentives that might encourage banking customers to use the drive-in at off-peak times?
3. A suggestion has been proposed to make airline tickets variable in price with the cost becoming more expensive as one approaches the time of departure. Comment.
4. What are some of the organizational problems that can arise from the use of part-time employees?
5. How can computer-based reservation systems be used to increase service capacity utilization?
6. Illustrate how a particular service has successfully implemented strategies for altering demand and controlling supply.
7. What are some possible dangers associated with developing complementary services?

EXERCISES

13.1 Reconsider the Surf Side Hotel example given that rising costs have resulted in a $100 opportunity loss due to a no-show. Assume the no-show experience has not significantly changed and the loss due to a guest being overbooked is still $100. Should Surf Side revise its no-show policy?

13.2 An outpatient clinic has kept a record of walk-in patients during the past year. The table below shows the expected number of walk-ins by day of the week.

Day	Expected number of walk-ins
Monday	50
Tuesday	30
Wednesday	40
Thursday	35
Friday	40

The clinic has a staff of 5 physicians and each can examine 15 patients a day on the average.
    (a) What is the maximum number of appointments that should be scheduled for each day if it is desirable to smooth out the demand for the week?
    (b) Why would you recommend against scheduling appointments at their maximum level?
    (c) If the majority of the walk-ins arrive in the morning, when should the appointments be made to avoid excessive waiting?

13.3 A commuter airline overbooks its flights by one passenger (i.e., the ticket agent will take seven reservations for an airplane which has only six seats). The no-show experience for the past 20 days is shown below:

No-shows	Frequency
0	6
1	5
2	4
3	3
4	2

Using the relationship $P(d \geq x) = L/(\pi + L)$, find the implied overbooking opportunity loss L if the profit π from a passenger is $20.

13.4 Crazy Joe operates a canoe rental on the Guadalupe River. He currently leases 15 canoes from a dealer in the nearby city at a cost of $10 per day. On weekends, when the water is high, he picks up the canoes and drives to a launching point on the river and rents canoes to white-water enthusiasts for $30 per day. Lately canoeists have complained about the unavailability of canoes. Crazy Joe records the demand for canoes and finds the experience below for the past 20 days.

Daily demand	Frequency
10	1
11	1
12	2
13	2
14	2
15	3
16	3
17	2
18	2
19	1
20	1

Recommend an appropriate number of canoes to lease.

13.5 The sheriff has been asked by the county commissioners to increase the weekend patrols in the lake region during the summer months. The sheriff has proposed the following weekly schedule, shifting deputies from weekday assignments to weekends:

Day	Su	M	Tu	W	Th	F	Sa
Assignments	6	4	4	4	5	5	6

(a) Can the sheriff staff this schedule with seven deputies?

(b) If not, what change(s) in the schedule would make it possible?

(c) Assume the sheriff is able to hire the extra deputies needed to staff the original proposal. Develop a complete schedule of tours, providing two consecutive days off per week for each officer.

CASELETTE: RIVER CITY NATIONAL BANK

River City National Bank has been in business for ten years and is a fast-growing community bank. The bank president, Gary Miller, took over his position five years ago in an effort to get the bank on its feet. He is one of the youngest bank presidents in the southwest and his energy and enthusiasm explain his rapid advancement. Mr. Miller has been the key factor behind the bank's increase in status and meeting of high standards. One of the reasons for this is that the bank customers come first in Mr. Miller's eyes. To him, one of the bank's main objectives is to serve its customers better.

The main bank lobby has one commercial teller and three paying and receiving teller booths. The lobby is designed to have room for long lines, should they occur. Attached to the main bank are six drive-in lanes (one commercial only) and one walk-up window off to the side of the drive-in. Owing to the bank's rapid growth, the drive-in lanes and the lobby were constantly overcrowded although the bank had some of the longest banking hours in town. The lobby is open from 9 a.m. until 2 p.m. Monday through Saturday and reopens from 4 to 6 p.m. on Friday. The drive-in is open from 7 a.m. until midnight Monday through Friday and on Saturday from 7 a.m. until 7 p.m. Several old and good customers were starting to gripe and complain. They did not like the long wait in line and also felt that the tellers were becoming quite unfriendly.

This all was very disheartening to Mr. Miller, despite the fact that the cause of it was an increase in the business the bank was doing. Thus, it was with his strong recommendation that the board of directors finally approved the building of a remote drive-in bank just down the street. The drive-in can be approached from two directions and has four lanes on either side, as seen in Figure 13.8. The first lane on either side is commercial only, and the last lane was built but is not operational. The banking hours for this facility are from 7 a.m. until 7 p.m. Monday through Saturday.

The bank employs both full-time and part-time tellers. The lobby tellers and the morning tellers (7 a.m. to 2 p.m.) are considered full-time employees, whereas the afternoon shift (2 p.m. to 7 p.m.) and the night-owl shift (7 p.m. to midnight) are considered part-time. The tellers perform normal banking services: cash checks, make deposits, verify deposit balances, sell money orders and traveler's checks, and cash government savings bonds.

At the present time, the overcrowding for the most part has been eliminated. The hardest problem in resolving that situation was making customers aware of the other facility. The remote drive-in tellers, after six months, are still having customers tell them, "I didn't realize ya'll were over here. I'm going to have to start coming to this drive-in more often!"

Now, instead of the overcrowding situation, the bank is finding it is having problems with fluctuating demand. River City National rarely experienced this problem until the extra capacity of tellers and drive-in lanes were added with the building of the remote bank.

Two full-time and four part-time tellers are employed at the remote drive-in Monday through Friday. Scheduling on Saturdays is no problem as all six tellers take turns rotating, with most working every other Saturday. On paydays and on Fridays, the remote drive-ins have cars lined up out to the street. A high

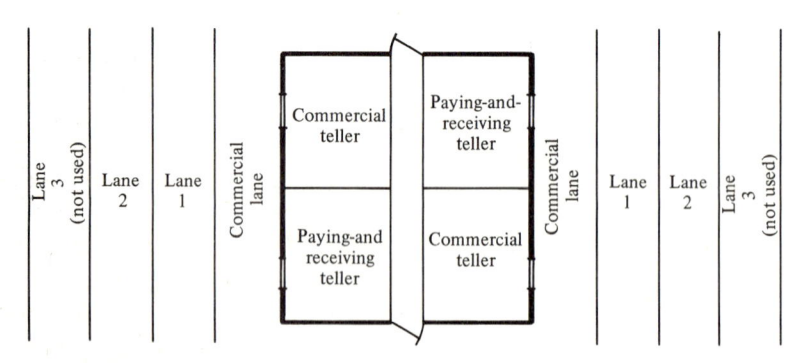

Figure 13.8 Layout of remote drive-in.

demand for money and service from the bank is the main reason for this dilemma, but certainly not the only one. Many customers are not ready when they get to the bank. They need a pen or a deposit slip, or they do not have their check filled out or endorsed yet. This, of course, creates idle time for the tellers. There are also problems with customers which take time, such as explaining that their accounts are overdrawn and, thus, their payroll checks must be deposited instead of cashed. Also, there is usually a handful of noncustomers trying to cash their payroll checks or personal checks who can become quite obstinate and take up a lot of time when they find they cannot cash their checks. The transactions take 30 seconds on the average. This ranges from 10 seconds for a straight deposit to 90 seconds for cashing a bond to about 3 minutes for making out traveler's checks. (The latter occurs very rarely.)

Compared with the peak banking days, the rest of the week is very quiet. The main bank stays busy, but not crowded. On the other hand, the remote drive-in is unusually slow. Mr. Miller's drive-in supervisor, Ms. Marilyn Powell, did a study on the number of transactions the remote tellers did on the average. The figures for a typical month are shown in Table 13.6.

Once again customers are starting to complain. When the tellers at the remote drive-in close out at 7:00 p.m. on Fridays, they are always turning people away while they are in the process of balancing. These customers have asked Mr. Miller to keep the new drive-in open at least until 9 p.m. on Friday. The tellers are very much against the idea, but the board of directors is beginning to favor it. Mr. Miller wants to keep his customers happy but he feels there must be some other way to resolve this situation. Therefore, he calls in Ms. Powell and requests that she please look into the problem and make some recommendations for a solution.

CASELETTE: GATEWAY INTERNATIONAL AIRPORT

Gateway International Airport (GIA) has experienced a substantial growth in both commercial and general aviation operations during the past several years (an operation is a landing or a takeoff). Because of the initiation of new commercial service at the airport (scheduled for several months in the future), GIA's manager has concluded that this increase in operations and the associated change in the hourly distribution of takeoffs and landings will require an entirely new work schedule for the current air traffic controller (ATC) staff. The manager feels that GIA may have to hire additional ATC personnel because the present staff of five will probably not be enough to handle the expected demand.

After examining the various service plans each commercial airline has submitted for the next six-month period, the manager's staff has developed an average hourly demand forecast of total operations (Figure 13.9) and a weekly forecast of variation from this average daily demand (Figure 13.10). GIA's assistant manager for operations is delegated the task of developing workforce

Table 13.6 Transactions for typical month at remote drive-in

Day of week	First week Morning shift	First week Afternoon shift	Second week Morning shift	Second week Afternoon shift	Third week Morning shift	Third week Afternoon shift	Fourth week Morning shift	Fourth week Afternoon shift	Fifth week Morning shift	Fifth week Afternoon shift
Monday	....	....	175	133	149	120	182	171	169	111
Tuesday	....	195	120	85	136	77	159	137	112	89
Wednesday	200	113	122	115	182	186	143	103	92	95
Thursday	156	210	111	100	172	152	118	99	147	163
Friday	223*	127	236*	225	215*	230	206*	197	259*	298
Saturday	142		103	98	147	150	170	156	....	....

* Most of these transactions occurred after 10 a.m.

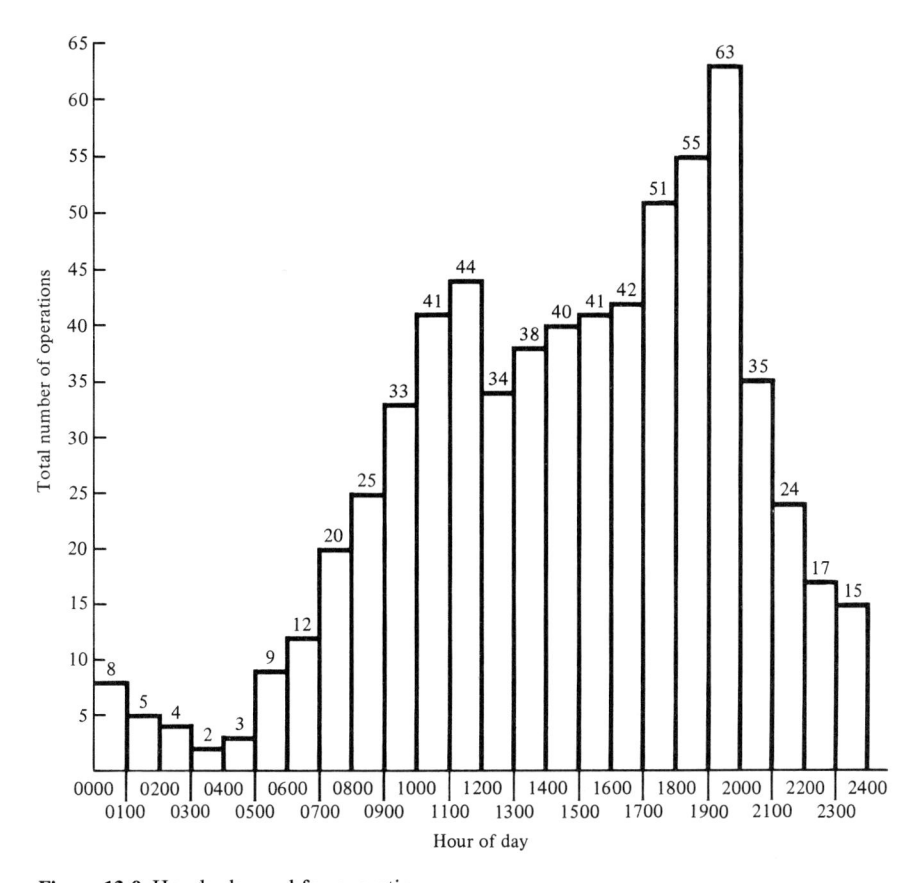

Figure 13.9 Hourly demand for operations.

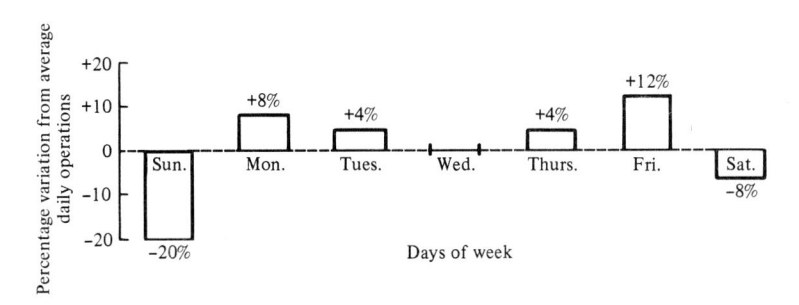

Figure 13.10 Daily demand variation from average.

requirements and schedules for the ATC staff so as to maintain an adequate level of operational safety with a minimum of excess ATC "capacity." The various constraints involved are:

1. Each controller will work a continuous eight-hour shift (ignoring any lunch break), which will always begin at the start of an hour at any time during the day (i.e., any and all shifts begin at X:00), and the controller must have at least 16 hours off duty before resuming duty.
2. Each controller will work exactly five days per week.
3. Each controller is entitled to two consecutive days off, with any consecutive pair of days being eligible.
4. Federal Aviation Administration (FAA) guidelines will govern GIA's workforce requirement, so that the ratio of total operations to number of available controllers in any hourly period cannot exceed 16.

Questions

1. Assume that you are the assistant manager for operations at GIA, and utilize the techniques of workshift scheduling to develop an analysis of the total workforce requirements and days-off schedule. For the primary analysis, you may assume that:
    a. Operator requirements will be based on a shift profile of demand (i.e., eight hours).
    b. There will be exactly three separate shifts each day with no overlapping of shifts.
    c. The distribution of hourly demand shown in Figure 13.9 is constant for each day of the week, but the levels of hourly demand vary during the week according to Figure 13.10.
2. On the basis of your primary analysis, discuss the potential implications for workforce requirements and days-off scheduling if assumptions *a* and *b* above are relaxed to permit analysis based upon the hourly demand for no preset number of shifts and shifts may overlap. In other words, discuss the effects of analyzing hourly demand requirements on the basis of each ATC position essentially having its own shift, which can overlap with any other ATC's shift to meet that demand.
3. Do you feel that this would result in a larger or smaller degree of difficulty in meeting the four general constraints? Why?
4. What additional suggestions could you make to GIA's manager that might tend to minimize the workforce requirements level and days-off scheduling difficulty?

SELECTED BIBLIOGRAPHY

Abernathy, W. J., N. Baloff, J. C. Hershey, and S. Wandel: "A Three Stage Manpower Planning and Scheduling Model–A Service Sector Example," *Operations Research,* May–June 1973, pp. 693–710.

———, ———, and ———: "The Nurse Staffing Problem: Issues and Prospects," *Sloan Management Review,* Fall 1971, pp. 87–99.

Baker, K. R., and M. J. Magazine: "Workforce Scheduling With Cyclic Demands and Day-Off Constraints," *Management Science,* vol. 24, no. 2, October 1977, pp. 161–167.

Buffa, E. S., M. J. Cosgrove, and B. J. Luce: "An Integrated Work Shift Scheduling System," *Decision Science,* vol. 7, no. 4, September 1973, pp. 1030–1047.

Drake, Alvin W., Ralph L. Keeney, and Philip N. Morse: "Improving the Effectiveness of New York City's 911," *Analysis of Public Systems,* MIT Press, Cambridge, Mass., 1972, chap. 9.

Mabert, Vincent A., and Alan R. Raedels: "The Detail Scheduling of a Part-Time Work Force: A Case Study of Teller Staffing," *Decision Science,* vol. 8, no. 1, January 1977, pp. 109–120.

Nautiyal, J. C., and R. L. Chowdhary: "A Suggested Basis for Pricing Campsites: Demand Estimation in an Ontario Park," *Journal of Leisure Research,* vol. 7, 1975, pp. 95–107.

Rising, E. J., R. Baron, and B. Averill: "A Systems Analysis of a University Health-Service Outpatient Clinic, *Operations Research,* September 1972, pp. 1030–1047.

Sasser, Earl W.: "Match Supply and Demand in Service Industries," *Harvard Business Review,* November–December 1976, pp. 133–140.

Warner, D. M., and J. Pranda: "A Mathematical Programming Model for Scheduling Nursing Personnel in a Hospital," *Management Science,* vol. 19, no. 4, December 1972, pp. 411–422.

Williams, Fred E.: "Decision Theory and the Innkeeper: An Approach for Setting Hotel Reservation Policy," *Interfaces,* vol. 7, no. 4, August 1977, pp. 18–30.

CHAPTER
FOURTEEN

SERVICE VEHICLE SCHEDULING AND ROUTING

"Consumer-server interactions"—we have used this phrase so often that it may seem trite. But we really cannot overemphasize the importance of these interactions to service organizations. And there is no better example of their impact upon operations than the routing of service vehicles.

If we reflect a moment, we can all generate a long list of examples where vehicles are dispatched to consumers to provide a service. For instance, consider school busing, refuse pickup, street sweeping, newspaper delivery, and numerous other commercial delivery and pickup operations. These examples have a common characteristic: servers must travel to geographically dispersed locations in order to render their services.

Vehicle routing involves determining which consumer locations are to be visited by a particular server and in which sequence the visitations are to be made. What criteria do you think are appropriate for setting these routes? The most frequently reported measure is vehicle distance traveled. That is, routes are determined so as to minimize the total distance traveled by all servers. Imagine how important this aspect of vehicle routing is becoming as fuel becomes scarce and its cost soars. For example, in 1976 the cost of school bus transportation for the state of New York was $150 million. And this was before the advent of the energy crunch! We can see that even a small percentage reduction in vehicle distance traveled would likely yield great dollar savings.

Other criteria may also be appropriate for vehicle routing. There are instances where we might want servers to visit as many consumers as possible within the constraints of time, distance traveled, and availability of vehicles. Or we might want to minimize the number of vehicles required to provide a specific level of service. These criteria are closely related to minimizing vehicle distance traveled.

This chapter provides an overview of the vehicle routing problem. A taxonomical structure is first developed that delineates the various types of routing problems. Techniques for vehicle routing are then described and illustrated. The techniques presented are heuristic methods that are efficient and provide reasonably good solutions. Finally, the logic of the IBM computer program VSP/X is shown. This program, which is readily available, is the most widely used vehicle routing computer software.

TAXONOMY OF VEHICLE ROUTING

Many terms and expressions used in routing problems come from network theory. This is to be expected because a map of consumer locations, server locations, and transportation routes can be represented by a network.

There are two basic components of a network. These are a set of nodes (small circles) that represent locations and a set of branches (lines connecting pairs of nodes) that represent transportation routes. When the flow between nodes must be in a specific direction, as with one way streets, the nodes are connected by an arrow. Figure 14.1 shows a small network. Imagine a depot located at node 0 and consumers located at the other nodes. Typically, service vehicles depart from the depot, visit each consumer location, and then return to the depot. The arrow between nodes 2 and 3 indicates one-directional flow.

In this chapter we shall focus on the *node routing* problem. This involves routing servers through the network such that specific nodes are visited. This is a common problem that occurs whenever consumers are located at specific geographic points. But there are other types of routing problems. For example, we might be interested in routing servers so that specific branches are traversed; consider street sweeping and snow plowing. This situation is known as *branch routing*. A mixture of branch routing and node routing, that is visiting

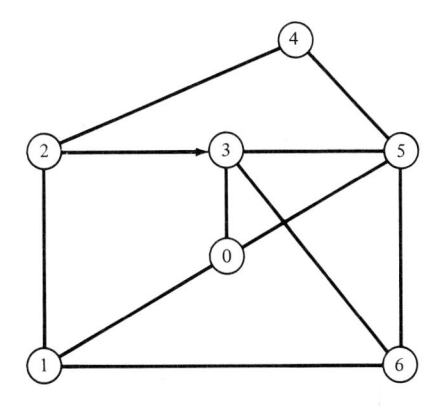

Figure 14.1 Network representation of a depot, consumer locations, and transportation routes.

314 MANAGING SERVICE OPERATIONS

```
                        ┌─────────────────┐
                        │ Vehicle routing │
                        │    problems     │
                        └─────────────────┘
           ┌────────────────┬──┴──────────────┬────────────────┐
    ┌──────────────┐ ┌──────────────┐ ┌──────────────┐ ┌──────────────┐
    │  Number of   │ │  Number of   │ │ Elements to be│ │ Direction of │
    │   vehicles   │ │    depots    │ │   visited    │ │   branches   │
    └──────────────┘ └──────────────┘ └──────────────┘ └──────────────┘
```

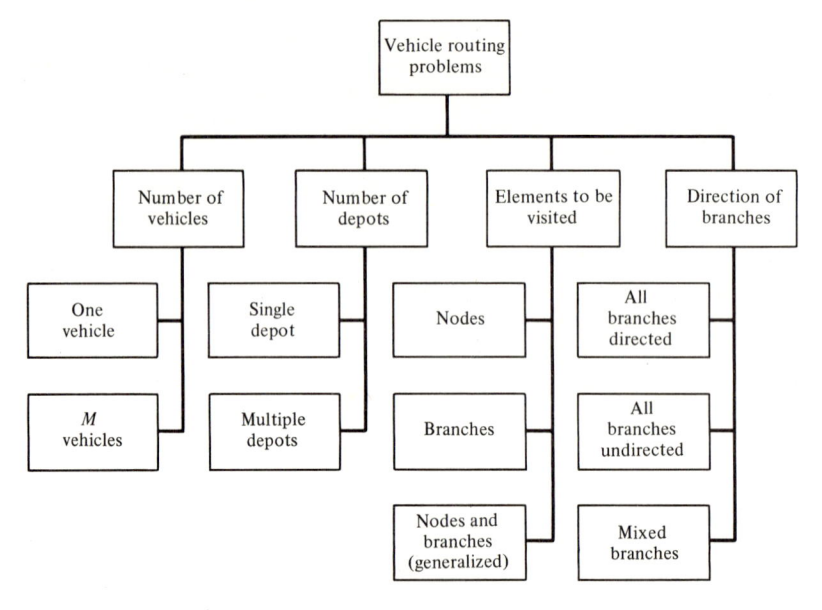

Figure 14.2 Classification of vehicle routing problems.

specific nodes and traversing specific branches, is known as the *generalized routing* problem.

Routing problems can be classified according to their underlying characteristics. We shall restrict our classification to non-real-time programs, that is, to problems where routes are fairly regular and routine.[1] Consequently, they are not under continuous review and readjustment. School bus routes and mail routes are examples of the many problems that fall into this non-real-time category.

Figure 14.2 gives the characteristics for classifying routing problems. The broad categories are:

1. *Number of vehicles.* Routing problems are classified as single vehicle or multiple vehicle (*m* vehicle).
2. *Number of depots.* There is either one depot from which vehicles are dispatched or multiple depots.
3. *Elements (nodes and branches) that are to be visited or traversed.* The classifications are node routing, branch routing, and generalized routing.
4. *Direction of flow for traversing branches.* Branches are categorized as directed (vehicles can travel in one direction only) or undirected (vehicles can travel in either direction).

---

[1] Real-time routing problems occur with police, fire, and emergency medical vehicles. The routes are subject to continuous adjustment, based upon the current location of vehicles and demand points.

In addition to the categories listed above, routing problems can be classified by constraints or side conditions imposed on the system. These might involve upper bounds on the length or duration of a route, capacities of service vehicles, and specific times at which consumers are to be visited (*time windows*).

A few routing problems have received considerable attention over the years. The most famous is the *traveling salesman* problem. This involves routing a single vehicle from a central depot to all nodes in the network and finally back to the depot. And this is to be achieved with minimum penalty, such as transportation cost or distance traveled. The traveling salesman problem is very easy to conceptualize; unfortunately, it is also very difficult and costly to solve for problems of practical size. Consequently, heuristic methods that provide good solutions are generally used, instead of optimizing techniques.

Routing a single vehicle over specified branches is known as the *Chinese postman* problem.[2] Assume that a postman is located at the central post office. He must traverse every road within a particular area delivering mail and then return to the post office. Again, this must be accomplished with minimum penalty. Similar situations are also found with snow plowing, trash pickup, street sweeping, and any services that are to be delivered over the length of branches.

Single-vehicle routing problems may not seem very realistic. After all, not many service systems involve routing only one vehicle. But there is a practical reason for concern over single-vehicle routing. Many solution methodologies for the m-vehicle problem and for the multiple-depot problem are built upon solutions to the single-vehicle problem. Therefore, we must deal with the one-vehicle problem before we can begin to handle more realistic and complex problems.

TECHNIQUES FOR VEHICLE ROUTING

Pin and String Method[3]

The pin and string method is a useful quick and dirty approach for vehicle routing. The basic "tools" needed for this heuristic method are straight pins, a tack, string, and a large highway map encompassing the sites to be visited. For example, the map might be of a scale 1 inch = 10 miles, but an even larger map would be preferable.

The pin and string method is very simple; it involves the following steps:

---

[2] This problem was first studied by Mei-Ko Kwan. "Graphic Programming Using Odd or Even Points," *Chinese Mathematics*, vol. 1, 1962, pp. 273–277.

[3] See, for example, W. W. Abendroth, "A Dirty Shirt Method for Scheduling Vehicles," *Transportation and Distribution Management*, vol. 12, no. 8, August 1972, pp. 24–26.

1. Insert the tack on the map at the depot from which the vehicles are to be dispatched. This shall be referred to as the *origin*.
2. Insert pins at the consumer locations to be visited.
3. Cut the string into lengths that represent full workshifts of travel. For example, if vehicles can travel an average of 25 miles per hour, and a workshift is 8 hours long, then a vehicle can travel an average of 200 miles during the workshift (8 hours × 25 miles/hour = 200 miles). If our highway map has a scale 1 inch = 10 miles, then a string 20 inches long represents a full workshift of travel for a single vehicle (200 miles/10 miles per inch = 20 inches).
4. Tack one end of a string at the origin. Pull the string tightly, without stretching, to a pin and fasten it. If an unattached length of the string still remains, then pull it tightly to a second pin and fasten it. This process is continued until the string is played out (if the vehicle does not have to return to the origin) or just enough string remains to reach back to the origin. It is highly unlikely that the full length of the string will be entirely used. The reason for this is that there may not be a route that requires exactly a full workshift. Consequently, there will be some slack remaining in the route and also in the string. Figure 14.3 shows a map with a single string. Note that the unpinned portion of string is not long enough to encircle another consumer location.
5. If some pins are still not encircled, then return to step 4 using an additional string. Each string represents a vehicle and the pins encircled by the string represent the consumer locations included in the vehicle's route.
6. Once all the pins are encircled, add together the length of the unpinned portions (slack) of each string. If this sum is less than the full length of a string (for example, less than 20 inches), then the routing is achieved with a minimum number of vehicles. Otherwise, it might be possible to reduce the number of vehicles (strings) by reconfiguring the strings around the pins. This can be attempted by trial and error.

The pin and string method is a relatively simple approach for determining vehicle routes. But is it too simple? After all, it relies upon unrealistic assumptions, such as straight-line distances and average speeds. Using this method, we cannot think in terms of optimal vehicle routing. However, the method frequently can give satisfactory and usable answers to complex routing problems. Equally important, it provides answers quickly, with little expense, and in a manner that can be easily understood by all concerned individuals.

But suppose that the pin and string method is not satisfactory. Perhaps it is not scientific or systematic enough. In this case, there are more rigorous heuristic techniques that can be used. The most widely adopted approach is the *Clarke-Wright* (C-W) *algorithm*.[4] While this algorithm has been modified by various users, the basic logic has remained unchanged. Routes are developed

---

[4] See G. Clarke and J. W. Wright, "Scheduling of Vehicles From a Central Depot to a Number of Delivery Points," *Operations Research*, vol. 12, no. 4, July–August 1964, pp. 568–581.

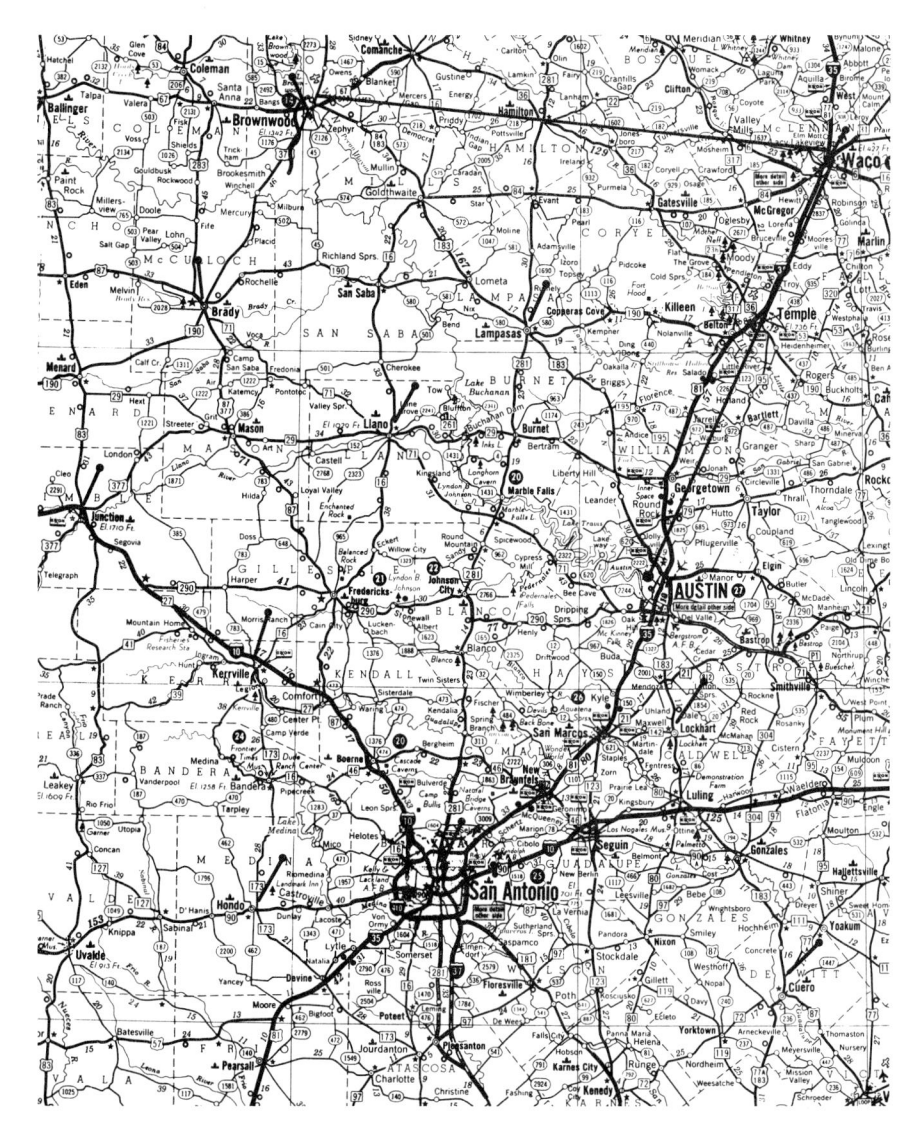

Figure 14.3 A pin and string solution to a vehicle routing problem.

by means of a *savings* concept. The C-W algorithm can be used for hand solutions to small routing problems. But, more importantly, its logic is readily available in computer software packages.

Savings Concept of the Clarke-Wright Algorithm

The C-W algorithm considers the savings that can be achieved by linking pairs of consumers (cities or locations) into a common route. To explain the savings concept, we shall assume that there are N geographically dispersed consumers that are to be visited by vehicles that are located at a central depot. The central depot generally is labeled 0. Initially, we shall assume that there are enough vehicles so that we can assign one to visit each consumer. That is, N vehicles are assigned to visit N consumers. Finally, we shall assume that the cost, distance, or penalty of traveling between locations is symmetric. The cost between locations i and j shall be labeled C_{ij}. By symmetric costs we mean that the cost is the same in going from i to j as from j to i.

What is the total cost of the initial assignment that uses N vehicles? The cost of visiting consumer 1 is $2C_{01}$. Similar costs are associated with the other $N-1$ consumers. This gives a total cost of visiting all N consumers:

$$\text{Total cost} = 2C_{01} + 2C_{02} + \cdots + 2C_{0N-1} + 2C_{0N}$$

$$= 2\sum_{j=1}^{N} C_{0j} \tag{1}$$

Now consider using the same vehicle to visit both location i and location j. The route of this vehicle would be $0-i-j-0$. Does this new route achieve any cost savings when compared with the initial assignment? We save one trip between i and 0, we save one trip between 0 and j, but we add a new trip between i and j. Let S_{ij} be the net savings achieved by linking locations i and j into the same route.

$$S_{ij} = C_{0i} + C_{0j} - C_{ij} \tag{2}$$

The net-savings calculation only uses the cost or penalty associated with traveling between locations. The C-W algorithm systematically considers the net savings associated with adding a new consumer location to a route. Routes are constructed by sequentially adding on locations that offer the greatest net savings.

Example 14.1: Branch banking A major urban bank has four branch offices in addition to its head office. Once a day a vehicle is dispatched from the head office to the branches to pick up checks. These checks are returned to the head office for processing. Figure 14.4 is a network that represents the relative locations of the branch offices and the head office. Distances between locations are given on the network.

The time required to collect the checks is directly proportional to the distance traveled by the collection vehicle. You are asked to determine the net savings that can be realized by linking pairs of branch banks into a common route.

Table 14.1 is a half-matrix whose elements are the shortest distances between the banks. For example, the distance between the head office and branch 2 is 15 miles. We use equation (2) to calculate net savings for every

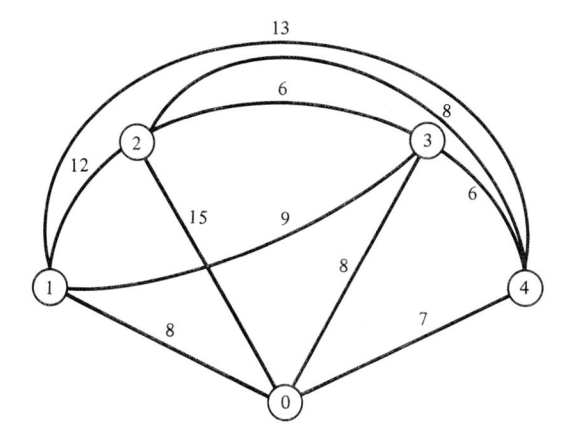

Figure 14.4 Network of bank home office and four branches with distances in miles.

pair of locations. To illustrate this, consider linking locations 1 and 2. The net savings is

$$S_{12} = C_{01} + C_{02} - C_{12}$$
$$= 8 + 15 - 12$$
$$= 11$$

Table 14.2 is a half-matrix whose elements are the net savings for all pairs of locations.

Notice from Table 14.1 that, if four vehicles are used to collect the checks (one goes to each branch bank), then the total distance traveled is 76 miles (2 × 38). This is the total distance associated with the initial solution. Can this be reduced by developing longer individual routes and using fewer vehicles? Which pair of locations will provide the greatest advantage if they are linked into a common route? The C-W algorithm specifically addresses these questions.

Table 14.1 Shortest distance half-matrix: miles between banks

		Branch banks			
		1	2	3	4
Head office	0	8	15	8	7
	1		12	9	13
Branch banks	2			6	8
	3				6

320 MANAGING SERVICE OPERATIONS

Table 14.2 Net savings between all pairs of banks

		\multicolumn{4}{c}{Branch banks}
		1	2	3	4
Head office	0	....	....	....	....
Branch banks	1		11	7	2
	2			17	14
	3				9

The Clarke-Wright (C-W) Algorithm

The C-W algorithm focuses on the net savings involved in developing a route. But it also considers any constraints inherent in the system. These constraints might involve the capacity of a vehicle and the length of a workshift.

We shall use a half-matrix whose elements are net savings. Also, let T_{ij} be an indicator as to whether or not location i and location j are *directly* linked in a route. This indicator can take on any one of three values:

$T_{0j} = 2$. A vehicle travels from the depot to location j and then returns to the depot.
$T_{ij} = 1$. A vehicle travels *directly* between location i and location j.
$T_{ij} = 0$. A vehicle does *not* travel *directly* between location j and location i.

The appropriate values of T_{ij} are recorded in the half-matrix and are circled to distinguish them from the net savings. Notice that most of the values of T_{ij} are zero. For convenience, when $T_{ij} = 0$, it is not recorded in the half-matrix. Therefore, a cell of the matrix without a circled value implies $T_{ij} = 0$.

For a particular location j ($j = 1, 2, \ldots, N$), the following relationship always holds:

$$\sum_{i=0}^{j-1} T_{ij} + \sum_{k=j+1}^{N} T_{jk} = 2 \qquad (3)$$

Equation (3) ensures that, if a vehicle arrives at j, it also departs. This condition is satisfied if the sum of the T values in column j plus the sum of the T values in row j equals 2. Table 14.3 illustrates the calculation of this relationship.

The C-W algorithm is surprisingly simple:

1. Develop an initial allocation of one vehicle to each consumer location. Thus, N vehicles are assigned to visit N consumers.
2. Calculate the net savings S_{ij} for each pair of locations and enter these values in the half-matrix.

Table 14.3 Calculating equation (3) for T values*

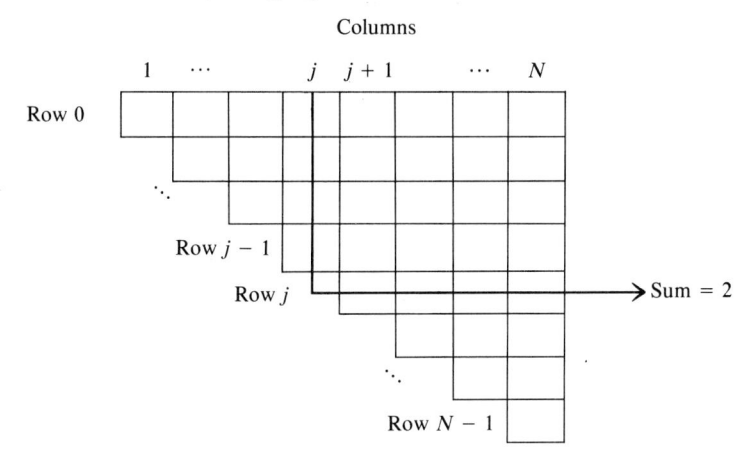

* For each column j, the sum of the T values in column j plus the sum of the T values in row j must equal 2 (i.e., for every location a vehicle must arrive and depart).

3. Enter the appropriate values of T_{ij} in the matrix and circle them.
4. Search the rows and columns of the half-matrix for the maximum net savings. If the maximum savings occurs in cell (i,j) of the matrix, then locations i and j can be linked if the following holds:
   a. T_{0i} and T_{0j} must be greater than zero.
   b. Location i and location j are not already on the same route.
   c. Linking i and j does not violate any system constraints.
5. If all conditions in step 4 are satisfied, set $T_{ij} = 1$. This joins locations i and j in the same route. Then adjust the other T_{ij} values so that equation (3) is satisfied. Return to step 4 using the next-highest net savings.
6. If the conditions in step 4 are not satisfied, then return to step 4 using the next-highest net savings.

The process (steps 1 to 6 above) is repeated until no other links are possible. Ties for the maximum net savings can be randomly broken.

Using the C-W Algorithm with No System Constraints

In Example 14.1 a vehicle travels from a bank's head office to four branch offices and then returns to the head office. We would like to develop a route for this vehicle that minimizes the total distance traveled. This, of course, is the classic traveling salesman problem.

Table 14.4A gives the half-matrix with the initial solution. The circled 2s indicate that a separate vehicle visits each of the four branch banks. The other values in the matrix are the net savings that we calculated in Table 14.2.

322 MANAGING SERVICE OPERATIONS

From Table 14.4A, we see that the largest net saving comes from linking locations 2 and 3 ($S_{23} = 17$). All the necessary conditions are satisfied. Consequently, set $T_{23} = 1$, and adjust the other values of T_{ij} to satisfy equation (3). Table 14.4B gives the revised half-matrix. Note that $T_{02} = 1$ and $T_{03} = 1$ so as to satisfy equation (3).

Table 14.4A Initial solution*

	1	2	3	4
0	②	②	②	② ....
1		11	7	2
2			17	14
3				9

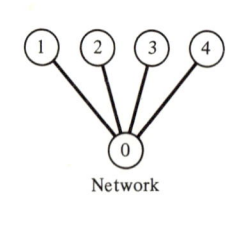

Network

* Routes: First vehicle: 0–1–0
        Second vehicle: 0–2–0
        Third vehicle: 0–3–0
        Fourth vehicle: 0–4–0

Table 14.4B First Iteration*

	1	2	3	4
0	②	①	①	② ....
1		11	7	2
2			① 17	14
3				9

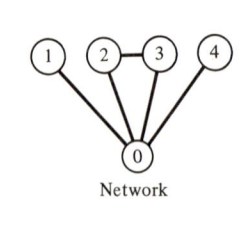

Network

* Routes: First vehicle: 0–1–0
        Second vehicle: 0–2–3–0
        Third vehicle: 0–4–0

Assignment

Develop a routing schedule that will incorporate the additional capacity constraint. How does this final solution compare with the previous two solutions with respect to operating costs and round-trip time?

SELECTED BIBLIOGRAPHY

Abendroth, W. W.: "A Dirty Shirt Method for Scheduling Vehicles," *Transportation and Distribution Management,* vol. 12, August 1972, pp. 24–26.

Bodin, Lawrence D., and Samuel J. Kursh: *A Computerized System for the Routing and Scheduling of Street Sweepers.* Program for Urban and Policy Sciences SUNY Stony Brook, N. Y., March 1976.

———: "A Taxonomic Structure for Vehicle Routing and Scheduling Problems," *Computer and Urban Society,* Pergamon Press, London, 1975, pp. 11–29.

Camp, Robert C., and Daniel W. DeHayes: "A Computer-Based Method for Predicting Transit Time Parameters Using Grid Systems," *Decision Sciences,* vol. 5, no. 3, July 1974, pp. 340–346.

Christofides, N., and S. Eilon: "An Algorithm for the Vehicle Dispatching Problem," *Operations Research Quarterly,* vol. 20, no. 3, 1969, pp. 309–318.

Clarke, G., and J. W. Wright: "Scheduling of Vehicles From a Central Depot to a Number of Delivery Points," *Operations Research,* vol. 12, no. 4, July–August 1964, pp. 568–581.

Cook, Thomas, and Robert Russell: "A Simulation and Statistical Analysis of Stochastic Vehicle Routing With Timing Constraints," *Decision Sciences,* vol. 9, no. 4, October 1978, pp. 673–687.

Gillett, Billy, and Jerry Johnson: "Multi-Terminal Vehicle-Dispatch Algorithm," *Omega,* Pergamon Press, London, vol. 4, no. 6, 1976, pp. 711–718.

——— and L. R. Miller: "A Heuristic Algorithm for the Vehicle-Dispatch Problem," *Operations Research,* vol. 22, no. 2, March–April 1974, pp. 340–349.

Golden, Bruce L.: "Evaluating a Sequential Vehicle Routing Algorithm," *AIIE Transactions,* vol. 9, no. 2, June 1977, pp. 204–208.

Krolak, Patrick, W. Felts, and J. Nelson: "A Man-Machine Approach Toward Solving the Generalized Truck-Dispatching Problem," *Transportation Science,* vol. 6, July 1972, pp. 149–169.

Magnanti, Thomas L., and Bruce L. Golden: "Transportation Planning: Network Models and Their Implementation," Management Science and Statistics Working Paper 77–008, University of Maryland, College Park, Md., 1977.

Marks, David H., and Robert Stricker: "Routing for Public Service Vehicles," *Journal of the Urban Planning and Development Division,* ASCE, vol. 97, no. UP2, December 1971, pp. 165–178.

Nace, G. E.: "Distributing Goods by VSP/360," *Software Age,* March 1969, pp. 8–29.

Orloff, C. S.: "Routing a Fleet of M-Vehicles to/from a Central Facility," *Networks,* vol. 4, 1974, pp. 147–162.

Pierce, J. F.: "Direct Search Algorithms for Truck-Dispatching Problems," *Transportation Research,* Pergamon Press, London, vol. 3, 1969, pp. 1–42.

Quon, Jimmie E., Tanaka Masaru, and Abraham Charnes: "Refuse Quantities and Frequency of Service," *Journal of the Sanitary Engineering Division,* ASCE, vol. 94, no. SA 2, April 1968, pp. 403–420.

Russell, Robert: "An Effective Heuristic for the M-Tour Traveling Salesman Problem With Some Side Conditions," *Operations Research,* vol. 25, no. 3, May–June 1977, pp. 517–525.

Svestka, Joseph A., and Vaughn E. Huckfeldt: "Computational Experience with an M-Salesman," *Management Science,* vol. 19, no. 7, March 1973, pp. 790–799.

Tillman, Frank A., and Harold Cochran: "A Heuristic Approach for Solving the Delivery Problem," *Journal of Industrial Engineering,* vol. 19, no. 7, July 1968, pp. 354–358.

—— and Thomas Cain: "An Upperbound Algorithm for the Single and Multiple Terminal Delivery Problem," *Management Science,* vol. 18, no. 11, July 1972, pp. 664–682.

Truitt, Marcus, Jon C. Liebman, and Cornelius Kruse: "Simulation Model of Urban Refuse Collection," *Journal of the Sanitary Engineering Division,* ASCE, vol. 95, April 1969, pp. 289–298.

Yellow, P. C.: "A Computational Modification to the Savings Method of Vehicle Scheduling," *Operations Research Quarterly,* vol. 21, no. 2, March–April 1970, pp. 281–283.

CHAPTER
FIFTEEN

PROJECT MANAGEMENT: PLANNING, SCHEDULING, AND CONTROLLING SERVICE ACTIVITIES

Dynamic organizations typically have several projects in process, while having several others on the drawing boards. For service organizations, these projects can vary widely in complexity, resource requirements, time needed for completion, and risk. Consider, for example, projects that might be undertaken by a passenger airlines: opening a new route, overhauling an aircraft, implementing a new marketing strategy, installing a new data processing system, purchasing a new fleet of aircraft, changing in-flight service, and installing a new inventory control system.

Similar lists of projects can be envisioned for financial institutions, retail stores, health care organizations, and virtually every other service organization. Managing these projects, of course, is important. But it has special significance for organizations that "sell" project management as their service. Such organizations exist to oversee many large-scale, complex projects, as in research and development, marketing, and construction.

The management of projects is also very important to organizations strapped for resources. For example, a small company is likely to have difficulty in raising funds and tapping the other resources necessary to carry out a project. And the risks inherent in project implementation can pose a threat to the survival of a company. Failure of even a single project can be fatal. The potential risks and rewards associated with a project are factors that enter into selecting a project and developing a strategy for implementation.

Project management is concerned with planning, scheduling, and controlling activities. It addresses issues such as:

1. What activities are required for completing a project?
2. In what sequence should the activities be performed?
3. When should the activities begin and end?
4. What activities are the most important for meeting project objectives?
5. How should resources be allocated to get the activities done?
6. What is the effect of changing the strategies for project implementation?
7. What is the likelihood of meeting project objectives?
8. Is project implementation on schedule?
9. How should project implementation be revised to get back on schedule?

This chapter focuses on the management of service projects. It begins with an overview of the functions that comprise a project management system. Traditional bar-chart methods for project management are then presented and discussed. As an alternative to these traditional methods, the popular network-based methods are described in detail and illustrated. Recent studies indicate that these network techniques are among the most widely accepted management science tools.

PROJECT MANAGEMENT: A CONCEPTUAL FRAMEWORK

Characteristics of Project Systems

We began this chapter with a list of some typical projects. These projects have several common characteristics that should be noted. First, they are relatively large-scale. That is, they involve a substantial commitment of resources over the period of implementation.

Another characteristic is that the projects are complex in terms of the number of activities and of the interdependence of the activities. The projects involve many activities that should be performed in a prespecified sequence. The sequence generally is dictated by technological or strategic considerations. Also, the time and resources required by the activities must be estimated. This is particularly difficult for activities that have never been performed previously, as often is the case with research and development projects.

A final characteristic is that the projects are relatively nonroutine. This means that the service organizations do not engage in a particular project in an ongoing, repetitive fashion. Consequently, each project has novel features that require customized managerial attention.

The Project Management System

Organizations initiate new projects for a variety of reasons, such as competitive pressures, new technologies, and changing demand. These are the catalysts

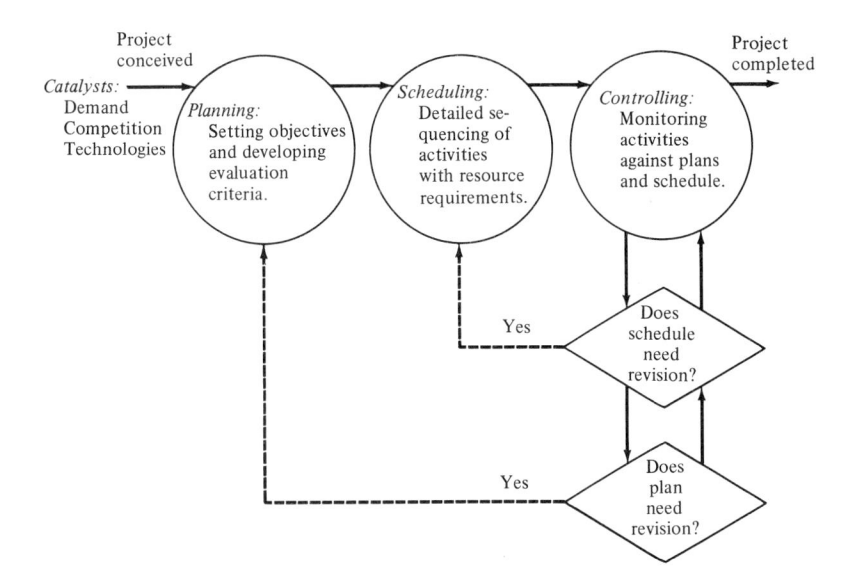

Figure 15.1 The project management system.

that lead to the conception of a new project. Figure 15.1 depicts three project management functions as they evolve from project conception to completion. *Planning* involves specifying objectives and evaluation criteria and developing a gross initial framework for project implementation. The plan outlines in aggregate terms the total resources required for achieving project objectives.

Once the initial plans are developed and accepted, a more detailed schedule is worked out. *Scheduling* begins with decomposing the project into individual activities. The sequencing of the activities is specified; also, time and resource requirements are estimated. The schedule is the basis upon which the project is implemented.

While the project is being implemented, the activities are monitored and controlled. *Controlling* is concerned with making sure that all aspects of project implementation are carried out according to the schedule and plan. If they are not, the schedule and plan are revised as necessary to ensure that project objectives are achieved.

TRADITIONAL TECHNIQUES FOR PROJECT MANAGEMENT

Gantt Project Charts

Before 1958, Gantt project charts were the most common managerial tool for planning, scheduling, and controlling large-scale projects. The chart bears the name of its originator, Henry Gantt, who was a contemporary of Frank Gilbreth, a pioneer of modern production and operations management.

The first step in using a Gantt chart is to break down the project into discrete, whole activities. "Discrete" means that the end of one activity can be identified from the beginning of succeeding activities.

After the project has been decomposed into its activities, the sequence of the activities is determined. This is easier said than done. It is likely that there will be several possible strategies for carrying out the project, and it may not be obvious which one is best. The skills of the project manager, along with the influences of other people interested in the project, ultimately determine the sequence adopted.

A Gantt chart also requires time estimates for each activity. The durations of the activities are assumed to be deterministic and known. This means that we presume to know exactly how long each activity will take. Of course, this is not realistic, but it does provide estimates that are helpful for managing a project.

A Gantt chart consists of a horizontal time axis and a vertical activity axis. The following symbols are commonly used:

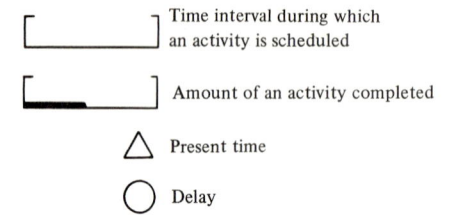

⌐⎯⎯⎯⎯⎯⌐   Time interval during which
⌐⎯⎯⎯⎯⎯⌐   an activity is scheduled

⌐⎯⎯⎯⎯⎯⌐   Amount of an activity completed

△   Present time

○   Delay

Example 15.1: Conducting a customer survey Consider an organization that is conducting a customer survey. Figure 15.2 is a Gantt chart that shows the time period during which each activity is to be carried out. Note that the present time is nine days into the project. The activity "administer questionnaire" is one day behind schedule, and the activity "arrange for keypunching" is delayed. The schedule may have to be rearranged in order to avoid a delay in presenting the final report.

Example 15.2: Servicing a Boeing 747 A Gantt chart also can be used to schedule repetitive operations. Consider the activities required during a routine 50-minute stopover of a Boeing 747 passenger aircraft. Figure 15.3 is a Gantt chart that displays the activities and also indicates crew responsibility. This chart can be used to pinpoint potential delays and to reschedule activities as needed to get back on schedule.

A Critique of Gantt Charts

Gantt charts have several appealing features that account for their continued acceptance. They are visual, easy to construct, and easy to understand. But, more importantly, they result in forced planning. In order to construct a chart, the project manager is compelled to think in detail about activity scheduling and resource requirements.

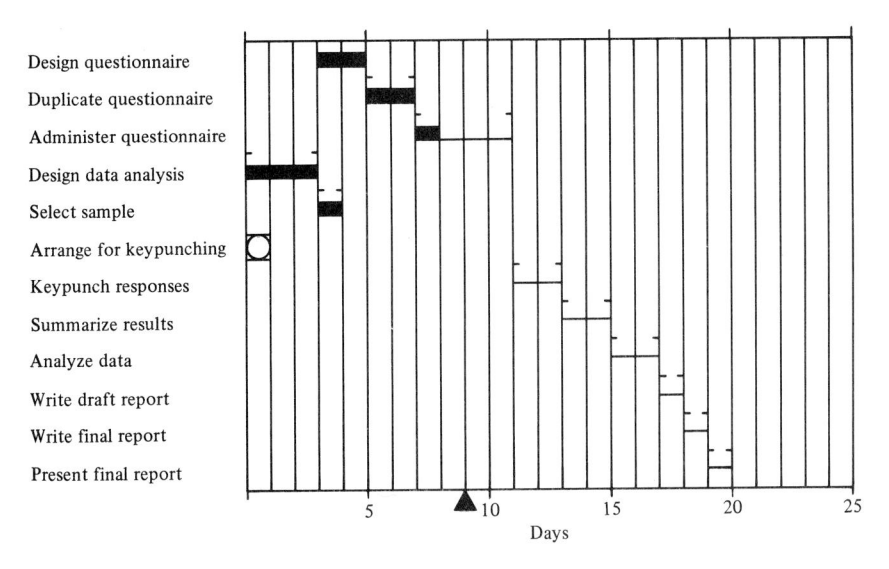

Figure 15.2 Gantt project chart: conducting a customer attitude survey.

Are Gantt charts a good enough tool for service project management? As just mentioned, they do have some appealing features. But for large-scale, complex projects these charts are inadequate. In particular, they do not clearly show the interdependence of activities. Consequently, it is difficult to evaluate the effects of changes in project implementation that may result from activity delays or changes in sequence. Also, these charts do not give any indication about the importance of activities for meeting project objectives. And the importance of activities often is the basis for allocating resources and managerial efforts. Gantt charts do not provide a quantitative measure for achieving this allocation. Consequently, they are ineffective and cumbersome when used with large, complicated projects. Network-based techniques were developed specifically to overcome the deficiencies of Gantt charts.

NETWORK TECHNIQUES FOR PROJECT MANAGEMENT

Network Techniques: A Brief History

In 1957, work was undertaken by the U. S. Navy's Special Projects Office to develop a means for managing large-scale, complex projects. This culminated in the technique known as PERT (Program Evaluation and Review Technique). PERT was applied in 1958 to the Polaris ballistic missile system, where it was credited with saving two years in development time. This research and development project was comprised of thousands of interdependent activities, whose durations were uncertain. Handling these uncertainties was a major concern in project management. Using PERT, it became possible to make probability statements with regard to project completion time.

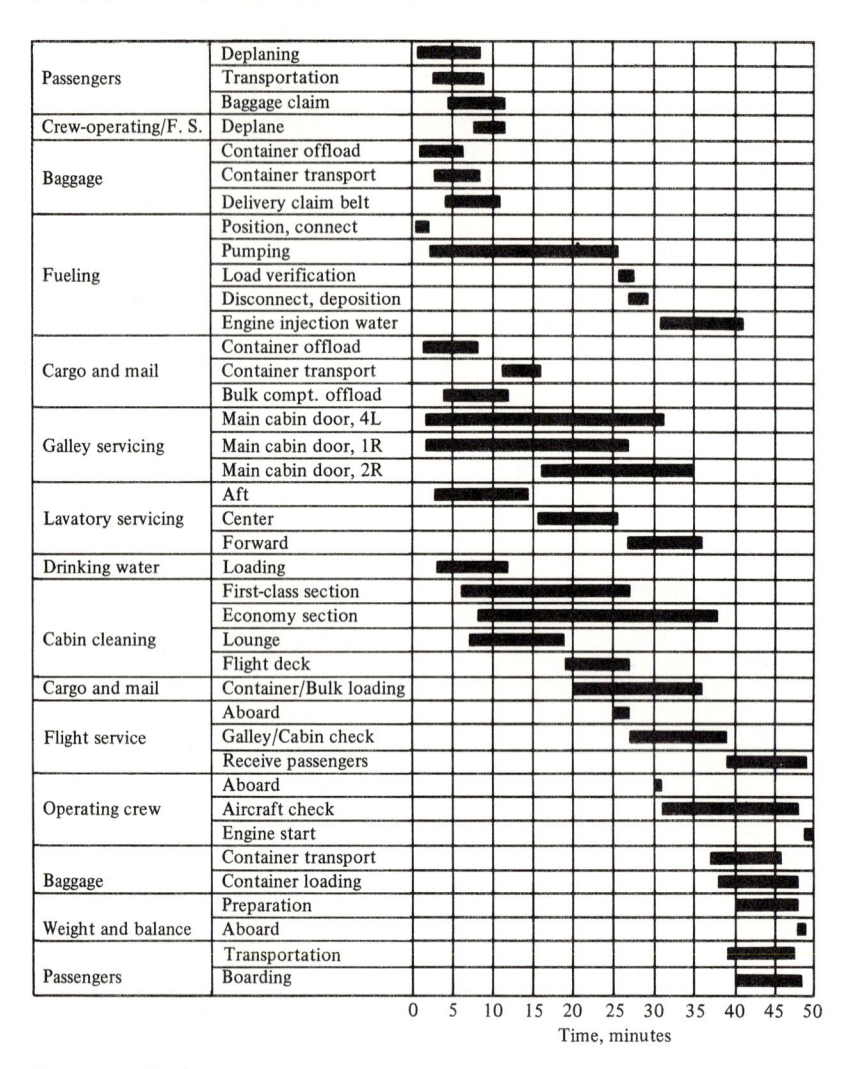

		0 5 10 15 20 25 30 35 40 45 50
Passengers	Deplaning	
	Transportation	
	Baggage claim	
Crew-operating/F. S.	Deplane	
Baggage	Container offload	
	Container transport	
	Delivery claim belt	
Fueling	Position, connect	
	Pumping	
	Load verification	
	Disconnect, deposition	
	Engine injection water	
Cargo and mail	Container offload	
	Container transport	
	Bulk compt. offload	
Galley servicing	Main cabin door, 4L	
	Main cabin door, 1R	
	Main cabin door, 2R	
Lavatory servicing	Aft	
	Center	
	Forward	
Drinking water	Loading	
Cabin cleaning	First-class section	
	Economy section	
	Lounge	
	Flight deck	
Cargo and mail	Container/Bulk loading	
Flight service	Aboard	
	Galley/Cabin check	
	Receive passengers	
Operating crew	Aboard	
	Aircraft check	
	Engine start	
Baggage	Container transport	
	Container loading	
Weight and balance	Preparation	
	Aboard	
Passengers	Transportation	
	Boarding	

Time, minutes

Figure 15.3 Service activities for Boeing 747.

At the same time that PERT was being developed, E. I. Du Pont de Nemours Company was working independently on a network technique called CPM (Critical Path Method). This method was developed in conjunction with a new plant construction project. A key difference between CPM and PERT is that CPM does not consider the uncertainties in the durations of activities. But, given the nature of construction projects, these uncertainties are not extremely important. CPM does allow for time-cost tradeoffs in performing activities. This enables managers to analyze the overall impact of reducing the duration of activities by increasing the resources directed at these activities.

PERT and CPM use very similar methodologies that make them equally good managerial tools. They were the forerunners of other network-based methods for project management. Acronyms such as PEP, SPERT, and IMPACT refer to project planning techniques that are similar to PERT and CPM. They all rely upon a common methodology that we shall call *critical path analysis*. This methodology involves constructing a project network, estimating activity durations, and determining the amount of time activities can be delayed without delaying project completion time.

Constructing a Project Network

A network consists of a set of circles called nodes and a set of arrows called arcs. The arcs connect the nodes to give a visual presentation of the sequence of activities. A project network is known as a *systems flow plan*.

There are two ways for constructing a systems flow plan. One method, known as *activities on nodes* (AON), has the nodes represent project activities, while the arcs indicate the activity sequence. The second method, known as *activities on arcs* (AOA), has the arcs represent project activities. The nodes are *events*, which are the starts or completions of activities. An event takes place at an instant of time, while an activity takes place over an interval of time. The AON and AOA methods are equally good for representing the sequence of activities, and both are widely used for project management.

A key assumption underlying PERT and CPM is that an activity cannot begin until *all* immediate predecessor activities are completed. Also, a systems flow plan generally has a single node that indicates the project beginning and a single node that indicates the project ending. PERT and CPM systems flow plans are *connected* and *acyclic*. The term "connected" means that it is possible to get to any network node by following arcs leaving the initial node. "Acyclic" means that the sequence of activities progresses uninterruptedly from the initial node to the completion node, without looping around in circles.

Nodes in a systems flow plan are numbered sequentially, beginning with the initial node. If a particular node *i* immediately precedes another node *j*, then *j* must have a larger number than *i*. A skip numbering system frequently is used. For example, the nodes might be numbered 0, 10, 20, and so forth. This allows the project manager to add activities into a revised network, without having to renumber every node. The following example illustrates both the AON and AOA methods for constructing a systems flow plan.

Example 15.3: Nutrition education project A state education agency received a federal grant to establish student learning objectives in the area of nutrition education. These objectives would set the minimum acceptable level of nutrition education for public school students from kindergarten through twelfth grade. The objectives should also incorporate the opinions of a broad spectrum of professionals with interests in nutrition. Table 15.1 lists the activities required for this project, along with sequence and duration.

Table 15.1 Nutrition education objectives

Activity description	Code	Immediate predecessor activity	Estimated duration, weeks
Review literature on nutrition learner objectives.	A	....	2
Form a task force of experts.	B	....	3
Form subgroups of task force members.	C	B	1
Conduct task force meeting.	D	A, B	1
Collate and analyze outcomes from meeting.	E	D	3
Send outcomes to subgroups.	F	C, E	0.5
Send outcomes to pilot school systems.	G	E	0.5
Send outcomes to 20 national experts.	H	E	0.5
Collect, collate, and analyze responses from all groups.	I	F, G, H	3
Develop final set of outcomes.	J	I	2
Mail out final set of outcomes to interested agencies.	K	J	1

Figure 15.4 is an AON systems flow plan for the project. Notice that the nodes represent the activities, while the arcs represent activity sequence. Node 0 indicates the beginning of the project, and Node 110 the completion.

Figure 15.5 is an AOA systems flow plan. The broken arcs joining node 10 with 20, node 40 with 50, and node 60 with 70 are referred to as *dummy activities*. Dummy activities do not consume time. Instead, they are included in a systems flow plan to maintain proper activity sequence. It should be clear that the AOA and AON systems flow plans describe the same sequence of activities.

Critical Path Analysis

Critical path analysis is the core of PERT and CPM. It involves determining the amount of time that activities can be delayed without delaying project completion time. Activities that cannot be delayed are called *critical activities*, owing to their importance for completing the project. Critical activities often receive top priority in the allocation of resources and managerial efforts. They are the focal points in the strategy for project implementation.

Critical path analysis involves some simple calculations. Table 15.2 lists

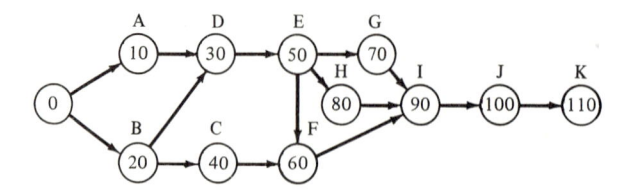

Figure 15.4 AON systems flow plan: nutrition education objectives.

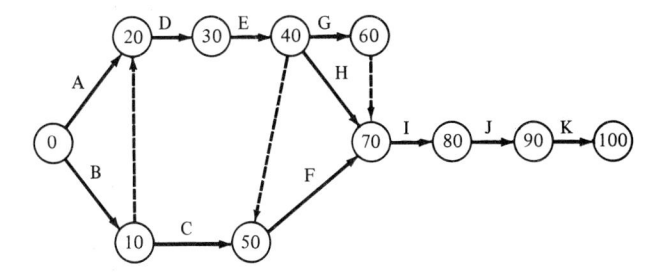

Figure 15.5 AOA systems flow plan: nutrition education objectives.

the notation used in the analysis. Notice that we have not indicated how the expected activity durations t_e are determined. In many cases, these values are assumed to be deterministic (constants) and are based upon expert judgement and past experience. In other cases, the expected durations are assumed to be the arithmetic means of known probability distributions. We shall discuss this case in more detail later.

Critical path analysis involves calculating early times (*ES* and *EF*), late times (*LS* and *LF*), and slack times (*TS* and *FS*). Early times are calculated for each activity beginning with the first activity and moving successively through the network. The early start for the first activity is set equal to zero. For a particular activity the early times are calculated as follows:

$$EF = ES + t_e \tag{1}$$

$$ES = EF_{\text{predecessor}} \tag{2}$$

Table 15.2 Notation for critical path analysis

Item	Symbol	Definition
Expected activity duration	t_e	The expected duration of an activity
Early start	ES	The earliest time an activity can begin if all previous activities are begun at their earliest times
Early finish	EF	The earliest time an activity can be completed if it is started at its early start time
Late start	LS	The latest time an activity can begin without delaying the completion of the project
Late finish	LF	The latest time an activity can be completed if it is started at its latest start time
Total slack	TS	The amount of time an activity can be delayed without delaying the completion of the project
Free slack	FS	The amount of time an activity can be delayed without delaying the early start of a subsequent activity

where $EF_{predecessor}$ is the early finish of an immediately preceding activity. When there are several immediate predecessors, then the one with the *largest* early finish time is used. The early finish for the last activity is the early finish for the project.

Late times are calculated for each activity, beginning with the last activity in the network. By convention, the late finish for the last activity is set equal to the early finish for the project. For the remaining activities, the late times are calculated as follows:

$$LS = LF - t_e \qquad (3)$$

$$LF = LS_{successor} \qquad (4)$$

where $LS_{successor}$ is the late start of an immediately succeeding activity. When there are several immediate successors, then the one with the *smallest* late start is used.

Slack times are determined from the early times and late times. Total slack for an activity can be calculated in either of two equivalent ways:

$$TS = LF - EF \qquad (5)$$

or

$$TS = LS - ES \qquad (6)$$

Total slack is one of the most important aspects of critical path analysis. Activities that have zero total slack are critical, meaning they cannot be delayed without delaying project completion time. A set of critical activities always forms a complete and unbroken path from the initial node to the completion node of the network. Such a path is referred to as the *critical path*. In terms of expected duration this is the longest path in the network. Every systems flow plan has *at least* one critical path.

Free slack is an important measure for identifying the impact of one activity upon succeeding activities in the project. It is calculated as follows:

$$FS = ES_{successor} - EF \qquad (7)$$

where $ES_{successor}$ is the early start time of an immediately succeeding activity. When there are several successor activities, the one with the *smallest* early start is used.

Free slack is always less than or equal to total slack. For example, it is possible for an activity to have zero free slack, while having positive total slack. In such a case, a delay in the activity will delay a succeeding activity, but it will not necessarily delay the completion of the project.

Example 15.4: Project scheduling calculations Figure 15.6 shows an AOA systems flow plan for a project. The expected durations of activities are written below each arc. The early times, late times, and slack times for each activity are recorded using the format shown at the top of the figure.

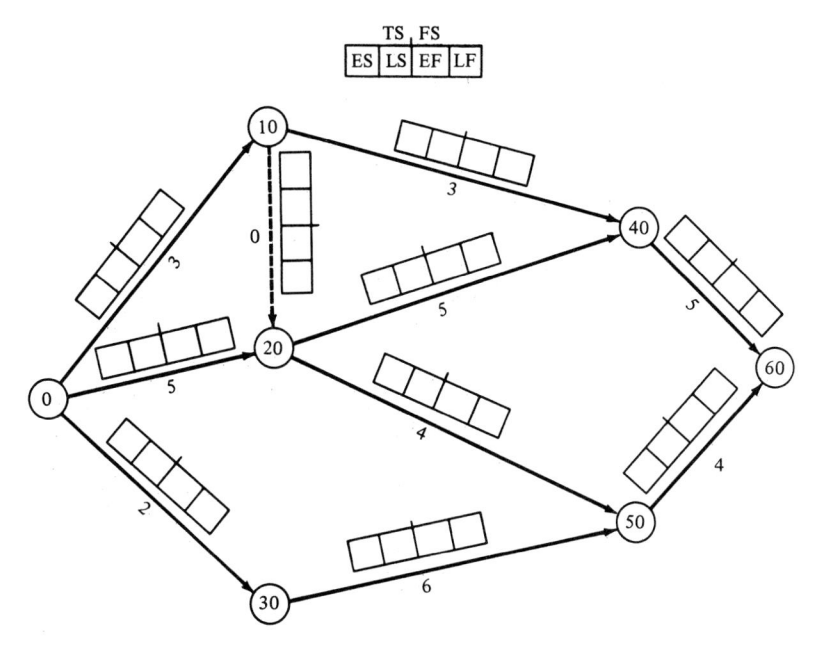

Figure 15.6 AOA systems flow plan.

Figure 15.7 shows the systems flow plan with the early times. These are calculated beginning with the first network activities. We see that the early completion of the project is 15 weeks.

Figure 15.8 shows the completed critical path analysis. Notice that the late finish was set equal to 15 weeks. This is the early completion time of the project. This value (15 weeks) is the starting point for calculating late times.

The critical activities have zero total slack. In this case, the critical path is determined by the nodes 0–20–40–60. Any delay in activities on this path will delay the completion of the project beyond the fifteenth week. But delays in other activities, within limits, can be tolerated. For example, activity 20–50 has two weeks of total slack. This means that this activity can be delayed by as much as two weeks without affecting project completion time. However, a delay in this activity will delay activity 50–60. We know this because 20–50 has zero free slack.

Of what value is the information provided by critical path analysis? First, we know which activities are likely to determine project completion time if everything goes according to plan. We have identified the activities that cannot be delayed and, consequently, require more intense managerial attention. We have also identified those activities that can be delayed, and, therefore, can be managed in a more casual fashion. Related to this, of course, is the allocation of

348 MANAGING SERVICE OPERATIONS

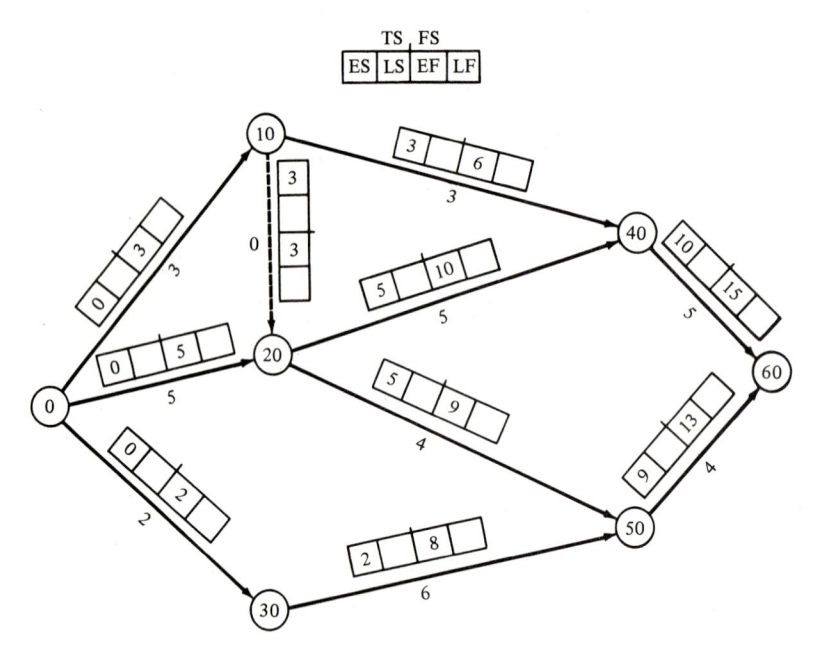

Figure 15.7 AOA systems flow plan with early time calculations.

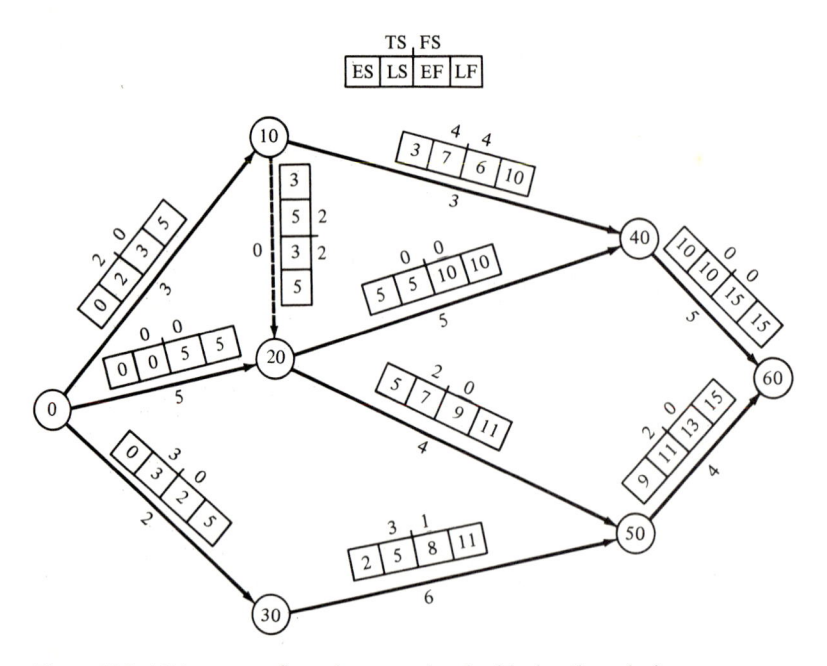

Figure 15.8 AOA systems flow plan: completed critical path analysis.

resources. Slack times are quantitative measures that can be used to set priorities for resource allocation. Resources might be shifted from activities with slack time to critical activities.

Estimating Activity Durations

In the previous example, we assumed that activity durations t_e were known constants. For many situations, this assumption is not practical owing to the uncertainties involved in carrying out the activities. These durations generally are random variables that have associated probability distributions. Therefore, we do not know in advance the exact durations of all activities. And, consequently, we cannot determine the exact completion time of the project.

PERT attempts to consider the uncertainties of activity durations. The durations are assumed to be random variables that follow a particular probability distribution known as the Beta distribution. Figure 15.9 shows a typical Beta distribution. PERT uses this distribution because, on the surface, it appears to be appropriate for many activity durations. But more importantly, it is used because it leads to some very simple formulas that facilitate critical path analysis. We shall describe how PERT uses the Beta distribution to consider the uncertainties in activity durations.

PERT requires three estimates of each activity duration. These are:

1. *Optimistic time* t_o. This is the duration of an activity if there are no complications or problems. As a rule of thumb, there should be about a 1 percent chance of the actual duration being less than t_o.
2. *Pessimistic time* t_p. This is the duration of an activity if extraordinary problems arise. As a rule of thumb, there should be about a 1 percent chance of the actual duration ever exceeding t_p.
3. *Most likely time* t_m. This is the duration that is most likely to occur. In statistical terms, t_m is the modal value.

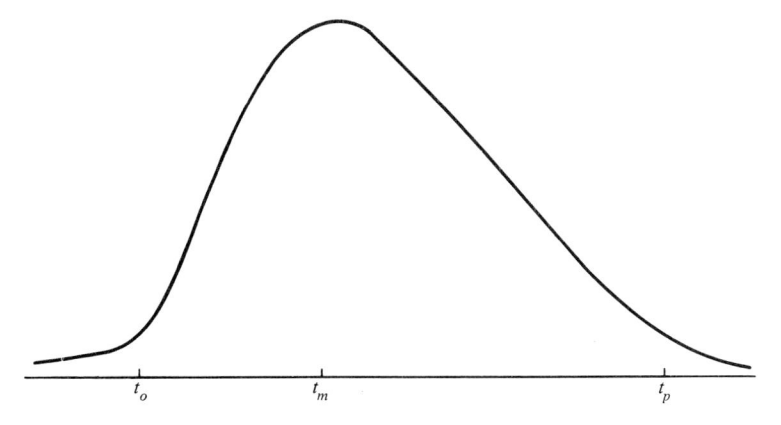

Figure 15.9 Typical Beta distribution.

The standard deviation σ of an activity duration is a measure of uncertainty. It indicates how widely dispersed the distribution is about the expected duration t_e. With PERT, we assume that the optimistic time t_o and the pessimistic time t_p are six standard deviations apart. This yields

$$\sigma = (t_p - t_o)/6 \tag{8}$$

Consequently, the variance of an activity duration is given by

$$\sigma^2 = (t_p - t_o)^2/36 \tag{9}$$

The variance given above can be substituted into a complex formula for the Beta distribution, and the expected activity duration can be calculated. The resulting formula for t_e is extremely simple:

$$t_e = (t_o + 4t_m + t_p)/6 \tag{10}$$

We now can easily calculate σ^2 and t_e for every activity in the systems flow plan. Equations (9) and (10) are central to PERT. The steps involved in the analysis are straightforward:

1. For every activity, obtain estimates of t_o, t_m, and t_p.
2. Use equation (10) to calculate t_e for the activities.
3. Perform critical path analysis using the expected activity durations t_e. This means that early times, late times, and slack times are calculated.
4. The expected project completion time $\bar{T}$ is assumed to be the sum of the expected durations of activities on the critical path.
5. The variance of project completion time σ_T^2 is assumed to be the sum of the variances of activities on the critical path. These variances are calculated by means of equation (9).
6. Project completion time is assumed to be normally distributed.[1]
7. Probabilities regarding project completion time can be determined from the available standard normal tables. (See Table C in the tables at the back of the book.)

Example 15.5: PERT calculations A project is described by the AOA systems flow plan given in Figure 15.10. The durations of the activities are random variables and three time estimates are recorded on each arc. You are asked to determine the expected project completion time, the variance of project completion time, and the probability of finishing the project within six months (24 weeks).

---

[1] This assumption is based upon a well-known statistical law called the central limit theorem. In loose terms, this theorem says that the sum of many independent random variables is a random variable that tends to be normally distributed. In this case, the project completion time is the sum of the individual durations of activities on the critical path.

Figure 15.10 AOA systems flow plan with uncertain activity durations.

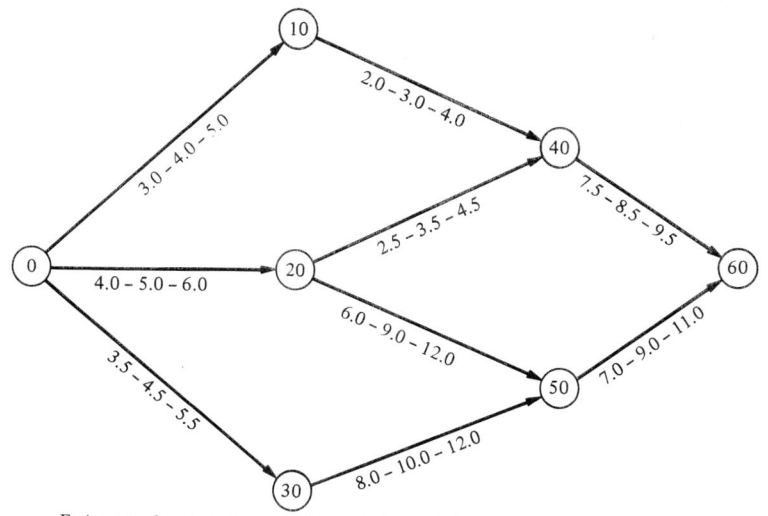

Estimates of activity durations (in weeks) recorded on arcs: $t_o - t_m - t_p$.

The variances and expected activity durations are calculated by means of equations (9) and (10) and are given in Table 15.3. Using the expected durations, critical path analysis then is performed. Figure 15.11 presents the completed analysis.

The critical path is 0–30–50–60. We would expect the activities on this path to take 23.5 weeks to be completed. This is the PERT expected project completion time $\bar{T}$. The variance of project completion time is calculated by summing the variances associated with the critical activities. This yields $\sigma_T^2 = \frac{1}{9} + \frac{4}{9} + \frac{4}{9} = 1$.

We can now use $\bar{T}$ and σ_T^2 to determine the probability of finishing the project within 24 weeks. The appropriate Z value (standard normal deviate) is

$$Z = \frac{24 - \bar{T}}{\sigma_T}$$

$$= \frac{24 - 23.5}{1}$$

$$= 0.5$$

This Z value has an associated probability that can be found in the standard normal table. Figure 15.12 shows the appropriate area under the normal curve. There is a 0.6915 probability of finishing the project within the 24 weeks.

352 MANAGING SERVICE OPERATIONS

Table 15.3 Variances and expected activity durations

Activity	t_o	t_m	t_p	Variance, σ^2	Expected durations, t_e
0–10	3.0	4.0	5.0	$\frac{1}{9}$	4.0
0–20	4.0	5.0	6.0	$\frac{1}{9}$	5.0
0–30	3.5	4.5	5.5	$\frac{1}{9}$	4.5
10–40	2.0	3.0	4.0	$\frac{1}{9}$	3.0
20–40	2.5	3.5	4.5	$\frac{1}{9}$	3.5
20–50	6.0	9.0	12.0	1	9.0
30–50	8.0	10.0	12.0	$\frac{4}{9}$	10.0
40–60	7.5	8.5	9.5	$\frac{1}{9}$	8.5
50–60	7.0	9.0	11.0	$\frac{4}{9}$	9.0

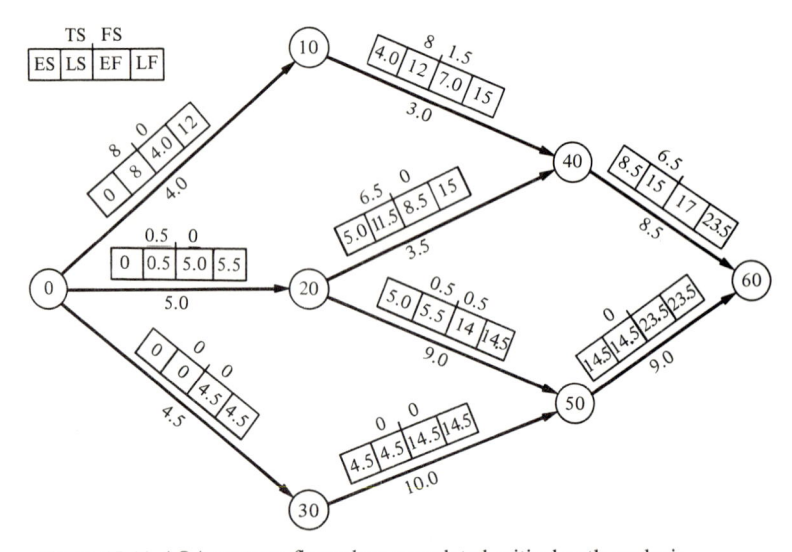

Figure 15.11 AOA systems flow plan: completed critical path analysis.

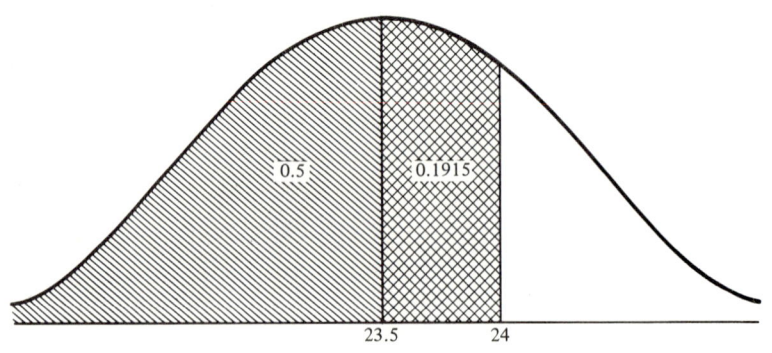

Figure 15.12 Area under normal curve.

The PERT Assumption: A Critique

The key assumption underlying PERT is that the critical path, as calculated from expected activity durations, will actually determine project completion time. How valid is this assumption? We know that the duration of the critical path is uncertain; it has a probability distribution associated with it. Likewise, the durations of other paths are uncertain. Consequently, it is possible for the critical path to take less time than expected, while some other path takes more time than expected. The net effect may be that a path which was not identified as being critical determines project completion.

The key PERT assumption has some important implications for the accuracy of the calculations. The PERT estimates of expected completion time and variance of completion time for the project are biased. For the variance, the bias can be either on the high or on the low side. But the expected project completion time is always optimistically biased. That is, the true expected completion time is always greater than or equal to the PERT estimate. Extensive studies of the PERT assumptions indicate the PERT expected time generally is in error by 5 to 10 percent. However, an example was constructed where the error was 172 percent. The latter example was developed to dramatize the effects of the PERT assumption.[2]

There is a simple guideline that can assist in giving a feel for the accuracy of the PERT estimates. If the expected duration of the critical path is much longer than that of any other path, the estimates are likely to be good. This is because it is likely that the critical path will actually determine project completion time. However, if there are paths with very little total slack time, then these paths may well affect project completion time. In such a case, the PERT estimates will be highly biased and inaccurate, and managerial attention should not be restricted to critical path activities. Attention should also be given to the *near* critical activities, that is, activities with little slack time.

Some analysts are not comfortable with the inherent biases of PERT. Consequently, alternative methods have been suggested for project network analysis that are more accurate, but they also require more sophisticated statistical analysis and greater computation time. For example, Monte Carlo simulations can be used to analyze project networks whose activity durations are stochastic. Simulation has the advantage of allowing any type of distribution for the durations of activities; it is not restricted to the Beta distribution. Also, it provides unbiased estimates of the expected project completion time and of the variance of project completion time. The accuracy of the Monte Carlo simulation estimates is a function of the number of realizations, that is, the sample size. The primary criticism leveled against using Monte Carlo simulation is the computation cost. It takes considerably more computation time than PERT. But as larger and faster computers become more readily available, techniques

---

[2] This example is described by K. R. MacCrimmon and C. C. Ryavec: "An Analytical Study of PERT Assumptions," *Operations Research,* vol. 12, no. 1, January–February 1964, pp. 16–37.

such as Monte Carlo simulation become more practicable. These techniques, are likely to make conventional PERT an obsolete project management method.

Problems with Implementing Critical Path Analysis

The mechanics of critical path analysis make the use of network models appear deceptively simple. After all, the calculations are straightforward. But network analysis does not resolve all of the problems inherent in project management. Two major concerns are developing the systems flow plan (network structure) and eliciting time estimates for activities.

The systems flow plan indicates the sequence in which the activities are to be performed. For most projects, there may be several different strategies that may be adopted. We mentioned before that technological factors along with the influences of people concerned with the project generally determine the strategy selected. But as the project is implemented, the systems flow plan is subject to review and possible revision. A revision may be needed because some activities get off schedule or resources may not be available.

Reviewing and revising the systems flow plan can be very time-consuming. Individuals involved in the project must be consulted with regard to anticipated changes. In most projects complete agreement to change is not possible, so a compromise revision of the plan is adopted. The process of reviewing and revising the systems flow plan is an ongoing process that can take a large amount of the project manager's time.

The second concern in using network models is eliciting time estimates for activities. Of course, poor estimates would result in poor project management. But it is difficult to get good time estimates. Some activities may involve several people who can affect the duration. How do you get a consensus of opinion with regard to the estimated duration? In some cases, a consensus may not be possible; the individuals just don't agree.

Another problem is bias introduced into estimates of activity durations. For example, an individual may actually expect to carry out an activity in eight days, but gives an estimate of ten days. That way, the individual provides for a few days of leeway—a form of protection. If many activity durations are biased to this extent, the critical path analysis will be of little value. It is important for the project manager to sort out as much bias as possible, but this can be extremely difficult.

SUMMARY

Managers of service organizations typically are immersed in the detailed operations of ongoing projects. They also are responsible for generating new projects. The vitality of an organization can be seen in the way projects are conceived and carried out. For dynamic organizations, project management has important dimensions. It involves planning, scheduling, and controlling the activities necessary to carry out a project successfully.

For small uncomplicated projects, Gantt charts are a good tool for assisting project managers. But for large projects that involve many interdependent activities, Gantt charts are cumbersome. Network techniques, such as CPM and PERT, were developed as tools for aiding managers of complex projects. Most network techniques use a similar methodology known as critical path analysis. PERT specifically addresses the problem of uncertain activity durations. It allows the manager to make probability statements with regard to meeting project objectives.

Network techniques are very important tools for project management. They indicate the activities that are likely to affect project completion. They also facilitate the evaluation of changes in project implementation. Furthermore, advances are being made with regard to the accuracy and efficiency of network approaches. This, in conjunction with the availability of faster and cheaper computer resources, will make network techniques even more valuable to service operations managers.

TOPICS FOR DISCUSSION

1. Consider a major urban bank. Give examples of large, complex projects undertaken by the bank that might benefit from project management techniques.
2. Project management is concerned with planning, scheduling, and controlling activities. Explain what each of these means in terms of project management.
3. Are Gantt charts still viable project management tools? Explain.
4. Determining activity sequence and estimating activity durations often are the most difficult aspects of PERT analysis. Explain.
5. Give a critique of the PERT assumptions.
6. The PERT estimate of expected project duration is always optimistic. Explain why this is so. Can we get any feel for the magnitude of the bias?
7. What are some typical problems with implementing critical path analysis?
8. Costs and resource utilization are major concerns of project management. Can you suggest methods for integrating these into critical path analysis?

EXERCISES

15.1 The following project to develop an orbiting solar collector has been funded by NASA as its contribution to the nation's energy crisis. Draw the network and identify the critical path activities.

Activity	Immediate predecessor	Optimistic	Most likely	Pessimistic
A	....	4	6	8
B	....	1	2	3
C	A	4	4	4
D	A	4	5	6
E	B	7	10	16
F	B	8	9	10
G	C	2	2	2
H	D, E, G	2	3	7
I	F	1	3	11

Activity duration, months

15.2 Electronic Protection Inc. is nearly finished with a project to produce a smoke detector. A reduction in required performance specifications will make the remaining work easier than originally planned. The following activities and revised time estimates will complete the project.

Activity	Time, days	Immediate predecessor	Description
A	1	....	Check total weight and approve.
B	2	....	Check power consumption.
C	2	....	Check temperature requirements.
D	2	A, B	Select detector.
E	4	A, C	Design transistor circuit.
F	1	C	Choose encapsulating material.
G	4	D	Ensure hermetic seal.
H	8	G, E, F	Perform final test.

(*a*) Draw a critical path scheduling diagram and indicate the critical path.
(*b*) Calculate the total slack and free slack for each activity.

15.3 The following activities are required for completing a project:

Activity	Immediate predecessor	Optimistic	Most likely	Pessimistic
A	....	3	6	15
B	....	2	5	14
C	A	6	12	30
D	A	2	5	8
E	C	5	11	17
F	D	3	6	15
G	B	3	9	27
H	E, F	1	4	7
I	G	4	19	28
J	H, I	1	1	1

(*a*) Draw a network diagram of this project showing the activities and their expected duration times.
(*b*) What is the critical path and the expected completion time of the project?
(*c*) What is the probability of completing the project in 41 days or less?

15.4 Slippery Rock College is planning a basketball tournament and has decided to use CPM to schedule the project. The following information has been collected on each activity in the project:

Activity	Description	Immediate predecessor	Time estimate, days
A	Select teams	....	3
B	Mail out invitations.	A	5
C	Arrange accommodations.	....	10
D	Plan promotion.	B, C	3
E	Print tickets.	B, C	5
F	Sell tickets.	E	10
G	Complete arrangements.	C	8
H	Develop schedules.	G	3
I	Practice.	D, H	2
J	Conduct tournament.	F, I	3

(a) Draw a network diagram of this project and label activities and events.
(b) Calculate the total slack and free slack for all activities. What is the critical path?
(c) When should the team selection begin if the tournament is scheduled to start on the morning of December 27 (include Saturday and Sunday as working days)?

15.5 The PERT network in Figure 15.13 and the table below show the expected number of weeks to complete each activity and the corresponding standard deviation:

Activity	Expected duration, weeks	Standard deviation, weeks
A	5	1
B	10	$\sqrt{2}$
C	4	1
D	7	1
E	6	$\sqrt{2}$
F	8	1
G	4	$\sqrt{2}$
H	3	1
I	5	1
J	7	$\sqrt{2}$
K	8	$\sqrt{3}$

(a) Determine the critical path and the earliest expected completion time.
(b) What is the probability of completing the project in 24 weeks or less?

15.6 You are asked to plan the following covert operation for the AIC.

Activity	Immediate predecessor	Optimistic	Most likely	Pessimistic
A	....	1	2	3
B	A	3	3	3
C	B	4	6	8
D	A	2	8	8
E	A	6	9	12
F	D, C	4	7	10
G	D	10	10	16
H	D, E	4	5	6
I	F, G, H	2	2	2

(a) Draw a network diagram for this project.
(b) Calculate the expected time and variance for each activity.
(c) Determine the critical path and expected project completion time.
(d) What is the probability of the project taking more than 25 days?

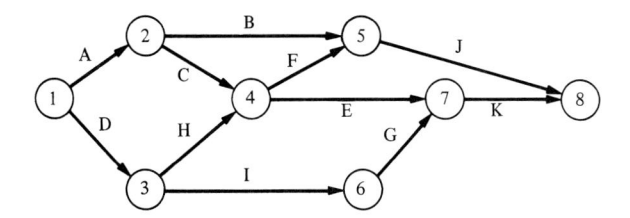

Figure 15.13 PERT network.

CASELETTE: WHITTIER COUNTY HOSPITAL

After some 50 years in the present location, Whittier County Hospital is beginning to make preparations to move into a new building sometime in the near future, when its construction and outfitting are completed. The hospital's board of directors has appointed a special management committee to control the entire procedure, including coordination with outside agencies as well as the internal departments. As a first step in its mission, the committee wishes to develop a base of information that will be used to (1) establish an initial sketch plan for proceeding through the detailed planning and moving phases and (2) provide a fundamental management and scheduling tool for day-to-day operations during the transition period.

The management staff believes that a PERT analysis of a sketch plan would be very helpful to the committee's understanding of the moving process and so begins to develop a network of activities and duration estimates for the task. After consultation with the general contractor at the building site, it is estimated that the completion of construction and checking of newly installed equipment will likely take 50 more days, with 40 and 60 days as the optimistic and pessimistic estimates. At this point the structure will be vacated by the contractor and turned over to the board.

Before this occurs, however, a detailed plan of action for each of the hospital departments must be drawn up for approval by the move committee (MC), as it is formally known. The staff estimates that this will take at least 10 days, perhaps as many as 20 days, and probably 15 days to develop and secure approval.

Once the detailed plan has received this initial go-ahead, the staff will have a number of activities to perform before a trial run and subsequent evaluation of the plan are made:

1. Develop and distribute an information newsletter to all hospital employees outlining the general procedures, with specific procedures attached for each department; it is estimated that this will take at least three, probably four, and at most seven days.
2. Develop information and generate media coverage for the upcoming events; this is estimated to take at least (and probably) two days and three days at most.
3. Negotiate with local EMS and private ambulance services for transferring the patients: at least 10, probably 14, and at most 20 days.
4. Negotiate with professional moving companies for transferring equipment, records, and supplies: four, five, and eight days.
5. Coordinate the procedures with and determine the responsibilities of the local police and fire departments: three, five, and ten days.
6. Coordinate the admissions and exchange procedures during the transition period with other hospitals in the surrounding area: two, three, and five days.

Once the construction and equipment checkout is completed, the new facility must be thoroughly cleaned by hospital staff before the actual move so that it will conform to the required levels for such institutions. Also, after the contractor vacates the premises, the employees can be oriented to the layout and workings of the new building. Because this orientation process is very important, the management staff wants to make sure it begins after the newsletter is distributed and is completed prior to the trial run of the move. The staff estimates that cleaning and orientation can occur at the same time without problems: cleaning will take at least two, probably three, and at most five days; the employee orientation will take four, five, and seven days, respectively.

Although the actual trial run will only take one day, the entire activity including evaluation is estimated to be likely to take three days (the minimum as well), with five days at most if serious problems are encountered. Once this step is finished, coordination of final plans and schedules with the patient and equipment carriers, local agencies, and area hospitals should take two days (at most three). Finally, the completed schedules and procedures will be discussed in each department throughout the hospital on the day prior to move day, and this discussion is expected to run the entire day owing to the normal work schedules and tasks all employees will be maintaining.

For move day, the staff has broken the entire process into seven different activities for the sketch plan:

Activity	Time estimate, days		
	Optimistic	Likely	Pessimistic
Administration, accounting, and business office	0.25	0.5	1
Library and medical/personnel records	0.25	0.5	0.75
Laboratory and purchasing/stores	0.3	0.8	1
Housekeeping and food services	0.5	0.75	1.3
Other equipment and supplies that must move same day as patients	0.8	1	1.2
Patients	0.4	1	1
Other equipment and supplies (noncritical) that will be moved after patients	1	2	2.5

The staff feels confident that basic operations will be fully underway at the new location once the first six activities above are complete, and that is the critical goal established by the hospital's board of directors. The new location will not, of course, be fully operational until the remaining, noncritical equipment and supplies are moved.

Questions

1. Assume that you are part of the management staff whose task is to develop this sketch plan. Develop the PERT network as outlined above and identify the critical path to reaching basic operational status. Determine the expected time to reach basic operational status at the new facility.

2. The board of directors has said that it would like to try to move on a Sunday to minimize interference with weekday traffic. If there are Sundays which fall 46, 53, 60, 67, and 74 days from now, determine the probability of reaching basic operational status at the new location on the two Sundays which are nearest the expected time you calculated previously (assume a normal distribution).
3. Briefly assess the potential problems you see in applying PERT analysis to the sketch plan for moving Whittier County Hospital.

CASELETTE: INFO-SYSTEMS, INC.

Info-Systems is a rapidly growing firm that specializes in information systems consulting. In the past, its projects have been of a relatively short-term nature, not requiring extensive project scheduling or close management surveillance. However, recently the firm was awarded a contract to develop and implement a large inventory system for a manufacturing firm.

During the initial proposal study, Info-Systems determined that the manufacturing firm's current hardware configuration was inadequate to meet the long-range needs of the company and new general hardware specifications were developed. Therefore, as a part of its assignment, Info-Systems is to perform a vendor evaluation and selection for the new hardware. The initial study also proposed that the system would comprise a combination of batch and on-line processing and estimated a minimum of one year to complete.

Info-Systems' management sees the project being divided into four major areas involving the activities to support (1) hardware selection and installation, (2) batch processing development, (3) on-line processing development, and (4) conversion from the old system to the new one.

Furthermore, management feels that the use of a project management system would be very beneficial in providing a more definitive estimate of the probable project completion, in controlling the project once it is underway, and in assigning personnel to the project at the appropriate times. Therefore, management assigned several of the senior staff to develop a detailed task list, which is presented in Table 15.4.

Assignments

1. Prepare a PERT network.
2. Prepare the following calculations: (*a*) total project duration, (*b*) earliest and latest start times for each activity, and (*c*) earliest and latest finish times for each activity.
3. Identify the critical path.
4. The elapsed time for delivery of the hardware is estimated at 90 days. Would the project completion be affected if the delivery of the hardware were delayed by 30 days? Would the critical path change?
5. With the original network and critical path, what strategies could management consider in order to complete the project on time if activity B were delayed by several weeks?
6. Discuss the advantages of using PERT or CPM for a professional service organization. What are some disadvantages?

Table 15.4 Activities list for inventory system project

Tasks	Duration, work days	Preceding activities
A. Evaluate and select hardware vendor	30	. . . .
B. Develop batch processing system requirements (i.e., data definition, transaction volume, etc.).	60	. . . .
C. Develop on-line processing requirements (i.e., volume, response times, etc.).	40	. . . .
D. Define specific hardware requirements; order and receive equipment.	100	A, B, C
E. Design report layouts for batch system.	30	B
F. Design input forms for batch system.	20	E
G. Design screen layouts for on-line system.	25	C
H. Design file layouts.	20	F, G
I. Prepare program specifications for *daily* batch cycle.	30	H
J. Prepare program specifications for *weekly* batch cycle.	20	H
K. Prepare program specifications for *monthly* batch cycle.	15	H
L. Prepare program specifications for on-line processing.	25	H
M. Install and test new hardware.	15	D
N. Code programs for *daily* batch cycle.	20	I
O. Code programs for *weekly* batch cycle.	15	J
P. Code programs for *monthly* batch cycle.	10	K
Q. Code programs for *on-line* cycle.	18	L
R. Document batch system.	35	I, J, K
S. Document on-line system.	25	L
T. Test *daily* cycle.	20	M, N
U. Test *weekly* cycle.	15	M, O
V. Test *monthly* cycle.	12	M, P
W. Test *on-line* processing.	15	M, Q
X. Test total system.	20	T, U, V, W
Y. Design conversion requirements, programs, and files.	30	H
Z. Prepare conversion programs.	20	Y
AA. Test conversion programs.	15	Z
BB. Run actual conversion.	3	X, AA
CC. Operate system in parallel and train users.	60	R, S, BB
DD. Gain user acceptance.	5	CC
EE. Implement production system.	5	DD

SELECTED BIBLIOGRAPHY

Buffa, E. S.: *Modern Production Management,* John Wiley and Sons, Inc., New York, 1977.

────: *Operations Management: The Management of Productive Systems,* John Wiley and Sons, Inc., New York, 1976.

Burt, J. M., and M. B. Garman: "Monte Carlo Techniques for Stochastic PERT Network Analysis," *Proceedings for the Fourth Conference on Applications of Simulation,* New York, December 1970, pp. 146–153.

Chase, R., and N. Aquilano: *Production and Operations Management,* Richard D. Irwin, Inc., Homewood, Ill., 1973.

Fulkerson, D. R.: "Expected Critical Path Lengths in PERT Networks," *Operations Research,* vol. 10, no. 6, November–December 1962, pp. 808–817.

Grubbs, F. E.: "Attempts to Validate Certain PERT Statistics or 'Picking on PERT'," *Operations Research,* vol. 10, no. 5, November–December 1962, pp. 912–915.

Hammersley, J. M., and D. C. Handscomb: *Monte Carlo Methods,* John Wiley and Sons, Inc., New York, 1965.

Hartley, H. O., and A. W. Wortham: "A Statistical Theory for PERT Critical Path Analysis," *Management Science,* vol. 12, no. 10, June 1966, pp. 469–481.

Hopewell, L.: "Trends in Data Communication," *Datamation,* August 1973, pp. 49–52.

Kleindorfer, G. B.: "Bounding Distributions for Stochastic Acyclic Networks," *Operations Research,* vol. 19, no. 7, November–December 1971, pp. 1586–1601.

MacCrimmon, K. R., and C. C. Ryavec: "An Analytical Study of PERT Assumptions," *Operations Research,* vol. 12, no. 1, January–February 1964, pp. 16–37.

Martin, J. J.: "Distribution of the Time Through a Directed Acyclic Network," *Operations Research,* vol. 13, no. 1, January–February 1965, pp. 46–66.

Pritsker, A. B., and W. W. Happ: "GERT: Graphical Evaluation and Review Technique, Part I: Fundamentals," *Journal of Industrial Engineering,* vol. 17, no. 5, May 1966, pp. 267–274.

Ringer, L. J.: "Numerical Operators for Statistical PERT Critical Path Analysis," *Management Science,* vol. 16, no. 2, October 1969, pp. 136–143.

Shore, B.: *Operations Management,* McGraw-Hill Book Company, New York, 1963.

Sullivan, R., and J. Hayya: "Alternatives to PERT for Stochastic Network Analysis," *Project Management Quarterly,* December 1978, pp. 13–18.

Van Slyke, R. M.: "Monte Carlo Methods and the PERT Problem," *Operations Research,* vol. 11, no. 5, September–October 1963, pp. 839–860.

Wiest, J. D., and F. K. Levy: *A Management Guide to PERT/CPM,* Prentice-Hall, Inc., Englewood Cliffs, N.J., 1969.

Withington, F. G.: "The Next (and Last?) Generation," *Datamation,* May 1962, pp. 71–74.

CHAPTER
SIXTEEN

MEASURING AND CONTROLLING SERVICE QUALITY

Quality can be viewed from two perspectives, design and conformance. Design quality is considered when the service package is conceived. As noted in Chapter 2, the service package is a bundle of goods and services consisting of a supporting facility, facilitating goods, explicit services, and implicit services. Once these features are defined, they become the requirements or standards for acceptable service performance.

Service managers and consumers alike expect consistency in service performance. For example, the airline flight attendant should treat each passenger in a courteous manner. Just as the consumer expects the pocket calculator to be identical to all others of the same model, so should service at motels in the same chain be consistent. Thus, controlling service quality is ensuring that service performance conforms to requirements. These requirements are attributes of the service and must be explicit and measurable. Measurements are taken on a regular basis to identify any nonconformance to requirements, which would indicate a lack of quality. Quality problems, therefore, are nonconformance problems.

If a three-star hotel conforms to the requirements set by management, then it is a quality hotel. If a budget hotel conforms to specified requirements, then it also is a quality hotel. Luxury or its absence is made explicit in the requirements. For services, these explicit and measurable requirements follow naturally from the service package.

But services are intangible. Therefore, how can service quality be measured? It takes imagination and creativity. Often surrogate measures, or substitutes for direct measurements, are made. For example, the quality of emer-

Table 16.1 Quality requirements for budget hotel

Service concept feature	Attribute or requirement	Measurement	Nonconformance corrective action
Supporting facility	Appearance of building	No flaking paint	Repaint unit
	Grounds	Green grass	Water
	Air conditioning and heating	Temperature maintained at 68° ± 2°	Repair or replace
Facilitating goods	TV operation	Reception clear in daylight	Repair or replace
	Soap supply	Two bars per bed	Restock
	Ice	One full bucket per room	Restock from ice machine
Explicit services	Room cleanliness	Stain-free rug	Shampoo
	Swimming-pool water purity	Marker at bottom of deep end visible	Change filter
	Room appearance	Drapes drawn to width of 3 ft	Instruct maid
Implicit services	Security	All perimeter lights working	Replace defective bulbs
	Pleasant atmosphere	Telling departing guests "Have a nice day"	Instruct desk clerk
	Waiting for room	No customer having to wait for a room	Review room cleaning schedule

gency ambulance service can be measured by its average response time or the quality of service at a drive-in bank can be evaluated by the waiting time of customers.

Table 16.1 presents some quality requirements and ways to measure these requirements for a budget hotel. These examples illustrate the need to define explicitly, in measurable terms, what constitutes conformance to requirements. They also are needed to trigger corrective actions for nonconformance. Quality control is action-oriented. When nonconformance occurs, a search is made to identify the cause and corrective action is then initiated.

The control of service quality fits the classic cybernetic model.[1] This model, shown in Figure 16.1, involves measurement of output, comparison with a standard, feedback of deviations, and corrective action to bring the system back into conformance with requirements. The theoretical foundation of service quality control is based on this model of communication and control. However, this mechanistic model must be supplemented with a concern for the behavioral aspect of service operations. Service personnel require motivation to perform their activities correctly the first time.

The central role of a positive quality attitude in service systems can be seen in airline travel. It is technically feasible to replace airline pilots with remote

---

[1] For a further study of cybernetic models, see W. Ross Ashby, *An Introduction to Cybernetics*, Chapman and Hall, Ltd., and University Paperbacks, London, 1971.

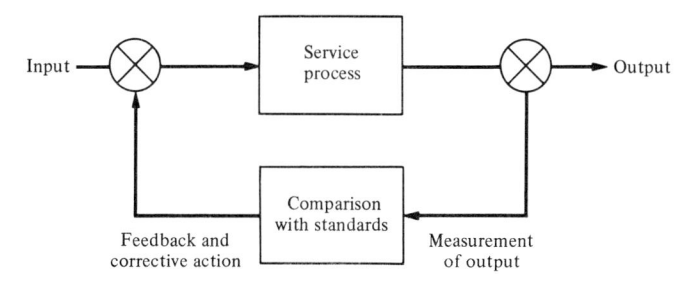

Figure 16.1 Cybernetic model.

control devices operated from the ground. However, such a cost-cutting move is unlikely because of the certain outcry from passengers. Understandably, passengers are reassured by the presence in the cockpit of someone with a vested interest in reaching the destination safely. Quality management is a systematic way of creating a sense of this personal involvement by developing the attitudes and controls that prevent quality problems from occurring.

The discussion of quality management begins with a cybernetic model of control. This model helps us to see the relationships among all the components of a quality management system. More importantly, the cybernetic view dispels any passive notions about quality; it shows that quality is assured only if there is action. With this foundation, the concept of achieving service quality by design is explored. Several approaches to measuring quality also are reviewed, including the use of quality control charts. Two quality management programs are presented, one dealing with the important concern for personnel training and development and the other illustrating a step-by-step program of quality improvement. Finally the issue of service liability is discussed.

SERVICE PROCESS CONTROL

The control of service quality can be viewed as a feedback control system. In a feedback system the output is compared to a standard. The deviation from the standard is communicated back to the input, and adjustments then are made to keep the output within a tolerable range. The thermostat in a home is a common example of feedback control. Room temperature is monitored continually; when the temperature drops below some preset value, the furnace is activated and operates until the correct temperature is restored. This temperature control system illustrates the five features of the basic control cycle:

1. *Sensor.* A mechanism that measures the output variable being monitored
2. *Goal setter.* The person who sets the standards of acceptable system performance, against which actual output is compared
3. *Discriminator.* A device that measures the difference between the current system performance and the standard

4. *Decision maker.* The person responsible for deciding what action should be taken
5. *Effector.* The person directed to take corrective action

Figure 16.2 shows these features of the basic control cycle in service quality control. The service concept establishes a basis for setting goals and defining measurements of system performance. The activities of sensing and discriminating are accomplished by monitoring conformance to requirements. Nonconformance to requirements is studied by the decision maker to identify its causes and to direct someone to take corrective action.

Unfortunately, it is difficult to implement an effective control cycle for service systems. Problems begin with the definition of service performance measures. While the intangible nature of services makes direct measurement difficult, it is not impossible. There are many surrogate measures of service quality. For example, the waiting time of consumers might be used as a measure of service quality. In some public services, the number of complaints received is used to measure quality.

Monitoring service performance is frustrated by the simultaneous nature of production and consumption. This close interface between consumer and provider prevents any direct intervention in the service process to observe conformance to requirements. Consequently, consumers may be asked to express their impression of service quality "after the fact" by filling out questionnaires. But monitoring only the final consumer impressions of service quality may be

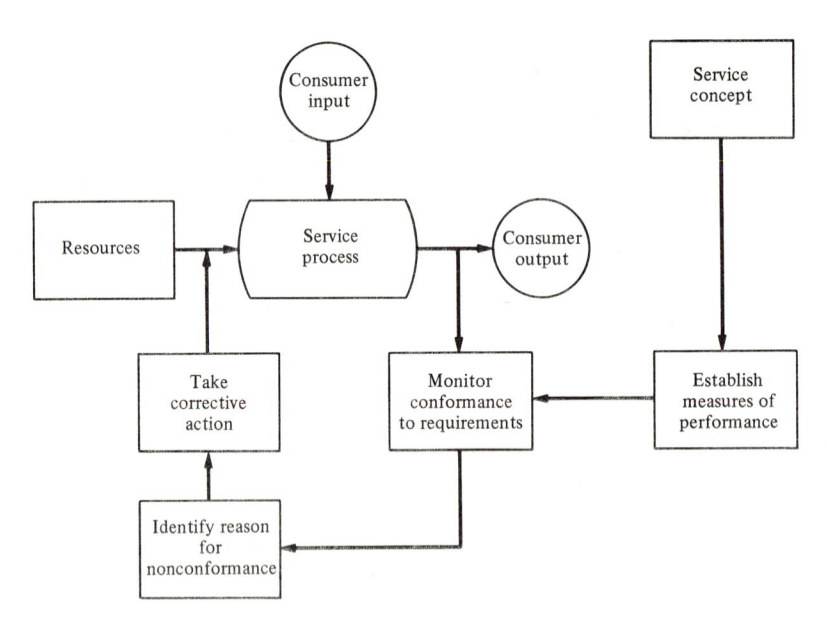

Figure 16.2 Cybernetic view of quality control.

too late to avoid lost future sales. These difficulties of controlling service quality are addressed by employing three strategies:

1. Designing quality into the service system
2. Developing creative service performance measures and monitoring programs
3. Motivating service personnel to be concerned personally about the quality of their work

Designing Quality into the Service

Quality is not inspected into a product or somehow added on. A concern for quality begins with the design of the service process. Again, consider the example of a budget hotel. How can quality be designed into this service? Some suggestions follow.

1. *Supporting facility*. Architecturally the building is designed of materials, such as brick, that are maintenance free. The grounds are watered by an underground sprinkler system. The air conditioning and heating system is decentralized so that any failure is confined to a small area.
2. *Facilitating goods*. Room furnishings are durable and easy to clean.
3. *Explicit services*. Maids are trained to clean and make up rooms in a standard manner. Every room has the same appearance, including such "trivial" matters as the opening of the drapes.
4. *Implicit services*. Individuals with a pleasant appearance and good interpersonal skills are recruited as desk clerks. Training in standard operating procedures (SOP) ensures uniform and predictable treatment for all guests. An on-line minicomputer keeps track of guest billing, reservations, and registration processing. This system allows guests to check out quickly and automatically notifies the cleaning staff when a room is free to make up.

Thus, service quality can be enhanced by prudent design. The underground sprinkler system facilitates keeping the grass green. The minicomputer indirectly facilitates the maid service through timely communication.

Recall the concept of limiting employee discretion illustrated by the McDonald's example in Chapter 7. The use of the french-fry scoop was seen as a design feature that ensured consistent quantity. But it also enhanced cleanliness and, hence, the quality of the service. Limiting employee discretion by physical design or by instituting SOPs is an important strategy in service quality control. Because it is difficult for management to intervene in the service process and impose an appraisal system (inspection and testing), limiting discretion and facilitating conformance through design often are used instead. It is interesting to note how these unobtrusive design features channel service behavior without the slightest hint of coercion. For example, keeping the maids posted on which rooms are available for cleaning allows this task to be spread throughout the day and thereby avoids a rush in the late afternoon which could result in potential quality degradation.

The success of franchising can be traced to several attractive features, such as the financial vehicle to raise capital from many small entrepreneurs and the ability to capture a market rapidly by locking up choice sites. Franchised services, such as fast foods and muffler repair, use the concept of standardization in design, operation, and pricing. Consumers expect identical service from any outlet, just as they make no distinction between products of the same brand. All franchise outlets benefit from this consistency in service because consumers develop brand loyalty which is not bound by geography. An American tourist in Munich, Germany, is treated to a Big Mac that is identical to those served in New York or San Francisco. Franchising represents an approach to controlling quality in services.

Measuring Service Performance

A comprehensive view of the service system is necessary to identify the possible measures of performance. For example, five dimensions for assessing the quality of care in the health field have been suggested.[2] These are content, process, structure, outcome, and impact. We will use these dimensions for developing measures of service quality.

Content Are standard procedures being followed? For example, is the dentist following accepted medical practices in extracting a tooth? For routine services, standard operating procedures generally are developed and service personnel are expected to follow these established procedures. In health care a formal peer review system, called Professional Standards Review Organization (PSRO), has been developed as a method of self-regulation. Physicians in a community set standards for their practices, and regular reviews are made to ensure compliance.

Process Is the sequence of events in the service process appropriate? The primary concern is the maintenance of a logical sequence of activities and a well-coordinated use of service resources. The interactions between the consumer and the service personnel are monitored. Also of interest are the interactions and communications among the service workers. Check sheets (see Figure 16.3) are common measurement devices. For emergency services, such as fire and ambulance, simulated disaster drills in a realistic setting are used to test a unit's performance. Problems with coordination and activity sequencing can be identified and corrected through these practice sessions.

---

[2] Willy De Geyndt, "Five Approaches for Assessing the Quality of Care," *Hospital Administration,* Winter 1970, pp. 21–42.

QUALITY CONTROL CHECK SHEET

Emergency Room

Unit _____ Room _____ Date _____ Time _____
Patient _____ Observer _____
Diagnosis _____ Date admitted _____

A. PATIENT WELFARE AND SAFETY

		Yes	No
1.	Is patient adequately attended?		
2.	Is patient receiving good emotional support from emergency personnel?		
3.	Have necessary restraints been applied for safety of patient?		
4.	Has wound been adequately cleaned and prepared for treatment?		
5.	Has patient been prepared for examination?		
6.	If sterile technique is indicated, are personnel following sterile procedures?		
7.	Have patient's personal belongings been given proper care?		
8.	Is identification tag complete and applied on patient's wrist?		
9.	Is equipment being used for patient functioning properly, and is necessary safety precaution in effect?		
10.	Has patient received instructions for follow-up care, and does he understand them?		
	Totals		

B. PATIENT COMFORT AND ACCESSIBILITY OF IMMEDIATE NEEDS

		Yes	No
1.	Are adequate measures being taken to make patient as comfortable as possible?		
2.	Is bed neatly made and comfortably positioned?		
3.	Are bed pan and urinal empty, rinsed with cover on, and positioned?		
4.	Has patient received adequate explanation of care and treatment he is receiving?		
5.	Have patient's relatives been given necessary information about patient?		
	Totals		

C. PATIENT ROOM CONDITION

		Yes	No
1.	Is room appearance satisfactory?		
2.	Is lavatory clean, orderly, and stocked?		
3.	Is noise level satisfactory?		
4.	Are lighting and ventilation adequate?		
5.	Are personnel being discreet in conversation and in presence of patient?		
	Totals		

Observer Comments (Reference Number)

Figure 16.3 Quality control check sheet for the emergency room. [*Reprinted from M. S. Blumberg and J. Drew, "A Quality Control Plan for Nursing Service and Methods for Assessing Nursing Care," with permission of Mr. Harold Buck, Commission for Administrative Services in Hospitals, Santa Ana, Calif.*]

Structure Are the physical facility and organizational design adequate for the service? The physical facilities and support equipment are only part of the structural dimension. The qualifications of the personnel and the organizational design are also important quality dimensions. For example, the quality of medical care in a group practice is enhanced by the on-site laboratory and x-ray facilities. But more importantly, the organization facilitates consultations among the doctors. Group medical practice also provides the opportunity for peer pressure to control the quality of care provided by its members.

The adequacy of the physical facilities and equipment can be compared to standards for quality conformance. A famous fast-food restaurant is known for its attention to cleanliness. Store managers are subjected to surprise inspections in which they are held responsible for the appearance of the parking lot and sidewalk, as well as the restaurant's interior. Personnel qualifications for hiring, promotion, and merit increases are also matters of meeting standards. University professors seldom are granted tenure unless they have published, because the ability to publish is considered evidence of the quality of research. A measure of organizational effectiveness in controlling quality would be the presence of active self-evaluation procedures and members' knowledge of their peers' performances.

Outcome What change in status has the service effected? The ultimate measure of service quality is a study of the end result. Is the consumer satisfied? We are all familiar with the cards placed at restaurant tables requesting our comments on the quality of the service. Complaints by consumers are one of the most effective measures of the outcome quality dimension. For public services, the assumption is often made that the status quo is acceptable, unless the level of complaints begins to rise. The concept of monitoring output quality by tracking some measure like the number of complaints is widely used. For example, the performance of a hospital is monitored by comparing certain measures. The number of hysterectomies per 1000 population might be used to identify hospitals that may be performing unnecessary surgery.

Clever approaches to measuring outcome quality often are employed. For example, the quality of trash pickup in a city can be documented by taking pictures of the city streets after the trash vehicles have made their rounds. One often forgotten measure of outcome quality is the satisfaction of the service personnel with their own performance.

Impact What is the long-range effect of the service on the life of the consumer? Are the citizens of a community able to walk the streets at night with a sense of security? The result of a poll asking that question would be a measure of the impact of police performance. The overall impact of health care is often measured by life expectancy, and the impact of education is measured by literacy rates and scores on nationally standardized tests. However, the impact also must include a measure of service availability and accessibility. Health care in the United States is criticized for the financial barriers to patient accessibility and for the lack of health care in rural areas. Measures of availability are usually quoted as population served in square miles. The impact of McDonald's hamburgers is displayed in neon lights in terms of the number of burgers sold.

Table 16.2 illustrates how these five quality dimensions can be applied to measuring the performance of a health clinic.

Quality Control Charts

The performance of a service is often judged on some key indicators. For example, the educational performance of a high school is measured by the Scholastic Aptitude Test (SAT) scores of its graduates, the effectiveness of a police department's crime prevention program is judged by the crime rate, and bank tellers' performances are judged by the accuracies of their end-of-day balances.

What happens if the service process is not performing as expected? Generally, an investigation is conducted to identify the cause of the problem and to suggest corrective action. However, performance variations may be the result of random occurrences and may not have a specific cause. The decision maker wants to detect true changes in the system's performance and to avoid the costs associated with poor service. On the other hand, making an unnecessary change in a system that is performing correctly must be avoided. Thus, there are two types of risks involved in controlling quality, as shown in Table 16.3.

Table 16.2 Measuring service performance for a health clinic

Performance dimension	Description	Possible measures
Content	Evaluation of medical practice	Review medical records for conformance with national standards of medical care.
Process	The sequence of events in the delivery of care and the interactions between patients and medical staff	Use checklists to monitor conformance with procedures. Conduct exit interviews with patients.
Structure	The physical facilities, equipment, staffing patterns, and qualifications of health personnel	Record times patients wait to see a doctor. Note ratio of doctors to registered nurses on duty. Record utilization of equipment.
Outcome	The change in the patient's health status as a result of care	Record deaths as a measure of failures. Note the level of patient dissatisfaction by recording the number of complaints. Record the number of diseased organs removed in surgery.
Impact	Appropriateness, availability, accessibility, and overall effect on the community of the health clinic	Note number of patients turned away because of lack of insurance or financial resources. Record the mode of travel and distance patients travel to reach the clinic.

372 MANAGING SERVICE OPERATIONS

Table 16.3 Risks in quality control decisions

True state of service	Quality control decision	
	Take corrective action	Do nothing
Process in control	Type I error (producer's risk)	Correct decision
Process out of control	Correct decision	Type II error (consumer's risk)

These risks have been given names to identify the injured party. If a process is deemed out of control when in fact it is performing correctly, a Type I error has occurred which is the *producer's risk*. If a process appears to be functioning properly when, in fact, it is out of control, a Type II error has occurred which is the *consumer's risk*.

Figure 16.4 is a quality control chart used to monitor ambulance response time. Similar control charts are used to help decision makers in many types of service organizations avoid errors in interpreting system performance. A control chart is a visual display of system performance over time. When a measurement falls outside the control limits, above the upper control limit (UCL) or below the lower control limit (LCL), the process is considered out of control. That is, the system is in need of attention. For our ambulance example, day 4 signaled a need for investigation by the supervisor. Why was there an excessive mean response time for that day? This was explained by the fact that a nearby ambulance was out of commission and our vehicle needed to travel longer distances. Since day 4, ambulance performance has remained within the control limits, so no action is required.

Constructing a control chart is similar to determining a *confidence interval* for the mean of a sample. Recall from statistics that the distribution of sample means tends to be normally distributed.[3] We know from standard normal tables that 99.7 percent of the normal distribution falls within ±3 standard deviations of the mean. Using representative historical data, the mean and standard deviation for some system performance measure are calculated. These are used to construct a 99.7 percent confidence interval for the mean calculated from samples. We expect future sample means to fall within this confidence interval. If they do not, then we conclude that the process has changed and the true mean has shifted.

The steps in constructing and using a quality control chart are summarized below:

1. Decide on some measure of service system performance.
2. Collect representative historical data from which estimates of the population mean and variance for the system performance measure can be made.

---
[3] This is based on the central limit theorem.

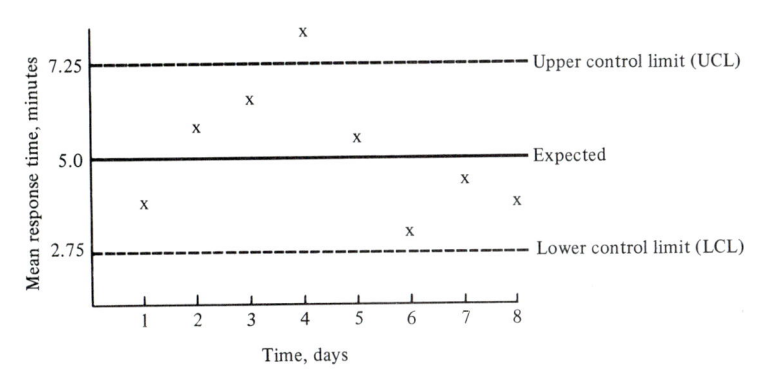

Figure 16.4 Quality control chart for ambulance response.

3. Using the standard normal tables, select a confidence level based on the desired Type I error.
4. Decide on a sample size and, using the estimates of population mean and variance, calculate the control limits based on a desired Type I error.
5. Graph the control chart as a function of sample means versus time.
6. Plot current sample means on the chart and interpret the results as:
   a. Process in control
   b. Process out of control requiring investigation and action
7. Update the control chart on a periodic basis and incorporate recent data.

Control charts for means fall into two categories based on the type of performance measure. A variable control chart ($\bar{X}$ chart) records measurements that permit fractional values, such as length, weight, or time. An attribute control chart (p chart) records discrete data, such as the number of defects or number of errors as a percentage. An example of each type of control chart follows.

Example 16.1: Control chart for variables: $\bar{X}$ chart The quality control chart for mean ambulance response time is an example of a variable measure. Assume that past records of ambulance system performance yield an estimate of population mean response time of 5.0 minutes, with an estimated standard deviation of 1.5 minutes. Furthermore, it has been decided to take a random sample of four ambulance calls each day to calculate a sample mean response time for monitoring performance. The usual confidence level of ±3 standard deviations is selected to guarantee a Type I error of less than 0.3 percent. Thus, there is a 0.3 percent chance of committing the error of taking corrective action when, in fact, the process is in control. This occurs because for a normal distribution, 0.3 percent of the sample values fall beyond ±3 standard deviations from the mean. Appropriate formulas for calculating the control limits for an $\bar{X}$ chart are given below:

$$\text{UCL} = \mu + Z_\alpha \sigma_{\bar{x}} \qquad (1)$$

$$\text{LCL} = \mu - Z_\alpha \sigma_{\bar{x}} \qquad (2)$$

where μ = population mean
σ = population standard deviation
Z_α = standard normal deviate for Type I error of α percent
n = size of periodic sample
$\sigma_{\bar{x}} = \sigma/\sqrt{n}$ standard error of the mean

For our example the control limits are:

$$\text{UCL} = 5.0 + 3\,(1.5/\sqrt{4}) = 5.0 + 3(0.75) = 7.25$$
$$\text{LCL} = 5.0 - 3\,(1.5/\sqrt{4}) = 5.0 - 3(0.75) = 2.75$$

Example 16.2: Control chart for attributes: p chart In some cases, system performance is classified as either good or bad. Of primary concern is the percentage of bad performance. For example, consider the operator of a mechanized sorting machine in a post office. The operator must read the ZIP code on a parcel and, knowing its location in the city, divert the package by conveyor to the proper route truck. From past records, the error rate for skilled operators is about 2 percent, or a fraction defective of 0.02. Management wants to develop a control chart to monitor new operators with 95 percent assurance that personnel unsuited for the job can be identified. The following formulas are used to construct a percentage, or p, chart:

$$\text{UCL} = \bar{p} + Z_\alpha \sigma_{\bar{p}} \qquad (3)$$
$$\text{LCL} = \bar{p} - Z_\alpha \sigma_{\bar{p}} \qquad (4)$$

where $\bar{p}$ = population fraction defective
Z_α = standard normal deviate for Type I error of α percent
n = size of periodic sample

$\sigma_{\bar{p}} = \sqrt{\dfrac{\bar{p}(1-\bar{p})}{n}}$ standard error of the percentage

The p chart control limits for the sorting operation will be calculated on the basis of random samples of 100 parcels drawn from the route trucks.

$$\text{UCL} = 0.02 + 1.96\,\sqrt{\frac{(0.02)(0.98)}{100}} = 0.02 + 1.96\,(0.014) = 0.047$$

$$\text{LCL} = 0.02 - 1.96\,\sqrt{\frac{(0.02)(0.98)}{100}} = 0.02 - 1.96\,(0.014) = -0.007$$

The p chart for this operation is shown in Figure 16.5. Several observations can be made. The selection of 1.96 for the Z_α value is found from Table C with the restriction that one-half of α must be in each tail. When the calculation of a LCL results in a negative number, the LCL is set equal to zero. Finally, the distribution of sample percentages is assumed to follow a normal distribution centered about the population percentage.

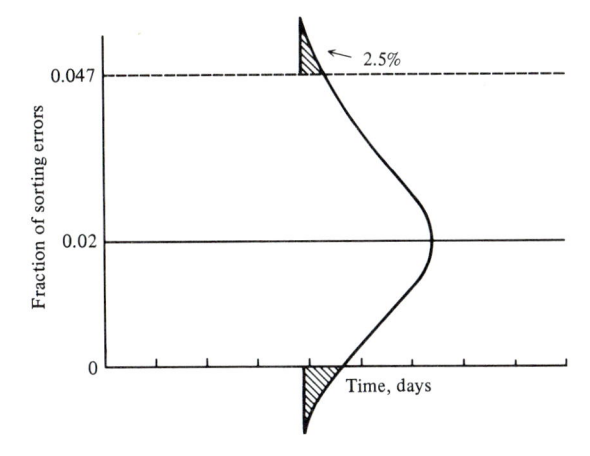

Figure 16.5 Control chart for sorting operation.

Characteristic Curves

A companion curve to a quality control chart is the characteristic curve. This curve plots the consumer's risk as a function of the true process mean. The characteristic curve measures the discriminating power of the quality control chart and, thus, indicates the exposure of consumers to out-of-control conditions.

The characteristic curve for the sorting operation control chart is shown in Figure 16.6. As expected, the probability of accepting samples with a 0.02 error rate is 0.975. If the true error rate were in fact 0.047, the value of the UCL, we see that 50 percent of the samples would still fall within the control limits and no corrective action would be taken. The characteristic curve thus displays the Type II error, or consumer's risk, for various levels of noncompliance. Table 16.4 shows the calculations for constructing the characteristic curve for various error rates. These calculations suggest two methods of reducing the level of consumer's risk. Either increase the sample size or reduce the control limit by accepting a larger producer's risk, or Type I error. We see that, as the sample size becomes larger, the characteristic curve becomes steeper and more discriminating. Management often selects some unacceptable noncompliance level, such as an error rate of 0.10, and establishes a desired consumer risk β for this level, say 5 percent. From Table 16.4 we see that the consumer's risk criterion has been met for the sorting operation.

Designing a sampling plan for quality control involves making decisions on the sample size, frequency of sampling, and selection of Type I and Type II errors. All these decisions require cost tradeoffs. For example, large sample size results in more discriminating plans, but with considerable cost. Infrequent sampling should only be advocated if out-of-control conditions do not result in expensive rework or serious consumer liabilities. The selection of small Type I errors could result in not detecting out-of-control conditions early enough. Allowing large Type II errors could result in loss of consumer goodwill or service liability costs.

376 MANAGING SERVICE OPERATIONS

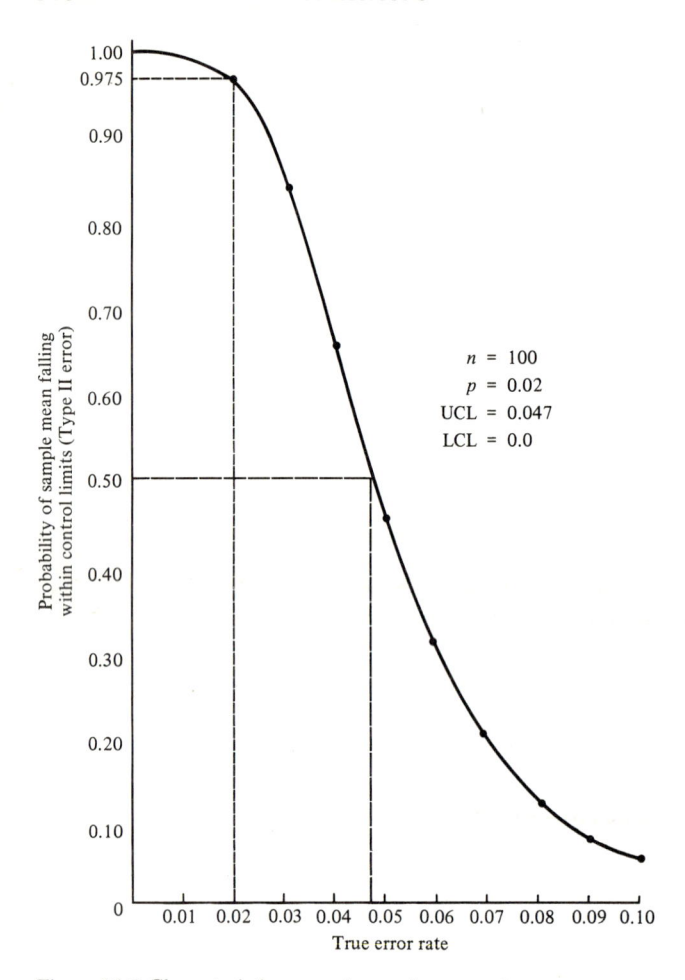

Figure 16.6 Characteristic curve for sorting operation.

$n = 100$
$p = 0.02$
UCL = 0.047
LCL = 0.0

Y-axis: Probability of sample mean falling within control limits (Type II error)
X-axis: True error rate

Table 16.4 Constructing characteristic curve for sorting operation

$\bar{p}$	$\sigma_{\bar{p}} = \sqrt{\dfrac{\bar{p}(1-\bar{p})}{100}}$	$\bar{p} - 0.047$	$Z = \dfrac{\bar{p} - 0.047}{\sigma_{\bar{p}}}$	Probability from Table C
0.03	0.017	−0.017	−1.00	0.84
0.04	0.020	−0.007	−0.35	0.64
0.05	0.022	0.003	0.14	0.44
0.06	0.024	0.013	0.54	0.30
0.07	0.026	0.023	0.88	0.19
0.08	0.027	0.033	1.22	0.11
0.09	0.029	0.043	1.48	0.07
0.10	0.030	0.053	1.77	0.04

PLANNING FOR SERVICE QUALITY

Service quality begins with people. All our measurements to detect nonconformance by means of statistically based control charts do not produce a quality service. Instead, quality begins with the development of positive attitudes among all people in the organization. How is this accomplished? Positive attitudes can be fostered through a coordinated program that begins with employee selection and progresses through training, initial job assignments, and other aspects of career advancements. To avoid complacency, an ongoing quality improvement program is required. These programs emphasize prevention of poor quality, taking personal responsibility for quality, and building an attitude that quality can be made certain. Programs like *"Zero Defects"*[4] that stress the theme "Do it right the first time" build a quality attitude so that error-free performance is possible.

Personnel Programs for Quality Assurance

Nationwide service organizations are faced with special problems of maintaining consistent service across all units. Consumers expect the same service from a motel unit in Chicago as they found at the unit located in New Orleans. In fact, the idea of "finding no surprises" is used as a marketing feature.

G. M. Hostage believes the success of the Marriott Corporation is due in part to personnel programs that stress training, standards of performance, career development, and rewards.[5] He finds that service quality is enhanced by the attitude the company takes towards its employees. The following eight programs have been the most effective.

Individual development Using programmed instruction manuals, new management trainees acquire the skills and technical knowledge for the entry-level position of assistant manager. For a geographically dispersed organization these manuals ensure that job skills are being taught in a consistent manner.

Management training Management personnel through the middle levels attend one management development session each year. A variety of professional management topics are addressed at two- and three-day seminars attended by lower-level managers from various operating divisions.

Manpower planning The kinds of people needed to fill key company positions in coming years are identified. An inventory of good prospects is created for future promotion. A key element of the plan is a periodic performance review of all management personnel.

---

[4] *A Guide to Zero Defects Quality and Reliability Assurance Handbook*, U.S. Department of Defense 4115.12, 1965.

[5] G. M. Hostage, "Quality Control in a Service Business," *Harvard Business Review*, vol. 53, no. 4, July–August 1975, pp. 98–106.

Standards of performance A series of booklets were developed to instruct employees in how to conduct themselves when dealing with guests and, in some cases, even in how to speak. *The Marriott Bellman* stresses how to make a guest feel welcome and special. *The Switchboard Operator* tells in detail how to speak with a guest and how to handle a variety of specific situations. *The Housekeeper* tells precisely how a room is to be made up, down to the detail of placing the wrapped soap bar on the proper corner of the washbasin with label upright. In many cases booklets are accompanied by an audiovisual film to demonstrate proper procedures. Adherence to these standards is checked by random visits from a flying squad of inspectors.

Career progression A job advancement program with a ladder of positions of increasing skill and responsibility gives employees the opportunity to grow with the company.

Opinion surveys An annual rank and file opinion survey is conducted by trained personnel at each unit. Subsequently the results are discussed at a meeting. This survey has acted as an early warning system to head off the buildup of unfavorable attitudes.

Fair treatment Employees are provided with a handbook of company expectations and obligations to its personnel. The formal grievance procedure includes access to an ombudsman to help resolve difficulties.

Profit sharing A profit sharing plan recognizes that employees are responsible for much of the company's success and deserve more than a paycheck for their efforts.

Quality Improvement Program

Philip Crosby suggests a 14-step quality improvement program that has been used successfully at the International Telephone and Telegraph Corporation.[6] These sequential steps are as follows:

1. *Management commitment.* The need for quality improvement is first discussed with members of management to gain their commitment. This raises the level of visibility and concern for quality at the highest levels and ensures everyone's cooperation.
2. *Quality improvement team.* Representatives from each department are selected to form a team. This team runs the quality improvement program and ensures each department's participation.
3. *Quality measurement.* The status of quality throughout the organization is audited. This requires that quality measurements be reviewed and established where they do not exist. Once quality becomes measurable, an ob-

---

[6] Philip B. Crosby, *Quality is Free,* McGraw-Hill Book Company, New York, 1979.

jective evaluation is made to identify nonconformance and monitor corrective action. Developing quality measures for services is a difficult task but it represents an opportunity for worker participation. Service personnel most often respond with enthusiasm and pride when asked to identify quality measures for their work.
4. *Cost-of-quality evaluation.* To avoid any bias in the calculations, the comptroller's office identifies the cost of quality. The cost of quality is composed of items such as litigation, rework, engineering changes, and inspection labor. Measuring the cost of quality provides an indication of where corrective action will be profitable for an organization.
5. *Quality awareness.* Communicate to supervisors and employees the cost of poor quality through the use of booklets, films, and posters. This helps change attitudes about quality by providing visible evidence of the concern for quality improvement.
6. *Corrective action.* A systematic process of facing problems, talking about them, and resolving them on a regular basis is needed. The habit of identifying quality problems and correcting them at the local level is encouraged.
7. *Establish a zero-defects program committee.* Select three or four members of the team to investigate the zero-defects concept and to implement the program. Impress upon the committee the literal meaning of the words "zero defects." The idea that everyone should do his or her work right the first time must be communicated to all employees.
8. *Supervisor training.* Conduct a formal orientation for all levels of management to enable them to explain the program to their people.
9. *Zero-defects day.* Create an event that employees can recognize as a turning point in the organization's attitude towards quality. From this day on zero defects will be the performance standard of the organization.
10. *Goal setting.* Encourage employees to think in terms of establishing improvement goals for themselves and their groups.
11. *Error-cause removal.* Ask people to describe any problem that keeps them from performing error-free work on a simple, one-page form. The appropriate department is asked to respond to the problem expeditiously.
12. *Recognition.* Establish award programs to recognize those who meet their goals. With genuine recognition of performance, continued support for the program results.
13. *Quality councils.* Bring together the quality professionals on a regular basis to discuss necessary actions for program improvement.
14. *Do it over again.* A typical program takes over a year, and, by then, turnover necessitates a new educational effort. The repetition makes the program a permanent part of the organization.

SERVICE LIABILITY

Caveat emptor, let the consumer beware, is rapidly becoming obsolete. Today, the consumer must be given attention. Shoddy workmanship, faulty products, and broken promises all carry a price. Type II errors can no longer be ignored because now their cost may be bankruptcy. For example, a gourmet soup company was forced out of business because of the recall cost when its vichyssoise was found to contain poison-producing botulism organisms. Announcements of automobile recalls for correcting defects are commonplace. Products can be returned, exchanged, or fixed, but what of faulty service?

Services are difficult for the consumer to evaluate before the fact, because they are intangible and consumed simultaneously with production. What recourse does the consumer of a faulty service have? Legal recourse! Medical malpractice law suits have been notorious for their large settlements. Although some cases of abuse have surely occurred, the possibility of malpractice litigation does promote a physician's sense of responsibility to the patient. The threat of a negligence suit might induce an irresponsible doctor to take more time in an examination, seek more training, or give up performing a procedure for which he or she is not competent. Unfortunately, the cost of medical care may have been increased by doctors practicing defensive medicine (e.g., ordering unnecessary tests).

No service has immunity from prosecution. For example, a Las Vegas hotel was sued for failing to provide proper security when a guest was assaulted in her room. Income-tax preparers can be fined up to $500 per return if a taxpayer's liability is understated because of negligence or disregard of internal revenue rules and regulations.

The control of service quality takes on new meaning in this age of consumerism. Systems under the most watchful control still experience unanticipated failures. In these events the service provider may need to use imagination to placate the consumer.

SUMMARY

Once service quality is defined as conformance to requirements, then quality can be controlled. Of course, this means that measurements of service quality must be made and compared with expectations. If nonconformance is observed, the cause is found and action is taken to bring service back into conformance. This control process is often implemented by using a quality control chart. Quality control charts are based on the statistical properties of sample means in which a tradeoff is made between the producer's risk and the consumer's risk. These tradeoffs are made in light of the cost of quality control programs, the potential costs associated with service liability, and the real costs of rework. Service quality begins with people, and thus a quality control program must include training and motivating people to do it right the first time.

TOPICS FOR DISCUSSION

1. Design a system of performance measures for a fire department using the service dimensions of content, process, structure, outcome, and impact.

2. Comment on the inadequacy of the industrial concept of quality control when applied to health care.
3. If continued financial rewards do not yield quality improvements, what can be done?
4. Could employee turnover in service be a blessing? Comment.
5. Suggest an automated training program using the latest multimedia technology for routine high-turnover service jobs, like waiting restaurant tables, retail store clerking, or hotel housekeeping.
6. Suggest methods of installing a sense of organizational esprit de corps.
7. As consumers take a more active part in the service process, how does this complicate the issue of service liability?

EXERCISES

16.1 In recent months several complaints have been sent to the police department of Gotham City regarding the increasing incidence of congestion in the city's streets. The complaints attribute the cause of these congestions to the lack of synchronization of the traffic lights in Gotham City. The traffic lights in Gotham City are controlled by a main computer system, and adjusting the program is costly unless there is a real need to do so.

The police department started to study a sample of 1000 intersections that were reported to have congestion in the past 12 months. For sample size of 1000 the data are:

Month	Congestion incidence
January	14
February	18
March	14
April	12
May	16
June	8
July	19
August	12
September	14
October	7
November	10
December	18

(a) Construct a control chart based on the above data.

(b) If during the next three months the reports of congestion at these 1000 intersections indicate the following, should the system be modified?

Month	Congestion incidence
January	15
February	9
March	11

16.2 The Speedway Clinical Laboratory is a scientific blood test laboratory that receives samples of blood from local hospitals and clinics. The blood samples are passed through several automated tests, and the results are printed out through a central computer that reads and stores the information about each sample of blood tested.

Management is concerned with the quality of the services it is providing and wants to establish quality control limits as a measure of the quality of the tests given. Such managerial practice is viewed as significant, because a wrong analysis of the sample can lead to a wrong diagnosis by the physician, which may cost the life of the patient. For this reason samples of size 100 were collected from the blood samples after they had gone through the testing. After performing the tests manually, the results were:

Day	Bad samples	Day	Bad samples
1	8	11	4
2	3	12	6
3	1	13	5
4	0	14	10
5	4	15	2
6	2	16	1
7	9	17	0
8	6	18	6
9	3	19	3
10	1	20	2

(a) Construct a control chart to be used in assessing the quality of the service described above.

(b) On the average, what is the expected number of samples that were tested and have wrong test results?

(c) Later, a sample of size 100 was taken. After inspecting the accuracy of the tests given, 10 samples were found to be tested wrongly. What is your conclusion about the quality of the service?

(d) Construct an OC curve for this control system.

16.3 The Long Life Insurance Company receives new applications to buy insurance from its salesmen, who are specially trained in selling insurance to new customers. After the applications are received, they are processed through a computer. The computer is programmed in such a way that it can print out messages whenever it runs through an item that is not consistent with company policies. The company is concerned with the accuracy of the training that its salesmen receive. It contemplates recalling them for more training if the quality of their jobs is below certain limits. Five samples of 20 applications that were received from specific market areas were collected and inspected. The results are:

Sample	No. of applications that had errors
1	2
2	2
3	1
4	3
5	2

(a) Estimate the standard deviation for the percentage of applications that need rework, from samples of size 20.

(b) Determine the upper and lower control limits for a p chart with sample size of 20.

(c) After the control limits were established, a sample of size 20 was taken. Four applications were found to have mistakes. What can we conclude from this?

16.4 The management of the Delight franchised restaurants is in the process of establishing quality control charts for the time that its service people give to each customer. Management thinks that the length of time each customer is given should remain within certain limits to enhance the quality of the service. A sample of six service people was selected, and the customer service observed 4 times. The activities that service people were performing were identified, and the time to service one customer was recorded:

	Service time, sec			
Service person	Sample 1	Sample 2	Sample 3	Sample 4
1	200	150	175	90
2	120	85	105	75
3	83	93	130	150
4	68	150	145	175
5	110	90	75	105
6	115	65	115	125

(a) Determine the upper and lower control limits of an $\bar{X}$ chart with a sample size of 6.

(b) After establishing the control chart, a sample of six service people was observed and yielded the following customer service times, in seconds:

$$180 \quad 125 \quad 110 \quad 98 \quad 156 \quad 190$$

Is corrective action called for?

16.5 The Last National Bank employs several tellers to work at the four-line drive-in facility that the bank provides for customers' convenience. An inspector collects a sample of 100 checking accounts and determines how many of them are overdrawn. The inspector decides that the bank will tolerate no more than one overdrawn account. If so, then the quality of job that a specific teller is doing is satisfactory, otherwise it is not.

(a) Construct the OC curve for this situation.

(b) What are the uses of the OC curve that you constructed above?

CASELETTE: CLEAN SWEEP, INC.

Clean Sweep, Inc., (CSI) is a custodial/janitorial services company specializing in contract maintenance of office space. Although not a large company in comparison with its primary competitors, CSI does have several major contracts to service some of the state government's offices. In order to enter and to stay in the custodial services business, CSI adopted the strategy of having a small workforce which performs high-quality work at a reasonably rapid pace. At present, CSI's management feels that it has a staff which is more productive on an individual basis than its competition. However, management recognizes that this single factor is the key to the company's success, and so maintaining a high level of worker productivity is critical.

Within the staff, the organizational structure is divided into four crews, each of which is composed of a crew leader and six to nine other crew members, and all crews are under the direction of a single crew supervisor. Within the state building complex, there are nine buildings included in CSI's contracts, and the custodial assignments have been distributed as shown in Table 16.5 to balance the workload distribution among crews (on the basis of gross square feet of floor space per member).

The responsibilities of each crew involve the following general tasks, listed in no order of importance: (1) vacuum carpeted floors, (2) empty trash cans and

Table 16.5 Custodial assignments

Crew	No. of members*	Buildings assigned gross sq ft	Total sq ft assigned
1	6	Bldg A, 30,000; Bldg C, 45,000; Bldg F, 35,000	110,000
2	8	Bldg B East, 95,000; Bldg H, 55,000	150,000
3	9	Bldg B West, 95,000; Bldg G, 85,000	180,000
4	8	Bldg D, 40,000; Bldg E, 75,000; Bldg I, 42,000	157,000

* Excludes crew leader.

place trash in industrial waste hoppers, (3) dry mop and buff marble floors, (4) clean rest rooms, (5) clean snack-bar area(s), and (6) dust desk tops.

Each crew works an $8\frac{1}{2}$-hour-long shift, during which it gets two 15-minute paid rest breaks and one 30-minute lunch break (unpaid). However, there is some variation among the crews in the flexibility of choosing break and lunch times, due primarily to the personalities of the crew leaders. The crew leaders of crews 2 and 3 are most strict in their supervision, while the leaders of crew 1 and crew 4, in particular, are least strict, according to the crew supervisor.

CSI's management is aware that the department of the state government which oversees the custodial service contracts makes periodic random inspections and rates the cleaning jobs CSI does. This department also receives any complaints about the custodial service from office workers. Table 16.6 contains the monthly ratings and number of complaints received (by building) during CSI's current contract. Because the time for renegotiation of CSI's contract is several months away, company management would like to maintain a high quality level during the remaining months to improve its competitive stance.

As is typical with custodial service operations, employee turnover in CSI's staff has been fairly high but still lower than many of its competitor's. Management attributes this to the higher pay scale CSI offers, relative to the competition. Even though individual staff costs are higher, the greater productivity levels of a smaller-than-average workforce has resulted in greater-than-average profits for the company. Nevertheless, there are problems reported by the crew supervisor, with complaints voiced by the crew members. These complaints fall into two general categories: (1) inequity in crew-leader attitudes and performance expectations and (2) lack of opportunities for personal advancement. Table 16.7 shows a historical distribution of monthly complaints from each crew according to these two categories for the same period as shown in Table 16.6.

Questions

1. Given the facts of the case and your conception of the custodial service industry, assess the service quality of CSI's crews.
2. Discuss possible ways to improve service quality.
3. Describe some potential strategies for reducing CSI's staffing problems.

Table 16.6 Complaints and ratings of cleaning crews*

Month	A	Be	Bw	Building C	D	E	F	G	H	I
1	2	5	7	3	2	3	2	4	3	4
	7	5	3	6	7	5	6	5	4	5
2	1	6	8	2	1	1	2	3	2	5
	7	5	3	6	6	5	6	5	5	4
3	0	6	8	1	0	2	2	4	0	1
	8	5	4	6	8	5	6	6	6	7
4	1	5	4	1	0	1	1	4	1	3
	7	5	5	8	8	6	7	5	6	6
5	1	3	2	2	0	1	1	3	1	2
	6	6	6	7	8	6	7	5	6	6
6	2	5	3	0	1	0	0	2	1	0
	7	6	6	7	7	8	6	5	5	7
7	0	4	2	1	0	0	0	0	0	1
	8	7	7	6	6	8	8	6	7	7
8	1	2	4	2	1	0	1	2	1	1
	6	6	5	7	7	8	7	5	6	7
9	1	2	4	1	1	0	1	1	3	0
	7	7	5	6	7	8	6	5	5	8

* First-row numbers for each month represent total number of complaints. Second-row numbers for each month represent ratings on a 1 to 10 scale; any rating under 5 is felt to be poor and 8 or above is good.

Table 16.7 Job related complaints from crew members

Month	Crew 1 Ineq-uity	Crew 1 No advance-ment	Crew 2 Ineq-uity	Crew 2 No advance-ment	Crew 3 Ineq-uity	Crew 3 No advance-ment	Crew 4 Ineq-uity	Crew 4 No advance-ment
1	0	1	3	3	4	3	0	2
2	0	0	2	1	1	1	0	1
3	1	0	2	1	2	2	1	2
4	0	0	1	2	3	1	0	2
5	1	1	3	1	2	1	0	2
6	1	0	1	2	2	1	0	1
7	0	1	1	1	1	3	0	1
8	0	0	2	2	1	2	1	1
9	0	0	2	1	2	2	0	2

SELECTED BIBLIOGRAPHY

Adam, Everett E., Jr.: "Behavior Modification in Quality Control," *Academy of Management Journal,* vol. 18, no. 4, December 1975, pp. 662–679.

A Guide to Zero Defects Quality and Reliability Assurance Handbook, U.S. Department of Defense 4115.12, 1965.

Ashby, W. Ross: *An Introduction to Cybernetics,* Chapman and Hall, Ltd., and University Paperbacks, London, 1971.

Bennigson, L. A., and A. I. Bennigson: "Product Liability: Manufacturers Beware!" *Harvard Business Review,* May–June 1974, pp. 122–132.

Crosby, Philip B.: *Quality is Free,* McGraw-Hill Book Company, New York, 1979.

De Geyndt, Willy: "Five Approaches for Assessing the Quality of Care," *Hospital Administration,* Winter 1970, pp. 21–42.

Hostage, G. M.: "Quality Control in a Service Business," *Harvard Business Review,* vol. 53, no. 4, July–August 1975, pp. 98–106.

van Gigch, John P.: *Applied General Systems Theory,* 2d ed., Harper and Row Publishers, Inc., New York, 1978.

CHAPTER
SEVENTEEN

MANAGEMENT INFORMATION SYSTEMS: THE NERVOUS SYSTEM OF SERVICE ORGANIZATIONS

Information is part of the resources of every organization that enables management to weave together plans, operations, and controls into a coordinated strategy for meeting organizational objectives. Viable information is needed for decision making at all levels within organizations.

Information systems have special significance for service organizations. In many cases, they directly contribute to the value of the service package. Savings banks, for example, maintain records of customer accounts that must be processed accurately and quickly. Banking services are delivered by information systems that allow interaction of customers with their accounts.

Information systems also enable organizations to provide better services. Think how real estate firms, travel agencies, investment companies, and many other organizations use information systems to improve existing services or to offer new services. Notice how the information system often is highlighted as part of a marketing strategy to provide an additional competitive advantage. For example, hotel chains have nationwide reservation systems to accommodate travelers on long trips. The system helps capture the customer's business for the entire trip.

Large service organizations, such as airlines, banks, and insurance companies, are known to generate huge volumes of information. This, of course, requires a sophisticated system for information management. But even small organizations are becoming information-oriented. Law firms, restaurants, and funeral homes are examples of the increasing number of small organizations benefiting from a formal, integrated information system.

Management information systems (MIS) generally refer to the people, equipment, and activities needed to collect data and to make the data useful for management decision making. But, in the 1980s we must think of MIS as computer-based systems for processing data and for supporting the functions of management. In this chapter, we discuss some basic concepts of computerized management information systems. We also give examples of information systems used in service organizations.

COMPUTERS: SOME BASIC CONCEPTS

Not long ago, computers were thought of as mysterious "black boxes," with which only analytical wizzards could grapple. And computers were so expensive that only large companies could afford the luxury of electronic data processing.

But the world has changed. Computers are no longer a luxury; they are a necessity for conducting daily operations and for achieving organizational objectives. Also, advances in technology have brought computers within the grasp of even the smallest organizations. Their uses have expanded tremendously. Computers assist in simple office chores, such as typing and word processing. But they also are used for maintaining inventory, personnel, and accounting records; for developing schedules of operations; and for forecasting and developing strategic plans. Computers are used to support decision making at all levels within organizations.

A computer system is made up of *hardware* (the electronic gadgetry) and *software* (programs and instructions). Let's look at these more closely.

Computer Hardware

There are four basic components of computer hardware. These are devices for getting data into the computer, devices for getting processed data out of the computer, devices for storing data, and devices for processing data. Figure 17.1 shows the interactions among components of a computer system.

Input devices The most familiar input device is the reader for standard 80-column punch cards. This device reads the data represented by holes punched in the card. Other input devices are typewriterlike terminals for direct input, punched-paper tape readers, magnetic tape drives, and magnetic disc drives. Data also can be read by magnetic-ink character recognition or optical character recognition.[1]

---

[1] Magnetic ink characters are used widely for check coding. Optical characters are found in the Universal Product Code (UPC) on many retail items, especially on packaged food: they are the mysterious black and white lines found on food labels.

MANAGEMENT INFORMATION SYSTEMS **389**

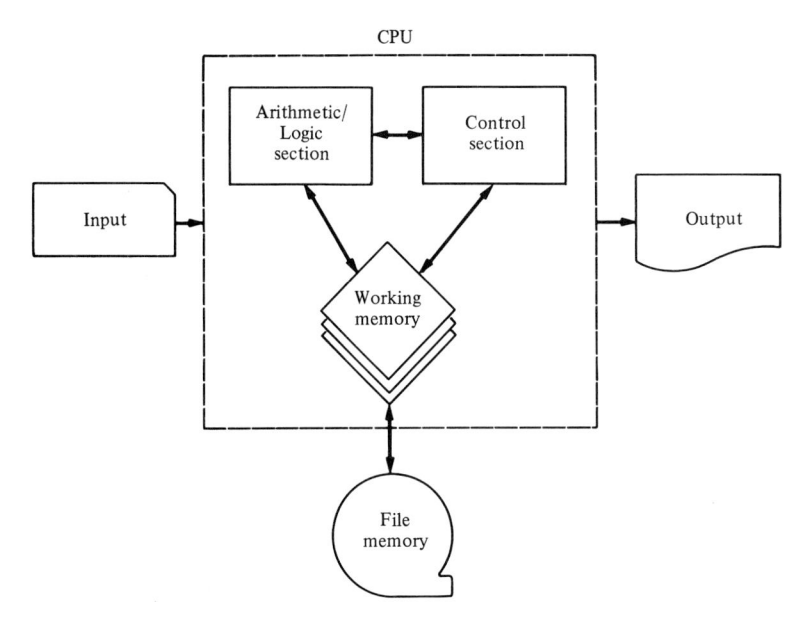

Figure 17.1 Hardware components of a computer.

Output devices Many of the devices for data input also can be used for data output. The most familiar output device is the printer. But output also can be displayed graphically on a televisionlike cathode-ray tube (CRT). The hardware for inputting and outputting data are collectively referred to as I/O devices.

Memory Data storage devices of computers are called memories. File memory is used to store large amounts of data. Common types of file memory are magnetic tape and magnetic disc. Data stored in files are outside the computer's central processing unit.

Working memory is an important part of the processing unit of the computer. This memory is divided into cells, called registers. Each register stores a specific number of objects or characters and has an address so that it can be accessed. Capacity and access time are principal concerns with storage.[2]

Central processing unit (CPU) The CPU is the most important hardware component of the computer. In addition to internal storage, the CPU contains an arithmetic/logic section and a control section. The arithmetic/logic section

---

[2] A common type of working memory is magnetic core, which consists of small rings of ferromagnetic material that can retain one of two polarities and thus represent either 0 or 1. Consequently, operations are carried out with binary representations of the data. Other types of working memory are semiconductor microcircuit memories (silicon chips), thin-film magnetized dots, and plated-wire magnetic memories. These forms of memory differ principally in access time, storage capacity, and cost.

performs operations, such as adding, dividing, and comparing. The control section directs and coordinates all operations called for by the instructions. This includes control of the I/O devices, control of memory files, and execution of instructions.

Computer Software

The programs that guide the computer operations are called software. They generally are written in an English-like language that is easy to use. BASIC, COBOL, FORTRAN, and PASCAL are examples of such programming languages. These languages require additional supporting software called *compilers* that translates the programs into a form (machine language) that the computer can process.

Many software programs are available to handle conventional business operations. Programs can be easily acquired for payrolls, inventory control, forecasting, and customer accounts. But for special operations software must be developed and tailored to the specific requirements. Many computer service companies specialize in developing computer software.

TRENDS AFFECTING MANAGEMENT INFORMATION SYSTEMS

During the past 30 years, there have been many evolving factors that affect the design and operation of MIS. Some of these factors are technologically based, others deal with attitudes of employees and consumers, and all the factors interact with each other. Consider the following.

Advances in Computer Hardware Technology

The first computers used vacuum tubes and could execute about 16,000 additions per second. Now, computers using microcircuitry embossed on silicon chips can execute more than 1,500,000 additions per second. Technological breakthroughs also have occurred with storage devices and I/O devices. These have led to the "small-computer" revolution. Minicomputers and microcomputers have greatly expanded capabilities and thus have become comparable to older, much larger computers.[3]

Advances in Computer Software

Software, of course, must be compatible with hardware. Improved software languages, such as BASIC and PASCAL, make programming much easier. In

---

[3] There is no firm definition of minicomputers and microcomputers. As a rule of thumb, "microcomputer" will refer to a system costing less than $3,000, and "minicomputer" to a system that costs between $3,000 and $15,000. Larger computers are referred to as *main frames*.

some cases, managers can learn to operate a computer comfortably after a few hours of instruction. Also, many "canned" programs are available for conventional business operations. These are programs provided by computer hardware and software companies that are not user specific. That is, many organizations can readily use canned programs without having to make extensive modifications. Significant advances also have been made in software development for small computers. For example, data-base management software for minicomputers is becoming a reality.

Reduced Costs of Computer Systems

The computer industry is one of very few industries where costs have been declining. This is not to say that computers are any cheaper. In fact, the costs of many large computers have risen. But, the costs relative to computation speed have fallen dramatically. During the past 30 years, the cost per computation has been reduced by a factor of 1000. Microcomputers have the same computation capabilities as the large, expensive systems of the 1960s.

Increased Number of Computer Systems Companies

Until the late 1960s, most organizations had to rely upon one major computer manufacturer for systems design and implementation. But since then there has been a proliferation of small, independent computer systems companies. These companies provide a variety of services, such as systems design and implementation, software development, and MIS personnel training.

Computer Orientation of Personnel and Consumers

Computers pervade our society. Consequently, many employees and consumers have grown up with a computer orientation. They do not fear the computer. On the contrary, they feel at ease when interacting with a computer system. Attitudes are such as to encourage the adoption of MIS. A computer system can improve employee attitudes toward work and can enhance consumer attitudes toward the service package.

Increased Number of Computer Installations

The number of new computer installations has continuously and dramatically grown. The increased capabilities and low cost of small computers have made them very popular for organizations of all sizes. By 1980, there were nearly 400,000 small computer systems in the United States. These are systems that cost less than $15,000. But many complex organizations still prefer a big centralized system. Virtually every organization can find a system to meet its MIS needs within its financial limits.

The Information Explosion

The volume of information available to and required by managers today is increasing at a phenomenal rate. Just consider the external operations of an organization. Data are continually being created that relate to all aspects of operations, and managers need information on the external environment. For example, data banks are becoming commonplace, and effective managers are able to use them for developing plans and policies. Informal information systems cannot keep up with this surge of information. The ability of managers to collect and to process data and to use the resulting information rests upon the design of the information system.

OVERVIEW OF MANAGEMENT INFORMATION SYSTEMS

Nature of Management Information

Management information is the body of information needed to achieve an organization's objectives. There is a tendency to think of information as a collection of data, such as inventory records and sales records. But information is more than this. It is data that have been collected and processed so as to be useful to management for decision making.

Figure 17.2 depicts the transformation of data into information. The data first are collected and recorded. This step is often the most crucial because it determines the quality and value of the information ultimately produced. It involves deciding what data to collect and how to code, classify, and verify the data.

Recorded data are transmitted to storage areas. Storage enables past data

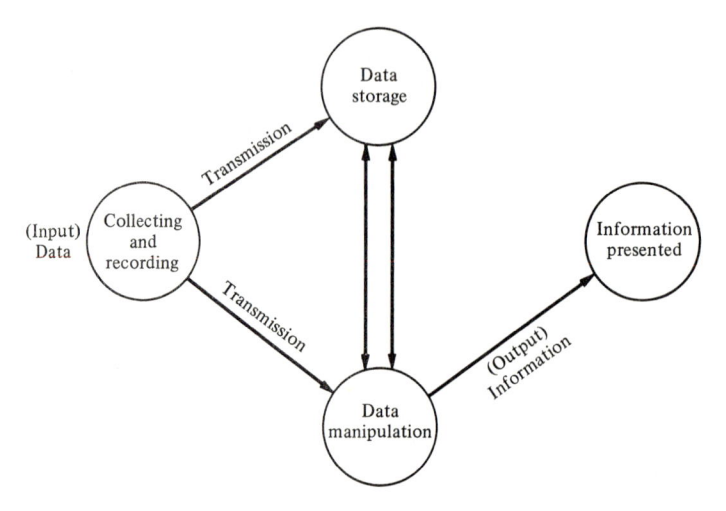

Figure 17.2 Transforming data into information.

to be retrieved and to be used for decision making. Important issues at this step are the capacity and cost of storage, and the ease with which the data can be retrieved (accessed).

Recently collected data are combined and manipulated with past data. This is the transformation step that converts data into useful information. The process can take any number of forms. For example, classifications of data can be updated, new classifications can be developed, and existing classifications can be combined. The purpose of the transformation process is to make the data useful to management. The information derived from the process then is presented in a format appropriate for management decision making.

Management information generally relates to money, personnel, materials, consumers, demand, facilities, and equipment. The information may involve the internal plans and operations of the organization, or it may involve competitors, the environment, and other external factors.

One can imagine the huge volume of data potentially available to management. Certainly, there are more data than can be collected, processed, and used in any reasonable fashion. In some cases, too much data can overwhelm management and impede the decision-making process. A challenge to management is to discern and process only data that can be transformed into useful information. And sorting the wheat from the chaff can be extremely difficult.

Value of Management Information

Management information improves decision making by reducing uncertainty. Uncertainty results from a lack of information regarding the current state of the organization, future events, and the relationship between various factors of concern to the organization.

Consider the current state of the organization and assume that there is no information on inventory levels and cash balances. How can management make decisions on replenishing inventory? Without information, making correct decisions would be just a matter of chance. The same is true with regard to the relationship between factors. For example, can management reasonably change the type of services provided without some information on consumer attitudes? It cannot! It may end up losing consumers.

Anticipating future events is crucial to all organizations. It is the basis for service design, capacity planning, facilities location, and virtually all the operational functions of service organizations. These operational functions cannot be properly performed without forecasts, that is, information regarding future events.

There are many factors that contribute to the value of management information. These include:

1. *Timeliness*. The information is available when it can be useful.
2. *Relevance*. The information is directly related to the concerns and objectives of the organization.

3. *Accessibility.* The information can be easily and efficiently retrieved.
4. *Objectivity.* The information is free from personal and other forms of bias.
5. *Comparability.* The information is in a format such that it can be displayed and used with other information.
6. *Accuracy.* The information is correct and precise within acceptable limits.
7. *Clarity.* The information can be easily understood.

MIS: A General Framework

In Chapter 2, we defined a system to be a set of elements that interact, that are interdependent, and that have common objectives. We also noted that a large system often consists of several integrated subsystems. This is the case for a management information system.

It is convenient to view MIS in the context of the planning, operating, and controlling subsystems of an organization. Figure 17.3 depicts the information flows linking these subsystems. Planning involves establishing organizational objectives and developing a strategy for achieving those objectives. To be successful, planning requires data that are relevant to the objectives and that assist in evaluating various alternative strategies. These data may concern past internal operations of the organization. They also may relate to the activities of competitors and to trends in the environment. The data are inputs into the planning subsystems. They are used to make forecasts of demand and projections of other factors that are the foundation for strategic planning.

The outputs of the planning subsystem are strategies and policies to be carried out at the operating level. The operating subsystem of MIS creates and delivers the service package. It involves such functions as inventory manage-

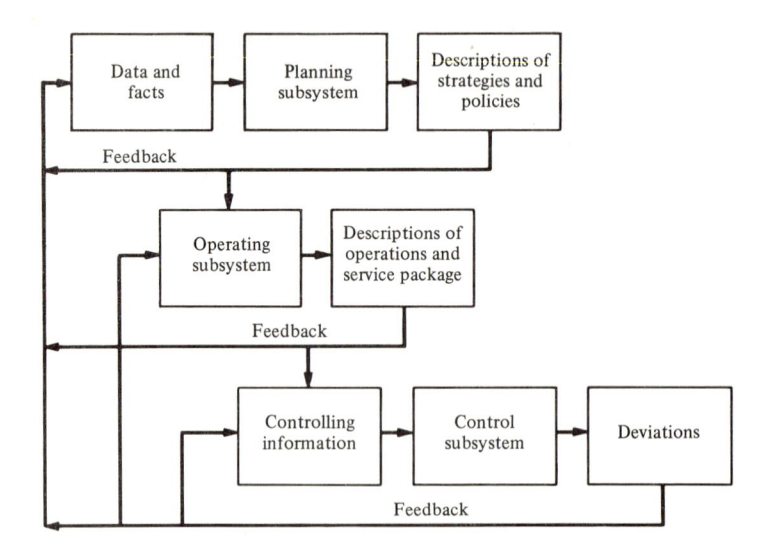

Figure 17.3 Information flows in MIS.

Table 17.1 Typical applications of MIS

Planning subsystem	Operating subsystem	Controlling subsystem
Cash budgeting	Purchasing	Cost accounting
Capital budgeting	Workshift scheduling	Credit control
Project planning	Payroll	Sales
Demand forecasting	Employee records	Quality control
Capacity planning	Inventory management	Sales analysis
Profit and loss projections	Transportation management	Plant and equipment control

ment,[4] workshift scheduling, vehicle routing, purchasing, and maintenance scheduling. The operating subsystem requires large amounts of data that must be manipulated in a timely fashion. That is, the timeliness of the resulting information to a great extent determines its value.

The operating function of an organization leads to the delivery of a service package. The operating subsystem of MIS yields data that describe all aspects of the operations and the service package. These are inputs into a control subsystem. The purpose of this subsystem is to monitor the operations and services. Standards of performance are set, and the operations and services are judged by these standards. When significant deviations are noted, this information is fed back to the planning subsystem and to the operating subsystem. Plans and operations are adjusted in response to the information emanating from the control subsystem.

Table 17.1 lists typical applications of MIS. These are grouped according to the information subsystems with which they are commonly associated. Note, however, that some applications can transcend several subsystems. For example, cash budgeting involves both planning and operating.

How Effective Managers Use MIS

It should be clear that an information system has potential far beyond that of simple data processing. Applications of information systems are becoming available that support the management decision process. This is in addition to the reporting and record-keeping functions often associated with *electronic data processing* (EDP).

EDP systems tend to be data-oriented. With these, the user receives periodic reports on standard operating functions. The system often carries out mechanical clerical activities. These activities involve the manipulation of past data into various reports that are routinely provided to management. The system requires little or no user interaction.

Innovative information systems are being developed that go beyond "data processing." These systems are management-decision-oriented. That is, a *de-*

---

[4] Inventory management is an important use of MIS. This topic is covered in Chapter 18.

cision support system (DSS) assists management in making and implementing decisions. Consequently, the user actively interacts with the system as part of the decision process.

Steven Alter categorizes computer systems by what the user does with them.[5] He suggests the following classifications that range from data-oriented uses to model-oriented uses.

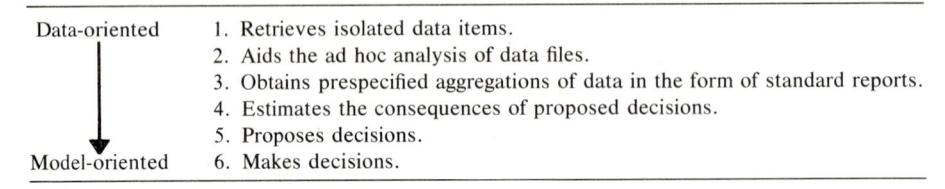

Data-oriented	1. Retrieves isolated data items.
↓	2. Aids the ad hoc analysis of data files.
	3. Obtains prespecified aggregations of data in the form of standard reports.
	4. Estimates the consequences of proposed decisions.
	5. Proposes decisions.
Model-oriented	6. Makes decisions.

A data processing system usually is associated with the third category, data aggregation and report generation. But the potential exists for expanding the uses of information systems into the other categories. These are the areas of application that improve the effectiveness of management by supporting the decision process. For example, computer-based models exist for evaluating alternatives for facilities location, facilities layout, and vehicle routing. The user can readily investigate different decision settings by changing some of the data used in the models. Sensitivity analysis is performed by the user posing various what-if questions and getting immediate feedback from the system. In this way, the information system supports the nonroutine decision-making functions of management.

Figure 17.4 shows the relative uses of DSS and EDP within the planning, operating, and controlling subsystems. We see that planning, which uses "fuzzy" or less-precise, data, should rely heavily upon DSS. However, the controlling subsystem processes routine data into reports, the typical EDP function.

[5] Adapted from Steven L. Alter, "How Effective Managers Use Information Systems," *Harvard Business Review,* November–December 1976, p. 98.

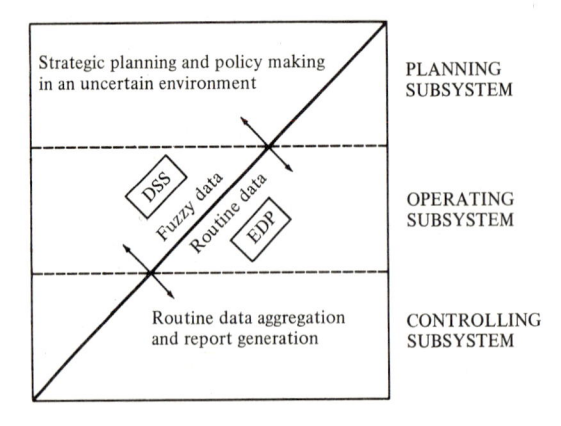

Figure 17.4 Relative amounts of fuzzy data and routine data used in the information subsystems.

Table 17.2 Comparison of EDP and DDS

Electronic data processing (EDP)	Decision support system (DSS)
Characteristics	
Passive clerical activities	Active line, staff, and management activities
Oriented toward mechanical efficiency	Oriented toward overall effectiveness
Focus on past	Focus on the present and future
Emphasis on consistency	Emphasis on flexibility and ad hoc utilization
Purposes	
Transaction processing	Decision making
Record keeping	Decision implementation
Business reporting	
Uses	
Obtain prespecified aggregations of data in the form of standard reports	Retrieve isolated data items
	Use as mechanism for ad hoc analysis of data files
	Obtain prespecified aggregations of data in the form of standard reports
	Estimate consequences of proposed decisions
	Propose decisions
	Make decisions

Source: Used by permission of the *Harvard Business Review*. Exhibit from "How Effective Managers Use Information Systems" by Steven L. Alter (*Harvard Business Review*, November–December 1976). Copyright © 1976 by the President and Fellows of Harvard College; all rights reserved.

There are many possibilities for extending MIS to support management decision making. They all entail making better use of the information system at the planning level. Management awareness and the initiative to innovate are required if the potential advantages of information systems are to be realized. Table 17.2 gives a more detailed comparison of DSS and EDP.

MIS IN SERVICE ORGANIZATIONS: SOME BRIEF EXAMPLES

Hospital Information System[6]

Most hospitals have adopted some form of computerized information system. Consider, for example, the case of Canyon General Hospital in Anaheim, California. Canyon has an advanced, doctor-oriented information system called CHAMPS (Canyon General Hospital Automated Medical Processing System). This system uses 10 minicomputers, along with discs, tapes, 60 CRTs (cathode-

---

[6] Adapted from D. M. Canen, "Multiple Minis for Information Management," *Datamation*, September 1975, pp. 54–58.

ray tubes), and assorted other hardware. It maintains patient records, handles the ordering of supplies and services, schedules the use of operating rooms and other facilities, and keeps track of accumulated patient charges.

To illustrate the capabilities of CHAMPS, assume that a doctor wants to schedule an appendectomy. The doctor dictates to a transcriptionist his or her name, the patient's name, and the type of surgery. This information is entered into a CRT that has been preformatted for surgical data. The computer also generates on the CRT a list of secondary orders typically associated with an appendectomy. Any of these secondary orders can be canceled.

Once the information has been verified by a registered nurse and transmitted, the computer schedules the operation and notifies the appropriate departments. The nursing floor receives orders for preoperative care, such as a surgical bath and no food for the patient after midnight. The central supply department receives orders to send a preoperative supply kit to the patient's floor and to provide patient transportation. The food service department is notified that no food will be served after midnight, and the laboratory receives orders for the required surgical and pathological services. As the various orders are carried out, the patient's records are updated on a CRT.

Investment Management Information System[7]

Investment firms for decades have made use of computer-based decision support systems. Consider the case of a particular New York brokerage house that uses the computer for research, as well as for conventional operations. The computer system continually monitors the major stock exchange transactions. Data on earnings, dividends and other basic indicators are entered into data files. Data transmissions and report generation are controlled by a set of analytical programs on a large scientific computer.

The system provides the information required to evaluate decision rules against historical or hypothetical company, market, and environmental conditions. It enables the user to test various what-if situations and to carry out sensitivity analyses. The investment environment for different situations are simulated on the system. This analysis involves ongoing computer-user interactions. It is carried out quickly and results in high-quality decision procedures. The computer in this case is viewed as a partner in the decision process.

Funeral Home Information System[8]

Mount Moriah Cemetery and Funeral Home in Kansas City, Missouri, innovated in the use of minicomputers. Moriah, which employs about 75 workers, operates two funeral homes, two cemeteries, a flower shop, and a nursery.

---

[7] Adapted from Arnold E. Amstatz, "The Computer—New Partner in Investment Management," *Management Science,* vol. 15, no. 2, October 1968, pp. B9–B99.

[8] Adapted from Layton McCartney, "Small Business Systems: They're Everywhere," *Datamation,* October 1978, pp. 91–93.

The minicomputer is used for conventional business chores, such as accounting and payroll. It also is used to monitor nursery operations. It assists in determining which types of plants are selling best and it is used for inventory control of nursery items. In addition to the conventional uses, the information system generates daily routing schedules for lawn care service at the cemeteries.

Professional Rodeo Information System[9]

The Professional Rodeo Association in Fort Collins, Colorado, is a major organizer of rodeos. The association relies upon livestock contractors to provide animals for particular rodeo events and to provide them at specified times. However, information on available animals was sometimes lacking and there was speculation that some contractors saved animals for their favorite cowboys.

The association purchased a small business computer to assist in information management. The information system keeps track of animals that cowboys are to ride in particular rodeos. It also randomly pairs performers with animals and maintains an ongoing record of members' point standings and yearly earnings. The MIS operates like a reservation system. A cowboy can call over a WATTS line to book a ride on a particular type of animal. Also, the contractors of animals have to provide information well in advance of a rodeo. The cowboys now have assurance that the computer, not the contractor, selects the animal.

Real Estate Information System

Real estate associations frequently maintain data banks on property available for sale within particular regions. The data banks contain all the vital statistics on property, such as location, price, and number of bedrooms. Real estate agents can access the data banks by way of a portable terminal.

A national real estate agency advertises its information system as part of a marketing strategy. This system is used to match potential buyers with available properties anywhere throughout the United States. The characteristics and desires of the buyers are compared with the characteristics of the properties. The system reassures both the buyers and the sellers of property that they have been treated fairly.[10]

Airlines Information System

One of the most important aspects of airline operations is the ability to make customer reservations quickly. And underlying these operations is a complex,

---

[9] Adapted from Layton McCartney, op. cit., pp. 91–93.
[10] This system has more marketing advantage than operational advantages. The data bank is updated voluntarily by real estate agents. But some agents will not contribute data on prime properties that they want to keep to themselves.

computerized reservation system. A typical airline reservation system works as follows.

An airline maintains a large central data base that contains all the information on flight schedules and on existing reservations. Reservation agents can interact instantaneously with the data base by way of terminals located at the sales counters. When a customer requests space on a particular flight, the agent keys in the request. If no space is available, the system lists alternative flights that have not been fully booked.

When an agent books a reservation, the agent enters the customer's name, where the customer can be contacted, when the tickets will be picked up, and other special instructions surrounding the particular reservation. For example, the system will automatically book reservations on connecting flights. And if a flight is canceled, the system will reassign passengers to the next available flights.

The reservation system provides a list of passengers just before takeoff. This can be used for passenger and seat control and for planning meals and drinks. The information also is used to analyze operations. For example, load factors, volume of traffic, and number of cancellations are compiled and used for operations planning and control.

SUMMARY

The plans and operations of an organization must be integrated if management objectives are to be realized. Information is the key for achieving this coordination. Management information systems have become a necessity for all organizations. They are formal, computer-based systems that surround the acquisition and transformation of data into useful information. This term "useful" must be emphasized.

Conventional information systems are used predominantly for routine data processing functions. But innovative information systems are being implemented that directly support the decision-making process. These extensions of MIS offer the greatest potential for improving the effectiveness of managers.

TOPICS FOR DISCUSSION

1. How can an information system enhance the consumer's perceptions of service quality?
2. In what ways can an information system facilitate the use of limited service capacity?
3. What are some possible changes in an organization that could result from the installation of a computerized information system?
4. The acceptance of an information system by an organization is directly related to its perception as an aid and indirectly related to its perception as a management control. Comment.
5. The ancillary benefits from an information system can often be more important than the intended purpose. Comment.
6. Explain why police officers object to the use of vehicle locator technology that helps dispatchers deploy patrol cars.

CASELETTE: LEMON COUNTY COMMISSIONER'S COURT

Within Lemon County, there are 28 primary and secondary agencies or charity organizations providing various services to many different segments of the populace. For example, some of the agencies which have received funding in previous years include the Better Business Bureau, the local chamber of commerce, Planned Parenthood, Inc., the local housing authority, several senior-citizen activity centers, an organization which counsels and aids rape victims, a drug-abuse counseling service, the Red Cross, a local community theater group, the Salvation Army, and a legal-aid clinic. Almost all of these service organizations are eligible to receive a portion of federal funds from several revenue-sharing programs created to channel funds to the local level in ways deemed appropriate at the local level. This is done by having annual blocks of federal money allocated to a local political body for further distribution at the discretion of that local body. The Lemon County Commissioner's Court has acted as this dispensing agent for several years.

Ned Kelly, one of the most budget-conscious commissioners, annually asks the county staff to compile a report containing the status of each funded-agency's progress in meeting its current goals with a cost-effectiveness analysis of the service. Applications from agencies that wish to be considered for funding from the next-year's block allocation are also included. The applications from each organization must include a requested funding level, goals for the upcoming year, and a proposed budget.

In the previous years, the staff relied heavily on individual reports from each agency, developed annually in response to the request for information on: the numbers of people and types of aid or assistance rendered, the organization's current goals and degree of success in achieving those goals, and the organization's personnel structure and operating budget. In addition, the agencies receiving funds from this program were required to submit quarterly reports on their use of the funds, giving information on the number of clients and types of aid given. Both the annual and quarterly reports were used to prepare a summary overview and interpretation of the organizations' capabilities for the commissioner's court.

It had become evident to Kelly that the existing procedure was not well equipped to suit his major purpose in asking for valid, comparable information on all of the applicants. There had been instances in which clients of some funded organizations had publicly complained of long waiting times between applying for and receiving assistance, mishandled paperwork, excessive interview requirements, and inconsistent standards for granting assistance among the agencies. For the most part, Kelly was sympathetic to these complaints, but he usually preferred to avoid judging the merits of each organization's approach solely on the basis of the personal opinions of the clients. Yet at the same time, it was necessary to make some judgments for the purpose of allocating the available funds.

Some months prior to the time of year when the county usually requested information and grant applications from the local service agencies, the county auditor's assistant had come to see Kelly about problems her staff perceived in the current method of collecting information. Ruth Leslie pointed out to the commissioner that there was no standard means of reporting the information Kelly really wanted to know on service quality, productivity, and cost. Each agency either responded with wordy descriptions of general types of service, rendered to present the most optimistic viewpoint possible, or simply provided poorly written and unsubstantiated reports on their level of performance. In addition, the agencies complained vociferously to the commissioner's court every year on the amount of time they were spending to develop the annual reports, and in some cases, the quarterly reports as well. Finally, Ms. Leslie noted that the process her staff went through to compile, to verify (to some degree), and to analyze the information in the reports was very time-consuming in itself and resulted in a product that was often criticized by Kelly for its incompleteness. As a result of the entire situation, Ms. Leslie observed that absolutely no one seemed to be satisfied with the current approach, and she suggested that the county initiate an integrated accounting and data collection system for the allocation and distribution of these funds.

Kelly was intrigued by the idea, but wanted to know more about the approach and how it would function to better serve the spectrum of interested parties. Consequently, he aked Ms. Leslie to prepare a short, *general* report outlining the concept of such a system as applied to the present circumstances. In particular, he wants her to address the potential effects upon the relationships among these service agencies (both private and public nonprofit in nature) and the county if such a system were put into practice. He is not interested in hardware requirements or any cost details until he is convinced that this approach is sound.

Assignments

1. Consider yourself to be in Ms. Leslie's position and develop an appropriate response to Kelly's request. Be sure to establish what a management information system should accomplish under the circumstances described above.
2. Describe how your concept would improve the quality of information available to the different participants of the system; speculate on how well it would be received by the service agencies and how successful it could be if implemented.
3. What potential stumbling blocks might impede the implementation of the system? Suggest priorities of activities for system implementation.

SELECTED BIBLIOGRAPHY

Alter, Steven L.: "How Effective Managers Use Information Systems," *Harvard Business Review,* November–December 1976, p. 98.

Amstatz, Arnold E.: "The Computer—New Partner in Investment Management," *Management Science,* vol. 15, no. 2, October 1968, pp. B9–B99.

Canen, D. M.: "Multiple Minis for Information Management," *Datamation*, September 1975, pp. 54–58.

Kanten, Jerome: *Management-Oriented Management Information Systems*, Prentice-Hall, Inc., Englewood Cliffs, N.J., 1972.

McCartney, Layton: "Small Business Systems: They're Everywhere," *Datamation*, October 1978, pp. 91–93.

McLean, Ephraim R., and John V. Soden: *Strategic Planning for MIS*, John Wiley and Sons, Inc., New York, 1977.

Murdick, Robert G., and Joel E. Ross: *Information Systems for Modern Management*, Prentice-Hall, Inc., Englewood Cliffs, N.J., 1971.

Trent, Robert H., and Thomas L. Wheeler: *Developments in Management Information Systems*, Dickenson Publishing Co., Inc., Enrico, Calif., 1974.

CHAPTER
EIGHTEEN

INVENTORY MANAGEMENT

Inventory management represents one of the earliest and most successful applications of computerized information systems. For example, basic inventory systems are used to maintain records of inventory balances and to indicate when an order for replenishment is needed. They also are used to determine an appropriate order quantity, to list possible vendors, and even to initiate a purchase requisition order. Software for inventory management is readily available for computers of all sizes.

There are several reasons why managers of service organizations need to understand inventory theory. First, many service organizations maintain large inventories. These may consist of items for sale, such as products in retail stores, or they may be stocks of items that eventually will be processed, such as food in a restaurant. Organizations also maintain inventories of spare parts used for equipment maintenance, as well as inventories of items needed to carry out daily operations, such as paper and pens. There may be a wide variety of different items (stock-keeping units or SKUs) maintained in inventory that require a large investment in capital. Management or mismanagement of inventories can significantly influence the profitability of an organization and determine the extent to which organizational objectives are achieved.

Another reason for understanding inventory theory is that capacities of some service organizations exhibit characteristics of inventories. Seats on an aircraft and rooms in a hotel are examples of these types of capacities. An understanding of inventory theory can contribute to better management of capacity.

INVENTORY THEORY

Functions of Inventory

Figure 18.1 depicts a simple inventory distribution system. Demand for inventory items is initiated as the service operations are carried out. Demand, of course, is a random variable with an associated probability distribution. As demand occurs, the items are withdrawn from the stocks of inventories. Eventually, the stocks must be replenished and an order is placed with the vendor, perhaps a wholesaler. During the time from initiating until receiving the order, the stock level continues to decline. This period is called the replenishment *lead time* and also is a random variable.

The above process illustrates one of the most important functions of inventories. Inventories allow the operations of the service organization to continue without interruption and somewhat independently of the vendor. This is known as the *decoupling function*. Without inventories, service operations would be inextricably linked to the operations and to the reliability of the vendor.

The vendor also maintains inventories that are periodically replenished from a factory warehouse. The stocks in the factory warehouse are replenished when new production runs are initiated. The service organization, the wholesaler, and the factory are stages in the inventory distribution system. Inventories serve to decouple the operations of each stage.

There are several different types of inventories. These are:

1. *Seasonal inventories*. Inventories that exist owing to seasonality in demand or in supply. Retailers of toys build large inventories in anticipation of the

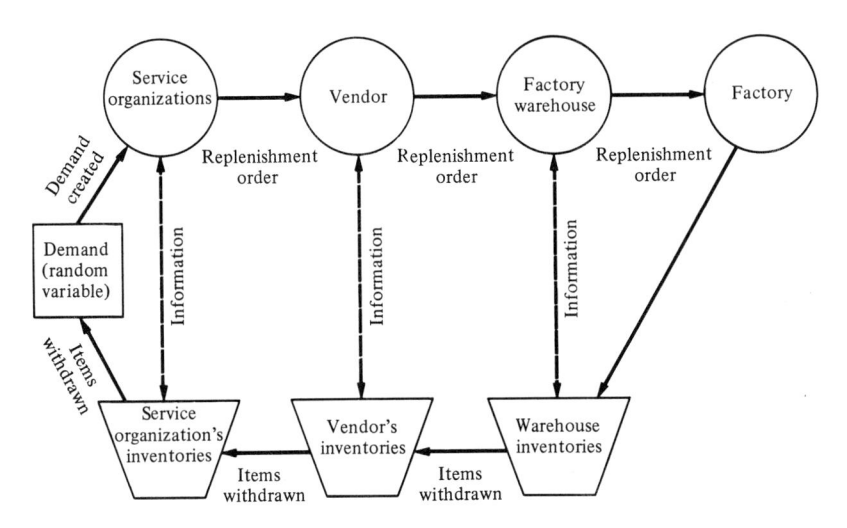

Figure 18.1 Simple inventory distribution system.

Christmas rush. Vegetable canning companies develop large inventories shortly after the harvest season.
2. *Speculative inventories.* Inventories that are acquired owing to anticipated increases in costs. It may be more economical to maintain a larger inventory now than to incur higher purchase costs at some later time.
3. *Cyclic inventories.* Inventories that result from the normal ordering cycle. Cyclic inventories are at their peak immediately after a replenishment is received.
4. *In-transit inventories.* Inventories that have been ordered, but that have not been received.
5. *Safety stocks.* Inventories that are maintained to guard against stockouts. These inventories are needed owing to the uncertainties in demand and in replenishment lead time.

Characteristics of Inventory Systems

Operations managers frequently are involved in designing and implementing an inventory control system. This requires an understanding of the characteristics of the stocks being maintained and of the characteristics of various alternative inventory systems. The following are some of the features of inventory systems that require consideration.

1. *Nature of demand for the inventory items.* Does demand have noticeable trends, cycles, or seasonality? Is demand stochastic, with an associated probability distribution? Is demand for some inventory items dependent upon demand for certain other inventory items (demand dependency)? Is demand discrete (integer-valued) or is it continuous? Is demand lumpy (batches of items are demanded)?
2. *Nature of relevant inventory costs.* What costs are relevant for inventory control? Do vendors offer quantity discounts? Are costs changing over time?
3. *Nature of replenishment lead time.* How long does it take to replenish inventory once an order is placed? Is lead time stochastic, with an associated probability distribution?
4. *Length of planning horizon.* How long will this type of inventory be maintained? Is there a time in the foreseeable future when this inventory will not be needed?
5. *Constraints on the inventory system.* What resources are required for maintaining the inventory? Are any of these resources limited? Do they impose constraints on the inventory system?

Relevant Costs of an Inventory System

The performance of an inventory system usually is gauged by its average annual cost. Several relevant costs typically considered are the holding costs, ordering costs, stockout costs, and the unit cost of the items. The inventory holding cost is the cost that varies directly with the number of items held in stock. The opportunity cost associated with capital tied up in inventory is a major component of the holding cost. Other components are insurance cost, obsolescence cost, deterioration cost, and direct handling cost. The ordering cost is the cost that varies directly with the number of orders placed. Paperwork and order expediting and receiving often contribute to the ordering cost. The stockout cost is the cost that varies directly with the number of units out of stock. This cost is difficult to identify because it involves lost customer goodwill and other intangible costs. The unit cost of the item is the unit price charged by the vendor.

Inventory management is concerned with three principal questions. These are:

1. What should be the *order quantity* when we place an order for replenishment?
2. What is the appropriate *reorder point* in terms of inventory balance or the appropriate replenishment interval?
3. How much *safety stock* should be maintained?

We shall see later that determining the reorder point and the safety stock are related issues. Both affect the service level. We would like to address all three questions in light of the average annual cost of the inventory system.

INVENTORY CONTROL SYSTEMS

Many different inventory control systems are used in practice. Most of these differ in the method for determining order quantity and in the method for determining the replenishment time. We shall restrict our discussion to three of the most common inventory control systems. These are the fixed-order-quantity system, the fixed-replenishment-interval system, and the (s, S) system.

Fixed-Order-Quantity System

Figure 18.2 depicts inventory balances for the fixed-order-quantity system. The inventory level decreases in a random fashion until it reaches a predetermined trigger level, known as the reorder point R. When the inventory balance reaches R, an order for replenishment is placed with the vendor. For this inventory system, the order quantity Q is fixed (i.e., Q units are always ordered each time an order is placed).

From the time the reorder point is reached until the replenishment is received, the inventory level continues to decline. Generally, there will be some inventory remaining just before the replenishment is received. The average inventory balance just before the replenishment arrives is the safety stock level,

R: Reorder point T: Replenishment lead time
B: Safety (buffer) stock Q: Fixed order quantity

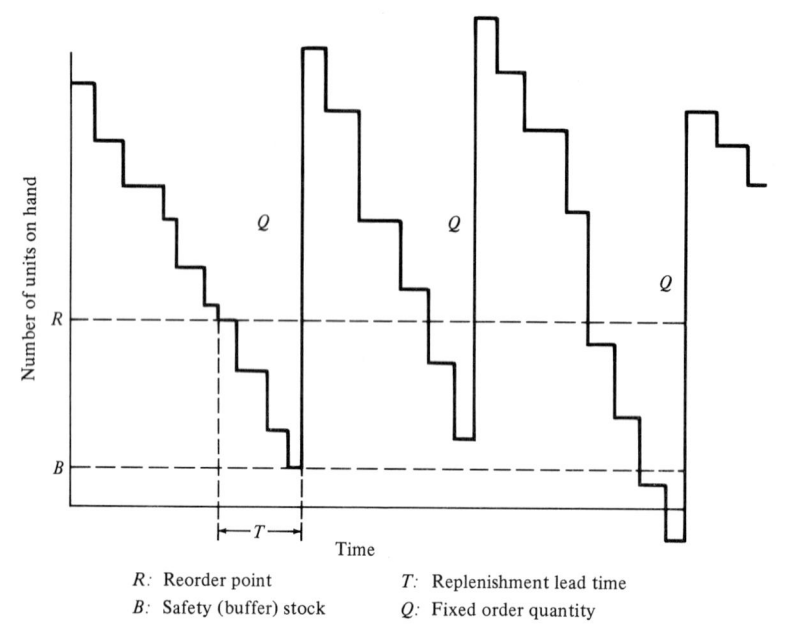

Figure 18.2 Fixed-order-quantity system.

or buffer stock B. This inventory is maintained to protect against stockouts that might result from unusually high demand levels and long replenishment lead time. Notice, however, that on occasion a stockout does occur. For this system, unsatisfied demand is backordered until the replenishment is received. What would "lost demand" look like for an inventory system?

The fixed-order-quantity system commonly is used with low-valued inventory items. These are items that can be ordered in large quantities without much managerial concern. A computerized information system can keep a perpetual record of inventory balances to indicate when the reorder point is reached.

Fixed-Interval System

Figure 18.3 depicts the inventory balances for the fixed-interval system. Orders for replenishment are placed at fixed intervals t. The order quantity varies and is enough to bring the total inventory (on hand plus on order) up to some predetermined maximum level. Notice that occasional backorders can occur with this system, just as with the fixed-order-quantity system. With the fixed-interval system, the order quantity varies in response to the demand rate, while the cycle time between orders is fixed. The primary issue with this system is determining the appropriate cycle time.

The fixed-interval system generally is used with high-valued inventory items. These are items for which inventory levels must be tightly controlled

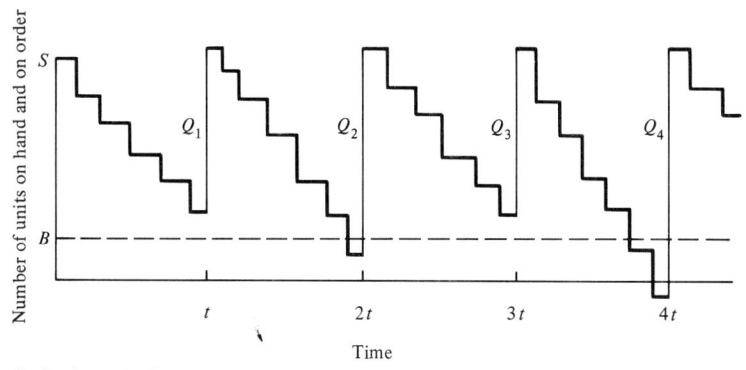

S: Predetermined maximum level of inventory (on hand plus on order)
t: Fixed review period
B: Safety (buffer) stock
Q: Variable order quantity

Figure 18.3 Fixed-interval system.

owing to the high cost. Frequent replenishment orders are placed with each order size being relatively small.

(s, S) Inventory Control System

The (s, S) system is a combination of the fixed-order-quantity system and the fixed-interval system. The inventory balances for the (s, S) system are depicted in Figure 18.4. The on-hand plus on-order inventory level is reviewed at fixed intervals of time t. If the total inventory level at the review time is above s (a trigger level), then *no* order is placed. If the inventory level is at or below s, then an order for replenishment is placed. The order quantity varies and is enough to bring the inventory balance up to a predetermined maximum level S. Of course, backorders also can occur with this system.

The (s, S) system has some of the characteristics of both the fixed-order-quantity system and the fixed-interval system. However, order quantities tend to be smaller than with the fixed-order-quantity system, while the number of times orders are placed is fewer than with the fixed-interval system. The (s, S) system often is used with moderately valued inventory items.

The ABC's of Inventory Control

We know that service organizations are not homogeneous with regard to their inventory systems. Some organizations maintain only a few items in stock, while other organizations maintain many thousands of different items. The value of individual items can be used to select an appropriate inventory control system.

Suppose we group inventory items into high-, medium-, and low-value ca-

410 MANAGING SERVICE OPERATIONS

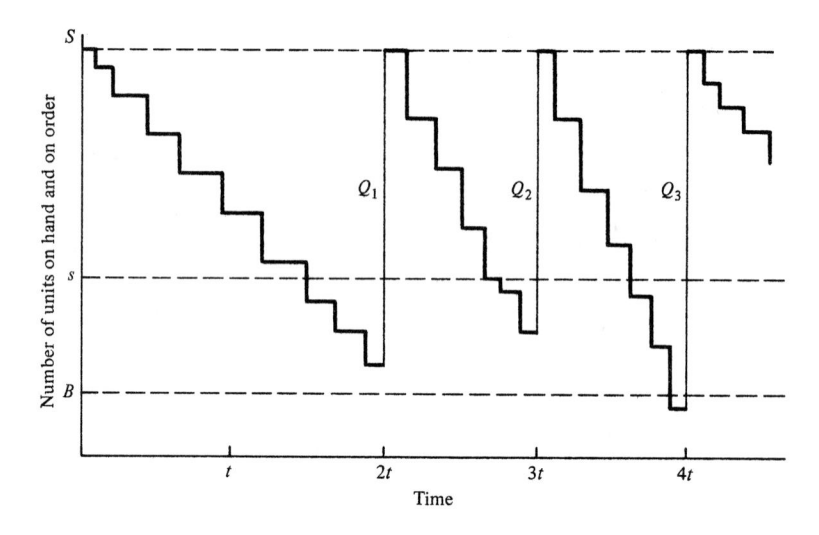

S: Predetermined maximum level of inventory (on hand plus on order)
s: "Trigger level"
t: Fixed review period
B: Safety (buffer) stock
Q: Variable order quantity

Figure 18.4 (s, S) inventory control system.

tegories. Figure 18.5 depicts these common groupings. Generally, a small percentage of the items (say 15 percent) accounts for a large percentage of the total value of the inventories (perhaps 75 percent). These are the A items and require special managerial attention. A fixed-interval control system might be used for these items.

Also, it is common for a large percentage of the items (say 50 percent) to account for a small percentage of the inventory value (perhaps 5 percent). These are the C items, and they can be managed in a more casual fashion. For these items, a fixed-order-quantity system might be used. The order quantities can be relatively large without incurring excessive costs. And a large safety stock also can be maintained.

The B classification is for the middle-valued items. They are not so costly as to require special managerial attention, but they are not so cheap that they can be overstocked. The (s, S) inventory control system might be used for these items.

INVENTORY MODELS

Inventory models are used to address the three principal questions of inventory control: How much to order? When to order? How much safety stock to maintain? There have been many models developed during the past 50 years. Most

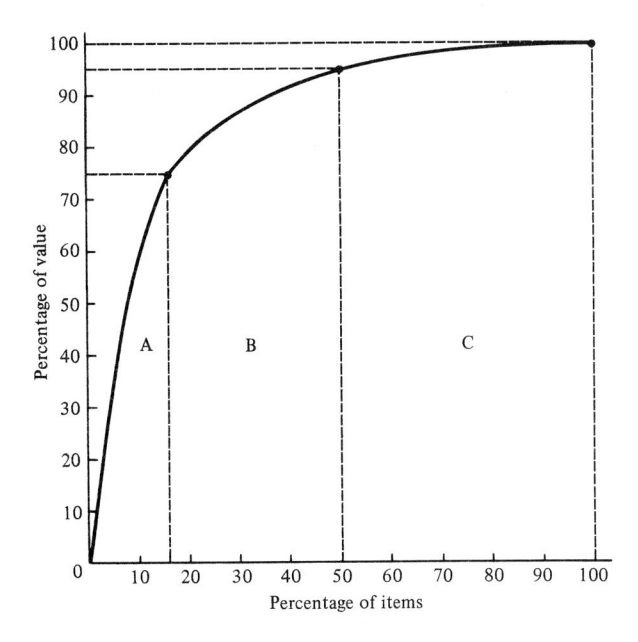

Figure 18.5 ABC classification of inventory items.

of these use relevant inventory costs as the criteria for gauging performance. For example, some models determine an *economic order quantity* (EOQ). This is the order quantity that minimizes the annual relevant costs of the inventory system. Other models focus on the replenishment cycle.

Most inventory models yield analytical solutions. That is, conventional optimization methods are used to determine optimal order quantities and cycle times. But descriptive simulation models also have been used. These models can contain more realistic details of the inventory system. For an assumed inventory system with specified order quantities and cycle times, simulation models estimate the performance of the system over an extended period. By trying different combinations of order quantities and reorder cycles, the best from the set can be identified.

The best known inventory model is the simple economic order quantity. We shall describe this in more detail.

Simple Economic Order Quantity

The simple EOQ requires many simplifying assumptions. For example, demand rate is assumed constant and known, and no stockouts are allowed. Figure 18.6 depicts the inventory balances over time for this simple system. We want to determine Q^*, the quantity that minimizes relevant costs.

There are no costs associated with stockouts because they do not occur. Also, because all demand must be satisfied, the annual cost of purchasing the item is a constant and is not affected by the order quantity. This leaves the inventory holding cost and inventory ordering cost. The relevant annual cost K

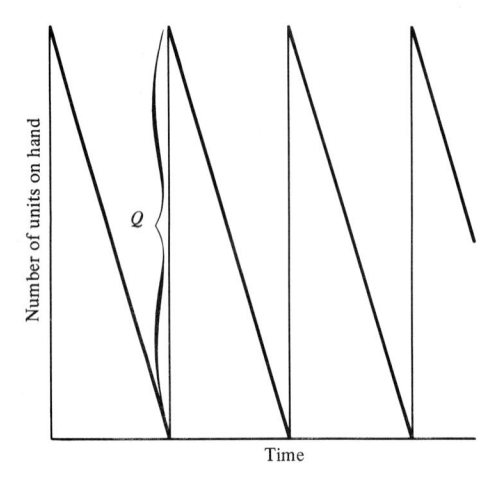

Figure 18.6 On-hand inventory for simple economic-order-quantity system.

for this inventory system is:

$$K = \text{ordering cost } plus \text{ average holding cost} \qquad (1)$$

We can express equation (1) in a more usable form. First, we define some notations:

D = average annual demand
i = annual inventory holding cost (expressed as a percentage of the cost of the item)
C = unit cost of the item
A = cost of placing an order for replenishment
Q = order quantity

The annual ordering cost is easy to derive. Because all demand D must be satisfied with orders of size Q, then D/Q orders are placed annually. Each of these orders cost A, and this gives an annual ordering cost of $(D/Q)A$.

The average annual holding cost also is easy to derive. If one unit is kept in inventory for one year, the holding cost would be iC. From Figure 18.6, we see that the maximum inventory balance is Q, while the minimum balance is zero. This gives an average inventory level of $Q/2$ units. Thus, the average inventory holding cost becomes $(Q/2)iC$.

We can now rewrite the relevant annual cost of the inventory system as

$$K = (D/Q)A + (Q/2)iC \qquad (2)$$

The holding cost and the ordering cost change with different values of Q. Figure 18.7 depicts these costs as a function of order quantity. Notice that there is a unique value of Q that gives a minimum annual cost for the inventory system. This value, of course, is the *economic order quantity* Q^*.

There are several ways to determine Q^*. For example, we can take the de-

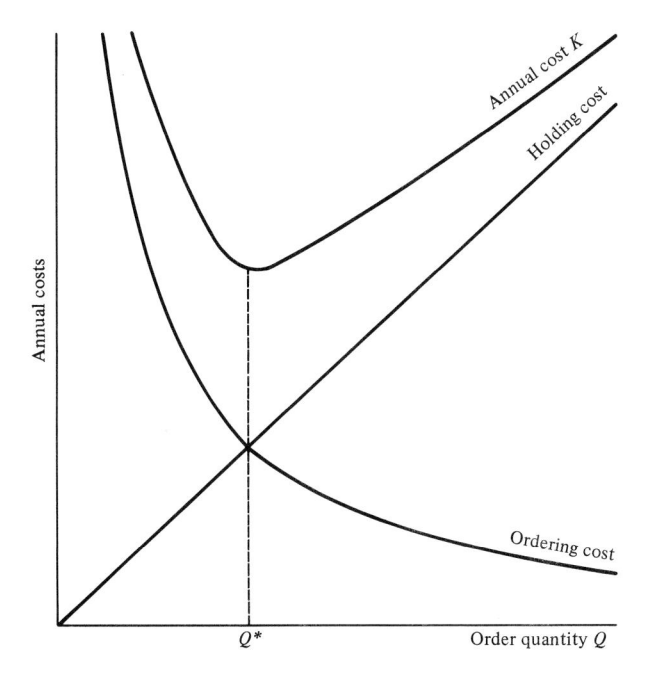

Figure 18.7 Annual costs: simple economic order quantity.

rivative of equation (2) with respect to Q, set the derivative equal to zero, and solve for Q^*. But there is another easier way to solve for Q^*. Observe that the minimum of K occurs where the inventory holding cost equals the ordering cost. Therefore, we can equate the two costs and solve for Q^*. No matter how we go about it, we ultimately will arrive at the well-known formula for economic order quantity:

$$Q^* = \sqrt{\frac{2DA}{iC}} \qquad (3)$$

Example 18.1: Central Airway's EOQ Central Airways (CA) maintains an inventory of spare parts that is valued at nearly $8 million. The inventory is composed of many thousands of different items (SKUs) used in aircraft maintenance, and the inventory balances are updated on a computerized information system.

Consider one particular inventory item: SKU 1001. Annual usage rate of SKU 1001 is relatively stable and averages 1000 units. CA purchases the item from the manufacturer at a cost of $20 per unit, delivered. An order for replenishment is placed whenever the inventory balance reaches a predetermined reorder point. The cost associated with placing an order is estimated to be $30. This includes the cost of paperwork, correspondence, and other things needed for processing an order. The replenishment quantity is determined using conventional economic-order-quantity formulas.

A financial accountant at CA estimates the annual inventory holding cost to be 30 percent of the average value of the inventory. This, of course, includes a 20 percent opportunity cost of capital. SKU 1001 is an essential item. Consequently, CA never wants to run out of stock for this item. We want to determine the replenishment order size for SKU 1001 that minimizes relevant inventory costs.

From the problem description we know the following:

$$D = 1000 \text{ units per year}$$
$$A = \$30 \text{ per order}$$
$$i = 30 \text{ percent per year}$$
$$C = \$20 \text{ per unit}$$

We can substitute values of Q into equation (2) to see what happens to cost K. From Table 18.1, we see that, as Q increases from 70 units, K decreases until it reaches a minimum at $600. From this point on, K increases. This is consistent with the general shape of the cost curve depicted in Figure 18.7.

Of course, we can calculate the economic order quantity directly by using equation (3). This gives

$$Q^* = \sqrt{\frac{2DA}{iC}}$$
$$= \sqrt{\frac{2(1000)(30)}{(0.3)(20)}}$$
$$= \sqrt{10{,}000}$$
$$= 100 \text{ units}$$

The annual relevant cost when $Q^* = 100$ units is $600.

Inventory Management under Uncertainty

The simple EOQ formula does not consider uncertainties in demand rate and uncertainties in replenishment lead time. But these uncertainties do exist and

Table 18.1 Tabulation of inventory costs

Order quantity Q	Order cost, $30	Inventory holding cost, 30%	Total cost K
70	$428.57	$210.00	$638.57
80	375.00	240.00	615.00
90	333.33	270.00	603.33
→ 100	300.00	300.00	600.00
110	272.73	330.00	602.73
120	250.00	360.00	610.00
130	230.77	390.00	620.77

INVENTORY MANAGEMENT **415**

may result in excess inventories during some periods and in stockouts during other periods. The inventory system needs to balance the likelihoods and costs associated with each of these occurrences.

The key to inventory management under uncertainty is the *service level* during the replenishment lead time, that is, the percentage of demand that occurs during the lead time that can be satisfied from inventory. Some analytical approaches for determining the optimal service level have been suggested. But, in practice service level is a policy decision. For one category of items, a 99 percent service level might be used, while, for another category of items, a 95 percent service level might be appropriate. Operations managers often play a major role in selecting service levels.

The service level is used to determine a *reorder point R*. The reorder point is set to achieve a prespecified service level. This, of course, requires information on the frequency distribution of demand during the replenishment lead time.

When we set the reorder point, we also are determining the *safety stock* level *B*. From Figure 18.8, we see that the reorder point equals the safety stock level plus the average demand during the lead time. That is,

$$R = B + \bar{d}_L \tag{4}$$

where $\bar{d}_L$ is the *average demand during the lead time*. We can rewrite equation (4) to solve for *B*:

$$B = R - \bar{d}_L \tag{5}$$

Example 18.2: Central Airway's reorder point Recall Central Airway's inventory item SKU 1001. CA's computerized information system has kept track of demand rate for item SKU 1001. Replenishment orders have been placed 20 times in the past with the same manufacturer. Table 18.2 gives the frequency distribution of demand during the lead time.

SKU 1001 is an important item for aircraft maintenance. It is a company policy to achieve a 95 percent service level for such items. What is the

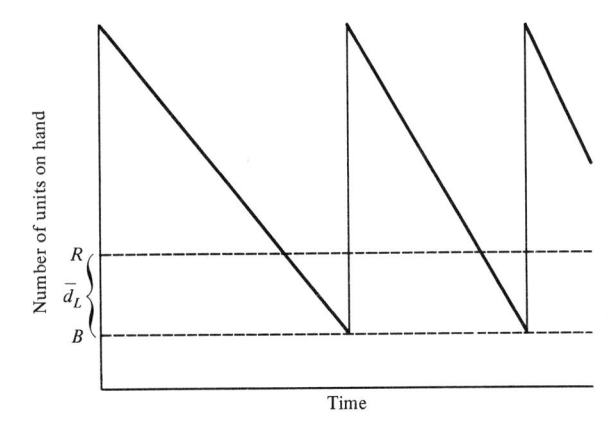

Figure 18.8 Reorder point and safety stock.

Table 18.2 Frequency distribution of demand during replenishment lead time

Demand	Frequency	% Frequency	Cumulative frequency, %
100	1	5	5
110	4	20	25
120	10	50	75
130	4	20	95
140	1	5	100
Total	20	100	

reorder point and safety stock level needed to yield a 95 percent service level?

From Table 18.2, we see that 95 percent of the time, demand is less than or equal to 130 units. Therefore, a reorder point of 130 units gives the desired 95 percent service level. We also calculate from Table 18.2 the average demand during the lead time. That is:

$$\bar{d}_L = [100(1) + 110(4) + 120(10) + 130(4) + 140(1)] \div 20$$
$$= 120 \text{ units}$$

Finally, the safety stock level associated with $R = 130$ is

$$B = R - \bar{d}_L$$
$$= 130 - 120$$
$$= 10 \text{ units}$$

AN EXAMPLE OF A COMPUTER-BASED INVENTORY SYSTEM

The techniques that underlie inventory management have been programmed for most computer systems, including the small computers popular with many service organizations. The inventory software (the computer programs) often is available in standard packages provided by computer manufacturers and by software companies. In some cases, however, the software is specifically developed to meet the unique needs of the customer. This was the case for McMahon Books, Inc., a medium-size book retailer.[1]

McMahon operates an IBM Series 1 computer system and uses computer programs developed by a local software company. The total system (both hardware and software) cost about $100,000. A major task in installing the new system was encoding the company's 24,000 book titles for the initial inventory records. This involved entering the inventory data into the computer system. Future plans include installing an optical reader to speed data entry for the inventory records and to reduce errors.

---

[1] This example was reported by P. D. Doebler, "The Computer in Book Distribution," *Publishers Weekly,* vol. 218, no. 11, September 12, 1980, p. 34.

The computerized inventory system has a number of benefits. It released two workers from the back office who previously had manually updated inventory files. The space where the files had been kept was cleared to make room for selling displays. The computer system also speeds book-order preparation by generating recommended orders for titles. The system compares sales records for each title during the most recent eight-week period. These records are used to pinpoint titles that might be running low. In a similar fashion, the system automatically recommends the return of slow-moving titles to publishers. In this case, the computerized system has additional advantages. All slow-moving titles that should be returned to the same publisher can be consolidated. This results in considerable cost savings in book handling and in freight.

The system developed for McMahon Books, Inc., also performs some of the more mundane office chores. These include purchase-order printing, accounting, check printing, and tabulating employee hours. As a result, more personnel time is available for selling, and this has led to increased sales. Better management of stocks has enabled sales personnel to answer questions about what titles are available and when new titles will be received. Consequently, better service is being provided to customers and McMahon Books, Inc. gains a competitive edge. In fact, the company has highlighted the enhanced service that results from the computerized inventory system in its advertising promotions.

SUMMARY

Inventory management can significantly influence the success of an organization. For some service organizations, the extent to which organizational objectives are achieved is affected by the inventory system adopted. Good inventory management is characterized by concern for inventory holding costs, inventory ordering costs, and shortage costs, as well as the purchase price of the items. Furthermore, the lead time for replenishment and the appropriate service level should be considered.

Most inventory systems are maintained by computers. This simplifies the manipulations of large amounts of data relevant to inventory decisions. These computerized information systems greatly facilitate inventory management.

TOPICS FOR DISCUSSION

1. Discuss the functions of inventory for a bank, for a hospital, and for a university.
2. Why is inventory management generally one of the first applications of a new data processing system?
3. Discuss the relevant costs for inventory management.
4. Compare and contrast a fixed-order-quantity inventory system with a fixed-interval system.
5. What are the managerial advantages of ABC analysis for inventory control.
6. Discuss the assumptions of the simple EOQ model. How valid are these assumptions?
7. Discuss the importance of service level for inventory management. Generally, how is service level determined for most inventory items?

8. What is the importance of safety stocks? Are safety stocks ever used? Explain.
9. What factors go into determining a reorder point?
10. Some noninventory items, such as seats on an aircraft, have the same characteristics as inventories. Give some service-related examples of these items. Can they be managed using inventory-type models?

EXERCISES

18.1 Annual demand for the notebook binders that Ted's Stationery Shop sells is 10,000 units. Ted operates his business on a 200-day working year. The unit cost of a binder is $2 and the cost of placing an order with his supplier is 40 cents. The cost of carrying a binder in stock for a year is 10 percent of its value.
   (a) What should be the economic order quantity?
   (b) How many orders are placed per year?
   (c) How many working days elapse between reorders?

18.2 Deep Six Seafoods, a restaurant that is open 360 days a year and that specializes in fresh Maine lobsters, is concerned about its purchase policy. Air freight charges have increased significantly to the point where it is costing Deep Six $48 to place an order. Because the lobsters are shipped live in a saltwater tub, the order cost is not affected by order sizes. The cost to keep a lobster alive until needed runs about 2 cents per day. The demand for lobsters during the one-day lead time is as follows:

Lead-time demand	Probability
0	0.05
1	0.10
2	0.20
3	0.30
4	0.20
5	0.10
6	0.05

   (a) Deep Six would like to reconsider its order size. What would you recommend as an economic order quantity?
   (b) The Maine distributor is willing to give Deep Six a 50-cent discount on each lobster, if orders are placed in lots of 360 each. Should Deep Six take the distributor up on this offer?
   (c) If Deep Six insists on maintaining a safety stock of two lobsters, what is the service level?

18.3 Dutch Farms imports cheese by the case from Holland for distribution to its Texas retail outlets. During the year (360 days) Dutch Farms sells 1080 cases of cheese. Owing to spoilage, Dutch Farms estimates that it costs the firm $6 per year to store a case of cheese. The cost to place an order runs about $10. The desired service level is 98 percent. The demand for cheese during the one-day lead time is shown below. (Note sales are in case lots only.)

Lead-time demand (cases)	Probability
0	0.02
1	0.08
2	0.20
3	0.40
4	0.20
5	0.08
6	0.02

(a) Calculate the EOQ for Dutch Farms.
(b) How many cases should Dutch Farms hold as safety stock against stockouts?
(c) Dutch Farms owns a refrigerated warehouse of 500-square-feet capacity. If each case of cheese requires 10 square feet and must be refrigerated, how much per year could Dutch Farms afford to spend on renting additional space?

18.4 The local distributor for Macho Heavy beer is reconsidering its inventory policy now that only kegs will be sold. The sales forecast for next year (360 days) is 1080 kegs. The cost to store a keg of Macho in a refrigerated warehouse is approximately $9 per year. Placing an order with the factory costs about $10. The demand for Macho during the one-day lead time is recorded below:

Lead-time demand (kegs)	Probability
0	0.03
1	0.12
2	0.20
3	0.30
4	0.20
5	0.12
6	0.03

(a) Recommend an economic order quantity for Macho Heavy.
(b) If orders are placed in carload lots of 200 kegs, the brewery is willing to give the local distributor a 25-cent discount on the wholesale price of a keg. Based on an analysis of total variable inventory costs, is this offer attractive?
(c) What is the recommended safety stock if Macho decides on an 85 percent service level?

CASELETTE: ELYSIAN CYCLES

Elysian Cycles (EC), located in a major southwestern city, is a wholesale distributor of bicycles and bicycle parts. Its primary retail outlets are located in eight cities within a 400-mile radius of the distribution center. These retail outlets generally depend on receiving orders for additional stock within two days after notifying the distribution center (if the stock is available). The company's management feels this is a valuable marketing tool that aids survival in a highly competitive industry.

EC distributes a wide variety of finished bicycles, but these are all based on five different frame designs, each of which may be available in several sizes. Table 18.3 gives a breakdown of the product options available to the retail outlets.

EC receives these different styles from a single manufacturer overseas, and shipments may take as long as four weeks from the time an order is made by telephone or telex. With the cost of communication, paperwork, and customs clearance included, EC estimates that each time an order is placed it incurs a cost of $65. The cost per bicycle is roughly 60 percent of the suggested list price for any of the styles available.

Demand for the bicycles is somewhat seasonal in nature, heavier in the spring and early summer and tapering off through the fall and winter seasons (except for a heavy surge in the six weeks prior to Christmas). A breakdown of

Table 18.3 Bicycles stocked

Frame style	Available sizes, in	No. of gears	Suggested list price (complete bicycle)
A	18, 21, 23	3	$ 99.95
B	18, 21, 23	10	124.95
C	18, 21, 23, 24.5	10	169.95
D	21, 23, 24.5	10	219.95
E	21, 23, 24.5	10 or 15	349.95

the previous year's business with the retail outlets usually forms the basis for EC's yearly operations plan. A growth factor (either positive or negative) is used to refine further the demand estimate by reflecting the upcoming yearly market for bicycle sales. By developing a yearly plan and updating it when appropriate, EC can establish some reasonable basis for obtaining any necessary financing from the bank. Last year's monthly demand for the different bicycle styles EC distributes is shown in Table 18.4.

Owing to the increasing popularity of bicycles for recreational purposes and for supplanting some automobile usage, EC believes that its market may grow by as much as 25 percent in the upcoming year. However, because there have been years when the full amount of expected growth did not materialize, EC has decided to base its plan on a more conservative 15 percent growth factor to allow for variations in consumer buying habits and to ensure that it is not excessively overstocked if the full market does not occur. Holding costs associated with inventory of any bicycle style is estimated to be about 0.75 percent of the unit cost of a bicycle per month.

Table 18.4 Monthly demand

Month	A	B	C	D	E	Total
January	0	3	5	2	0	10
February	2	8	10	3	1	24
March	4	15	21	12	2	54
April	4	35	40	21	3	103
May	3	43	65	37	3	151
June	3	27	41	18	2	91
July	2	13	26	11	1	53
August	1	10	16	9	1	37
September	1	9	11	7	1	29
October	1	8	10	7	2	28
November	2	15	19	12	3	51
December	3	30	33	19	4	89
Total	26	216	297	158	23	720

Assignment

Develop an inventory control plan for Elysian Cycles to use as the basis for its upcoming yearly plan. Be sure to justify your reasons for choosing a particular type (or combination of types) of inventory system(s). On the basis of your particular plan, specify the safety stock requirements if EC institutes a policy of maintaining a 95 percent service level.

SELECTED BIBLIOGRAPHY

Arrow, Kenneth J., Samuel Karlin, and Herbert Scarf: *Studies in the Mathematical Theory of Inventory and Production,* Stanford University Press, Stanford, Calif., 1958.

Austin, L. M.: "Project EOQ: A Success Story in Implementing Academic Research," *Interfaces,* vol. 7, no. 4, August 1977, pp. 1–12.

Brown, R. G.: *Decision Rules for Inventory Management,* Holt, Rinehart, and Winston, Inc., New York, 1967.

Buffa, Elwood S.: *Modern Production/Operations Management,* 6th ed., John Wiley and Sons, Inc., New York, 1980.

———, and J. G. Miller: *Production-Inventory Systems: Planning and Control,* 3d ed., Richard D. Irwin, Inc., Homewood, Ill., 1979.

Buffa, F. P.: "A Model for Allocating Limited Resources When Making Safety-Stock Decisions," *Decision Sciences,* vol. 8, no. 2, April 1977, pp. 415–426.

Doebler, P. D.: "The Computer in Book Distribution," *Publishers Weekly,* vol. 218, no. 11, September 12, 1980, p. 34.

Hadley, G., and T. M. Whitin: *Analysis of Inventory Systems,* Prentice-Hall, Inc., Englewood Cliffs, N.J., 1963.

Magee, J. F., and D. M. Boodman: *Production Planning and Inventory Control,* 2d ed., McGraw-Hill Book Company, New York, 1967.

Naddor, Eleizer: *Inventory Systems,* John Wiley and Sons, Inc., New York, 1966.

Peterson, R., and E. A. Silver: *Decision Systems for Inventory Management and Production Planning,* John Wiley and Sons, Inc., New York, 1979.

Starr, M. K., and D. W. Miller: *Inventory Control: Theory and Practice,* Prentice-Hall, Inc., Englewood Cliffs, N.J., 1962.

PART FIVE

TRANSITION

CHAPTER
NINETEEN

SERVICE, CULTURE, AND SOCIETY

Our society is in transition from an industrial economy to a service economy, from consumers to individual producers. We have provided service operations managers with tools of analysis and with models for control, many adapted from successful applications in manufacturing. Service managers should find this material helpful during this transition period. However, there are developments in information and communication technology that, together with a highly educated population, suggest a major change in the structure of how work will be accomplished in the future. A new role for the service operations manager is emerging.

The developments in information technology, the importance of the invisible economy, the metamorphosis of the consumer into a producer, and the rise in self-help organizations will be examined. The implications of these developments on the changing role of the operations manager will also be explored.

INFORMATION AND COMMUNICATIONS TECHNOLOGY

In many occupations, people no longer need work together physically. Indeed, for years salespeople have worked out of their homes, visiting the office only occasionally. But now it is possible for computer programmers, investment counselors, file clerks, and even secretaries to work at home. Advances in computer technology and communications have led to distributive information systems. Access to the main computer and to data files can be made from remote terminals via ordinary telephone lines. CRT (cathode-ray tube) terminals allow information to be displayed, updated, and entered from a keyboard with direct access to the computer files. Computer programmers can compose their programs at the terminal and test-run routines at any hour of the day from home or office. It is common to see professors and graduate students leaving campus with an additional attache case these days. The compact, silent (the newest versions use heat-sensitive printing), and portable terminal allows work to be done during off-peak evening hours, holidays, and weekends. The computer is never shut down, only physical access to it is restricted by working hours.

The computer now becomes no farther away than the nearest telephone. Thus, people are free to work wherever they please. For example, people with children can work at home updating insurance claim files. An investment counselor can access financial information from the client's office or home.

The advent of word processing increases the possibilities. Word processing is the ability to store, manipulate, and process data as needed in the preparation of letters and reports using CRT terminals. The secretary of the future may take dictation at home; type the text on a home terminal; wire an electronic copy to its addressee, at whose facility a hard copy is printed on company stationery; print a copy for the boss; and file a magnetic copy with the customer's computerized record account.

The implications of a dispersed workforce are many. Avoiding the commuting costs of gasoline and travel time alone may ensure the demise of the centralized downtown office. People will have much more freedom in where they may live. For example, a recent University of Texas graduate unwilling to leave Austin, Texas, arranged with a Chicago employer to perform everyday market-research duties by telephone at home in Texas and meet periodically with superiors in Chicago.

For the operations manager this means that personnel must assume more responsibility for accomplishing their work. Direct supervision will no longer be practical. Traditionally the operations manager has been responsible for the physical and human resource inputs to the production process. Now we find that information resources must also be considered. The service process design is not complete without considering the communications network and supporting information technology.

FROM CONSUMER TO PROSUMER[1]

The economy that politicians worry about and that economists measure is composed of the output of goods and services sold in the marketplace. There exists a growing invisible economy composed of all the unpaid work done directly by

---

[1] The term "prosumer" was coined by Alvin Toffler, author of *The Third Wave,* William Morrow and Co., Inc., New York, 1980.

people for themselves, for their families, or for their communities. Examples are pumping your own gasoline at a self-service station, installing insulation in the attic, and manning a rape crisis hotline. The invisible economy is growing rapidly for several reasons. The increased availability of leisure time provides the opportunity. Uncontrolled inflation provides the incentive to cut expenses. Experiences with shoddy workmanship and with unresponsive servers reinforce the idea that if you want it done right, then do it yourself. A subtle reason also exists to promote unpaid work; it is rational from an economic perspective. For example, calling a plumber out to the house to unstop a sink might cost $20. If the homeowner does the work, the homeowner could earn the equivalent of perhaps $40. This would be the case if the homeowner were in the 50 percent income tax bracket. In other words the homeowner would need to earn $40 to pay the plumber $20. Ben Franklin's advice "a penny saved is a penny earned" could be recast as "a dollar's worth of self-service is worth two dollars in taxable wages."

The do-it-yourselfer is the vanguard of the modern self-service ethic, which no longer looks down upon working with one's hands but considers it a sign of pride and self-reliance. Still more importantly, the self-service ethic represents freedom from dependence upon others to supply our needs. The self-service ethic also represents a blow to the market economy that has separated the activities of consumption from production. The self-service ethic is fueled by a better-educated, information-rich society, provided with home-based technology, such as automobile repair tools, pregnancy-test kits, and power tools for lawn, garden, and workshop. To this are being added the home microcomputer and expanded cable television.

The implications for service operations managers are twofold. Some services, such as routine automobile maintenance, will have a declining market. This may also be the case for routine medical checkups now that people are becoming more concerned with preventive medicine. The self-serve blood pressure machine has joined the scales at the neighborhood pharmacy. An entire self-help movement has spawned organizations to help overeaters, smokers, gamblers, drug abusers, and others. Under the guidance of a counselor, the participants share their experiences and provide support for each other. The underlying concept is that each individual must cure himself or herself through discipline and behavior changes. Again the reliance is on self-help and not on the consumption of professional mental health care.

On the other hand, the self-service ethic represents an opportunity for service operations managers. More can be expected of consumers. It was physically impossible for the telephone company to keep up with increasing demand just by adding operators. So the company turned to the consumer for assistance by introducing direct dialing. Banks, overwhelmed at the drive-in facility, are turning to automatic tellers. The Whirlpool Corporation has inaugurated a new approach to appliance repair. Its system, called Cool-Line, consists of a toll-free 800 number that customers can call to talk directly with a service technician about problems with their appliances. Using the model number, the technician refers to the appropriate drawings and talks the customer through the necessary repair. This concept of involving the consumer in the process is possible because the self-service ethic makes it acceptable. Creative operations managers will look to the *prosumer* as a productive resource to be integrated into the service process and managed along with the other human and physical resources. With the use of prosumer labor together with new information technology, imaginative new service delivery systems are possible.

A SERVICE SOCIETY

In a service society the distinction between work and leisure becomes irrelevant. Wages earned working for the market have the same currency as unpaid work for self. The routine of the traditional eight-to-five job forced upon employees by the rhythm of manufacturing will no longer be required. Even today employees are demanding freedom from regimentation. The concept of flextime gives employees the freedom to choose their arrival and departure times within limits, provided the assigned work is accomplished. The idea of shared jobs, in which two qualified people share the same position, is a response to the desire for freedom to pursue other activities. Lifestyles based on working part-time for wages in the market and at other times engaging in prosumer activities could become a reality for a sizeable segment of the population. A labor force desiring part-time hours will challenge the service operations manager's coordination and scheduling skills.

More importantly, service operations managers must nurture and invest in their human capital because the skill, dexterity, and knowledge of this resource is essential to the well-being of the organization. Exploiting the knowledge, skills, imagination, ideas, and insights of service personnel creates the competitive advantage that leads to growth and prosperity. Operations managers who are able to create a challenging working environment that motivates personnel to perform at their best will be eagerly sought.

IMPROVING SERVICE SECTOR PRODUCTIVITY

As has been the case in manufacturing, service operations managers are responsible in the final analysis for the productivity of the organization. The transformation of the United States economy, once dominated by manufacturing, to a service economy has created new opportunities for operations managers. Some economists have stated that the productivity problem in the United States is caused by this growth of the service sector. They view the service sector as labor-intensive and capital-poor, with an output difficult to measure. This was the state of manufacturing that Frederick Taylor faced almost a century ago.

Today a new breed of operations managers views the service sector as the new frontier of the profession. Transferring the appropriate technology developed in past years for manufacturing to services is part of the productivity solution. But service operations are sufficiently different from manufacturing; they require new approaches to improve productivity. For example, recent advances in computer-based information systems and in communications technology provide opportunities for productivity gains in the information-rich service operations. Imaginative operations managers skilled in the use of this electronic technology will be the process engineers designing new service delivery systems. Improved information processing should lead to better utilization of service capacity and thus to increased productivity.

The fact that the consumer is part of the process, and, thus, a potential productive resource is unique to services. In this context, the entire society is actively contributing to the gross national product in everyday self-service activities. This is possible in today's society because of the improved level of education. As recently as 1957 fewer than half of the labor force had finished high school and only 9 percent had finished college. By 1978, three out of four workers had finished high school, and a third had attended college, had obtained a college degree, or had attended graduate school.[2] This factor adds another dimension to the design of innovative service delivery systems and presents a challenge for the service operations manager. Unlike their manufacturing colleagues, service operations managers must be concerned with the consumer-provider interface and the perception the consumer gains from the total service experience. This illustrates the difficulty of measuring service productivity because the output is viewed by the consumer as a bundle of perceptions—a service package.

Productivity in services also must be placed in the context of today's better-educated society that expects more from work than just a paycheck. Service operations managers must be sensitive to the desire for personal commitment and challenge in order to motivate personnel to achieve excellence in the work place.

CAPSTONE CASE: THE UNIVERSITY STUDENT UNION

In October 1982, Susan Welsh reported to work as the new assistant manager of the University Student Union (USU). Susan recently received her MBA degree from a prestigious east-coast business school, where she developed an interest in service organizations. She felt that the USU offered an opportunity to use her knowledge and skill in managing service operations.

On her first day at work, Susan was briefed on her responsibilities by the USU manager, Greg Bloom. Greg wanted Susan to be exposed to every aspect of the USU operations. These include service planning, financial management,

[2] Eli Ginzberg and George J. Vojta, "The Service Sector of the U.S. Economy," *Scientific American*, vol. 244, no. 3, March 1981, pp. 48–55.

inventory control, personnel management, facilities planning, and quality control. Initially, Susan was to concentrate on becoming familiar with the USU operations. Consequently, Greg asked her to spend her first week conducting a management audit. Specifically, she was to provide a written report that outlined the current status of operations, that indicated management priorities, and that suggested directions that should be taken in managing the operations of the USU. The written report was due by the end of October.

The Union

The USU is an integral part of the university and caters to many of the community needs of 46,000 students. The union provides for the services, conveniences, and amenities that members of the university community need in their daily lives on campus. It provides dining services, study rooms, recreational facilities, and cultural activities. Some of these activities are revenue producing, such as the dining services. However, many others do not generate revenue and are paid for from other sources. All students are assessed a fee upon registration that is used for the operation of the union.

The objectives of the USU are typical of most university unions. They involve the following:

1. Providing effective, high-quality programs and activities for the university community
2. Providing relevant and popular services for the university community
3. Providing and maintaining adequate, appealing, and efficiently managed facilities
4. Satisfying the needs and wants of a diverse community
5. Recruiting, training, and evaluating high-quality paid staff
6. Recruiting, training, and evaluating high-quality volunteer workers
7. Keeping operations financially sound
8. Gaining recognition for the contribution of the union to campus life

USU Operations

Susan spent three days making observations on various aspects of the operations of the USU. She was told that the union building had recently been renovated at a cost of $1.5 million. The remodeling efforts were directed primarily at the dining facilities, which were greatly expanded and diversified. In addition to a bar-type lounge that offers soft drinks and beer, there are hamburger/hot dog sections, salad bars, and pizza sections, as well as more traditional food sections. Susan made the following notes on various operations of the union.

Layout of facilities Since the renovation, there have been many changes in the layout of the dining facilities. These changes have been made on the basis of the observations of the service manager with respect to student attitudes, length of waiting lines, and popularity of various services. For example, the Steer Here Hamburger Stand originally provided sandwiches with lettuce and tomato, but without mustard and ketchup. The process was changed so that customers could add the lettuce and tomato at a convenient condiment table. The process and layout were changed again so that all the condiments (including mustard and ketchup) would be added by the staff instead of the customer. It appeared that the service manager was not sure what strategy to adopt.

Quality control Quality control is a major concern of the management of the USU. Various forms of inspection by the service manager constitute the backbone of the quality control system. However, Greg Bloom expressed concern that the inadequate staff levels for the food service operations hamper quality assurance. Ideally, food is tasted in the kitchen and then tested routinely by food supervisors. Two samples of each food type are kept for several days in the event of problems, such as food poisoning. An important aspect of quality is the delivery of the food from the kitchens to the customers. The quality must be maintained and the appearance must be aesthetically appealing.

Personnel management Personnel management is concerned with staff recruiting and training. More than one-half of the paid staff of the USU are part-time students. They are employed in low-skill jobs in the kitchen and dining areas. Part-time workers are paid minimum wage and most work during the rush hours of the day. High turnover is prevalent among the part-time workers, and this necessitates continuous recruiting and training of new personnel.

The USU previously had a formal training program for new workers. However, Greg Bloom felt that the tenure of most workers was so short that such a training program was not worthwhile. Therefore, new workers learn their tasks on the job under the direction of their supervisors.

Student workers have some additional advantages that contribute to the service of the USU. These workers tend to be self-motivated and friendly. In addition, they quickly develop good relations with customers, who are their colleagues in the university community. Student workers are a great asset to the USU.

Inventory control The USU uses two inventory systems. The first is the university-wide system that controls furnishings and properties valued at $200 or more. The union has no control over this system. The second inventory system is for food services. One area of the union is reserved for food storage, and items are dispensed when a standard requisition form is completed by a food supervisor. Inventory records are maintained on a computerized system. When prespecified reorder points are reached, orders for replenishments are placed.

The vendors for various food items are determined at the beginning of each academic year on the basis of low bids. This created some unusual problems during the high inflationary periods of 1980 and 1981. Several vendors demanded readjustment of contracts for various staple foods owing to increasing costs. The union accepted the higher rates rather than risk interruption of food services.

Financial management As previously indicated, the USU offers some services that are revenue-producing and other services that are not revenue-producing. Greg Bloom is intent upon keeping the union financially sound. This means that the revenues from services and from student fees must cover expenses. But financial pressures have been building. The cost of labor increased drastically with changes in the minimum-wage law. Also, employers are required to make larger payments to social security on behalf of employees. On top of increased labor costs, the costs of all utilities have jumped. To cover these costs, the price of food was raised. But this caused demand to slacken. In another attempt to increase revenues, Greg Bloom proposed to university officials that student fees be increased. But such an increase is politically unpopular. The university already has instituted a major increase in tuition, and any additional levies on students would not go over well.

Alternatives to Consider

Susan was surprised by the complexity of problems facing the USU. Everywhere she turned, there were pressing issues that appeared to need immediate attention. But Susan decided to restrict her attention to the tasks given her by Greg Bloom. She wanted to make an appraisal of the current operations, to rank-order management priorities, and to suggest directions that should be taken in managing the operations of the USU.

Questions

1. What aspects of service operations management that you studied in this textbook apply specifically to the USU? Explain their relevancy.
2. What are the unique features of the USU that make operations management particularly difficult? Explain how you might deal with these problems.
3. Outline a report that Susan Welsh could submit to Greg Bloom.

TABLES

Table A Single-payment present worth factors

				Interest or discount rates				
n	0.04	0.05	0.06	0.08	0.10	0.15	0.20	n
1	0.9615	0.9524	0.9434	0.9259	0.9091	0.8696	0.8333	1
2	0.9246	0.9070	0.8900	0.8573	0.8264	0.7561	0.6944	2
3	0.8890	0.8638	0.8396	0.7938	0.7513	0.6575	0.5787	3
4	0.8548	0.8227	0.7921	0.7350	0.6830	0.5718	0.4823	4
5	0.8219	0.7835	0.7473	0.6806	0.6209	0.4972	0.4019	5
6	0.7903	0.7462	0.7050	0.6302	0.5645	0.4323	0.3349	6
7	0.7599	0.7107	0.6651	0.5835	0.5132	0.3759	0.2791	7
8	0.7307	0.6768	0.6274	0.5403	0.4665	0.3269	0.2326	8
9	0.7026	0.6446	0.5919	0.5002	0.4241	0.2843	0.1938	9
10	0.6756	0.6139	0.5584	0.4632	0.3855	0.2472	0.1615	10
11	0.6496	0.5847	0.5268	0.4289	0.3505	0.2149	0.1346	11
12	0.6246	0.5568	0.4970	0.3971	0.3186	0.1869	0.1122	12
13	0.6006	0.5303	0.4688	0.3677	0.2897	0.1625	0.0935	13
14	0.5775	0.5051	0.4423	0.3405	0.2633	0.1413	0.0779	14
15	0.5553	0.4810	0.4173	0.3152	0.2394	0.1229	0.0649	15
16	0.5339	0.4581	0.3936	0.2919	0.2176	0.1069	0.0541	16
17	0.5134	0.4363	0.3714	0.2703	0.1978	0.0929	0.0451	17
18	0.4936	0.4155	0.3503	0.2502	0.1799	0.0808	0.0376	18
19	0.4746	0.3957	0.3305	0.2317	0.1635	0.0703	0.0313	19
20	0.4564	0.3769	0.3118	0.2145	0.1486	0.0611	0.0261	20
21	0.4388	0.3589	0.2942	0.1987	0.1351	0.0531	0.0217	21
22	0.4220	0.3418	0.2775	0.1839	0.1228	0.0462	0.0181	22
23	0.4057	0.3256	0.2618	0.1703	0.1117	0.0402	0.0151	23
24	0.3901	0.3101	0.2470	0.1577	0.1015	0.0349	0.0126	24
25	0.3751	0.2953	0.2330	0.1460	0.0923	0.0304	0.0105	25
26	0.3607	0.2812	0.2198	0.1352	0.0839	0.0264	0.0087	26
27	0.3468	0.2678	0.2074	0.1252	0.0763	0.0230	0.0073	27
28	0.3335	0.2551	0.1956	0.1159	0.0693	0.0200	0.0061	28
29	0.3207	0.2429	0.1846	0.1073	0.0630	0.0174	0.0051	29
30	0.3083	0.2314	0.1741	0.0994	0.0573	0.0151	0.0042	30
31	0.2965	0.2204	0.1643	0.0920	0.0521	0.0131	0.0035	31
32	0.2851	0.2099	0.1550	0.0852	0.0474	0.0114	0.0029	32
33	0.2741	0.1999	0.1462	0.0789	0.0431	0.0099	0.0024	33
34	0.2636	0.1904	0.1379	0.0730	0.0391	0.0086	0.0020	34
35	0.2534	0.1813	0.1301	0.0676	0.0356	0.0075	0.0017	35
40	0.2083	0.1420	0.0972	0.0460	0.0221	0.0037	0.0007	40
45	0.1712	0.1113	0.0727	0.0313	0.0137	0.0019	0.0003	45
50	0.1407	0.0872	0.0543	0.0213	0.0085	0.0009	0.0001	50

Source: Christopher K. McKenna, *Quantitative Methods for Public Decision Making,* McGraw-Hill Book Company, New York, 1980.

Table B Uniform-series present worth factors

	\multicolumn{7}{c}{Interest or discount rates}	
n	0.04	0.05	0.06	0.08	0.10	0.15	0.20	n
1	0.962	0.952	0.943	0.926	0.909	0.870	0.833	1
2	1.886	1.859	1.833	1.783	1.736	1.626	1.528	2
3	2.775	2.723	2.673	2.577	2.487	2.283	2.106	3
4	3.630	3.546	3.465	3.312	3.170	2.855	2.589	4
5	4.452	4.329	4.212	3.993	3.791	3.352	2.991	5
6	5.242	5.076	4.917	4.623	4.355	3.784	3.326	6
7	6.002	5.786	5.582	5.206	4.868	4.160	3.605	7
8	6.733	6.463	6.210	5.747	5.335	4.487	3.837	8
9	7.435	7.108	6.802	6.247	5.759	4.772	4.031	9
10	8.111	7.722	7.360	6.710	6.144	5.019	4.192	10
11	8.760	8.306	7.887	7.139	6.495	5.234	4.327	11
12	9.385	8.863	8.384	7.536	6.814	5.421	4.439	12
13	9.986	9.394	8.853	7.904	7.103	5.583	4.533	13
14	10.563	9.899	9.295	8.244	7.367	5.724	4.611	14
15	11.118	10.380	9.712	8.559	7.606	5.847	4.675	15
16	11.652	10.838	10.106	8.851	7.824	5.954	4.730	16
17	12.166	11.274	10.477	9.122	8.022	6.047	4.775	17
18	12.659	11.690	10.828	9.372	8.201	6.128	4.812	18
19	13.134	12.085	11.158	9.604	8.363	6.198	4.843	19
20	13.590	12.462	11.470	9.818	8.514	6.259	4.870	20
21	14.029	12.821	11.764	10.017	8.649	6.312	4.891	21
22	14.451	13.163	12.042	10.201	8.772	6.359	4.909	22
23	14.857	13.489	12.303	10.371	8.883	6.399	4.925	23
24	15.247	13.799	12.550	10.529	8.985	6.434	4.937	24
25	15.622	14.094	12.783	10.675	9.077	6.464	4.948	25
26	15.983	14.375	13.003	10.810	9.161	6.491	4.956	26
27	16.330	14.643	13.211	10.935	9.237	6.514	4.964	27
28	16.663	14.898	13.406	11.051	9.307	6.534	4.970	28
29	16.984	15.141	13.591	11.158	9.370	6.551	4.975	29
30	17.292	15.372	13.765	11.258	9.427	6.566	4.979	30
31	17.588	15.593	13.929	11.350	9.479	6.579	4.982	31
32	17.874	15.803	14.084	11.435	9.526	6.591	4.985	32
33	18.148	16.003	14.230	11.514	9.569	6.600	4.988	33
34	18.411	16.193	14.368	11.587	9.609	6.609	4.990	34
35	18.665	16.374	14.498	11.655	9.644	6.617	4.992	35
40	19.793	17.159	15.046	11.925	9.779	6.642	4.997	40
45	20.720	17.774	15.456	12.108	9.863	6.654	4.999	45
50	21.482	18.256	15.762	12.233	9.915	6.661	4.999	50

Source: Christopher K. McKenna, *Quantitative Methods for Public Decision Making,* McGraw-Hill Book Company, New York, 1980.

Table C Areas of a Standard Normal Distribution

An entry in the table is the proportion under the entire curve which is between $z = 0$ and a positive value of z. Areas for negative values of z are obtained by symmetry.

z	0.00	0.01	0.02	0.03	0.04	0.05	0.06	0.07	0.08	0.09
0.0	0.0000	0.0040	0.0080	0.0120	0.0160	0.0199	0.0239	0.0279	0.0319	0.0359
0.1	0.0398	0.0438	0.0478	0.0517	0.0557	0.0596	0.0636	0.0675	0.0714	0.0753
0.2	0.0793	0.0832	0.0871	0.0910	0.0948	0.0987	0.1026	0.1064	0.1103	0.1141
0.3	0.1179	0.1217	0.1255	0.1293	0.1331	0.1368	0.1406	0.1443	0.1480	0.1517
0.4	0.1554	0.1591	0.1628	0.1664	0.1700	0.1736	0.1772	0.1808	0.1844	0.1879
0.5	0.1915	0.1950	0.1985	0.2019	0.2054	0.2088	0.2123	0.2157	0.2190	0.2224
0.6	0.2257	0.2291	0.2324	0.2357	0.2389	0.2422	0.2454	0.2486	0.2517	0.2549
0.7	0.2580	0.2611	0.2642	0.2673	0.2703	0.2734	0.2764	0.2794	0.2823	0.2852
0.8	0.2881	0.2910	0.2939	0.2967	0.2995	0.3023	0.3051	0.3078	0.3106	0.3133
0.9	0.3159	0.3186	0.3212	0.3238	0.3264	0.3289	0.3315	0.3340	0.3365	0.3389
1.0	0.3413	0.3438	0.3461	0.3485	0.3508	0.3531	0.3554	0.3577	0.3599	0.3621
1.1	0.3643	0.3665	0.3686	0.3708	0.3729	0.3749	0.3770	0.3790	0.3810	0.3830
1.2	0.3849	0.3869	0.3888	0.3907	0.3925	0.3944	0.3962	0.3980	0.3997	0.4015
1.3	0.4032	0.4049	0.4066	0.4082	0.4099	0.4115	0.4131	0.4147	0.4162	0.4177
1.4	0.4192	0.4207	0.4222	0.4236	0.4251	0.4265	0.4279	0.4292	0.4306	0.4319
1.5	0.4332	0.4345	0.4357	0.4370	0.4382	0.4394	0.4406	0.4418	0.4429	0.4441
1.6	0.4452	0.4463	0.4474	0.4484	0.4495	0.4505	0.4515	0.4525	0.4535	0.4545
1.7	0.4554	0.4564	0.4573	0.4582	0.4591	0.4599	0.4608	0.4616	0.4625	0.4633
1.8	0.4641	0.4649	0.4656	0.4664	0.4671	0.4678	0.4686	0.4693	0.4699	0.4706
1.9	0.4713	0.4719	0.4726	0.4732	0.4738	0.4744	0.4750	0.4756	0.4761	0.4767
2.0	0.4772	0.4778	0.4783	0.4788	0.4793	0.4798	0.4803	0.4808	0.4812	0.4817
2.1	0.4821	0.4826	0.4830	0.4834	0.4838	0.4842	0.4846	0.4850	0.4854	0.4857
2.2	0.4861	0.4864	0.4868	0.4871	0.4875	0.4878	0.4881	0.4884	0.4887	0.4890
2.3	0.4893	0.4896	0.4898	0.4901	0.4904	0.4906	0.4909	0.4911	0.4913	0.4916
2.4	0.4918	0.4920	0.4922	0.4925	0.4927	0.4929	0.4931	0.4932	0.4934	0.4936
2.5	0.4938	0.4940	0.4941	0.4943	0.4945	0.4946	0.4948	0.4949	0.4951	0.4952
2.6	0.4953	0.4955	0.4956	0.4957	0.4959	0.4960	0.4961	0.4962	0.4963	0.4964
2.7	0.4965	0.4966	0.4967	0.4968	0.4969	0.4970	0.4971	0.4972	0.4973	0.4974
2.8	0.4974	0.4975	0.4976	0.4977	0.4977	0.4978	0.4979	0.4979	0.4980	0.4981
2.9	0.4981	0.4982	0.4982	0.4983	0.4984	0.4984	0.4985	0.4985	0.4986	0.4986
3.0	0.4987	0.4987	0.4987	0.4988	0.4988	0.4989	0.4989	0.4989	0.4990	0.4990

Source: Donald H. Sanders, A. Franklin Murph, and Robert J. Eng, *Statistics—A Fresh Approach,* McGraw-Hill Book Company, New York, 1976.

Table D Uniformly distributed random numbers

0.06785	0.39867	0.90588	0.17801
0.81075	0.87641	0.67964	0.43877
0.98544	0.51653	0.44093	0.79428
0.31479	0.75057	0.28248	0.26863
0.12484	0.88287	0.78805	0.00907
0.23882	0.82137	0.51759	0.24723
0.23897	0.93060	0.94078	0.44676
0.40374	0.57000	0.33415	0.90000
0.73622	0.85896	0.36825	0.31500
0.36952	0.39367	0.09426	0.79517
0.14510	0.05047	0.01535	0.46997
0.12719	0.35159	0.55903	0.01268
0.99407	0.53816	0.64881	0.64309
0.32694	0.57237	0.74242	0.68045
0.42780	0.54704	0.63281	0.92243
0.00633	0.87197	0.90597	0.95629
0.38490	0.27804	0.06567	0.49591
0.22363	0.96354	0.25298	0.88459
0.54105	0.62235	0.93190	0.66122
0.31786	0.84724	0.04084	0.98260
0.47556	0.38855	0.52135	0.34085
0.70850	0.55051	0.86505	0.21192
0.64791	0.89438	0.83997	0.00898
0.21424	0.34592	0.77920	0.16675
0.77524	0.41976	0.08429	0.71506

INDEX

Abendroth, W. W., 315*n*., 335
Abernathy, W. J., 164, 165, 182, 310
Activities on arcs (AOA), 343, 350–352
Activities on nodes (AON), 343, 344
Adam, E. E., Jr., 386
Affirmative action, 213–214
Airport Services, Inc., caselette, 333–335
ALCOVE Corporation caselette, 157–159
Algorithms:
　defined, 11
　use of, 298
　(*See also specific algorithms, for example:* Clarke-Wright algorithm; Greedy adding algorithm; Simplex algorithm)
Alter, S., 396, 397, 402
American Institute of Architects, 189
American Telephone and Telegraph (AT&T), 213
Amstatz, A. E., 398*n*., 402
Analog models, 59
Aquilano, N., 142, 362

Arcs, activities on (AOA), 343, 350–352
Areal unit, 166
Armour, G. C., 201*n*., 202, 209
Arrival process, 241–245, 259
　(*See also* Poisson distribution)
Arrow, K. J., 421
Ashby, W. R., 364*n*., 386
Athol Furniture, Inc., caselette, 179–182
Atkinson, G. A., 188, 209
Austin, L. M., 421
Averill, B., 243, 246, 252, 256, 270*n*., 284, 288, 289*n*., 311

Babbage, C., 214
Backorder, 408, 409
Baker, K. R., 299, 310
Balking in queuing systems, 241, 249
Baloff, N., 310
Baron, R., 243, 246, 252, 256, 270*n*., 284, 288, 289*n*., 311
Barzel, Y., 240, 255
BASIC computer language, 390

Basic variable, 96–97
Batch (job shop) service operation, 147
Bell, D., 4, 6, 14
Benefit-cost (*see* Cost-benefit analysis)
Benihana of Tokyo, 300
Bennet, K. W., 233
Bennigson, A. I., 386
Bennigson, L. A., 386
Berg, S. V., 154*n*., 159
Bergman, L., 183
Berry, W. L., 141
Beta distribution, 349–350, 353
Bleuel, W. H., 284
Blood, M. R., 233
Blum, E. H., 22*n*., 28, 57
Blumberg, M. S., 369
Bodin, L. D., 335
Boodman, D. M., 421
Box, G. E., 141
Branch routing, 313
Branches, 313
Brewer, G. D., 159
Bright, J., 141
Brown, L. A., 166*n*., 182
Brown, P. M., 203*n*., 210
Brown, R. G., 142, 421
Buck, H., 369
Budnick, F. S., 113, 255, 284

439

440 INDEX

Buffa, E. S., 142, 199*n*., 201*n*., 202, 209, 210, 295, 310, 361, 421
Buffa, F. P., 142, 421
Burt, J. M., 362
Butler, W. F., 142

Cain, T., 336
Calling population, 241–242, 259, 273
Camp, R. C., 335
Canen, D. M., 397*n*., 403
Canyon General Hospital (Anaheim, Calif.), 397
Capacity:
  adjustable, 300
  and demand, 192, 269, 275
  and inventory theory, 404–407
  and process layout, 197
  service (*see* Service capacity)
  sharing, 301
Capacity planning, 257, 269–270, 275
Cathode-ray tube (CRT), 389, 397–398, 426
Causal forecasting models, 115, 130–133
  econometric models, 131–133
  regression models, 131–133
Caveat emptor, 379
Cedar Valley Community College caselette, 283
Census tracts, 166
Central limit theorem, 350
Chambers, J. C., 142
CHAMPS (Canyon General Hospital Automated Medical Processing System), 397–398
Chandrasekaran, R., 142
Characteristic curve, 375, 376
Charnes, A., 335
Chartrand, P. J., 233
Chase R. B., 142, 153*n*., 154, 155, 159, 362
Chinese postman problem, 315
Chowdhary, R. L., 290, 311
Christofides, N., 326*n*., 335

Church, R., 175, 182
Churchman, C. W., 39, 57
Clark, C., 3, 14
Clark-Fisher hypothesis, 3
Clarke, G., 316*n*., 335
Clarke-Wright (C-W) algorithm, 316–326
  with constraints, 320–321
  without constraints, 321
  net savings, 320–321, 323
  savings concept, 317
  traveling salesman problem, 321–324
  (*See also* VSP/X)
Clean Sweep, Inc., caselette, 383–385
COBOL computer language, 390
Cochran, H., 336
Cohen, R. C., 22*n*., 28
Communication, substitution of, for transportation, 175
Communications technology, 425, 429
Compilers, 390
Computers:
  compilers, 390
  costs, 391
  hardware (*see* Hardware, computer)
  languages, 60–62, 390
  microcomputers, 390, 427
  minicomputers, 390, 397–399
  number in use, 391
  processing capability, 390
  software (*see* Software, computer)
  technological advances, 388, 390–392, 425–426, 429
Confidence interval, 372–373
Connors, M. M., 209
Constrained optimization models, 82–92
  goal programming, 81, 101–103
  graphical solution, 92–94
  integer programming, 88–90
  linear programming, 60, 81–82, 84
  network models, 90–92

Constraint functions, 83
  (*See also* Objective function coefficients; Right-hand-side constraints)
Consumer(s):
  and computers, 391
  contact operations, 153–155
  participation of, 27, 151–153, 240, 300
  perceptions of, 19, 27, 184, 214, 264
  protection of, 35
  relationship to employees, 24, 211, 312
  role in services, 12–14, 21, 26, 235, 429
  waiting, 257
Consumer's risk, 372, 375
Consumption, relationship of, to production, 21–23, 116–117, 235, 366, 380, 427
Continuous-flow system, 192–193
  job specialization, 193
  line balancing problem, 195–197
  operations flow diagram, 193–195
  process charts, 193–194
  and product layout, 191–193
Conway, R. W., 250*n*., 255
Cook, T., 335
Cooper, B. S., 46*n*., 57
Coquille Refinery Corporation caselette, 78–79
Cosgrove, M. J., 295, 297, 310
Cost-benefit analysis, 33, 39–51
  defensive driving program study, 48–50
  direct benefits in, 46
  human life as intangible benefit in, 47
  indirect benefits in, 46
  intangible benefits in, 47
  negative benefits in, 47
Cost effectiveness, 40, 164
  kidney disease treatment study, 50, 51

County General Hospital caselette, 231–233
CPM (*see* Critical Path Method)
Crabill, T. B., 284
CRAFT (Computerized Relative Allocation of Facilities Technique), 201–203
Critical Path Method (CPM), 342–354
 critical path, 346–353
 early times, 345–350
 late times, 345–350
 notation, 345
 slack times, 345–350, 353
 (*See also* Program Evaluation and Review Technique)
Crosby, P. B., 378, 386
Cross-impact analysis, 135
Cross-training employees, 301
CRT (cathode-ray tube), 389, 397–398, 426
Customers (*see* Consumers)
Cybernetic model, 364–366
 decision maker, 366
 discriminator, 365–366
 effector, 366
 goal setter, 365–366
 sensor, 365–366

Daley Monthly Car Pool caselette, 332–333
Darukhanavala, P., 142
Data:
 collection of, 392–393
 manipulation of, 393–395
 storage of, 392–393
Data bank, 399
Data base, 400
Data-base management software, 391
Davis, L. E., 233
Decision support system (DSS), 395–397
 and electronic data processing, 397
Decoupling function, 405
Degenerate solution, 96
DeGeyndt, W., 368*n.*, 386
DeHayes, D. W., 335
Delphi method, 134–135

Demand:
 and capacity, 192, 269, 275
 cyclical, 295
 and facility design, 186–187
 and facility layout, 191
 and inventories, 405–406
 spatial, 166–167
 (*See also* Service demand)
Demand forecasting, 116–117, 295–297
Demand smoothing, 22–23, 26, 116, 152, 287–289, 295
 off-peak, 291
 partitioning, 288–289
Deviational variables, 102
Deviational weights, 102
Differential pricing, 289–291
Discount rate, effect of, on project selection, 43
Discrete-event simulation, 61, 67
Dissatisfaction-avoidance by workers, 225
Distributions:
 beta, 349–350, 353
 Erlang, 258
 exponential, 242–244, 259, 263, 273
 geometric probability, 261
 normal, 350, 352–353, 372–374, 437
 Poisson (*see* Poisson distribution)
 standard normal, table, 437
Distributive information systems, 425–426
Division of labor, 150
Doebler, P. D., 416*n.*, 421
Donnelly, J. H., 176, 182
Dorfman, R., 57
Drake, A. W., 13, 284, 310
Drew, J., 369
DSS (decision support system), 395–397
Dummy activities, 344
Dupont de Nemours, E. I., Company, 342
Durham, N., 80
DYNAMO computer language, 60–61

E. I. Dupont de Nemours Company, 342
Early times in critical path analysis, 345–350
Econometric models, 131–133
Economic activity:
 industrial world, 3
 invisible economy, 427
 OPEC countries, 3
 stages of, 3–4
 third world, 3
 United States, 428–429
Economic order quantity (EOQ), 407, 411–414
Economies of scale, 23, 264
EDP (*see* Electronic data processing)
Eilon, S., 326*n.*, 335
Electronic data processing (EDP), 388, 395–397
 and decision support system, 397
Elshafei, A. N., 209
Elysian Cycles caselette, 419–421
Emery, F. E., 233
Employees:
 relationship of, to consumer, 24, 211, 312
 scheduling of (*see* Work scheduling)
 in service organizations, 211, 426
 (*See also* Workers; Workforce; *entries beginning with term:* Job)
Energy consumption and facility design, 189–190
Eng, R. J., 437
Engel, C., 6
English, R. A., 16, 29
Eppen, G. D., 114
Equal Employment Opportunity Act, 213
Erlang distribution, 258
Esquire Department Store caselette, 207–209
Euclidian metric travel distance, 161–162, 170–171
Evaluation of service operations, 33–57
 implementation of, 39
 objectives, 34, 36
 the process, 34–39

442 INDEX

Evaluation of service operations *(Cont.)*:
 system paradigm, 37
 validation, 39
Ewen, R. B., 233
Explicit services in service package, 17–19, 148, 363, 366
Exponential distribution, 242–244, 259, 263, 273
Exponential smoothing, 123–124
 with seasonal adjustment, 126–129
 with trend adjustment, 124–126
Exxon Company, 187

Facilitating goods in service package, 16–18, 20, 148, 363, 366
Facilitating services, 16–17
Facility design, 21, 185–190
 aesthetics, 187
 and capacity planning, 275
 costs, 188–190
 and energy consumption 189–190
 environment, 187–188
 flexibility, 186–187
 and land, 186
 relation to facility layout, 191
Facility layout, 184–185, 191
 process layout (*see* Process layout)
 product layout (*see* Product layout)
 relation to facility design, 191
Fair Labor Standards Act, 213
Farr, J. L., 233
Federal Aviation Agency, 292
Federal Minimum Wage Law, 213
Feedback control system, 365
Felts, W., 335
First-come, first-served rule (FCFS), 247, 249–250, 260
Fitzsimmons, J. A., 22*n*., 28, 35*n*., 57, 183, 245, 256

Fixed-order-quantity system, 407–408
Fixed-replenishment-interval system, 408–409
Flex-time, 428
Foote, B. L., 220, 284
Foote, N. N., 3, 14
Forecasting, 115–121
 characteristics of methods of, 121
 demand, 116–117, 295–297
 importance of, 116–117
 selection of methods of, 117–121
Forecasting horizon, 119
Forecasting models:
 causal, 115, 130–133
 subjective, 115, 133–136
 time series, 115, 121–129
Forrester, J. W., 60, 61*n*., 80
FORTRAN computer language, 390
Foster, R. N., 142
Fourier models, 133
Franchising, 368
Francis, R. L., 209
Fuchs, V. R., 14, 28
Fulkerson, D. R., 362
Fusfeld, A. R., 142

Gantt, H., 339
Gantt project charts, 339–341
Garman, M. B., 362
Gartner, A., 14, 29
Gateway International Airport caselette, 307–310
Geometric probability distribution, 261
Gershung, J. L., 14
Gersuny, C., 14
Gibson, C. H., 233
Gilbreth, F., 214, 339
Giles, W. F., 233
Gillett, B., 335
Ginzberg, E., 14, 429*n*.
Gnomial Functions, Inc., caselette, 140–141
Goal programming, 81
 preemptive priorities in, 101–103
Golden, B. L., 324*n*., 335
Gordon, G., 65, 80

Gould, F. S., 114
GPSS computer language, 61
Graen, G. B., 233
Grant, E. L., 57
Gray, P., 175, 183
Greedy adding (GA) algorithm, 175
Gross, D., 284
Grubbs, F. E., 362
Gudapati, D., 142
Guerts, M. D., 142

Hackman, R. J., 233
Hadley, G., 421
Hakimi, S., 183.
Half-matrix, 319–323, 325
Hall, E. T., 256
Hammersley, J. M., 362
Handscomb, D. C., 362
Happ, W. W., 362
Hardware, computer, 388–390
 central processing unit (CPU), 389–390
 input devices, 388
 memory, 389
 output devices, 389
Hartley, H. O., 362
Hasenfeld, Y., 16, 29
Hatt, P. K., 3, 14
Hayya, J., 362
Health Maintenance Organization (HMO):
 (A) caselette, 179
 (B) caselette, 206
 (C) caselette, 207
Helmer, O., 134
Hershey, J. C., 164, 165, 182, 310
Herzberg, F., 224–225, 227, 230, 233
Heuristic technique, 198
 Clarke-Wright (C-W) algorithm (*see* Clarke-Wright algorithm)
 computer program, 296
 CRAFT, 201–203
 operations sequence analysis, 199–201
 pin and string method, 315–317
Hierarchy of needs, 222–224
Hierarchy of services, 163

Hillier, F. S., 114, 209, 284
Hinrichs, H. H., 57
Historical analogy, 135–136
Hodgswon, A., 142
Holiday Inn, 185
Holmes, J., 166n., 182
Hopewell, L., 362
Hoppock R., 222
Horizontal loading, 223–224
Hostage, G. M., 25n., 29, 377, 386
Houston Port Authority caselette, 282–283
Howell, M. A., 233
Huckfeldt, V. E., 335
Huff, D. L., 171, 173, 183
Hulin, C. L., 233
Human engineering, 215
Human service organizations, typology of, 16
Hygiene factors, 225–227

Ibrahim, I. B., 142
Iconic models, 59
IMPACT, 343
Implicit services in service package, 19, 148, 363, 366
Industrial society, characteristics of, 5
Info-Systems, Inc., caselette, 360–361
Information explosion, 392
Innovation in services, 25
Interactive routing programs, 329–330
Intermittent-flow system, 197
International Business Machines (IBM) Corporation, 313, 326
Inventories:
 cyclic, 406
 in-transit, 406
 safety stocks, 406–407, 411–416
 seasonal, 405–406
 speculative, 406
Inventory distribution system, 405
Inventory management:
 computer software for, 404
 in management information systems, 394–395

Inventory management (Cont.):
 (See also Inventory systems)
Inventory models, 410–416
 economic order quantity (EOQ), 407, 411–414
 inventory management under uncertainty, 414–416
Inventory systems:
 computer-based, 416–417
 constraints on, 406
 costs of, 406–407, 411–414
 demand for items, nature of, 406
 fixed-order-quantity system, 407–408
 fixed-replenishment-interval system, 408–409
 planning horizon, 406
 reorder point, 407, 415–416
 replenishment, 404–409, 411
 (s,S) inventory control system, 409
 and service capacity, 404
 and service level, 415
Inventory theory, 404–407
Inverse transformation method, 66
Invisible economy, the, 426–427
I/O (input/output) devices in computer systems, 389–390
Ireson, W. G., 57

Jenkins, G. M., 141, 142
Jewell, W. S., 269n.
Job enlargement, 223
Job enrichment, 224–228
Job rationalization, 214–215
Job sharing, 428
Job shop (batch) service operation, 147
Jockeying in queue configuration, 247
Johnson, J., 335
Johnson, T., 227, 234

Kahn, R. L., 222

Kaiman, L., 209
Kanten, J., 403
Karlin, S., 421
Kaufmann, F., 159
Kavesh, R. A., 142
Keeney, R. L., 13, 57, 284, 310
Kendall, D. G., 258
Kendall notation, 258–259
Kernan, J. B., 210
Khumawala, B. M., 183
Kilbridge, M. D., 234
Klarman, H. E., 57
Kleindorfer, G. B., 362
Kopelman, R. E., 234
Krohler Supermarkets caselette, 76–78
Krolak, P., 335
Kruse, C., 336
Kursh, S. J., 335
Kwan, M., 315n.

Labor, division of, 150
Labor force (see Workforce)
Labor unions, effect of, on work design, 212
Lanford, H. W., 142
Late times in critical path analysis, 345–350
Lawler, E. E., 224, 234
Lead time, 405–406, 415
Least squares regression, 131
Lee, R. C., 209
Lee, S. M., 114
Leibman, J., 183
Leisure and the invisible economy, 427–428
Lemon County Commissioner's Court caselette, 401–402
Levitt, T., 149n., 159, 234
Levy, F. K., 362
Lew, P., 203n., 210
Lewis, R., 14
Lieberman, G. J. 114, 284
Liebman, J. C., 336
Lindblom, C. E., 57
Line balancing problem in continuous flow system, 195–197
Line (flow shop) service operation, 147–148

444 INDEX

Linear programming
  60, 81–82, 84
  constrained optimization models, 82
  goal programming, 81, 101–103
  graphical solution, 92–94
  integer programming, 88–90
  network models, 90–92
Little, J. D. C., 269n.
Location set covering problem, 172
Locke, E. A., 233
Lopez, D. A., 175, 183
Lower control limit (LCL), 372–374
Luce, B. J., 295–297, 310

m-vehicle routing problem, 315
Mabert, V. A., 141, 142, 301n., 311
McBride, C. C., 13
McBridge, R., 22n., 28
McCartney, L., 398n., 399n., 403
MacCrimmon, K. R., 353n., 362
McDonald's Hamburgers, 149–150, 367–368, 371
McKenna, C. R., 435, 436
McLean, E. R., 403
McPherson, K., 210
MAD (mean absolute deviation), 118–119
Magazine, M. J., 284, 299, 310
Magee, J. F., 421
Magnanti, T. L., 335
Makridakis, S., 142
Malpractice, 380
Man-machine charts (see Worker-machine charts)
Management information systems (MIS), 388–395
  accessibility, 394
  accuracy, 394
  applications, 395
  clarity, 394
  comparability, 394
  and computer technology, 390–392

Management information systems (MIS) (Cont.):
  controlling subsystem, 394
  data-oriented, 396
  and decision making, 393
  model-oriented, 396
  objectivity, 394
  operating subsystem, 394–395
  planning subsystem, 394
  relevance, 393–394
  timeliness, 393–395
  (See also Decision support system)
Management training, 377
Manpower planning (see Workforce planning)
Manufacturing operations management, relationship of, to services, 13, 15
Marcus, M., 141
Marginal analysis, 275
Marks, D. H., 183, 335
Marriott, J. W., 25
Marriott Corporation, 377–378
Marriott Hotels, 25
Martin, J. J., 362
Martino, J. P., 142
Masaru, T., 335
Maslow, A., 222–223
Mathematical models, 59–60
  analysis of, 60
  deterministic, 59
  dynamic, 59
  static, 59
  stochastic, 59–60
  (See also Linear programming; Systems simulation)
Matrix:
  in Clarke-Wright algorithm: half-matrix, 319–323, 325
  in facilities layout: cost, 201
    flow, 199
    interdepartmental flow, 201
    triangularized, 199
Maximal covering location problem, 175
Maximal service distance, 172

Maxwell, W. L., 250n., 255
Mayo, E., 222
$M/D/1$ queuing model, 263
Mean absolute deviation (MAD), 118–119
Mean square deviation (MSD), 118–119
Metropolitan metric travel distance, 161–162, 168–170
$M/G/\infty$ general self-service queuing model, 267, 279–280
$M/G/1$ queuing model, 262, 278
Microcomputers, 390, 427
Miller, D. W., 421
Miller, J. G., 142
Miller, L. R., 335
Miller, L. W., 250n., 255
Milton, E. F., 142
Mincer, J., 142
Minicomputers, 390, 397–399
MIS (see Management information systems)
Miserly County Transportation Authority caselette, 53–57
$M/M/c$ queuing model:
  finite-queue, 267, 274, 279
  standard, 263, 268, 270–271, 273, 278, 296n.
$M/M/1$ queuing model:
  finite-queue, 261, 277
  standard, 259, 262–263, 265, 277
Models, 59, 81
  analog, 59
  constrained optimization, (see Constrained optimization models)
  cybernetic, 364–366
  econometric, 131–133
  forecasting (see Forecasting models)
  Fourier, 133
  iconic, 59
  inventory, 410–416
  mathematical, 59–60
    (See also Linear programming; Systems simulation)
  network, 90–92, 354

Models (Cont.):
 queuing (see Queuing models)
 regression, 131–133
 schematic, 59
Mojena, R., 113, 255, 284
Monte Carlo simulation, 64–68, 353–354
Moore, J. M., 209
Moore, L. J., 70n., 71, 80
Morrison, D., 142
Morse, P. N., 13, 284, 310
Most-likely time, 349
Mount Moriah Cemetery and Funeral Home (Kansas City, Mo.), 398–399
MSD (mean square deviation), 118–119
Mullick, S. K., 142
Multiphasic testing laboratory, 150
Multiple-depot routing problem, 315
Multiple-server system, 264, 267, 274
Multisite location problem, 160
Munich Delicatessen caselette, 110–111
Murdick, R. G., 403
Murph, A. F., 437
Muther, R., 210

N-period moving average, 122
Nace, G. E., 326n., 327, 335
Naddor, E., 421
National Broadcasting Company, 213
Nautiyal, J. C., 290, 311
Naylor, T., 80
Nelson, C. R., 142
Nelson, J., 335
Net savings:
 in Clarke-Wright algorithm, 320–321, 323
 in VSP/X, 328
Network models, 90–92, 354
Network theory, 313–315
Networks:
 components of, 313
 project management techniques, 341

Networks, project management techniques (Cont.):
 (See also Project management)
 systems flow plan (project network), 343, 350, 352, 354
 transportation, 326
 (See also Vehicle routing problems)
Node routing problem, 313
Nodes, activities on (AON), 343, 344
Nonbasic variable, 96–97
Nonconformance problems in service quality, 363–364, 366
Nonsatisfaction of workers, 225
Normal distribution, 350, 352–353, 372–374
Normal element times, 216
Norman, A. H., 80
Nugent, C. E., 210

Oak Hollow Evaluation Center caselette, 138–140
Objective function coefficients, 83
 ranging, 98–99, 102
Ofer, G., 14
Oldham, G. R., 233
Olsen, P. R., 29
O'Neal, C. R., 142
Ongoing process service operation, 147–148
Operations-flow diagram, 193–197
Operations management (see Service operations management)
Operations sequence analysis, 199–201
 CRAFT, 201–203
Opportunity cost, 97
Optimal solution, 84, 92–95
Optimistic time, 349–350
Optimization criteria, 163–165
Organizational structure, 211
 (See also Work design)
Orloff, C. S., 335

Overbooking, 292–294

p-chart (attributes control chart), 374
Pan American Airlines, 300
Panico, J. A., 244n., 256
Parallel-server queuing models, 258–259
Parallel-server system, 263–264, 270
Parameters, 83
Parikh, S. C., 284
Part-time employees, 301–302, 428
PASCAL computer language, 390
Paul, W. J., 234
Payne, R., 187n., 210
Pegden, C. D., 80
PEP, 343
Performance rating, 215
Personalization in service package, 197
PERT (see Program Evaluation and Review Technique)
Pessimistic time, 349–350
Peterson, R., 421
Phillips, R. J., 188, 209
Pierce, J. F., 335
Pin and string method for vehicle routing, 315–317
Platt, R. B., 142
Poisson distribution, 243–244, 259, 265, 267–268, 271, 273
Pooling services, 264–267
Postindustrial society:
 characteristics of, 5–7, 9
 development of, 5
Pranda, J., 311
Prasow, P., 234
Predecessor activity, 343
Preemptive priorities, 101
Preindustrial society, characteristics of, 4–5
Present-value analysis, 41–45
Prest, A. R., 57
Pricing, differential, 289–291
Pritsker, A. B., 80, 362
Private-sector location analysis, 164

Probability distributions (*see* Distributions)
Process charts, 193–194
Process layout, 191, 197
  influencing factors, 191
  intermittent-flow system, 197
  operations sequence analysis, 199–201
  and personalization of services, 197
  relative-location problem, 198–201
Producer's risk, 372
Product layout, 191
  continuous-flow system, 192–193
  efficiency, 191–193
  job specialization, 193
  line process, 195
  parallel configuration, 192
  series configuration, 192
Production and consumption (*see* Consumption, relationship to production)
Production-line approach to service, 149–151
Productivity:
  and consumers, 13, 240
  growth in, 11
  and job rationalization, 215
  as measure of economic efficiency, 11
  and salaries, 12–13
  in service organizations, 12
  and worker motivation, 222–224
Professional Rodeo Association (Fort Collins, Colo.), 399
Professional service organization (PSO), 228–229
Professional Standards Review Organization (PSRO), 368
Program Evaluation and Review Technique (PERT), 341–354
  activity duration, 349–353
  activity time estimates, 349–350
  assumptions, 352–354
  dummy activities, 344

Program Evaluation and Review Technique (PERT) (*Cont.*):
  implementation problems, 354
  network diagrams, 343–344
  project completion time, 350–353
Project completion time in PERT, 350–353
Project management, 338–362
  functions, 339
  Gantt project charts, 339–341
  network techniques for, 341
  project systems, 338
  traditional techniques for, 339–341
  (*See also* Critical Path Method; Program Evaluation and Review Technique)
Project service operation, 146–147
Prosumer, 426, 428
Pseudo-random numbers, 65
Public-sector location analysis, 164
Public Utilities Commission, 271

Quality, 363–386
  attributes control chart (*p* chart), 374
  characteristic curve, 375, 376
  and conformance, 363–364, 366
  consumer's risk, 372, 375
  control of, 15, 364
  control charts, 369, 371, 373
  and design, 363, 367
  improvement program, 377–379
  management of, 365
  measurement of, 368
  producer's risk, 372
  service liability, 379–380
  Type I error, 372–375
  Type II error, 372, 375, 380

Quality (*Cont.*):
  variable control chart ($\bar{X}$ chart), 373–374
Queuing models:
  $M/D/1$, 263
  $M/G/\infty$ general self-service, 267, 279–280
  $M/G/1$, 262, 278
  $M/M/c$ (see $M/M/c$ queuing model)
  $M/M/1$ (see $M/M/1$ queuing model)
  queue configuration, 241, 245–249, 259
  queue discipline, 241, 249–250, 260
  (*See also* Waiting time)
Quon, J. E., 335

Raedels, A. R., 301*n*., 311
Raiffa, H., 57
Rand Corporation, 134
Random numbers, 65–66, 438
Random variables, 349–350, 405
Real-time routing problems, 314*n*.
Rectangular displacement travel distance (*see* Euclidian metric travel distance)
Regression models, 131–133
  econometric models, 131–133
  Fourier models, 133
Reisman, A., 142
Relative-location problem, 198–201
Reneging in queuing systems, 241, 248, 269
Research and development (R&D), 9
  General Motors, 9
  International Business Machines, 9
  U.S. Steel Corporation, 9
Reservation systems, 292, 399–400
Retail location model, 171
Revelle, C., 175, 182, 183
Rice, D. P., 46*n*., 57
Riessman, F., 14, 29

INDEX 447

Right-hand-side (RHS) constraints, 83, 96–98
   ranging, 99–101
Ringer, L. J., 362
Rising, E. J., 243, 246, 252, 256, 270n., 284, 288, 289n., 311
River City National Bank caselette, 305–307
River City Planning Commission caselette, 53
Robertson, K. B., 234
Rochberg, R., 142
Rosengren, W., 14
Ross, J. E., 403
Routine service organization (RSO), 228–230
Ruml, J., 210
Russell, R., 335
Ryavec, C. C., 353n., 362

Saaty, T. L., 268, 271n., 284
Sacksman, H., 142
Sanders, D. H., 437
Sasser, E. W., 29, 311
Satisficing, 101
Savas, E. S., 57, 183
Savings concept of Clarke-Wright algorithm, 317–319
Scarf, H., 421
Schainblatt, A. H., 39, 57
Scheduling:
   of consumers, in intermittent-flow system, 197
   of work (see Work scheduling)
Schematic models, 59
Scholastic Aptitude Test (SAT), 371
Schwartz, B., 237n., 256
Self-service ethic, 427
Self-service operations (see Consumer)
Sensitivity analysis, 48, 96, 98
Sequoia Airlines caselette, 111–113
Service capacity, 22–23, 116, 152, 235–236, 240, 257, 263–264, 266, 269–270, 272, 287

Service delivery system (SDS), 211
Service demand, 22–23, 26, 116, 287–292
Service Employees International Union, 212
Service facility:
   location analysis, 160–177
   site selection, 23, 165
   (See also Facility design; Facility layout)
Service level, 415
Service liability, 379–380
Service operations:
   characteristics of, 20, 176
   classification of, 146–147
   definition of, 26, 116
   design of, 146
   evaluation of (see Evaluation of service operations)
   and marketing, 26
   open-systems view of, 26
Service operations management, 6, 9, 11–14
   forecasting in (see Forecasting; Forecasting models)
   new role for managers, 425, 427–428
   origin of, 115
   relationship of, to manufacturing, 13, 15
Service organizations:
   design of facilities (see Facility design)
   employees in, 211, 426
   human, typology of, 16
   and inventories (see Inventories; entries beginning with term: Inventory)
   layout of facilities (see Facility layout)
   technological innovation, 154–156, 214
Service package, 15–20, 148, 184, 211–214, 363, 395
   explicit services, 17–19, 148, 363, 366
   facilitating goods, 16–18, 20, 148, 363, 366
   implicit services, 19, 148, 363, 366

Service package *(Cont.)*:
   personalization, 197
   supporting facility, 16, 18, 148, 363, 366
Service process, 241, 250–253, 260
   design of, 426
   role of consumers in, 12–14, 21, 26, 235, 429
Services:
   classification of, 16–17
   as collective good, 33
   complementary, 291
   hierarchy of, 163
   innovation in, 25
   measurement of, 25
   quality of (*see* Quality)
   relationship of: to agriculture, 7
      to computer information systems, 12
      to consumers, 12–13
      to employment, 8, 9
      to environment, 15
      to GNP, 8
      to manufacturing, 7
      to personal income, 7
      to productivity, 12
      to technology, 12, 146
      to United States economy, 7
   standardization of, 151, 195, 368, 378
   system design, 34, 148–154
Shadow price, 97, 100
Shift scheduling, 86–88, 295–299
   part-time employees, 301–302, 428
   (*See also* Work scheduling)
Shore, B., 362
Shortest-processing-time (SPT) rule, 249–250
Silver, E. A., 421
Simplex algorithm, 96
SIMSCRIPT computer language, 61
Simulation (*see* Systems simulation)
Single-payment present worth factor, 41, 435
Single-server system, 263–264, 266

Slack times in critical path analysis, 345–350, 353
Slack variable, 94, 97
SLAM computer language, 62
Smith, D. D., 142
Smith, H., 236, 256
Smith, P. C., 233
Smith, V. K., 80
Smith, W. F., 50*n*., 51, 57
Soden, J. V., 403
Software, computer, 388, 390–391
  for data-base management, 391
  for inventory management, 404
Sommers, M. S., 210
Sorrentino, C., 14
Southwest Center for Urban Research, 187
Spatial demand, 166–167
SPERT, 343
Standard cycle time, 216
Standard element times, 216
Standard normal distribution, table, 437
Standard operating procedures (SOP), 367
Standardization of service, 151, 195, 368, 378
Starr, M. K., 421
Steady-state system, 259, 262–263, 267, 272
Stidham, S., Jr., 269*n*.
Stinson, J. E., 227, 234
Stock-keeping unit (SKU), 404, 413–415
Stockout costs, 407–408
Stricker, R., 335
Subjective forecasting models, 115, 133–136
  cross-impact analysis, 135
  Delphi method, 134–135
  historical analogy, 135–136
Sullivan, R. S., 35*n*., 57, 362
Supporting facility in service package, 16, 18, 148, 363, 366
Surplus variable, 94
Surrogate measures, 363, 368
Svestka, J. A., 335
Swain, R., 183
System performance, 372

Systems, 26
  closed, 26
  concept, 33–34
  continuous-flow (*see* Continuous-flow system)
  design, 34, 148–154
  intermittent-flow, 197
  multiple-server, 264, 267, 274
  open, 26–27
  parallel-server, 263–264, 270
  single-server, 263–264, 266
  steady state, 259, 262–263, 267, 272
  transient state, 259
  (*See also* Queuing models)
Systems flow plan, 343, 350, 352, 354
Systems simulation, 60–62, 270
  continuous, 60–61
  discrete-event, 61, 67
  hybrid, 62
  methodology, 62–64
  Monte Carlo simulation, 64–68, 353–354
  validation, 64

Taha, H. A., 114
Target population, 66
Taylor, B., 70*n*., 71, 80
Taylor, F. W., 15, 214, 221, 428
Taylor, G. M., 57
Teamsters Union, 212
Technology:
  of computers, advances in, 388, 390–392, 425–426, 429
  innovation in, 154–156, 214
  role of, 9, 146
  substitution of, for people, 150–151
Thomas, D. R. E., 159
Thompson, P. H., 234
Thornton, R., 22*n*., 28
Thrifty-Rent-A-Car caselette, 254–255
Tillman, F. A., 336

Time series forecasting models, 115, 121–129
  exponential smoothing, 123–124
  exponential smoothing with seasonal adjustment, 126–129
  exponential smoothing with trend adjustment, 124–126
  N-period moving average, 122
Time study, 215
Time windows, 315
Toffler, A., 426*n*.
Toregas, C., 183
Transactional analysis, 25
Transient state, 259
Transportation models (*see* Network models)
Traveling salesman problem, 315, 321–324
Trent, R. H., 403
Triage, 250
Trist, E. L., 233
Truitt, M., 336
Turvey, R., 57
Two-factor theory for motivating employees, 224, 227
Type I error, 372–375
Type II error, 372, 375, 380

Uniform-series present worth factor, 42, 436
Uniformly distributed random numbers, table, 438
Unions, effect of, on work design, 212
United Airlines, 213
U.S. Navy Special Projects Office, 341
United States of America Bank (of Chicago), 240
University Student Union capstone case, 429
Upper control limit (UCL), 372–375
Utilization factor, 263–264

van Gigch, J. P., 29, 386
Van Slyke, R. M., 362

Variables:
 basic, 96–97
 decision, 83
 dependent, 131
 deviational, 102
 independent, 131
 nonbasic, 96–97
 random, 349–350, 405
 slack, 94, 97
 surplus, 94
Vehicle routing problems, 312–336, 395
 Chinese postman problem, 315
 Clarke-Wright (C-W) algorithm (see Clarke-Wright algorithm)
 classification of, 314
 constraints, 315
 interactive routing programs, 329–330
 m-vehicle problem, 315
 multiple-depot problem, 315
 pin and string method, 315–317
 single-vehicle problem, 315
 traveling salesman problem, 315, 321–324
 VSP/X (see VSP/X)
Vojta, G. J., 14, 429
Volgyesi, A. S., 210
Vollman, T. E., 113, 201n., 202, 210, 255, 284
VSP/X, 313, 326–330
 advantages, 329
 barriers, 328
 coordinate method, 327–328
 flowchart, 327
 net savings, 328
 options, 328–329
 true-distance method, 327–328
 zones, 327–328

Wagner, H. M., 114
Waiting, 236
 economics of, 239
 as psychological punishment, 237
 as ritual insult, 238
 as social interaction, 239
 time, 257, 264, 266, 269–274
Waiting
 (See also Queuing models)
Walby, K., 166n., 182
Walker, C. R., 222
Wandel, S., 310
Warner, D. M., 311
Watts, D. G., 142
Weber, A., 171n.
Weber problem, 171n.
Webster, D. B., 80
Wheeler, T. L., 403
Wheelwright, S. C., 142
White, J. A., 209
White, T., 22n., 28
Whitin, T. M., 421
Whittier County Hospital caselette, 358–360
Whybark, D. C., 142
Wiest, J. D., 362
Wildavsky, A., 57
Williams, F. B., 166n., 182
Williams, F. E., 311
Withington, F. G., 362
Word processing, 426
Work cycles, 215–219
Work design:
 affirmative action, 213–214
 definition of, 211
 and education, 212
 and job enlargement, 223
 origin of, 214, 221–222
 for service organizations, 227–230
 and unions, 212
Work measurement:
 activity charts, 220–221

Work measurement (Cont.):
 time study, 215
 work sampling, 216–219
 worker-machine charts, 219
Work methods charts:
 activity charts, 220–221
 worker-machine charts, 219
Work sampling, 216–219
Work scheduling, 15, 295–299, 395
 part-time employees, 301–302, 428
 (See also Shift scheduling)
Work simplification, 215
Worker-machine charts, 219
Workers:
 dissatisfaction-avoidance by, 225
 motivation of, 222–224
 (See also Employees; Workforce; entries beginning with term: Job)
Workforce:
 dispersion of, 426
 distribution of, by occupation, 10
Workforce planning, 88–90
 (See also Project management)
Wortham, A. W., 362
Wright, J. W., 316n., 335
Wyckoff, D. D., 29

$\bar{X}$ chart (variable control chart), 373–374

Yellow, P. C., 336
Youngmann, C., 166n., 182

Zartler, R. L., 210
Zero-based budgeting, 34
Zero Defects program, 377